The Invention of Christian Discourse
Volume I

Rhetoric of Religious Antiquity
Series

Editors

Vernon K. Robbins
Duane F. Watson

Deo Publishing

The INVENTION *of* CHRISTIAN DISCOURSE

Volume I

Vernon K. Robbins

deo
PUBLISHING

BLANDFORD FORUM

Rhetoric of Religious Antiquity series, 1

ISSN 1574 3926

Published by Deo Publishing
P.O. Box 6284, Blandford Forum, Dorset DT11 1AQ, UK

Art featured on the cover: Rick A. Robbins, "His LifeLine" (42" x 50" acrylic on canvas, 2002). Online: http://home.comcast.net/~rick1216/LifeLine/LifeLine5.htm

Cover design: Bernard Madden

Printed by Cromwell Press Group, Trowbridge, Wiltshire

British Library Cataloguing-in-Publication data
A catalogue record for this book is available from the British Library

ISBN 978-90-5854-021-8

To

Deanna
Rick
Chimene and Michael
Nicholas, Sophia, and Anastasia

My love and appreciation

Contents

Chapter 5
Christian Wisdom Rhetorolect
Part II: Solomon, Wisdom in Divine History, and the New Testament

Chapter 6
Christian Prophetic Rhetorolect
Part I: Kingdom, Confrontation, Abraham, Moses, and Samuel

Chapter 7
Christian Prophetic Rhetorolect
Part II: Story-Lines in the New Testament

Chapter 8
Christian Apocalyptic Rhetoric
Part I: Empire, Destruction, and Transformation

Chapter 9
Christian Apocalyptic Rhetoric
Part II: Flesh and Blood versus Cities, Military Power, and Wealth in First Century Christian Apocalyptic Rhetorolect

Chapter 10
Conversations and Prospectives

Preface

It is a daunting task to write a book for a research group. In many ways it is exceptionally rewarding; in other ways, it is exceedingly challenging. It is rewarding to meet with international colleagues in different venues at various times each year to participate in ongoing conversation and debate concerning how to refine one's procedures and to receive remarkable new scholarly resources for one's work as people encounter new publications and send references to them over the email list for the research group. But it is also exceptionally challenging. While other scholarly colleagues are writing books of various lengths, a person writes one research essay after another for edited volumes, while the book for the research group gets longer and longer, because it seems necessary to address a wide range of questions and suggestions that arise in meeting after meeting.

It all began in November, 1997, at the SBL meeting in San Francisco, when Duane F. Watson came to me and asked if I would lead the way in developing a rhetorical approach to interpret the literature and traditions of the religions of Mediterranean Antiquity. My immediate response was that this was an overwhelming task. His counter response was that my sixteen years in Classics and Religious Studies at the University of Illinois at Urbana-Champaign before moving to the Department and Graduate Division of Religion at Emory University in Atlanta, Georgia, gave me a reach of experience with Mediterranean Antiquity that could take the rhetorical strategies of analysis and interpretation he had learned under the mentorship of George A. Kennedy a significant step forward. It was less clear to me then than it is now with the arrival of *Words Well Spoken: George Kennedy's Rhetoric of the New Testament*[1] how I have been blending Kennedy's work with the rhetorical practices I learned under the mentorship of Thomas M. Conley at the University of Illinois, and the special experiences I had

[1] Edited by C. Clifton Black & Duane F. Watson (Studies in Rhetoric and Religion 8; Waco, TX: Baylor University Press, 2008).

with Burton L. Mack, Ronald F. Hock, Edward N. O'Neil, and Robert C. Tannehill at the Institute for Antiquity and Christianity in Claremont, California, during Spring, 1982.

As Duane and I entered into plans with David E. Orton, who had proposed the idea of a series on the Rhetoric of Religious Antiquity (RRA), I faced my first surprise. The first task was to write commentary on the writings in the New Testament! I had thought that various "hymns" probably would be the place to begin: Cleanthes' *Hymn to Zeus*; Isidorus' four *Hymns to Isis*; the *Hymn to Demeter*, etc. Then we could go on to the oracles at Delphi and Dodona, the healings of Asclepius, etc. Instead, our task was to begin with the NT. In the context of the broader literature and inscriptions I envisioned as the subject matter of our challenge, it became obvious to me that the "special" rhetorical nature of the NT writings had to do with their "Jewishness." But what was that special rhetorical nature? Through a long process of research, analysis, discussion, debate, and disagreement, the idea I had in 1996 about six major "rhetorical dialects" (rhetorolects) in first century Christian discourse, which can also be understood as "forms of life" or "belief systems," gradually took full form. This meant that a major alternative to Greco-Roman rhetoric, with its focus on only three modes – judicial, deliberative, and epideictic – had to be developed, and this would be very objectionable to most of the colleagues with whom I enjoyed significant collegiality as a New Testament scholar who used Greco-Roman rhetoric!

The first question was how to proceed. My own search through areas of biblical studies brought into view the website on Constructions of Ancient Space that James W. Flanagan had pioneered for Hebrew Bible studies.[2] This site introduced me to Critical Spatiality Theory, which has proven to be very important for sociorhetorical interpretation (SRI).[3] With the help of L. Gregory Bloomquist, I became aware of Conceptual Blending/Integration Theory in the cognitive sciences.[4] Gradually this has led me to the field of "embodied cognition" and the

[2] Online: http://www.cwru.edu/affil/GAIR/Constructions/Constructions.html. See Jon L. Berquist and Claudia V. Camp (eds.), *Constructions of Space I: Theory, Geography, Narrative* (Library of Hebrew Bible/Old Testament Studies 481; New York/London: T. & T. Clark, 2007).

[3] David M. Gunn and Paula M. McNutt (eds.), *"Imagining" Biblical Worlds: Studies in Spatial, Social and Historical Constructs in Honor of James W. Flanagan* (London: Sheffield Academic Press, 2002).

[4] Gilles Fauconnier and Mark Turner, *The Way We Think: Conceptual Blending and the Mind's Hidden Complexities* (New York: Basic Books, 2002).

special branch of "grounded cognition"[5] that is providing the means to analyze and interpret the spaces, places, and situations at work in the religious literature and traditions of Late Mediterranean Antiquity. My conclusion is that six major social-cultural-religious frames guided first century Christian rhetoric: wisdom, prophetic, apocalyptic, precreation, priestly, and miracle.[6]

The second question concerned the places where we should present and test our work. Duane and I began our work in the venue of three ongoing contexts. The most immediate context was the international conferences Thomas H. Olbricht had nurtured, beginning in Heidelberg, Germany, in 1992.[7] We thank Thomas and all those who hosted, wrote papers, participated, and edited volumes in particular for the conferences in Florence, Italy, in 1998;[8] Lund, Sweden, in 2000;[9] Heidelberg, Germany, in 2002;[10] and Pretoria, South Africa in 2005.[11] These conferences contributed in innumerable ways to our ongoing search for ways to perform SRI of religious texts and traditions in Mediterranean Antiquity.

The second context for our work was the international SRI Seminar in the Studiorum Novi Testamenti Societas. I thank Samuel Byrskog, who co-chaired the seminar with me, and those who wrote papers and participated in the meetings in Pretoria, South Africa (1999), Tel Aviv (2000), Montreal (2001), Durham, UK (2002), and Bonn (2003).

The third context was the annual SBL meetings. I am deeply grateful to the leaders of the SBL who welcomed our work and to all who participated in the Steering Committee and the sessions of the Rheto-

[5] Lawrence W. Barsalou, "Grounded Cognition," in *Annual Review of Psychology* 59 (2008) 617-45; idem, Aron K. Barbey, W. Kyle Simmons, and Ava Santos, "Embodiment in Religious Knowledge," *Journal of Cognition and Culture* 5 (2005) 14-57.

[6] Cf. Vernon K. Robbins, "The Dialectical Nature of Early Christian Discourse," *Scriptura* 59 (1996) 353-62, online: http://www.religion.emory.edu//faculty/robbins/dialect/dialect353.html.

[7] See an account of the conferences in Vernon K. Robbins, "From Heidelberg to Heidelberg: Rhetorical Interpretation of the Bible at the Seven 'Pepperdine' Conferences from 1992 to 2002," in *Rhetoric, Ethic, and Moral Persuasion in Biblical Discourse: Essays from the 2002 Heidelberg Conference* (ed. T.H. Olbricht and Anders Eriksson; ESEC 11; New York/London: T. & T. Clark, 2005) 335-77. Online: http://www.religion.emory.edu/faculty/robbins/Pdfs/HeidelbergJuly2002.pdf.

[8] S.E. Porter and T.H. Olbricht (eds.), *Rhetorical Criticism and the Bible: Essays from the 1998 Florence Conference* (JSNTSup 195; Sheffield: Sheffield Academic Press, 2002).

[9] Anders Eriksson, Thomas H. Olbricht, and Walter Übelacker (eds.), *Rhetorical Argumentation in Biblical Texts: Essays from the Lund 2000 Conference* (ESEC 8; Harrisburg, PA: Trinity Press International, 2002).

[10] See n. 8.

[11] *Rhetoric(s) of Body Politics and Religious Discourse* (ed. G. van den Heever; *Scriptura* 90:3; Stellenbosch: University of Stellenbosch, 2005).

ric in the NT Section during its beginnings in 1991-1996. My appreciation extends to Duane F. Watson and L. Gregory Bloomquist who led the Section diligently and creatively in succession after 1996 when my term as chair ended. A special volume, and then a special session in Denver in 1999 on the rhetoric of apocalyptic,[12] gave us the first taste of the benefits of working together on the rhetoric of a particular kind of discourse. Next came the special session on miracle discourse in Denver in 2001, from which a collection of essays is soon to appear.[13] Then came the special session on priestly discourse organized by L. Gregory Bloomquist (San Antonio 2004), from which there also will soon be a forthcoming volume.[14]

On Friday, November 22, 2002, the day before the official beginning of the sessions in the SBL at Toronto, the RRA group started a new practice of meeting for a full day of presentations and discussion before the annual meetings. This practice continued in Atlanta (2003), San Antonio (2004), Philadelphia (2005), Washington, DC (2006), and San Diego (2007), and it continues this year in Boston. By 2004, the work of the group had become robust enough that David A. deSilva agreed to submit a proposal for the existence of an official RRA Seminar in the SBL. I am deeply grateful to David not only for launching this Seminar, but also to him and the administration of Ashland Theological Seminary for providing free housing and generous hosting of the RRA group during summer meetings since June, 2002. These meetings have been a key to our ongoing work on the project, giving us an opportunity to organize our activities before bringing them to the annual SBL meetings in November each year. I am also grateful to him for special sessions he organized in the seminar on story-lines in the NT, from which some essays have already been published in various places; on precreation discourse, from which a volume is forthcoming;[15] and on rhetography, which created the context and the title of my essay that explains most clearly so far the relation of my approach to the work of George Kennedy.[16]

[12] Greg Carey and L. Gregory Bloomquist (eds.), *Vision and Persuasion: Rhetorical Dimensions of Apocalyptic Discourse* (St. Louis, MO: Chalice Press, 1999); Duane F. Watson (ed.), *The Intertexture of Apocalyptic Discourse in the New Testament* (Symposium 14; Atlanta, SBL, 2002).

[13] Duane F. Watson (ed.), *The Role of Miracle Discourse in the Argumentation of the New Testament* (Symposium; Atlanta: SBL, 2009).

[14] Tentatively entitled *Priestly Discourse and Sacrifice in Early Christianity* (Symposium; Atlanta: SBL).

[15] In *Religion and Theology* (Pretoria: UNISA Press/Leiden: Brill).

[16] V.K. Robbins, "Rhetography: A New Way of Seeing the Familiar Text," in *Words Well Spoken,* 81-106.

As a result of L. Gregory Bloomquist's special interest in SRI, which began at the 1995 London Rhetoric Conference sponsored by Thomas Olbricht, his energetic work has made St. Paul University at Ottawa a major center for the emergence of Ph.D. dissertations that have contributed to the application and development of this interpretive analytics.[17] I thank him from the bottom of my heart (as my mother used to say!) for his generosity, his encouragement, his commitment to our approach, his careful work with his students, and his special role in bringing Conceptual Blending/Integration into our strategies of interpretation.[18] After Duane Watson's term as Chair of the Rhetoric of the New Testament Section, Greg was the natural successor to carry the Section to a new place, which he has done with great skill and hard work. In addition, he organized special sessions at Ottawa in connection with oral defenses of Ph.D. dissertations, and convinced the administration of St. Paul University to provide generous housing and other accommodations for meetings of the group at Ottawa in the summers of 2006 and 2007. I am deeply grateful to Greg, to the administration at St. Paul University, and to numerous Ph.D. students who accepted special responsibilities and burdens to make our visits a success.

There is much yet to learn and even more to analyze and interpret. The "opening" volume of the RRA series has become Volume 1 of a two-volume work. I apologize for its length. I wish I could have presented the approach in a succinct and clear manner in the opening volume. I am finding my way with much briefer presentations in my classes at Emory University, and I look forward to a volume that condenses the approach to a form similar to *Exploring the Texture of Texts*.[19] But the condensed volume must wait a few years to appear. In the meantime, my Socio-Rhetorical Interpretation web site must function as the more simplified environment for the use of this interpretive analytics.[20]

[17] An interpretive analytics approaches texts as discourse and "sees discourse as part of a larger field of power and practice whose relations are articulated in different ways by different paradigms." The rigorous establishment of the relations of power and practice is the analytic dimension. The courageous writing of a story of the emergence of these relations is the interpretive dimension. See Vernon K. Robbins, *The Tapestry of Early Christian Discourse: Rhetoric, Society and Ideology* (London/New York: Routledge, 1996) 12, quoting Hubert L. Dreyfus, *Michel Foucault: Beyond Structuralism and Hermeneutics* (2nd ed.; Chicago: University of Chicago Press, 1983) 199.

[18] Vernon K. Robbins, "Conceptual Blending and Early Christian Imagination," in *Explaining Christian Origins and Early Judaism: Contributions from Cognitive and Social Science* (ed. Petri Luomanen, Ilkka Pyysiäinen, and Risto Uro; Biblical Interpretation Series 89; Leiden/Boston: Brill, 2007) 161-95. Online: http://www.religion.emory.edu/faculty/robbins/Pdfs/BlendingFinland2007.pdf.

[19] (New York: Continuum International Publishing Group, 1996).

[20] Online: http://www.religion.emory.edu/faculty/robbins/SRI/index.html.

The long period of gestation for this volume has created an expansive list of people to whom I owe great debts of gratitude. I have felt overwhelmed as I have contemplated how I can properly thank them, and I am certain I will still miss thanking some key people. My gratitude is exceptionally deep to H.J. Bernard Combrink, who welcomed me regularly at the University of Stellenbosch, South Africa, beginning in 1996, wrote programmatic essays applying SRI,[21] and guided Th.D. students in dissertations that used SRI. I must also thank Hendrik Bosman, Elna Mouton, Jan Botha, Johan Thom, and others at the University of Stellenbosch; Charles A. Wanamaker and his students at nearby University of Capetown; Gerhard van den Heever, Johannes N. Vorster, and colleagues at UNISA; and colleagues and friends at the University of Pretoria.

Beyond this, I owe a great debt of thanks and appreciation:

To David B. Gowler, who spearheaded the Festschrift,[22] along with the devoted support of L. Gregory Bloomquist and Duane F. Watson, and organized the SBL session in Atlanta in 2003 that celebrated the volume, as well as the wonderful banquet at the Abbey Restaurant afterwards. They are extraordinary friends and true professionals.

To Robert von Thaden for his expert help first as my Teaching Assistant and then as my Research Assistant during the last years of his Ph.D. program at Emory University. Many portions of this volume are deeply indebted to his expert work with library resources, as well as his outstanding dissertation using Conceptual Blending/Integration Theory.[23]

To Bart B. Bruehler not only for his exceptional use of social-spatial theory in his Ph.D. dissertation,[24] but also for his remarkable ability to critique the ongoing research of fellow students and other colleagues.

To those who participated in our monthly research sessions on SRI at Emory during 2005-2007: Rob, Bart, David Armstrong-Reiner, Juan Hernandez, and Mary R. Huie-Jolly. They helped to create a lively, cordial, and highly productive scholarly environment.

To colleagues at the *Helsinki Collegium for Advanced Studies*, Finland, who invited me to give a paper at the international symposium on "Body, Mind, and Society in Early Christianity," in August-September, 2005. This allowed me to formulate a systematic statement

[21] Online: http://www.religion.emory.edu/faculty/robbins/SRS/Combrink/index.htm.

[22] *Fabrics of Discourse: Essays in Honor of Vernon K. Robbins* (ed. D.B. Gowler, L.G. Bloomquist, and D.F. Watson; Harrisburg/London/New York: Trinity Press International, 2003).

[23] Robert von Thaden, "Fleeing *Porneia*: 1 Corinthians 6:12–7:7 and the Reconfiguration of Traditions," Ph.D. dissertation, Emory University, 2007.

[24] Bart B. Bruehler, "The Public, the Political, and the Private: The Literary and Social-Spatial Functions of Luke 18:35–19:48," Ph.D. dissertation, Emory University, 2007.

of my thinking about conceptual blending and first century Christian discourse at a strategic time in the project.[25]

To Gordon D. Newby, my trustworthy friend and deeply committed colleague, with whom I co-taught the Introduction to Sacred Texts at Emory from 1994 until 2007.

To Laurie L. Patton as an ongoing supporter of my life and work both as Chair of the Department of Religion and co-teacher along with Gordon Newby and me from 1997 until 2000.

To Dana Odwazny, who designed Power Points for learning SRI with support from the SIRE program in Emory College, along with William S. Bradford who took the project further by integrating audio into them as well. Their work in succession has made an outstanding contribution that is being enjoyed by current students and others who find these tools for learning on the web site.

To my former students Russell B. Sisson and Wesley H. Wachob, who bring me joy every time they call.

To Roy R. Jeal, who has become a special friend through our early morning walks during the regular meetings of the RRA.

To special graduate students at St. Paul University, Ottawa: Olu Jerome Megbelayin, Priscilla Geisterfer, Tete Delali (Eloi) Gunn, Alexandra Gruca-Macaulay, Gaetane Forget, Francois Beyrouti, Timothy Beech, and others whose names are beyond my reach at the moment.

To an especially energetic group of RRA members during its most recent phase: Fredrick J. Long, Dennis Sylva, Robert L. Webb, Richard S. Ascough, B.J. Oropeza, and Robert Hall; they pushed me to ever greater clarity and understanding.

To Emory University as a context for my ongoing work, including Dean Robert Paul and the current Chair of the Department, Gary Laderman; and to the many students at the college, M.A., and Ph.D. levels who have participated and/or assisted with energy and purpose in classes I have taught, and have written various kinds of papers. This includes faculty and staff in the Department and Graduate Division of Religion, colleagues in the Department of Middle Eastern and South Asian Studies, and special contributions by Antoinette Denapoli, Abbas Barzegar, Tony Olimpio, Meghan Henning, and Thomas Fabisiak. All of these people together make a treasured environment for my life and work.

[25] "Conceptual Blending and Early Christian Imagination," in *Explaining Christian Origins and Early Judaism: Contributions from Cognitive and Social Science* (ed. Petri Luomanen, Ilkka Pyysiäinen, and Risto Uro; Biblical Interpretation Series 89; Leiden/Boston: Brill, 2007) 161–95. Online: http://www.religion.emory.edu/faculty/robbins/Pdfs/Blending Finland2007.pdf.

Extraordinary thanks to Brandon Wason for work beyond proper measure on the indices for this volume, plus many other editorial matters.

Many thanks to David E. Orton and his staff at Deo Publishing for ongoing support and encouragement which is very much appreciated.

Special gratitude to people at Central Presbyterian Church, Atlanta, and the Decatur-Dekalb YMCA, with special mention of John and Anne Huss, Jack and Jo Alice Halsell, Gary Charles, the John Nix family, Carol Pitts, Betty Bolander, Morgan, Eley, Rick, Bernard, Charles, Stacey, Bill, Safiyah, Panos, Jerry, Parthi, Lisa, the Wallace Nelms family, our Nicola's community of friends, and many others too numerous to mention here, but which also must include Nancy Baxter, for their expressions of love and support.

Beyond all words, I thank my dear wife Deanna and our immediate family: Rick, Chimene, Michael, Nicholas, Sophia, and Anastasia, to whom I dedicate this volume.

And just to be complete, I should not omit all who have smiled while looking generally in my direction, greeted me with a kind word, nodded approvingly, thought of me positively, or in any other way have shown their support during the writing of this volume!

All Saints Day, 2008
Atlanta, GA

Glossary

For further definition and discussion of terms, see Vernon K. Robbins, *Exploring the Texture of Texts* (New York: Continuum, 1996) and *The Tapestry of Early Christian Discourse* (New York/London: Routledge, 1996). Online, see the Dictionary of Socio-Rhetorical Terms: http://www.religion.emory.edu/faculty/robbins/SRI/defns/

Apocalyptic rhetorolect: One of six major first century Christian **rhetorolects**, alternatively called belief systems or forms of life, which is a localization of Mediterranean visual **mantic** (divine communication) **discourse**. Apocalyptic rhetorolect blends human experiences of the emperor and his imperial army (**firstspace**) with God's heavenly temple city (**secondspace**), which can only be occupied by holy, undefiled people. In the space of blending, God functions like a heavenly emperor who gives commands to emissaries to destroy all evil in the universe and create a cosmic environment where holy bodies experience perfect well-being in the presence of God. A primary goal of the blending is to call people into action and thought guided by perfect holiness (**thirdspace**). Apocalyptic redemption, therefore, means the presence of all of God's holy beings in a realm where God's holiness and righteousness are completely and eternally present.

Argumentative texture: see **Rhetology**

Blending, Conceptual: A process of conceptual mapping and integration through which humans develop emergent structure in their minds that is related to creative products of thinking. Presupposing that people think by integrating individual items and vital relations through cross-mapping from different domains of thought, cognitive scientists who work with this theory begin with a presupposition that a mental space is a small conceptual packet assembled for purposes of thought and action (Gilles Fauconnier and Mark Turner, *The Way We Think: Conceptual Blending and the Mind's Hidden Complexities* [New York:

Basic Books, 2002]). Through analysis and interpretation of inputs into mental spaces, they reach a conclusion that a conceptual integration network connects an array of mental spaces in the mind. From their perspective, a conceptual integration network contains one or more blended or integrated mental spaces. One of the special emphases is that the blended or integrated spaces develop emergent structure that is not available from the inputs that go into the blended, integrated space.

Critical Spatiality Theory (CST): A special form of cultural geography studies that guides sociorhetorical interpreters as they study the relation of the geophysical places people experience (**firstspace**) to the mental spaces humans create and manipulate in their minds (**secondspace**) to understand and give order to their experiences throughout life (**thirdspace**). The work of Edward Soja on firstspace, secondspace, and thirdspace is currently of particular importance for **SRI** in relation to conceptual **blending** and integration (Jon L. Berquist and Claudia V. Camp (eds.), *Constructions of Space I: Theory, Geography, and Narrative* [New York/London: T. & T. Clark, 2007]).

Eisegesis: see **Exegesis**

Enthymeme, enthymematic-argumentative structure: argumentation from sure assumptions of social and cultural reasoning, which are probable assumptions considered to be likelihoods. **SRI** regularly displays the inductive-deductive-abductive structure of enthymematic argumentation by identifying Rule, Case, Result, rather than Major Premise, Minor Premise, Conclusion characteristic of the syllogism in formal logic.

Exegesis: The term regularly used for "higher critical" interpretation that keeps its focus on "leading" [-*egesis*] ideas "out of" [*ex*] a text that are in the text itself, rather than on reading one's own ideas "into" [*eis*] a text (*eisegesis*).

Firstspace: A concept within **critical spatiality theory** (**CST**) in which experienced spaces, locations, and situations are primary spaces in which people develop and perpetuate special pictures and memories in their minds. See **Secondspace**; **Thirdspace**.

ICM (Idealized Cognitive Model): A complex structured whole, a gestalt (see **Rhetorolect**), which uses four kinds of structuring principles: (1) propositional structure, in **SRI** called argumentative-enthymematic structure (see **Enthymeme**; **Rhetology**); (2) image-schematic structure, in SRI called descriptive-narrative structure (see **Rhetography**); (3) **metaphoric mappings**; and (4) **metonymic mappings** (George Lakoff, *Women, Fire, and Dangerous Things: What Categories Reveal about the Mind* [Chicago: University of Chicago Press, 1987]).

Ideological texture: The particular alliances and conflicts nurtured and evoked by the language of a text, the language of interpretations of a text, and the way a text itself and interpreters of the text position themselves in relation to other individuals and groups. The four sub-textures of ideological **texture** are the individual locations of writers and readers, i.e., their presuppositions, dispositions, and values; relationships to groups, in which membership influences readers and writers; modes of intellectual discourse, which provide the particular perspective readers follow as they raise questions and set boundaries around their readings; and spheres of ideology, which concern the particular points of view inscribed in a text that invite people to analyze it in particular ways.

Inner texture: The various ways a text employs language to communicate. This includes various types of linguistic patterns within a text (progressive and repetitive **textures**); structural elements of a text (narrational and opening-middle-closing textures); the specific ways a text attempts to persuade its readers (**argumentative texture**); and the ways the language of a text evokes feelings, emotions, or senses that are located in different parts of the body (sensory-aesthetic texture).

Integration, Conceptual: see **Blending, Conceptual**

Interpretive analytics: An approach to texts as discourse, in which discourse is part of a larger field of power and practice whose relations are articulated in different ways by different paradigms. The rigorous establishment of the relations of power and practice is the analytic dimension. The courageous writing of a story of the emergence of these relations is the interpretive dimension.

Intertexture: A text's representation of, reference to, and use of phenomena in the world outside the text being interpreted. This world includes other texts (oral-scribal intertexture); other cultures (cultural intertexture); social roles, institutions, codes, and relationships (social intertexture); and historical events or places (historical intertexture).

Invention: The **topical**, figurative (**rhetography**), and argumentative resources (**rhetology**) people use to create their speech, action, and thought.

Mantic discourse: A form of speech, thought, and belief focused on divine communication to humans. In the Mediterranean world, mantic discourse featured oracles, spoken and interpreted by mediums, and visions told to people for the purpose of communicating divine messages that regularly required interpretation because their contents could be understood in different ways with different results. See **Apocalyptic rhetorolect**; **Prophetic rhetorolect**.

Metaphor, metaphoric mapping: The transporting of aspects of one conceptual domain to another conceptual domain. Many cognitive scientists now think human cognition at its foundations is metaphorical, namely through cross-mapping between conceptual domains humans create language, establish complex social structures and relationships, initiate and perpetuate cultural frames of understanding, and participate **ideologically** in life.

Metonym, metonymic mapping: Using one well-understood or easy-to-perceive aspect of something to stand either for the thing as a whole or for some other aspect or part of it. An example could be to say, "We need a faster glove on third base," when the person means they need a person who can more quickly catch a baseball that has been hit and throw the ball to first base to put the batter out. In the study of first century Christianity, a writer may use the term "resurrection" to refer to an entire system of **apocalyptic** thinking whereby God raises people from death to life as a way of transporting them from "this age," which is dominated by evil and wickedness, into "the coming age," which will be governed by God's goodness, righteousness, and holiness.

Miracle rhetorolect: One of six major first century Christian **rhetorolects**, alternatively called belief systems or forms of life, which is a localization of Mediterranean healing **ritual discourse**. First century Christian miracle rhetorolect has a primary focus on human bodies afflicted with paralysis, malfunction, or disease. In this context, a malfunctioning body becomes a site of social geography. Miracle belief features a bodily agent of God's power who renews and restores life, producing forms of new creation that oppose powers of affliction, disruption, and death. The location of importance for early Christian miracle belief, therefore, is a space of relation between an afflicted body and a bodily agent of God's power (**firstspace**). In this belief system, social, cultural, political, or religious places on earth are simply places where bodies may be. A bodily agent of God's power, wherever it may be, is a location where God can function as a miraculous renewer of life (**secondspace**). A major goal of miracle belief is to effect extraordinary renewal within people that moves them toward speech and action that produces communities that care for the well-being of one another (**thirdspace**).

Multistability: A rich dimension of discourse in which hearers, readers, and interpreters understand assertions within a range of conceptual systems. The context of meanings and meaning effects does not lead to instability, namely a completely disordered range of possibilities for understanding. Rather, the rhetorical effect of multistability is to introduce a multiple range of relationships among persons, objects, and places that create contexts for lively discussion, debate, and disagreement concerning the particular cultural frame or frames of understanding that should be accepted as guides to understanding.

Philosophy, **Philosophical discourse**: Speaking and writing that investigates, teaches, and aims to guide people to live according to wisdom. Two major streams are moral philosophy (**wisdom** based on the visible world) and speculative philosophy (belief systems based on invisible phenomena like primordial things, **precreation**).

Politics of invitation: Inviting people into conversation and debate over interpretation of texts and other cultural artifacts, with a presupposition that the people invited into the conversation will contribute significantly alternative insights as a result of their particular experiences, identities, and concerns.

Precreation rhetorolect: One of six major first century Christian **rhetorolects**, alternatively called belief systems or forms of life, which is a localization of Mediterranean speculative **philosophy**. Precreation rhetorolect interprets the invisible, while wisdom rhetorolect (a localization of moral philosophy) interprets the visible world. Precreation rhetorolect blends human experiences of divine emperors (like Roman emperors) and their households, which people hear about but often do not see (**firstspace**) with God's cosmos (**secondspace**). A special presupposition in this **blending** is that God has an eternal, primordial status as a loving heavenly emperor with a household and community populated by loving people. The result of this blending is the presence of the loving Emperor Father God in God's heavenly household before all time and continually throughout God's non-time. God's Son existed with God during non-time before time began with the creation of the world. This eternal Son does what His Father asks him to do, and heirs and friends of the eternal emperor and his eternal son receive eternal benefits from their relation to this eternal household and community. In the space of blending (**thirdspace**), people establish relationships with the love of God the eternal heavenly Emperor Father by believing, honoring, and worshipping not only God but also his eternal Son. Precreation belief, then, features love that is the source of all things in the world and the means by which people may enter into God's eternal love. In this belief system, God's light is embodied love that provides the possibility for entering into eternal love, rather than being limited to light in the form of wisdom that is the basis for the production and reproduction of goodness and righteousness. The goal of the blending in precreation belief is to guide people towards community that is formed through God's love, which reflects the eternal intimacy present in God's precreation household and community.

Priestly rhetorolect: One of six major first century Christian **rhetorolects**, alternatively called belief systems or forms of life, which is a localization of Mediterranean sacrificial and mystery ritual discourse. First century Christian priestly belief blends human experiences in sacrificial and mystery temples (**firstspace**) with a concept of God's cosmos and temple city (**secondspace**). In the space of **blending** (**thirdspace**), people enact rituals that are perceived to activate special benefits for humans from God. Things like food, possessions, and money but also things like comfort and honor may be given up to God in ritual actions. Some of these things may be given to God by giving them to other people on earth, or by allowing other people to take things like honor or fame away without protest. The greatest offering people can give to God, of course, is their entire life. Much early Christian priestly belief somehow relates to Jesus' giving of his life on the cross, but other dimensions of it relate to entering into the mysteries of God through prayer, blessing, singing, and praise. The goal of the conceptual blending is to create people who are willing to engage in complex ritual actions to receive special divine benefits that come to them, because these ritual actions are perceived to benefit God as well as humans. In other words, ritual actions by humans create an environment in which God acts redemptively among humans in the world.

Prophetic rhetorolect: One of six major first century Christian **rhetorolects**, alternatively called belief systems or forms of life, which is a localization of Mediterranean oracular **mantic** (divine communication) **discourse**. First century Christian prophetic belief blends experiences in a "kingdom" that has political boundaries on earth (**firstspace**) with God's cosmos (**secondspace**), with the presupposition that God transmits God's will in special ways into the speech and action of prophets. The reasoning in the belief system presupposes that the prophet has received a divine message about God's will. The prophet speaks and acts in contexts that envision righteous judgments and actions by kings, who should be God's leaders who establish justice on the earth. As a result of the nature of God's message, the prophet regularly experiences significant resistance, and often explicit rejection and persecution. In the space of **blending** (**thirdspace**), people establish various identities in relation to God as heavenly King over his righteous kingdom on earth. The nature of prophetic belief is to confront religious and political leaders who act on the basis of human greed, pride, and power rather than God's justice, righteousness, and mercy for all people in God's kingdom on the earth. The goal of prophetic belief is to create a governed realm on earth where God's righteousness is enacted among all of God's people in the realm with the aid of God's specially transmitted word in the form of prophetic action and speech (**thirdspace**).

Rhetography: The progressive, sensory-aesthetic, and/or argumentative texture of a text (**rhetology**) that invites a hearer/reader to create a graphic image or picture in the mind that implies a certain kind of truth and/or reality.

Rhetology: The argumentative texture of a text, which makes assertions supported by reasons and rationales; clarified by opposites and contraries; energized by analogies, comparisons, examples (**rhetography**); and confirmed by authoritative testimony in a context either of stated conclusions or of progressive texture that invites a hearer/reader to infer a particular conclusion.

Rhetorolect: Alternatively called a belief system or form of life. A form of language variety or discourse (abbreviation of "rhetorical dialect") identifiable on the basis of a distinctive configuration of themes, images (**rhetography**), **topics**, reasonings, and argumentations (**rhetology**). From the perspective of cognitive science, a rhetorolect is an **idealized cognitive model** (**ICM**). By their nature, rhetorolects blend with one another, interacting like dialects do when people from different dialectical areas converse with one another. The **blending** of rhetorolects in first century Christian discourse created new configurations of speech, belief, thought, and action as the movement grew. Six major rhetorolects are prominent in first Christian discourse: **wisdom**, **prophetic**, **apocalyptic**, **precreation**, **priestly**, and **miracle** discourse. Whatever rhetorolects, belief systems, or forms of life people enact either consciously or unconsciously as speakers, writers, or interpreters, the choice exhibits distinctive socio-rhetorical features of their discourse, beliefs, dispositions, and actions.

Ritual discourse: Speech and writing that describes or directs people to perform a sequence of actions, usually accompanied by speech, considered to evoke beneficial exchange between human beings and divine beings or powers. See **Miracle rhetorolect**; **Priestly rhetorolect**.

Sacred texture: The manner in which a text communicates insights into the relationship between the human and the divine through **inner texture**, **intertexture**, **social and cultural texture**, and **ideological texture**. This texture includes aspects concerning deity, holy persons, spirit beings, divine history, human redemption, human commitment, religious community (e.g., ecclesiology), and ethics.

Secondspace: People's cognitive and conceptual interpretation of geophysical spaces as social, cultural, religious, and **ideological** places. In **SRI**, people's **blending** of geophysical spaces with God's cosmos is a special aspect of secondspace. See **Critical Spatiality Theory**.

Social and cultural texture: The social and cultural nature of a text as a text. The configuration of language in a text evokes a particular view the world (specific social **topics**), participates in general social and cultural attitudes, norms, and modes of interaction known to people at the time of composition of the text (common social and cultural topics) and establishes a relation to the dominant cultural system (final cultural categories), either sharing in its attitudes, values, and dispositions at some level (dominant and subcultural rhetoric) or rejecting these attitudes, values, and dispositions (counterculture, contraculture, and liminal culture rhetoric).

(SRI) Sociorhetorical interpretation: An approach to literature that focuses on values, convictions, and beliefs both in the texts we read and in the world in which we live. It views texts as performances of language in particular historical and cultural situations. The "socio-" refers to the rich resources of modern social, cultural, and cognitive sciences. The "rhetorical" refers to the way language in a text is a means of communication among people. SRI presupposes that a text is a tapestry of interwoven **textures**, including **inner texture**, **intertexture**, **social and cultural texture**, **ideological texture**, and **sacred texture**. A major goal of socio-rhetorical interpretation is to nurture an environment of interpretation that encourages a genuine interest in people who live in contexts with values, norms, and goals different from our own.

Syllogism: see **Enthymeme**.

Texture: Emerging from a metaphor of figuration as weaving, the concept of texture in relation to a text derives from Latin *texere* (to weave) that produces an arrangement of threads in the warp and woof of a fabric. **SRI** extends the metaphor of texture to the metaphor of tapestry, approaching a text as a thick network of meanings and meaning effects that an interpreter can explore by moving through the text from different perspectives. This approach has led to special focus in SRI on **inner texture**, **intertexture**, **social and cultural texture**, **ideological texture**, and **sacred texture** in texts.

Thirdspace: Spaces, places, and situations in which people negotiate their daily lives in ongoing contexts of sensory-aesthetic experiences that are "spaces of blending." In **SRI**, thirdspace is a dynamic space in which readers, interpreters, and writers negotiate possible alternative identities on a daily basis in relation to **firstspaces** and **secondspaces**. See **Blending, Conceptual**; **Critical Spatiality Theory**.

Topos, Topoi (pl.), **Topics:** A place to which an arguer, problem solver, or thinker may mentally go to find arguments. Thus, topoi (plural) are landmarks on the mental geography of thought which themselves evoke a constellation of networks of meanings as a result of social, cultural, or **ideological** use. A topos contains a pictorial dimension, which **SRI** calls its **rhetography**, and an argumentative dimension, which SRI calls its **rhetology**.

Wisdom rhetorolect: One of six major first century Christian **rhetorolects**, alternatively called belief systems or forms of life, which is a localization of Mediterranean moral **philosophy**. Wisdom rhetorolect interprets the visible world, while precreation rhetorolect (a localization of speculative philosophy) interprets the invisible. First century Christian wisdom rhetorolect blends human experiences of the household, one's intersubjective body, and the geophysical world (**firstspace**) with the cultural space of God's cosmos (**secondspace**). In the lived space of **blending** (**thirdspace**), people establish identities in relation to God who functions as heavenly Father over God's children in the world. People perceive their bodies as able to produce goodness and righteousness in the world through the medium of God's wisdom, which is understood as God's light in the world. In this context, wisdom belief emphasizes "fruitfulness" (productivity and reproductivity) in the realm of God's created world.

Introduction: Interpreting the Expressible in Early Christian Discourse

Introduction

The New Testament is remarkably graphic and argumentative at the same time. Verse after verse creates a vivid picture in the mind of the hearer. The pictures create frames of understanding that are highly persuasive to the hearer or reader. In the context of the verbal pictures, the verses regularly contain assertions supported by reasons and rationales beginning with "for," "since," or "because." In addition, the verses present conclusions that begin with words commonly translated as "therefore" or "thus." There have been various attempts to develop a mode of interpretation that investigates and explains the function of this combination of the picturesque and the persuasive in biblical interpretation. Some, for example, consider the term "parable" especially helpful for describing the function of New Testament literature. Others, in turn, consider "metaphor" to be a special mode of thinking that guides New Testament literature and the modes of belief that emerge after it. Still others consider the most appropriate terminology for the combination of picture and argumentation in the New Testament to be "myth."

A Major Problem with Current Rhetorical Interpretation of the New Testament

Rhetorical interpretation holds the promise of analyzing and interpreting the dynamic interrelation of the picturing and argumentation in the New Testament and other early Christian literature. But there is a major problem. Rhetorical interpretation, as it was re-introduced to New Testament interpretation during the last half of the twentieth century used an incorrect picturing of the situations underlying the argumentation in the New Testament. Hans Dieter Betz, Wilhelm Wuellner, and George A. Kennedy, who led the way, all used the classical categories of judicial (forensic), deliberative (symbouletic), and epideictic (demonstrative) rhetoric as the gateway into rhetorical interpretation of the New Testament.[1] The problem is that the picturing of the conventional situations underlying classical rhetoric is incorrect for the conventional situations underlying the rhetoric in the New Testament.

Classical rhetoric pictures the major rhetorical situations in the life of people on the basis of the city-state understood as a city. From the perspective of classical rhetoric, there are three primary settings that guide the training of an orator and that serve the public at large by their skillful contribution to society. The first kind of classical rhetoric envisions the law court, where a judge and a jury make decisions about the guilt or innocence of someone whom a prosecutor says has committed a crime and whom a defendant says is innocent of the charge. The picturing of a law court underlies judicial (or forensic) rhetoric in classical rhetorical interpretation. The goal is to persuade the audience (the judge and jury) to reach a decision of guilty or acquitted. Regularly, this kind of rhetoric is focused on action in the past that someone claims caused improper damage or death and someone else claims was necessary or accidental. The second kind of classical rhetoric envisions the political assembly, where a leader in the city speaks to the gathered population of the city to convince them to take an action like going to war or building a wall around the city. The picturing of a political assembly underlies deliberative (or symbouletic) rhetoric in classical rhetorical interpretation. The goal is to persuade the audience either to take a particular action (like going to war) or not to take a particular action (for example, not going to war). This kind of rhetoric is focused on the future, where people are in a position to make a decision to engage in a particular kind of action, not to engage in that particular action, or to engage in some other kind of action. The third kind of classical rhetoric envisions the civil ceremony, where a speaker delivers a funeral oration or a speech to dedicate the launching of a new ship, the completion of a new harbor, or some other public accomplishment or experience of disaster. The picturing of a civil ceremony underlies epideictic (or demonstrative) rhetoric in classical rhetorical interpretation. The goal is to use praise and blame to address a series of topics in a manner that will confirm and strengthen people's commitment to conventional values of that which is right and wrong, good and bad, acceptable and unacceptable. Hans Dieter Betz, Wilhelm Wuellner, George A. Kennedy, and their contemporaries and successors in Klaus Berger, Robert Jewett, Duane F. Watson, Frank Witt Hughes, Elisabeth Schüssler-Fiorenza, Margaret M. Mitchell, and others have all begun with picturing the alternative underlying situations in New Testament literature from classical rhetoric, which is based on

[1] Duane F. Watson, *The Rhetoric of the New Testament: A Bibliographic Survey* (Tools for Biblical Study series 8; Blandford Forum: Deo Publishing, 2006) 18-53.

conventional social situations in the city-state and subsequently the city in Hellenistic and Roman times.

The problem is that argumentation in the New Testament does not presuppose that the law court, political assembly, and civil ceremony work positively for Christian belief and practice. These conventional social institutions in cities throughout the Roman empire regularly created problems, suffering, conflicts, persecution, imprisonment, and even death for early Christians. To counter these institutions, early Christians developed argumentation that used picturing based on social interaction related to households, political kingdoms, imperial armies, imperial households, temples, and individual bodies of people. This picturing of multiple social situations created Christian rhetorical discourse in the form of wisdom, prophetic, apocalyptic, precreation, priestly, and miracle argumentation during the first century CE. During the second century, Christians began to envision Christianity as a city, and in this context they began to develop discourse of Christian legal decision (judicial rhetoric based on Christian law courts), Christian political action (deliberative rhetoric based on Christian assemblies), and Christian public display of honor and shame (epideictic rhetoric based on Christian public ceremonies). During the third and fourth centuries CE, many Christians were directly appropriating the categories of city-based classical rhetoric. Thus, it is appropriate to use the categories of classical rhetoric for Christian discourse during the third and fourth centuries CE and onwards. It is, however, necessary to blend these categories with the inner workings of wisdom, prophetic, apocalyptic, precreation, priestly, and miracle rhetoric as they developed during the first century CE and continued throughout the centuries until today.

Sociorhetorical Interpretation as an Interpretive Analytic

This book uses rhetorical analysis and interpretation based on both oral and literary dynamics within social, cultural, ideological, and religious contexts of interaction during the first century CE to interpret New Testament literature. The overall scope of the book includes insights that span a period of time from 1000 BCE through the emergence of Islam and the Qur'an during the seventh century CE. The primary focus, however, is on the seventy year period from the death of Jesus (ca. 30 CE) to the end of the first century (100 CE). The traditional name for this mode of interpretation is sociorhetorical interpretation (regularly abbreviated SRI by its proponents).[2] This mode of interpretation began

[2] Ibid., 86–88; Vernon K. Robbins, "Beginnings and Developments in Socio-Rhetorical Interpretation": http://www.religion.emory.edu/faculty/robbins/Pdfs/SRIBegDevRRA.pdf; David B. Gowler, L. Gregory Bloomquist, and Duane F. Watson (eds.), *Fabrics of*

during the last half of the 1970s and was first named in 1984 in my *Jesus the Teacher: A Socio-Rhetorical Interpretation of the Gospel of Mark.*[3]

In many ways, the present book is my way of working with issues that Anthony C. Thiselton introduced to New Testament interpreters in 1980 in the chapters in *The Two Horizons* where he interwove a discussion of the writings of Ludwig Wittgenstein with the writings of Heidegger, Bultmann, and Gadamer.[4] I worked through those chapters in detail in 1985, but my location in a department and graduate division of religion, rather than a department of religion and philosophy, led me to address the heavily philosophical issues through the writings of other colleagues in the field rather than through direct engagement with Thiselton's writings.[5] The present volume is an additional step in addressing the linguistic turn, the pictorial turn, and the embodiment of language that Thiselton continually addresses in the name of hermeneutics in his work.[6]

The immediate goal of the present book is to provide tools, insights, and strategies for commentators to interpret the New Testament as a creative mode of discourse within first century Mediterranean society. In this regard, it is important to know that a key dynamic of sociorhetorical criticism, in contrast to literary-historical-theological methods of the 19th and 20th centuries, is its nature as an interpretive analytic.[7] Sociorhetorical criticism, properly understood and applied, is not a method. A method uses a limited number of analytical strategies for the purpose of reaching a conclusion that is superior to the use of the analytical strategies of another method. The goal of a method is to exclude the analytical strategies of

Discourse: Essays in Honor of Vernon K. Robbins (Harrisburg/London/New York: Trinity Press International, 2003).

[3] Philadelphia: Fortress Press, 1984; pbk, Minneapolis: Fortress Press, 1992. See David B. Gowler, "The Development of Socio-Rhetorical Criticism," in Vernon K. Robbins, *New Boundaries in Old Territory: Form and Social Rhetoric in Mark* (ESEC 3; New York: Peter Lang, 1994) 1-36; online: http://userwww.service.emory.edu/%7Edgowler/chapter.htm. See "Socio-Rhetorical Criticism" in W. Randolph Tate, *Interpreting the Bible: A Handbook of Terms and Methods* (Peabody, MA: Hendrickson, 2006) 342-46.

[4] Anthony C. Thiselton, *The Two Horizons: New Testament Hermeneutics and Philosophical Description* (Grand Rapids, MI: Eerdmans, 1980) 24-47, 357-445.

[5] See, however, Vernon K. Robbins, "Where is Wuellner's Anti-Hermeneutical Hermeneutic Taking Us? From Schleiermacher to Thistleton (sic) and Beyond," in (eds.), *Rhetorics and Hermeneutics* (ed. James D. Hester and J. David Hester; ESEC 9; New York/London: T & T Clark International, 2004) 105-25.

[6] Anthony C. Thiselton, *New Horizons in Hermeneutics: The Theory and Practice of Transforming Biblical Reading* (Grand Rapids, MI: Zondervan, 1992); idem, *Thiselton on Hermeneutics: Collected Works with New Essays* (Grand Rapids, MI/Cambridge, UK: Eerdmans, 2006); idem, *The Hermeneutics of Doctrine* (Grand Rapids, MI/Cambridge, UK: Eerdmans, 2007).

[7] Vernon K. Robbins, *The Tapestry of Early Christian Discourse: Rhetoric, Society and Ideology* (London/New York: Routledge, 1996) 11-17.

another method by using superior strategies for reaching a particular desired and limited goal. An interpretive analytic, in contrast to a method, applies analytical strategies for the purpose of inviting other analytical strategies where those other strategies could illumine something the first set of strategies did not find, exhibit, discuss, and interpret.

In political terms, literary-historical-theological methods apply either a politics of exclusion, with a presupposition that the excluded is inferior, or a politics of inclusion that reduces the identity of those included to an identity that contributes to the point of view of the person applying the strategies of analysis and interpretation. In contrast, a sociorhetorical interpretive analytic applies a politics of invitation, with a presupposition that the people invited into the conversation will contribute significantly new insights as a result of their particular experiences, identities, and concerns. In other words, a sociorhetorical interpretive analytic presupposes genuine team work: people from different locations and identities working together with different cognitive frames for the purpose of getting as much insight as possible on the relation of things to one another.[8]

In the final analysis, then, the difference between a method and an interpretive analytic is philosophical. The philosophy of a method is grounded in a belief that the true nature of something is "in something itself." In contrast, the philosophy of an interpretive analytic is grounded in a belief that the true nature of something is exhibited in the way it relates to all other things. This is a difference between a philosophy of essence or substance and a philosophy of relations.[9] The presupposition underlying the approach in this volume is that while the 19th and 20th centuries benefited immensely from philosophies that guided people toward the particularities of different things, a primary task for the 21st century is to guide people toward a robust understanding of the relation of things to one another. The goal is not, "You are included on my terms," but "You are included on your own terms." This is a difficult philosophy to apply and to fulfill as a result of multiple self-oriented philosophies based on philosophies of essence and

[8] Robbins, "Where is Wuellner's Anti-Hermeneutical Hermeneutic Taking Us?", 105-25.

[9] Vernon K. Robbins, "The Rhetorical Full-Turn in Biblical Interpretation and Its Relevance for Feminist Hermeneutics," in *Her Master's Tools? Feminist and Postcolonial Engagements of Historical-Critical Discourse* (ed. Caroline Vander Stichele and Todd Penner; Global Perspectives on Biblical Scholarship 9; Atlanta: SBL and Leiden: Brill, 2005) 110-14. I am deeply grateful for the insights of my colleague Martin J. Buss, for his insights on relational philosophy; see Martin J. Buss, *Biblical Form Criticism in its Context* (JSOTSup 274; Sheffield: Sheffield Academic Press, 1999) 156-66; idem, *The Concept of Form in the Twentieth Century* (Sheffield: Sheffield Phoenix Press, 2008); Timothy J. Sandoval and Carleen Mandolfo (eds.), *Relating to the Text: Interdisciplinary and Form-Critical Insights on the Bible* (JSOTSup 384; Sheffield: Sheffield Academic Press, 2003).

substance, but it is a goal, we submit, that we must try to emulate in our research, analysis, and interpretations during the 21st century.

A long-range goal of the present book is to provide insights into the ways Christian thinking, reasoning, and believing work internally and in relation to other kinds of thinking, reasoning, and believing. The immediate data, therefore, is the New Testament literature in its Mediterranean context during the first century. Regularly, however, the discussion concerns the entire Bible, Jewish and Hellenistic-Roman literature outside the Bible at the time of the emergence of Christianity, and Christian tradition down through the seventh century, when some people and topics of New Testament tradition were presented dynamically in the official version of the Qur'an overseen by Muhammad's secretary Zayd b. Thâbit and authorized by the caliph 'Uthmân.[10] All of this data will help us to understand the nature of Christian discourse both in the context of its emergence during the first century of the Christian era and in the context of its relation to other discourse.

A basic presupposition of the approach is that although first century Christians lived in a culture we regularly describe as "traditional," they found ways to weave new dimensions into existing modes of Mediterranean discourse. The study concludes that early Christians reconfigured multiple forms of preceding and contemporary discourse by blending pictorial narrative with argumentative assertions in ways that created distinctive social, cultural, ideological, and religious modes of understanding and belief in the Mediterranean world. This book moves beyond *The Tapestry of Early Christian Discourse* and *Exploring the Texture of Texts*,[11] therefore, by focusing on sociorhetorical analysis and interpretation of conventional forms of discourse. The previous two books presented strategies for interpreting the inner texture, intertexture, social and cultural texture, ideological texture, and sacred texture of texts without raising the issue of conventional form. The purpose was to organize sociorhetorical strategies of analysis and interpretation in a manner that showed their relationship to one another and encouraged people to use them in programmatic ways to perform sociorhetorical exegesis.[12] As the

[10] See "Qur'ân" in Gordon D. Newby, *A Concise Encyclopedia of Islam* (Oxford: Oneworld, 2002) 178–80.

[11] Vernon K. Robbins, *The Tapestry of Early Christian Discourse: Rhetoric, Society and Ideology* (London and New York: Routledge, 1996); idem, *Exploring the Texture of Texts: A Guide to Socio-Rhetorical Interpretation* (Harrisburg, PA: Trinity Press International, 1996).

[12] Exegesis is the term regularly used for "higher critical" interpretation that keeps its focuses on phenomena "in" the text itself (thus, leading [-*egesis*] ideas "out of" [*ex*] the text on the basis of what is in the text), rather than on reading one's own ideas "into" the text (*eisegesis*). Sociorhetorical interpretation is intentionally designed to keep interpreters exegetically focused as they analyze and interpret multiple textures of a text.

analysis and interpretation proceeded, different but interrelated socio-rhetorical modes of early Christian discourse began to appear.

Rhetorical Dialects (Rhetorolects) in Early Christian Discourse

The special terminology this book uses for different forms of conventional discourse is "rhetorolect" (pronounced rhetórolect). This term is a contraction of "rhetorical dialect." A rhetorolect or rhetorical dialect is "a form of language variety or discourse identifiable on the basis of a distinctive configuration of themes, topics, reasonings, and argumentations."[13] The primary thesis of this book is that six conventional modes of discourse (rhetorolects) – wisdom, prophetic, apocalyptic, precreation, priestly, and miracle – contributed dynamically to the creativity in early Christian speaking and writing.[14] Early Christians blended these rhetorolects into one another in the three literary modes contained in the New Testament: biographical historiography (Gospels and Acts), epistle, and apocalypse (Revelation to John). These six rhetorolects began to appear when sociorhetorical interpreters expanded their area of focus to the entire New Testament, beyond simply the letters of Paul, the Gospels, and the Acts of the Apostles, which were the focus of earlier rhetorical interpreters. Different narrational patterns blend with different argumentative strategies in wisdom, prophetic, apocalyptic, precreation, priestly, and miracle rhetorolect. Gradually the conclusion has emerged that six rhetorolects functioned as prototypical modes of discourse that assisted early Christians in their energetic work of creating dynamic, adaptable, and persuasive modes of discourse within Mediterranean society and culture.[15] Other modes of discourse beyond

[13] Vernon K. Robbins, "The Dialectical Nature of Early Christian Discourse," *Scriptura* 59 (1996) 353-62, online: http://www.religion.emory.edu/faculty/robbins/dialect/dialect353.html; idem, "Argumentative Textures in Socio-Rhetorical Interpretation," in *Rhetorical Argumentation in Biblical Texts* (ed. A. Eriksson, T.H. Olbricht, and W. Übelacker; ESEC 8; Harrisburg: Trinity Press International, 2002) 356; cf. M.M. Bakhtin, "The Problem of Speech Genres," in M.M. Bakhtin, *Speech Genres and Other Late Essays* (trans. V.W. McGee; ed. C. Emerson and M. Holquist; Austin: University of Texas Press, 1986) 60-102, esp. 78-84.

[14] Robbins, "The Dialectical Nature," 27-65.

[15] Insights from the chapter entitled "Lexicon Rhetoricae" in Kenneth Burke, *Counter-Statement* (Berkeley: University of California Press, 1968, c1931) 123-83 have guided sociorhetorical interpretation from its beginnings; see Vernon K. Robbins, *Jesus the Teacher: A Socio-Rhetorical Interpretation of Mark* (Minneapolis: Fortress Press, 1992, c1984) 5-12. The special focus on six conventional modes of discourse in early Christianity emerged through use of insights from Burke, *Counter-Statement*, pp. 124-130 in a comparative environment of interpretation that has included Hebrew Bible, Old Testament Apocrypha and Pseudepigrapha, Hellenistic Jewish writings, Qumran literature, New Testament Apocrypha, Mishnah, *Pirke de Rabbi Eliezer*, Hellenistic Roman literature, and the Qur'an. Additional Muslim, Hindu, and Buddhist sacred texts also have

these six were indisputably at work in first century Christian discourse. The thesis of these two volumes is that at least these six functioned as primary modes of discourse during the first seventy years (30-100 CE) of the existence of Christianity. Perhaps other interpreters will gather evidence to suggest that one or more additional modes of discourse also were primary. The burden of proof for these two volumes will be that at least the six modes identified above functioned in a primary manner during the first century and contributed to the more complex speech genres that emerged in the subsequent centuries.[16]

One of the special goals of sociorhetorical interpretation is to nurture a "full-body" mode of interpretation, rather than to continue a tradition of body-mind dualism in interpretation. Special focus on the body has drawn attention to different experiences of the body in different geo-physical places in the six rhetorolects. This has led to the use of two recent theories that give special insight into the ways in which humans experience places where they live and blend their experiences with their thinking and reasoning. First, critical spatiality theory, a special form of cultural geography studies, guides sociorhetorical interpretation of the relation of the geophysical places people experience with the mental spaces humans create and manipulate to understand and give order to their experiences throughout life.[17] Second, conceptual blending theory (alternatively called conceptual integration theory),[18] guided by conceptual metaphor theory grounded in empirical findings in cognitive science,[19] guides sociorhetorical interpretation of the blending of the six rhetorolects in early Christian writings. In other words, these two theories help sociorhetorical interpreters give a new account of unity and diversity in early Christian life and discourse. In turn, this account creates the opportunity to describe and understand

played a comparative role as a result of team teaching since the middle 1990s with Professors Gordon D. Newby and Laurie L. Patton.

[16] For a discussion of primary and secondary speech genres, cf. Bakhtin, *Speech Genres*, 60-63.

[17] The most immediate source for critical spatiality theory is the online site maintained by James W. Flanagan and Jon L. Berquist: http://www.cwru.edu/affil/GAIR/Constructions/Constructions.html. See a sociorhetorical use of cultural geography theory in Bart B. Bruehler, "The Public, the Political, and the Private: The Literary and Social-Spatial Functions of Luke 18:35–19:48," Ph.D. dissertation, Emory University, 2007.

[18] G. Fauconnier and M. Turner, *The Way We Think: Conceptual Blending and the Mind's Hidden Complexities* (New York: Basic Books, 2002). For conceptual blending interpretation in a sociorhetorical framework, see Robert von Thaden, "Fleeing *Porneia*: 1 Corinthians 6:12–7:7 and the Reconfiguration of Traditions," Ph.D. dissertation, Emory University, 2007. Also Vernon K. Robbins, "Conceptual Blending and Early Christian Imagination," in *Explaining Christian Origins and Early Judaism: Contributions from Cognitive and Social Science* (ed. Petri Luomanen, Ilkka Pyysiäinen, and Risto Uro; Biblical Interpretation Series 89; Leiden/Boston: Brill, 2007) 161-95.

[19] George Lakoff and Mark Johnson, "Afterword, 2003," in idem, *Metaphors We Live By* (2nd ed.; Chicago/London: University of Chicago Press, 2003) 243-76.

Christian life and discourse in subsequent centuries, including the present day, in substantively new ways.

Orality and the Body in Early Christian Discourse

Attention to a full-body mode of interpretation has made it necessary to begin with the sounds that came out of the mouths of people who spoke about the speech, action, and thought of Jesus of Nazareth during the first centuries of the Common Era. The sounds people produced in contexts where they made gestures and other movements of the body evoked meanings that the discourse conveys through narrational procedures focused on action and speech in time and space. The focus on the sounds exhibits itself in the use of "rhet-" words throughout this volume. The Greek root "*rhēt-*" refers to that which is expressible, i.e., that which can be communicated by being stated.[20] People who believed that Jesus was the Messiah began with "expressible language" (*rhētē glōssa*), "utterance" in M.M. Bakhtin's terminology,[21] to describe the ways in which they considered Jesus to be special. The field of study that specializes in analysis and interpretation of "the expressible," i.e., expressive language in a concrete utterance, is rhetoric.[22] Thus, the field of rhetorical studies is foundational for the full-body sociorhetorical approach that guides this volume.

At present, many inquiries in the field of early Christian studies are dominated by attention to printed words and historical objects, without significant attention to the sounds people articulated as they gestured and moved their bodies in space and time to communicate their attitudes, hopes, fears, beliefs, and arguments. With the aid of multiple efforts, interpretation attentive to the oral activity of early Christians has begun to move toward the center of the field.[23] Once interpreters began to focus on

[20] See the "*rhēt-*" words in Polybius, *Histories* 32.6.7 (to give a stated [*rhētēn*] answer); Plato, *Theatetus* 205d, 205e (syllables are expressible [*rhētai*]); *Epistles* 341c (subject matter that admits of verbal expression [*rhēton*]), 341d (things which can be stated [*rhēta*]).

[21] Bakhtin, *Speech Genres*, 84-102.

[22] Patricia Bizzell and Bruce Herzberg, eds., *The Rhetorical Tradition:Readings from Classical Times to the Present* (Boston : Bedford Books of St. Martin's Press, 1990).

[23] Werner Kelber, *The Oral and Written Gospel* (Philadelphia: Fortress, 1983); idem, "Jesus and Tradition: Words in Time, Words in Space," *Semeia* 65 (1994) 139-67; Paul Achtemeier, "Omnes verbum sonat: The New Testament and the Oral Environment of Late Western Antiquity," *JBL* 109 (1990) 3-27; Ian Henderson, "Didache and Orality in Synoptic Comparison," *JBL* 111 (1992) 283-306; John Miles Foley, *The Theory of Oral Composition, History and Methodology, Folkloristics* (Bloomington: Indiana University Press, 1988); idem, *The Singer of Tales in Performance* (Bloomington: Indiana University Press, 1995); Joanna Dewey (ed.), *Orality and Textuality in Early Christian Literature* (Semeia 65; Atlanta, GA: Scholars Press, 1994); Richard A. Horsley and Jonathan A. Draper, *Whoever Hears You Hears Me: Prophets, Performance, and Tradition in Q* (Harrisburg: Trinity Press

the orality of early Christian discourse, a major challenge emerged to overcome an artificial division between "the living oral tradition" and "the dead written tradition."[24] Rhetorical studies have helped us to understand the difference between an "oral culture" and a "rhetorical culture."[25] People in an oral culture have never seen their language written with signs, like an alphabet. For them, their "language" is a sequence of sounds. People in a rhetorical culture, in contrast, know that "writings" exist, even if they themselves depend completely on sounds for their communication. Early Christians were aware that writings existed. This knowledge of writing means they lived in a rhetorical rather than oral culture. When people spoke, they often referred to written speech, and on occasion they recited written speech. When people wrote, they regularly composed oral speech that they attributed to various people, and they imitated oral speech in their own narration. Extensive portions of the Gospels and Acts are exercises in producing oral speech in written form.[26] In addition, it is likely that Paul spoke his letters, and one or more scribes composed written communication out of his oral speech.[27] When these written compositions were transported to various communities, people in those contexts read Paul's letters to people who gathered to hear them. Even the Gospels and Acts would have been experienced by people orally as a person performed a written composition in their midst.[28] The Revelation to John explicitly presupposes that the people who receive blessing from it will receive blessing in a context where it is read aloud (Rev 1:3).[29] Overall, the NT writings emerged in a context where people knew that writings existed, even if

International, 1999); Jonathan A. Draper (ed.), *Orality, Literacy, and Colonialism in Antiquity* (Semeia Studies; Atlanta: SBL, 2004); idem (ed.), *Orality, Literacy, and Colonialism in Southern Africa* (Semeia Studies; Atlanta: SBL, 2004); Richard A. Horsley (ed.), *Oral Performance, Popular Tradition, and Hidden Transcript in Q* (Semeia Studies 60; Atlanta: SBL, 2006).

[24] Kelber's initial book promulgated a view that living discourse died when it was written down, but Kelber himself has gradually revised this point of view.

[25] Vernon K. Robbins, "Oral, Rhetorical, and Literary Cultures: A Response," *Semeia* 65 (1994) 75-91.

[26] Vernon K. Robbins, "Interfaces of Orality and Literature in the Gospel of Mark," in *Performing the Gospel: Orality, Memory, and Mark* (ed. R.A. Horsley, J.A. Draper, and J.M. Foley; Minneapolis: Fortress Press, 2006) 125-46; idem, "Oral Performance in Q: Epistemology, Political Conflict, and Contextual Register," in Horsley, *Oral Performance*, 109-122.

[27] Pieter J.J. Botha, "Living Voice and Lifeless Letters: Reserve towards Writing in the Greco-Roman World," *Hervormde Teologiese Studies* 49 (1993) 742-59; idem, "The Social Dynamics of the Early Transmission of the Jesus Tradition," *Neot* 27 (1993) 205-31; idem, "The Verbal Art of the Pauline Letters: Rhetoric, Performance and Presence," in *Rhetoric and the New Testament: Essays from the 1992 Heidelberg Conference* (ed. S.E. Porter and T.H. Olbricht; Sheffield: JSOT Press) 409-28.

[28] Whitney Shiner, *Proclaiming the Gospel: First-Century Performance of Mark* (Harrisburg, PA: Trinity Press International, 2003); ibid., "Memory Technology and the Gospel of Mark," in Horsley, Draper, and Foley, *Performing the Gospel,* 147-65.

[29] According to Rev 1:3, both those who read the words aloud will be blessed and those who hear the words and do them.

they could neither read nor write, and where a majority of people created new compositions by dynamically interrelating oral and written discourse, whether they were speaking or writing.

It is important, then, to approach early Christian writings as compositions that emerged in contexts where orality was dynamically at work in practices of writing. This is such a daunting task that Bernard Brandon Scott and Margaret Dean started a program of "sound mapping" of early Christian literature for the purpose of "ear training" that might allow interpreters to appropriate at least some insights that can inform our work.[30] It is necessary to perform various exercises with the New Testament writings to draw as closely as possible to them as compositions that have not gone through the stages of modern production of books, magazines, newspapers, and newsletters.

Another dimension that must inform a full-body mode of interpretation is the social, cultural, ideological, and religious geography of early Christian discourse. The sounds early Christians produced in contexts of gestures and movements of the body occurred not simply in "natural" geographical locations but in places formed and nurtured as social, cultural, ideological, and religious spaces. This requires extensive use of the social sciences in the context of rhetorical analysis and interpretation[31] and particular use of the tools of "critical spatiality theory" and "conceptual blending theory" referred to above (nn. 17-19). Many guidelines for use of the social sciences in sociorhetorical interpretation are present in the chapters on social, cultural, and ideological texture in *The Tapestry of Early Christian Discourse* and *Exploring the Texture of Texts*.[32] Additional guidelines emerge in this volume.

The reconceptualization of early Christian culture as a rhetorical culture with multiple social, cultural, and ideological contexts has deep ramifications for our work. Averil Cameron has helped to pave the way for our work with her Sather Lectures published in 1991. She reveals in

[30] Bernard Brandon Scott and Margaret E. Dean, "A Sound Mapping of the Sermon on the Mount," in *Treasures New and Old: Contributions to Matthean Studies* (ed. D.R. Baur & M.A. Powell; SBLSS 1; Atlanta: Scholars Press, 1996) 311-78; C. Clifton Black and Duane F. Watson (eds.), *Words Well Spoken: George Kennedy's Rhetoric of the New Testament* (Waco: Baylor University Press, 2008); Margaret E. Dean, "The Grammar of Sound in Greek Texts: Toward a Method for Mapping the Echoes of Speech in Writing," *Australian Biblical Review* 44 (1996) 53-70.

[31] John H. Elliott, *What Is Social-Scientific Criticism?* (Minneapolis: Fortress Press, 1993); Bruce J. Malina, *The New Testament World: Insights from Cultural Anthropology* (Revised edition; Louisville: Westminster/John Knox Press, 1993); Jerome H. Neyrey (ed.), *The Social World of Luke-Acts: Models for Interpretation* (Peabody, MA: Hendrickson, 1991); David A. deSilva, *Honor, Patronage, Kinship & Purity: Unlocking New Testament Culture* (Downers Grove, IL: InterVarsity Press, 2000).

[32] Robbins, *Tapestry*, 144-236; idem, *Exploring*, 71-119.

her opening words that she understands the deep relation of spoken and written discourse to historical interpretation:

> It is no longer a novelty to hold that societies have characteristic discourses or "plots," or that the development and control of a given discourse may provide a key to social power, or even that an inquiry into the dissemination of knowledge by oral or written means ought to be high on the agenda for historians.[33]

To this she adds:

> Finding suitable terminology is difficult. Rather than a single Christian discourse, there was rather a series of overlapping discourses always in a state of adaptation and adjustment, and always ready to absorb in a highly opportunistic manner whatever might be useful from secular rhetoric and vocabulary.[34]

The topic of the book you are reading is the earliest period of the creation of these overlapping discourses by early Christians. In rhetorical terms, this means that the book focuses on the "invention" of early Christian discourse. The term invention is used here in its technical rhetorical sense: the topical, figurative, and argumentative resources early Christians used to create their speech, action, and thought.[35]

In a book entitled *Dying for God*, Daniel Boyarin has taken additional steps that help us to conceptualize the issues more deeply. He begins by exploring relationships between Judaism and Christianity in terms of "family resemblance as a semantic, logical category."[36] He proposes a "wave theory of Christian-Jewish history," built on an assumption that "an innovation takes place at a certain location and then spreads like a wave from that site to others, almost in the fashion of a stone thrown into a pond."[37] In the terms of Bakhtin, humans use discourses in ways that send them centrifugally out from local contexts into multiple contexts throughout inhabited regions of the world.[38]

As Boyarin sets the stage for his analysis and interpretation, he recites and interprets an account in the Babylonian Talmud that his teacher, Professor Saul Lieberman, had connected with the well-known talmudic story of the excommunication of Rabbi Eli'ezer. The story is as follows:

> On that day, Rabbi Eli'ezer used every imaginable argument, but they did

[33] Averil Cameron, *Christianity and the Rhetoric of Empire: The Development of Christian Discourse* (Sather Classical Lectures, 56; Berkeley: University of California Press, 1991) 1.

[34] Cameron, *Christianity*, 5.

[35] George A. Kennedy, *New Testament Interpretation through Rhetorical Criticism* (Chapel Hill: University of North Carolina Press, 1984) 13-23.

[36] Daniel Boyarin, *Dying for God: Martyrdom and the Making of Christianity and Judaism* (Figurae: Reading Medieval Culture; Stanford: Stanford University Press, 1999) 1-8.

[37] Boyarin, *Dying*, 9.

[38] Bakhtin, *Speech Genres*, 60-67.

> not accept it from him. He said: If the law is as I say, this carob will prove it. The carob was uprooted from its place one hundred feet. Some report four hundred feet....A voice came from heaven and announced: The law is in accordance with the view of Rabbi Eli'ezer. Rabbi Yehoshua' stood on his feet and said "it [the Torah] is not in heaven." *Baba Metsi'a* 59a[39]

Boyarin suggests that "it was precisely the manner of Rabbi Eli'ezer's support for his position, via quasi-prophetic or magical means, that so enraged the Rabbis."[40] This is, in my view, a keen insight into the nature of the relation of Jewish and Christian discourse by the end of the 1st century CE. In the terms I use for sociorhetorical analysis and interpretation, Rabbi Eli'ezer's response interwove miracle, prophetic, and apocalyptic rhetorolect in a manner highly characteristic of early Christian argumentation. When he did this, the Rabbis recognized that he enacted a discursive practice characteristic of the sector of Judaism associated with Jesus the Nazarene, rather than characteristic of "rabbinic discourse." In other words, my thesis is that a particular blending of multiple rhetorolects is the distinctive sociorhetorical characteristic of early Christian discourse.

The preceding discussion means that in the midst of the new social, cultural, rhetorical, and ideological modes of interpretation that have emerged during the last three decades, sociorhetorical interpretation has accepted a special challenge. The challenge is to analyze, exhibit, and interpret the manner in which early Christians reconfigured biblical, Jewish, and Greco-Roman modes of discourse into their own distinctive, dynamic, and multivalent mode of discourse. From one angle, the NT writings exhibit an invasion of Hebrew Bible discourse into Mediterranean biographical historiography, epistle, and apocalypse. From another angle, they exhibit an invasion of Mediterranean biographical historiography, epistle, and apocalypse into Hebrew Bible discourse. This happened because, written in Greek, these Christian compositions emerged out of dynamic interaction among multiple kinds of oral and written discourses in the Mediterranean world during the first century CE. The view in this book is that wisdom, prophetic, apocalyptic, precreation, priestly, and miracle rhetorolects were primary mediators of this process. During the first century, early Christians filled these modes of discourse with action, speech, and thought attributed to God, Jesus Christ, Holy Spirit and the followers of Jesus to negotiate social, cultural, and ideological relationships in the contexts in which they lived. This new discourse functioned as a major resource for second and third century discourse, which helped to set the stage for an

[39] Boyarin, *Dying*, 33.
[40] Boyarin, *Dying*, 32.

empire-wide Christian culture that emerged in multiple forms from the fourth century through the Medieval period.

The Social, Cultural, and Ideological Geography of Earliest Christianity

In addition to its focus on the expressible (*rhetical*) nature of early Christian discourse, i.e., its use of that which is conventional (meaningful) to express that which is distinctive, sociorhetorical interpretation focuses on the social, cultural, ideological, and religious geography of early Christian discourse. This "geography" of early Christian discourse emerges in the context of two special axes of God's confrontation of humans: God's created world, which exists in God's time, and the inhabited world, which exists in human chronological time. In other words, in contrast to the social geography of classical discourse, which featured the courtroom, the political assembly, and the civil ceremony in local city-state contexts, early Christian discourse features the social, cultural, ideological, and religious geography of the overall context of intersubjective bodies, households, villages, synagogues, cities, temples, kingdoms, and empires in which they lived and which they imagined.[41] It was not decisions and declarations in courtrooms, political assemblies, and civil ceremonies that established the sociorhetorical discourse of early Christians, but the decisions and declarations of God concerning intersubjective bodies, households, country-villages, synagogues, cities, temples, kingdoms, and empires.[42] In other words, the "institutionalized" human realm they experienced in the Mediterranean world was not dominated by the institutions of the Greek city-state but by basic institutions of life in the Mediterranean world. Early Christians expressed themselves in terms that were meaningful in the "everyday" social, cultural, ideological, and religious contexts in which they lived in the inhabited realm of God's world.

[41] Jon L. Berquist distinguishes between large-scale spaces (region, empire, world), medium-sized spaces (household, village, city) and small-scale spaces (body) in "Theories of Space and Construction of the Ancient World," AAR/SBL Constructs of Social and Cultural Worlds of Antiquity Group, November 20, 1999: http://www.cwru.edu/affil/GAIR/papers/99papers/jberquist.html.

[42] See Vernon K. Robbins, "The Social Location of the Implied Author of Luke-Acts," in *The Social World of Luke-Acts: Models for Interpretation* (ed. J.H. Neyrey. Peabody, MA: Hendrickson, 1991) 305-32; cf. Jerome H. Neyrey, *2 Peter, Jude* (AB 37C; New York: Doubleday, 1993) 32-42, 128-42. In Bakhtin's writings, these time-space categories are "chronotopes": M.M. Bakhtin, "Forms of Time and of the Chronotope in the Novel," in M.M. Bakhtin, *The Dialogic Imagination: Four Essays* (ed. M. Holquist; trans. C. Emerson and M. Holquist; Austin: University of Texas Press, 1981) 84-258; Roland Boer (ed.), *Bakhtin and Genre Theory in Biblical Studies* (Semeia Studies 63; Atlanta: SBL, 2007).

A major reason early Christians created distinctive rhetorolects was that they could not depend on civil courtrooms, political assemblies, and ceremonies to "hear their cases" equitably, exhort people to make decisions that would protect environments in which they could live safely and happily, and celebrate values that would affirm, nurture, and inspire people to think and act in ways that would build positive relationships and actions in the contexts in which they lived. All too often, the civil locations of courtroom, political assembly, and civil ceremony brought punishment, defeat, and celebration of values that threatened rather than nurtured their lives and their households. In this context, early Christians created discourses that "thought beyond and outside"[43] the local contexts of the courtroom, political assembly, and civil ceremony to the location of the inhabited world in God's cosmos.[44] When early Christians were being taken before a civil judge and jury, they had their own discourse that enabled them to think and speak beyond this local context. When they were hearing political speeches designed to mobilize people to rebel or to begin a new political movement, they were thinking beyond this local context to God's leadership of them in the "everyday" social, cultural, and ideological institutions of the Mediterranean world. When they were seeing and hearing civil ceremonies that celebrated the birthday of the emperor, dedicated a temple to a Hellenistic-Roman deity, or commemorated the death of a general, they were thinking beyond these local contexts to celebrations of God's creation of intersubjective bodies, of God's guidance of households, of God's feeding of villages, of God's redistribution of goods in cities, of God's establishment of new leadership in kingdoms, and of God's establishment of a new empire. These alternative modes of believing and reasoning nurtured, strengthened, and sustained them in a world where major alternative value systems guided other people in the contexts in which they lived.

This means that first-century Christians, living in the context of Mediterranean society and culture, created a new paideia by shifting the topography of their argumentation from local courtrooms, political assemblies, and civil ceremonies to the broad conceptual contexts of intersubjective bodies, households, villages, synagogues, cities, temples, kingdoms, and empires in the inhabited human world. The phrase "to-

[43] See James D. Hester, "Creating the Future: Apocalyptic Rhetoric in 1 Thessalonians," *R & T* 7 (2000) 192-212.

[44] See Galatians as described by J. Louis Martyn, *Galatians: A New Translation and Commentary* (AB 33A; New York: Doubleday, 1997) 21: "The oral communication for which the letter is a substitute would have been an argumentative sermon preached in the context of worship – and thus in the acknowledged presence of God – not a speech by a rhetorician in a courtroom."

pography"[45] of argumentation builds on the insight that different rhetorolects contain different configurations of specific, common, and final "topics" (*topoi*) or "locations of thought and action" (*loci*) to negotiate the social, cultural, and ideological contexts in which they functioned. Classical rhetoric was formulated on the basis of "the speech" delivered in the institutionalized contexts of the city state: courtroom, political assembly, and civil ceremony. Hellenistic-Roman rhetoric broadened its compositional focus beyond the speech to epistle, historiography, chreia, fable, narrative, maxim, essay, and declamation.[46] In this context, Hellenistic-Roman rhetoricians began to expand their conceptual location of social geography beyond the courtroom, political assembly, and civil ceremony. The view in this book is that early Christian discourse developed a spectrum of primary social locations that included intersubjective bodies, households, villages, synagogues, cities, temples, kingdoms, and empires. Presuppositions and logics about these social locations functioned in ways that informed the theological, Christological, and ecclesiological discourse they used to negotiate their social, cultural, and ideological relationships in the Mediterranean world.

Rhetology and Rhetography in Early Christian Discourse

Once interpretation begins to focus on bodies and geophysical locations, it becomes obvious that it is necessary not only to interpret reasoning in argumentation but also to interpret picturing of people and the environments in which they are interacting. This means that interpreters must work not only with rhetology (the logic of rhetorical reasoning) but rhetography (the graphic picturing in rhetorical description).[47] Very different kinds of persuasion are in process when a speaker calls a person a teacher, a prophet, a priest, a military general, a

[45] For this terminology, see James D. Hester, "A Fantasy Theme Analysis of 1 Thessalonians," in *Rhetorical Criticism and the Bible* (ed. S.E. Porter and D.L. Stamps; JSNTS 195; Sheffield: Sheffield Academic Press, 2002) 518.

[46] Cf. Klaus Berger, *Formgeschichte des Neuen Testaments* (Heidelberg: Quelle und Meyer, 1984); ibid., "Hellenistische Gattungen im Neuen Testament," in H. Temporini and W. Haase (eds.), *ANRW* 25.2; Part 2, *Principat*, 25.2 (Berlin and New York: Walter de Gruyter, 1984) 1031-1432, 1831-1885; Stanley K. Stowers, *Letter Writing in Greco-Roman Antiquity* (Philadelphia: Westminster, 1986); D.A. Russell and N.G. Wilson, *Menander Rhetor* (Oxford: Clarendon Press, 1981); George A. Kennedy, *Progymnasmata: Greek Textbooks for Prose Composition and Rhetoric* (WGRW 10; Atlanta, SBL, 2003); Watson, *The Rhetoric of the New Testament*, 17-53.

[47] Vernon K. Robbins, "Rhetography: A New Way of Seeing the Familiar Text," in *Words Well Spoken: George Kennedy's Rhetoric of the New Testament* (ed. C. Clifton Black and Duane F. Watson; Waco: Baylor University Press, 2008) 81-106; W.J.T. Mitchell, *Picture Theory: Essays on Verbal and Visual Representation* (Chicago/London: University of Chicago Press, 1994).

heavenly ruler, or a liar, a deceiver, a fornicator, a wolf, or a beast. In other words, the picture an argument evokes (its rhetography) is regularly as important as the reasoning it presents (its rhetology).

Classical rhetoric is helpful as a beginning point for thinking about rhetography and rhetology, since its focus on speaker (*ēthos*), speech (*logos*), and audience (*pathos*) concerns not only reasoning but picturing of the situation, the speaker, and the audience. Yet interpreters have not taken full advantage of this threefold approach. The speaker and audience are integral parts of the rhetography, working interactively and dynamically with the reasoning (rhetology) in the speech. The reasoning in the speech, however, also will use vivid picturing (rhetography) to create its effects. It is essential to work comprehensively with the interrelation of rhetology and rhetography in analysis and interpretation of early Christian argumentation.

Analysis of rhetography in early Christian discourse has produced an awareness of the differences when a speaker uses language associated with households, kingdoms, imperial armies, imperial households, temples, and intersubjective bodies of people. Each picture evokes special configurations of meanings that are important for persuading or convincing people to do certain things and not to do other things. Each rhetorolect contains its blending of rhetography and rhetology. A household is a place of nurturing and instructing people to live good and productive lives (wisdom rhetorolect). A kingdom is a place where bold speakers need to confront leaders and the larger populous to lead lives that bring justice to all (prophetic rhetorolect). An imperial army is sent out with a task of destroying regions of the empire that are perceived to be rebellious, for the purpose of creating peace and salvation throughout the empire (apocalyptic rhetorolect). An imperial household is a place where an emperor, who regularly is worshipped through special rituals, may have a son who performs tasks of patronage, benefit, and friendship throughout the empire (precreation rhetorolect). A temple is a place where priests oversee sacrifices to gods that bring benefits to humans (priestly rhetorolect). Individual bodies of people are "locations" where illness, suffering, and death may be removed to restore malfunctioning bodies into positively functioning, socially integrated, and miraculously renewed people of service and well-being (miracle rhetorolect). Rhetography, then, is as important as rhetology in rhetorical analysis and interpretation. Sociorhetorical interpretation as presented in this book programmatically correlates rhetography and rhetology in a text as it performs its analysis and interpretation.

Unity and Diversity in Earliest Christianity

One of the characteristics of first-century Christian discourse was to give an experience of "kinship"[48] in a context of substantive diversity. Many of their images of kinship are grounded in the patronage system that created networks for distributing goods and benefits throughout the Mediterranean world.[49] This study proposes that the overall kinship or "unity" grounded in patronage in New Testament discourse emerged from the multiple ways early Christians negotiated socially, culturally, and ideologically with people both inside and outside their groups and communities. Using conventional modes of discourse, they referred to God, Jesus, and holy spirit as primary agents who distributed goods and benefits throughout the world, and they gradually referred in their discourse to more and more followers of Christ as additional agents and mediators of those goods and benefits. Thomas H. Olbricht states it as follows:

> In the Christian view, the world is the arena in which God (through God's Son and the Spirit) carries out divine purposes among humans. In popular Greek thinking, the gods also acted, but since there were many gods, there were many goals, often at cross-purposes. In Aristotle's view, God had no involvement in human life, and therefore, "humanity is the measure of all things" (*Nic. Eth.* 10.8). All truths, proofs, and positions are in the final analysis human. In the Christian rhetoric, in contrast, a recitation of the acts of God in the community of believers plays a major role, affecting proofs, arrangement, and style. That which is eternal is not so much immutable laws but the once-for-all actions of God.[50]

Multiplicity in New Testament discourse is grounded in the complexity of God's attributes and actions as Christians attribute multiple kinds of speech and actions to Jesus of Nazareth and his earliest followers, and attribute diverse functions to holy spirit in multiple contexts. Unity in New Testament discourse is grounded in a conviction that Jesus is the primary agent and mediator of the attributes, actions, and power of God, with holy spirit and followers of Christ in supportive

[48] K.C. Hanson, "Kinship," in *The Social Sciences and New Testament Interpretation* (ed. R.L. Rohrbaugh; Peabody, MA: Hendrickson, 1996) 62-79; deSilva, *Honor, Patronage, Kinship & Purity*, 157-239.

[49] Moses I. Finley, *The Ancient Economy* (Berkeley/Los Angeles: University of California Press, 1973); Richard P. Saller, *Personal Patronage under the Early Empire* (Cambridge: Cambridge University Press, 1982); John H. Elliott, "Patronage and Clientage," in Rohrbaugh, *The Social Sciences and New Testament Interpretation*, 144-56; deSilva, *Honor, Patronage, Kinship, & Purity*, 95-156.

[50] Thomas H. Olbricht, "An Aristotelian Rhetorical Analysis of 1 Thessalonians," in *Greeks, Romans, and Christians: Essays in Honor of Abraham J. Malherbe* (ed. D.L. Balch, E. Ferguson, and W.A. Meeks; Minneapolis: Fortress, 1990) 226.

roles in the human realm of life.[51] Among first century Christians, there was no overall agreement about the specific attributes and actions of Jesus that best revealed the attributes and actions of God and holy spirit. Thus, there was no overall Christological or ecclesiological agreement among the diverse groups that constituted first-century Christianity. There was, however, an agreement that God, holy spirit, and followers of Christ were the initiators, enablers, and powers through whom Jesus of Nazareth and the resurrected Lord Jesus Christ worked to redeem the human and cosmic realms.

By the end of the third century, Christians had used New Testament writings and other literature and traditions as resources for establishing a Christological base for unity in Christianity. During the fourth century, they argued that to understand the nature of God and holy spirit it was necessary to understand Christ as the center of the Godhead. The Christological unity that emerged during the fourth century marginalized substantive portions of early Christianity, with a history that comes down to the present day.[52] Even Christians who are marginalized, however, regularly appeal to the New Testament to describe themselves as "Christian." The New Testament continues to function today as a resource for diversity, for unity, for unity within diversity, and for diversity within unity. As a result of the nature of New Testament discourse, the kinds of unity and the kinds of diversity among Christians has the potential to shift rather dramatically in different times and places. It is the goal of this study to help the reader understand how this is possible.

Conclusion

There are traditions of interpretation that presuppose that the creativity of early Christian discourse lies in the arena of its mysteries, its areas of inexpressibility. In other words, the creative, radical nature of NT discourse lies in the things to which it points but is unable to express.[53] This volume takes an alternative approach, namely, that the creativity of early Christian discourse lies in its ability to express in new and creative ways that which early Christians experienced and imagined.

[51] Cf. James D.G. Dunn, *Unity and Diversity in the New Testament: An Inquiry into the Character of Earliest Christianity* (Second Edition; Philadelphia: Trinity Press International, c1977, 1990); John Reumann, *Variety and Unity in New Testament Thought* (Oxford: Oxford University Press, 1991).

[52] Cf. Wilhelm Baum and Dietmar Winkler, *Die apostolische Kirche des Ostens: Geschichte der sogenannten Nestorianer* (Klagenfurt: Kitab, 2000).

[53] One thinks here of the hymn (by Bernard of Clairvaux?), "Jesus, the very thought of thee": "But what to those who find? Ah, this no tongue nor pen can show. The love of Jesus – what it is – none but who love him know." Called to my attention by David A. deSilva.

The thesis is that early Christians expressed what others might have considered to be inexpressible by blending and reconfiguring conventional Mediterranean modes of discourse in new ways. In the context of this blending and reconfiguring, traditional concepts acquired new meanings, conventional poetics acquired new forms, and authoritative rhetorics acquired new meaning effects. The challenge for sociorhetorical analysis and interpretation is to exhibit the processes by which this expressibility (rheticality) occurred.

It is not enough for a commentator to submit to the rhetorics of the NT. Rather, it is important for commentators to analyze and interpret the means by which its rhetorics have attained their power to influence, persuade, and convince readers, hearers, and commentators over the centuries, and do so still today. This volume proposes that the rhetorical power of the NT does not lie so much in those things to which it points but is unable to express. Rather, its power lies in its ability to express in believable ways things which others may consider to be inexpressible, and therefore unbelievable.

1

Story and Argument in Christianity and Its Context

Introduction

The overall conclusion of this book is that early Christians created a new, distinctive mode of discourse through the particular way they focused on the relation of "an overall story" to "belief arguments" (convictions). Christians distinguished themselves from various "Greco-Roman" religious believers and from Rabbinic Judaism by embedding "their beliefs" in "their story" in a particular way. Greek and Roman religions, rabbinic Judaism, and Christianity are so complex that any summary of their patterns of belief is a serious reduction of their richness and multiplicity. It is possible, however, to get an initial glimpse of some trends among religious traditions in the Mediterranean world by looking at some texts that summarize, in one way or another, some basic points of view in the overall setting. Christianity emerged in the context of multiple kinds of religion in the Mediterranean world. The major focus of chapters four through nine will be on the first century of the Common Era, when the earliest Christian texts emerged. To set the stage for those chapters, we will focus on five Mediterranean religious texts that emerged during the second through the fifth century CE, namely when Christian discourse was emerging as a distinctive mode of discourse among various kinds of Greek and Roman religions and an emergent Rabbinic Judaism.

Let us start with two texts that present summaries of Christian belief during the third through the fifth centuries CE: the Apostles' Creed and the Nicene-Constantinopolitan Creed. These summaries give clues to the manner in which Christianity set forth an "authoritative" storyline that produced an alternative "culture of religious wisdom" that presented a set of "belief arguments" in the Mediterranean world. These summaries are, of course, simplifications that significantly obscure many of the complexities of Christianity and its patterns of belief. They can, however, be a good beginning point for moving into some of those complexities.

The Apostles' Creed

The first text for our consideration is commonly called the Apostles' Creed. Its ancient title was *symbolum apostolorum*, Symbol of the Apostles, a title that arose from the tradition that the Twelve Disciples formulated the creed before they separated from each other and went into various regions to spread the Gospel after Jesus ascended into heaven and all had received the Holy Spirit.[1] The account written by Rufinus (d. 410) reads as follows:

When they [the Apostles] were on the point of taking leave of each other, they first settled on a common form for their future preaching, so that they might not find themselves, widely dispersed as they would be, delivering divergent messages to the people they were persuading to believe in Christ. So they all assembled in one spot and, being filled with the Holy Spirit, drafted this short summary, as I have explained, of their future preaching, each contributing the clause he judged fitting: and they decreed that it should be handed out as standard teaching to converts.[2]

This story is, of course, early Christian apocrypha.[3] There is no suggestion of this activity in NT literature nor even during the second or third century CE. Scholarship has revealed that the Apostles' Creed developed out of a third century Roman baptismal creed, regularly called the Roman Symbol.[4] Many of the statements in the creed have a close relation to creedal statements in the New Testament.[5] The creed itself, however, appears to have developed out of a tradition of asking questions about the Trinity in the context of baptism. Hippolytus presented the baptismal tradition (ca. 210 CE) as follows:

> Do you believe in God, the Father Almighty?
> – I believe.
> Do you believe in Christ Jesus, Son of God,
> who was born of Holy Spirit and the Virgin Mary
> who was crucified under Pontius Pilate, and died [and was buried]
> and rose the third day living from the dead,
> ascended into the heavens,
> and sat down at the right hand of the Father

[1] Acts 1:8, 21-26.

[2] J.N.D. Kelly, *Rufinus: A Commentary on the Apostle's Creed* (Westminster, MD: Newman and London: Longmans, Green and Co., 1955) 29-30.

[3] For Christian apocryphal writings, see J.K. Elliott (ed.), *The Apocryphal New Testament* (Oxford: Clarendon Press, 1993).

[4] P. Smulders, "Some Riddles in the Apostles' Creed," *Bijdragen* 31 (1970) 240-50; Liuwe H. Westra, *The Apostles' Creed: Origin, History, and Some Early Commentaries* (Turnhout, Belgium: Brepols, 2002).

[5] See J.N.D. Kelly, *Early Christian Creeds* (London/New York/Toronto: Longmans, Green and Co., 1952) 1-29.

and will come to judge the living and the dead?
– I believe.
Do you believe in the Holy Spirit,
and (or: in) the Holy Church,
and the resurrection of the flesh?
– I believe.[6]

By the end of the fourth century, when tradition had emerged that each of the apostles had contributed a clause to a "Symbol of the Apostles," interpreters began to interpret this "Apostles' Creed" from the perspective of twelve "articles" of faith:[7]

1. I believe in God the Father Almighty, creator of heaven and earth;
2. and in Jesus Christ, His only Son, our Lord,
3. who was conceived by the Holy Spirit, born from the Virgin Mary,
4. suffered under Pontius Pilate, was crucified, dead and buried, [descended into hell,]
5. on the third day he rose again from the dead,
6. and ascended to heaven,
7. and sits at the right hand of God the Father almighty;
8. from thence he shall come to judge the living and the dead.
9. I believe in the Holy Spirit,
10. the holy catholic church, the communion of saints,
11. the forgiveness of sins,
12. the resurrection of the body, and the life everlasting.[8]

On the basis on its relation to the baptismal tradition in Hippolytus, it is clear that the Apostles' Creed has been influenced by a Trinitarian view of God.[9] Article 1 focuses on God the Father, articles 2-8 focus on the Son, and articles 9-12 focus on the Holy Spirit. Interpreters also have observed that fewer variations arose in articles 4-8, which recount a sequence of events from the crucifixion of Jesus to his coming in the future, than in any other part of the creed.

For our purposes, it is necessary to observe something about the Apostles' Creed that few interpreters have discussed. Articles 1-8 present "basic" items in a "Christian" story-line about the history of the world:

(1) God's creation of heaven and earth;

[6] Smulders, "Some Riddles," 242; for a recent discussion see Westra, *The Apostle's Creed*, 21-72.

[7] See Westra, *The Apostles' Creed*, 11-12.

[8] The twelve article contents, according to Westra, *The Apostles' Creed*, 12.

[9] See a discussion of the Textus Receptus in Kelly, *Early Christian Creeds*, 368-71. For the Trinitarian nature of the creed, see Smulders, "Some Riddles," 240-50.

(2-4) Jesus' existence on earth as a result of conception by the Holy Spirit, birth to the Virgin Mary, suffering under Pontius Pilate, crucifixion, death, and burial (and perhaps descent into hell);

(5-8) Jesus' existence after death as a result of resurrection from the dead, installation in a position of power at the right hand of God, and task of coming in the future to judge the living and the dead.

It is notable, first, that this story-line skips over all of God's activity with Israel. In other words, a biblical creed could potentially include reference to people like Abraham, Moses, David, or the prophets. Instead, the Apostles' Creed moves directly from God's creation of heaven and earth to conception of Jesus by the Holy Spirit. Second, it is notable that the beginning and ending of the story-line basically coincide with the beginning and ending of the biblical story from Genesis through Revelation. The overall scope of the traditional biblical canon, then, appears to have a relation to the overall scope of the Apostles' Creed.

Next, it is important to observe that articles 9-12 emerge as "beliefs" out of the basic story-line in articles 1-8. The creed captures this dynamic when it contains "I believe in" twice in the creed: (1) at the very beginning; and (2) before the list of beliefs at the end. In other words, Christian belief is a dynamic process of believing in a basic story-line, which gives rise to beliefs that are perceived to be implied by that story-line. This means that a change in the story-line could change a "belief" statement, and the change of a "belief" statement could change the story-line. For example, if conception "by the Holy Spirit" (article 3) were not part of the story-line, it might not be essential to believe "in the Holy Spirit" (article 9), unless there were some other event in the story-line that supported it. One can imagine that if a Christian were challenged about belief in the Holy Spirit, and there were no statement about "conception by the Holy Spirit" in the story-line, that Christian might immediately point to the coming of the Holy Spirit into the Church as it is recounted in Acts 2. In other words, the natural instinct of a Christian would be to recount an event in the Christian story-line that would support the belief. For another example, if it did not say in the story-line that Jesus "rose from the dead" (article 5), there would be significant question about belief "in the resurrection of the body" (article 12; see 1 Cor 15). Moreover, if Jesus does not really sit at the right hand of God and have a task of coming in the future to judge the living and the dead (articles 7-8), it might not be essential to believe "in the life everlasting" (article 12). In other words, specific episodes in the story-line are a basis for specific Christian beliefs. Therefore, after recounting "belief" in a basic story-line in articles 1-8, a Christian recounts "additional beliefs" based on the story-line in articles 9-12. This means that the overall structure of the Apostles' Creed is:

1. I believe in a basic story-line about God the Father and His only Son, Jesus Christ, Our Lord, who was conceived by the Holy Spirit.
2. Therefore, I believe in the Holy Spirit, the holy catholic church, the communion of saints, the forgiveness of sins, the resurrection of the body, and the life everlasting.

First, then, the internal dynamic of the Apostles' Creed is argumentative. The creed does not simply contain a sequence of beliefs, nor does it simply contain a story-line. It contains a story-line that has an "I believe, therefore I believe ..." structure. Second, the underlying, driving force of the Apostles' Creed is a "particular" story. If a person replaced "God the Father Almighty" with "ever omnipotent Zeus," or "His only Son" with "Isis, mistress of every land," both the content of the story and the subject matter of the argumentation would move decisively into an alternative culture of religious belief. Third, however, we will see below that there are certain aspects of Christian belief argumentation that have a dynamic relation to argumentation in summaries of Rabbinic and Greek and Roman points of view. This raises intriguing and important issues about the relation of the "rhetoric" of Christian discourse and the "rhetoric" of Rabbinic Judaism and of various Greek and Roman religions. These interrelationships establish the context for detailed investigations of the "rhetoric of religious antiquity,"[10] which is the topic for the series in which this book has its home. Thus, the issues that underlie this book concern the relation of Christian discourse to a wide variety of alternative religious discourses in the Mediterranean world during the time when Christianity emerged.

The underlying thesis of this book is that early Christians created a distinctive mode of religious discourse by setting forth a particular "argumentative story." An interpreter discovers very soon, however, that there are substantive variations among Christians as they tell "the Christian story-line," and these variations introduce significantly alternative kinds of argumentation in Christianity. Thus, in a context of a certain kind of unity among Christians there is extensive diversity.[11] The question is what kind of unity and what kind of diversity. This book approaches this question through an investigation of two phenomena that continually are related to one another: (1) various Christian story-lines in an overall Christian story-line; and (2) multiple kinds

[10] See online: http://www.deopublishing.com/rhetoricofreligiousantiquity.htm.

[11] See Dunn, *Unity and Diversity in the New Testament*; Reumann, *Variety and Unity in New Testament Thought.*

of Christian argumentation in an overall context of Christian "belief argument." Let us begin this process by comparing a longer Christian creed with the Apostles' creed, to see what happens when some fourth century Christians expanded statements that were in some earlier Roman creeds.

Comparison of the Apostles' Creed and the Nicene-Constantinopolitan Creed

As Christians in positions of leadership and authority during the fourth century established "orthodox" statements of belief in the context of the Church Councils at Nicea (325 CE) and Constantinople (381 CE), a Nicene-Constantinopolitan Creed (often simply called the "Nicene Creed") emerged.[12] For our purposes in this book, comparison of the twelve articles in the Apostles' Creed (hereafter AC) with statements in the Nicene-Constantinopolitan Creed (hereafter NCC) can help us to see some of the specific issues at stake in the "Christian story-line" in the context of argumentation about "Christian beliefs" during the fourth century (see table opposite).

For the issues under consideration in this book, the NCC addition in article 1 of "all things visible and invisible" is highly important. The Apostles' Creed asserts what is present in Gen 1:1: "God made heaven and earth." The NCC expands the statement to include God's creation of both visible and invisible things. Something in addition to the Hebrew Bible account of creation, then, appears in the expanded version of article 1 in NCC. Exploring the New Testament, we can readily imagine that the expansion concerns belief in things that have never been seen by anyone. In John 20:29, for example, Jesus tells Thomas: "Blessed are those who have not seen and yet believe." But more than this is at stake in the addition to article 1 in the NCC. First Timothy 1:17 asserts: "To the King of the ages, immortal, invisible, the only God, be honor and glory forever and ever. Amen." According to this verse, one of the attributes of God, alongside of immortality, is invisibility. Rom 1:20 asserts an additional attribute: "Ever since the creation of the world his [God's] eternal power and divine nature, invisible though they are, have been understood and seen through the things he has made." Both God's divine nature and God's eternal power are invisible. One of the effects of God's power, however, is to make and do things in the world that can be seen, i.e., that are visible.

As Christians include a "New Testament" point of view about both visible and invisible things in article 1 of the NCC, the expansion adds more than a "belief argument." The expansion adds an "event" to the

[12] Kelly, *Early Christian Creeds*, 344-67; cf. Luke Timothy Johnson, *The Creed: What Christians Believe and Why It Matters* (New York: Doubleday, 2003) 32-38.

Apostles' Creed	Nicene-Constantinopolitan Creed
(1) I believe in God the Father Almighty, creator of heaven and earth;	(1) We believe in one God, the Father all mighty, maker of heaven and earth, of all things visible and invisible;
(2) and in Jesus Christ, His only Son, our Lord,	(2) and in one Lord Jesus Christ, the only-begotten Son of God, Begotten from the Father before all time, Light from Light, True God from True God, begotten not made, of the same substance as the Father, through whom all things were made;
(3) who was conceived by the Holy Spirit, born from the Virgin Mary,	(3) who for us men and for our salvation came down from heaven and was incarnate by the Holy Spirit and the Virgin Mary, and became human.
(4) suffered under Pontius Pilate, was crucified, dead and buried, [descended into hell],	(4) He was crucified for us under Pontius Pilate, and suffered, and was buried,
(5) on the third day he rose again from the dead,	(5) and rose on the third day, according to the scriptures,
(6) and ascended to heaven	(6) and ascended to heaven,
(7) and sits at the right hand of God the Father almighty;	(7) and sits on the right hand of the Father,
(8) from thence he shall come to judge the living and the dead.	(8) and will come again with glory to judge the living and the dead. His kingdom shall have no end.
(9) I believe in the Holy Spirit,	(9) and in the Holy Spirit, the Lord and Giver of life, who proceeds from the Father, who together with the Father and Son is worshiped and glorified, who spoke through the prophets;
(10) the holy catholic Church, the communion of saints,	(10) and in one, holy, catholic, and apostolic church.
(11) the forgiveness of sins,	(11) We confess one baptism for the forgiveness of sins.
(12) the resurrection of the body, and the life everlasting.	(12) We look forward to the resurrection of the dead and the life of the world to come.

biblical story of creation that prepares the way for the story to be "specifically Christian." The additional biblical "event" is God's creation of invisible things, before he made "visible things" (heavens, earth, light, etc: Gen 1). It is important to say "prepares the way," since the "additional" event in the creation story is present in the LXX [Greek] version of Gen 1:2. While the Hebrew version says that the earth was *tohu*, without form, the Greek version says the earth was "invisible [*aoratos*]." In other words, for the LXX, the earth was not simply without form, but it actually could not be seen until God created light (Gen 1:3). Among other things, this creates the possibility that God might have created other invisible things (e.g., wisdom or Jesus as word or wisdom), before God created visible things.

The expansion of article 1 in the NCC establishes a context for expansion of article 2 beyond the AC statement about "Jesus Christ, His only Son, our Lord" into: "the only-begotten Son of God, begotten from the Father before all time, Light from Light, True God from True God, begotten not made, of the same substance as the Father, through whom all things were made." It would appear that NCC article 2 is related to Col 1:15-16: "He [God's Son] is the image (*eikōn*) of the invisible God, the first-born of all creation; for in him all things in the heavens and on earth were created, things visible and invisible...." Expansion of article 1 so it includes the creation of things both visible and invisible, then, has a dynamic relation to Christian argumentation about the participation of both God and God's Son Jesus Christ in creating and sustaining all visible and invisible things in the world. First, if Jesus was begotten "before all time," his most inner nature is invisible rather than visible. This coheres with Col 1:15, which asserts that Jesus is "in the image of the invisible God." If Jesus were begotten after time began, he could, of course, have both invisible and visible nature. But if Jesus existed before time, he would have been invisible, since nothing visible existed until "at the beginning," when time began (Gen 1:1). Second, if Jesus existed before all time, then he must be "begotten" and not "made." If Jesus were "made" by God, he could, theoretically, have been made invisible before God made him visible. But Jesus was "begotten," not "made," because Jesus was not "created." He was not part of creation, but the agent through which creation occurred. Jesus was "begotten before time." Therefore, he was invisible; because things were made visible only at the "time" of creation. Third, Jesus' "begotten" inner nature is "in the image of the invisible God," while humans' "created" inner nature is somewhat different, even though humans are "created in the image of God" (Gen 1:26-27). The nature of humans has to be different in some way, since humans were visible from the moment they came into being. Fourth, it should be obvious that the difference lies in the knowledge that Jesus is "of the same substance of the Father," while humans have a "created substance," a substance somehow related to all other created things rather than completely to God. Fifth, if the Son is of the same substance as the Father, then the Son is "True God from True God." Sixth, if the Son is true God from true God, then the Son can be the one "through whom all things are made." Seventh, if all things were made through the Son and the first thing God made was light (Gen 1:3), then it could be reasonable to think that the Son was invisible "Light from Light" before the time when "created light" was "made visible" in the world that was created.[13]

[13] For a detailed discussion of these issues, see Lewis Ayres, *Nicaea and its Legacy: An Approach to Fourth-Century Trinitarian Theology* (Oxford: Oxford University Press, 2004) 133-221; cf. Vernon K. Robbins, "Conceptual Blending and Early Christian Imagina-

If a person adds an additional "event" or "era" to the biblical creation story, namely the presence of invisible things "before all time," then a lengthy chain of argumentation seems entirely appropriate (might one say "reasonable"?) for "belief." In this volume, we refer to Christian reasoning and argumentation about this era before creation as early Christian "precreation" rhetorolect. The addition of expanded belief arguments in articles 1-2 of the NCC implies an era of "non-time" before the "biblical" story-line in Genesis 1 that is very important for the Christian story-line of the world. The presence of a "non-time era" introduces a dynamic mode of elaboration of additional Christian belief arguments. In this instance, the presence of invisible things before all time gives rise to God's creation of all things through his "Son," who was invisibly "begotten" from God before creation. God's begetting of his Son would not be an "event," because no events would occur prior to time. So there was some kind of "timeless begetting emanation" prior to the event of creation. But this emanation was not one or more "event," because events only began with creation, which was the beginning of time.[14] Humans, of course, cannot think of "emanation" outside of time, but perhaps there is no difficulty for God's inner nature to have "timeless emanation" within itself. The point is that "addition" to the story-line is dynamically related to "elaboration" of belief argumentation. The chain of argumentation in articles 1-2 of the NCC is dynamically related to additions to the biblical story of creation. Christians must believe, and therefore defend, both the additions to the story-line and the chain of argumentation related to it.

The next important additions in the NCC for our purposes occur in articles 5 and 9. In article 5, the NCC adds "according to the scriptures."[15] Then, in article 9 concerning the Holy Spirit the NCC adds: "the Lord and Giver of Life, who proceeds from the Father, who together with the Father and Son is worshipped and glorified, who spoke through the prophets." First, let us notice the additions of "according to the scriptures" and "who spoke through the prophets." We noticed above that the AC skipped from God's creation of the world to the conception of Jesus Christ by the Holy Spirit, omitting all events concerning God's relation to Israel. The NCC "corrects" this omission in articles 5 and 9 by referring both to "the scriptures" and to "the

tion," in Petri Luomanen, Ilkka Pyysiäinen, and Risto Uro (eds.), *Explaining Christian Origins and Early Judaism: Contributions from Cognitive and Social Science* (Biblical Interpretation Series 89; Leiden/Boston: Brill, 2007) 161-95.

[14] Cf. Ayres, *Nicaea and its Legacy*, 88-92, 236-240.

[15] One may want to say it substitutes "from the dead" with "according to the scriptures." Overall it is obvious that articles 4-5 in NCC were influenced by 1 Cor 15:4.

prophets." The addition of "the scriptures" in article 5, which concerns the resurrection of the Son Jesus Christ, has the potential for bringing Luke 24:44-48 into Christian reasoning and argumentation:

Then he [Jesus] said to them, "These are my words that I spoke to you while I was still with you – that everything written about me in the law of Moses, the prophets, and the psalms must be fulfilled." Then he opened their minds to understand the scriptures, and he said to them, "Thus it is written, that the Messiah is to suffer and to rise from the dead on the third day, and that repentance and forgiveness of sins is to be proclaimed in his name to all nations, beginning from Jerusalem."

The presence of the assertion about the scriptures is, without doubt, a direct assault on Marcionism, which excluded "Old Testament" scriptures from Christian scripture. Marcion had omitted the references to scripture from these verses in Luke 24, making it read: "44a And he said to them, "These are the words that I spoke to you while I was still with you, [omit 44b-46a] 46b that thus it was necessary for the Messiah to suffer and to rise from the dead on the third day ...."[16] The addition of "who spoke through the prophets" in article 9 in the NCC supports, in particular, the unity between the Old and the New Testament by asserting that the same Holy Spirit who spoke through the prophets is also the "Giver of Life" (through the conception of Jesus in Mary's womb).[17] Returning to the topic of the Christian story-line, we can see a "Christian filling in" of the story-line that includes the entire story of Israel. With two small additions among the belief arguments, an unlimited number of biblical events now may enter into the Christian story.

At this point, it is important for us to relate what we have seen in the Apostles' Creed and the Nicene-Constantinopolitan Creed to the project of sociorhetorical analysis and interpretation that is the task of this book. It was observed in the Introduction that sociorhetorical interpretation has brought six prototypical rhetorolects to light in first century Christian literature. An extended discussion of three of the rhetorolects occurs in chapters 4-9 in this book. It will be helpful, however, to make a few observations now, even if some of the assertions may not seem fully obvious to the reader at this point.

Two of the six early Christian rhetorolects are wisdom and precreation. The socially experienced basis for wisdom rhetorolect, it will be argued, is a blending of God's heaven and earth with "household," which is the place where God's wisdom is taught to children on earth, and with "people's bodies," so these bodies are able to go forth and multiply "the fruit" of goodness and righteousness in the world. In wisdom rhetorolect, God functions as Father, a term closely related to

[16] Tertullian, *Adv Marc* IV.43.

[17] See Smulders, "Some Riddles," 255-56.

the head of a household who provides nurture, food, and wisdom to "children" who are to become productive of "good" like God produced a "good" creation (Gen 1). Article 1 in the AC and the NCC begins with Christian wisdom rhetorolect. As we noticed above, however, article 1 in the NCC adds an assertion that the "one Lord Jesus Christ" was begotten from the Father "before all time." With the addition of this "begetting" prior to the event of creation of the world, the NCC moves beyond wisdom rhetorolect to precreation rhetorolect. The socially experienced basis for precreation rhetorolect, it will be argued, is a blending of God's created world with the household of an emperor, since the emperor's household "reigns" over an "empire." This "reigning household" has an eternal nature. In Christian rhetorolect, this "precreation household" is characterized by a utopian, intimate relation understood as "love" (*agapē*) between the emperor Father and his only Son. First the Father "begets" the Son; second the Father creates the world "through" this Son; third the Father "sends" the Son into the world as light to save the world; fourth the Son "glorifies" the Father by doing what he sees his Father doing before and after the world is made; fifth people who "believe" the Son so they become "friends" with the Son gain access through friendship into the emporer's household, which exists eternally; and sixth the Father took the Son back up into his eternal household. The additions in articles 1-2 in the NCC move the argumentation beyond wisdom rhetorolect into precreation rhetorolect. Since precreation rhetorolect is an expansion of wisdom rhetorolect, the preferred names for God and Jesus still are Father and Son. Both terms, however, have more extended meanings in articles 1-2 in the NCC, as we have explored above.

Christian prophetic rhetorolect is also important in early Christian discourse. The "socially experienced" basis for prophetic rhetorolect is the blending of God's cosmos with a person who confronts one or more leaders of a political kingdom to enact "God's will," rather than their own personal desires, for the benefit of the people in the kingdom. In prophetic rhetorolect, then, the goal is enactment of God's righteousness and justice on earth as a means of establishing a "special king" on earth. In other words, prophetic rhetorolect emerges in contexts where "prophets" confront "rulers" whom they "know" are "God's rulers" on earth. The authoritative nature of the rulers whom the prophet encounters, and the authoritative nature of the will of God for these rulers, calls forth the title "King" both for God and for the ruler. The goal is for God to have a special king who enacts God's kingship on earth. Article 9 in the NCC introduces Christian prophetic rhetorolect specifically when it refers to the Holy Spirit speaking through the prophets. In Christian rhetorolect, the Holy Spirit is the special representative of God who anoints God's prophets and kings for the purpose of creating "God's kingdom" on earth.

Christian priestly rhetorolect is present in article 11 in both creeds, which asserts the "remission" or forgiveness of sins. The "socially experienced" basis for priestly rhetorolect is the blending of God's world with God's Temple or "house of worship" on earth and with people who offer sacrifices to God for the purpose of beneficial exchange between God and humans. In other words, in the context of priestly rhetorolect, people's bodies can be perceived to be "temples of the Lord." The title "priest," of course, plays a strong role in this rhetorolect as action is taken to call forth God's forgiveness of sin. It is noticeable that neither creed asserts that Christ died "for our sins." Interpreters have observed that these creeds were formulated before extensive discussions of atonement emerged in Christian argumentation. Priestly rhetorolect is close at hand, however, in the "belief" about remission or forgiveness of sins in article 11. When a believer is guided by a theory of atonement, a dynamic relation naturally exists between the assertion about Christ's death in article 4 and the assertion about forgiveness or remission of sins in article 11.

Christian apocalyptic rhetorolect is present in article 8 in both creeds and specifically in article 12 in the NCC. The socially experienced basis for apocalyptic rhetorolect is the blending of God's function as almighty emperor over the earth with many heavenly assistants (angels and some humans whom God made into heavenly beings) and a large army (host) to establish peace and salvation throughout the empire. God's special dwelling place in the heavens is a place of purity and holiness like a temple. In this context, bodies of people can be perceived as microcosmic temples on earth, which can either be corrupted or kept pure and holy. A major goal of God is to destroy corruption and establish divine holiness throughout the created world. God, in the role of an emperor who can be called "the Most High" or "the Almighty" (*pantokratōr*),[18] sends Jesus, who is regularly called the Son of man but can also be called "the King of Kings and Lord of Lords."[19] God also sends other emissaries, some who bring special messages to humans, some who destroy evil in God's creation, and some who bring holy bodies into God's presence. God's presence is so powerful and holy that it creates a temple-like environment wherever it manifests itself, destroying impurity and evil and establishing purity and holiness throughout the entire context (Rev 21:22).

Christian miracle rhetorolect lies in the background in both creeds when they appeal to God as "Almighty" in article 1 of both creeds and

[18] Rev 1:8; 4:8; 11:17; 16:7, 14; 19:6, 15; 21:22.
[19] Rev 17:14; 19:16.

in article 7 in the AC. It is noticeable, however, that there is no explicit and direct focus on healing or restoration of individual bodies of people on earth, as in the Gospels and Acts in the New Testament. In other words, if there is an implication in the creeds that "all things are possible with God," this implication is embedded in apocalyptic rhetorolect rather than miracle rhetorolect. As in Revelation[20] and the writings of Paul, so in these two creeds, miracle rhetorolect may be implied but is not an explicit focus of God's work through Christ, through creation, and through faith.

Mishnah, *Sayings of the Fathers* (*Pirke Aboth*)

Let us now compare the Christian AC and the NCC with the highly focused "story-line" of Israel in "The Sayings of the Fathers" in the Rabbinic Mishnah. A major reason for moving to this next text is that Rabbinic Judaism, like Christianity, builds its convictions in particular ways on the biblical story. Also like Christianity, it adds various items to the biblical story, all in a spirit of elaborating what the biblical story says and implies, to create its patterns of Jewish belief. There are, however, major differences of emphasis and focus between the rabbinic story-line in *Pirke Aboth* 1 and the Christian story-line in the Apostles' Creed and the Nicene-Constantinopolitan Creed.

By 200 CE, Jewish leaders who came to be known as Rabbis were establishing "Jewish rabbinic culture" as an alternative to Christian culture through their production of the Mishnah.[21] In this context a "special story-line" emerged that gave authoritative status to rabbinic tradition alongside the Tanakh (Torah/Prophets/Writings), which Christians were beginning by this time to call their "Old" Testament. The Rabbinic story, as it is told in Mishnah, *Pirke Aboth* 1 unfolds in the following manner:

I. Biblical story-line: Moses to the Great Synagogue

(1) Moses received the Law from Sinai and committed it to Joshua, and Joshua to the elders,[22] and the elders to the Prophets;[23] and the Prophets com-

[20] D.A. deSilva, "Toward a Socio-Rhetorical Taxonomy of Divine Intervention: Miracle Discourse in the Revelation to John," in *Fabrics of Discourse: Essays in Honor of Vernon K. Robbins* (ed. D.B. Gowler, L.G. Bloomquist, and D.F. Watson; Harrisburg/London/New York: Trinity Press International, 2003) 303-16.

[21] See Jack N. Lightstone, *Mishnah and the Social Formation of the Early Rabbinic Guild: A Socio-Rhetorical Approach* (Studies in Christianity and Judaism/Études sur le christianisme et le judaïsme 11; Waterloo: Wilfrid Laurier University Press for the Canadian Corporation for Studies in Religion/Corporation Canadienne des Sciences Religieuses, 2002).

[22] Joshua 24:31.

[23] Jeremiah 7:25.

mitted it to the men of the Great Synagogue.[24] They said three things: Be deliberate in judgment, raise up many disciples, and make a fence around the Law.

II. From Priestly Observance to Study in Households: Simeon the Just to Shemaiah and Abtalion

(2) Simeon the Just was of the remnants of the Great Synagogue. He used to say: By three things is the world sustained: by the Law, by the [Temple-] service, and by deeds of loving-kindness.

(3) Antigonus of Soko received [the Law] from Simeon the Just. He used to say: Be not like slaves that minister to the master for the sake of receiving a bounty, but be like slaves that minister to the master not for the sake of receiving a bounty; and let the fear of Heaven be upon you.

(4) Jose b. Joezer of Zeredah and Jose b. Johanan of Jerusalem received [the Law] from them. Jose b. Joezer of Zeredah said: Let thy house be a meeting-house for the Sages and sit amid the dust of their feet and drink in their words with thirst.

(5) Jose b. Johanan of Jerusalem said: Let thy house be opened wide and let the needy be members of thy household; and talk not much with womankind. They said this of a man's own wife: how much more of his fellow's wife! Hence the Sages have said: He that talks much with womankind brings evil upon himself and neglects the study of the Law and at the last will inherit Gehenna.

(6) Joshua b. Perahyah and Nittai the Arbelite received [the Law] from them. Joshua b. Perahyah said: Provide thyself with a teacher and get thee a fellow [-disciple]; and when thou judgest any man incline the balance in his favor.

(7) Nittai the Arbelite said: Keep thee far from an evil neighbor and consort not with the wicked and lose not belief in retribution.

(8) Judah b. Tabbai and Simeon b. Shetah received [the Law] from them. Judah b. Tabbai said: Make not thyself like them that would influence the judges; and when the suitors stand before thee let them be in thine eyes as wicked men, and when they have departed from before thee let them be in thine eyes as innocent, so soon as they have accepted the judgment.

(9) Simeon b. Shetah said: Examine the witnesses diligently and be cautious in thy words lest from them they learn to swear falsely.

(10) Shemaiah and Abtalion received [the Law] from them. Shemaiah said: Love labor and hate mastery and seek not acquaintance with the ruling power.

(11) Abtalion said: Ye Sages, give heed to your words lest ye incur the penalty of exile and ye be exiled to a place of evil waters, and the disciples that come after you drink [of them] and die, and the name of Heaven be profaned.

III. Torah School Houses: Hillel and Shammai

(12) Hillel and Shammai received [the Law] from them. Hillel said: Be of the disciples of Aaron, loving peace and pursuing peace, loving mankind and bringing them nigh to the Law.

[24] "A body of 120 elders, including many prophets, who came up from exile with Ezra...": *Tif. Yis.*

(13) He used to say: A name made great is a name destroyed, and he that increased not decreases, and he that learns not is worthy of death, and he that makes worldly use of the crown shall perish.

(14) He used to say: If I am not for myself who is for me? and being for mine own self what am I? and if not now, when?

(15) Shammai said: Make thy [study of the] Law a fixed habit; say little and do much, and receive all men with a cheerful countenance.

IV. Sages and Disciples: Gamaliel I and Simeon

(16) Rabban Gamaliel[25] said: Provide thyself with a teacher and remove thyself from doubt, and tithe not overmuch by guesswork.

(17) Simeon his son said: All my days have I grown up among the Sages and I have found naught better for a man than silence; and not the expounding [of the Law] is the chief thing but the doing [of it]; and he that multiplies words occasions sin.

(18) Rabban Simeon b. Gamaliel said: By three things is the world sustained: by truth, by judgment, and by peace, as it is written, "Execute judgment of truth and peace" (Zech 8:16).

Aboth 1 presents a summary of the underlying story-line for Rabbinic Judaism. Rather than focusing on the creation of the world, it focuses on the creation of a particular "people" who will live according to God's ways in the world. The story begins with Moses, to whom God gave both the written and oral Law. The story unfolds by recounting the people who, after Moses, faithfully transmitted both the written and oral Law to others. The story reaches its conclusion with Rabbis who approach the written and oral Law in such a manner that it creates a world of truth, discernment, and peace.

The chapter begins with people who represent the beginning, middle, and end of the "biblical" transmission of the written and oral Law (1:1). Moses stands at the beginning of the story. He received both the written and oral Law at Mount Sinai. A chain of people stands in the middle of the story: Joshua, the elders, the prophets. Emphasis on the sequence that creates authoritative transmission creates "chain-link repetition." In other words, just like a chain is connected by means of the linking point at the beginning and the linking point at the end of the link, so the wording in the middle part of the verse is mentioned twice, namely at the beginning of the link and the end of the link. This creates a repetitive "double-step" in the wording: "... to *Joshua, Joshua* to *the elders, the elders* to *the prophets, the prophets* to ...." In contrast to Moses, who was the beginning of the chain, Joshua, the elders, and the prophets are both beginnings and endings. Each person played a role of "receiving" the written and oral Law from someone else. This was the "beginning" of their time of special responsibility. At the end of their

[25] Grandson (or possibly son) of Hillel.

time of responsibility, they transmitted what they knew and learned to the next person or group. These beginning and ending points create a chain-link story-line of authoritative transmission as told by the Bible.[26]

The "men of the Great Synagogue" represent the end of the "biblical" story-line of transmission. This final "event" in the story-line is not specifically recounted in the Bible itself. Rather, it is an "implication" the Rabbis drew from the biblical story. The Rabbis described the Great Synagogue in the following manner: "A body of 120 elders, including many prophets, who came up from exile with Ezra; they saw that prophecy had come to an end and that restraint was lacking; therefore they made many new rules and restrictions for the better observance of the Law" (*Tif. Yis.*). It is important to notice the emphasis on "many new rules and restrictions for the better observance of the Law." The authoritative story-line continues by adding "new rules and restrictions" as they are spoken by authoritative transmitters of God's Law. This "new" dimension creates a context for "better" observance of God's Law. In other words, the new dimension is not like the Christian story, where "events" in the life and death of a "new" person exhibit the "further unfolding" of the story of God's actions in and with the world. Rather, the "story" unfolds in the emergence of additional rules and restrictions that clarify how people can successfully live according to God's Law in "new" situations, namely contexts not present either in the wilderness, where God gave the Law to Moses, Joshua, and the elders; during the time of the initial kingdom of Israel; or in the time immediately after the return from exile. As the people of Israel face the historical, political, and religious changes of Persian rule, Greek rule, and Roman rule, it is necessary to study the Law anew to determine how it applies to these new situations. New times in the story, therefore, call for new rules and restrictions that enable better observance of God's Law.

After the "biblical" chain of authoritative transmission, *Pirke Aboth* 1:2-11 presents a chain from the men of the Great Synagogue to Shemaiah and Abtalion, who set the stage for the "Houses" of Hillel and Shammai. Simeon the Just is featured as the authoritative link between the men of the Great Synagogue and the Hasmonean-Maccabean period down to the coming of Roman rule. Sirach 50 features Simeon (Simon II) as the glorious high priest of the temple. At the same time that

[26] The biblical account is understood in Rabbinic tradition to recount Joshua's receiving of the Law from Moses and transmission of the Law to the elders in Josh 24:31, since this verse asserts that Israel "served the Lord" both during the time of Joshua and during the time of the elders. In turn, Jer 7:25 supports the transmission of the Law by the prophets when the Lord of hosts, the God of Israel (7:1) says: "From the day that your ancestors came out of the land of Egypt until this day, I have persistently sent all my servants the prophets to them, day after day."

Simeon "received the portions from the hands of the priests," "all the sons of Aaron in their splendor held the Lord's offering in their hands before the whole congregation of Israel" (Sir 50:12-13). In other words, Simeon was the leader of all the "sons of Aaron," embodying the tradition of holiness in Israel through the priesthood established by Moses (Exod 28:1). The description ends with Simeon coming down from the temple and raising his hands "over the whole congregation of Israelites, to pronounce the blessing of the Lord with his lips, and to glory in his name" (Sir 50:20). Simeon the Just, then, is not simply one who studied Law. He embodied the holiness of Israel as high priest in the temple. For this reason, *Aboth* 1:2 ends with the saying of Simeon: "By three things is the world sustained: by the Law, by the [Temple-] service, and by deeds of loving kindness." Simeon places temple worship in the center of the list, as the bridge from the Law to deeds of loving kindness. Only the blessing of God, and the glory of God's name, in a context of worship of God, can enable a person to move from knowledge of the Law to performance of deeds of loving kindness. Simeon, the high priest of the temple during the coming of Greek rule during 219-196 BCE, provides the authoritative "chain-link" between the men of the Great Synagogue and the interpreters who continued to transmit the Law down to Shemaiah and Abtalion, who transmitted the Law to Hillel and Shammai, the founders of the famous "Schools" in Jerusalem.

Aboth 1:12-15 focuses on Hillel and Shammai. The initial saying of Hillel focuses on Aaron, the priestly brother of Moses: "Be of the disciples of Aaron, loving peace and pursuing peace, loving mankind and bringing them nigh to the Law" (1:12). As study of the Law enters the time of Roman rule, then, the dynamics of priestly life enter into the teacher-disciple relation that produces enactment of the Law. The goal when studying the Law, according to Hillel, is to become a disciple of Aaron. Such a disciple loves and pursues peace (*shalom*), loves the people in God's world, and brings God's people near to the Law. The result of "priestly" study of the Law, then, is love and pursuit of peace. This coheres with Sir 50:23, where a concluding benediction includes: "May he [the God of all] give us gladness of heart, and may there be peace in our days in Israel, as in the days of old." Loving and pursuing peace, one who studies the Law loves people in God's world and brings them into this "peace" by bringing them into the knowledge and enactment of God's Law. A saying of Shammai ends this unit: "Make thy [study of the] Law a fixed habit; say little and do much, and receive all men with a cheerful countenance" (*Aboth* 1:15). Here we see the "cheerful countenance" related to the "gladness of heart" in the benediction in Sir 50:23. The goal of regular study of the Law is "action," and this action is characterized by receiving "all men with a cheerful countenance." Peace and cheerfulness, then, can emerge as inner attributes and actions of people who study the Law, even, and perhaps especially, during times when there is no "nation" of Israel, but the people of Israel are governed by foreign rulers.

Aboth 1:16-18 end the chapter with a focus on Gamaliel I and Simeon his son, who continue the chain of transmission that eventually comes to Judah the Patriarch (2:1), who compiled the Mishnah. Gamaliel emphasizes the importance of finding a teacher and "removing thyself from doubt" (1:16). With this saying, one sees the other side of the emphasis with which the chapter starts. In 1:1, the men of the Great Synagogue tell those who study the Law to "raise up many disciples." At an earlier time in history, the emphasis was on the importance of those who knew the written and oral Law to create settings for teaching others. *Aboth* 1:16 at the end of the chapter features Rabbi Gamaliel telling members of the community to provide themselves with teachers. The presupposition appears to be that, as a result of the founding of "Schools" for study and interpretation of the Law, many teachers exist among God's people. Now the task must be to find oneself a teacher who can lead one beyond doubt about what God can do into a life of faithfulness according to the Law, which can bring God's blessings into one's life. The chapter ends with sayings of Gamaliel's son Simeon that emphasize doing the Law and, by this means, producing truth, judgment, and peace that sustain the world. The final saying of Simeon recites a verse from the Bible, exhibiting how the transmission of God's Law is alive and well at the end of the authoritative chain that comes down to Judah the Patriarch. Simeon provides biblical testimony for his saying about truth, judgment and peace by asserting, "As it is written, 'Execute judgment of truth and peace'," which is a recitation of Zech 8:16. From a rabbinic perspective, then, one must understand that even the prophets presented commandments of the Law. One must know that sayings of Rabbis many years after the Bible authoritatively transmit the deepest insights of all of the Bible in the form of new statements of the Law.

Rather than beginning with God's creation of the world, like the Christian story-line, the story-line of Rabbinic Judaism begins with Moses, to whom God gave both the written and oral Law as a means to create a special "people of Israel" who would live according to God's ways in the world. Since the focus is on the creation of a particular "people" through commandments, Moses is the one who, in the beginning, launches the authentic human "chain of tradition" that moves authoritatively down to Judah the Patriarch, compiler of the Mishnah. Every person in the "chain" is a reliable transmitter of authoritative tradition that was given to him by a reliable person. Instead of transmitting an authoritative "argumentative story," therefore, the story-line presents an authoritative chain of reliable transmission of God's Law from its beginnings in Moses to the present.

For Rabbinic Judaism, then, wisdom rhetorolect is the story of Torah wisdom. The "special" story about God is God's creation of the people of Israel through the transmission of God's Law to God's people. Since the Law is both written and oral, the story moves beyond the "written" Law in the "scriptures" (writings) through an authoritative chain of transmission of both written and oral Law from the Bible to the Mishnah, which is the foundation for both the Jerusalem and Babylonian Talmuds, which consist of Mishnah plus interpretation (gemara). As "Torah" wisdom unfolds, it blends prophetic and priestly discourse into its conceptuality and language. The prophets provide the bridge from the elders to the men of the Great Synagogue. While the temple still existed, the temple service was the bridge between knowing and doing the Law. After the destruction of the temple, study, interpretation, and enactment of the Law stood at the foundations of authentic, priestly worship of God. In turn, priestly holiness also stands at the center of study, interpretation, and enactment of the Law. In the study of God's Law, wisdom and holiness are one, each totally embedded in the other.

Looking back at first century Christian discourse in relation to emergent rabbinic discourse, it is interesting to note that Moses is the most frequently cited Hebrew Bible person in the New Testament.[27] The frequent reference to Moses in the New Testament functions as a dynamic way of "embedding" the story of Moses into the argumentative Christian story. In the context of this "Moses" story-line, there is no apocalyptic discourse, unless one interprets "Gehenna" in (5) within an apocalyptic frame of meaning. Also, there is no precreation discourse, even though Proverbs 8 in Tanakh and Sirach 1 and 24 in particular create such a possibility for Torah wisdom to exist with God prior to the creation of the heavens and the earth. One also notices the absence of miracle discourse in the story-line. Rather, wisdom, prophetic, and priestly frames blend together in the presentation of a chain of people from Moses to Rabban Simeon ben Gamaliel. As the story-lines embedded in the six early Christian rhetorolects unfold in these two volumes, it will be informative to see the particular ways early Christians understood the story-line from Moses to Jesus, in contrast to the Rabbinic story-line from Moses to the time of the Mishnah.

[27] 69 times. It is interesting, and important, to note that Moses is also the most frequently cited Hebrew Bible person in the Quran (137 times).

Cleanthes' *Hymn to Zeus*

Christianity emerged, of course, in the context of the Mediterranean world, which included the mainland areas of northern Egypt, the eastern Syria-Decapolis-Galilee-Judea (plus) regions, Asia Minor, Macedonia-Greece, and the Roman peninsula. These areas contained multiple kinds of worship of gods and goddesses. As a beginning point to move beyond the relation of Christian discourse to rabbinic discourse, we will take a brief look at Cleanthes' *Hymn to Zeus* and a *Hymn to Isis* by Isidorus. This will help us to invite additional discourses from the wide-reaching religious sphere of the Mediterranean world into our discussion of Christian discourse. These explorations can give us some important initial glimpses into additional patterns and arguments in the extended environment in which Christianity emerged.

We will begin with Cleanthes' *Hymn to Zeus*. Especially through the influence of Stoicism, Zeus came to be viewed in ways that are highly significant for understanding Christianity during its earliest centuries. Cleanthes (331-232 BCE), who became head of the Stoic school in 262 BCE, is attributed with a *Hymn to Zeus* which is displayed here according to an outline of the hymn formulated by Johan C. Thom:[28]

I. Invocation: Praise of Zeus
A. Zeus as ruler
1 Noblest of immortals (*athanatōn*), many-named, always all-powerful (*pankrates*)
Zeus, first cause and ruler (*archēge*) of nature, governing everything with your law (*nomou*), greetings!
B. Corresponding human reaction: praise
3 For it is right for all mortals (*thnētoisi*) to address you:
for we have our origin (*genos*) in you, bearing a likeness (*mimēma*) to god,
5 we, alone of all that live (*zōei*) and move as mortals on earth (*thnēt' epi gaian*).

II. Argument: Zeus' rule and human recalcitrance
A. Description of Zeus' rule
1. Obedience of nature
6 Therefore I shall praise you constantly and always sing of your rule (*kratos*).
For this whole universe, spinning around the earth,
obeys you wherever you lead, and is readily ruled (*krateitai*) by you;
such a servant do you have between your unconquerable hands (*chersin*),
10 the two-edged, fiery (*puroenta*), ever-living thunderbolt (*keraunon*).
For by its strokes (*plēgēis*) all works (*erga*) of nature <are guided>.
With it you direct the universal reason (*logos*), which permeates
everything, mingling with the great and the small lights.

[28] Johan C. Thom, "The Problem of Evil in Cleanthes' *Hymn to Zeus*," *Acta Classica* 41 (1998) 48; cf. idem, *Cleanthes' Hymn to Zeus* (Studies and Texts in Antiquity and Christianity 33; Tübingen: Mohr Siebeck, 2005) 40-41.

Because of this you are so great, the highest (*hypatos*) king (*basileus*) for ever.
2. Contrast: human folly
15 Not a single deed (*ergon*) takes place on earth without you, God,
nor in the divine celestial sphere nor in the sea
except what bad people (*kakoi*) do in their folly (*anoiais*).
B. Zeus creates harmony out of conflict
18 But you know how to make the uneven even
and to put into order the disorderly; even the unloved is dear to you.
For you thus join everything into one, the good with the bad,
that there comes to be one ever-lasting rational order (*logos*) for everything.
C. Human recalcitrance
1. Rejection of universal reason
22 This all mortals (*thnētōn*) that are bad (*kakoi*) flee from and avoid,
the wretched, who though always desiring to acquire good things (*agathōn*),
neither see nor hear God's (*theou*) universal law (*nomon*),
obeying which they could have a good life with understanding.
2. Continual quest for diverging objects
26 But they immediately rush without understanding, each after something else,
some with a belligerent eagerness for glory (*doxēs*),
others without discipline intent on profits,
others yet on indulgence and the pleasurable actions of the body.
<They desire the good,> but they are borne now to this, then to that,
while striving eagerly that the complete opposite of these things happen.

III. Prayer: Deliverance and insight
A. Plea for deliverance from ignorance and for insight
32 But all-bountiful (*pandōre*) Zeus, cloud-wrapped ruler of the thunderbolt (*archikeraune*),
deliver (*hryou*) human beings from their destructive ignorance;
disperse it from their souls, Father (*pater*); grant that they obtain
the insight on which you rely when governing everything with justice (*dikēs*) –
B. Goal of deliverance and insight: praise
36 so that we, having been honored (*timēthentes*), may honor (*timēi*) you in return,
constantly praising your works (*ta sa erga*), as befits
one who is mortal (*thnēton*). For there is no other greater honor for mortals
or for gods (*theois*) than always to praise the universal law (*nomon*) with justice (*dikēi*).[29]

[29] The translation is from Johan C. Thom, "Cleanthes' *Hymn to Zeus* and Early Christian Literature," in A.Y. Collins and M.M. Mitchell (eds.), *Antiquity and Humanity: Essays on Ancient Religion and Philosophy presented to Hans Dieter Betz on his 70th Birthday* (Tübingen: Mohr Siebeck, 2001) 477-99; cf. A.A. Long & D.N. Sedley, *The Hellenistic Philosophers. Volume 1: Translations of the Principal Sources, with Philosophical Commentary* (Cambridge/New York/Melbourne: Cambridge University Press, 1997) 326-27; Thom, *Cleanthes' Hymn to Zeus*, 34-41.

The hymn opens with reference to Zeus as "noblest of immortals" (1: *kudist' athanatōn*). This opening establishes a hierarchical relation between Zeus, the most highly honored, eternal, immortal deity, and humans on earth, who are mortal (*thnētoi*: 3, 5, 22, 38) and may be bad people (17, 20, 22: *kakoi*). Zeus is both Father (34: *pater*) over human beings and highest King forever (14: *hypatos basileus dia pantos*) over the world. Zeus is all-powerful (1: *pankrates*), ruling the world with unconquerable hands (9: *anikētois meta chersin*). Zeus has two assistants: (1) his universal law (2, 24, 39: *koinos nomos*); and (2) his two-edged, fiery, ever-living thunderbolt (10: *amphēkē puroenta aeizōonta keraunon*). The universal law that assists Zeus emerges from his attribute as *archēgos* (2): originator[30] and ruling leader[31] of nature.[32] The entire cosmos obeys (8: *peithetai*) wherever Zeus leads (8: *agēis*) and is readily ruled (8: *ekōn ... krateitai*) by Zeus. With the aid of his universal law and his fiery thunderbolt, Zeus joins all things, good and bad, into one, bringing one eternal *logos* (rational order) into being.[33]

While the cosmos is obedient to Zeus, some humans are not. This creates a special, and unusual, problem for all-powerful Zeus.[34] Humans are the only living beings on earth that bear a likeness (*mimēma*) to Zeus, because they have their origin (*genos*) in him (4-5). Yet they may turn away from Zeus' rule and leadership. Instead of seeking the *logos* Zeus brings into being, some people flee from it (22) and act in folly (17: *anoias*). They flee from the eternal *logos* Zeus brings into being, and they do not see and hear God's universal law (24: *theou koinon nomon*). As a result, they pursue first one thing and then another without any discipline or understanding (26-31). In contrast, people who see and hear Zeus' law, and turn towards Zeus' *logos*, receive honor through Zeus' justice (35-36). People who know this honor Zeus in return, singing constantly of his works (37) and singing forever with justice of his universal law (39).

Cleanthes' *Hymn to Zeus* leads us into philosophical dimensions of Christian discourse. This hymn is argumentative in ways that are similar to certain belief arguments of Christians. A major difference from the Christian story lies in the manner in which the hymn stays with an implicit story of Zeus' creation and governing of the world. The hymn does not introduce events after Zeus' creation of the world that verify and clarify Zeus' attributes and actions as Father and King of the uni-

[30] The one who established (led forth: *agō*) the beginning (*archē*) of things.

[31] The ruler (*archōn*) who leads (*agō*).

[32] Thom, "Cleanthes' *Hymn*" translates *archēge* with "first cause and ruler"; Long & Sedley, *The Hellenistic Philosophers*, I:326 translate it with "prime mover."

[33] (21: *hena gignesthai pantōn logon aien eonta*).

[34] See Thom, *Cleanthes' Hymn to Zeus*, 69-142.

verse. In other words, this hymn remains fully argumentative within a conceptuality of Zeus' bringing forth of the universe and its order. The hymn does not move beyond this into events that create a specific story-line related to specific belief arguments. Instead, it presents a specific argument about Zeus as originator and ruler of the universe in a context where a hymnist argues that humans have a right to address Zeus and, in fact, have a duty to return to Zeus the honor Zeus offers to humans.

The opening invocation sets forth the basis for the belief arguments in the hymn through its assertions that Zeus is "noblest of immortals," "many-named," "always all-powerful," "first cause and ruler of nature," and "one who governs everything with his law" (1-2). Yet the initial argument of the hymn is that humans have the right to speak directly to Zeus, since they alone of all things that live on earth bear a likeness to their originator (3-5). On the basis of this argument, the hymnist launches into praise of Zeus, convinced that it is appropriate to do so (6).

In the context of the initial argument about the right of humans to address Zeus, the hymn presents an argument about Zeus and humans that unfolds in two steps: (1) a positive argument concerning Zeus' power to rule; and (2) an elaborated argument from the contrary that even though Zeus rules over every deed that takes place in the cosmos, bad people do not obey Zeus' rule. First, the hymnist asserts that he will constantly sing of Zeus' rule (*kratos*), since the entire universe obeys his leadership and readily accepts his rule (6-8). Zeus is able to rule in this manner with the assistance of his two-edged, fiery, ever-living thunderbolt, since the strokes of this thunderbolt guide all the works of nature and direct the universal reason (*logos*) which permeates everything as Zeus brings it into being (9-13). Because Zeus is able to rule in this manner, with the aid of his fiery thunderbolt, it is only proper to conclude that he is the highest king forever (14).

Second, the hymnist turns to a contrary argument, namely an argument that, although everything in the universe obeys Zeus, everything does not actually obey him. On the one hand, not a single deed takes place on earth, in the divine celestial sphere, or in the sea without Zeus (15-16). On the other hand, there are things that bad people do in their folly (17). To be sure, Zeus himself knows (18: *epistasai*) how to deal with everything in the universe. He knows how to make the uneven even, to put order into the disorderly, since even the unloved is dear to him (18-19). Indeed, through this knowledge he joins the good and bad together and causes one ever-lasting rational order (*logos*) to come into being (20). The problem is that bad mortals flee from and avoid this rational order (*logos*). Even though they desire to acquire good things (*agathōn*), they neither see nor hear God's universal law, which could bring them, if they obeyed it, a good life with understanding (23-25). Instead, bad people rush without understanding after all kinds of things, some with lustfulness seeking glory, others without discipline wanting profits, and still others with indulgence wanting pleasures of the body (26-29).

In this context, the hymnist launches a plea to Zeus to deliver human beings from their destructive ignorance. The hymnist addresses "All-Giving" Zeus as Father and pleas with him to scatter the ignorance from the souls of bad people and grant them the insight on which Zeus himself relies as he governs everything with justice (32-35). If Zeus will honor humans in this way by granting them deliverance from ignorance, then humans may honor Zeus in return, praising his works as befits mortals (36-37); because there is no greater honor for mortals and gods than always to praise with justice the universal law (38-39).

The emphasis on insight and understanding that removes ignorance signals a strong presence of wisdom rhetorolect in Cleanthes' *Hymn to Zeus*. Zeus uses this insight to bring *logos* (rational order) to being throughout the universe. The emphasis, however, is on the presence of this wisdom in Zeus' rule of the world. The Hymn is dominated, therefore, with "kingdom" rhetorolect, which is called prophetic rhetorolect in this book as a result of the focus on justice in it. Justice is something that both god and humans must enact if there is to be successful kingship and kingdom. Zeus works toward justice with the assistance of universal law (*koinos nomos*) and his eternal, two-edged fiery thunderbolt. Zeus' use of fire here is reminiscent, on the one hand, of the "fire of God" that comes down on the cities named in Amos 1–2. On the other hand, this fiery instrument reminds one of Moses' assertion to the Israelites that "Your God is a devouring fire" (Deut 4:24). Also, the interchange between God and Abraham over the nature of righteousness and justice when God rains sulfur and fire down on complete cities (Gen 18:16–19:29) is reminiscent of the hymnists' reminding of Zeus that he governs everything with justice (35). In a context of praise of Zeus, the Hymn ends with an assertion that implicates both mortals and gods in an intermingling of praise of the universal law with justice (39). Universal law is like wisdom. It is "justice wisdom" (35). This justice wisdom is the agency through which Zeus brings *logos* into being throughout the universe. Bad people flee from the *logos*, that which Zeus brings into being. The hymnist prays for Zeus to give humans the "insight" Zeus uses when he governs everything with justice (35). This insight, it appears, can allow humans to praise the universal law with justice. For this reason, it appears, the pears, the Hymn ends with praise of the universal law, rather than praise of Zeus himself.

The presence of this kind of "philosophical" belief in the Mediterranean world about the highest King and Father of the universe is important for understanding many dynamics of Christianity. At the base of Christian belief lies a particular story-line from creation through the story of Jesus. But Christians understand this story-line in at least "semi-philosophical" ways. As a result, their "belief arguments" have philosophical dimensions as well as implications for how one tells the "story" of God's world. It is also informative that Zeus uses "assistants" as he runs the world. Zeus' law (*nomos*) and Zeus' bringing of universal reason (*logos*) into being are especially interesting in relation to the function both of wisdom (*sophia*) and word-wisdom (*logos*) in Christianity. In addition, the role of Zeus' two-edged, fiery, every-living thunderbolt has an uncanny relation both to the Holy Spirit that can come as tongues of fire into the Christian community (Acts 2) and to the Son of Man in Rev 1:14-16 who has eyes "like a flame of fire" and a "sharp, two-edged sword" that comes from his mouth. The presence of these accompanying agents of the highest God, who is King and Father of all, creates a context that has very special dynamics in relation to Christianity.[35]

Isidorus' *Hymn to Isis*

Next we will look at a hymn to Isis, a goddess who became widely known and worshipped in the Mediterranean world by 200 CE. Through a blending of Greek and Egyptian religion, worship of the goddess Isis spread throughout the Mediterranean world in the centuries prior to and during the emergence of Christianity. During the Hellenistic period, the role of the Egyptian goddess Ma'at (truth, justice, order) was transferred to Isis, wife of Osiris and mother of King Horus.[36] According to Diodorus Siculus "her birth was everlasting and ancient."[37] With her husband Osiris, Isis established the process for agricultural productivity in the world. In addition, Isis established justice in human society:[38]

> Isis also established laws ... in accordance with which people regularly

[35] For further insights, see Thom, "Cleanthes' *Hymn*," and H.-J. Klauck, *The Religious Context of Early Christianity: A Guide to Graeco-Roman Religions* (trans. B. McNeil; Edinburgh: T & T Clark, 2000) 351-57.

[36] Howard Clark Kee, *Miracle in the Early Christian World: A Study in Sociohistorical Method* (New Haven/London: Yale University Press, 1983) 113-14.

[37] Diodorus Siculus, *Library* 1.1-4, trans. C.H. Oldfather, LCL (New York: Putnam, 1933).

[38] Kee, *Miracle*, 114.

> dispense justice to one another and are led to refrain through fear of punishment from illegal violence and insolence; and it is for this reason also that the early Greeks gave Demeter the name Thesmophorus, acknowledging in this way that she had first established laws.[39]

After Isis and Osiris establish order in Egypt, Osiris "turned over supreme power to Isis his wife."[40] Part of this supreme authority was to receive the names of other deities: Demeter, Thesmophorus, Selene, Hera.[41]

It will be helpful to look at a *Hymn to Isis* attributed to Isidorus, which scholars think probably was written between 88 and 80 BCE:[42]

I. Invocation
Giver of wealth (*ploutodoti*), Queen of the gods (*basileia theōn*), Lady Hermouthis,
All-powerful (*pantokrateira*), Good Fortune (*tychē agathē*), Isis of the Great Name,
most high (*hypsistē*) Deo, Discoverer of all life (*zōēs pasēs*),

II. Rehearsal of Isis' Mighty Works
You put Your hand to mighty works of all kinds (*pantoiōn ergōn*), so as to give
life and an ordered society to all mankind (*anthrōpoisi hapasi*),
You introduced laws (*thesmous*) so that there might be a measure of justice (*eudikiē*),
You revealed sciences so that men might live decently,
You discovered the flowering nature of all fruitful plants (*karpōn*).

III. Created World is Domain of Isis' Power
For You the sky came into being, the whole earth,
the breath of the breezes, the Sun with its welcome radiance.
By Your power (*dynamei*) the streams of the Nile are all filled full
at the summer season, and its water pours turbulent
over the whole land so that the crop may never fail.

IV. All Earthly Mortals Worship Isis
All mortals (*brotoi*) who live (*zōousi*) on the limitless earth,
Thracians, Greeks, and foreigners (*barbaroi*) as well,
utter Your Glorious Name which all honor (*polytimēton para pasi*),
each in his own language, each in his own land.
Syrians call You Astarte, Artemis, Nanaea,
the tribes of Lycia call you Queen Leto,
men in Thrace call you Mother of the Gods (*mētera theōn*),
Greeks call you Hera of the lofty throne (*megalothronon*), and Aphrodite,
kindly Hestia, Rheia, and Demeter.

[39] Diodorus Siculus, *Library* 1.13.4-5.
[40] Diodorus Siculus, *Library* 1.17.3.
[41] Diodorus Siculus, *Library* 1.25.1.
[42] V.F. Vanderlip, *The Four Greek Hymns of Isidorus and the Cult of Isis* (American Studies in Papyrology 12; Toronto: A.M. Hakkert, 1972) 12-13.

Egyptians call you Thiouis because You, being One (*mounē*), are all
the other goddesses (*theai*) named by all peoples.

V. Hymnist Sings Because Isis Rescues All People
My Lady, I shall not stop hymning your Mighty Power (*megalēn dynamin*),
Immortal Saviour (*sōteir' athanatē*), goddess of the many names (*polyōnmenoi),*
almighty (*megistē*) Isis,
rescuing (*hrymenē*) from war cities and all of their citizens,
men, their wives, possessions and dear children.
All who are held in the destiny of Death (*moirais thanatou*), all in bondage,
all who are racked with pain which will not let them sleep,
all men journeying in a foreign country,
all who sail on the great sea in stormy weather,
when ships are wrecked and men lose their lives
all these find salvation (*sōzonth'*) if they pray (*epeuxamenoi*) for Your present help.

VI. Personal Plea
Hear my prayers (*euchōn*), You whose Name has Mighty Power (*megalosthenes*),
be propitious to me and free (*anapauson*) me from all affliction.[43]

Many of the attributes of Isis are attributes of Zeus expressed in a feminine mode. Instead of Father and King, Isis is Mother (20) and Queen (1). Like Zeus, she is immortal (26: *athanatē*), all-powerful (2: *pantokrateira*), many-named (26), and the most high (3: *hypsistē*). She is honored by everyone (16), and she is known for her mighty works of all kinds (4). But there are also ways in which she is different.

In contrast to Cleanthes' *Hymn to Zeus,* Isidorus' *Hymn to Isis* elaborates in detail the manner in which Isis is "many-named." Because all people, civilized and barbarian, both utter and honor her glorious name in their own language, she is known not only as Isis but as: Astarte, Artemis, Nanaea, Queen Leto (18-19); Mother of the Gods, Hera of the lofty throne, Aphrodite, kindly Hestia, Rheia, Demeter, and Thiouis (20-23). In addition, she has attributes that call forth additional names: Giver of wealth, Queen of the gods, Lady Hermouthis, All-powerful, Good Fortune, Most High Deo, Discoverer of all life (1-3); and Immortal Savior (26). The listing of specific names in addition to special attributes exhibits an aspect that is not emphasized so emphatically with Zeus. In Cleanthes' hymn, Zeus appears to be many named as a result of his status as Father and King of the universe. In other words, as the highest god, people honor his unsurpassed attributes and deeds with a wide array of names that exhibit his rank above all other gods. In Isidorus' hymn, there is an emphasis that Isis has

[43] For the Greek, see Vanderlip, *The Four Greek Hymns*," 17-18.

many names, but she is "one" (23: *mounī*). She is "the one" manifestation of all other major goddesses among all other peoples. The emphasis in the two hymns, then, moves in opposite directions. Zeus is well known as the highest of gods; as a result, people use many names to honor his status. Isis may be viewed by some people simply as a local goddess of Egypt or somewhere else; she is in fact the One Almighty, Immortal Queen and Mother of all gods who has manifested her powers through all other goddesses whom people know. In other words, while Zeus manifests his power through law, the thunderbolt, and *logos*, Isis manifests her power as one goddess through all other goddesses.

Among the names for Isis, Immortal Savior emerges as especially important (26): an indication of her mighty power (25) and of her activity of rescuing people from various kinds of circumstances (27). Her function as Immortal Savior leads to a list of particular kinds of rescues she performs: (1) cities and all their citizens from war; (2) all who are held in the destiny of death; (3) all in bondage; (4) all in pain that will not let them sleep; (5) all journeying in a foreign country (31); (6) all sailing on the great sea in stormy weather; and (7) when ships are wrecked and men lose their lives (27-33). All of the people in these situations, the hymn asserts, may find salvation (*sōzonta*), if they pray to Isis for help in their circumstance (34). For this reason, Isis also is called Good Fortune (2: *tychē agathē*), rather than, perhaps, simply Fortune. Isis does not punish, like Zeus might. Rather, she brings good fortune to people if they pray to her.

Isis, like Zeus, works with justice. But her justice is limited to activities among humans, rather than a principle that functions throughout the inner processes of the cosmos itself. Zeus is All-Giving (*Hymn to Zeus* 32). In contrast, Isis is Giver of wealth (*Hymn to Isis* 1), a mode of giving limited to the sphere of human life in the cosmos. Isis introduced social laws (*thesmous*) so that beneficial justice (*eudikiē*) could operate among humans (6). These laws appear not to be universal law (*koinos nomos*), which people should see and hear, and which can be guided by some special force, like an eternal, fiery thunderbolt, to bring into being one, everlasting universal rational order (*hena pantōn logon aien eonta*).[44] Indeed, Isis appears not to be the originator and ruler of all things in the universe. Rather, "for her sake" (*sou charin*) the sky, the whole earth, the breath of the breezes, and the sun with its welcome radiance came into being (9-10). The special realm of her power, and the special domain in which she can act beneficially, is the created cosmos. She is the "discoverer" (3: *euretria*) of all life rather than its

[44] *Hymn to Zeus* 21.

originator and ruler. But in this context, her mighty works give life and an ordered society, introduce laws to produce justice, reveal technologies so people may live respectably, and find the flowering nature of all fruitful plants (4-8). Isis, then, is a "personal" deity; one who oversees personal benefits of all human beings in the world.

The hymn ends with a personal plea by the hymnist that Isis hear the hymnist's prayers, act beneficially toward the hymnist and give the hymnist rest from all affliction (*lypēs*). The hymnist does not simply pray for all mortals, like the hymnist in Cleanthes' *Hymn to Zeus* (32-39) but for personal benefit (Isis Hymn: 35-36).

In contrast to Cleanthes' *Hymn to Zeus*, there is very little "governing" rhetorolect in Isidorus' *Hymn to Isis*. Isis is interested in justice (6), but she does not oversee and enact a system of justice like Zeus does. Her participation in justice has more kinship with wisdom rhetorolect, which focuses on order in the universe that provides an environment for productivity rather than destruction.[45] According to the Hymn, Isis gives an ordered society to people through her mighty works (4-5). She introduced laws, revealed sciences, and discovered the flowering nature of all fruitful plants (6-8). These activities participate in the creation and ordering of the world, and the inner processes are related to Zeus' use of universal law and production of rational order (*logos*). Thus, in basic ways the attributes and activities of Isis have a relation to wisdom rhetorolect.

The dominant rhetorolect in Isidorus' *Hymn to Isis*, however, is miracle rhetorolect. All-powerful Isis uses her power beneficially in the realm of human life, not only giving wealth (1), good fortune (2), and never-failing crops from the water of the Nile (11-13). She functions in a special way as Immortal Savior (26) who responds to people's needs in times of crisis. When all hope appears to be gone in times of war, death, bondage, pain, travel in a foreign country, stormy weather on the sea, and shipwreck (27-33), Isis responds and brings salvation if people pray to her for help (34). For this reason, the hymnist prays to Isis in the final two lines for personal benefit and rest from all affliction (35-36). These are the dynamics and concerns of miracle rhetorolect.

In the two hymns, then, we see two important movements in Mediterranean religious discourse. On the one hand, "philosophical" religion may work through one or more of the pantheon of gods to articulate a cosmic system whereby humans may receive benefits from the gods. This approach moves toward wisdom and prophetic rhetorolect in a manner that envisions precreation rhetorolect, namely, rational order that transcends the order and disorder of the created

[45] See John J. Collins, *Jewish Hellenism in the Hellenistic Age* (OTL; Louisville, KY: Westminster John Knox Press, 1997) 203-204 on "Wisdom and Isis."

world. On the other hand, a particular religion may energetically, or even aggressively, "incorporate" other gods or goddesses to become a (or "the") Highest God. One way to achieve this is through miracle rhetorolect, where one god manifests the powers and actions of multiple deities and uses these powers to respond to personal crises of people who live in the created world. Especially in the Gospels and Acts in the NT, Christian discourse enters these discursive worlds associated with Isis. We will see in the forthcoming chapters that Christianity participates in most of the ways of understanding divinity and humanity in the universe that are present in Cleanthes' *Hymn to Zeus* and Isidorus' *Hymn to Isis* presented above. As Christianity reconfigured Jewish understanding of the God of Israel and Hellenistic-Roman understandings of gods, goddesses, and the cosmos and their traditions, rites, and hymns, Christianity created a dynamic, versatile mode of religious thought, belief, and action in the Mediterranean world.

Conclusion

This chapter has provided a brief glimpse into the Mediterranean world in which Christianity emerged. The thesis of the chapter is that Christianity established a distinctive mode of discourse and a distinctive belief culture by introducing a new argumentative story-line through special interaction with emerging Rabbinic Judaism in the context of a wide variety of Hellenistic-Roman religions. While the rabbinic story-line focused on new interpretations that provided the means for better observance of God's Law, the Christian story-line focused on a new sequence of events in the world that provided a better means for receiving the benefits of God's forgiveness and love. In relation to Zeus the almighty and eternal Father and King, assisted by universal law and the eternal, fiery thunderbolt in the production of universal *logos*, the Christian story-line featured God the Father as the almighty, eternal King, assisted by his only-begotten Son Jesus Christ (the *logos*), and the Holy Spirit, the Giver and Sustainer of life. In relation to Egyptian-Hellenistic Isis, through whom the attributes and deeds of all divine goddesses throughout the ages brought civilization, language, healing, and salvation, the Christian story-line presented triune divinity that brought grace, peace, miraculous healing, and salvation to a sinful world.

A key to the power of the argumentative Christian story-line is its comprehensive reach from eternity before the world began to eternity after the world ends. Embedding the story of Jesus in this never-ending story line creates a context where Christians can potentially interpret time in any century as "Christian time" related both to "heaven and earth time" and to God's realm outside of time. Since, however, additional events in the story-line are intimately related to Christian belief arguments, Christians continually develop ways to identify the "true" argumentative story over against various kinds of "less true" or "false" presentations of the argumentative story. This dynamic was at work during the beginnings of early Christianity, and it is constantly at work among different kinds of Christian traditions throughout the world to-day.

A key to the power of Rabbinic Judaism is its infinite capacity to be extended into another century in another time and place where it is necessary to be faithful to God's Law. Rabbis, and indeed all "devoted" Jews in every century, are invited to step into the chain of transmission of God's written and oral Law and participate in it. Participation in God's Law means studying it both in teacher-disciple contexts and in teacher-teacher contexts, where teaching and debate can sharpen understanding in a context of multiple points of view and traditions. Participating in God's Law means studying it, interpreting it, understanding it, and doing it. This is a never-ending process – a process that can extend into any place and any time, including beyond time!

A key to Greco-Roman religion is the ability of various gods to manifest the attributes and deeds of other gods. Zeus as the eternal, "many-named," all-powerful Father and King over all the universe maintains a position of superiority to all other gods, controlling the fate of all other gods and of all humans. Yet, a goddess like the "many-named" Isis can manifest all the attributes and deeds of all other goddesses, which includes activities often attributed to Zeus. This almost unlimited ability of certain deities to manifest the deeds and attributes of other deities creates a context where all kinds of "local" deities can be integrated into higher deities as these deities manifest additional deeds and attributes through a process of gaining additional names.

As these religions functioned in this manner in the Mediterranean world, they participated in various ways in wisdom, prophetic, apocalyptic, precreation, miracle, and priestly rhetorolect. As we move through the chapters in this book and the subsequent volume, we will move through these six rhetorolects in early Christian discourse.

The stage has now been set for the next chapter, which focuses on the relation of the argumentative Christian story to the Christian Bible, which begins with the creation of the world (Genesis) and ends with an eternal city that comes down from heaven when heaven and earth come to an end (Revelation). The challenge before sociorhetorical interpretation in this volume is to analyze, display, and interpret the ways in which Christianity both incorporated and transformed the "Old Testament" story and the conceptualities about deities in the Mediterranean world into the "Christian" biblical story. This is a goal that most literary-historical interpreters during the last half century, at least, have not set for themselves.[46] Therefore, it is important to find a way, in the midst of the rich heritage of literary-historical interpretation, to move toward a mode of interpretation that can exhibit and interpret the inner processes of the story-argument formation that occurred during the period of time when Christian discourse was emerging in the Mediterranean world.

[46] Northrop Frye, *The Great Code: The Bible and Literature* (New York: Harcourt, Brace, Jovanovich, 1982) was a major exception, and recently Jack Miles, *God: A Biography* (New York: Alfred A. Knopf, 1995); idem, *Christ: A Crisis in the Life of God* (New York: Vintage Books, 2001).

2

Argumentative Christian Story and the Bible

Literary Poetics from the Hebrew Bible to the Quran

Literary Poetics in the Hebrew Bible

The perspective that drives the analysis, research, and interpretation for this book and the series in which it appears concerns the persuasive nature of religious discourse from the Hebrew Bible through the New Testament to the Quran in the seventh century CE. Paul Ricoeur helped to inaugurate the approach in this book and in this series with his essay in 1980 entitled "Toward a Hermeneutic of the Idea of Revelation."[1] In this essay, he discusses five discourses in the Hebrew Bible: prophetic, narrative, prescriptive, wisdom, and hymnic discourse.[2] Ricoeur's approach helped to move biblical interpretation beyond historical and theological issues into an appreciation of the Hebrew Bible from the perspective of the literary poetics it made conventional in Jewish tradition. This means, for Ricoeur, that there are five conventional "poetics" in the Hebrew Bible. In each instance there are two or more entire books in the Hebrew Bible that contain a conventional poetics. Ricoeur does not list them, but it is easy to see the literary home of prophetic poetics in the major and minor prophets; the literary home of narrative poetics in Genesis through Exodus 19, Joshua through 2 Kings, Ezra-Nehemiah through 1-2 Chronicles, and perhaps Ruth; the literary home of prescriptive poetics in Exodus 20–40, Leviticus, and Deuteronomy; the liter-

[1] Paul Ricoeur, *Essays on Biblical Interpretation* (Philadelphia: Fortress, 1980) 75-85. Subsequently, David Tracy built on Ricoeur's insights in *Plurality and Ambiguity: Hermeneutics, Religion, Hope* (San Francisco: Harper & Row, 1987). Also see Gerald O. West, *Biblical Hermeneutics of Liberation: Modes of Reading the Bible in the South African Context* (2nd, revised ed.; Maryknoll, NY: Orbis Books and Pietermaritzburg: Cluster Publications, 1995).

[2] From my perspective, Ricoeur does not give substantive consideration to apocalyptic discourse when he refers to it simply as "subsequently grafted on to the prophetic trunk" (77). His lack of attention results, of course, from his focus on the HB, where there is so much prophetic literature and the earliest images of destruction during the "last days" occur in this literature. Nevertheless, his typology of five kinds of discourses is a good place to begin in an assessment of discourses in the NT.

ary home of wisdom poetics in Proverbs, Qoheleth, and Job; and the literary home of hymnic poetics in Psalms and Song of Solomon. This was an important advance in biblical interpretation, because it called attention to the power of biblical literature to create poetic modes that functioned as conventional ways to construct responsible, creative images of human life in the world.

Literary Poetics in the Dead Sea Scrolls

The literary forms in the Dead Sea Scrolls exhibit a close relation to the literary poetics of the Hebrew Bible. In a context where scribes were copying and recopying multiple versions of all the writings in the Hebrew Bible except Esther, they built new literary modes deeply influenced by literary poetics in the Hebrew Bible. Accordingly, Qumranites adapted Psalms into Thanksgiving Hymns,[3] apocryphal and noncanonical psalms,[4] and songs for the burnt offering on the sabbath.[5] In addition, they created wisdom poems that blend proverbial wisdom with psalmic verse, lamentation, beatitude, and exorcism against demons.[6] Also, they adapted covenant legislation in the Torah into the Manual of Discipline, the Damascus Document, a halakic letter and other halakic texts.[7] They adapted the accounts of the holy wars of Israel against its neighbors into the War Scroll and the Temple Scroll.[8] In other ways they enacted literary poetics of the writings in the Hebrew Bible either by writing line-by-line commentaries on them or by weaving biblical verses with others into a florilegium.[9] Beyond this, there is "re-written Hebrew Bible," plus other writing related to Hebrew Bible.[10] The literature at Qumran, then, exhibits a deep literary poetic relation to the writings in the Hebrew Bible.

Literary Poetics in the Old Testament Apocrypha

In the context of Greek and Latin translation and transmission of the Bible, the Hebrew Bible corpus expanded with the addition of a number of entire books and with a number of additions to books. These additions are commonly called the Old Testament Apocrypha.[11] Five of

[3] Geza Vermes, *The Complete Dead Sea Scrolls in English* (New York: Penguin Books, 1997) 243-300; Florentino García Martínez, *The Dead Sea Scrolls Translated: The Qumran Texts in English* (2d ed.; Grand Rapids: Eerdmans/Leiden: Brill, 1996) 317-70.

[4] Vermes, *Complete Dead Sea Scrolls*, 301-18; Martínez, *Dead Sea Scrolls*, 303-16.

[5] Vermes, *Complete Dead Sea Scrolls*, 321-30; Martínez, *Dead Sea Scrolls*, 419-31.

[6] Vermes, *Complete Dead Sea Scrolls*, 395-425; Martínez, *Dead Sea Scrolls*, 371-404, 432-42.

[7] Vermes, *Complete Dead Sea Scrolls*, 97-160, 220-39; Martínez, *Dead Sea Scrolls*, 3-92.

[8] Vermes, *Complete Dead Sea Scrolls*, 161-219; Martínez, *Dead Sea Scrolls*, 95-128, 154-84.

[9] Vermes, *Complete Dead Sea Scrolls*, 460-504; Martínez, *Dead Sea Scrolls*, 185-216.

[10] Vermes, *Complete Dead Sea Scrolls*, 431-59, 507-95; Martínez, *Dead Sea Scrolls*, 218-99.

[11] David A. deSilva, *Introducing the Apocrypha: Message, Context, and Significance* (Grand Rapids: Baker Academic, 2002).

the books are additions to the narrative poetics in the Hebrew Bible (Tobit; Judith; *3 Ezra* [1 or 3 Esdras]; 1-2 Maccabees), plus two of the additions to Daniel (Susanna; Bel and the Dragon). Two of the OT Apocrypha books add distinctively to the wisdom poetics in the Hebrew Bible: Ben Sira (Sirach or Ecclesiasticus) and the Wisdom of Solomon. In addition, the middle part of Baruch contains a wisdom poem (3:9–4:4). The Prayer of Azariah and the Song of the Three Young Men elaborate the prayers and doxologies in Dan 2:20-23; 3:28; 4:3, 34-35, 37; and 6:26-27 with hymnic discourse.[12] Also, Baruch includes hymnic discourse as it ends with a poem of consolation (4:5–5:9), part of which (4:36–5:9) resembles *Psalms of Solomon* 11:1-7.

It is of special interest as one moves toward the New Testament that two books in the OT Apocrypha present themselves as epistolary discourse: the Epistle of Jeremiah and Baruch. The Epistle of Jeremiah is a seventy-two or seventy-three verse exhortation from Jeremiah to Jews in Babylon not to fear or worship idols. It imitates the act of letter writing in Jer 29:1-23 to the same people in exile, and Jer 10:1-6 is a notable resource for its subject matter.[13] In turn, the narrative introduction to Baruch (1:1-9) presents the composition as a letter sent by Jeremiah's secretary and friend, Baruch, to the priests and people of Jerusalem from his location in Babylon, where he was in exile early in the sixth century BCE.

The letter writing in the Old Testament Apocrypha extends a literary poetic that is embedded in various books in the Hebrew Bible. According to D. Pardee, there are eleven Hebrew letter fragments reported in direct speech in the Hebrew Bible.[14] Beyond this, contents of various letters and decrees occur in indirect speech in Esth 1:22; 3:13; 9:21; 2 Chr 30:1. In addition to the Hebrew letter fragments, Paul E. Dion has identified seven Aramaic letters in the Hebrew Bible.[15] The Epistle of Jeremiah and Baruch, then, are extensions of an epistolary poetic embedded in various other poetics in the Hebrew Bible, rather than the emergence of a new poetic.

In addition to the Epistle of Jeremiah and Baruch in the OT Apocrypha, the six Greek expansions of Esther called the *Additions to Esther* include two versions of an official letter from King Artaxerxes to the

[12] This is an extension of the common practice of inserting poetic compositions into prose works (cf. 1 Sam 2; 2 Sam 22) in the process of editing the OT works.

[13] Also see Ex 20:3-5; Deut 4:27-28; 5:7-9; 32:8-9; Pss 115:3-8; 135:15-18; Isa 40:18-20; 44:9-20; 46:1-7.

[14] D. Pardee, "Hebrew Letters," *ABD* 4:285: 2 Sam 11:15; 1 Kgs 21:9-10; 2 Kgs 5:6; 10:2-3, 6 (two letters); 19:10-13 = Isa 37:10-13; Jer 29:4-23, 26-28 (two letters); Neh 6:6-7; 2 Chr 2:11-15; 21:12-15.

[15] Paul E. Dion, "Aramaic Letters," *ABD* 4:285: Dan 3:31-33; 6:26-28; Ezra 4:11-16, 17-22; 5:7b-17; 6:6-12; 7:12-26.

governors of the hundred twenty-seven provinces from India to Ethiopia and to the officials under them (Add Esth B13:1-7; E 16:1-24 [HCSB]). These letters are official decrees by the king informing the officials in the provinces that Jews must be permitted to live according to their own laws, with instructions concerning their right to defend themselves if attacked. 1 Maccabees contains eight letters. Two of the letters present information from one group of people to another (8:23-32; 12:5-18), one letter is from a King to a group of people (10:25-45), and five are letters from one individual to another (10:18-20; 11:30-37; 11:57; 12:19-23; 13:36-40). They range in length from a one-sentence letter from King Antiochus VI to Jonathan (11:57) to a 21-verse decree from King Demetrius I to the nation of the Jews (10:25-45).[16] 2 Maccabees contains two prefixed letters: 1:1-9 from the Jews in Jerusalem and the land of Judea to the Jews in Egypt; and 1:10-2:18 from the people of Jerusalem, Judea, the senate and Judas to Aristobulus and the Jews of Egypt. In addition, it contains a letter from Antiochus IV to the Jewish citizens in 9:19-27 and four letters in chapter 11.[17] 3 Maccabees contains two letters: 3:12-29 is a letter from King Ptolemy Philopator to his generals and soldiers in Egypt and all its districts and 7:1-9 is a letter from King Ptolemy Philopator to the generals in Egypt and all in authority in his government. 1 Esdras contains six letters, decrees, or references to the writing of letters.[18] 1 Esdr 6:8-22 is of special interest, since it includes a narrative report of events with attributed speech. Thus, in addition to the two books in the OT Apocrypha where the

[16] 1 Macc 8:23-32 = a letter written on bronze tablets by Romans and sent to Jerusalem (8:22); 10:18-20 = a letter from King Alexander Epiphanes (Balas) to his brother Jonathan (8:17-18); 10:25-45 = a written "message" from King Demetrius I to the nation of the Jews (10:25); 11:30-37 = a letter from King Demetrius II to Jonathan; 11:57 = a one-sentence letter from King Antiochus VI to Jonathan; 12:5-18 = The high priest Jonathan, the senate of the nation, the priests, and the rest of the Jewish people to the Spartans; 12:19-23 = a letter from King Arius of the Spartans to High Priest Onias; 13:36-40 = a letter from King Demetrius II to Simon.

[17] From Lysias to the Jews in 11:16-21; from Antiochus V to Lysias in 11:22-26; from Antiochus V to the senate of the Jews and other Jews in 11:27-33; from envoys of the Romans to the Jews in 11:34-38.

[18] 1 Esdras 2:3-7 = a proclamation of King Cyrus of Persia; 2:17-24 = a letter from Bishlam, Mithridates, Tabeel, Rehum, Beltethmus, the scribe Shimshai, and the rest of their associates living in Samaria and other places to King Artaxerxes of Persia against those living in Judea and Jerusalem (2:16); 2:26-29 = King Artaxerxes' reply to the people in Samaria and its surroundings; 4:47 = reference to King Darius writing letters to all going to build Jerusalem (4:48-57 reports the contents of the letter in indirect quotation); 6:8-22 = a letter from Sisinnes the governor of Syria and Phoenicia, Sathrabuzanes, and their associates the local rulers in Syria and Phoenicia to King Darius (includes narrative report of events with attributed speech); 6:24-26, 28-31 = decrees to build the house of the Lord in Jerusalem and begin the rituals in it.

opening narration presents them as letters, there are 22 or 23 letters embedded in the books that are additions to the Hebrew Bible.

Some of the books in the OT Apocrypha exhibit a growing tendency to interweave multiple literary poetics together in one composition. Baruch, for example, is a letter that is to be read aloud as a confessional liturgy at festivals and appointed seasons (1:14). After the initial confession (1:15–2:10) and a prayer (2:11–3:8), the middle of the writing contains a wisdom poem (3:9–4:4). Then, the writing ends with a poem of consolation (4:5–5:9), part of which (4:36–5:9) resembles *Psalms of Solomon* 11:1-7. Probably written somewhere between 200 and 60 BCE, Baruch exhibits how writers were interweaving various modes of biblically-influenced discourse in compositions they presented as letters.

Finally, *4 Ezra* (2 Esdras) is not present in the oldest Greek codices of the LXX, so it is regularly considered by interpreters to be among the books of the OT Pseudepigrapha. It was, however, often included in the Vulgate during the Middle Ages, and can usually be found in an appendix to the Latin Bible, after the NT. The Apocrypha of the Church of England and many Protestant churches included it. The variation in the inclusion or exclusion of it is of special interest, of course, since *4 Ezra* is an apocalypse. No book in the Hebrew Bible is an apocalypse, but Daniel 7–12 is regularly considered to represent the genre of apocalypse in the Bible.[19] The first part of the apocalypse (Dan 7:1-28) is in Aramaic, and the remainder is in Hebrew.

In the OT Apocrypha, then, one sees narrative, wisdom, and hymnic discourse related to discourse in the Hebrew Bible. There is no significant addition to prescriptive discourse, like Leviticus and Deuteronomy. Some of the additions to prophetic discourse are more like hymnic discourse than prophetic oracle. Other additions to prophetic discourse are epistolary, a phenomenon of special interest for the NT corpus. In addition, there is a move toward apocalyptic discourse with the inclusion of *4 Ezra* in many Latin Bibles during the Medieval Period and in the Church of England and many Protestant Bibles in the OT Apocrypha. The presence of apocalyptic on the horizons of the OT Apocrypha is, of course, of special interest in relation to the literary poetics of books in the NT.

Literary Poetics in the New Testament

When an interpreter moves to the New Testament, it is obvious that there is no book of Psalms and no book of Prophetic oracles in it. This means there is no entire book containing hymnic or prophetic discourse. Also, there is no entire book containing extended prescriptive

[19] John J. Collins, "Apocalypses and Apocalypticism," *ABD* 1:279.

discourse like Exodus 20–40, Leviticus, or Deuteronomy. In addition, there is no book of Proverbs in the New Testament. But this does not mean there is no entire book containing wisdom discourse. The Epistle of James is regularly considered wisdom discourse. It is different in many ways from Proverbs, Qoheleth, and Job in the Hebrew Bible; but it has important relationships with Sirach and Wisdom of Solomon in the OT Apocrypha. There are five biographical-historiographies in the NT: the four Gospels and the Acts of the Apostles. In Ricoeur's terminology, all of these books are some kind of "narrative." After the five biographical-historiographies, a reader finds twenty-one letters in the New Testament, commonly referred to by the term "epistle" to indicate that they are somehow more formal than everyday letters. Then, the New Testament ends with an apocalypse, which we have seen embedded in Daniel in the Hebrew Bible and on the horizons of the OT Apocrypha with *4 Ezra*.

In many ways, what one might call an invasion of epistolary poetics into scripture becomes most noticeable in the New Testament. In addition to the twenty-one books that are presented as epistles, there are two letters in the Acts of the Apostles (15:22-29; 23:25-30)[20] and seven in the Apocalypse of John (2:1–3:22). In fact, the nature of the opening and closing of the Apocalypse gives it the framework of an ancient letter.[21] In the New Testament, then, the literary poetics of biographical historiography, epistle, and apocalypse take center stage. This is a decisive move away from the literary poetics of the Hebrew Bible, except for the dominance of biographical historiography (Gospels and Acts) at the beginning of the corpus.

Literary Poetics in the New Testament Apocrypha

Christian literature written in the literary genres of the New Testament, regularly called NT Apocrypha, were never collected discretely into a corpus for religious reading. Rather, the New Testament Apocrypha is a modern, scholarly collection of Christian writings related to the literary poetics of the NT. For these purposes, most scholars have used four primary categories: gospels, acts, epistles, and apocalypses. J.K. Elliott includes eleven manuscripts he considers to be apocryphal Gospels; nine papyrus fragments; a discussion of ten lost gospels (including fragments in early Christian writings); various sayings attributed to Jesus called "agrapha"; and a discussion of approximately fifteen other pieces of writing he considers to be related to "apocryphal gospels." He includes manuscripts of six apocryphal Acts; three manuscripts of "secon-

[20] Roman Christians report in Acts 28:21 that they have received no letters from Judea about Paul.

[21] Adela Yarbro Collins, "Revelation, Book of," *ABD* 5:696-699.

dary apocryphal Acts"; and portions of eight other apocryphal Acts. Then he includes nineteen apocryphal epistles: Abgar to Jesus; Jesus to Abgar; Letter of Lentulus; To the Laodiceans; fourteen Paul and Seneca letters; and the Epistle of the Apostles. Last, he includes the extended text of five apocryphal Apocalypses and information about nine other apocalypses in Christian literature.[22] Overall, one sees Christian writings throughout the subsequent centuries that extend the poetics of New Testament writings, rather than writings that return to Hebrew Bible modes of writing.

Literary Poetics in the Quran

During the seventh century of the Common Era, biblical tradition emerged in a new form in Quranic discourse. The Quran contains one hundred fourteen surahs or chapters, organized basically on the principle of the longest to the shortest. Most scholars describe the nature of its discourse as rhyming prose. The nature of the Quran is important for this book on the sociorhetorical nature of the NT, since the Quran represents a later, major reconfiguration of biblical discourse that functions as "sacred writing" for another distinctive religious tradition in the world, namely Islam. A general preview of some items may suffice at this point to suggest the importance for the project in this book of keeping the Quran in view on the horizons.

The Quran was produced in a milieu significantly influenced by both Jewish and Christian traditions.[23] An interpreter of biblical tradition can see this in Surah 1, which has been called "the Islamic equivalent of the Lord's Prayer in Christianity."[24] In fact, Surah 1 exhibits a fascinating blending of aspects characteristic of the Lord's Prayer with aspects characteristic of Psalm 1 in the Hebrew Bible.

After Surah 1 comes the longest chapter in the Quran, and one of the most complex. In Michael Sells's description, "For those familiar with the Bible, it would be as if the second page opened with a combination of legal discussions in Leviticus, the historical polemic in the book of Judges, and apocalyptic allusions from Revelation, with the

[22] J.K. Elliott, *The Apocryphal New Testament: A Collection of Apocryphal Christian Literature in English Translation* (Oxford: Clarendon Press, 1993); cf. Stephen J. Patterson, "New Testament Apocrypha," *ABD* 1:295-296.

[23] Gordon D. Newby, *A History of the Jews of Arabia: From Ancient Times to Their Eclipse Under Islam* (Columbia: University of South Carolina Press, 1988); idem, *The Making of the Last Prophet: A Reconstruction of the Earliest Biography of Muhammad* (Columbia: University of South Carolina Press, 1989); Bernard Lewis, *The Jews of Islam* (Princeton: Princeton University Press, 1984); Neal Robinson, *Christ in Islam and Christianity* (Albany: SUNY Press, 1991).

[24] Michael Sells, *Approaching the Quran: The Early Revelations* (Ashland, OR: White Cloud Press, 1999) 43.

various topics mixed together and beginning in mid-topic."[25] Using Ricoeur's language and our observations about the NT, the reader encounters prescriptive discourse blended with narrative and apocalyptic discourse in ways that move abruptly and energetically both from one topic to another and back and forth among topics.

The thesis of this book is that blending of multiple topics and modes of discourse already occurs in the New Testament. In fact, one of the major reasons the NT has a distinctive nature in relation to the Hebrew Bible is the intensive manner in which it reconfigures biblical discourse by blending it energetically and dynamically in a new context. It is also a thesis of this book that it is not sufficient to remain in the domain of literary poetics to describe the achievement of either the NT or the Quran. Rather, it is necessary to adopt an approach that is alert both to social and rhetorical phenomena in their discourse.[26]

Rhetorics in the Hebrew Bible

Walter Brueggemann moved analysis and interpretation of the Hebrew Bible beyond its literary poetics into its "rhetorics"[27] in his *Theology of the Old Testament: Testimony, Dispute, Advocacy*.[28] This is a very significant move, since it embeds the poetics of the Hebrew Bible in its oral power to effect change within human community. It is well known that throughout Mediterranean antiquity people did not regularly read texts individually, like we do today. Rather, people experienced written text as a flow of sounds in a context where someone performed the text orally. Biblical text, then, was first and foremost an oral performance for people.[29] During and after the fourth century CE, certain people began

[25] Sells, *Approaching*, 3.

[26] Vernon K. Robbins and Gordon D. Newby, "A Prolegomenon to the Relation of the Quran and the Bible," in *Bible and Qur'ān: Essays in Scriptural Intertextuality* (ed. J.C. Reeves; Symposium Series 24; Atlanta: SBL, 2003) 23-42.

[27] For the importance of the term and concept of "rhetorics," see Wilhelm Wuellner, "Hermeneutics and Rhetorics: From 'Truth and Method' to 'Truth and Power'," *Scriptura* S 3 (1989) 1-54; cf. Vernon K. Robbins, "Where is Wuellner's Anti-Hermeneutical Hermeneutic Taking Us? From Schleiermacher to Thiselton and Beyond," in *Rhetorics and Hermeneutics: Wilhelm Wuellner and His Influence* (ed. James D. Hester and J. David Hester; ESEC 9; New York/London: T & T Clark, 2004) 105-25.

[28] Walter Brueggemann, *Theology of the Old Testament: Testimony, Dispute, Advocacy* (Minneapolis: Fortress, 1997).

[29] See John Miles Foley, *The Theory of Oral Composition, History and Methodology, Folkloristics* (Bloomington: Indiana University Press, 1988); idem, *The Singer of Tales in Performance* (Bloomington: Indiana University Press, 1995); Werner H. Kelber, *The Oral and Written Gospel* (Philadelphia: Fortress, 1983); idem, "Jesus and Tradition: Words in Time, Words in Space," *Semeia* 65 (1994); Bernard Brandon Scott and Margaret E. Dean, "A Sound Mapping of the Sermon on the Mount," in *Treasures New and Old: Contributions to Matthean Studies* (ed. D.R. Bauer & M.A. Powell; SBLSS 1; Atlanta: Scholars Press, 1996) 311-78;

to read the Bible individually. Still to our present day, however, many people experience the Bible primarily through oral performance of it in public settings.

Brueggemann's analysis and interpretation of the Hebrew Bible brings to life the multiple rhetorics of testimony to God. The core testimony of Israel features: (a) verbal sentences (pp. 145-212); (b) adjectives (characteristic markings of Yahweh: pp. 213-228); (c) nouns (Yahweh as constant: pp. 229-266); and (d) Yahweh fully uttered (pp. 267-303). The countertestimony of Israel features: (a) cross-examining Israel's core testimony (pp. 317-332); (b) the hiddenness of Yahweh (pp. 333-358); (c) ambiguity and the character of Yahweh (pp. 359-372); and (d) Yahweh and negativity (pp. 373-399). The unsolicited testimony of Israel features: (a) Israel as Yahweh's partner (pp. 413-449); (b) the human person as Yahweh's partner (pp. 450-491); (c) the nations as Yahweh's partner (pp. 492-527); and (d) creation as Yahweh's partner (pp. 528-551). The embodied testimony of Israel features: (a) the Torah as mediator (pp. 578-599); (b) the king as mediator (pp. 600-621); (c) the prophet as mediator (pp. 622-679); and (d) the sage as mediator (pp. 680-694). This is a rhetorical theology of the Hebrew Bible that contributes directly to the sociorhetorical analysis and interpretation of early Christian discourse that follows. The major question for us is how first century Christians appropriated and reconfigured conventional rhetorics in the Mediterranean world, which included the rhetorics in the Hebrew Bible.

Social Rhetorics from the New Testament to the Quran

Social Rhetorics in the New Testament

My proposal is that, with the aid of three major literary modes – biographical historiography (Gospels and Acts); epistles; and apocalypse – first century Christians blended at least six rhetorolects[30] – wisdom, prophetic, apocalyptic, precreation, priestly, and miracle – into a distinctive, dynamic, and multivalent mode of discourse in the Mediterranean

Margaret E. Dean, "The Grammar of Sound in Greek Texts: Toward a Method for Mapping the Echoes of Speech in Writing," *Australian Biblical Review* 44 (1996) 53-70; Richard A. Horsley and Jonathan A. Draper, *Whoever Hears You Hears Me: Prophets, Performance, and Tradition in Q* (Harrisburg: Trinity Press International, 1999); Jonathan A. Draper (ed.), *Orality, Literacy, and Colonialism in Antiquity* (Semeia Studies; Atlanta: SBL, 2004).

[30] Vernon K. Robbins, "The Dialectical Nature of Early Christian Discourse," *Scriptura* 59 (1996) 353-62. Online: http://www.religion.emory.edu/faculty/robbins/dialect/dialect353.html. For basic insights into the argumentative nature of each rhetorolect, see idem, "Argumentative Textures in Socio-Rhetorical Interpretation," in *Rhetorical Argumentation in Biblical Texts* (ed. A. Eriksson, W. Übelacker, and T.H. Olbricht; ESEC 8; Harrisburg: Trinity Press International, 2002) 27-65.

world. Perhaps now it will be appropriate to extend the discussion of rhetorolect, which we first introduced in chapter 1.

> A rhetorolect is a form of language variety or discourse identifiable on the basis of a distinctive configuration of themes, topics, reasonings, and argumentations... By their nature, rhetorolects interpenetrate one another and interact with one another like dialects do when people from different dialectical areas converse with one another. The interaction of rhetorolects in early Christianity created new configurations of speech as the movement grew. Every early Christian writing contains a configuration of rhetorolects that is somewhat different from every other writing. These differences, interacting with one another, create the overall rhetorical environment properly called early Christian discourse.[31]

In order to understand each rhetorolect, it is necessary to understand the nature of rhetorical discourse. Ancient rhetorical treatises teach us that rhetorical discourse elaborates *topoi* in two ways: (1) pictorial-narrative; and (2) argumentative-enthymematic.[32] Identification and interpretation of *topoi* in NT literature received considerable attention during the last part of the twentieth century.[33] Abraham J. Malherbe and his associates have made extensive investigations of the amplificatory function of *topoi* of the hellenistic moralists in NT literature.[34] Their focus on these *topoi* reveals that early Christians participated actively in first century Mediterranean wisdom discourse. In addition, members of the Context Group have identified the presence of common social and cultural topics and values in all the writings in the NT.[35]

[31] Robbins, "Dialectical," 356.

[32] This understanding underlies Aristotle's discussion of paradigm and enthymeme in *Rhet.* 1.2.8-10. Cf. Wilhelm H. Wuellner, "Toposforschung und Torahinterpretation bei Paulus und Jesus," *NTS* 24 (1978) 467; Walter J. Ong, *Orality and Literacy: The Technologizing of the Word* (New York: Routledge, c1988, 1995) 110-11. See the less explicitly rhetorical approach to "motifs" in F. Gerald Downing, "Words as Deeds and Deeds as Words," *BibInt* 3 (1995) 129-43.

[33] Abraham J. Malherbe, "Hellenistic Moralists and the New Testament," *ANRW* 2.26.1 (1992) 320-25 [originally completed in 1972]; Wilhelm H. Wuellner, "Toposforschung und Torahinterpretation bei Paulus und Jesus," *NTS* 24 (1978) 463-83; Johan C. Thom, "'The Mind is Its Own Place': Defining the Topos," in *Early Christianity and Classical Culture: Comparative Studies in Honor of Abraham J. Malherbe* (ed. J.T. Fitzgerald, T.H. Olbricht, and L.M. White; NovTSup 110; Leiden: Brill, 2003) 555-73.

[34] Malherbe, "Hellenistic Moralists," 320-5; idem, *Moral Exhortation, A Greco-Roman Sourcebook* (Library of Early Christianity; Philadelphia: Westminster, 1986) 144-61; idem, "The Christianization of a *Topos* (Luke 12:13-34)," *NovT* 38 (1996) 123-35.

[35] For the basic range of these topics, see Bruce J. Malina, *The New Testament World: Insights from Cultural Anthropology* (rev. ed.; Atlanta: John Knox Press, 1993); John H. Elliott, *What Is Social-Scientific Criticism?* (Minneapolis: Fortress, 1993); John J. Pilch and Bruce J. Malina (eds.), *Handbook of Biblical Social Values* (Peabody, MA: Hendrickson, 1993); John J. Pilch, *The Cultural Dictionary of the Bible* (Collegeville, MN; Liturgical

A beginning point for us can be to understand that *topoi* are related to well-known social, political, cultural, and religious locations of thought and action in the Mediterranean world. A major task for NT interpreters is to analyze and interpret both the pictorial-narrative function and the argumentative-enthymematic function of *topoi* in which first century Christians found a conceptual home in the Mediterranean world. The author of this volume and the forthcoming companion volume has accepted the challenge to show the reader that first century Christians nurtured widespread Mediterranean *topoi* into at least six prototypical Christian rhetorolects. The language of "prototypical" comes from cognitive science findings about conceptual metaphor, which will be explained in the next chapter. The prototypical Christian rhetorolects exhibit the presence of human bodies both in physical and conceptual domains of household (wisdom), kingdom (prophetic), empire (apocalyptic; precreation), intersubjective body (miracle), and temple (priestly).[36] Synagogue, country-village, and city are three additional contexts that early Christians experienced firsthand, and other interpreters may explore the functions of these places in early Christian discourse. In the view of the author of these two volumes, synagogue does not function as a prototypical location for first century Christian discourse, even though synagogues are very important places in the Gospels and Acts, since imagery related to the Jerusalem temple was so prototypically dominant in first century Christian thought that it drove synagogue into the margins of Christian discourse. In turn, country-village imagery does not function as a prototypical location for first century Christian discourse, even though country-villages are especially important in the Gospels, since imagery of the heavenly temple-city dominates over it, especially in Colossians, Ephesians, Hebrews, and Revelation. The earthly city becomes a dominant location for Christian thought and action during the second to fourth centuries CE, rather than during the first century, and these cities become the location for the classical creedal Christian rhetorolect that emerges in the fourth and fifth centuries CE.[37]

Press, 1999); cf. Robbins, *Tapestry*, 159-66; idem, *Exploring*, 75-86. For publications of the Context Group see online: http://www.contextgroup.org.

[36] Vernon K. Robbins, "Conceptual Blending and Early Christian Imagination," 163-72; cf. idem, "Argumentative Textures in Socio-Rhetorical Interpretation," in *Argumentation in the Bible* (ed. Anders Eriksson, Walter Übelacker, and Thomas Olbricht; ESEC 8; Harrisburg: Trinity Press International, 2002) 353-62; cf. idem, "The Dialectical Nature of Early Christian Discourse," *Scriptura* 59 (1996) 353-62. Online: http://www.religion.emory.edu/faculty/robbins/dialect/dialect353.html.

[37] See Ayres, *Nicaea and its Legacy*.

Social Rhetorics in Rabbinic Literature

Second through fifth century rabbinic discourse bypassed the influences of first century Christian rhetorics as it developed its special rhetorics for rabbinic tradition. Jack Lightstone's sociorhetorical analysis of discourse in Mishnah, Tosefta, Semachot, and the Talmuds,[38] alongside of Daniel Boyarin's *Dying for God*,[39] show how Judaism developed a distinctive mode of discourse alongside emergent and developing Christian discourse.[40]

Jack Lightstone has presented a sociorhetorical analysis and interpretation of the other major alternative discourse that emerged out of Hebrew Bible discourse by the end of the second century, namely the discourse of Mishnah-Tosefta.[41] In contrast to early Christian discourse, rabbinic discourse focused on the Torah as the agent of God's attributes and actions. Lightstone considers early Rabbinic Rhetoric to be grounded in "Priestly-Scribal Bureaucratic Virtuosity." In contrast, we may describe Christian discourse in terms of "Apostolic Coalitional Faithfulness." Rather than priestly-scribal activities standing at the center, early Christians placed apostleship – being sent into the world to perform specific tasks – at the center. Some form of "*apostel-*" or "*apostol-*"occurs in twenty-two of the twenty-seven books in the NT.[42] In addition, a comprehensive investigation by James L. Kinneavy has

[38] J.N. Lightstone, *The Rhetoric of the Babylonian Talmud, Its Social Meaning and Context* (Studies in Christianity and Judaism/Études sur le christianisme et le judaïsme 6; Waterloo: Wilfrid Laurier University Press for the Canadian Corporation for Studies in Religion/Corporation Canadienne des Sciences Religieuses, 1994); idem, *Mishnah and the Social Formation of the Early Rabbinic Guild: A Socio-Rhetorical Approach* (Studies in Christianity and Judaism/Études sur le christianisme et le judaïsme 11; Waterloo: Wilfrid Laurier University Press for the Canadian Corporation for Studies in Religion/Corporation Canadienne des Sciences Religieuses, 2002).

[39] Daniel Boyarin, *Dying for God: Martyrdom and the Making of Christianity and Judaism* (Figurae: Reading Medieval Culture; Stanford: Stanford University Press, 1999).

[40] Kenneth L. Vaux's *Being Well* (Challenges in Ethics; Nashville: Abingdon, 1997) is suggestive for understanding how the succeeding centuries in Western culture built upon four major traditions of discourse: Hebrew, Greek, apocalyptic, and Christian. A person might think that apocalyptic should simply be embedded in Christian discourse. In sociorhetorical terms, his analysis reveals that Christian discourse interwove wisdom, miracle, prophetic, priestly, apocalyptic, and precreation discourse into a religious mode that domesticated apocalyptic thought in the context of precreation thought. Following the lead of Paul Ramsey, Kenneth L. Vaux's *Birth Ethics: Religious and Cultural Values in the Genesis of Life* (New York: Crossroad, 1989) proposes "genetic apocalyptic" discourse to confront the dynamics of technology, health, and the body during the 21st century.

[41] Jack N. Lightstone, *Mishnah and the Social Formation of the Early Rabbinic Guild: A Socio-Rhetorical Approach* (ESCJ 11; Waterloo: Wilfred Laurier Press, 2002); cf. idem., *The Rhetoric of the Babylonian Talmud, Its Social Meaning and Context* (ESCJ 6; Toronto: Canadian Corporation for Studies in Religion [Wilfred Laurier University Press], 1994).

[42] Only 2 Thessalonians, Philemon, James, and 2-3 John do not contain "apostle" vocabulary.

called to our attention that the noun *pistis* and the verb *pisteuein* occur 491 times in the NT, and in every NT writing except 2-3 John.[43] Moreover, his investigation concludes that "a substantial part of the concept of faith found in the New Testament can be found in the rhetorical concept of persuasion, which was a major meaning of the noun *pistis* (to believe) in Greek language at the period the New Testament was written."[44] He also observes that "The trust, assent, and knowledge of the model of faith have important similarities to the ethical, pathetic, and logical elements of the model of persuasion."[45]

Social Rhetorics in Second and Third Century Christianity

An essay by Karen Jo Torjesen helps us to move a step further in our understanding of the rhetorics of first century Christian discourse. In addition to the apocryphal literature, she explains, second and third century Christians produced literature that configured first century Christian discourse into five major christological discourses: (1) Jesus as divine wisdom (*sophia*), exhibiting the context of worship; (2) Jesus as victor over death, exhibiting the context of martyrdom; (3) Jesus as divine teacher (*didaskalos*), exhibiting the contexts of catechetical instruction and Christian schools; (4) Jesus as cosmic reason (*logos*) exhibiting the context of the Christian scholar's study; and (5) Jesus as world ruler (*pantocratōr*), exhibiting the context of the basilica.[46] Her conclusions show that the NT functioned not only as a resource for a new literary poetics but also as a rhetorical resource for christological descriptions of Jesus that functioned dynamically in multiple contexts of Christian belief, teaching, worship, and practice.

From the perspective of NT discourse, Jesus as divine wisdom (*sophia*), Jesus as divine teacher (*didaskalos*), and Jesus as cosmic reason (*logos*) are elaborations of paraenetic and precreation wisdom discourse in the NT; Jesus as victor over death and the powers is a blend of miracle, priestly, and apocalyptic discourse; and Jesus as world ruler (*pantokratōr*) is a blend of apocalyptic and precreation wisdom discourse. This means that second through fourth century Christians found multiple ways to expand and differentiate wisdom discourse for its own purposes, and this was a strategic development in a culture where philosophy had become a fully public mode of discourse.[47] In addition, second

[43] James L. Kinneavy, *Greek Rhetorical Origins of Christian Faith: An Inquiry* (New York: Oxford University Press, 1987) 109-19.

[44] Kinneavy, *Christian Faith*, 143.

[45] Kinneavy, *Christian Faith*, 145.

[46] E.g., Karen Jo Torjesen, "You Are the Christ: Five Portraits of Jesus from the Early Church," in *Jesus at 2000* (ed. M.J. Borg; Boulder, CO: Westview, 1997) 73-88.

[47] Troels Engberg-Pedersen, "The Hellenistic *Öffentlichkeit*: Philosophy as a Social Force in the Greco-Roman Empire," in *Recruitment, Conquest, and Conflict: Strategies in*

through fourth century Christians maintained a dynamic, interactive relation with multiple kinds of NT discourse as they moved their speech, actions, beliefs, and thoughts energetically out into the world of the Roman empire and beyond.

Torjesen's analysis exhibits how Christian discourse became centrally christological during the second and third centuries. This helps to clarify that NT discourse is in a stage of progression from theological discourse grounded in the attributes and actions of God toward christological discourse, where Christ becomes central in the reasoning. During the first century, early Christian discourse finds its coherence in a consensus that Jesus Christ and holy spirit are agents of the attributes and actions of God. During the second and third centuries, the emphasis shifts towards Christ as the dynamic center of the Godhead. Prior to the second and third centuries, one must understand the innermost dynamics of God in order to understand Jesus Christ and holy spirit. By the end of the third century, one must understand the innermost dynamics of Jesus Christ in order to understand God. A significant amount of NT interpretation during the last half of the twentieth century has been unable to explore the full range of NT discourse as a result of a view that this discourse is christological rather than theological in its grounding.

Social Rhetorics in the Quran

The Quran contains substantive miracle, wisdom, prophetic, and apocalyptic discourse. Precreation discourse is implicit rather than explicit in the Quran. In decades after the death of the prophet Muhammad, the Quran itself became a dynamic subject of precreation discourse, in particular in the controversy about whether the Quran was created or uncreated. In a context where Christians were arguing that Jesus existed with God prior to creation as the Logos, and Jesus was never created, many Muslims argued that the Quran existed with God prior to creation and was never created. In turn, Jewish tradition in contemporaneous midrashic works, for example, *Pirqe de Rabbi Eliezer*, argued that seven things existed with God prior to creation: Torah; Gehinnom, the garden of Eden, the throne of glory, the temple, repentance, and the name of the messiah. The Quran does not develop priestly discourse characteristic of Christianity. Six verses in the Quran assert that the prophets were wrongfully slain.[48] Opposition in Islamic belief to the Christian belief that Jesus was slain is so strong that priestly discourse is not prominent in Quranic discourse.

Judaism, Early Christianity, and the Greco-Roman World (ed. Peder Borgen, Vernon K. Robbins, and David B. Gowler; ESEC 6; Atlanta: Scholars Press, 1998) 15-37.

[48] Q 2:61, 91; 3:21, 112, 181; 4:155.

Miracle Discourse in the Quran

Miracle discourse is prominent in the Quran. Thirty-six times in the Quran the clause "Allah is (Thou art/He is) able to do all things" occurs.[49] In addition, ten verses refer to Allah as "Almighty,"[50] and forty-eight verses refer to Allah as "Mighty."[51] In Quranic discourse, the miraculous power of Allah is grounded in Allah's creation of the heavens and the earth. As Q 50:38 says: "And verily We created the heavens and the earth, and all that is between them, in six Days, and naught of weariness touched Us."[52] Since Allah produced all creation originally, Allah has the power to reproduce it.[53] Indeed, God's ability to produce and reproduce creation is easy,[54] and people can easily see the evidence that God produced it by "travelling in the land" (Q 29:20). In addition, God has no difficulty giving life to humans, and resurrecting them to new life, since humans are one of God's creations out of dust. As Q 64:7 says: "Those who disbelieve assert that they will not be raised again. Say (unto them, O Muhammad): Yea, verily, by my Lord! ye will be raised again and then ye will be informed of what ye did; and that is easy for Allah."[55] The emphasis on humans as made of earth occurs clearly in Q 30:19: "He brings forth the living from the dead, and He brings forth the dead from the living, and He revives the earth after her death. And even so will you be brought forth."

In the Hebrew Bible, narratives about Moses, Elijah, and Elisha describe scenes with dramatic miracle discourse. The Quran refers to Moses more than any other person in the Bible or anywhere in the world[56] (137 times), and there are a significant number of words in the context of these references that qualify as miracle discourse. In the context of nine

[49] Q 2:20, 106, 109, 148, 259, 284; 3:26, 29, 165, 189; 5:17, 19, 40, 120; 6:17; 8:41; 9:39; 11:4; 16:77; 18:46[45]; 22:6; 24:45; 29:20; 30:50; 33:27; 35:1; 41:39; 42:9; 46:33; 48:21; 57:2; 59:6; 64:1; 65:12; 66:8; 67:1.

[50] Q 3:6, 18; 12:39; 13:16; 14:48; 22:40, 74; 40:16; 57:25; 58:21.

[51] Q 2:129, 209, 220, 228, 240, 260; 3:62, 126; 4:56, 157, 165; 5:38, 118; 6:96; 8:10, 49, 63, 67; 9:40, 71; 14:4; 16:60; 27:9, 78; 29:16, 42; 30:27; 31:9, 27; 34:27; 35:2, 44; 36:38; 39:1; 40:8; 45:2, 37; 46:2; 48:7, 18; 57:1; 59:1, 24; 60:5; 61:1; 62:1, 3; 64:18; 67:2.

[52] Cf. Q 7:54; 10:3; 11:7; 25:59; 32:4; 57:4.

[53] Q 10:3-4, 34; 27:64; 30:11, 19; 50:11; 85:13.

[54] Q 29:19; 30:27.

[55] Cf. Q 2:73, 260; 3:27; 6:35, 95, 111; 7:57; 10:31; 21:21; 22:6; 25:3; 30:50; 36:12, 33; 41:39; 42:9; 50:3, 11, 43.

[56] One might think the Quran would refer to Muhammad more times than anyone else. Since many verses in the Quran address Muhammad directly, *The Glorious Quran* (trans. Muhammad M. Pickthall; New York: Mostazafan Foundation of New York, 1984) adds Muhammad's name in parentheses so often that a concordance search exhibits 277 occurrences of his name. However, the name Muhammad occurs only four times in the Arabic text of the Quran (3:144; 33:40; 47:2; 48:29).

references to Moses, there is explicit mention of clear proofs or miracles,[57] a term that occurs fifty times in the Quran.[58] There are seventy-four references to Pharaoh in the Quran, and most of these references recount, speak directly about, or evoke dynamics of Moses' confrontations with Pharaoh. A number of these verses use constructions like "when we did deliver you" (2:49) "we rescued you" (2:50), "and we drowned the folk of Pharaoh" (2:50) to communicate God's miraculous activity of leading the people of Israel out of Egypt. Q 7:133 refers to the flood, locusts, vermin, frogs, and blood as a succession of clear signs or miracles which Pharaoh and his people did not heed.

The Quran articulates no discourse with an emphasis on miracle either for Elijah or Elisha. Reference to Elisha occurs only twice in Quranic discourse: once he is listed with Ishmael, Jonah, and Lot as people whom God preferred among God's creatures (6:86[87]); and once he is listed with Ishmael and Dhu'l Kifl as of the chosen (38:48). There is no emphasis on miracle in either context referring to Elijah or Elisha.

The Quran refers to Elijah three times. Q 6:85(86) lists Elijah along with Zechariah (father of John the Baptist), John (the Baptist), and Jesus as among the righteous. While there is no emphasis on miracle in this context, Quranic discourse about Zechariah and Jesus includes an emphasis on miracle, and John's birth is miraculous. Thus, in an implicit manner the grouping of Elijah with Zechariah, John, and Jesus may be perceived to evoke an image of righteous people around whom God's miraculous powers were at work in a special way. One should mention again, however, that the emphasis in the context is on these men as "of the righteous," without any reference to God's miraculous work in the world. The other two references to Elijah occur in Q 37:123, 130, where the discourse attributes speech to Elijah as one who was sent to warn. Since the content of Elijah's speech is apocalyptic in tone, discussion of these references is present in the section below on apocalyptic discourse.

Unlike the Quran's reference to Elijah only three times, the New Testament refers to Elijah 29 times[59] in comparison to 66 references to Elijah in the Hebrew Bible. Luke 4:25-26 and James 5:16-17 summarize episodes in which God's miraculous power worked through Elijah, and Jesus' raising of the son of the widow of Nain from death in Luke

[57] Q 2:92; 4:153; 7:85, 104-105; 11:17; 17:101; 20:70-72; 29:39; 40:28.

[58] In addition to the references in n. 49, Q 2:87, 185, 209, 213, 253; 3:86, 105, 183, 184; 5:32, 110; 6:57, 157; 7:101; 8:42(2); 9:70; 10:13, 74; 11:28, 53, 63, 88; 14:9; 16:44; 20:133; 30:9; 35:25, 40; 40:22, 34, 50, 66, 83; 43:63; 47:14; 57:25; 61:6; 64:6; 98:1, 4.

[59] Matt 11:14; 16:14; 17:3, 4, 10, 11, 12; 27:47, 49; Mark 6:15; 8:28; 9:4, 5, 11, 12, 13; 15:35, 36; Luke 1:17; 4:25, 26; 9:8, 19, 30, 33; John 1:21, 25; Rom 11:2; Jas 5:17.

7:11-17 is a reconfiguration of Elijah's raising of the son of the widow of Zarephath in 1 Kings 17:17-24.[60] In addition, the Elijah-Elisha stories in the Hebrew Bible functioned for early Christians as a prefiguration of Jesus' miracles and played a highly formative role in the narrative portrayal of those activities in the Gospels of Mark and Luke.[61] Moreover, the one explicit reference to Elisha in the New Testament (Luke 4:27) focuses on his healing of Naaman the Syrian from his leprosy.[62]

There are 79 references to Moses in the New Testament.[63] Only Rev 15:3, however, comes close to associating Moses with miraculous discourse when the song of Moses and the Lamb begins with "Great and amazing are your deeds." John 6:32 refers to Moses' giving of the bread out of heaven to the people, but it is doubtful that there is any emphasis on the miraculous in the assertion. In contrast, the miracle is "the true bread from heaven which the Father gives." One could almost say, then, that the New Testament and the Quran exhibit a reversal of emphasis on miracle in the context of Elijah and Moses. For the New Testament, Elijah is the prominent miracle prophet in the story of Israel, and Elisha is included in this emphasis; for the Quran, Moses is the prominent miracle prophet in the story of Israel rather than Elijah and Elisha.

The other person whom Quranic discourse associates explicitly with miracles is Jesus, son of Mary. Q 2:87 emphasizes that Jesus followed after Moses with "clear proofs", and God supported Jesus with the holy spirit.[64] Once the Quran clearly groups Moses and Jesus together (2:136), and once Moses and Jesus are grouped together at the end of a list of four prophets including Noah and Abraham (33:7). Jesus is the only one in the Quran, besides God himself, who is given the power to raise the dead. Jesus raises the dead with God's permission (3:49; 5:110) alongside of his creating a live bird out of clay, healing the blind, and healing the leper. Quranic discourse refers to these activities respectively as Jesus' coming with a sign (3:49) and with clear proofs (5:110).

The Quran refers to Jesus twenty-five times,[65] exactly the same number of times it refers to Adam.[66] No miracles are attributed to

[60] A similar story is recounted of Elisha in 2 Kgs 4:32-37.

[61] Wolfgang Roth, *Hebrew Gospel: Cracking the Code of Mark* (Oak Park, IL: Meyer-Stone Books, 1988). Thomas L. Brodie, *The Crucial Bridge: The Elijah-Elisha Narrative as an Interpretive Synthesis of Genesis-Kings and a Literary Model for the Gospels* (Collegeville: Liturgical Press, 2000).

[62] The Hebrew Bible contains 86 references to Elisha in comparison with 66 references to Elijah.

[63] The Hebrew Bible refers to Moses more than 700 times.

[64] Cf. Q 2:92, 253.

[65] Q 2:87, 136, 253; 3:45, 52, 55, 59, 84; 4:157, 163, 171; 5:46, 78, 110, 112, 114, 116; 6:85; 19:34; 33:7; 42:13; 43:63; 57:27; 61:6, 14.

Adam, but the Quran asserts that "the likeness of Jesus with God is as the likeness of Adam. He created him of dust, then He said unto him: Be! and he is" (Q 3:59). Like Adam, Jesus was human; but also like Adam, God created Jesus simply by saying, "Be!" As the angel explained to Mary, "So (it will be). God creates what He will. If He decrees a thing, He says unto it only; 'Be!' and it is" (Q 3:47).

Wisdom Discourse in the Quran

Since "God creates what He will" (5:17) and is able to do all things, there could be great difficulty if Allah's will were arbitrary. To the good fortune of all, Allah's power and will are grounded in wisdom, which includes mercy and forgiveness. Forty-eight times the Quran refers to Allah as "(Al)mighty, Wise"[67] and seven times as "Knower, Powerful" or "Mighty, Knower."[68] In the Quran, God's knowledge is fully as great as God's power. Words referring to knowing, knowledge, and knower occur, on the basis of Pickthall's version, 692 times in the Quran. Thirty-two times the Quran refers to God as "Knower, Wise."[69] Thirteen times the Quran says that God is "the Knower of all things."[70] God knows the invisible and the visible,[71] the things hidden,[72] the unseen.[73] God knows what is in the breasts of people,[74] and God knows sins.[75]

The Quran also refers to God in a manner Pickthall rendered as "Aware." God is aware of "all who are in the heavens and the earth" (17:55). Indeed, God is "Aware of all things."[76] The Quran refers to God six times as "Wise, Aware,"[77] four times as "Knower, Aware,"[78] four times

[66] Q 2:31, 33, 34, 35, 37; 3:33, 59; 5:27; 7:11, 19, 26, 27, 31, 35, 172; 17:61, 70; 18:50; 19:58; 20:115, 116, 117, 120, 121; 36:60.

[67] Q 2:129, 209, 220, 228, 240, 260; 3:6, 18, 62, 126; 4:56, 158, 165; 5:38, 118; 6:96; 8:10, 49, 63, 67; 9:40, 71; 14:4; 16:60; 27:9, 78; 29:26, 42; 30:27; 31:9, 27; 34:27; 35:2, 44; 36:38; 39:1; 40:8; 45:2, 37; 46:2; 48:7, 19; 57:1; 59:1, 24; 60:5; 61:1; 62:1, 3; 64:18; cf. 42:51 (Exalted, Wise); 41:42 (Wise, Owner of Praise).

[68] Q 16:70; 30:54; 40:2; 41:12: 42:3, 50; 43:9.

[69] Q 2:32; 4:11, 17, 24, 26, 92, 104, 111, 170; 6:18; 8:71; 9:15, 28, 60, 97, 106, 110; 12:6, 83, 100; 22:52; 24:18, 58, 59; 33:1; 43:84; 48:4; 49:8; 51:30; 60:10; 66:2; 76:30.

[70] Q 2:29, 282; 4:32, 176; 5:97; 8:75; 24:35, 64; 33:54; 42:12: 57:3; 58:7; 64:11; cf. 4:70 (Knower); 36:79 (Knower of every creation); 15:86 (all wise Creator); 4:12; 22:59 (Knower, Indulgent).

[71] Q 6:73; 9:105; 19:9; 23:92; 32:6; 39:46; 59:22; 62:8; 64:18; cf. 18:26.

[72] Q 5:109; 9:78; 34:48.

[73] Q 34:3; 35:38; 72:26; cf. 6:50.

[74] Q 57:6; 67:13; 3:29, 119, 154; 5:7; 8:43; 11:5; 28:69; 31:23; 35:38; 39:7; 42:24; 57:6; 64:4.

[75] Q 17:17; 15:58.

[76] Q 2:231; 6:101; 9:115; 21:81; 29:62; 33:40; 48:26; 49:16; cf. 35:14.

[77] Q 6:73, 83, 128, 139; 15:25; 27:6; 34:1; cf. 11:1 (Wise, Informed); 24:10 (Clement, Wise).

[78] Q 4:35; 31:34; 49:13; 66:3.

as "Subtle, Aware,"[79] and twice as "Responsive, Aware."[80] God is aware of what all people do:[81] both the good things of those who go aright[82] and those who do evil or wrong.[83] God is aware of all that is hidden in human breasts.[84]

God is aware of all these things, and knows them, because God both hears and sees all things. God is the Hearer, Knower.[85] As part of this, of course, God is the Hearer of Prayer.[86] In addition, God sees all things (67:19). God is the "Hearer, Seer."[87] God sees "what you (pl.) do"[88] and "what they do."[89]

In the Quran, Joseph, son of Jacob, and the Quranic personage Luqman are the people most closely associated with wisdom, with Solomon and David also included. Joseph received wisdom and knowledge (12:22) from God for his task on earth. This made Joseph a lord of knowledge (12:76). In turn, Joseph is called "the truthful one" (12:46: *ayyuha*). This wisdom even enables Joseph to make his father Jacob a wise seer who can say: "Said I not unto you that I know from Allah that which ye know not" (12:96). In the Surah titled Luqman, God is "the True" (31:30) and there is an emphasis that God gave Luqman wisdom (31:12). In the context of Joseph and Luqman, there is an emphasis on God as true. In turn, God gave David and Solomon wisdom (judgment and knowledge). This made them wise in judgment and understanding (21:78-79).

The Quran does not contain a separate "wisdom" section, but rather, embeds wisdom, attributed to God, throughout many of the surahs. The wise, who submit to God's will, who become Muslim, are those who see the wisdom within the Quranic discourse itself.

[79] Q 6:103; 22:63; 31:16; 33:34; 67:14; cf. 4:39 (ever Aware).
[80] Q 2:158; 4:147.
[81] Q 2:283; 13:33; 17:54; 22:68; 23:51; 48:11; 58:13; 63:11; 64:8.
[82] Q 2:215; 3:92, 115; 4:127; 6:53; 9:44; 16:125; 17:84; 24:30, 41; 28:56; 39:70; 53:30, 32.
[83] Q 2:95, 187, 246; 3:63; 6:58, 119; 9:47; 10:36, 40; 12:19; 19:70; 20:104; 23:96; 26:188; 28:85; 35:8; 39:70; 46:8; 53:30; 62:7; 68:7.
[84] Q 3:119, 169, 154; 11:5; 29:10; 31:23; 35:38; 42:24; 64:4; cf. 60:1.
[85] Q 2:127, 137, 181, 224, 227, 244, 256; 3:34, 35, 121; 4:148; 5:76; 6:13, 115; 7:200; 8:17, 42, 53, 61; 9:98, 103; 10:65; 12:34; 21:4; 24:21, 60; 29:5, 60; 31:28; 41:36; 44:6; 49:1; 58:1; cf. 34:50 (Hearer, Nigh).
[86] Q 3:38; 14:39; 37:75.
[87] Q 4:58, 134; 17:1; 22:61, 75; 40:56, 20; 42:11; cf. 17:96 (Knower, Seer); 18:26 (clear of sight, keen of hearing).
[88] Q 2:110, 232, 237, 265; 3:156, 163; 11:112; 33:9; 34:11; 41:40; 48:24; 49:18; 57:4; 60:3; 64:2; cf. Knower of what you used to do (16:28); Seer of his bondsmen (3:15, 20; 42:27) and Seer of his slaves (35:31, 45).
[89] Q 2:96; 5:71; 8:39, 72.

Prophetic Discourse in the Quran

Everyone knows there is prophetic discourse in the Quran, since Muslim tradition emphasizes that Muhammad is the final, most authoritative prophet. Readers of the Quran will know, however, that the word *messenger* (*rasul*) is even more frequent than the word *prophet* (*nabi*), and that Muslims refer first and foremost to Muhammad as The Messenger. The Quran refers a total of 78 times to a prophet.[90] The New Testament refers to a prophet 150 times,[91] which is almost twice as many times as the Quran. In contrast, the word messenger occurs 368 times in the Quran (Pickthall: 243 times in the singular and 125 times in the plural). This is almost 2.5 times as often as the word prophet occurs in the New Testament and almost 4.75 times more than the word prophet occurs in the Quran.

The remarkable frequency of the word *messenger* in the Quran indicates that, for this revelational discourse, God sent messengers at various times to people with various combinations of abilities.[92] They are sent as miracle workers; as people who transmitted God's wisdom, knowledge, and truth; as people who announced God's good news; and as special warners of the terrible things that will happen to disbelievers. The concept of prophet is closely related to messenger, since God sends prophets. In Quranic discourse, however, God sends all kinds of messengers, and only certain ones are regularly referred to as prophets. God sends only certain messengers with miracles to confirm what they do. There are signs that accompany all of God's messengers, since God's creation presents signs of God's powerful activity every day. These signs function only for believers as portents that reveal the remarkable beneficence and mercy of God, of course. For unbelievers, these signs are simply natural functions of the universe and not anything that especially reveals the nature and magnificence of God.

Surah 21, entitled The Prophets (*al-Anbiya'*), recounts circumstances around eleven Hebrew Bible people (Noah, Abraham, Lot, Ishmael, Isaac, Jacob, Moses, Aaron, David, Solomon, Job), one New Testament person (Zechariah, father of John the Baptist), and three other prophets (Idris [Enoch], Dhu'l-Kifl [Ezekiel or Job], Dhu'n-Nun [Jonah]). In addition to Surah 21, which is devoted entirely to prophets, there are lists of prophets in various verses in the Quran. Jesus is most noticeably absent from Surah 21, since he is included in lists of prophets among Abraham, Ishmael, Isaac, Jacob, and Moses in 2:136; 3:84; 4:163-164 and among Noah, Abraham, and Moses in 33:7. Many consider Jonah

[90] 57 times in the singular; 21 times in the plural.

[91] 64 times in the singular; 86 times in the plural.

[92] A current web-site contains an article arguing for the introduction of 19 scriptures by 19 successive prophets: http://www.submission.org/Quran-19.html.

(*Yunus*) to be present in Dhu'n-Nun in Surah 21. Jonah (*Yunus*) appears only once in a list of prophets (4:163-164), but he has wonderful company there: Noah, Abraham, Ishmael, Isaac, Jacob, Moses, Aaron, David, Solomon, Job, and Jesus. In addition, Jonah appears among Ishmael, Elisha, and Lot in 6:86; receives special recognition in 37:139-148 after Noah (37:75-82), Abraham (37:83-111); Isaac (37:112-113), Moses and Aaron (37:114-122), Elijah (37:123-132), and Lot (37:133-138); and there is a Surah named Jonah (10: *Yunus*).

The term *prophethood* and the singular or plural of *prophet* occurs eighty-three times in the Quran. There is no verb that Pickthall interprets in English as "to prophesy." God promises 117 times. Prophets transmit God's knowledge, wisdom, truth, and good news; and they warn. Prophets in the Quran do not prophesy. Thus, the Quran makes no references to prophecies, and it does not describe anyone as prophesying. Both God and Satan promise (2:268). This would seem to fit the Islamic contention that Muhammad ends prophecy.

Apocalyptic Discourse in the Quran

Apocalyptic discourse is highly present in the Quran. References to the day of judgment occur 14 times,[93] to those who believe in God and the last day 27 times,[94] and things that will happen on the day of resurrection 71 times.[95] Norman O. Brown, following the lead of Louis Massignon, has called Surah 18 the "Apocalypse of Islam." "Surah 18," he says, "is the apocalypse of Islam: the heart of its message, not displayed on the surface, is the distinction between surface and substance, between *Zahir* and *batin*."[96] What Brown asserts about Surah 18 is true for most of the Quran. Almost the entire presentation of themes in the Quran involves either an implicit or explicit reference to the Eschaton. As we have indicated elsewhere, the very presentation of time is focused on a compression of the period from Creation to the Last Day, with a resulting emphasis of making all temporal events affected by a sense of the End.[97] In this context, one of the tasks of God's messengers

[93] Q 1:4; 15:35; 26:82; 37:20; 38:78; 51:12; 56:56; 68:39; 70:26; 74:46; 82:15, 17, 18; 83:11.

[94] Q 2:8, 62, 126, 177, 228, 232, 264; 3:114; 4:38, 39, 59, 136, 162; 5:69; 7:45; 9:18, 19, 29, 44, 45, 99; 24:2; 29:36; 33:21; 58:22; 60:6; 65:2.

[95] Q 2:85, 113, 174; 3:55, 77, 161, 180, 185, 194; 4:87, 109, 141, 159; 5:14, 36, 64; 6:12; 7:32, 167, 172; 10:60, 93; 11:60, 98, 99; 16:25, 27, 92, 124; 17:13, 58, 62, 97; 18:105; 19:95; 20:100, 101, 124; 21:47; 22:9, 17, 69; 23:16; 25:47, 69; 28:41, 42, 61, 71, 72; 29:13, 25; 30:56; 32:25; 35:14; 39:15, 24, 31, 47, 60, 67; 41:40; 42:45; 45:17, 26; 46:5; 58:7; 60:3; 75:1; 75:6.

[96] Norman Oliver Brown, *Apocalypse and/or Metamorphosis* (Berkeley and Los Angeles: University of California Press, 1991) 81.

[97] Gordon D. Newby, "Quranic Texture: A Review of Vernon Robbins' *The Tapestry of Early Christian Discourse* and *Exploring the Texture of Texts*," *JSNT* 70 (1998) 93-100.

is to warn people about the rewards of belief and the consequences of disbelief.

Apocalyptic discourse in the Quran sets up the alternative of gardens and paradise for believers and fire for disbelievers. The gardens and paradise as humans' reward for good action are mentioned 130 times.[98] These gardens, modeled on the garden of Eden in Gen 2–3, have much in common with the heavenly garden-city as it is depicted in Rev 22:1-5. Fire, the reward of those who sin, is mentioned 148 times,[99] and there are 103 references to hell.[100] This means that 64 surahs refer explicitly to the Fire, with one more implying it (Q 42). Forty-two surahs appear not to contain a reference to the fire for unbelievers or allude to it.[101] Surah 2: *al-Baqarah*, the longest surah in the Quran, has 14 or 15 references to the fire, more references than any other surah. Surah 3: *Al-Imran* has eleven references to the Fire. Surah 101: *al-Qar'iah* ends with the words "raging fire." It is unusual that the phrase "the fire of God" appears only once in the Quran (104:6), since fire is intimately associated with the nature of God in the Bible.[102] The Quran appears to present fire much more like the

[98] Q 2:25, 82, 221, 266; 3:15, 136, 195, 198; 4:13, 57, 122; 5:12, 65, 85, 119; 6:99; 7:40, 42, 43, 44, 46, 49, 50; 9:21, 72, 89, 100, 111; 10:9, 26; 11:23, 108; 13:23, 35; 14:23; 15:45; 16:31, 32; 17:91; 18:31-34, 40; 19:61, 63; 20:76; 22:56; 23:19; 25:15, 24; 26:85, 90; 29:58; 30:15; 31:8; 32:19; 34:15-16; 35:33; 36:34; 37:43; 38:50; 39:73-74; 40:8, 40; 42:7, 22; 43:70, 72; 44:25, 52; 46:14, 16; 17:5, 15; 48:5, 17; 50:9, 31; 51:15; 52:17; 53:13; 54:54; 55:46, 54, 62; 56:12, 89; 57:12, 21; 58:22; 59:20; 61:12; 64:9; 65:11; 66:8, 11; 68:17, 34; 69:22; 70:35, 38; 71:12; 74:40; 76:12; 78:16, 32; 79:41; 80:30; 81:13; 85:11; 88:10; 89:30; 98:8.

[99] Q 2:24, 39, 80, 81, 119, 126, 167, 174, 201, 217, 221, 257, 266, 275; 3:10, 16, 24, 103, 116, 131, 151, 162, 185, 191, 192; 4:10, 14, 30, 56, 145; 5:29, 27, 72, 86; 6:27, 128; 7:36, 44, 47, 50; 8:14; 9:17, 35, 63, 68, 81, 109, 113; 10:8, 27; 11:16, 17, 83, 98, 106, 113; 13:5, 35; 14:30, 50; 16:62; 18:29, 53; 21:39; 22:19, 51, 72; 23:104; 24:57; 27:90; 28:41; 29:24; 32:20; 33:64, 66; 34:12, 42; 35:6, 36; 38:27, 59, 61, 64; 39:8, 16, 19; 40:6, 41, 43, 46, 47, 49, 72; 41:19, 24, 28, 40; (42:45); 45:34; 46:20, 34; 47:12, 15; 51:13; 52:13, 14, 18, 27; 54:48; 55:35; 56:94; 57:15, 19; 58:17; 59:3, 17, 20; 64:10; 66:6, 10; 69:31; 70:15; 71:25; 72:15, 23; 73:12; 74:31; 76:4; 84:12; 85:5; 87:12; 88:4; 90:20; 92:14; 98:6; 100:2; 101:11; 102:6; 104:6; 111:3.

[100] Q 2:119, 206; 3:12, 197; 4:55, 93, 97, 115, 121, 140, 169; 5:10, 86; 7:18, 41, 179; 8:16, 36–37; 9:35, 49, 63, 68, 73, 81, 95, 109, 113; 11:119; 13:18; 14:16, 29; 15:43; 16:29; 17:8, 18, 39, 63, 97; 18:100, 102, 106; 19:68, 86; 20:74; 21:29, 98; 23:103; 25:34, 65; 26:91; 29:54, 68; 32:13; 35:36; 36:63; 37:23, 55, 64, 68, 163; 38:56, 85; 39:32, 60, 71–72; 40:7, 49, 60, 76; 43:74; 44:47, 56; 45:10; 48:6; 50:24, 30; 52:13, 18; 54:48; 55:43; 56:94; 57:19; 58:8; 66:9; 67:6; 69:31; 70:15; 72:15, 23; 78:21; 79:36, 39; 81:12; 82:14; 83:16; 85:10; 89:23; 96:18; 98:6; 102:6.

[101] Q 1, 12, 15, 17, 19-20, 25-26, 30-31, 36-37, 43-44, 48-50, 53, 60-63, 65, 67-68, 75, 77-83, 86, 89, 91, 93-97, 99, 103, 105-110, 112-114.

[102] E.g., Num 16:35; Deut 4:24, 33, 36; 5:4, 5, 22, 24, 26; 9:3; 18:16; 32:22; 1 Kgs 18:24, 38; 2 Kgs 1:10; Job 1:16; Pss 18:8; 29:7; 50:3; 78:21; 79:5; 89:46; 97:3.

Revelation to John, where fire is explicitly an instrument of God, but not identified so intimately with the internal nature of God.[103]

In a context where people face an alternative between gardens of delight and the raging fire on the basis of belief or disbelief, a major task of God's messengers is to warn people about the rewards of belief and the consequences of disbelief. It was noted above in the section on miraculous discourse how the Quran emphasizes the role of Elijah as warner about the consequences of disbelief, rather than as agent of God's miraculous power. Q 37:123-132 evokes Elijah's confrontation with the worshippers of Baal with reference to the doom that awaits them, rather than with reference to the manifestation of God's power in fire that came down and consumed the offerings (1 Kgs 18:36-39; see also 2 Kgs 1:10).

In addition, a number of surahs in the Quran vividly present details of the day of judgment in a manner reminiscent of Mark 13, Matt 24, Luke 21, and Rev 20–21 in the New Testament. Quran 82: ("The Cleaving" [*al-Infitar*]) presents in only 19 verses the splitting of the heavens, the dispersing of the planets, the raging of the seas, and the overturning of the graves that will occur on the day of judgment. Quran 75 ("The Rising of the Dead" (*al-Qiyamah*) presents in detail the sequence of events at the end, including the darkening of the sun and moon (cf. Mark 13:24 par.), when the righteous will be resurrected.

Noah and Jonah are apocalyptic prophets. In many ways, their discourse brings coherence to all of Quranic discourse, which, as we mentioned above, seems apocalyptic in its overall nature while at the same time using a variety of discourses.

Conclusion

To achieve sociorhetorical analysis and interpretation of books in the NT, it is necessary to move beyond literary poetics, and even beyond literary rhetoric, into the social rhetorics of multiple kinds of discourse in the corpus. One of the most noticeable features of NT literature is its overall reduction of literary poetics to biographical-historiography, epistle, and apocalypse. Another feature of this literature, however, is the energetic reconfiguration and blending of discourses characteristic of the Hebrew Bible, the OT Apocrypha, the OT Pseudepigrapha, and Mediterranean literature outside these cultural arenas. In order to produce sociorhetorical commentary on NT literature, then, it is necessary to enact strategies of rhetorical analysis and interpretation that focus on the blending of multiple rhetorolects in social, cultural, ideological, and

[103] Rev 1:14; 2:18; 3:18; 4:5; 8:5, 7, 8; 9:17, 18; 10:1; 11:5; 13:13; 14:10, 18; 15:2; 16:8; 17:16; 18:8; 19:12, 20; 20:9, 10, 14, 15; 21:8.

religious contexts where people are using reconfigured and reoriented literary poetics.

3

Social Location and Conceptual Blending in Early Christian Story

Introduction

A major challenge for interpretation of New Testament literature lies in the multiple ways in which argumentation occurs in the twenty-seven compositions that constitute the corpus. Within a half century after their first appearances in the Hellenistic-Roman world, early Christians were using blended rhetorolects[1] that could be transported into multiple "local" places. Early Christian discourse was able to shift the topography of Christian argumentation to multiple local places as a result of a consensus that Jesus, holy spirit, and followers of Christ were agents of God's attributes and actions in the inhabited world. When they shifted the topography of their discourse from household to kingdom, they were shifting from wisdom discourse to prophetic discourse, and regularly they were blending them together. When they shifted the verbal picturing from temple to body, regularly they were blending priestly discourse with wisdom and miracle discourse, and possibly with apocalyptic discourse. When they shifted to imperial discourse, they were moving either to apocalyptic or precreation discourse, or a dynamic blend of the two. New Testament literature exhibits multiple ways in which this shifting and blending of topographies occurred in first century Christianity. Certainly the shifting and blending occurred in many ways not available to us, since the NT writings are a small sample of the ways the earliest Christians used language to communicate their picturing of God's world and to persuade others that their picturing was reasonable and truthful. The NT writings present a sample of how early Christian discourse could shift and blend in biographical historiography, epistle, and apocalypse. The shifting and blending in the twenty-seven NT writings seemed to be so "foundational" for the way in which many fourth century Christians

[1] Vernon K. Robbins, "The Dialectical Nature of Early Christian Discourse," *Scriptura* 59 (1996) 353-62. Online: http://www.religion.emory.edu/faculty/robbins/dialect/dialect353.html.

viewed the world and spoke about it that the twenty-seven writings currently in the NT officially became the "classics" for early Christian discourse. From this time on, as Christians either agreed or disagreed with one another, they regularly "touched bases" in one way or another with one or more of these twenty-seven writings. Thus, this small corpus can be a good starting point for our analysis and interpretation. It must, however, be only a starting point. We must investigate many things that were earlier, many things that were in the overall Mediterranean world at the time, and many things that came later. Only in this way can we begin to understand the inner workings of early Christian discourse and Christian discourse as it works today.

Careful analysis of the twenty-seven writings in the NT shows that there is no one way in which argumentation proceeded in earliest Christianity. The thesis of this chapter is that NT literature exhibits a rhetorical process that created multiple modes of argumentation during the first century and still creates multiple modes today. This first century process is characterized by centripetal (inner-directed) rhetorical movement that, at one time and another, places wisdom, prophetic, apocalyptic, precreation, miracle, and priestly rhetorolect at the center; and centrifugal (outer-directed) rhetorical movement that, at one time and another, drives each rhetorolect out into other rhetorolects in literary contexts of biographical historiography, epistle, and apocalypse.[2]

The major task is to describe not only the literary process at work in first century Christianity, but also the rhetorical process. At present, dominance of the literary paradigm in biblical studies works against this type of rhetorical analysis and interpretation. In order to see the rhetorical process at work, it is necessary to keep in mind that literary discourse is a particular kind of rhetorical discourse, a kind that has been written according to certain literary conventions. Rhetorical discourse is much broader than written discourse, since it emerges in contexts where sounds from the mouth and gestures from the body move other persons toward action or a new configuration of feeling, attitude, worldview, belief, and understanding.[3]

Inventing a New Discourse

In rhetorical theory, invention heads the list of five parts of rhetoric:

[2] Bakhtin, *Speech Genres*, 60-67; cf. Robbins, "The Dialectical Nature," 353-62; Daniel Grossberg, *Centipetal and Centrifugal Structures in Biblical Poetry* (SBLMS 39; Atlanta: Scholars Press, 1989).

[3] See Patricia Bizzell and Bruce Herzberg, eds., *The Rhetorical Tradition:Readings from Classical Times to the Present* (Boston : Bedford Books of St. Martin's Press, 1990); Horst Ruthrof, *The Body in Language* (London/New York: Cassell, 2000).

(1) invention; (2) arrangement; (3) style; (4) memory; and (5) delivery.[4] Arrangement, also known as *dispositio* or *taxis*, has been a primary focus in NT interpretation as a result of the pioneering leadership both of Hans Dieter Betz and George A. Kennedy. Sociorhetorical interpretation places primary emphasis on invention and embeds insights concerning arrangement or *dispositio* in the framework of invention.

Invention "deals with the planning of a discourse and the arguments to be used in it."[5] But even more important, invention is a primary site of "epistemic and generative powers."[6] "In the Platonic world of Being, invention can only be discovery, but in the Aristotelean world of Becoming, it can also be creation; novelty and innovation are possible."[7] In other words, the presence in the conceptual framework of both the natural and the social world, where things emerge, change, and sometimes disappear, introduces dynamic processes of interaction where recreation can occur through reconfiguration.

A major task for sociorhetorical interpretation is to integrate social theory with rhetorical analysis and interpretation. As Margaret Zulick has stated: "… an opportunity exists to supplement the work of social theory from the vantage point of rhetoric. To set the spiral of social invention in full motion, it is advisable to look for those specific discursive processes that enable social invention to occur, within, across, and among multiple discourses."[8] "Social" means movement back and forth, which introduces change. Change is less perceptible as chronological sequence than as alternate contextualizations, different constellations, and new configurations. As Zulick asserts: "An understanding of the generative role of rhetoric in producing social change requires a more explicit and more complex theory of how the materiality of discourse

[4] George A. Kennedy, *New Testament Interpretation through Rhetorical Criticism* (Chapel Hill and London: University of North Carolina Press, 1984) 13-14.

[5] Kennedy, *New Testament*, 13.

[6] Carolyn R. Miller, "The Aristotelean *Topos:* Hunting for Novelty," in *Rereading Aristotle's Rhetoric* (ed. Alan G. Gross & Arthur E. Walzer; Carbondale and Edwardsville: Southern Illinois University Press, 2000) 130: "Robert Scott introduced this notion explicitly in 1967 and a few years later led a committee of the National Developmental Project on Rhetoric to characterize invention as 'a productive human thrust into the unknown'." See Robert L. Scott, "On Viewing Rhetoric as Epistemic," *Central States Speech Journal* 18 (1967) 9-17; idem, James L. Andrews, Howard H. Martin, J. Richard McNally, William F. Nelson, Michael M. Osborn, Arthur L. Smith, and Harold Zyskind, "Report of the Committee on the Nature of Rhetorical Invention," in *The Prospect of Rhetoric: Report of the National Developmental Project* (ed. Lloyd F. Bitzer and Edwin Black; Englewood Cliffs, NJ: Prentice Hall, 1971) 228-36, esp. 229.

[7] Miller, "*Topos*," 137.

[8] Margaret D. Zulick, "Generative Rhetoric and Public Argument: A Classical Approach," *Argument and Advocacy* 33 (1997) 110.

reflects back on its own preconditions, altering and reconfiguring everything it represents."[9]

It will be helpful now to return to the work of Averil Cameron, to which we referred in the introduction She observes that a key to the success of Christians was the manner in which their discourse "made its way in the wider world less by revolutionary novelty than by the procedure of working through the familiar, by appealing from the known to the unknown."[10] She also observes: "Out of the framework of Judaism, and living as they did in the Roman Empire and in the context of Greek philosophy, pagan practice, and contemporary social ideas, Christians built themselves a new world. They did so partly through practice – the evolution of a mode of living and a communal discipline that carefully distinguished them from their Jewish and pagan neighbors – and partly through a discourse that was itself constantly brought under control and disciplined."[11] The apostle Paul was very important, Cameron asserts: "Paul, who had never seen Jesus and whose writings are earlier than the first of the Gospels, established the precedent that Christianity was to be a matter of articulation and interpretation. Its subsequent history was as much about words and their interpretations as it was about belief or practice."[12] Thus, "As Christ 'was' the Word, so Christianity was its discourse or discourses;[13] … the successful formation of a religious discourse was one of early Christianity's greatest strengths."[14]

Cameron emphasizes, on the one hand, that the "rhetoric" of early Christian discourse lies in a close relation between the visual and the verbal,[15] the relation of language to picture that we are calling rhetography. On the other hand, she indicates that early Christians engaged in argumentation, even to the point of using various kinds of "reasoning" or "logic," which we are calling rhetology. As she states: "In practice … it was quite impossible not to resort to logical argument, and as I have argued above, all the writers from Paul onward who argued for the primacy of faith over logic did so through the medium of rhetorical argument."[16] The best means of persuasion, of course, "is through that which is already known."[17] This was especially important since, as we

[9] Zulick, "Generative Rhetoric," 110.

[10] Averil Cameron, *Christianity and the Rhetoric of Empire: The Development of Christian Discourse* (Sather Classical Lectures, 56; Berkeley: University of California Press, 1991) 25.

[11] Cameron, *Christianity*, 21.

[12] Cameron, *Christianity*, 11-12.

[13] Cameron, *Christianity*, 32.

[14] Cameron, *Christianity*, 42.

[15] Cameron, *Christianity*, 13, 21-23.

[16] Cameron, *Christianity*, 49.

[17] Cameron, *Christianity*, 40.

know, Mediterranean society was traditional in nature. That which was new had to emerge inherently out of that which was old. For early Christians, the rhetorical "commonplace" was "the old," but recontextualization, recombination, and reconfiguration of the old regularly created "the new."[18] Thus, "new" commonplaces emerged[19] and were the means by which early Christians formulated concepts and beliefs that others considered "new and different," yet somehow familiar and true.

The Topos as a Tool of Creativity within Rhetorical Invention

A major task for NT interpreters now is to produce rhetorical analysis and interpretation both of the pictorial-narrative function and the argumentative-enthymematic function of the topoi and values in all six major kinds of NT discourse: wisdom, prophetic, apocalyptic, precreation, priestly, and miracle.[20] A beginning point for bringing together Wuellner's insight into the twofold nature of topoi, the rich investigations by Malherbe and his associates, and research and interpretation by the Context Group is understanding that certain "specific (*idioi*) topoi" attain the status of "common (*koinoi*) topoi" in particular regional, ethnic, and imperial environments. In Walter J. Ong's words:

> From at least the time of Quintilian, *loci communes* was taken in two different senses. First, it referred to the 'seats' of arguments, considered as abstract 'headings' in today's parlance, such as definition, cause, effect, opposites, likenesses, and so on (the assortment varied in length from one author to another). Wanting to develop a 'proof' – we should say simply to develop a line of thought – on any subject, such as loyalty, evil, the guilt of an accused criminal, friendship, war, or whatever, one could always find something to say by defining, looking to causes, effects, opposites, and all the rest. These headings can be styled the 'analytic commonplaces'. Secondly, *loci communes* or commonplaces referred to collections of sayings (in effect, formulas) on various topics – such as loyalty, decadence, friendship, or whatever – that could be worked into one's own speech-making or writing. In this sense the *loci communes* can be styled 'cumulative commonplaces'. Both the analytic and the cumulative commonplaces, it is clear, kept alive the old oral feeling for

[18] Robbins, *The Tapestry of Early Christian Discourse*, 97-108, 121-124 and idem, *Exploring the Texture of Texts*, 40-52.

[19] Conceptual blending theorists refer to this as "emergent principles and logic": Todd V. Oakley, "Conceptual Blending, Narrative Discourse, and Rhetoric," *Cognitive Linguistics* 9.4 (1998) 341: "Blends are elaborated by imaginative simulation according to its emergent principles and logic." Cf. Fauconnier and Turner, *The Way We Think*, 42-44.

[20] Vernon K. Robbins, "Argumentative Textures in Socio-Rhetorical Interpretation," in *Argumentation in the Bible* (ed. A. Eriksson, W. Übelacker, and T.H. Olbricht; ESEC 8; Harrisburg: Trinity Press International, 2002) 27-65; cf. idem, Vernon K. Robbins, "The Dialectical Nature of Early Christian Discourse," *Scriptura* 59 (1996) 353-62. Online: http://www.religion.emory.edu/faculty/robbins/dialect/dialect353.html.

> thought and expression essentially made up of formulaic or otherwise fixed materials inherited from the past. To say this is not to explicate the whole of the complex doctrine, which itself was integral to the massive art of rhetoric.[21]

The topoi Malherbe and his associates analyze are not the analytic topoi Aristotle listed; they are specific topoi in the domain of cumulative commonplaces in the writings of the Hellenistic moralists. Participants in the Context Group have broadened the range of cumulative commonplaces to focus on topoi characteristic of ancient, pre-industrial society and culture.

In sociorhetorical terms, the twofold function of topoi (pictorial and argumentative) in early Christian discourse produced multiple "rhetorolects," because topoi emerge from a variety of conceptual locations with a "richness and connectedness of knowledge available for recombination" and function as "a source of patterns and relationships" within "the habits of thought, value hierarchies, forms of knowledge, and cultural conventions of the host society."[22] Enthymematic argumentation functions as an important means of persuasion in this context, since it moves from probable premises to a probable conclusion, regularly "start[ing] with the conclusion (or 'question') and ... searching for an argument to warrant thinking the subject and the predicate terms, or to warrant dissociating them if what one needs is a negative answer."[23] The issue is not one of "formal logic" or of "formal validity," nor is it the presence or absence of all three parts of a dialectical syllogism. The issue is argumentation from "signs," which are considered to be "sure assumptions," or from "likelihoods," which are considered to be probable assumptions, rather than from decontextualized philosophical thinking. Topoi reside at the base of enthymemes, since topoi function persuasively in descriptive and explanatory discourse on the basis of pattern recognition.[24] The experience of "recognizing the pattern" gives credibility to the topos, evoking a conviction that the pattern is "sure" (based on a "sign") or "probable" (based on "likelihood"). This credibil-

[21] Walter J. Ong, *Orality and Literacy: The Technologizing of the Word* (New York : Routledge, c1988, 1995) 110-11. I am grateful to Russell Sisson for this quotation.

[22] Carolyn R. Miller, "The Aristotelean *Topos:* Hunting for Novelty," in *Rereading Aristotle's Rhetoric* (ed. Alan G. Gross & Arthur E. Walzer; Carbondale and Edwardsville: Southern Illinois University Press, 2000) 141-42.

[23] Walter J. Ong, "Introduction" to "A Fuller Course in the *Art of Logic* (1672)," in *Complete Prose Works of John Milton. Volume VIII: 1666-1682* (ed. Maurice Kelley; New Haven and London: Yale University Press, 1982) 161; cf. David Hellholm, "Enthymemic Argumentation in Paul: The Case of Romans 6," in *Paul and His Hellenistic Context* (ed. Troels Engberg-Pedersen; Minneapolis: Fortress, 1995) 119-79.

[24] Barbara Warnick, "Two Systems of Invention: The Topics in *Rhetoric* and *The New Rhetoric*," in *Rereading Aristotle's Rhetoric* (ed. Alan G. Gross & Arthur E. Walzer; Carbondale and Edwardsville: Southern Illinois University Press, 2000) 110.

ity undergirds enthymematic argumentation, which moves in an inductive-deductive-abductive manner.[25] Thus, a topos is not simply a probable or sure "idea" or "theme"; it is "a nexus for enthymemes."[26] The inductive-deductive-abductive nature of enthymematic argumentation creates an invitation to interpreters to identify and display the constituents that function as Rule, Case, and Result, rather than Major Premise, Minor Premise, and Conclusion.[27]

As a person plans a discourse and its arguments, rhetorical topoi or "common places" are a key. In Carolyn Miller's terms:

> The *topos* is a conceptual space without fully specified or specifiable contents; it is a region of productive uncertainty. It is a "problem space," but rather than circumscribing or delimiting the problem, rather than being a closed space or container within which one searches, it is a space, or a located perspective, from which one searches. I am thinking here of the linguistic notion of "semantic space".... Such semantic networks may be conditioned both by the peculiarities of community history and by apparently logical relationships (like opposition and inclusion)....[28]

Elaborating a topos creates spaces for bringing in other topoi. Regularly, the end result of an elaboration of a topos is a new combination of topoi, what sociorhetorical interpretation calls recontextualization and reconfiguration. For rhetorical analysis and interpretation, it is important to understand that: "Once a topical pattern has developed into common use, it will be used over and over in various manifestations and will be effective by virtue of its recognizability."[29] This recognizability sometimes is distinctive of a particular kind of culture in a particular region of the world. Abraham J. Malherbe and his associates have made

[25] Richard L. Lanigan, "From Enthymeme to Abduction: The Classical Law of Logic and the Postmodern Rule of Rhetoric," in *Recovering Pragmatisms's Voice: The Classical Tradition, Rorty, and the Philosophy of Communication* (ed. Lenore Langsdorf and Andrew R. Smith; Albany, NY: SUNY Press, 1995) 49-70.

[26] I am grateful to L. Gregory Bloomquist for helping to nurture this insight; cf. Miller, *Topos*, 136; Greg Carey and L. Gregory Bloomquist (eds.), *Vision and Persuasion: Rhetorical Dimensions of Apocalyptic Discourse* (St. Louis, MO; Chalice Press, 1999) 11, 13.

[27] Vernon K. Robbins, "Enthymemic Texture in the Gospel of Thomas" (SBL Seminar Papers, 1998; Atlanta: Scholars Press, 1998) 343-66. Online: http://www.religion.emory.edu/faculty/robbins/enthymeme/enthymeme343.html; idem, "From Enthymeme to Theology in Luke 11:1-13," in *Literary Studies in Luke-Acts: A Collection of Essays in Honor of Joseph B. Tyson* (ed. R.P. Thompson and T.E. Phillips. Macon, GA: Mercer University Press, 1998) 191-214. Online: http://www.religion.emory.edu/faculty/robbins/Theology/theology191.html; idem, "Progymnastic Rhetorical Composition and Pre-Gospel Traditions: A New Approach," in *The Synoptic Gospels: Source Criticism and the New Literary Criticism* (ed. Camille Focant; BETL 110; Leuven: Leuven University Press, 1993) 111-47.

[28] Miller, "*Topos*," 141.

[29] Warnick, "Two Systems," 110.

extensive investigations of the amplificatory function of many topoi of the hellenistic moralists in NT literature.[30] "Friendship" is a major topos, associated with flattery and frankness of speech.[31] Stanley K. Stowers has used the topos of friendship to interpret the special dynamics of Paul's letter to the Philippians,[32] and Alan C. Mitchell has discussed the social function of friendship in Acts 2:44-47 and 4:32-37.[33] Another topos is covetousness or greed.[34] Malherbe has analyzed the Christianization of this topos in Luke 12:13-34.[35] Still another topos is household management, which already has attracted studies in NT literature and promises more.[36] Other topoi are *philotimia* (love of honor or fame); *homonoia* (concord or harmony); and *eusebeia* or *pietas* (piety). Analysis of these topoi in NT literature reveals that early Christians participated actively in first century Mediterranean discourse of the Hellenistic moralists."[37] For the sociorhetorical project envisioned in this presentation, it is necessary to extend analysis and interpretation beyond the topoi that occupied the Hellenistic moralists into topoi that were central to other groups and movements as well.

[30] Abraham J. Malherbe, "Hellenistic Moralists and the New Testament," *ANRW* 2.26.1 (1992) 320-5; idem, *Moral Exhortation, A Greco-Roman Sourcebook* (Library of Early Christianity; Philadelphia: Westminster, 1986) 144-61. See an overall summary and discussion of the topos in Johan C. Thom, "'The Mind is Its Own Place': Defining the Topos," in *Early Christianity and Classical Culture: Comparative Studies in Honor of Abraham J. Malherbe* (ed. J.T. Fitzgerald, T.H. Olbricht, and L.M. White; NovT Sup 110; Leiden: Brill, 2003) 555-73.

[31] John T. Fitzgerald (ed.), *Friendship, Flattery, and Frankness of Speech: Studies on Friendship in the New Testament World* (NovTSup 82; Leiden: Brill, 1996); idem (ed.), *Greco-Roman Perspectives on Friendship* (SBLSBS 34; Atlanta, GA: Scholars, 1997); David Konstan et al, *Philodemus: On Frank Criticism* (SBLTT 43; Atlanta, GA: Scholars, 1998).

[32] Stanley K. Stowers, "Friends and Enemies in the Politics of Heaven: Reading Theology in Philippians," in *Pauline Theology. Volume 1: Thessalonians, Philippians, Galatians, Philemon* (ed. Jouette M. Bassler; Minneapolis: Fortress, 1991) 105-21.

[33] Alan C. Mitchell, "The Social Function of Friendship in Acts 2:44-47 and 4:32-37," *JBL* 111 (1992) 255-72.

[34] Malherbe, *Moral Exhortation*, 154-57.

[35] Abraham J. Malherbe, "The Christianization of a *Topos* (Luke 12:13-34)," *NovT* 38 (1996) 123-35.

[36] Hermann von Lips, "Die Haustafel als '*Topos*' im Rahmen der Urchristlichen Paränese: Beobachtungen Anhand des 1. Petrusbriefes und des Titusbriefes," *NTS* 40 (1994) 261-80; Voula Tsouna-McKirahan, *The Ethics of Philodemus* (Oxford/New York; Oxford University Press, 2007).

[37] Cf. Abraham J. Malherbe, "The *Virtus Feminarum* in 1 Timothy 2:9-15," *Renewing Tradition: Studies in Texts and Contexts in Honor of James W. Thompson* (ed. M.H. Hamilton, T.H. Olbricht, J. Peterson; Princeton Theological Monograph Series; Eugene: Pickwick, 2006) 50-51 [45-65]. In a lecture entitled "Paul among Stoics and Cynics in Corinth," Malherbe refers to this environment as "the ecology of ancient Christianity and its world," which means that "[t]he two elements brought into relationship with each other must each be viewed in terms of its own environment, and then not be viewed statically."

Bruce J. Malina, John H. Elliott, Jerome H. Neyrey, Richard Rohrbaugh, John J. Pilch, Philip F. Esler, Halvor Moxnes, and other members of the Context Group have moved beyond a focus on the Hellenistic moralists by identifying the presence of common social and cultural topics and values in all the writings in the NT.[38] David A. deSilva's *Honor, Patronage, Kinship & Purity* shows that the topoi of the Hellenistic moralists, addressed by Malherbe and his associates, are intrinsic to the topics and values addressed by the Context Group: honor and shame; patronage, reciprocity, and grace; kinship and the household of God, and purity and pollution in the New Testament.[39] John J. Pilch, in particular, has analyzed social and cultural dimensions of NT miracle discourse.[40] In the midst of this work, Jerome H. Neyrey has moved beyond social and cultural topoi to the topos of "without beginning of days or end of life," which he calls a topos for a true deity.[41] From the perspective of sociorhetorical interpretation, Neyrey's essay contains initial insights into analysis and interpretation of a central topos in precreation discourse. Thus, various works by members of the Context Group have identified, analyzed, and interpreted social and cultural topoi other than those present in the writings of the Hellenistic moralists visible in NT discourse.

The Home of the Topos in Rhetology and Rhetography

The presence of two dimensions in topoi, the pictorial descriptive and the enthymematic argumentative, creates a special challenge for a biblical interpreter. One of the problems is an absence of terminology for interpreting the visual texture of a text, namely the rhetoric of a text that invites people to recruit images and pictures in the mind. Despite all the attention to history and narrative in the Bible, which regularly

[38] For the basic range of these topics, see Bruce J. Malina, *The New Testament World: Insights from Cultural Anthropology* (3d ed.; Louisville: John Knox Press, 1993); Jerome H. Neyrey, *The Social World of Luke-Acts: Models for Interpretation* (Peabody, Mass.: Hendrickson, 1991); John H. Elliott, *What Is Social-Scientific Criticism?* (Minneapolis: Fortress, 1993); Bruce J. Malina and Richard Rohrbaugh, *Social-Science Commentary on the Synoptic Gospels* (Philadelphia: Fortress, 1992); John J. Pilch and Bruce J. Malina (eds.), *Handbook of Biblical Social Values* (Peabody, MA: Hendrickson, 1993); John J. Pilch, *The Cultural Dictionary of the Bible* (Collegeville, MN; Liturgical Press, 1990); cf. Robbins, *Tapestry*, 159-66; idem, *Exploring*, 75-86. For publications of the Context Group see online: http://www.contextgroup.org/.

[39] David A. deSilva, *Honor, Patronage, Kinship & Purity: Unlocking New Testament Culture* (Downers Grove, IL: InterVarsity, 2000).

[40] John J. Pilch, *Healing in the New Testament: Insights from Medical and Mediterranean Anthropology* (Minneapolis: Fortress, 2000).

[41] Jerome H. Neyrey, "'Without Beginning of Days or End of Life' (Hebrews 7:3): *Topos* for a True Deity," *CBQ* 53 (1991) 439-55.

create story images and pictures in the mind, theology, philosophy, literary interpretation, and rhetorical interpretation do not have vocabulary ready at hand to describe, analyze, and interpret the visual texture of a text. In bodily terms, this nonexistent vocabulary suppresses the "lower" realm of bodily image and activity in a context of highlighting the "higher" reasoning realm of the mind, which one presumes to have a greater truth value as a result of its more generalized, abstract forms of thinking.

The absence of vocabulary for interpreting the visual texture of a text becomes readily apparent in interpretation of many domains of knowledge about early Christian literature. In the realm of Christology, for instance, there is an emphasis on christo-logos, the argumentative-enthymematic realm of belief that Jesus is the Messiah (Christ). What is missing from interpretation of this domain in NT literature is a concept of Christography, the pictorial-narrative realm of belief that Jesus is the Messiah. Many interpreters are unhappy with a definition of the NT Gospels as biographies. From a sociorhetorical perspective, the Gospels are Christographies. Christography amplifies the concept, "Jesus is the Messiah," through picture and narration that depicts "messianic actions and speech" by Jesus. First Corinthians 1:30-31 presents Christology, i.e. reasoning about Jesus as Christ: "God is the source of your life in Christ Jesus, who became for us wisdom from God, and righteousness and sanctification and redemption, in order that, as it is written, 'Let the one who boasts, boast in the Lord.' In contrast, Matt 9:20-22 presents Christography, i.e., narration of Jesus acting as Christ: "Then suddenly a woman who had been suffering from hemorrhages for twelve years came up behind him and touched the fringe of his cloak, for she said to herself, 'If I only touch his cloak, I will be made well'. Jesus turned, and seeing her he said, 'Take heart, daughter; your faith has made you well'. And instantly the woman was made well." Our interpretive vocabulary regularly develops dimensions of the rhetology, but it regularly lacks good terminology to interpret the rhetography.

Another realm close to hand is theology. Supposedly we all know that theology is reasoning (argumentative-enthymemic discourse) about God or the divine. We have substantive discussions concerning how theological discourse should be constructed, and these discussions and their results are highly productive. What is missing from this discussion is theography,[42] description and narration of God and God's activities. Daniel 7:9 presents theography: "As I watched, thrones were set in place, and an Ancient One took his throne, his clothing was white as snow, and the hair of his head like pure wool; his throne was fiery flames, and its wheels were burning fire." Biblical interpreters know this

[42] See Jack Miles, *Biography of God*, p. 11.

is vivid description of God, but there is no conventional terminology to guide analysis and interpretation of it. The natural terminology to describe this discourse is theography. Another instance of theography occurs in Rev 4:2-3: "At once I was in the spirit, and there in heaven stood a throne, with one seated on the throne! And the one seated there looks like jasper and carnelian, and around the throne is a rainbow that looks like an emerald." Once interpreters begin to analyze the dynamic, interactive relation between rhetology and rhetography in biblical literature, a new era of interpretation can emerge. Until then, rhetological vocabulary will continue to suppress rhetographical dimensions of biblical discourse and the absence of rhetographical vocabulary will continue to weaken the analytical and interpretive procedures of commentators.[43]

The absence of vocabulary to describe rhetography throughout biblical interpretation is ubiquitous. If we repair this deficiency, we can begin to clarify and exhibit more fully the nature of the multivalency of biblical discourse. Beyond the arenas of Christology and theology, the arenas of eschatology and apocalyptic will become much clearer if we use both rhetography and rhetology. Indeed, the implications for repairing the vocabulary through biblical interpretation is staggering. In truth, what is needed is a complete set of terms to describe rhetography and rhetology throughout biblical tradition. It is doubtful, however, that many interpreters or readers would welcome the overhaul that is necessary. Therefore, we will introduce new terminology only in relation to a few well-established terms. It would be helpful, for example, to analyze and interpret eschatography – verbal description of vivid events concerning the end-time. In addition, biblical interpreters regularly discuss cosmology. Decisively new dimensions of understanding will emerge if we engage in sociorhetorical analysis and interpretation of cosmography – vivid description of regions of the cosmos. In truth, analysis of certain dimensions of biblical rhetography have been emerging in biblical interpretation during the last thirty years.[44] If we name these dimensions more clearly, we can analyze and interpret them with much greater insight, understanding, and clarity.

The corpus of the NT readily exhibits dynamic, dialogical interaction between rhetology and rhetography in the basic outline of the

[43] For this reason, the sociorhetorical commentaries in the Rhetoric of Religious Antiquity series will begin interpretation of a section of text by analyzing its visual texture. Cf. V.K. Robbins, "Rhetography: A New Way of Seeing the Familiar Text," in *Words Well Spoken: George Kennedy's Rhetoric of the New Testament* (ed. C.C. Black and D.F. Watson; Studies in Rhetoric and Religion, 8; Waco: Baylor University Press, 2008) 81-106.

[44] Special mention must be made in this regard of the Blackwell Bible Commentaries edited by John Sawyer, David M. Gunn, Judith Kovacs, and Christopher Rowland, online: http://www.blackwellpublishing.com/seriesbyseries.asp?ref=BC.

books in it. The Gospels and Acts feature rhetography, displaying sequences of picturesque scenes that create stories. Whatever rhetology they contain is embedded in their rhetography. The epistles, in contrast, have explicit rhetology, displaying argumentation supported by reasons and antecedent, authoritative testimony, and clarified through contraries, opposites, and analogies. Whatever rhetography they contain is embedded in their rhetology.

The Revelation to John is a fascinating merger of rhetology and rhetography, since it features seven letters (grounded in rhetology) in the opening chapters in the context of fully-developed picturesque discourse. When picture and story become so thoroughly blended with reasoning that the reasoning evokes the pictures and the story, and the pictures and the story evoke the reasoning, then the discourse has become truly remarkable and powerful. Christian discourse had attained a highly forceful status by the end of the first century. We must analyze more thoroughly the means by which it achieved this status.

From Historical Time and Space to Critical Spatiality

In the context of analysis and interpretation of the rhetology and rhetography in early Christian literature, pictorial narration and reasoning associated with particular social, cultural, and religious locations have emerged as highly significant. Focus on these locations has drawn more detailed attention to the "social" in sociorhetorical interpretation. It became obvious, first of all, that a major characteristic of early Christian discourse is its pictorial narrational and enthymematic argumentative patterns related to people's bodies, households, villages, synagogues, cities, temples, kingdoms, and empires. In other words, the cognitions and reasonings were emerging from "lived experiences" in specific places in the first century Mediterranean world. This has led to the use of "critical spatiality theory" in sociorhetorical interpretation. This area of study, located in the field of cultural geography studies, builds in particular on writings by Henri Lefebvre,[45] Robert D. Sack,[46] Pierre Bourdieu,[47] Edward W. Soja,[48] and Stephen Toulmin.[49] James W.

[45] H. Lefebvre, *The Production of Space* (Oxford: Blackwell, 1991 [1974]).

[46] R.D. Sack, *Human Territoriality: Its Theory and History* (Cambridge: Cambridge University, 1986); idem, *Homo Geographicus: A Framework for Action, Awareness, and Moral Concern* (Baltimore: Johns Hopkins, 1997).

[47] P. Bourdieu, "Social Space and Symbolic Power", *Sociological Theory* 7 (1989) 14-25.

[48] E.W. Soja, *Postmodern Geography: The Reassertion of Space in Critical Social Theory* (New York: Verso, 1989); idem, "Postmodern Geographies and the Critique of Historicism", in *Postmodern Contentions: Epochs, Politics, Space* (ed. J.P. Jones III, W. Natter, and T.R. Schatzki; New York: Guildford, 1993) 113-36; idem, *Thirdspace: Journeys to Los Angeles and Other Real-and-Imagined Places* (Cambridge, MA: Blackwell, 1996).

Flanagan has been especially instrumental in bringing critical spatiality theory into biblical study.[50] In 1991, Robbins used Robert D. Sack's *Human Territoriality* for sociorhetorical analysis of "images of empire" in Acts[51] and T.F. Carney's *The Shape of the Past*[52] for the social location of the implied author of Luke-Acts.[53] Jerome H. Neyrey has applied strategies for interpreting the social location of the implied author to Jude and 2 Peter,[54] Luke's social location of Paul,[55] the Gospel of John,[56] and Paul's writings.[57] Since 2000, Roland Boer has written an important study on "the production of space" in 1 Samuel 1–2,[58] Michael McKeever an analysis of "refiguring space" in the Lukan passion narrative,[59] Claudia V. Camp an important essay on "storied space" in Sirach,[60] Victor H. Matthews an important discussion of physical, imagined, and "lived" space in ancient Israel,[61] and Thomas B. Dozeman an

[49] S. Toulmin, *Cosmopolis: The Hidden Agenda of Modernity* (Chicago: University of Chicago Press, 1990).

[50] J.W. Flanagan, "Ancient Perceptions of Space/Perceptions of Ancient Space", *Semeia* 87 (1999) 15-43. Online: http://www.cwru.edu/affil/GAIR/constructions/constructions.html. See his 'Constructions of Ancient Space' site online: http://guildzone.org. See David M. Gunn and Paula M. McNutt, *"Imagining" Biblical Worlds: Studies in Spatial, Social and Historical Constructs in Honor of James W. Flanagan* (London: Sheffield Academic Press, 2002).

[51] V.K. Robbins, "Luke-Acts: A Mixed Population Seeks a Home in the Roman Empire", *Images of Empire* (ed. L. Alexander; Sheffield: JSOT Press, 1991) 202-21. Online: http://www.religion.emory.edu/faculty/robbins/Pdfs/MixedPopulation.pdf.

[52] T.F. Carney, *The Shape of the Past: Models and Antiquity* (Lawrence, KS: Coronado Press, 1975).

[53] V.K. Robbins, "The Social Location of the Implied Author of Luke-Acts", *The Social World of Luke-Acts: Models for Interpretation* (ed. J.H. Neyrey; Peabody, MA: Hendrickson, 1991) 305-32.

[54] J.H. Neyrey, *2 Peter, Jude* (AB 37C; New York: Doubleday, 1993) 32-42, 128-42.

[55] J.H. Neyrey, "Luke's Social Location of Paul: Cultural Anthropology and the Status of Paul in Acts", *History, Literature, and Society in the Book of Acts* (ed. B. Witherington III; Cambridge: Cambridge University Press, 1996) 251-79.

[56] J.H. Neyrey, "Spaces and Places, Whence and Whither, Homes and Rooms: 'Territoriality' in the Fourth Gospel", *BTB* 32 (2002) 60-74; idem, "Spaced Out in John: Territoriality in the Fourth Gospel", *HervTeoStud* 58 (2002) 633-63.

[57] Jerome H. Neyrey, "The Social Location of Paul", *Fabrics of Discourse: Essays in Honor of Vernon K. Robbins* (ed. D.B. Gowler, L.G. Bloomquist, and D.F. Watson; Harrisburg/London/New York: Trinity Press International, 2003) 126-64.

[58] R. Boer, "Sanctuary and Womb: Henri Lefebvre and the Production of Space", presented to the AAR/SBL Constructions of Ancient Space Seminar, 2000. Online: http://www.cwru.edu/affil/GAIR/papers/2000papers/Boer.html.

[59] M.C. McKeever, "Refiguring Space in the Lukan Passion Narrative", Constructions of Ancient Space, 2000. Online: http://www.cwru.edu/affil/GAIR/papers/2000papers/mckeever.htm.

[60] C.V. Camp, "Storied Space, or, Ben Sira 'Tells' a Temple", in Gunn and McNutt, *"Imagining" Biblical Worlds*, 64-80.

[61] V.H. Matthews, "Physical Space, Imagined Space, and 'Lived Space' in Ancient Israel", *BTB* 33 (2003) 12-20.

essay on "Ezra-Nehemiah".[62] In addition, Bart B. Bruehler has analyzed local political space in Luke.[63] Critical analysis of social and cultural places and spaces in early Christian literature, as well as in first century Mediterranean material culture, needs to be incorporated into sociorhetorical commentary on the NT writings.

From Radical Rhetorics to Early Christian Rhetorolects (Rhetorical Dialects)

In the context of critical spatiality theory, which deepens, broadens, and expands the horizons of analysis and interpretation of places and spaces in early Christian literature, debate about judicial, deliberative, and epideictic rhetoric in New Testament literature, which focuses primarily on courtrooms, political assemblies, and civil ceremonies seems a highly limited approach. George A. Kennedy dealt with this issue by introducing the concept of radical rhetorics. By radical rhetoric, he meant that early Christians did not follow principles of "worldly rhetoric," supporting theses simply or even primarily with "logical" reasons, but introduced assertions based on external authority. Some of his discussion implicitly shifted the rhetorical frames in New Testament literature from judicial, deliberative, and epideictic rhetoric to wisdom, prophetic, and miracle rhetoric, but his own analysis and the analysis of the students who followed his lead stayed with the three classical rhetorical locations and modes. Careful analysis of Kennedy's comments about NT rhetoric either implicitly or incidentally brings into view the six major rhetorolects that will be discussed in this volume and the subsequent one: wisdom, prophetic, apocalyptic, precreation, priestly, and miracle.[64]

First, one notices statements by Kennedy that evoke the conventional call and activities of a prophet in the context of a kingdom. In an unexpected context, God confronts a person, calls the person to a prophetic task, provides the person with a "word of God" that must be pronounced before the king, groups of official leaders, and assemblies of the people in the kingdom. Kennedy refers to this kind of prophetic rhetoric as "the doctrine that the speaker is a vehicle of God's will."[65] He describes this kind of rhetoric in Paul in the following way:

> The radical rhetoric which Paul more willingly acknowledges [than the

[62] T.B. Dozeman, "Geography and History in Herodotus and in Ezra-Nehemiah", *JBL* 122/3 (2003) 449-66.

[63] Bart B. Bruehler, "The Public, the Political, and the Private: The Literary and Social-Spatial Functions of Luke 18:35-19:48," Ph.D. dissertation, Emory University, 2007.

[64] Robbins, "Rhetography."

[65] Kennedy, *New Testament Interpretation through Rhetorical Criticism*, 7-8.

rhetoric with worldly characteristics] is something external to himself, characterized by authority, power, and direct illumination, and its mode of expression is gentler, though in Paul's case perhaps a constrained gentleness. This tension of gentleness and anger in Christian rhetoric is doubtless a reflection of the tension of love and mercy in Christian theology.[66]

This is the nature of prophetic rhetoric, which evokes a picture of God calling and sending a prophet to perform a specific set of tasks associated with a kingdom. Equipped with powerful words and actions authorized by God, the prophet confronts the king, leaders in official positions of authority, and the people in the kingdom to act according to guidelines introduced by God for creating a context for well-being and long life on the earth. The tension of gentleness and anger to which Kennedy refers is the result of the presence of both blessings and woes in prophetic discourse. An excellent example of the juxtaposition of blessings and woes exists in Luke 6:20-26, and it is even more clearly evident when one juxtaposes Luke 6:20 and 11:42:

> Blessed are you who are poor, for yours is the kingdom of God. (Luke 6:20)
>
> But woe to you Pharisees! For you tithe mint and rue and herbs of all kinds, and neglect justice and the love of God; it is these you ought to have practiced, without neglecting the others. (Luke 11:42)

Biblical prophetic discourse evokes the context of a kingdom of God with specific boundaries on earth. God chose a special region of land, arranged for anointed kings to rule over it, and called prophets to confront the leaders and the people when they were not living according to God's covenantal guidelines.[67] Early Christian prophetic discourse evoked the context of a kingdom of God on earth and accepted the premise that God had called and specially authorized certain people within the community to confront its leaders and overall members with blessings and woes as words from God. In early Christian speech and writing, the regional boundaries of God's kingdom expand beyond the land of Israel to an area that spans from Rome (Acts 28:16) to Ethiopia (Acts 8:27-39), with a plan of expanding from Rome to Spain (Rom 15:24, 28). In this context, early Christian prophetic rhetorolect reconfigures God's promise of land to God's promise of "an inheritance" (*klēronomos*).[68] The power of early Christian prophetic argumentation

[66] Ibid., 96.

[67] For an excellent example of analysis of biblical prophetic discourse that provides rich data for understanding the nature of early Christian prophetic rhetoric, see Mark Roncace, *Jeremiah, Zedekiah, and the Fall of Jerusalem* (LHBOTS [JSOTS] 423; New York/London: T. & T. Clark, 2005) esp. 5-25, 146-73.

[68] E.g., 1 Cor 6:9-10; 15:50; Gal 3:18, 29; 4:1, 7, 30; 5:21; Rom 4:13, 14; 8:17.

resides as fully in the authoritative picture it evokes of God's calling of the speaker as it does in the reasons, rationales, analogies, precedents, and arguments from contraries and opposites in the discourse itself.

Second, Kennedy introduces statements that evoke conventional contexts of miraculous healing in Mediterranean antiquity. Kennedy especially identifies this in the Gospel of Mark:

> "Immediately" is one of Mark's favorite words and gives a forward movement to his account. The truth is immediately and intuitively apprehended because it is true. Some see it, others do not, but there is no point in trying to persuade the latter. This is the most radical form of Christian rhetoric. When Jesus performs his first miracle, the witnesses are "amazed" (1:27); they recognize truth but do not comprehend it rationally. The miracle is a sign of authority, as the crowd at once admits.[69]

While miraculous healing of the body regularly leads to sanctuaries of healing in the Mediterranean world, in early Christian discourse it presupposes interaction between Jesus' body and the body of a person with a malfunctioning body. In other words, in early Christian discourse the context for understanding this emerges from miraculous recoveries of illness, ailment, or death in the body itself. The geophysical context for early Christian miracle discourse is the body itself in relation to the body of the healer. An excellent example is the healing story just after the verse to which Kennedy refers:

> [30] Now Simon's mother-in-law was in bed with a fever, and they told him about her at once. [31] He came and took her by the hand and lifted her up. Then the fever left her, and she began to serve them. (Mark 1:30-31)

The occurrence of the miracle in a house is incidental. The healing could occur alongside a road, by the sea, on a mountain, or anywhere. The important thing is the presence of Jesus' body in relation to the body of the woman who is ill. In early Christian discourse, the hand of the healer is often central, but it need not be. The essential context for the discourse is a relationship between the body of the healer and the body of the person who is ill or otherwise afflicted. Kennedy notices that "the witnesses are 'amazed' (1:27); they recognize truth but do not comprehend it rationally. The miracle is a sign of authority, as the crowd at once admits."[70] Here Kennedy has identified early Christian miracle rhetoric, regularly presented in the form of a story that features an extraordinary transformation of a malfunctioning person into a healthy and well-ordered social being. This is radical rhetoric, but it is

[69] Kennedy, *New Testament Interpretation through Rhetorical Criticism*, 105.
[70] Ibid., 105.

well-understood rhetoric with a history that focuses on Elijah and Elisha in biblical tradition and on Asklepios in Mediterranean tradition.[71]

Third, Kennedy observes argumentation that evokes worldly wisdom discourse, but even this discourse often occurs in a form of "parables, which are directly apprehended."[72] In other words, what Kennedy calls "worldly rhetoric" is properly identified as early Christian wisdom discourse. He observes wisdom discourse especially in Matthew and the letters of Paul, but also in other portions of the NT:

> [E]ven in the first century a process was underway of recasting expressions in enthymematic form, thus making sacred language into premises which are supported, at least in a formal sense, by human reasoning.[73] … [T]here is need for some knowledge of classical rhetoric in reading the New Testament. To cite cases discussed in this book, it is not clear that readers of the New Testament have grasped that the rhetorical function of the Beatitudes, *as they stand in the text of Matthew*, is that of a proem, or that narrative passages in the Bible are often ethical proofs, or that Paul regularly enunciates a proposition which is worked out in a series of topics.[74]

In the context of the strategies of worldly rhetoric, as Kennedy calls it, careful investigation reveals that imagery of the family household lies at the base of early Christian wisdom discourse. The ideal teacher is a father figure who teaches his children how to live, because he cares for them. This imagery blends with a concept of God as Father over the created world, making it into a household where God provides food, shelter, and clothing for all who live in it, like a father provides for the needs of his family. In early Christian discourse, the function of God as father finds its beginnings in God's creation of the universe and provision of light as a means for productivity in it. In this conceptual domain, the light of God is God's wisdom, which guides people to live generously and harmoniously with their neighbors. Luke 11:33-36 is a very interesting passage in this regard, evoking many aspects of the picturing central to early Christian wisdom discourse:

> [33] No one after lighting a lamp puts it in a cellar, but on the lampstand so that those who enter may see the light. [34] Your eye is the lamp of your body. If your eye is healthy, your whole body is full of light; but if it is not healthy, your body is full of darkness. [35] Therefore consider

[71] Wendy Cotter, *Miracles in Greco-Roman Antiquity: A Sourcebook for the Study of New Testament Miracle Stories* (London: Routledge, 1999); cf. V.K. Robbins, "Sociorhetorical Interpretation of Miracle Discourse in the Synoptic Gospels," in *The Role of Miracle Discourse in the Argumentation of the New Testament* (ed. D.F. Watson; Symposium; Atlanta: SBL and Leiden: Brill, 2009).

[72] Kennedy, *New Testament Interpretation through Rhetorical Criticism*, 105.

[73] Ibid., 159.

[74] Ibid., 160.

> whether the light in you is not darkness. 36 If then your whole body is full of light, with no part of it in darkness, it will be as full of light as when a lamp gives you light with its rays. (Luke 11:33-36)

This wisdom discourse evokes the context of a family household. The imagery of the lighting of a lamp and the placing of the lamp in the household brings to mind the location where parents teach their children wisdom in the context of caring for their bodies from early childhood. The goal is to bring the light of God's wisdom into their bodies, so they may function as the good, productive world God created at the beginning of time. The eye is the special vehicle for this knowledge. Learning to see in the visible world the light of God's goodness and learning to let the eye shine this light into the body creates a person who is able to produce goodness and righteousness in the world.[75]

Kennedy observes that there is a radical nature even to the wisdom discourse in the NT, especially in the Gospel of Mark. He contrasts Mark with Matthew and Luke in the following manner:

> No effort is made to include any picture of Jesus' early teaching as seen in the Sermon on the Mount and the Sermon on the Plain. This kind of explanation is irrelevant to Mark. When Jesus preaches in Mark it is in parables, which are directly apprehended.[76] ... Mark very likely represents the survival of a continuous tradition of radical rhetoric in the early Church, long associated with the apostleship of Peter.[77]

On the one hand, it is a natural characteristic of wisdom rhetoric to feature parables and analogies that are directly apprehended. Analogies with the created world and other simple techniques are meant to present knowledge that people accept as self-evident. On the other hand, many early Christian wisdom passages come to the hearer or reader as radical wisdom. Kennedy asserts that "[t]his is characteristic not only of some individual pericopes, but of entire books such as the Gospel of Mark."[78]

Early Christian wisdom rhetoric naturally unfolds according to patterns and principles Kennedy assigned to rationally oriented, worldly rhetoric in his study of NT literature. The rhetography in this rhetoric blends the household and its members with God's created world and the vegetative productivity in it. In addition, virtually everything in a

[75] John H. Elliott, "The Evil Eye and the Sermon on the Mount: Contours of a Pervasive Belief in Social Scientific Perspective," *BibInt* 2 (1994) 51-84; John J. Pilch and Bruce J. Malina (eds.), *Handbook of Biblical Social Values* (Peabody, MA: Hendrickson, 1998) 68-72.

[76] Kennedy, *New Testament Interpretation through Rhetorical Criticism*, 105.

[77] Ibid., 106.

[78] Ibid., 7.

household and in God's created world functions by analogy in relation to one another. God the Father of the created world is like the father in a household and people in the world are children of God, like the little people in a household are children of the parents. In addition, people may be like animals (sheep, wolves, doves, serpents) or like trees that bear good or bad fruit. Nevertheless, much of this, as Kennedy says, is radical rhetoric. We will return to the radicality even of early Christian wisdom discourse below.

Fourth, Kennedy makes statements that lead an early Christian interpreter to the nature of precreation rhetoric in early Christian discourse:

> John's Gospel is radical Christian rhetoric in its demand for immediate and direct response to the truth, but John makes far more demands than Mark on his readers in approaching the truth they are to perceive. He uses the forms of logical argument not so much as proof, as does Matthew, but as ways of turning and reiterating the topics which are at the core of his message.[79]

Kennedy's insights lead a person to precreation rhetoric, a kind of radical rhetoric that presupposes that Jesus' knowledge is in Jesus as a result of the intimate relation he, as the only begotten Son of God, has had with God since before creation. The experiential base of this was knowledge about the imperial household, which for most early Christians was far away and never seen by them. Blending the imperial household with the household of God, the Gospel of John evokes an imperial primordial household outside of time and space with an intimate relation between the emperor Father and his son. The Father sends his son out into his empire to distribute the benefits of his eternal wealth to those who profess unconditional loyalty and friendship to the son. By this means, friendship with the son enacts a relationship with the father that yields benefits from the realm of eternal peace, salvation, and life.[80]

The Gospel of John, then, evokes the context of an imperial realm with a son of the emperor who goes throughout the empire to distribute primordial benefits that only an emperor can bestow. Everything Jesus does and says is primordial wisdom and action. God's creation of the world only made God's wisdom partially visible to human beings. Jesus' action and speech present the unfathomable wisdom of God to humans in terms that are comprehensible only with truly exceptional insight into the nature of God. In this instance, then, the radical rheto-

[79] Ibid., 113.

[80] For an initial exploration of the imperial nature of the discourse in the Gospel of John, see Gerhard van den Heever, "Finding Data in Unexpected Places (Or: From Text Linguistics to Socio-Rhetoric): A Sociorhetorical Reading of John's Gospel," *SBL Seminar Papers, 1998* (2 vols.; SBLSP 37; Atlanta: Scholars Press, 1998) 2:649-76.

ric evokes a picture of Jesus with God before the creation of the world. Jesus, as the only begotten Son who listened carefully to everything God the Father said to him, and who watched carefully everything his Father did, uses extraordinary images and arguments, regularly in the form of logical argument, to communicate the extraordinary knowledge available to him from God's primordial sphere. When God sends Jesus to earth to speak to people, Jesus uses unusual images and performs extraordinary signs among them. As Kennedy says: "John makes far more demands than Mark on his readers in approaching the truth they are to perceive. He uses the forms of logical argument not so much as proof, as does Matthew, but as ways of turning and reiterating the topics which are at the core of his message."[81] In early Christian discourse, this is precreation wisdom that gains plausibility for the hearer through blending with the scope of divine powers and benefits inherent in the emperor and his household.

Kennedy leads us incidentally to a fifth and sixth major kind of radical rhetoric in early Christian discourse when he discusses "topics," topoi or *loci*, which are "the 'places' where [the speaker] looks for something to say about his subject."[82] He presents the following example of "past fact leading to the topic of degree":

> "While we were yet sinners Christ died for us. Since, therefore, we are now justified by his blood, much more shall we be saved by him from the wrath of God" (Rom. 5:8-9). This type of *a fortiori* argument is commonly known as "the more and the less."[83]

With this example, Kennedy incidentally introduces the two other major contexts of reasoning evoked by early Christian speech and writing, namely priestly and apocalyptic discourse. The statement about being justified by Christ's blood when he died evokes priestly reasoning associated with a temple containing a sacrificial altar. Then the statement about being saved from the wrath of God evokes apocalyptic reasoning associated with the power of an emperor to destroy rebellious, "impure" people with legions of his imperial army. In this conceptual domain, the impurity of the people is regularly a result of an unwillingness to participate in ritual worship of the emperor and the emissaries the emperor sends out to perform certain tasks in his empire.

The picturesque nature of early Christian priestly discourse reaches its fullest form in a passage like Heb 9:11-12:

> 11 But when Christ came as a high priest of the good things that have come, then through the greater and more perfect tent (not made with

[81] Kennedy, *New Testament Interpretation through Rhetorical Criticism*, 113.
[82] Ibid., 20.
[83] Ibid., 20.

> hands, that is, not of this creation), [12]he entered once for all into the Holy Place, not with the blood of goats and calves, but with his own blood, thus obtaining eternal redemption. (Heb 9:11-12)

This discourse evokes the context of a sacrificial temple and blends this context with the conceptual realm of God in the heavens. Jesus is the high priest in God's temple in the heavens who offers himself as the perfect sacrifice. This is radical reasoning, but it is reasoning based on Mediterranean understanding of the process and benefits of offerings on an altar in a temple designed for sacrificial ritual.[84] The image of the context in the mind of the hearer enacts a conceptual domain in which the assertions can be understood as reasonable. The blend of radicality and reasonableness in it again is a rhetorical characteristic Kennedy identified both appropriately and skillfully.

The picturesque nature of early Christian apocalyptic discourse also will be fully evident to the reader. Among the many texts a person could choose, perhaps the following text is informative in this context:

> [8]The second angel blew his trumpet, and something like a great mountain, burning with fire, was thrown into the sea. [9]A third of the sea became blood, a third of the living creatures in the sea died, and a third of the ships were destroyed. (Rev 8:8-9)

The picturesque action in this episode evokes the image of the power of an imperial military army. Following instructions that have been relayed from the emperor to the trumpet blower, the trumpeter sounds the signal that enacts massive destruction of a portion of the empire that has been determined to be impure. Again, purity in apocalyptic rhetoric is based primarily on the willingness of people to participate in ritual obedience and worship of the emperor and obedience to the legions of representatives and military personnel who go throughout the empire to maintain peace, salvation, and well-being. The people and regions that are determined to be impure and rebellious must be destroyed. The might of the emperor's army is so great that it can lay waste not only entire cities but also vast regions of land. It can also destroy ships in the sea, discharging the people's bodies into the water and sending the cargo afloat to pollute the water. As the water turns to blood and the creatures in the sea die, the rebellious forces meet their end in a mass of destruction and pollution. The imagery is grotesque, but it is understandable to the hearer; radical but plausible in the context of the Mediterranean world.

[84] For an excellent analysis of biblical priestly discourse that provides rich data for analysis of early Christian priestly rhetoric, see William K. Gilders, *Blood Ritual in the Hebrew Bible: Meaning and Power* (Baltimore: Johns Hopkins University Press, 2004).

Apocalyptic rhetoric features "pronouncements" from the heavens in the midst of unfolding pictures of God's rescue of obedient, faithful, and righteous members of his empire and destruction of certain portions that are rebellious, unfaithful, and wicked. Just as an emperor has large numbers of people to perform the tasks he wants to be accomplished, so heavenly agents play key roles in bringing the present chaos to an end and a new world order into existence. The rhetography in this rhetoric blends the concept of an emperor with extraordinary military power at his disposal with God's power and creates a context for voices and actions that bring about a newly created order.

From the perspective of sociorhetorical interpretation, Kennedy's approach to radical rhetoric is a key for understanding the nature of the rhetoric in the NT writings. Kennedy's approach does not move us fully into rhetorical analysis of early Christian rhetoric, however, because it brings a system of "rational rhetoric" to the NT writings and describes the "nonrational rhetorical" aspects of the NT in terms that are oppositional to "real rhetoric," which he calls worldly rhetoric. In contrast to an approach that uses worldly rhetoric as a normative standard for real rhetoric, the goal of a rhetorical interpreter must be to use the insight that the NT writings blend rational and nonrational, worldly and radical, rhetoric together. Careful analysis of the rhetography in this discourse brings into view the multiple kinds of rhetoric in early Christian discourse.

Beyond Form and Genre to Frame and Prototype

As soon as an interpreter identifies multiple kinds of rhetoric in early Christian discourse, an issue emerges concerning the inner nature of each kind and the nature of the boundaries among them. Until very recently, it has been conventional in biblical studies to discuss the relation of kinds of discourse in terms of form and genre, and this has led to vigorous disputes about the relation of one genre to another. The foreground of the debates exhibits a presupposition that forms and genres are types of biblical discourse so different from one another that they do not easily merge with one another. Discussion of generic "mixtures" has regularly led to a genetic description of the influence of one form or genre on another and to discussions of "hybrid" forms. The absence of the story-line of Israel's history in Proverbs[85] led to an assertion that wisdom discourse was such a different form of biblical dis-

[85] Cf. John J. Collins, *Jewish Wisdom in the Hellenistic Age* (OTL; Louisville, KY: Westminster John Knox Press, 1997), 2: "The subject matter of Proverbs also stands in sharp contrast to most of the biblical tradition. The people of Israel and its history and destiny are not even mentioned."

course that it could not easily merge with forms focused on the story of Israel.[86] But then, of course, there is Ben Sira, which embeds a storyline of famous "men" of Israel (Sir 40–48) in its presentation of wisdom[87] and the Wisdom of Solomon, which tells the story of how Wisdom guided the leaders of Israel from Adam through the conquest of the land of Canaan (Wis. 10–12).[88] In a context where a majority of scholars presupposed that apocalyptic emerged out of influence from Persian dualism, Gerhard von Rad argued that it had its roots in wisdom literature.[89] Then Otto Plöger and Paul Hanson argued that biblical prophetic literature contained proto-apocalyptic texts.[90] Recently, these kinds of discussions have led to a volume entitled *Conflicted Boundaries in Wisdom and Apocalypticism*,[91] and an essay by Werner H. Kelber on the Coptic *Gospel of Thomas* as a hybrid gospel.[92]

Recent discussions make it pertinent to ask if a form and genre approach that presupposes that the different thought worlds of each genre naturally separate them from one another is the best way to approach the issue. The sociorhetorical approach in this volume moves beyond traditional form and genre criticism into frame and prototype criticism, which has extensive empirical evidence that human cognition presupposes at its most basic levels the transporting of aspects of one conceptual domain to another conceptual domain. In other words, at its foundations human cognition is metaphorical. Humans continually use reasoning in one domain to sort through cognitive items in another domain. This means that throughout the millennia humans have continually used forms, which cognitive scientists now call "frames," in one conceptual domain to understand and interpret forms in another domain. This view of semantic frames underlies the argument in this volume about early Christian rhetorolects. The argument is that the six early Christian rhetorolects investigated and interpreted in this volume and the next volume are cultural-religious frames that introduce multi-

[86] Roland E. Murphy, "Wisdom in the OT," *ABD* 6:920-31.

[87] Ibid., 97-111.

[88] Ibid., 213-21.

[89] Gerhard von Rad, *Wisdom in Israel* (trans. J.D. Martin; Nashville: Abingdon, 1972).

[90] Otto Plöger, *Theocracy and Eschatology* (trans. S. Rudman; Richmond, VA: John Knox, 1968); Paul Hanson, *The Dawn of Apocalyptic* (Philadelphia: Fortress Press, 1979); Stephen L. Cook, *Prophecy and Apocalypticism: The Postexilic Social Setting* (Minneapolis: Fortress Press, 1995) 1-9.

[91] Benjamin G. Wright III and Lawrence M. Wills (eds.), *Conflicted Boundaries in Wisdom and Apocalypticism* (Symposium 35; Atlanta: SBL, 2005).

[92] Werner H. Kelber, "The Verbal Art in Q and *Thomas*: A Question of Epistemology," in *Oral Performance, Popular Tradition, and Hidden Transcript in Q* (ed. R. Horsley; SBL Semeia Studies 60; Atlanta: SBL, 2006) 25-42; Vernon K. Robbins, "Oral Performance in Q: Epistemology, Political Conflict, and Contextual Register," in Horsley, *Oral Performance*, 109-13 [109-22].

ple networks of thinking, reasoning, and acting that were alive and dynamic in early Christian thought, language, and practice.

The foundational language about frames that underlies the work of modern cognitive science theorists has been developed energetically by Charles J. Fillmore at the University of California at Berkeley. His study of frame semantics is currently "a research program in empirical semantics which emphasizes the continuities between language and experience."[93] This group defines a frame as:

> any system of concepts related in such a way that to understand any one concept it is necessary to understand the entire system; introducing any one concept results in all of them becoming available.[94]

The sociorhetorical analysis and interpretation in this volume and the particular focus on rhetorolects as frames presuppose this approach to language, even though the sociorhetorical research was not a result of participation in this research movement. In frame semantics, a word represents "a category of experience," and researchers attempt to uncover "reasons a speech community has for creating the category represented by the word and including that reason in the description of the meaning of the word."[95]

In frame semantics, a companion term to frame is "prototype." According to Petruck, a prototype is "a fairly large slice of the surrounding culture against which the meaning of a word is defined and understood."[96] As she explains, the concept of prototype "provides a useful approach to the boundary problem for linguistic categories." Humans think prototypically, and our argument is that first century Christian discourse energetically reconfigured at least six prototypical networks of reasoning and acting in the Mediterranean world. Christians did this by reconfiguring people's perspective on what was "typical" and what was "atypical" in at least six conceptual domains. Empirical studies have shown that people's reasoning and acting are highly influenced by what they consider to be typical and atypical phenomena. In many areas of the world, for example, people consider robins and sparrows to be "typical" of the category bird, but ostriches and penguins to be "atypical." Early Christians reconfigured, this volume argues, what large numbers of Mediterranean people considered to be "typical" wisdom, prophetic, apocalyptic, precreation, priestly, and miracle conceptuality. This means that by the year 100 CE, Christians had developed a com-

[93] Miriam R.L. Petruck, "Frame Semantics," in *Handbook of Pragmatics: Manual* (ed. J. Verschueren, J-O. Östman, J. Bloomaert, and C. Bulcaen; Philadelphia/Amsterdam: J. Benjamins, 1997) 1; online: http://framenet.icsi.berkeley.edu/papers/miriamp.FS2.pdf.

[94] Ibid., 2.

[95] Ibid.

[96] Petruck, "Frame Semantics," 2.

plex system of things that were "typical" in the world, which many other people would, on first blush, consider "atypical." How did early Christians do this? This is the burden of this volume on wisdom, prophetic, and apocalyptic discourse, and the subsequent volume on precreation, priestly, miracle, and creedal discourse.

A beginning place for our procedure can be Miriam R.L. Petruck's listing of three practical matters of frame semantics as she saw them in 1997: "determining the contents of a frame, determining the boundaries of any particular frame; and determining how frames interact."[97] These are the challenges that lie before an assertion that six major rhetorolects, namely, six socio-cultural-ideological-religious frames, contributed substantively to the creativity in first century Christian discourse. The following chapters begin the process of identifying, analyzing, and interpreting the contents of six rhetorolects in first century Christian literature in which semantic frames functioning through prototyping modes of conceptuality established certain networks of thinking within certain frames, introduced boundaries among multiple frames of thinking through repetitive focus on certain prototypical phemonena, and produced dynamic interaction among these prototypically based frames with the aid of concepts that bridged from one frame to another and aspects of conceptual domains that easily blended with one another.

It will help us to raise some questions for a moment about how interpreters at various levels from the most unassuming believer to the most highly oriented scholar may think about certain aspects of the Hebrew Bible. Why is it that the Joseph story in Gen 38–50 is regularly not considered to be wisdom discourse? Gerhard von Rad, among others, has observed that "wisdom from God" is a central feature of the discourse in the Joseph story.[98] Nevertheless, "Proverbs, Qoheleth, and Job in the Hebrew Bible, and the apocryphal or deuterocanonical books of Ben Sira (Ecclesiasticus) and the Wisdom of Solomon"[99] are considered to be "typical" wisdom literature. The Joseph story, then, is "atypical" wisdom literature, and so, it appears, are "Psalms of wisdom."[100] Why also, one might ask, are the Elijah and Elisha stories not regularly considered to be "typical" prophetic literature? Interpretation of the Hebrew Bible regularly refers to narrative accounts of prophets

[97] Ibid., 6.

[98] Gerhard von Rad, "The Joseph Narrative and Ancient Wisdom," in idem, *The Problem of the Hexateuch and Other Essays* (trans. E. Dicken; Edinburgh and New York: McGraw Hill, 1966) 292-300.

[99] John J. Collins, *Jewish Wisdom in the Hellenistic Age* (OTL; Louisville, KY: Westminster John Knox Press, 1997) 1.

[100] James Limburg, "Book of Psalms," *ABD* 5:533-34 lists Pss 37, 49, 73, 112, 127, 128, 133 as Wisdom psalms and Pss 1, 19, and 119 as Torah Psalms.

as the "Former Prophets" (Joshua, Judges, 1–2 Samuel, 1–2 Kings), while the Latter Prophets, which are writings dominated by prophetic oracles, are often called the "classical" or "canonical" prophets.[101] In a context of the discovery of the Dead Sea Scrolls, which produced vigorous analysis, retranslation, and discussion of apocalyptic literature, Paul D. Hanson investigated "proto-apocalyptic" oracles in Isaiah 55–66, "early apocalyptic" oracles in Zechariah 9–10 and Isaiah 24–27, and "full-blown apocalyptic" in Zechariah 11–14.[102] His analysis, he asserted, demonstrates that "the sources of apocalyptic eschatology lie solidly within the prophetic tradition of Israel,"[103] in contrast to an approach like von Rad's, which asserts the emergence of apocalyptic out of wisdom tradition. Thus, what is wisdom tradition, prophetic tradition, and apocalyptic tradition? Should this be a question focused on form, genre, history, literature, theology, sociological worldview, or still something else?

After the work of Paul Hanson and others on apocalyptic in prophetic writings, John J. Collins led an SBL Apocalypse Group studying apocalyptic as a genre among other genres (parable, pronouncement story, miracle story, letter, and apocalypse) in the context of the emergence of Christianity during the first century CE.[104] In his later book, Collins gives a definition of "apocalypse" and lists a series of writings in which "[t]his definition can be shown to apply to various sections": *1 Enoch*, Daniel, *4 Ezra*, *2 Baruch*, *Apocalypse of Abraham*, *3 Baruch*, *2 Enoch*, *Testament of Levi* 2-5, the fragmentary *Apocalypse of Zephaniah*, and with some qualification *Jubilees*, the *Testament of Abraham* (both of which also have strong affinities with other genres), a fairly wide body of Christian and Gnostic literature and to some Persian and Greco-Roman material.[105] Are the apocalyptic semantic frames in these writings present in a "prototypical" manner in the apocalyptic discourse of first century Christian literature? The answer presented in this volume is that first century Christian discourse reconfigured what was "prototypical" in apocalyptic literature in significant ways. Placing Jesus Christ, whom God had resurrected from the dead, in a central place in its apocalyptic discourse, it created an intensely focused "apocalyptic frame" with a constellation of networks that highlighted the authority of the Lord Jesus Christ over God's kingdom until Christ ruled entirely

[101] John J. Schmitt, "Preexilic Hebrew Prophecy," *ABD* V:483.

[102] Paul D. Hanson, *The Dawn of Apocalyptic: The Historical and Sociological Roots of Jewish Apocalyptic Eschatology* (Philadelphia: Fortress Press, 1975) 26-28.

[103] Ibid., 29.

[104] John J. Collins (ed.), *Apocalypse: The Morphology of a Genre* (Semeia 14; Missoula: MT: Scholars Press, 1979).

[105] John J. Collins, *The Apocalyptic Imagination: An Introduction to Jewish Apocalyptic Literature* (2nd ed.; Grand Rapids, MI/Cambridge, UK: Eerdmans, 1998, c1984) 5.

over it, and then he would hand "his" (Christ's) kingdom over to God. But this is only part of the reconfiguration. Into this apocalyptic frame, the apostle Paul embedded a story-line from Abraham and a story-line from Adam. When Christian discourse embedded these two additional story-lines into the overall story-line focused on the heavenly Lord Jesus Christ, a significantly new "environment of prototypical apocalyptic writings" emerged in the Mediterranean world (including an *Apocalypse of Paul*). In this context, Ezek 1 and Dan 7–12 became "typical" apocalyptic, along with highly selective portions of *1 Enoch* and *4 Ezra*. In addition, the story of Sodom and Gomorrah and the Ten Plagues in Egypt became "typical" apocalyptic events for first century Christians, but less clearly the story of Noah and the Flood. What conceptual frames were at work, bringing about the "typical" reasoning of early Christians. Many portions of the apocalyptic writings listed by Collins above became "atypical" apocalyptic thinking for first century Christians. The issue in this volume is the manner in which first century Christian discourse established their new environments of frame and prototype in the context of the many frames and prototypes operative in their Mediterranean context.

Another issue for early Christians was Torah Law. Why is it that Christians regularly consider the Decalogue and the Book of the Covenant in Exodus and Deuteronomy to be authoritative Jewish Law, and not the laws governing priestly activities and the building of the tabernacle and temple in Exodus and Leviticus? The argument in this volume will be that first century Christians focused on wisdom from God in such a manner that Torah Law became "Torah Wisdom" rather than Torah Halakah. What were the processes at work in the creation of a "wisdom" frame for Torah Law, rather than a fully developed "halakah" frame for it? The answer lies in the ways in which humans correlate frames and prototypes as they think "in the context of their bodies" in particular places and spaces in the Mediterranean world. Society, culture, ideology, religion, and politics, as well as many other endeavors, are constructed and nurtured through an interaction between frames and prototypes as people experience the places and spaces in which they live. The focus, then, is on "embodied conceptualization and action," and this leads us to the recent work by cognitive scientists on conceptual metaphor and conceptual blending (integration) theory.

A Rhetorolect as an Idealized Cognitive Model (ICM)

In the process of moving beyond form and genre into frame and prototype analysis and interpretation, it gradually has become evident that the sociorhetorical concept of a "rhetorolect" is, from the perspective of cognitive science, some kind of Idealized Cognitive Model (ICM).[106] There will not be a frame semantics analysis in this volume to demonstrate the case, but the dimensions of rhetorolects that have appeared through sociorhetorical analysis suggest a highly close relationship to what the cognitive scientists call "ICMs." An ICM, according to George Lakoff, is "a complex structured whole, a gestalt, which uses four kinds of structuring principles":

a. propositional structure, as in Fillmore's frames;
b. image-schematic structure, as in Langacker's cognitive grammar;
c. metaphoric mappings, as described in Lakoff and Johnson;
d. metonymic mappings, as described by Lakoff and Johnson.[107]

It is noticeable, first of all, that Lakoff starts with the propositional structure of an ICM. The propositional structure of an ICM concerns the argumentative-enthymematic dimension of topoi in rhetorolects.[108] A key internal aspect of each rhetorolect is its network of arguments, which sociorhetorical analysis has exhibited in the form of rhetorical syllogisms called enthymemes since the concept was introduced in 1996. Wilhelm Wuellner had identified two dimensions in a topos: (1) argumentative-enthymematic; and (2) descriptive-narrative.[109] For this reason, sociorhetorical interpretation will use the terms argumentative-enthymematic structuring and image-descriptive structuring for Lakoff's propositional structure and image-schematic structure. Kennedy pursued the enthymematic nature of NT discourse quite extensively in his study of *The New Testament through Rhetorical Criticism*.[110] The initial essay on the "dialectical nature" of early Christian discourse exhibited examples of reasoning and argumentation in rhetorolects which were named as wisdom, miracle, apocalyptic, opposition, death-resurrection,

[106] George Lakoff, *Women, Fire, and Dangerous Things: What Categories Reveal about the Mind* (Chicago/London: University of Chicago Press, 1987) 68-76.

[107] Ibid., 68.

[108] For propositional assertions in NT literature, see Anthony C. Thiselton, *The Two Horizons: New Testament Hermeneutics and Philosophical Description* (Grand Rapids, MI: Eerdmans, 1980) 96-97, 166-68, 195-96, 354-55, 359-70, 433-37, 443-45; idem, *New Horizons in Hermeneutics: The Theory and Practice of Transforming Biblical Reading* (Grand Rapids, MI: Zondervan, 1992) 323-25 *et passim*.

[109] Wilhelm H. Wuellner, "Toposforschung und Torahinterpretation bei Paulus und Jesus," *NTS* 24 (1978) 467.

[110] Kennedy, *New Testament Interpretation through Rhetorical Criticism*, 7, 16-17, 49-61, 103-108, 118-42 *et passim*.

and cosmic.[111] Wisdom discourse exhibited a sequence of thesis, rationale, and summary containing arguments from analogies to plants and animals and arguments from example.[112] Miracle discourse, in contrast, placed stories at the center of its argumentation and developed theses, rationales, and summaries inductively from the stories. The theses, rationales, and summaries were focused on all things being possible for God, on the importance of faith in God, and on prayer.[113] Apocalyptic discourse, in turn, features dramatic images of God and his agents acting in decisive ways to preserve purity and righteousness and to destroy evil. The theses, rationales, and conclusions either picture or assert the action of God and his agents to achieve these ends.[114] Opposition (later called prophetic) discourse features attacks on specific behaviors and beliefs as a context for asserting the nature of the will of God for humans, which includes a necessity that people change their actions so they may receive the blessings God wills to give to them.[115] Death-resurrection (later called priestly) discourse, in addition, presents an argument that regularly presupposes a thesis that Christ died for people's sins, a confirmation of the thesis on the basis of the burial, resurrection, and post-resurrection appearance of Jesus, and proof from ancient testimony in the scriptures.[116] Cosmic (later called precreation) discourse is thoroughly epideictic in nature, exhibiting the authority of Jesus by placing him in a position of power alongside God in the cosmic order prior to the creation of the world and using Jesus as the agent for the creation of the world.[117]

After essays appeared on enthymemes in Luke and the Gospel of Thomas,[118] a programmatic essay for the 2000 Rhetoric Conference in Lund on argumentative textures in first century Christian discourse exhibited noticeably different "enthymematic" modes of argumentation in the six major rhetorolects in NT discourse. In the context of revised nomenclature for the rhetorolects as wisdom, miracle, apocalyptic, prophetic, suffering-death, and pre-creation,[119] enthymematic dimensions of the alternative conceptual domains in each rhetorolect were exhibited

[111] Thiselton, *The Two Horizons*, 357-61.

[112] Robbins, "The Dialectical Nature of Early Christian Discourse," 357-58.

[113] Ibid., 358-59.

[114] Ibid., 359-60.

[115] Ibid., 360.

[116] Ibid., 360.

[117] Ibid., 360-61.

[118] Vernon K. Robbins, "Enthymemic Texture in the Gospel of Thomas" (*1998 Society of Biblical Literature Seminar Papers*; Atlanta: Scholars Press, 1998) 343-66; idem, "From Enthymeme to Theology in Luke 11:1-13," in *Literary Studies in Luke-Acts: A Collection of Essays in Honor of Joseph B. Tyson* (ed. R.P. Thompson and T.E. Phillips; Macon, GA: Mercer University Press, 1998) 191-214.

[119] Robbins, "Argumentative Textures in Socio-Rhetorical Interpretation."

with "Rule, Case, Result," rather than "Thesis, Rationale, and Conclusion or Summary." The outcome of the rule, case, result analysis was an awareness that the rhetorolects not only use "classic" rhetorical assertions of thesis, rationale, contrary or opposite, analogy, example, citation of ancient authority, and exhortative conclusion in highly different ways, but also that some of the rhetorolects formulate "general theses" on the basis of narrative assertions rather than general principles (e.g., prophetic, suffering-death, precreation).[120] This result began to call attention to the second structuring principle Lakoff identifies in an ICM.

Lakoff identifies the second structuring principle in an ICM as "image-schematic structure, as in Langacker's cognitive grammar."[121] This concerns the second aspect of an enthymeme, which Wuellner identified as its "descriptive-narrative" dimension.[122] This aspect of sociorhetorical analysis and interpretation has gradually emerged in an awareness that the "rhetography" of Mediterranean discourse was leading the way in a determination of the content, boundaries, and interaction of early Christian rhetorolects.[123] The strategies Ronald Langacker uses to analyze image-schematic structure in discourse are significantly different, of course, from the strategies used in sociorhetorical analysis and interpretation. A major focus of his work, however, has been on the relation of image schemas in the mind to reasoning. Langacker (1986) discovered that "[m]any, if not most, of the details of syntactic constructions are consequences of the meanings of the constructions."[124] In addition, he discovered that it is still possible, "[w]ithin a theory that contains basic-level concepts and image schemas" … "to have rules of semantic composition that form more complex concepts from less complex ones."[125] The question for Lakoff, then, actually raised by Rudolf Arnheim in *Visual Thinking*,[126] is: "Do we reason imagistically?"[127] Lakoff proposes that "on the image-schema view, the answer could be yes."[128] This is a very important issue for analysis and

[120] Ibid., 44-65.

[121] George Lakoff, *Women, Fire, and Dangerous Things: What Categories Reveal about the Mind* (Chicago/London: University of Chicago Press, 1987) 68; Ronald Langacker, *Foundations of Cognitive Grammar* (vol. 1; Stanford: Stanford University Press, 1986).

[122] Wuellner, "*Toposforschung*," 467.

[123] Robbins, "Rhetography"; cf. Thiselton, *The Two Horizons*, 362-70.

[124] Lakoff, *Women, Fire, and Dangerous Things*, 291.

[125] Ibid., 280.

[126] Rudolf Arnheim, *Visual Thinking* (Berkeley: University of California Press, 1974).

[127] Lakoff, *Women, Fire, and Dangerous Things*, 456.

[128] Ibid.; with compliments of Roy Jeal, see Roger B. Nelsen, *Proofs without Words: Exercises in Visual Thinking* (Washington, DC: The Mathematical Association of America, 1993); idem, Proofs Without Words II: More Exercises in Visual Thinking (Washington, DC: The Mathematical Association of America, 2000); for an online example of visual thinking see: http://www.math.umd.edu/~gfleming/JIM/PtPww/PtPwwFrame.html. Also see Christian Leborg, *Visual Grammar* (New York: Princeton Architectural Press, 2006).

interpretation of first century Christian discourse, which contains extensive imagistic and pictorial narration. If image-schemas as well as basic-level concepts are operative in reasoning, then analysis and interpretation of the interaction of rhetology and rhetography, to use the terms of sociorhetorical interpreters, is important for understanding the new conceptual views and understandings that came into the Mediterranean world through NT discourse.

The third structural principle in an ICM as Lakoff presents it is: "metaphoric mappings, as described in Lakoff and Johnson."[129] During 2002, sociorhetorical interpreters began to work seriously with critical spatiality theory, with special focus on "2nd space" conceptualization, where metaphorical reasoning blends "1st space" experiential knowledge of places and spaces in the Mediterranean world with the cosmos, where it is presupposed that God dwells. This led, in turn to the inclusion of "conceptual blending (integration) theory" to analyze and interpret the nature of early Christian discourse. Using the foundational work of Gilles Fauconnier and Mark Turner in *The Way We Think: Conceptual Blending and the Mind's Hidden Complexities,*[130] the merger of conceptual blending theory with critical spatiality theory began to clarify the relation of the rhetorolects to one another on the basis of social, cultural, ideological and religious places and spaces in early Christian rhetorolects.[131] According to Fauconnier and Turner: "Conceptual integration always involves a blended space and at least two inputs and a generic space."[132] To these insights, Seana Coulson in particular has added the insight that organizing, cultural frames are continually operative, either as background or foreground, in conceptual blending.[133] Sociorhetorical analysis and interpretation of rhetorolects proceeds, therefore, on the presupposition that places and spaces dynamically inform conceptual blending through the presence of cultural frames, which Lakoff calls ICMs and which this book calls rhetorolects. Rhetorolects organize pictures of people and locations together in ways that nurture special cultural memories. Certain words and phrases evoke these memories in a manner that frames the reasoning about

[129] Ibid., 68.

[130] G. Fauconnier and M. Turner, *The Way We Think: Conceptual Blending and the Mind's Hidden Complexities* (New York: Basic Books, 2002). The use of this book for sociorhetorical commentary is the result of an e-mail by L.G. Bloomquist on Dec. 4, 2002, which called attention to the relation of conceptual blending theory to early Christian blending of rhetorolects, which was a topic of discussion at the Rhetoric of Religious Antiquity meetings prior to the AAR/SBL sessions at Toronto in November, 2002.

[131] See Robert von Thaden, "Fleeing *Porneia*: 1 Corinthians 6:12–7:7 and the Reconfiguration of Traditions," Ph.D. dissertation, Emory University, 2007.

[132] Fauconnier and Turner, *The Way We Think,* xv, 279.

[133] Seana Coulson, *Semantic Leaps: Frame-Shifting and Conceptual Blending in Meaning Construction* (Cambridge: Cambridge University Press, 2001).

topics the discourse introduces to the hearer. As the discourse creates pictures in the mind of special social, cultural, religious, and ideological places, it creates movements in the mind of association, dissociation, admiration, dislike, love, anger, courage, fear, etc. Figure 1 presents an abstract table that displays the presence of cultural frames (rhetorolects or ICMs), generic spaces (highly multiple cognitive activities), experience spaces (firstspace/input 1); conceptualized spaces (secondspace/input 2); and spaces of blending (thirdspace) that are dynamically related to one another in early Christian rhetorolects.

Figure 1: Conceptual Blending of Frames and Spaces in Rhetorolects

Cultural Frames (Rhetorolects or ICMs)	Conventionally organized mental networks in Mediterranean culture and tradition
Generic Spaces	Conceptual mental spaces
Experienced Spaces (Firstspace)	Experiences of the body in social places
Conceptualized Spaces (Secondspace)	Sensory-aesthetic and cognitive experiences creating cultural, religious, and ideological places
Spaces of Blending (Thirdspace)	Debate, reconciliation, elaboration, and avoidance in relation to cultural, religious, and ideological places

People's words and phrases cause people to recruit conventional discourse frames (rhetorolects or ICMs) that invite pictures of spaces and actions that exist in cultural memory. Sensory-aesthetic experiences of the body in various social places in the world – like household, village, city, synagogue, kingdom, temple, and empire – are the "firstspace" contexts in which people develop and perpetuate special pictures and memories in their minds. People activate cognitive and conceptual abilities to interpret these social places and actions as "secondspace" cultural, religious, and ideological places. In addition, people use processes of part-whole, similar-dissimilar, opposite, etc. to relate pictures, actions, and reasonings (in "generic" spaces) to one another. In the context of these activities, people negotiate their daily lives in ongoing contexts of sensory-aesthetic experiences which are "thirdspace" "spaces of blending." Sociorhetorical interpreters are accepting the challenge of analyzing and interpreting six rhetorolects that invite people to recruit organizing, cultural frames that blend places and spaces in special networks of reasoning and argumentation in particular ways: wisdom, precreation, prophetic, miracle, priestly, and apocalyptic. Figure 2 opposite presents an initial display of important places and spaces in the six primary first century Christian rhetorolects.

Figure 2: Blended Spaces and Locations in Early Christian Rhetorolects

Cultural Frames (Rhetorolects)	Wisdom	Prophetic	Apocalyptic	Precreation	Miracle	Priestly
Social, Cultural, & Physical Realia (1st Space)	Household, Vegetation, Living Beings	Political Kingdom, prophet's body	Political Empire, Imperial Temple, Imperial Army	Political Empire & Emperor's Household	Human Body & Unexpected Phenomena & Transformations in the natural world	Altar, Temple & Temple City
Visualization, Conceptualization, & Imagination of God's World (2nd Space)	God as Father-Creator (Progenitor), Wisdom (light) as Mediator, People as God's children, Jesus as God's Son	God as King, God on kingly throne in heavenly court, Selected humans as prophets, Selected people as God's kingdom, Jesus as Prophet-Messiah selected and sent by God	God as Almighty (*Pantokratōr*), Jesus as King of King and Lord of Lords, multiple heavenly assistants to God	God as Eternal Emperor-Father, Jesus as God's Eternal Son	God as Transforming Power, Selected humans as agents of God's transforming power, People as Healed and transformed by God, Jesus as Healer & Miracle-Worker	God as Holy and Pure, God on priestly throne in heavenly temple, Selected humans as priests, People as God's holy & pure priestly community (assembly, city, kingdom), Jesus as Priest-Messiah
Spaces of Mental Conception (Generic Spaces)	Cause-effect, change, time, identity, intentionality, representation, part-whole Formal argumentative topics: opposites, grammatical forms of the same word, correlatives, more and less, time, turning back upon the opponent, definition, varied meanings, division, induction, previous judgment, parts, consequence, contrast, openly and secretly, analogy, same result, before and after, purpose as cause, for and against, implausible probabilities, contradictions, cause of false impression, cause and effect, better, doing contrary to what has been done, mistakes, meaning of a name.*					
Ongoing Bodily Effects and Enactments: Blending in Religious Life (3rd Space = Space of Blending)	Human body as Producer of Goodness & Righteousness	Human body as Distributor and Receiver of justice (food, bodily needs, honor)	Human body as Receiver of resurrection & eternal life in a "new" realm of well-being	Human body as Receiver of eternal life through friendship (belief & loyalty) with God's eternal Son	Human body as Healed and amazingly Transformed	Human body as Giver of sacrificial offerings and Receiver of beneficial exchange of holiness and purity between God and humans

* Aristotle, *Rhetoric* II.23.1-29 (1397a-1400b); G.A. Kennedy, *Aristotle, On Rhetoric: A Theory of Civic Discourse* (New York, Oxford: OUP, 1991) 190-204.

Early Christian wisdom rhetorolect blends human experiences of the household, one's intersubjective body, and the geophysical world (firstspace) with the cultural space of God's cosmos (secondspace). In the lived space of blending (thirdspace), God functions as heavenly Father over God's children in the world, whose bodies are to produce goodness and righteousness through the medium of God's wisdom, which is understood as God's light in the world. In this context, wisdom rhetorolect emphasizes "fruitfulness" (productivity and reproductivity). The goal of wisdom rhetorolect is to create people who produce good, righteous action, thought, will, and speech with the aid of God's wisdom.

Early Christian prophetic rhetorolect blends human experiences of a kingdom (a territory of land with specific boundaries) and the speech and action of a prophet's body (firstspace), and the concept of a "kingdom of God" either on the earth or somewhere else in God's cosmos (secondspace). The reasoning in the rhetorolect presupposes that the prophet has received a divine message about God's will. The prophet speaks and acts on the basis of this message in a context of significant resistance, and often explicit rejection and persecution. In the space of blending, God functions as heavenly King over his righteous kingdom on earth. The nature of prophetic rhetorolect is to confront religious and political leaders who act on the basis of human greed, pride, and power rather than God's justice, righteousness, and mercy for all people in God's kingdom on the earth. The goal of prophetic rhetorolect is to create a governed realm on earth where God's righteousness is enacted among all of God's people in the realm with the aid of God's specially transmitted word in the form of prophetic action and speech (thirdspace).

Early Christian apocalyptic rhetorolect blends human experiences of the emperor and his imperial army (firstspace) with God's heavenly temple city filled with myriads of pure and holy heavenly beings (secondspace). In the space of blending, God functions as a heavenly emperor who gives commands to emissaries to destroy all the evil in the universe and to create a cosmic environment where holy bodies experience perfect well-being in the presence of God. Apocalyptic rhetorolect, then, features destruction of evil and construction of a cosmic environment of perfect well-being. The goal of this blending is to call people into action and thought guided by perfect holiness. The presupposition of the rhetorolect is that only perfect holiness and righteousness can bring a person into the presence of God, who destroys all evil and gathers all holiness together in God's presence. Apocalyptic redemption, therefore, means the presence of all of God's holy beings in a realm where God's holiness and righteousness are completely and eternally present.

Early Christian precreation rhetorolect blends human experiences of the emperor (like the Roman emperor) and his household (firstspace) with the cosmos (secondspace), with the presupposition that God has an eternal status as a loving heavenly emperor with a household populated by loving people. The result of this blending is the presence of the loving Emperor Father God in God's heavenly household before all time and continually throughout God's "non-time." God's Son existed with God during "non-time" before time began with the creation of the world. This "eternal" Son does what His Father asks him to do, and heirs and friends of the eternal emperor and his eternal son receive eternal benefits from their relation to this eternal household. In the space of blending (thirdspace), God functions as heavenly Emperor Father who possesses eternal blessings He will give people as a result of his love for the world and the people in it. People may enter into this love by believing, honoring, and worshipping not only God but also his eternal Son and members and friends whom God sends out with a message of eternal blessings. Precreation rhetorolect, then, features love that is the source of all things in the world and the means by which people may enter into God's eternal love. In this rhetorolect, God's light is love that provides the possibility for entering into eternal love, rather than being limited to light that is the basis for the production and reproduction of goodness and righteousness. The goal of the blending in precreation rhetorolect is to guide people towards community that is formed through God's love, which reflects the eternal intimacy present in God's precreation household.

Early Christian miracle rhetorolect has a primary focus on human bodies afflicted with paralysis, malfunction, or disease. In this context, a malfunctioning body becomes a "site" of "social geography." Miracle rhetorolect features a bodily agent of God's power who renews and restores life, producing forms of "new creation" that oppose powers of affliction, disruption, and death. The "location" of importance for early Christian miracle rhetorolect, therefore, is a "space of relation" between an afflicted body and a bodily agent of God's power (firstspace). In this rhetorolect, there is no focus on any particular social, cultural, political, or religious "places" on earth. A bodily agent of God's power, wherever it may be, is a "location" where God can function as a miraculous renewer of life (secondspace). A major goal of miracle rhetorolect is to effect extraordinary renewal within people that moves them toward speech and action that produces communities that care for the well-being of one another (thirdspace).

Early Christian priestly rhetorolect blends human experiences in a temple or other place of worship (firstspace) with a concept of temple city and God's cosmos (secondspace). Reasoning in priestly rhetorolect presupposes that ritual actions benefit God in a manner that activates divine benefits for humans on earth. In the space of blending (thirdspace), people make sacrifices by giving up things that give them well being in the form of giving them to God. Things like food, possessions and money but also things like comfort and honor may be given up to God. Some of these things may be given to God by giving them to other people on earth, or by allowing other people to take things like honor or fame away without protest. The greatest sacrifice people can offer to God, of course, is their entire life. Usually, in contrast, a person gives up only certain highly valued things in life. Much, though not all, early Christian priestly rhetorolect somehow relates to Jesus' death on the cross. Priestly rhetorolect features beneficial exchange between God and humans in a context of human sacrificial action. The goal of the conceptual blending is to create people who are willing to give up things they highly value in exchange for special divine benefits that come to them, because these sacrifices are perceived to benefit God as well as humans. In other words, sacrificial actions by humans create an environment in which God acts redemptively among humans in the world.

In the context of the use of conceptual blending (integration) theory, which presupposes that basic level, constitutive aspects of cognition are metaphorical, metonymy is the fourth "structural principle" in an ICM.[134] A major metonymic dimension of each of the rhetorolects is the nomenclature itself that is used to refer to each rhetorolect. Since the name for each of the rhetorolects is metonymic, it is natural that half of the names have changed since 1996 and that routinely one colleague or another recommends different nomenclature for one or more of the rhetorolects. A major reason for the instability of the names for the rhetorolects is that the names themselves are metonymic: the names refer to the conceptual domain of a rhetorolect by referring to some sector of the domain rather than to the entire domain. Since a rhetorolect has at least four major aspects when it is perceived to be some kind of ICM, it is virtually impossible to find terminology that refers to the entire conceptual domain of any rhetorolect. Rather, a significant sector will be chosen to refer to the entire domain. It is natural, then, that one scholar's choice will emphasize one sector of the domain when another scholar would prefer emphasis on another sector of it.

[134] Lakoff, *Women*, 68; see his discussion of metonymy, p. 77: "It is extremely common for people to take one well-understood or easy-to-perceive aspect of something and use it to stand either for the thing as a whole or for some other aspect or part of it."

The metonymic nature of the terminology for the rhetorolects has the potential to lead us closer to some of the metonymic dimensions internal to the rhetorolects themselves. Therefore we will look at some of the issues involved in the choice of the terminology for some of them. The initial name for precreation rhetorolect was "cosmic."[135] Subsequently, some colleagues continue to recommend the name "cosmological," while others recommend "protological," and still others recommend "pre-existent" for this rhetorolect. The problem with three of these terms, from the perspective of sociorhetorical interpretation, is that they all emphasize the rhetology of this rhetorolect in a context where the interpretive task is to identify and interpret the interaction between the rhetology and rhetography in it. Both cosmological and protological covertly show their emphasis on rhetology by the presence of "-logical" at the end of the word. In turn, the word pre-existent is a noticeably philosophical word, inviting the hearer or reader to recruit meanings in the arena of philosophical thought. It would not be satisfactory, as an alternative, to create new names such as cosmographical or protographical, since this would unduly imply a prominence of rhetography in the rhetorolect, when the rhetorolect itself does not not exhibit that prominence. The decision has been to use the term "precreation," as a way to refer to a primordial realm prior to the creation of the universe. A major weakness in the use of this term is that the "pre-" implicitly introduces temporality, "a time before," when a constitutive part of the rhetorolect is "non-time" conceptuality. This weakness has proven quite easy to overcome, however, with one or two sentences of explanation. Therefore, after a short period of uncertainty about the best nomenclature to use, "precreation" has become the term of choice for the rhetorolect that was originally referred to as cosmic.

Significant debate also has emerged over the choice of "apocalyptic" for the name of a rhetorolect. A major criticism has been its focus on the "revelational" aspect of this rhetorolect, which in some people's view makes it overlap with prophetic discourse so profoundly as to make them indistinguishable. The major alternative I have heard is to call this rhetorolect "eschatological." If an "eschat-" term were to be chosen for this mode of discourse, it would be preferable, in my view, to call it "eschatographical," because of its vividly picturesque nature. The term eschatological would again emphasize the rhetology of the discourse, when one of the most noticeable features of the discourse is its rhetography. Another problem with the term eschatological is that, in my view, early Christians made all six of the rhetorolects investigated in these two volumes eschatological by 100 CE. In other words, one of the characteristics of first century Christian discourse is the manner in

[135] Robbins, "The Dialectical Nature of Early Christian Discourse," 360-61.

which not only apocalyptic and prophetic discourse functioned as eschatological modes, but also wisdom, precreation, priestly, and miracle discourse. The word eschatological is not, therefore, a distinctive enough term to identify special features of the conceptual domain referred to as apocalyptic rhetorolect in this volume. A reason to prefer the term apocalyptic is the presence of the word "*apokalypsis*" at the beginning of the Revelation to John (1:1). While this is a reason some scholars would not choose it, since the use is so "Christian," this is precisely a reason in its favor in this volume on the invention of Christian discourse. Once the Revelation to John is a writing present in early Christian circles so that there may be an argument for or against using it as an "authoritative" writing, the "Christian" conceptual domain of "apocalyptic" is configured in a manner that gives prominence to the "revelational" aspect of apocalyptic discourse. More will be said about this in chapters eight and nine in this volume.

A somewhat different challenge emerged with the rhetorolects at first called "opposition" and "death-resurrection" in 1996.[136] In both instances, the choice of nomenclature focused on a sector of the conceptual domain that was too limited. Opposition discourse, it turned out, was confrontational "prophetic" discourse, and death-resurrection discourse was "priestly" discourse. In these instances, the nomenclature referred to a frame that was too small to invite the hearer or reader to recruit the entire rhetorolect, which has the scope of an ICM. The initial nomenclature invited people to recruit a frame like "courageous speech against leaders" or "vindication through death," rather than a cultural frame with interconnected networks of meaning that explained the authoritative nature of the speech for the former and the beneficial exchange between the divine and human realm for the latter. Through a period of trial and error, responding to criticism, and programmatic analysis during an eleven-year period (1996-2007), the current nomenclature has emerged of wisdom, prophetic, apocalyptic, precreation, priestly, and miracle. One important factor among others has been the frequency of certain words and word groups (like wise/wisdom, prophet[ess]/prophecy/prophesy, reveal/revelation, etc.) in the writings in the New Testament. Another factor has been a conclusion that a major achievement of first century Christian discourse was to create a particular kind of "Jewish" discourse that used Greek words that rather easily had "some kind of meaning" in Mediterranean culture. An emphasis on "some kind of meaning" is the key, since often an important part of the process was significant struggle over "more precisely what" the words might mean and over "who possessed the best meanings" of the words. One of the ways first century Christians established a "Jewish"

[136] Ibid., 360.

identity for their discourse was through reference to "biblical" people like Adam, Abraham, Moses, David, etc. Another way was to communicate "biblical" story-lines. On the one hand, first century Christian discourse refers to some biblical story-lines in a manner that either supports or teaches what one might call "conventional understanding" of those story-lines. On the other hand, the discourse contains some "argumentative presentations" of particular biblical story-lines, like Paul's interpretation of Jesus' "genealogical" relation to Abraham as "Abraham's seed" (Gal 3:15-20) and Jesus' "eschatological" relation to Adam as "the second Adam" (1 Cor 15:20-28; Rom 5:12-21). The biblical nature of the rhetorolects, albeit "biblical" in ways that participate regularly in widespread Mediterranean modes of conceptuality, makes it preferable, in the final analysis, to choose conventional biblical or Jewish terminology for the first century rhetorolects, rather than terminology generated out of some other conceptual sphere. A major challenge for first century Christians was to communicate their "new" ideas in the context of traditional culture, in which anything new was suspect, meaningless, unimportant, or all three. The view in this volume is that early Christians used well-known concepts, traditions, and stories "with a Jewish cast" to communicate their patterns of belief, action, and worldview in the Mediterranean world. The particular ways in which they were able to do this are the topic of this volume.

Conclusion

Sociorhetorical interpretation began in the 1970s with an attempt to explain special characteristics of language in the accounts of voyaging on the sea in Acts and in Jesus' calling, gathering, teaching, and sending out of disciples in the Gospels. In both instances, the goal was to understand the language of New Testament literature in the context of Mediterranean literature, both religious and non-religious. Also, the goal was to understand the use of language in relation to social, cultural, ideological and religious environments and relationships in the Mediterranean world. During the 1980s, the rhetorical treatises entitled *Progymnasmata* (Preliminary Exercises) played a major role in the interpretation of abbreviation, expansion, addition, rebuttal, commendation and elaboration in biblical and Mediterranean literature before and during the time of the emergence of early Christianity. During the 1990s, sociorhetorical interpretation identified multiple textures of texts for the purpose of reading and re-reading them in ways that activated a wide range of literary, rhetorical, historical, social, cultural, ideological, and religious "webs of signification" in texts. This led to a display of strategies of interpretation for five textures of texts: inner texture, intertexture, social and cultural texture, ideological texture, and sacred texture. During the last half of the 1990s, sociorhetorical interpretation gradually moved toward analysis of different rhetorolects in early Christian discourse. Gradually, six early Christian rhetorolects have appeared: wisdom, prophetic, apocalyptic, precreation, priestly, and miracle. Having initially gravitated toward wisdom rhetorolect during the 1980s and early 1990s, sociorhetorical interpreters focused specifically on apocalyptic and miracle rhetorolect during the last half of the 1990s. Two books on rhetorical interpretation of apocalyptic rhetorolect appeared during the late 1990s, and each includes essays that explicitly display sociorhetorical strategies of interpretation.[137] A session on rhetorical analysis and interpretation of miracle rhetorolect was held at an SBL meeting in 2001, and a book containing essays from the session is forthcoming.[138] A Festschrift appeared in 2003 that reviewed many of the developments in sociorhetorical interpretation and featured contributions to the approach from various angles.[139] Sociorhetorical interpreters still face major challenges of analyzing and interpreting prophetic, precreation and priestly rhetorolect in early Christian writings. In addition, they face the challenge of writing programmatic commentary that displays the manifold ways in which early Christian writings blend early Christian rhetorolects together. Work is under way to display this kind of sociorhetorical commentary in this series, entitled Rhetoric of Religious Antiquity.[140]

The particular focus on rhetorolects in this volume emerges primarily out of a conviction that all words and all thinking work with boundaries. In other words, meanings must have some kind of form or structure at the same time that they are continually dynamic and changing. At a time when analysis and interpretation of different modes of discourse in early Christian literature was exhibiting an interweaving of conceptual textures and patterns, L. Gregory Bloomquist identified a relation between sociorhetorical interpretation and conceptual blending theory in Fauconnier and Turner, *The Way We Think*.[141] The special focus of this book on the place of vital relations in conceptuality[142] and

[137] Greg Carey and L. Gregory Bloomquist (eds.), *Vision and Persuasion: Rhetorical Dimensions of Apocalyptic Discourse* (St. Louis, MO: Chalice Press, 1999); Duane F. Watson (ed.), *The Intertexture of Apocalyptic Discourse in the New Testament* (Symposium Series 14, Atlanta: SBL, 2002).

[138] Duane F. Watson (ed.), *The Role of Miracle Discourse in the Argumentation of the New Testament* (Symposium Series, Atlanta: SBL/Leiden: Brill).

[139] David B. Gowler, L. Gregory Bloomquist, and Duane F. Watson (eds.), *Fabrics of Discourse: Essays in Honor of Vernon K. Robbins* (Harrisburg/London/New York: Trinity Press International, 2003).

[140] Online: http://www.deopublishing.com/rhetoricofreligiousantiquity.htm.

[141] Gilles Fauconnier and Mark Turner, *The Way We Think: Conceptual Blending and the Mind's Hidden Complexities* (New York: Basic Books, 2002).

[142] Ibid., 89-112.

on the special efforts of humans to achieve "human scale" in their thinking[143] has provided keen guidance for the analysis of early Christian rhetorolects. The focus on vital relations requires continual inquiry about the contextual nature of the reasoning in the rhetorolects, and the focus on human scale requires continual search for modes of understanding in antiquity that made the reasoning in the rhetorolects plausible, rather than simply radical, namely unrelated to experiential living in the world.

The inclusion of conceptual blending theory and critical spatiality theory in sociorhetorical interpretation allows an interpreter to construct a topology of spaces in early Christian rhetorolects and to interpret the rhetorical power of the blending of spaces in these rhetorolects. Since each of the rhetorolects presents social, cultural, religious, and ideological language, story-telling and argumentation that evoke specific pictures, emotions, cognitions and reasonings, each rhetorolect made vital contributions in distinctive ways to a new culture of discourse that was emerging during the first century. Since many of the social places present in early Christian discourse (like household, village, places of sacred ritual, city, etc.) continue to exist to the present day in some reconfigured form, early Christian discourse continually functions anew in places believers perceive to be similar in social, cultural and religious function. Some believers locate their thinking primarily in one rhetorolect at a time, blending aspects of other rhetorolects into this one rhetorolect for very specific purposes. Other believers locate their thinking in a particular blend of multiple rhetorolects, inviting selective aspects of other rhetorolects in implicit, subtle, and nuanced ways. The variations produce a dynamic conceptual, cognitive, and verbal system of Christian discourse that is highly adaptive to multiple contexts and cultures. Figure 3 below exhibits the dominant social, cultural and ideological rhetoric internal to each rhetorolect.

Dynamic blending of the six early Christian rhetorolects created a richly variegated culture of early Christian discourse by the end of the first century. Believers blended each rhetorolect dynamically with the other rhetorolects either by blending multiple rhetorolects into one dominant rhetorolect or by blending particular rhetorolects together in a particularly forceful manner. The dynamics of these blendings throughout the verbal culture of early Christianity produced a continually increasing combination of cognitions, reasonings, picturings, and argumentations. This interactive process continued in Christian discourse throughout the centuries, and it continues in our present day.

[143] Ibid., 322-24, 324-48, 376-80.

Figure 3: Rhetoric Internal to Each Rhetorolect

Wisdom	Apocalyptic	Precreation	Prophetic	Miracle	Priestly
Speech of God, Christ, and believers produces fruitfulness	Christ's initial coming produced a new beginning and Christ's return will produce a new world	God's and Christ's primordial existence produces eternal life in believers	God calls people, including Christ, to call and exhort people to be a righteous kingdom	God's power working in and/or through Christ and believers produces bodily transformation	Sacrifice by Christ and believers produces glorification of God and holy benefit for believers

In relation to the issues discussed above, the conclusions of George Lakoff about frames, prototypes, propositional and image-schematic structure, metaphoric mappings, and metonymic mappings are substantive for undergirding the sociorhetorical analysis and interpretation in this volume. He has made the concept of frame especially well known both in single-authored books[144] and co-authored books.[145] His work, along with the work of Mark Johnson, Mark Turner, and Gilles Fauconnier, have caused conceptual metaphor theory and conceptual blending (integration) theory to influence many areas of study, including the study of religion. Instead of a focus on "form and content," which has been central for most modern approaches to biblical interpretation, conceptual metaphor and blending theory focuses on the highly complex conceptual relationships between source domains and target domains at the foundations of language. The approach not only builds on empirical evidence from studies of the brain that our ordinary conceptual system is fundamentally metaphorical in nature, but it also proceeds on empirical evidence that this metaphorical system is grounded in everyday experiences of life and action.[146] This means that another emphasis is the "embodiment" of all human conceptuality.[147] All

[144] George Lakoff, *Women, Fire, and Dangerous Things: What Categories Reveal about the Mind* (Chicago: University of Chicago Press, 1987); idem, *Moral Politics* (Chicago: University of Chicago Press, 1996); idem, *Don't Think of an Elephant: Know Your Values and Frame the Debate* (White River Junction, VT: Chelsea Green Publishing, 2004).

[145] George Lakoff and Mark Johnson, *Metaphors We Live By* (Chicago/London: University of Chicago Press, c1980, 2003); idem and Mark Turner, *More than Cool Reason: A Field Guide to Poetic Metaphor* (Chicago: University of Chicago Press, 1989); idem and Mark Johnson, *Philosophy in the Flesh* (New York: Basic Books, 1999); idem and R. Núñez, *Where Mathematics Comes from: How the Embodied Mind brings Mathematics into Being* (New York: Basic Books, 2000).

[146] Lakoff and Johnson, *Metaphors We Live By*, 3.

[147] Mark Johnson, *The Body in the Mind: The Bodily Basis of Meaning, Imagination, and Reason* (Chicago/London: University of Chicago Press, 1987); George Lakoff and Mark Johnson, *Philosophy in the Flesh: The Embodied Mind and Its Challenge to Modern Thought* (New York: Basic Books, 1999).

human thinking is related to the body in which it occurs, and the experiences of that body in the world are integral to the conceptual frames operative in the thinking, reasoning, feeling, believing, and action of the person. Central to the experiences of the body are its relation to other humans in the world, in addition to its relation to all other kinds of phenomena in the world: material, biological, intellectual, imaginative, spiritual, etc.

Lakoff's use of the new theory of categorization called prototype theory, which argues on the basis of empirical data that "human categorization is essentially a matter of both human experience and imagination – of perception, motor activity, and culture on the one hand, and of metaphor, metonymy, and mental imagery on the other,"[148] is central for understanding the sociorhetorical strategies of analysis and interpretation in this volume. The empirical data undergirding his approach means that "[t]he properties relevant to the description of categories are *interactional properties*, properties characterizable only in terms of the interaction of human beings as part of their environment. Prototypical categories are sometimes describable in terms of *clusters* of such interactional properties. These clusters act as gestalts: the cluster as a whole is psychologically simpler than its parts."[149] The definition given to the term rhetorolect in 1996 was: "a form of language variety or discourse identifiable on the basis of a distinctive configuration of themes, topics, reasonings, and argumentations."[150] The language of "a distinctive configuration" points to a "cluster" that acts as a "gestalt," which "as a whole is psychologically simpler than its parts." It is likely that early Christian rhetorolects are what Lakoff identifies as "cluster ICMs."[151] They appear to contain clusters of topoi related to networks of meanings that configure first century Christian discourse in ways that are, at one and the same time, linked to multiple meaning networks in Mediterranean culture and distinctive of people with particular experiences in particular places and spaces in the Mediterranean world.

Approaching first century Christian writing with insights from researchers like Lakoff, Fauconnier, and Turner makes it clear that believers have the potential to blend all kinds of rhetorolects with other kinds of rhetorolects either on the terms of a dominant rhetorolect or in a conceptual environment of a blend of rhetorolects. Multiple kinds of blendings create vibrant, interactive systems of discourse in any cultural context. First century Christians, it is argued in this volume, created a system of discourse that was able to address issues and topics concern-

[148] Lakoff, *Women, Fire, and Dangerous Things*, 8.
[149] Ibid., 56.
[150] Robbins, "The Dialectical Nature of Early Christian Discourse," 356.
[151] Lakoff, *Women, Fire, and Dangerous Things*, 74-76, 203.

ing individual human bodies, households, villages, synagogues, cities, temples, kingdoms, empires, the created world, and God's uncreated realm. The ability of this discourse to address microcosmic details about individual bodies on earth as well as macrocosmic details about God's uncreated realm prepared Christianity not only to function in contexts where it would become the official religion of the Roman empire but also to function in contexts almost anywhere in the world. This discourse was able to do this, because it was interactive with topoi that addressed issues, concerns, emotions, insights, knowledge, and mysteries that cover a spectrum reaching from mundane daily activities to the widest reaches of God's unknown realm of being. To be sure, there are many topics and issues first century Christian discourse did not address. Nevertheless, the spectrum was so wide-reaching that it successfully launched a new culture of discourse in the Mediterranean world that expanded and became continually more nuanced and complex throughout twenty centuries in the history of the world.

4

Christian Wisdom Rhetorolect
Part I: Household and God's Productive World

Introduction

Picturesque and argumentative wisdom makes early Christian discourse accessible to people almost anywhere in the world. The primary internal dynamic of early Christian wisdom was fruitfulness. Just as God created the world to be fruitful, so God created humans to be fruitful. The special task of human beings is to produce the fruit of goodness and righteousness in the world. From the perspective of this rhetorolect, humans are able to do this by acting on God's wisdom.

Early Christian wisdom rhetorolect moves toward its goals by blending together human experiences of the household, the geophysical world within God's cosmos, and the intersubjective body in which people live.[1] In this conceptual blending, God functions as heavenly Father over God's children in the world. The blending of these three spaces conceptually presents a goal for people's intersubjective bodies to produce goodness and righteousness through the medium of God's wisdom, which is understood as God's light in the world. In this way, wisdom rhetorolect emphasizes "fruitfulness" (productivity and reproductivity). The goal of wisdom rhetorolect is to create people who produce good and righteous action, thought, will, and speech with the aid of God's wisdom.

The effect of wisdom rhetorolect in early Christian discourse was the production of a new *paideia* in the Mediterranean world by the fourth century CE. Building on the tradition of Hebrew Bible wisdom discourse, Christianity produced stories, sayings, letters, biographical-historiography, and finally, creeds, that blended Biblical, Jewish, Hellenistic-Roman, and "new messianite" ("early Christian")[2] wisdom traditions

[1] The terminology of intersubjective bodies comes from Couze Venn, *Occidentalism: Modernity and Subjectivity* (London: Sage, 2000) esp. 72-106.

[2] The term "messianite," rather than "Christian," best describes the nature of first century Christian discourse. The most definitional aspect of the early Jesus movement, which was located in first century Judaism, was its focus on Jesus as a messianic personage. During the earliest decades, there was no agreed upon perspective on what it meant to be a

dynamically together. When Christianity was adopted as the religion of the Roman empire during the fourth century, it functioned dynamically as a new form of wisdom and instruction, in Greek terms a new *paideia*, in the Roman world.[3]

There are four basic rhetorical resources for early Christian wisdom rhetorolect: (1) Torah wisdom; (2) wisdom story; (3) proverbial wisdom, and (4) argumentative wisdom. The resource for Torah wisdom lies primarily in statements that God told to Moses and Moses told to Israel. Resources for the wisdom story-line lie in Genesis, the Deuteronomic literature, literature attributed to Solomon, the psalms, the prophetic literature, and common knowledge about people who sow grain, bake bread, herd sheep, sweep their houses, and tend vineyards. Resources for proverbial wisdom lie in traditions about Solomon and other people like Job in the Hebrew Bible, in Hellenistic Jewish literature both inside and outside the OT Apocrypha, and in Hellenistic-Roman moral philosophical literature of various kinds. Resources for argumentative wisdom are especially rich in the sphere of Hellenistic literature, both Jewish and Hellenistic-Roman. The resources for early Christian wisdom rhetorolect, therefore, are both deep and wide in the Hebrew Bible, in Hellenistic Jewish literature, and in Hellenistic-Roman literature contemporary with early Christianity.

One of the basic characteristics of early Christian wisdom rhetorolect is to turn scriptural discourse into proverbial speech. This occurs either by selecting only part of a verse for recitation or by omitting words from the biblical verse to make it shorter. A classic instance is Habakkuk 2:4, which Paul recites as, "The one who is righteous will live by faith" (Rom 1:17; Gal 3:11), but which exists in Hab 2:4 as: "Look at the proud! Their spirit is not right in them, but the righteous live by their faith." Early Christian wisdom rhetorolect shortens the scriptural verse into an easily remembered and transmitted proverb: "The one who is righteous will live by faith." Another instance is Lev 19:18, which New Testament writings recite as "You shall love your neighbor as yourself"[4] (Matt 19:19; 22:29; Mark 12:31; Rom 13:9; Gal 5:14; Jas 2:8). Leviticus 19:18 actually

follower of Jesus, beyond a general agreement that he was "somehow" a person who had been "anointed" ("christened") by God to perform a special task on earth in relation to God's will, action, and goals.

[3] Werner Jaeger, *Early Christianity and Greek Paideia* (Cambridge: Harvard University Press, 1961); Averil Cameron, *Christianity and the Rhetoric of Empire: The Development of Christian Discourse* (Sather Classical Lectures, 56; Berkeley: University of California Press, 1991) 202-21.

[4] Cf. Matt 5:43; Mark 12:33; Luke 10:27.

states: You shall not take vengeance or bear a grudge against any of your people, but you shall love your neighbor as yourself: I am the Lord."[5]

Christianity gave its foundational wisdom discourse distinctive features by embedding it in a holy family of God the Father, Jesus the only Son of God, and Mary the earthly mother of Jesus. This configuration of a holy family blends the concept of an earthly household containing a mother and a son with the concept of a world created by God, who is Father both of the universe and of the Messiah (*christos*) Jesus, from whom the followers of Jesus received the name Christian (*christianoi*: Acts 11:26; 26:28; 1 Pet 4:16). When this family discourse blends with God's created world, the concept of Holy Spirit blends with Mary, the mother of Jesus, especially through the stories of Jesus' birth, where Jesus is "from the Holy Spirit" (Matt 1:18, 20; cf. Luke 1:35). This blending creates a framework of belief that gradually overmaps the initial concept of the holy family with the Trinity of Father, Son, and Holy Spirit[6] in the Christian creedal rhetorolect of the fourth century.

Wisdom Speech Genres, Typical and Atypical Biblical Wisdom Literature, Wisdom Discourse, and Early Christian Wisdom Rhetorolect

As we begin to discuss first century CE Christian wisdom discourse, it is important to distinguish between wisdom speech genres (both oral and written), typical and atypical biblical wisdom literature, wisdom discourse, and early Christian wisdom rhetorolect.

A wisdom speech genre (oral or written) is a particular form of speech emerging from everyday life[7] that presents reflective insights about the nature of the created world and human life in it.[8] In Israel, the primary wisdom speech genres were proverb or aphorism (*mashal*) and positive and negative admonitions.[9] Centripetal movement[10] in Israelite culture

[5] For the overall trend to make Torah wisdom into proverbial wisdom, see Chapter 1 on Mishnah, *Pirke Aboth* 1:1.

[6] See how the concept of the holy family of Father, Son, and Holy Mary is still present in conversation and dialogue in Qur'an 5:116.

[7] M.M. Bakhtin, *Speech Genres and Other Late Essays* (trans. Vern W. McGee; Austin: University of Texas Press, 1986, 78-81.

[8] Walter Brueggemann, *Theology of the Old Testament: Testimony, Dispute, Advocacy* (Minneapolis: Fortress Press, 1997) 680-82; James L. Crenshaw, *Urgent Advice and Probing Questions: Collected Writings on Old Testament Wisdom* (Macon, Ga.: Mercer University Press, 1995).

[9] Roland E. Murphy, "Wisdom in the OT," *ABD* VI:921.

[10] M.M. Bakhtin, *The Dialogic Imagination: Four Essays* (ed. Michael Holquist; trans. Caryl Emerson and Michael Holquist; Austin: University of Texas Press, 1981) 272: Centripetal movement is "verbal-ideological centralization and unification" that produces

produced wisdom literature that contained large amounts of these primary speech genres. John J. Collins lists "Proverbs, Qoheleth, and Job in the Hebrew Bible, and the apocryphal and deuterocanonical books of Ben Sira (Ecclesiasticus) and the Wisdom of Solomon" as the writings scholars regularly identify as wisdom literature.[11] He explains that a major reason for calling them "wisdom literature" is the presence of more than half of the occurrences of the Hebrew word for wisdom (*hokmah*) in Proverbs, Qoheleth, and Job.

Proverbs, Qoheleth, Job, Ben Sira, and Wisdom of Solomon are all so complex that they are what Bakhtin called secondary, rather than primary, genres.[12] Over a period of time, these literary works became "typical" instances[13] of biblical wisdom literature in Israelite culture. These typical instances contain "a repertoire"[14] of wisdom speech genres (oral and written) that traveled "centrifugally"[15] out into Israelite culture. This centrifugal movement created "biblical wisdom discourse" in the Mediterranean world, making these wisdom speech genres available to writers who could include them in other biblical literature, in apocryphal or deuterocanonical and pseudepigraphical literature, in Qumran literature, in Hellenistic Jewish literature, and in Mediterranean works outside the sphere of "biblical" tradition (e.g., Pseudo-Phocylides).

Typical Hebrew Bible wisdom literature contains a combination of didactic and speculative wisdom. Speculative wisdom probed beyond the boundaries of that which was visible (God's created world) to the invisi-

stratification "into languages that are socio-ideological: languages of social groups, 'professional' and 'generic' languages, languages of generations and so forth."

[11] John J. Collins, *Jewish Wisdom in the Hellenistic Age* (Louisville, KY: Westminster John Knox Press, 1997) 1.

[12] "The vast majority of literary genres are secondary, complex genres composed of various transformed primary genres (the rejoinder in dialogue, everyday stories, letters, diaries, minutes, and so forth). As a rule, these secondary genres of complex cultural communication *play out* various forms of primary speech communication" (Bakhtin, *Speech Genres*, 98; cf. 61-62, 72-76, 98-99).

[13] Eleanor Rosch, "Cognitive Representations of Semantic Categories," *Journal of Experimental Psychology (General)* 104 (1975) 192-233; idem, "Principles of Categorization," in *Cognition and Categorization* (ed. E. Rosch and B. Lloyd; Hillsdale, NJ: Lawrence Erlbaum, 1978) 27-48; Carol A. Newsom, "Spying out the Land: A Report from Genology," in *Bakhtin and Genre Theory in Biblical Studies* (ed. Roland Boer; Semeia Studies 63; Atlanta: SBL, 2007) 19-30.

[14] Bakhtin, *Speech Genres,* 80.

[15] Bakhtin, *The Dialogic Imagination*, 272: Centrifugal movement is the result of "the uninterrupted processes of decentralization and disunification" by which utterances partake in "social and historical heteroglossia… [T]his active participation of every utterance in living heteroglossia determines the linguistic profile and style of the utterance to no less a degree than its inclusion in any normative-centralizing system of a unitary language… The authentic environment of an utterance, the environment in which it lives and takes shape, is dialogized heteroglossia, anonymous and social as language, but simultaneously concrete, filled with specific content and accented as an individual utterance."

ble (that which lay "beyond" God's visible, created world). The special characteristic of Israelite speculative wisdom was its attempt to probe "temporally" beyond wisdom to a sphere of "non-time." In the Hebrew Bible, wisdom literature contains more searching toward non-time that existed before the beginning of time than that which will exist after the end of time. We will see that Jewish apocalyptic literature is that kind of wisdom literature that searches for special wisdom "both during and beyond the end of time."

The presence of both "created-world time" and "non-time before created-world time" in Hebrew Bible wisdom literature supports the view both of James L. Crenshaw and George W. E. Nickelsburg that central to wisdom is "searching and seeking" for understanding.[16] Israelite wisdom literature not only contains proverb or aphorism and positive and negative admonitions, but it also contains a story of wisdom with God prior to and during the time of creation, and the continuation of the story of wisdom during created-world time. This "speculative wisdom story" in the Hebrew Bible created the context for what we call "precreation rhetorolect" in early Christian discourse. The present chapter focuses on "didactic" or instructional wisdom, which we call "wisdom rhetorolect" in the sphere of early Christian discourse. Two chapters in the next volume will probe deeply into the nature of biblical precreation discourse and its presence as an important rhetorolect in first century Christian discourse.

By the second century BCE, biblical wisdom literature contained multiple kinds of discourses. More and more, "active searching" became a characteristic of this tradition. Ben Sira, writing during the first quarter of the second century BCE, presupposed that Torah was wisdom: "All this is the book of the covenant of the Most High God, the law that Moses commanded us as an inheritance for the congregations of Jacob" (Sir 24:23). Bar 4:1 says something very similar: "She is the book of the commandments of God, the law that endures forever." But this was simply the tip of the iceberg, so to say. Gerald T. Sheppard has documented that all scripture was becoming "wisdom" by the beginning of the Common Era.[17] In a context where the question had become, "What are all the places a person should look to find wisdom?", one of the major answers was "scripture," which gradually meant all of the Hebrew Bible. Ben Sira helped to set the stage well when he described the activities of the sage who studied Torah wisdom in the following manner:

[16] James L. Crenshaw, *Old Testament Wisdom: An Introduction* (Atlanta: John Knox Press, 1981) 17; George W.E. Nickelsburg, "Response to Sarah Tanzer," in *Conflicted Boundaries in Wisdom and Apocalypticism* (ed. B.G. Wright III and L.M. Wills; Symposium 35; Atlanta: SBL, 2005) 51-54.

[17] Gerald T. Sheppard, *Wisdom as a Hermeneutical Construct: A Study in the Sapientializing of the Old Testament* (BZAW 151; Berlin: Walter de Gruyter, 1980).

> On the other hand he who devotes himself
>   to the study of the law of the Most high
> will seek out the wisdom of all the ancients,
>   and will be concerned with prophecies;
> he will preserve the discourse of notable men
>   and penetrate the subtleties of parables;
> he will seek out the hidden meanings of proverbs
>   and be at home with the obscurities of parables. (Sir 39:1-3 RSV)[18]

This meant that by the first century CE biblical wisdom speech genres had expanded beyond proverbs or aphorisms and positive and negative admonitions to commandments of Moses, psalms of wisdom, prophetic oracles, and parables.

As a result of this "sapientializing" of biblical discourse, by the time of the rise of Christianity Deuteronomy was functioning as an additional instance of wisdom literature in the Hebrew Bible.[19] It is important that the LXX contains two occurrences of *sophos* in the first chapter of Deuteronomy. The first occurs when Moses tells the people that God earlier had told him: "Choose for each of your tribes individuals who are wise (*sophous*), discerning (*epistēmonas*), and reputable (*synetous*), and I will appoint them as your leaders over you" (1:13). Then Moses tells them: "So I took from you the wise (*sophous*), discerning (*epistēmonas*), and reputable (*synetous*), and I appointed them to lead you ..." (1:15). Moses repeats this emphasis in Deut 4:6. After telling the Israelites he will now teach them statutes and ordinances (4:5), he says:

> You must observe them diligently, for this will show your wisdom (*sophia*) and discernment (*synesis*) to the peoples, who, when they hear all these statutes (*dikaiōmata*), will say, "Surely this great nation is a wise (*sophos*) and discerning (*epistēmōn*) people!" (4:6).

Then in Deut 16:19, Moses teaches them: "You must not distort justice; you must not show partiality; and you must not accept bribes, for a bribe blinds the eyes of the wise (*sophōn*) and subverts the cause of those who are in the right." Later, in the midst of the Song of Moses, Moses recites the words: "Do you thus repay the Lord, O foolish (*mōros*) and not wise (*ouchi sophos*) people? Is not he your father, who created you, who made you and established you?" (Deut 32:6). An emphasis on wisdom both frames and punctuates the teaching of Moses in Deuteronomy. Moreover, there is an emphasis that this wisdom is related to God as the father who created them. Early Christians present Jesus as finding the wisdom he, as the son of God, needs from Deut 6:13, 6:16, and 8:3 to

[18] As quoted by Nickelsburg in Wright and Wills, *Conflicted Boundaries*, 52.
[19] Cf. Collins, *Jewish Wisdom*, 15, 54-55.

overcome the tests of Satan (Matt 4:1-11/Luke 4:1-13).[20] Moreover, the concept of God as father permeates the NT writings, appearing in all of them except 3 John. We will discuss more of this in the next chapter.

In order for any kind of discourse to become prominent in a cultural setting, people must value the kind of person who produces the speech genres central to it. For wisdom, the scholarly term for the person to be valued is "sage," and the more common term is "teacher."[21] Valuing a person who produces these kinds of speech genres is related to "indexing" in language, culture, and literature.[22] Within Israel, the sage or teacher was indexed as a person who could mediate knowledge about God's created world and human life in it. As Walter Brueggemann has indicated, there were multiple "agents" in Israel who mediated knowledge about God.[23] As our investigation proceeds, we will identify six major agents and the rhetorolects in which first century Christians "indexed" them as highly valuable for understanding the nature of the benefits, dangers, and responsibilities of living in God's created world.

A major question the interpreter of first century Christianity faces concerning early Christian wisdom rhetorolect is: "What was the primary social-cultural-ideological location and institution that produced a valuing of the teacher/sage?" A wide range of evidence points to the household, where parents were the teachers of children and Christians gathered to learn how to live a life that included Jesus (Christ) as a major mediator of wisdom about God's world.[24] In a cultural context where Greece had made philosophy (the love of wisdom) a public possession,[25] first century Christians placed a high value on wisdom in the households that provided the primary institutional base for their existence and ex-

[20] Vernon K. Robbins, "The Socio-Rhetorical Role of Old Testament Scripture in Luke 4–19," in *Z Noveho Zakona /From the New Testament: Sbornik k narozeninam Prof. ThDr. Zdenka Sazavy* (ed. Hana Tonzarova and Petr Melmuk; Prague: Vydala Cirkev ceskoslovenska husitska, 2001) 81-93: online: http://www.religion.emory.edu/faculty/robbins/SRS/vkr/vkr01-05/index.htm.

[21] Brueggemann, *Theology*, 680.

[22] William K. Gilders, *Blood Ritual in the Hebrew Bible: Meaning and Power* (Baltimore and London: Johns Hopkins University Press) 8-11, 78-84, 101-104, 139-41, 186-91, building on insights in Nancy Jay, *Throughout Your Generations Forever: Sacrifice, Religion, and Paternity* (Chicago: University of Chicago Press, 1992).

[23] Brueggemann, *Theology*, 567-704.

[24] Halvor Moxnes (ed.), *Constructing Early Christian Families: Family as Social Reality and Metaphor* (London: Routledge, 1997); Ekkehard W. Stegemann and Wolfgang Stegemann, *The Jesus Movement: A Social History of Its First Century* (Minneapolis: Fortress Press, 1999) 277-80; cf. Brueggemann 1997: 682-83.

[25] Troels Engberg-Pedersen, "The Hellenistic *Öffentlichkeit*: Philosophy as a Social Force in the Greco-Roman World," in *Recruitment, Conquest, and Conflict: Strategies in Judaism, Early Christianity, and the Greco-Roman World* (ed. P. Borgen, V.K. Robbins, and D.B. Gowler; ESEC 6; Atlanta: Scholars Press, 1998) 15-37.

pansion.[26] Early Christians nurtured their special wisdom through the structure and value of parents and teachers who functioned as "father/teachers" over "brothers" and "sisters" in households. A passage in 2 Timothy sums up the valuing of the father/teacher from childhood to adulthood and the manner in which all scripture had become wisdom when it says:

> 14 But as for you, continue in what you have learned and firmly believed, knowing from whom you learned it, 15 and how from childhood you have known the sacred writings that are able to instruct you (*sophisai*) for salvation through faith in Christ Jesus. 16 All scripture is inspired by God and is useful for teaching (*didaskalian*), for reproof, for correction, and for training (*paideian*) in righteousness, 17 so that everyone who belongs to God may be proficient, equipped for every good work. (2 Tim 3:14-17 NRSV)

As indicated earlier, a major result of the emergence of Christianity was the creation of a new paideia.[27] This "new utterance"[28] was an alternative to other "Jewish" and Greco-Roman language-worlds of wisdom belief in the Mediterranean world. This means that early Christian wisdom is a form of "disputation" discourse.[29] Each thesis it presents is a "potential dispute" with other modes of thinking. The primary dispute emerged over the insertion of Jesus into the system. In other words, each early Christian thesis presupposed that Jesus (Christ) somehow was an important participant in the presentation of "true wisdom" about God, God's created world, and human life in the world.

Sociorhetorical interpretation uses the term "rhetorolect" to communicate the particular nature of early Christian communication in the Mediterranean world.[30] As indicated in the previous chapter, after a decade of analysis and interpretation of six early Christian rhetorolects, a discovery was made that a rhetorolect is, in the language of cognitive science, an "idealized cognitive model" containing four structuring principles. In the context of sociorhetorical interpretation, these structuring principles internal to rhetorolects are: (1) argumentative-enthymematic structuring; (2) image-description structuring; (3) metaphoric mapping; and (4) metonymic mapping. The argumentative-enthymematic structur-

[26] The word wisdom (*sophia*) occurs fifty times, wise (*sophos*) twenty times, and to make wise (*sophizō*) twice (2 Tim 3:15; 2 Pet 1:16).

[27] Werner Jaeger, *Early Christianity and Greek Paideia* (Cambridge, Mass.: Harvard University Press, 1961); Robert L. Wilken, "Wisdom and Philosophy in Early Christianity," in *Aspects of Wisdom in Judaism and Early Christianity* (ed. R.L. Wilken; Notre Dame and London: University of Notre Dame Press, 1975) 143-68.

[28] Amos N. Wilder, *Early Christian Rhetoric: The Language of the Gospel* (Cambridge, Mass.: Harvard University Press, 1964) 1-17.

[29] Brueggemann, *Theology*, 690.

[30] Robbins, "The Dialectical Nature of Early Christian Discourse."

ing in early Christian wisdom rhetorolect is deeply related to "the complete argument" in Mediterranean rhetoric.[31] This means that it regularly proceeds through some or all of a pattern of thesis, rationale, opposite or contrary, analogy, example, authoritative judgment, and exhortative conclusion. George A. Kennedy referred to these patterns as "worldly rhetoric" in *New Testament Interpretation through Rhetorical Criticism.*[32] The image-description structuring in early Christian wisdom rhetorolect emphasizes household relationships that feature father, mother, brother, sister, and extended members of the household like servants, teachers, workers, etc. The metaphoric mapping features a reciprocal blending of household imagery with God's created world and God's created world with members of a household. This metaphoric mapping creates the context for metonymic mapping, where reference to God as father, humans as God's children, people's actions as good fruit or bad fruit, or wisdom as light has the rhetorical force to evoke the entire language-world or belief system[33] of people being guided (or not being guided) by God's wisdom as they live in God's created world.

The time-space (chronotope)[34] of early Christian wisdom rhetorolect is "household-created world" time. In this context, wisdom time is production-reproduction time. This is "seasonal" time focused on "productivity" in an ongoing cycle of "birth-growth-death." One of the characteristics internal to this "wisdom" belief system is to place ethical expectations on humans in relation both to their time in the cycle of life and to their location in God's created world. Thus, different things are expected from full-grown adults, elderly people, young adults, and children, as well as different things from householders, leaders, overseers, stewards, servants, workers, strangers, and dependents. God's time as "productivity" time, therefore, holds humans responsible for their words and deeds in relation both to "the season of their life" and to their location in God's created world.

In NT writings, major wisdom speech genres are unattributed sayings (proverbs, gnomic sayings), attributed sayings (chreiai), parables, and

[31] Vernon K. Robbins, "Progymnastic Rhetorical Composition and Pre-Gospel Traditions: A New Approach," in *The Synoptic Gospels: Source Criticism and the New Literary Criticism* (ed. Camille Focant; BETL 110; Leuven: Leuven University Press, 1993) 111-47.

[32] Kennedy, *New Testament Interpretation*; see Robbins, "Rhetography."

[33] See Bakhtin, *The Dialogical Imagination*, 385-86, 425 for belief system as "the circle of one's vision" or "conceptual horizon" (425). A world view "becomes only one of the participants in a dialogue of languages … capable of internally dialogic resistance to new authorial intentions…" (386).

[34] Ibid., 84-258, 425-26; Bula Maddison, "Liberation Story or Apocalypse? Reading Biblical Allusion and Bakhtin Theory in Toni Morrison's *Beloved*," in *Bakhtin and Genre Theory in Biblical Studies* (ed. Roland Boer; Semeia Studies 63; Atlanta: SBL, 2007) 161-74, also see 201-203.

commandments.[35] These speech genres presented wisdom discourse as an alternative both to Jewish "pre-rabbinic" wisdom and to Hellenistic-Roman wisdom. The epistle of James, the Sermon on the Plain (Luke 6:20-49), and the Sermon on the Mount (Matt 5–7) are the result of centripetal forces in early Christian culture that brought wisdom speech genres into extensive patterned elaborations in the secondary literary genres of letter and Gospel. The force of wisdom speech patterns was strong enough to function as a "form-shaping ideology" only on the literary genre of letter in first century Christianity. The narrative orientation of the secondary literary genre of Gospel during the first century CE was strong enough to resist early Christian wisdom speech genres as a "form-shaping ideology." The presence of early Christian wisdom rhetorolect created a context in which wisdom speech genres functioned as a form-shaping ideology in Gospels during the second and third centuries CE (e.g., *Gospel of Thomas*, *Secret Book of James*, *Dialogue of the Savior*, and *Gospel of Mary*).[36] It also played a strong enough role that wisdom writings like the *Sentences of Sextus*[37] and the *Teachings of Silvanus* emerged during the second and third centuries.[38]

Centrifugal forces in first century Christian culture produced a presence of some wisdom rhetorolect in almost all the NT writings. One of the symptoms of its centrifugal presence is the occurrence of some form of the Greek stem *soph-* (wise or wisdom) in 13 of the 27 NT writings.[39] We will argue in the next volume that the absence of *soph-* terminology in the Gospel of John and the epistles of 1, 2, and 3 John is a symptom of the centripetal rhetorical force of precreation rhetorolect on the language-world/belief system that dominates their discourse. In turn, it is noticeable that prophetic rhetorolect does not invite *soph-* terminology in Galatians, priestly rhetorolect does not invite *soph-* terminology in Hebrews, and apocalyptic rhetorolect does not invite *soph-* terminology in 1-2 Thessalonians and Jude. To be sure, wisdom rhetorolect may be pre-

[35] Wilder, *Early Christian Rhetoric*, esp. 1-54, 71-88; William A. Beardslee, "The Wisdom Tradition and the Synoptic Gospels," *JAAR* 35 (1967) 231-40; idem, *Literary Criticism of the New Testament* (Minneapolis: Fortress Press, 1970) 30-41; Robert C. Tannehill, *The Sword of His Mouth* (Philadelphia: Fortress Press and Missoula, Mont.: Scholars Press, 1975); Vernon K. Robbins, "The Chreia," in *Greco-Roman Literature and the New Testament: Selected Forms and Genres* (ed. D.E. Aune; SBL Sources for Biblical Study 21; Atlanta: Scholars Press, 1988) 1-23; Bernard Brandon Scott, *Hear Then the Parable: A Commentary on the Parables of Jesus* (Minneapolis: Fortress Press, 1989) 7-62.

[36] Robert J. Miller (ed.), *The Complete Gospels* (San Francisco: HarperSanFrancisco, 1994) 301-66.

[37] Wilken, "Wisdom and Philosophy in Early Christianity."

[38] William R. Schoedel, "Jewish Wisdom and the Formation of the Christian Ascetic," in Wilken, *Aspects of Wisdom*, 169-99.

[39] Matthew, Mark, Luke, Acts, Romans, 1-2 Corinthians, Ephesians, Colossians, James, 2 Timothy, 2 Peter, Revelation.

sent in a writing without the presence of *soph-* terminology. As we recall, John Collins noticed the presence of half of the occurrences of Hebrew Bible "wisdom" terminology in Proverbs, Qoheleth, and Job.[40] Early Christian wisdom rhetorolect functioned centripetally enough in one letter in the NT (James) that a new "atypical" member of the literary genre "wisdom" exists in the NT canon. In the Gospels, a centripetal presence of wisdom is especially noticeable in the Sermon on the Plain (Luke 6:20-49) and the Sermon on the Mount (Matt 5–7). Otherwise, wisdom rhetorolect functions centrifugally in NT writings in a context of the strong presence of other early Christian rhetorolects.

Wisdom literature was a widespread phenomenon in the Mediterranean world long before Christianity came on the scene. Wisdom literature featuring proverbs and various kinds of short stories were present in Egypt and Babylonia in particular, but also in other regions as well. In addition, law codes, legal decrees, and "guidelines" for behavior became an internal part of Mediterranean wisdom literature. By the second century BCE, wisdom writings had become central to the Bible. By the first century CE, writings like Pseudo-Phocylides, Epictetus, the Kyriai Doxai, and other wisdom writings were promulgating "wisdom" views of the world.[41] When early Christianity emerged during the first century CE, it participated vigorously in a cultural environment in which wisdom discourse was pervasively present and highly valued. One of the special effects of the particular wisdom culture of first century Christians was the emergence of a particular, episodic story-line of biblical wisdom beginning with the creation of the world. We turn now to this story.

The Early Christian Story-Line of Biblical Wisdom

The writings of the New Testament exhibit a selectivity from the Hebrew Bible that emphasizes three key moments in which God gave wisdom to people in the world:

1. God's creating of the world;
2. God's giving of Torah wisdom to Moses;
3. God's giving of wisdom to Solomon.

The beginning of this Christian story occurs in God's speech that created light in the world. Early Christian discourse presupposes an analogy between God's wisdom and light. When children receive wisdom from parents in a household they are receiving God's light. For the Christian wisdom story, this is the beginning of the world as well as the beginning

[40] Collins, *Jewish Wisdom*, 1.

[41] Walter T. Wilson, *Love without Pretense: Romans 12.9-21 and Hellenistic-Jewish Wisdom Literature* (WUNT 2. Reihe, 46; Tübingen: J.C.B. Mohr (Paul Siebeck), 1991) 1-148.

of the knowledge of "goodness" in the world. All people who see God's created world should be able to know the nature of goodness both in the world and in God. After God created humans, according to the Christian wisdom story, God's speech created commandments that guided people toward a fruitful life. These commandments become present in the world first of all through Moses, who was given "writings" that contained the major commandments of God.[42] After God had given commandments to Moses, God gave special wisdom to Solomon, son of King David. Solomon's wisdom, contained in proverbs rather than commandments, emphasizes the nature of parental speech both as a lamp and as light.[43] Early Christian wisdom discourse blends commandment wisdom with proverbial wisdom. We will show below that this is a blending of the geography of the household with the biblical geography of God's created world. With this move, wisdom discourse reaches into the innermost nature of God, the divine creator of the world, and blends the relation of God to the world with the relation of parents to their children.

In order for the biblical story of God's creation of the world to function as a "self-evident" mode of persuasion, there had to be a place where humans experienced the "truth" firsthand about the nature of God's created world. Recent theories about humans and their relation to spaces and places call these places "Firstspace."[44] In the biblical tradition, and in early Christian tradition, this Firstspace of wisdom discourse was the household. Christian speakers and writers built early Christian wisdom rhetorolect by blending together Firstspace images and reasoning related to the household with Secondspace in God's created world. When biblical tradition blended household with God's created world in wisdom rhetorolect,[45] it pictured God as father and people on earth as children who received God's instruction. Activities and relationships in households throughout the Mediterranean world provided social, cultural, and ideological geography for early Christian wisdom discourse.[46] Activities and relationships in households blended "naturally"[47] with places of vegetation like gardens, vineyards, and fields in God's created world. All of these

[42] According to Jewish tradition, the Torah contains 613 commandments.

[43] The Gospel of John speaks of Christ as light (1:4-5, 7-9; 3:19-21; 5:35; 8:12; 9:5; 11:9-10; 12:35-36, 46) and John the Baptist as a lamp (5:35).

[44] David M. Gunn and Paula M. McNutt, *"Imagining" Biblical Worlds: Studies in Spatial, Social and Historical Constructs in Honor of James W. Flanagan* (JSOTS 359; Sheffield: Sheffield Academic Press, 2002) 14-50.

[45] Household is input 1 and God's created world is input 2, following Fauconnier and Turner, *The Way We Think,* 131-35, 179-80, 182-83, 186-87, 189-91, 305, 340-45, 353-60, 389-93.

[46] In the terminology of critical spatiality theory, households would be Firstspace and created world Secondspace.

[47] This blending concerns nature.

geographical and human arenas of growth, productivity, and responsibility provide analogies for the production of good in God's world.

Once household reasoning merged comfortably with reasoning about God's created world, this blended reasoning traveled naturally into reasoning about the intersubjective body as Thirdspace. Every human body becomes a special microcosm of God's created world in a network focused on the production of good things. Like God's created world, the human body is designed to be a place where good things are fruitful and multiply. Humans are to bear good fruit by producing good and righteous thoughts and actions as they grow and mature in wisdom and knowledge. Early Christian wisdom rhetorolect, therefore, is a network of reasoning that focuses on the production of good and righteous thoughts, actions, and results in God's world.

Households, Vegetation, and Living Beings as Spaces and Places for Wisdom Rhetorolect

Religious Blending	Wisdom Rhetorolect
Social, Cultural, & Physical Realia (1st Space)	Households, Vegetation, Living Beings
Visualization, Conceptualization, & Imagination of God's World (2nd Space)	God as Father-Creator (Progenitor), Wisdom (light) as Mediator, People as God's children, Jesus as God's Son
Ongoing Bodily Effects and Enactments: Blending in Religious Life (3rd Space)	Human body as Producer of Goodness & Righteousness

The Hebrew Bible begins with a story that describes God's creation of the world. In the reasoning of early Christians, this story presented an account of the beginning of a realm of time and a realm of light where things were visible. Before God's creation of the world, there was no time and there was darkness. In both Judaism and Christianity, the realm of "no-time" became a positive concept, namely an "era" that existed before time began and that will continue after time ends. In other words, the realm of "no-time" became a realm of "eternity" that always existed and always will exist. The era "beyond time" will become important in the discussion of prophetic, apocalyptic, and precreation rhetorolect in succeeding chapters. Early Christian wisdom belief, reasoning, and argumentation did not focus predominantly on a realm of non-time beyond this world. Rather, its "wisdom" was grounded in observations about living in the sequential moments of time in God's created world. This focus was possible as a result of God's light in the world. God's creation of light caused plants to grow, brought forth animals and humans, and produced an ordered world of day, night, weeks, months, seasons, and years.

The light from God is God's visible wisdom. According to Christian wisdom rhetorolect, God's world reveals God's wisdom if a person looks at it carefully. But once a person has looked, one must be willing to walk according to God's ways, to think and speak the thoughts of God, and to produce goodness and righteousness as fruits of God's wisdom. The reasoning and argumentation in early Christian wisdom rhetorolect, then, is concerned with what people do with their feet, hands, mouths, ears, and eyes here in this world. It is concerned, so to speak, with "on the ground" activities. With this focus, it directs people's heads towards daily duties in the family household and regular activities in God's created world. This is the nature of corporeal, conceptual blending in Christian discourse. Multiple "frames" of conceptuality blend together as people use their bodies and the locations of their bodies to understand the world in which they live and to tell others their reasoning about their lives in God's world. Early Christian wisdom rhetorolect uses its reasoning about the family household and God's created world to formulate guidelines for a way of life in the world that co-participates with God in the production of goodness and righteousness and persuades others to adopt these ways of living for the purpose of fulfilling the inner purposes of God.

Beginnings of Biblical Wisdom in Creation: Genesis 1–3 as a Fruitfulness Network

Genesis 1–3 presents the most basic biblical story about the beginning of the world. The present chapter explains how this biblical story represents the frame that grounds early Christian wisdom rhetorolect. Returning again and again to the nature of the world as people observed and experienced it, early Christian wisdom rhetorolect was grounded in people's experiences of what we often call the "mundane" things of everyday life. An underlying presupposition of this Christian discourse is that God created this world. This creates a persistent blending of concepts of God's created world with every individual part of this world. Thus, every part of the world in which a Christian lives is, in essence, a microcosm of the macrocosm that God created.

As is well known, the pictorial narration of God's creating of the world in Gen 1–3 features God's creating of light through speech (Gen 1:3). Less well known, perhaps, are the precise inner processes by which God makes the created world productive by means of speech and light. Once God creates light, the reader is told that God sees that the light is good (1:4). God does not pronounce the light good; God "sees" that it is good. This is an important detail, since light enables one to see. But more than this, light enables God to see that which is good, which is the internal nature of wisdom. Wisdom is enabled by light which allows God, and persons made in the image of God, to identify that which is good and to act upon it in a manner that produces additional good.

The process of creation begins, then, with a speaking agent who is able to see, because the primary thing speech creates is light. The seeing described in the story is the kind of seeing that knows what it sees. The seeing is not simply a matter of glancing at something or observing it, as though it simply "caught God's eye." God's seeing knows what it sees. At its most primary level, God's speech creates light, which creates the ability to "know" that something is good. Speech-light, then, creates a self-perpetuating environment of knowing (wisdom), which is continually transmitted to other speaking-seeing beings. Speech-light is the source and inner process of wisdom. Speech-light identifies that which is good for the purpose of creating additional good through speech that creates light. The process continues through speech-light, which is the continual transmission of wisdom. God, who is a speaking agent, and other beings created as speaking agents in the image of God (Gen 1:26-27), transfer light-wisdom to one another through speech. This transfer of light-wisdom creates an environment of identifying good for the purpose of making good productive of itself. Seeing, perceiving, and knowing good are the inner processes of God's created world and also the inner processes of wisdom in God and in the world.

A natural beginning place for wisdom argumentation, as a result of its deep relation to the biblical creation story, is an assertion of the good, namely the placement of a "thesis" in the form of a proverb, commandment, or exhortation before the ears and eyes of a hearer-seer. Early Christian discourse is filled with assertions that focus on the good: "You are the salt of the earth" (Matt 5:13); "You are the light of the world" (Matt 5:14); "Love your enemies" (Luke 6:27); "Give to everyone who begs from you" (Luke 6:30); "Be merciful, just as your heavenly Father is merciful" (Luke 6:36). The foundation of wisdom argumentation is speech that creates "light" in the form of focusing on that which is good for the purpose of reproducing good in the world.

After God sees that light is good, God separates light from darkness (Gen 1:4). God's differentiation between light and darkness is a second step, not the first step of creation or of wisdom. The primary task of wisdom is identifying and focusing on the good, which results in "placing" that which is good in front of one's eyes, thoughts, and actions. A result of focusing on that which is good, however, is the "pushing" of other things away from the good. The nature of these other things, "the darkness," is not clear, and they are not the focus either of God's activities or of God's wisdom in Gen 1. But God's action of separating the light from the darkness (Gen 1:4b) creates a negative in the form of an "opposite," that which is "not" light.

Argument from the opposite is a natural definitional step in wisdom discourse. That which is good can be defined, rather than simply identified, by juxtaposing good with its opposite, that which is not good. It is natural in wisdom discourse, therefore, to juxtapose a positive assertion with an opposite one. Rom 12:14, for example, asserts, "Bless those who persecute you; bless and do not curse them." The goodness of blessing a person while that person is inflicting harm on oneself is defined more sharply by setting the act of blessing alongside its opposite, the act of cursing someone. Only a few things, however, have direct opposites. Usually there are a number of alternatives one faces in contexts of the decisions one must make in life. For this reason, wisdom discourse usually introduces "contraries," which can be any number of alternatives, rather than opposites. Things are good or not good in relation to other things which may also be good or perhaps not so good. Rom 12:16, for example, asserts, "Live in harmony with one another; do not be haughty, but associate with the lowly; do not claim to be wiser than you are." Two contraries of living in harmony with one another are being haughty and claiming to be wiser than you are, and one good way of living in harmony is to associate with the lowly. The assertion about associating with the lowly occurs in such a manner that it functions as an adversative, a statement introduced with "but." Both opposites and contraries naturally function as adversatives in wisdom discourse, helping to focus and sharpen one's understanding of choices that are either good in themselves or that create environments that produce good. Wisdom discourse, then, contains positive assertions, opposites, contraries, and adversatives. This multiplicity of relationships has an intrinsic relation to the multiplicity of relationships in God's creation. As the story of creation unfolds in Gen 1-3, multiple relationships emerge as part of the internal nature of the world God created. The unfolding story, therefore, gradually exhibits the inner dynamics and challenges of wisdom discourse as it appears before the ears and eyes of the hearer-seer of the story.

A beginning point in wisdom discourse, then, is reasoning and argumentation based on identification and differentiation. Identities and differences are assumed, asserted, or explained by using opposites, contraries, and adversatives. These emerge internally from the story of God's creation of the world. When God creates light, God sees that it is good. The concept of good introduces a value that not only evokes an opposite (bad or evil) but also has the potential to create a hierarchical system where certain things are better than other things.[48] The concept of bad or evil does not emerge in the creation story until Gen 2–3. Genesis 1 exhibits, instead, a complex system of differences. God separates light from darkness and names light day and darkness night (1:4-5). This separating and naming creates a picture of opposites occupied by light/darkness (non-

[48] See "final cultural categories" in Robbins, *Exploring,* 86-89 and idem, *Tapestry,* 167-74, 182-89.

light) and day/night (non-day). Through the actions of creation, separation, and naming, God creates contraries (light is "not" water, earth, or vegetation) which can be referred to as adversatives (light is not water "but" light). Creating a dome, God separates waters above from waters below, and then gathers waters under the sky into one place in relation to dry land (1:6-10). These waters are not opposites (waters/non-waters). Rather, they are contraries differentiated from one another (waters above, waters below, and waters separated from dry land). As God's created world emerges, therefore, the internal dynamics of wisdom discourse emerge, namely identification and differentiation based on opposites (light/non-light) and contraries (waters above, waters below, and waters below separated from dry land) which create contexts for adversatives (not this "but" this). Contraries and adversatives continue to emerge as God creates plants yielding seed and fruit trees that bear fruit with seed in it (1:11-12).

Next God creates lights in the dome of the sky (1:14). On the one hand, these lights create an opposite by separating the day from the night. On the other hand, they create contraries by establishing signs, seasons, days, and years (1:14). God's creation of the sun and moon is grounded in a blend of contrary and hierarchical reasoning: the sun is the greater light to rule the day; the moon is the lesser light to rule the night. This is hierarchical reasoning. This reasoning blends with a system of contraries occupied by the sun, the moon, and the stars (1:16-18). This system extends to living creatures as God differentiates between creatures that come forth from the water, including sea monsters and swarming water creatures, birds that fly across the dome of the sky (1:20-22), and creatures that come forth from the land: cattle, creeping things, wild animals (1:24-26).

When God creates humans, a new feature emerges in the story of creation, namely reasoning by analogy. This reasoning enters in two ways. First, God asserts that humans are somehow "like" God. Humans are not beings who exist simply on their own terms. They are somehow "similar" to God. Second, humans share with the sun, moon, and stars, which are manifestations of light, a position of ruling over things in the created world. Humans are to "have dominion" over the fish of the sea, birds of the air, and every living thing that moves on the earth (Gen 1:28), which is somehow related to the dominion of the sun, moon, and stars over light, darkness, times, seasons, and years. Thus, God creates humans with a function related by analogy both to God and to multiple manifestations of light God created in the world.

Early Christian wisdom discourse extends its reasoning by analogy about humans to reasoning by analogy about many other things in God's created world. Humans are not only like God in certain ways, as in "Be merciful, just as your heavenly Father is merciful" (Luke 6:36), and like the sun, moon, and stars in certain ways, as in "You are the light of the world" (Matt 5:14). Humans are to be good trees who bear good fruit (Matt 6:16-20; Luke 6:43-44). Also, humans can be like ravenous wolves or sheep among wolves, or they may have wisdom like serpents or be innocent like doves (Matt 10:15-16). In other words, the story of creation creates reasoning by analogy that goes forth and multiplies and fills the reasoning within wisdom discourse. Early Christian wisdom rhetorolect exhibits a wide range of reasoning and argumentation by analogy both with God and with phenomena in God's created world. We will see in later chapters how reasoning by analogy even with phenomena beyond the natural order plays a substantive role in other early Christian rhetorolects.

Gen 1 ends with God's blessing of humans (1:28). This introduces "being blessed" into wisdom discourse. God's blessing comes on humans as both a pronouncement that enables them to be fruitful and multiply and a command that directs them to be fruitful and multiply (1:28). Then God adds to this blessing the assertion that humans are to have dominion over fish, birds, and every other living thing on the earth. In addition, God asserts that humans may eat every plant yielding seed on the earth and every tree with seed in its fruit. God gives every green plant for food to every beast of the earth, bird of the air, and everything that creeps on the earth – indeed, everything that has breath of life in it. God differentiates humans from other living beings, however, by asserting that they may have food that either yields seed or has seed in its fruit.

After God blesses humans, God blesses the seventh day and makes it holy (2:3). Why? What is special about this seventh day? The presentation of this blessing creates the opportunity for the one and only rationale in the account of the creation story that ends in Gen 2:4. Rationales appear often in wisdom discourse. It is noticeable that no rationale appears thoughout all of Gen 1. The entire chapter focuses on actions of God interwoven with short narrational comments that what God said happened,[49] and that a succession of days occurred.[50] Gen 2:1-4a presents a conclusion that summarizes the story. Gen 2:1-2 emphasize that God completed what he set out to do (*synetelesthēsan* ... *synetelesen* ...). Then it repetitively emphasizes God's "works" in 2:2-3: (2: his works which he did ... all his works which he did ... 3: all his works, which God had begun to do ...).[51] This construction of the conclusion emphasizes works (deeds: *erga*), emphasizes works that have been "done" (*epoiēsen*), and emphasizes works that have been completed (*synetelesen*). God, then, has

[49] And there was light (1:30); and it was so (1:7, 11, 15, 24, 31).

[50] First day (1:5); second day (1:8); third day (1:13); fourth day (1:19); fifth day (1:23); sixth day (1:31).

[51] 2: *ta erga autou ha epoiēsen* ... *pantōn tōn ergōn autou hōn epoiēsen* ...3: *pantōn tōn ergōn autou hōn ērxato ho theos poiēsai*.

been very active doing deeds that produced good things. What might be "the lesson" here for humans created in the image of God? Might it also be expected that humans will do works that will produce good things? When the seventh day came, God blessed it and made it holy. Why? Because a set of deeds God had set out to do had produced good to a point of completion. When the production of good reaches a state of completion, God can enter into "rest."

Having noticed the emphasis on works done by God which might in some way function by analogy with works humans are expected to do, let us explore the function of light and darkness in Gen 1. The relation of light to darkness in Gen 1 functions by analogy to humans in wisdom discourse, as well as to their relation to what is good and not good. As it says in Luke 11:35-36: "Therefore consider whether the light in you is not darkness. If then your whole body is full of light, with no part of it in darkness, it will be as full of light as when a lamp gives you light with its rays." According to wisdom discourse, it is important for humans to see the difference between light and darkness, and they must also learn to distinguish between what is good and not good, since these distinctions underlie all that God did during the creation of the world. This leads us to God's relation to light and darkness.

In Gen 1, there is a decisive difference between God's power over light and God's power over darkness. God creates the light but not the darkness. Darkness was already in the cosmos, covering the face of the deep (1:2). God commands light, light does what God tells it to do, and God evaluates light as good (1:4). Not so with darkness. Darkness is already there. God does not command it. First, God separates the light from the darkness (1:4). Second, God names the darkness night (1:5). In other words, God's actions with darkness exhibit a limit that God's actions do not have with light. God does not change darkness into something different, nor does God command darkness to produce something. Rather, God names darkness as something to be distinguished from light. Darkness is visible as a result of the creation of light. When darkness becomes visible, it becomes distinguishable from other things. God names the darkness night and the light day. God not only evaluates light as good (1:4), but God evaluates the separation of light from darkness as good (1:18). God does not differentiate things from one another in the darkness, nor does God create anything out of darkness. Is it possible that God does not deal more directly and decisively with darkness, because God is not able to do so?

A fundamental issue for wisdom discourse is the nature of darkness. In Gen 1, which is a primary resource for the pictures and reasoning in wisdom discourse, God does not see darkness as good, but God does not name darkness evil. Darkness simply is part of the cosmos. Darkness is a place where God creates light. Once God creates light, the natural goodness of light is visible, and its separation from darkness is good. Some interpreters associate darkness in Gen 1 with chaos. It is not clear that this is the best term to describe the darkness in Gen 1. Gen 1:2 associates darkness with formlessness, a mixing of things that does not allow one thing to be distinguished from another. Gen 1:2 also associates this formlessness with deep waters. Is this chaos? It depends on what one means by chaos. The emphasis, again, appears to lie on formlessness, something that is all mixed together so it has no distinctive quality and nature. It is not clear what lurks in the darkness, except water. While it is possible that the deep waters contain chaos, the story in Gen 1 emphasizes that the waters contain earth, and both water and earth can bring forth creatures.

After Gen 1:1-5 focuses on the creation of light, Gen 1:6-10 focuses on water. God does not create water, just like God does not create darkness. In contrast to darkness, which God simply separated from light, God restrains water to two major places and starts to do things with it. First, God creates a dome to restrain water. This dome separates the waters above the sky from the waters below the sky (1:6-8). Here one sees reasoning from contraries. The waters above the sky stand in a contrary relation to the waters under the sky. Second, God commands the waters under the earth to gather into one place (1:9). This means that waters under the earth be in places of relation to land and possibly to other things. There are many contraries with water. The opposite of water is not clear from the creation story. Rather, the alternatives to water are earth, dry land, air, sky, and wind. The opposite of light is darkness, and the opposite of darkness is light. In contrast, the waters, and most other things in God's created world, are contraries rather than opposites (e.g., fish are not horses, but this does not make them the opposite of horses, but a contrary of horses).

God limits the power of the waters above the sky by creating a force against them, but God does not establish dominion over them by commanding them to do something. The narration says God's action of creating the dome is successful (1:7), but it does not say that God sees this restraint of the waters on its own as decisively good. After creating the dome that establishes a separation between waters above the sky and waters under the sky, God commands the waters under the sky and they obey (1:9). God's command of these waters allows dry land to appear (1:9), and this dry land is the source of every living plant and animal on earth (1:11-25). One of the things that lurks unseen in the water, therefore, is dry land! When God establishes control over the waters under the sky, which allows the dry land in the waters to appear, the narration tells the reader that God sees the result as good (1:10).

There is a dramatic shift in the process of creation at Gen 1:11 when God commands the earth to put forth vegetation that yields seed and fruit. Up to this point, the acts of creation have separated light from darkness, waters from waters, and seas from dry land. Beginning in Gen 1:11, the things God has created begin themselves to participate in the process of creation by producing new things. In other words, Gen 1 exhibits a remarkable sequence from God's commands for things to come into existence to God's commands for things to themselves become productive. Herein lies the basic dynamic of wisdom discourse. Wisdom discourse concerns the nurturing and productivity of life and goodness on the earth. The beginning of all things good is God's creation of light (1:3). This begins a process of creating, separating, and naming that reaches a stage where God commands the things he has created to produce new things, and then God commands those things to be fruitful and multiply. The entire movement of the narrative, then, is toward productivity, fruitfulness; and there is a sequence from the creating activity of God to the creating activity of things God has created. In the biblical story of creation, therefore, God transmits to created things themselves God's own, divine ability to create. In turn, all of this creative, productive ability is part of the inner fabric of wisdom discourse, which focuses on God's production of goodness and righteousness, and on God's transmitting of the ability to produce goodness and righteousness to the things and humans God created in the world.

When the earth produces vegetation of all kinds, the discourse introduces the concept both of plants yielding seed and of plants bearing fruit with seed in it (1:11-12). In other words, at this point the productivity of creation focuses on the perpetuation of species through seed. To create this environment, God establishes lights in multiple manifestations and forms throughout the created world. God creates lights in the dome of the sky, the two great lights, plus the stars to "rule over" day and night and to separate light from darkness (1:14-18). This episode introduces yet another topos, "ruling over": various forms of light rule over the day and the night, they separate all seasons and days and years from one another, and they give light upon the earth. Various forms of light, which emerge ultimately from God's speech that creates light, rule over all time in God's created world. As wisdom tradition develops interactively with God's speech and with light, various forms of speech from God and from people become authoritative. This means that, at various times throughout history, speech from God comes into the world in various forms and through various people to "rule." This "ruling" activity of God sometimes brings blessing and sometimes brings punishment. As we will see in the next chapter, this aspect of wisdom discourse bridges to prophetic discourse, which features special wisdom about God's will that God transmits to special people with the task of confronting certain people with this information. When God sees, in the creation story, how the lights govern over day, night, and all the times and seasons on the earth, God sees that it is good (1:18). Through the lights, God rules over all times, seasons, and places on the earth. When wisdom tradition blends the conceptuality of God's light with God's wisdom, then God's wisdom, in the various forms in which it comes into the world, also rules over all times, seasons, and places on the earth.

After God creates the lights in the dome of the sky, God commands the waters under the sky to bring forth swarms of living creatures, and the waters create every living thing that moves (1:20). Then God commands the earth to put forth living creatures of every kind, and it does (1:24). The narration interprets these acts of productivity by the waters and by the earth as God's acts of creating (1:21, 25). Yet this productivity is different from God's creation of the light and the dome, because both the waters and the earth not only do something in response to God's command, but they themselves produce things different from themselves. Both the waters and the earth become producers of creation, in contrast to light, which creates the context for productivity but does not itself produce things directly out of itself. Light, as a manifestation of God's speech, goes where God tells it to go, does what God tells it to do, and takes the forms God tells it to take. By this means, light enables the waters and the earth to produce created things. And God sees, with the aid of light, that this is good (1:25).

In the context of the creation of living creatures, a new feature emerges in the biblical story: God blesses the living creatures in the waters and the sky (1:22). God's blessing takes the form of a command to be productive. God tells them to be fruitful, like God tells the earth to put forth vegetation (1:11), and the waters (1:20) and the earth (1:24) to bring forth living creatures. Then God's blessing tells the living creatures to "multiply" (1:22). In other words, they are to produce "more of their own kind," rather than something different from themselves. The blessing to the sea creatures is to "be fruitful and multiply and fill" the waters in the seas (1:22). This commands not only the fruitfulness already associated with plants and earth creatures, but also a process of "filling" a region of God's created world. While previous commands caused something to come into being for a specific purpose, to go somewhere in the created world for a specific purpose, or to produce something in a form different from itself for a specific purpose, the commands associated with "blessing" concern the production of large numbers of "one's own kind" and to sea creatures the command includes filling an entire region of God's created world with their kind. As wisdom discourse emerges out of the biblical story of creation, it contains an internal challenge to be fruitful and multiply and fill the earth. By analogy to God's blessing that enables and commands productivity of its own kind, wisdom discourse enables and commands productivity of good for the purpose of filling the earth with goodness and light, which means filling the earth with wisdom that produces more goodness and wisdom.

It is noticeable that God does not bless the living creatures the earth produces (1:24-25). Rather, God commands the earth to produce living creatures (1:24) and leaves the earth creatures without blessing, just like God commands the earth to bring forth vegetation (1:11) and does not bless the vegetation. There is no blessing of the living creatures on earth, no command that they be fruitful and multiply, and no command that they fill the earth. Instead, the story moves directly forward to the creation of humankind. Will other things emerge whom God will bless? If so, what will be the content of the blessing? Will things besides the earth (1:11-12, 24), the waters (1:20), and living creatures in the waters and the sky (1:22) become producers of created things through God's commands? The reader can only anticipate what will happen next.

After the waters and the earth produce living things of every kind, God speaks a command to create humankind "according to our likeness" (1:26).[52] One of the roles of humankind will be to share a position analogous to the two greater lights in the dome of the sky that "rule over the day and the night," and "separate the light from the darkness" (1:18). Humankind shall "have dominion over the fish of the sea, and over the birds of the air, and over the cattle, and over all the wild animals of the earth, and over every creeping thing that creeps upon the earth" (1:26). In other words, humankind is to rule over every "living creature" in a manner somehow analogous to the rule of the "two greater lights" over the day and the night (1:18). Will humankind also "separate" living creatures as the two greater lights separate the day from the night (1:14, 18)? The answer will be that humankind will separate living creatures both by naming them and by distinguishing between clean and unclean among them. In addition, humankind will be responsible for separating light from darkness, namely to distinguish between that which is good and that which is not good.[53]

Immediately after creating humankind, God blesses them (1:28). The blessing is like the blessing to the creatures in the waters: "Be fruitful and multiply and fill" (1:22). In other words, instead of commanding the living creatures produced by the earth to fill the earth (cf. 1:24-25), God

[52] God's command to create humankind "in our image" (1:26) is a very important topic, upon which we must not linger in this context. When humankind is created male and female (1:27), this exhibits deep insight into the nature of God and God's creation as an intermingling of male and female modes of productivity.

[53] At this point in the story, "that which is not good" is not yet named "evil."

commands humankind to fill the earth. So far, we see analogy at five major points in the biblical story. First, as the two greater lights in the dome of the sky rule over the day and the night under the sky, so humankind rules over all living creatures under the sky. As the task is important, so is the sphere in which the task is performed. The two greater lights are expected to rule only in the sphere under the sky, not over all of God's domain. Likewise, humankind is to rule only in the sphere under the sky, and not over all heaven and earth. Second, as other living creatures are to multiply, so humankind is to multiply. Third, as vegetation (1:11-12) and sea creatures (1:22) are to bear fruit, so is humankind (1:28). Fourth, as creatures in the sea and birds of the air are blessed by God, so is humankind. Fifth, as sea creatures are to fill the domain in which they live, so humans are to fill the earth.

By this point in the story, a person sees various analogies and contraries, and a primary opposite, light and darkness. Also, a person sees certain things valued as good or blessed, while other things are not. Once this range of "wisdom reasoning" begins, it reverberates throughout every sphere that comes within the purview of wisdom thought and discourse. This means that, in certain ways, wisdom discourse pervades every other form of discourse. The power of wisdom discourse is to correlate by analogy, opposite, contrary, and valuation almost every aspect of the spheres it blends together.

There is yet another command from God in Gen 1. In addition to having "dominion" over the fish of the sea, birds of the air, and every living thing that moves upon the earth, humankind is to "subdue" the earth (1:28). In turn, God gives "every plant yielding seed" and "every tree with seed in its fruit" to humankind for food (1:29). Also, God gives "every green plant for food" to every beast of the earth, every bird of the air, everything that creeps on the earth, "everything that has the breath of life" (1:30). All vegetation, then, is meant to be food for the living creatures, including humankind, in God's world. Perhaps this is the reason God does not bless the vegetation, and perhaps this is the reason humans should bless vegetation before they eat it. In addition, there appears to be an emphasis in Gen 1-3 that, while "vegetation" is for all living creatures, seed-bearing and fruit-bearing plants are especially for humankind. Thus, just as humankind is to be seed-bearing and fruit-bearing, so the food of humankind is seed-bearing and fruit-bearing.

In Gen 1:27, God creates humans in the "image" of God. God can create humans in the image of God only if there is light that allows an image to appear. In other words, creation of humans in God's image presupposes an intimate relation between God and light. If there is light within God, an image of God may somehow be "visible," which could enable God to create humankind in God's image. But God does more than this. Through God's acts of creation, God makes light external to God. Light becomes a force that rules over night and day and creates the context for productivity in the world. God creates light in multiple forms through a series of actions of separation. Then God creates humans in the image of God. What can be the implications of being created in the image of God in Gen 1? Are humans able to create light in multiple forms? If so, what are the forms of this light?

As wisdom discourse unfolds in biblical tradition, it expands the focus beyond the specific episode of God's creation of humans in Gen 1:26-29 to the entire creation story that includes Gen 2-3, and finally to the story of God's interaction with humankind throughout history. From the perspective of wisdom discourse, God invites humans to be co-creators of light in the world by speaking it to others, by thinking it, by memorizing it, and by acting it out in a manner that allows others to "see that it is good." In other words, in the human realm speech, thought, memory, and action become light that nurtures people in the production of goodness. God is the subject of action twenty-four times in Gen 1 prior to God's action of creating humans in 1:26. To be created in the image of God is to be created as a being who commands, separates, and names things in the created world. These actions create a context for productivity in the world. The major fruitfulness humans are to produce is "that which is good." Humans are to "see" how God creates and they are to create in a similar manner. In other words, the narrative itself produces a sequence that hearers are to envision in their minds and imitate. Humans are to use speech to create light, separate things, and name things; use their eyes and minds to identify and evaluate that which is good, and use their mouths to command those things which are created to participate in creation and be productive. As we will see below, when humans create and produce that which God sees as good, wisdom discourse calls them trees that bear good fruit. In fact, they become trees of life.

But before we move to exhortations that people become trees of life, we must be aware that there is more to the creation story than we have analyzed thus far. The story of creation moves to God's creation of wisdom on earth in Gen 2-3. This occurs through a puzzling, problematic, and troubling sequence of events that starts with Gen 2:9:

> Out of the ground the Lord God made to grow every tree that is pleasant to the sight (*hōraion eis horasin*) and good (*kalon*) for food, the tree of life also in the midst of the garden, and the tree of the knowledge (*gnōston*) of good (*kalou*) and evil (*ponērou*).

This verse blends together sight, that which is good for food, life, and the knowledge of good and evil. Seeing, eating, nurturing or attaining life, and the ability to distinguish between good and evil all emerge out of the ground! In other words, the productivity of the earth (*hē gē*) that focuses on "bringing forth life" in 1:24, moves in Gen 2-3 toward productivity out of the earth (*ek tēs gēs*) that "brings forth wisdom," namely the knowledge of good and evil. In other words, God caused "wisdom itself" and "life itself" to grow out of the earth! This wisdom was not only visible but was "pleasant to the sight," not only good but "good for food," and did not only bring forth life but brought forth the knowledge of good and evil. Even though God "taught" the man that the tree was the "food" of the knowledge of good and evil (2:17),[54] the man could not "picture" the knowledge of good and evil in his mind. In other words, neither the man nor the woman could actually "know" the good and evil in the tree, because they could not "see" it. In contrast to God, who "knows" good immediately when God sees it, humans cannot immediately create a picture of good and evil in their minds that gives them the ability to distinguish between good and evil. In humans, this ability needs to be "cultivated": planted, watered, and nurtured into mature wisdom. In other words, when God created humans in the image of God, there was not a complete transference of the ability to see and know. Therefore, when the serpent asked the woman about the tree, she only knew that it was a tree "in the middle of the garden" (3:3). Her "picture" of the tree did not include the "(in)sight" that it was the tree of "the knowledge of good and evil"! The serpent, however, had a cleverness that "knew" it. The serpent taught the woman that the fruit of the tree would "open her eyes" so she could be "like God, knowing good and evil" (3:5). She learned a cleverness that brought a certain level of "sight inside her." This cleverness allowed her to "see" the knowledge of good and evil, but, as we will see below, it did not actually allow her to attain God's level of the knowledge of good and evil.

Here is a remarkable story of the birth of wisdom and the nature of it! Wisdom concerns the nurturing of life and the ability to see what is good and evil as one is nurturing life. Once the serpent had "taught" the woman, she was able to "see" that the tree was not only good for food and a delight to the eyes, but it "was to be desired to make one wise (*tou katanoēsai*)." But she still had to "take it in." This is exactly what she did. The woman took some of the fruit (*karpou*) and ate it, and gave some also to the man, who ate it (3:6), and their "eyes" were opened and they "knew" (*egnōsan*). What they knew, we all know, was that they were naked. And this is the usual focus of interpretation. What we must not miss is the attaining of wisdom through fruit from the earth that nurtures both life and knowledge. But we also must not miss the emphasis that "wisdom" is not only hard to see, but once one sees it it readily leads to desire which one shares with others and which creates great problems for

[54] God taught this to the man like a parent teaches a child that a stove is hot by saying, "Do not touch that hot stove because it will badly burn you"!

humans in the world. Wisdom, then, is a very puzzling, problematic thing. Though it comes from the same source as life itself, it not only leads to life but to desire, curse, and death! It is a "special" thing humans have as a result of "being like God," but this special attribute is an incredible burden to bear!

Once we are clear that wisdom is attained through the fruit of the earth, that it must be "seen," and that it is very problematic, it is important to turn to the opposites, contraries, and hierarchies in Gen 2–3. In the context of the story in Gen 3, good and evil emerge as opposites in the midst of informative contraries and hierarchies. The serpent is the "most crafty" (*phronimōtatos*) of all wild animals (3:1), a certain kind of hierarchy of wisdom. The serpent offers the woman the possibility of having knowledge like God, which surely is a form of knowledge even higher than the serpent's. The source of this knowledge lies in the midst of contrary kinds of fruit in the garden: (1) the fruit of trees all around in the garden; (2) the fruit of the tree of the knowledge of good and evil; and (3) the fruit of the tree of life. The man and woman can eat of the fruit of the trees all around in the garden (2:16; 3:2). But they must not eat of the tree of the knowledge of good and evil in the middle of the garden (2:17; 3:3); because, if they do, the Lord God is concerned that they will also eat from the tree of life and live forever (3:22). The fruit the humans can eat, then, is "undifferentiated fruit." This fruit is all around in the garden. One can imagine that as the humans ate it, they might begin to see differences and give different names to different kinds of fruit, like the man gave names to the animals God brought before him (2:19-20). The fruit the humans must not eat is differentiated by God, and both fruits introduce opposites. First, there is the fruit of the knowledge of good and evil (2:17; 3:6). Second, there is the fruit of the tree of life, which introduces the opposites of living forever (3:22) or dying (2:17; 3:3).

The presence of the two differentiated trees in Gen 2–3 introduces contrary knowledges: (1) knowledge of good and evil; and (2) knowledge of eternal life and death. The serpent focuses on the knowledge of good and evil, asserting to the woman that she would live in a world of analogy with God, namely she would be like God, if she has "knowledge" based on the opposites of good and evil. The opposites of good and evil, then, would bring benefit to humans rather than harm. Focusing on good and evil, the serpent caused the woman to see "the good" of eating from the tree. The tree was not only good for food, and good for the eyes to see ("a delight"), but it would make a person wise (3:6). The woman accepted the serpent's focus, ate of the fruit, and also gave some of the fruit to her husband to eat. The Lord God presents an alternative set of opposites as a result of the eating. In the Lord God's view, when humans attain the knowledge of good and evil, which makes them like God, they will try to eat from the tree of life and live forever (3:22). Instead of focusing only on the means by which humans become like God, namely knowledge of good and evil, the Lord God focuses on the ability of humans to bypass God's control of their life and death by eating of the tree of life.

Focusing on life and death rather than on good and evil, the Lord God prevents the man from eating of the tree of life and living forever by driving him out of the garden "to till the ground from which he was taken" (3:23). While God and God's creation provide humans the means to distinguish between good and evil, God retains dominion over life and death. Humans must cultivate the ground to produce an ongoing source of life. In this context, they have wisdom, the knowledge of good and evil which God has given them through the processes and products of creation. But they do not have the means to attain eternal life. They must focus on life, working continually to sustain life from day to day. They only know life, however, as an opposite to death, like light is related to darkness. Humans have all kinds of differentiated knowledge about life on earth, much like light is present in differentiated manifestations in God's created world. This differentiated knowledge is the inner content of their wisdom. Death, however, is undifferentiated in wisdom primarily as an opposite to life. Like darkness in wisdom discourse, death is not a place to create, to be productive. Rather, the knowledge of death in wisdom discourse is that it is not life. It is an opposite of life, rather than a differentiated conceptual arena which is a resource for creativity and productivity of the good. We will see that prophetic and apocalyptic discourse dramatically change the conceptual arena of death, and thus the conceptual arena of darkness, making both death and darkness highly differentiated arenas that invite significantly new resources and significantly different actions by God. In wisdom discourse, humans have an ongoing responsibility to be "productive" of the resources of life, growth, and well-being. In this context, they attain significant knowledge of evil and death as opposites of good and life. But the focus is on multiple ways of nurturing life and producing good toward the goal of a life of well-being in God's created world.

It is now time to turn to the topic of nakedness in the story of creation, which is a central topic of traditional discussion even though it occupies only a few verses in the story. When the man and woman eat of the tree of the knowledge of good and evil, their eyes are opened, they "know" (*egnōsan*) they are naked, and they cover themselves with fig leaves they sew together as loincloths (3:7). Why do the man and woman cover their nakedness? Do they cover it as a result of shame in the presence of one another? Is it to be understood as "modesty" rather than shame? The text does not say. When the Lord God walks through the garden, the man and the woman are afraid, "because they are naked" (3:10). Why does their nakedness cause them fear in the presence of the Lord God? What is the nature of this fear and its relation to good and evil? Is this a clue concerning another difference between humans and God? Do humans alone have shame and fear. Do shame and fear emerge first and foremost in a context of differentiation between males and females among humans, or does it emerge primarily in the relation of differentiated humans to God? Young children are not born with shame and fear over their nakedness. This is "knowledge" their parents and others teach them. And there is special shame and fear in the context of different genders of humans. Women have less fear and shame of nakedness in the context of other women, and men have less shame and fear of nakedness in the context of other men. But men and women are "expected" to have shame of their nakedness in the presence of one another except when they are married! Does God have ways of dealing with nakedness that do not produce shame or fear in God? The text raises many questions without giving answers. Wisdom discourse wrestles deeply with the relation of women and men to one another, and with the relation of the differentiation between women and men to God. This chapter on wisdom discourse will not present significant answers to the questions that emerge from this part of the story of God's creation of the world and the living beings in it. It has been considered important to identify some of the questions the story raises, but it will be necessary for the reader to look elsewhere for substantive exploration of these issues.[55]

Gen 3:14-19 presents a remarkable sequence of events after the man and the woman attain the knowledge of good and evil, which brings a recognition of their nakedness. First they see the Lord God curse the serpent; second the woman experiences an assertion from God that she will have increased pain in childbearing and a lesser status in relation to her husband; and third the man experiences God cursing the ground from which he must now grow food and asserting that the man must toil continually to produce food until he returns to the dust of the earth from which he was produced. Christian discourse has some very interesting ways to interpret this part of the story. We will pursue only some of these ways in this chapter.

To understand the inner nature of wisdom discourse, it is important to know that there are ways humans are like God in addition to their knowing good and evil! We recall, for instance, that in Gen 2:19 the Lord God allows the man to name every living creature. God brings every living creature before the man, "to see what he would call it." In

[55] For a significant discussion of many of the issues, see Robert von Thaden, "Fleeing *Porneia*: 1 Corinthians 6:12–7:7 and the Reconfiguration of Traditions," Ph.D. dissertation, Emory University, 2007.

other words, the man "sees" it and calls it a name, and God "sees" what the man calls it, and that is its name (2:19-20). The Lord God invites the man "to see" and "to name" the things God has made, just as God has seen and named all things from the beginning of the story. It is important to notice the "seeing." The visibility of things makes it possible for both God and humans to "know" things in such a way that they can distinguish one thing from another. The ability to see things is the foundational premise for wisdom. But seeing things is not enough. One must be able to see, to distinguish, to name, and then to live out the knowledge this seeing, distinguishing, and naming brings.

The nature of wisdom, according to the biblical story, is incredibly complex. One not only learns it from others, but it somehow comes from the ground from which we ourselves come and which produces the food that nurtures our life. Wisdom, then, lies at the very source of our lives and the nurturing of our lives. We will see below that both the Moses story and the proverbs of Solomon "domesticate" the location of wisdom, namely they relocate the story from the Garden of Eden to the family household. But the story never loses touch with God's created world. The special power of wisdom discourse lies in the manner in which it evokes Firstspace images of the household in which a person was born, nurtured, and raised, blends the space of the household with the Secondspace of God's created world, and then transports this blended space into the Thirdspace of the intersubjective body of every person on earth.

Torah Wisdom: Deuteronomy 5–8 as the Teachings of Moses

After the story-line of Christian wisdom rhetorolect begins with God creating the world and Adam and Eve eating fruit from the tree of the knowledge of good and evil, it continues with Moses. The book of Deuteronomy in the Hebrew Bible is a special resource for early Christian wisdom rhetorolect, since it presents "the words that Moses spoke to all Israel" (Deut 1:1). From the perspective of early Christian discourse, then, Deuteronomy is a book of the wisdom of Moses.

Early Christian wisdom rhetorolect as it appears in the New Testament selects and reconfigures the ten commandments especially as they function in the broader context of Deuteronomy. Regularly, interpreters give the primary reference for these commandments as Exodus 20. It is important, however, to look first in the context in Deuteronomy, second in Leviticus 19, and thirdly in the application of Torah in prophetic literature to interpret the meanings of the ten commandments in early Christian wisdom rhetorolect. The range of interest in early Christian wisdom rhetorolect focuses primarily on six of the ten commandments in the Decalogue. These six commandments appear as follows in Deut 5:16-21 (cf. Exod 20:12-17):

> [Moses said,] "Honor your father and your mother, as the LORD your God commanded you, so that your days may be long and that it may go well with you in the land that the LORD your God is giving you.[56]
> 17 You shall not murder.
> 18 Neither shall you commit adultery.
> 19 Neither shall you steal.
> 20 Neither shall you bear false witness against your neighbor.
> 21 Neither shall you desire[57] your neighbor's wife.
> Neither shall you desire your neighbor's house, or field, or male or female slave, or ox, or donkey, or anything that belongs to your neighbor.[58]

The synoptic Gospels portray various contexts where selections from God's commandments to Israel as presented in Deuteronomy play a substantive role.[59] In Mark 10:17-22/Matt 19:16-22/Luke 18:18-23, Jesus recites five or six commandments to a man who addresses Jesus either as "teacher" (Matt 19:16) or "good teacher" (Mark 10:17/Luke 18:18) and asks him what he must do to inherit[60] eternal life. In Luke 18:18, Jesus responds by reciting five commandments, placing adultery at the head of the list and honoring father and mother at the end, with murder, theft, and false witness in the middle. Mark 10:19 features Jesus responding with six commandments, placing murder at the beginning of the list and honoring father and mother at the end, with "do not defraud" (Lev 19:13) between the final commandment and commandments about adultery, theft, and false witness. In turn, Matt 19:18-19 also portrays Jesus reciting six commandments, but in a different way from Mark 10:19. Like Mark 10:19, Matt 19:18 features Jesus beginning with the commandment against murder and continuing with adultery, theft, and false witness.[61] Like Luke 18:20, Matt 19:18 does not contain "do not defraud," which is not in Deut 5.[62] After the commandment to honor one's father and mother, however, Matt 19:19 adds, "and love your neighbor as

[56] A shorter form of this commandment, which exists in the MT of Exodus 20:12, was expanded to read the same as Deut 5:16 in the LXX. It is very possible that this expansion was the result of early Christian usage of the LXX.

[57] Regularly translated "covet."

[58] The NRSV translates Exod 20:17 as: "You shall not desire your neighbor's house; you shall not desire your neighbor's wife, or male or female slave, or ox, or donkey, or anything that belongs to your neighbor." For a detailed discussion of the variations in Exodus and Deuteronomy, and in various Hebrew and Greek manuscripts, see William Loader, *The Septuagint, Sexuality, and the New Testament: Case Studies on the Impact of the LXX in Philo and the New Testament* (Grand Rapids/Cambridge, U.K.: Eerdmans, 2004) 8-11.

[59] See Loader, *The Septuagint, Sexuality, and the New Testament,* 5-9, 15-19 for a detailed account of the special influences of Deuteronomy on Jewish and Christian tradition.

[60] Or "have" (Matt 19:16).

[61] Matt 5 also features Jesus addressing commandments in the Decalogue in the order of murder (5:21), then adultery (5:27).

[62] See Deut 24:14; cf. Jas 5:4.

yourself," which is an abbreviation of Lev 19:18. Thus, the Matthean version, in contrast to Mark and Luke, ends with a focus on the man's relation to his neighbor rather than to his father and mother.

The differences arise from a shift of focus on the household, where a child learns Torah wisdom, to one's relation to neighbors, where an adult has the responsibility to live according to Torah wisdom. Mark 10:17-22 and Luke 18:18-23 exhibit a focus on doing what your mother and father have taught you. The basis for this lies in Deut 6:6-7:

> Keep these words that I am commanding you today in your heart. [7] Recite them to your children and talk about them when you are at home and when you are away, when you lie down and when you rise.

Mothers and fathers are expected to teach their children how to live properly in the world. The beginning "household era" of every person's life grounds wisdom discourse in primary, elemental knowledge every person learns during the initial years of time on earth. When the man asks Jesus what he must do to inherit eternal life, Jesus recites six commandments to him in an order that places "Honor your father and mother" in emphatic final position (10:19). The effect is to say: Do these five commandments to fulfill what you were taught by your father and mother! The text directly exhibits this effect. The man says, "Teacher, I have kept all these since my youth." In other words, he says that he has properly learned and done what his parents taught him! This focus on the household is noticeable even in the broader context of Mark 9:33–10:31, with its emphasis on the house in 9:33, the little child in 9:36-37, the little ones in 9:42, marriage and divorce in 10:2-12,[63] the little children in 10:13-16, Jesus' address to his disciples as children in 10:24, and Jesus' discussion of house, brothers, sisters, mothers, fathers, and fields in 10:29-30. Likewise, Luke 18:18-23, which proceeds in the same manner as Mark 10:17-22 with the same effect, is preceded by a discussion of infants in Luke 18:15-17 and followed by a discussion of homes, wife, brothers, parents, and children in 18:28-30.

A similar focus on the household teaching of Torah is present in Mark 7:9-13/Matt 15:3-5, where Jesus responds to Pharisees and scribes about eating with defiled hands. When Jesus speaks about "rejecting" the commandments, the topic is "honoring your father and mother." When the emphasis on father and mother is emphasized in early Christian wisdom rhetorolect, it can be natural to add the statement of Torah wisdom in Exod 21:16: "Whoever speaks evil of father or mother will surely die" (Exod 21:16 LXX).[64] The effect is that whoever does not do what their

[63] Notice how Jesus' discussion of divorce occurs "in the house" (10:10).

[64] It is important to notice that Jesus does not recite Torah "law" here, but Torah "wisdom." Torah law about this is found in Lev 20:9: "All who curse father or mother shall be put to death; having cursed father or mother, their blood is upon them."

parents taught them to do acts in a manner that speaks evil against, or even curses, one's father and mother. Mark 7:11-13/Matt 15:3-5 develop this reasoning toward a context where sons are engaging in action of "fulfilling Torah" through Corban, a special gift to God, in a manner that directly avoids honoring one's parents through financial support. They give a gift to God for the specific purpose of avoiding their responsibilities for their parents. Jesus calls this a way of making void "the word of God," which their parents taught them from their youth. The issue is whether they follow Torah as it came to them from their parents or Torah that is coming to them from adults who are devising ways to avoid responsibility for the well-being of their parents.

A similar focus is also present in Eph 6:1-3, which recites Deut 5:16 in the context of guiding children to obey their parents "in the Lord." The narrator supports the reasoning that people should honor their father and mother with a rationale that "this is right (just: *dikaios*)." In other words, having been born, nurtured, and raised by one's parents, it is only "just" to honor them. If a person honors them, that person receives a promise that it may be well with them and they may live long on the earth (Eph 6:3/Deut 5:16).

The version of Jesus' recitation of the commandments in Matt 19:16-22 exhibits the shift from an emphasis on the household, where one initially learns Torah, to the adult world where one's relation to one's neighbors is the primary issue in early Christian wisdom rhetorolect. In Matt 19:19, Jesus does not end his rehearsal of the commandments with "Honor your father and mother," but with: "Also, you shall love your neighbor as yourself." This calls forth a different response from the man. Instead of saying, "Teacher, I have kept all these things from my youth" (Mark 10:20/Luke 18:21), in Matt 19:20 the man says, "I have kept all these: what do I still lack?" The emphasis is on what the man has accomplished as an adult, rather than on the manner in which his actions have honored his father and his mother from his youth. Now, honoring his father and mother is simply one among other things he must do to fulfill his adult responsibilities. In other words, his parents essentially become like neighbors, whom he must love as himself. And if his parents are no longer alive, he must learn to embody the honor he had for them during their lifetime in selfless actions toward his neighbors. At this point, Jesus refers to "completion" (often translated "perfection") of the man's keeping of the commandments. The commandments Jesus recites can be completed by transferring the focus from obtaining the possessions the man has received through his parents, both during their lifetime and after their deaths, to "love" in the adult world in which one lives in relation to one's neighbors. The "completion" of the Torah one has learned in the household, then, must occur in the world of the adult person, namely the world of "neighbors" in which adults live.

The focus on neighbors in Matt 19:16-22 is developed in additional ways in Matt 5:43-48. Living as an adult in relation to Torah wisdom is not a matter of loving one's neighbor and hating one's enemy (Matt 5:43). Rather, one must love one's enemies and pray for those who persecute you. The effect of this is to move one's allegiance from one's household father, the context in which one was born and raised, to "the Father in heaven" (Matt 5:45), in the created world in which one lives as an adult. This shift is grounded in the Shema, which occurs in Deut 6:4-5:

> Hear, O Israel: The LORD is our God, the LORD alone. [5]You shall love the LORD your God with all your heart, and with all your soul, and with all your might. [6]Keep these words that I am commanding you today in your heart.

After their youth, the time when people are children of their earthly father, people must become during their adult life "children of their Father in heaven" (Matt 5:45). In Matthew the "fulfillment" of one's honoring of father and mother occurs in one's acceptance, during their adult life, of their "heavenly Father." If one greets only the brothers and sisters who are their kinfolk from the household of their childhood, one is not fulfilling one's responsibility to Torah wisdom. Even the Gentiles greet their brothers and sisters (Matt 5:47)! The completion of Torah wisdom must occur in God's wide-reaching created world, which is populated not only by Gentiles but also by enemies and people who persecute you. Here one must "complete" the goals of Torah wisdom, namely one must live in a relation of love to one's "neighbors," a relation God "completes" through blessings like forgiving those who forgive others (Matt 6:14) and giving to everyone who asks (Matt 7:8). God's relation to the created world is "complete" (perfect) in God's actions of "making his sun rise on the evil and on the good, and sends rain on the righteous and on the unrighteous" (Matt 5:45). Adults who live according to Torah wisdom in God's created world must also bring their actions to completion (perfection) by loving their enemies and by praying for those who persecute them (Matt 5:44, 48).

The completion of an adult life according to Torah wisdom becomes fully expressed in early Christian wisdom rhetorolect in Romans 12:9–13:10. Beginning with "Let love be genuine; hate what is evil, hold fast to what is good; love one another with mutual affection; outdo one another in showing honor" (12:9-10), it explores multiple aspects of "living with one's neighbor" until it concludes with:

> Owe no one anything, except to love one another; for the one who loves another has fulfilled the law. [9]The commandments, "You shall not commit adultery; You shall not murder; You shall not steal; You shall

> not covet"; and any other commandment, are summed up in this word, "Love your neighbor as yourself." [10] Love does no wrong to a neighbor; therefore, love is the fulfilling of the law. (Rom 13:8-10)

The conclusion recites four commandments of the Decalogue and "Love your neighbor as yourself" (Lev 19:18), which "sums up" (*anakephalaioutai*) the law (Rom 13:9). The first three commandments occur in the order in which Jesus begins the list of commandments to the man in Luke 18:20: one must not commit adultery, murder, or theft. Rom 13:9, however, does not contain a commandment against false witness or fraud, nor does it contain an exhortation to honor one's father and mother, all of which occur in one or another of the synoptic stories. Rather Rom 13:9 contains "Do not desire (covet)" (Deut 5:21/Exod 20:17) at the end of the list as a transition to "Love your neighbor as yourself" (13:9).

Paul's inclusion of the command, "Do not desire (*epithymēseis*)," is the "tip of an iceberg" in Pauline discourse, and indeed in early Christian discourse more broadly.[65] Either some form of the verb *epithymeō* or some form of noun (*epithymia*; *epithymētēs*) meaning "desire" occurs twenty-five times in letters attributed to Paul.[66] "Desire" was the emotion-fused thought of the first woman toward the tree that could make one wise in the garden (Gen 3:6). After Paul asserts in Gal 5:14 that the whole law is summed up in "You shall love your neighbor as yourself," he asserts: "Do not gratify (complete: *telesēte*) the desire (*epithymian*) of the flesh, for what the flesh desires is opposed to the Spirit, and what the Spirit desires is opposed to the flesh; for these are opposed (*antikeitai*) to each other, to prevent you from doing what you want" (Gal 5:16b-18). In Paul's way of thinking, "the desire" of the flesh is opposed to "the fruit" of the spirit (Gal 5:22). Paul establishes the desire of the flesh and the fruit of the spirit as opposites, and this creates a context for a long list of contraries on each side. Paul's list of "desires of the flesh" begins with what appears to be a reconfiguration of "Do not desire your neighbor's wife" (Deut 5:21/Exod 20:21), namely "fornication" (Gal 5:19),[67] and continues with impurity, licentiousness, idolatry, sorcery, enmities, strife, jealousy, anger, quarrels, dissensions, factions, envy, drunkenness, and carousing (Gal 5:19-21). The contraries of the fruit of the spirit are: love, joy, peace, patience, kindness, generosity, faithfulness, gentleness, and self-

[65] Kathy L. Gaca, *The Making of Fornication: Eros, Ethics, and Political Reform in Greek Philosophy and Early Christianity* (Berkeley/Los Angeles/London: University of California Press, 2003) 152-94; Loader, *The Septuagint, Sexuality, and the New Testament*, 15-25.

[66] *epithymeō*: Rom 7:7; 13:9; 1 Cor 10:6; Gal 5:17; 1 Tim 3:1; *epithymētēs*: 1 Cor 10:6; *epithymia*: Rom 1:24; 6:12; 7:7, 8; 13:14; Gal 6:16, 24; Eph 2:3; 4:22; Phil 1:23; Col 3:5; 1 Thess 2:17; 4:5; 1 Tim 6:9; 2 Tim 2:22; 3:6; 4:3; Tit 2:12; 3:13.

[67] See Robert von Thaden, "Fleeing *Porneia*."

control (Gal 5:22). Beginning, then, with "Honor your father and mother," early Christian Torah wisdom adopts "Love your neighbor as yourself" as a summary of Torah. Once the focus moves to the neighbor in the context of commandments not to murder, commit adultery, steal, bear false witness, or defraud, attention shifts from "Honor your father and mother" to "Do not desire." Desire then becomes a topos for all kinds of sins. In other words, if "Love your neighbor as yourself" is a positive summary of the law, "Do not desire" becomes a summary of how to avoid sin.[68]

Before turning to a discussion of "desire as the cause of sin," let us notice that the injunction to complete Torah wisdom in the adult world of neighbors is grounded, as noted above, in the content of the Shema that emphasizes "You shall love the LORD your God with all your heart, and with all your soul, and with all your might" (Deut 6:5). This grounding underlies the statement in Rom 12:11 to "serve the Lord" and the reference to "those who love him" in Jas 1:12. Thus, in early Christian wisdom rhetorolect, the focus on the completion of Torah wisdom in the commandment, "Love your neighbor as yourself" (Lev 19:18) is closely related to keeping the words "in your heart" that Moses taught[69] (Deut 6:6). This means that adults should be able at any time to recite the Shema "by heart," as well as other prominent parts of Torah wisdom. The synoptic gospels feature various contexts where people are able to do this.

When a person called a scribe (*grammateus*: Mark 10:28) or a lawyer (*nomikos*: Matt 22:35) comes to Jesus asking him which is the greatest commandment, Jesus recites the Shema. In Mark 12:29-30, Jesus recites it in its entirety in the form:

> Hear, O Israel: the Lord our God, the Lord is one; [30]you shall love the Lord your God with all your heart, and with all your soul, and with all your mind, and with all your strength.

In Matt 22:37, Jesus recites a shorter form that does not include the "Hear, O Israel" verse or the final phrase "with all your strength." Jesus' ability in Mark and Matthew to recite the Shema exhibits to the reader that Jesus has properly memorized it "by heart" and is able to recite it on request or command. Again, this fulfills Deut 6:6-7, which commands:

> Keep these words that I am commanding you today in your heart. Recite them to your children and talk about them when you are at home and when you are away, when you lie down and when you rise.

[68] Gaca, *The Making of Fornication*, 152-57; Loader, *The Septuagint, Sexuality, and the New Testament*, 19-24.

[69] Deut 6:1: *didaxai*.

An alternative approach appears in Luke 10:25-28. When a lawyer comes to Jesus and asks him what he must do to inherit eternal life, Jesus asks him "what is written in the Torah." The man responds with a shortened version, like Jesus' recitation in Matt 22:37, except that it inserts "with all your strength" (cf. Mark 10:30) before "and with all your mind." In Luke 10, then, the emphasis is on the lawyer's ability to recite the Shema, rather than on Jesus' ability to recite it.

There is an additional phenomenon in all the synoptic versions of the story, however. Whether Jesus, the scribe, or the lawyer recites the Shema, the reciter adds the abbreviated version of Lev 19:18 that is well known in early Christian Torah wisdom as "Love your neighbor as yourself." When Jesus recites it, he calls it the "second" greatest commandment (Mark 12:31/Matt 22:39), and he includes the opening phrase, "You shall" (love your neighbor as yourself). When the lawyer recites the shorter version (like Matt 22:36) of the Shema, he includes "and your neighbor as yourself" at the end, as though it were an integral part of Deut 6:5.

The Lukan version of the story, where the lawyer rather than Jesus recites the Shema along with "Love your neighbor as yourself," continues with Jesus' challenge of the lawyer to understand the meaning of the parable of the Good Samaritan. In other words, Jesus challenges his ability to love the Lord God "with all his mind," which is the final phrase the lawyer recites prior to the injunction about the neighbor. After the story in which Jesus tells about a Samaritan who responds to the needs of a "half-dead" man alongside the road, with "all his heart, soul, mind, and strength,"[70] Jesus asks the lawyer, "Which of these three (priest, Levite, Samaritan), do you think, was a neighbor to the man who fell into the hand of robbers?" (Luke 10:36). When the lawyer says, "The one who showed mercy," Jesus says to him, "Go and do likewise" (10:37).

Three things in the Lukan story are important for understanding early Christian wisdom rhetorolect. First, wisdom about how to live properly in the world is grounded in Torah wisdom. Therefore, people must know basic Torah wisdom "by heart" and be able to recite it on proper occasions. Second, it is not enough simply to "know" Torah wisdom and be able to recite it. One must also be willing "to do it." For this reason, Jesus asserts to the lawyer, when he answers the first question correctly about what is written in Torah: "Do this and you will live" (10:28). Then when the lawyer answers Jesus' second question correctly about the people in

[70] See Vernon K. Robbins, "The Sensory-Aesthetic Texture of the Compassionate Samaritan Parable in Luke 10," in *Literary Encounters with the Reign of God* (ed. S.H. Ringe and H.C. Paul Kim; New York/London: T & T Clark, 2004) 247-64; online: http://www.religion.emory.edu/faculty/robbins/Pdfs/Samaritan.pdf.

the story about the "half-dead man," Jesus concludes his conversation with an exhortative conclusion to the lawyer, "Go and do likewise." Third, early Christian wisdom rhetorolect includes "parables," stories that teach by example, analogy, puzzlement, shock, and paradox. Breaking through one's stereotypes, prejudices, presuppositions, and desires, early Christian wisdom rhetorolect presents surprising and even offensive views of God and God's world. It is necessary, in the reasoning internal to this discourse, that people know this wisdom by heart, that they know how to recite it on proper occasions, and that they do it in the adult world where people are neighbors.

It is now appropriate that we return to the topic of "desire (coveting) as the cause of sin" in early Christian wisdom rhetorolect. The manner in which desire functions as the cause of sin, according to early Christian wisdom, is clearly stated in Jas 1:12-16. Desire, it claims, works through temptation in a context where blessing is presented as the opposite of death. The wisdom argumentation in James begins with a thesis about being blessed, followed by a rationale that describes the form of the blessing:

> *Thesis:* Blessed is anyone who endures temptation.
> *Rationale:* Such a one has stood the test and will receive the crown of life that the Lord has promised to those who love him. (1:12).

The thesis about being blessed is grounded in Torah wisdom as it is expressed in Deut 28:1-6:

> [Moses said,] "If you will only obey the LORD your God, by diligently observing all his commandments that I am commanding you today, the LORD your God will set you high above all the nations of the earth; [2] all these blessings shall come upon you and overtake you, if you obey the LORD your God:
> [3] Blessed shall you be in the city, and blessed shall you be in the field.
> [4] Blessed shall be the fruit of your womb, the fruit of your ground, and the fruit of your livestock, both the increase of your cattle and the issue of your flock.
> [5] Blessed shall be your basket and your kneading bowl.
> [6] Blessed shall you be when you come in, and blessed shall you be when you go out."

Deuteronomy envisions a state of well-being it describes as "blessedness" (*eulogēmenos*), describing it as a condition that grows or spreads from the well-being of people themselves to everything related to them and, indeed, to the places they go. The key to this blessedness, according to Deut 28:1, is obeying all the Lord's commandments, and the reward for doing so is that "God will set you high above all the nations of the earth." Jas 1:12 reconfigures the issue from "being set high above all the nations" to "receiving the crown of life," which would be a crown that not only rules over nations but over death.[71] Jas 1:12 describes blessedness (*makarios*) in relation to those who endure testing or temptation. This condition comes "to those who love him" (1:13). This blessing comes, then, upon those who fulfill Deut 6:5, which asserts that one "must love the Lord ..." People who live according to the Torah wisdom in Deut 6:5 will be blessed in many ways, according to Deut 28:1-6. They will be blessed in the city and the field. The fruit of the womb, the ground, the livestock, the basket, and the kneading bowl will be blessed. People will be blessed when they come in and when they go out. Jas 1:12 begins with this presupposition of Torah wisdom and applies it to insights about testing and temptation. The high point of Moses' teaching about enduring testing or temptation is in Deut 8:2:

> Remember the long way that the LORD your God has led you these forty years in the wilderness, in order to humble you, testing you to know what was in your heart, whether or not you would keep his commandments.

Jas 1:12 explores "what is in the heart" in the context in which people are tested or tempted. Jas 1:13 explains what is in the heart by what "comes out of the mouth," something we will explore later in this chapter. Introducing an argument from the opposite that uses a general example, the narrator presents a syllogism that concludes that desire causes sin. The syllogism, since it begins with a statement about a person rather than a "philosophical" principle, presents the Case (minor premise) first, followed by the Thesis (major premise) and Result:

> *Negative Case:* No one, when tempted, should say, "I am being tempted by God";
> *Rationale/Thesis:* for God cannot be tempted by evil and he himself tempts no one.
> *Contrary:* [14] But one is tempted by one's own desire, being lured and enticed by it;
> *Result/Case:* [15] then, when that desire has conceived, it gives birth to sin,
> *Result:* and that sin, when it is fully grown, gives birth to death.

In a characteristic mode of wisdom argumentation, Jas 1:13-15 elaborates the thesis and rationale in 1:12 through an argument from example supported by rationale, opposites, and contraries that move to a conclusion. The Case (example/minor premise) is a negative one in which a person speaks improperly saying "I am being tempted by God."

[71] Cf. Wis 4:2; Rev 2:10; 3:11. It is called a crown of righteousness in 2 Tim 4:8 and a crown of glory in 1 Pet 5:4. See Martin Dibelius, *James: A Commentary on the Epistle of James* (rev. H. Greeven; trans. M. A. Williams; Hermeneia; Philadelphia: Fortress Press, 1976) 88-90; Johnson, *James*, 188; C. Freeman Sleeper, *James* (ANTC; Nashville: Abingdon Press, 1998) 56.

The Rationale (thesis/major premise) that "proves" that it is inappropriate for a person to talk this way is that "God cannot be tempted by evil and he himself tempts no one" (1:13). The nature of wisdom rhetorolect is to introduce "incontrovertible" principles.[72] Often these principles are undeniable insights based on experience, like "Fig trees do not bear grapes." When the wisdom teacher takes the reasoning into the realm of God, it is expected that the hearer will accept the reasoning about God as undeniable. The narrator presupposes that everyone should know that God cannot be tempted by evil and he himself tempts no one. We will see in a later chapter that Job confronts God precisely on principles that a majority of people, including his "close friends," consider to be undeniable. But the epistle of James does not present this kind of "rebellious" wisdom. The narrator expects the hearer to accept the principle that God is neither tempted by evil, nor does God tempt anyone. This leads to the assertion of a contrary: "One is tempted by one's own desire, being lured and enticed by it" (1:14). This is a contrary, not an opposite. An argument from the opposite would be that "No one is really tempted, but only imagines that they are." When a person enters the world of contraries, there are many options. Potentially a person could be tempted by beauty, happiness, leisure, fame, or many other things. Instead, Jas 1:14 asserts that people are tempted by their own desires. The basis for this observation appears to lie in God's commandment to Israel through Moses, "Do not desire (covet)" (Deut 5:21).[73] The word for covet in the Greek LXX of the commandment is the verb *epithymeō*, to desire. Early Christian discourse, as noted above, extends the verb to the noun *epithymia*, desire. Jas 1:14 first speaks of "one's own desire" as something that lures and entices us. Then 1:15 conceptualizes desire in terms of a pregnant womb. Once desire is conceived, like a child is conceived, it gives birth to sin. When desire is fully grown, it gives birth to death. Here is the "reproductive" dynamic of wisdom rhetorolect on the opposite side of that which is good. The narrator envisions the "productivity" of sin through a process like the production and growth of children from conception through birth and growth to adulthood. Rather than producing growth into "life," desire (coveting) gives birth to sin, which grows up into "adult sin," which gives birth to death.

How could such a "multiplication of desire" be based on Torah wisdom? Here a return to the commandment not to desire can be helpful. In contrast to murder, adultery, theft, and false witness against one's

[72] Wisdom statements are supposed to be self-evident, since they exist, as it were, in the "fabric" of the universe itself.

[73] Gaca, *The Making of Fornication*, 153-54; Loader, *The Septuagint, Sexuality, and the New Testament*, 23-24.

neighbor, which appear to be "single" in manifestation, "desiring" (coveting) manifests itself in multiple ways. In Torah, this commandment stands out for its "elaboration." One should not covet one's neighbor's wife, house, field, male or female slave, ox, donkey, "or anything that belongs to your neighbor" (Deut 5:21). The list is long, but it could be made even longer! Desire has the potential for never ending. Thus, desire is reproductive of evil, just like light is productive of good. Light (wisdom) and desire are "competing" reproductive forces in the world, according to early Christian wisdom rhetorolect. Jas 1:17 explains that every generous and perfect gift is from above, from the Father of lights. Jas 1:18 explains that the Father of lights gave us birth by the word of truth, so that we would become a kind of first fruits of his creatures. In other words, when God caused the word of light (the word of the "image" of God) to be conceived as a human in the world, humans became "first fruits" of all the creatures to whom "the earth gave birth through the word of light." The blending of spheres is exceptionally dynamic in this reasoning. Word appears to be "born" of light; the earth "conceived" the word of truth and gave birth to humans as "first fruits." Here the hierarchical thinking we noticed above in Gen 1–3 appears to be playing a role. God created a world that produces all kinds of fruit. The "first fruits" of the word of truth from the Father of lights are humans. This first fruit, of course, is meant to be life and to give life. How sad if, instead of giving birth to life, this first fruit becomes filled with "desire" that gives birth to sin and this sin gives birth to death. The result, of course, is the opposite of what God desires for humans in the world.

We noticed above that all the synoptic gospels portray Jesus as able to recite five or six of the ten commandments of the Decalogue, and Matthew and Mark present him reciting the Shema ("Hear, O Israel ...") plus "Love your neighbor as yourself" from Torah wisdom. Matthew and Luke go even further in the story of the devil's testing of Jesus in the wilderness before he begins his adult ministry. In both versions of the story, the devil tests Jesus three times. Each time, Jesus recites Torah wisdom to the devil. These recitations are from Deut 6-8. Why does Jesus recite verses from these chapters? Early Christian wisdom rhetorolect envisions Jesus' knowledge of Torah wisdom as the basis for his knowledge about the poor, the rich, the boastful, the humble; about forgiveness and mercy; about asking and receiving, and about being blessed or being cursed. A primary basis for this knowledge is Deut 5–8, which contains not only the commandments of the Decalogue (Deut 5) but the Shema (Deut 6:4-5) and the elaboration of the Shema in Deut 6–8. When the devil tests Jesus by telling him to turn stones into loaves of bread, Jesus responds with Deut 8:3: "One does not live by bread alone, but by every word that comes from the mouth of God" (Matt 4:4; cf. Luke 4:4).[74] When the devil tests Jesus by telling him to throw himself down from the temple, Jesus says, "Do not put the Lord your God to the test" (Deut 6:16; Matt 4:7; Luke 4:12). When the devil tests Jesus by telling him to bow down and worship him and he will give him all the kingdoms of the world, Jesus replies, "It is written, 'Worship the Lord your God, and serve only him'" (Deut 6:13; Luke 4:8; Matt 4:10). It is important to notice that two of Jesus' responses are from the chapter in Deuteronomy that features Moses' teaching of the Shema to Israel (6:13, 16). Closer attention will reveal that 6:13 presents a "positive" thesis in relation to "Love the Lord your God ..." (6:5) as a "restatement of the Shema." This restatement stands at the end of a rehearsal of how the Lord God will bless them when they come into the land God has promised to them:

> When the LORD your God has brought you into the land that he swore to your ancestors, to Abraham, to Isaac, and to Jacob, to give you – a land with fine, large cities that you did not build,
> 11 houses filled with all sorts of goods that you did not fill, hewn cisterns that you did not hew, vineyards and olive groves that you did not plant – and when you have eaten your fill,
> 12 take care that you do not forget the LORD, who brought you out of the land of Egypt, out of the house of slavery.
> 13 The LORD your God you shall fear; him you shall serve, and by his name alone you shall swear" (6:13).

In characteristic fashion, early Christian wisdom rhetorolect features an abbreviated version that functions as a "proverb" in form and force: "Worship the Lord your God and serve only him." Moreover, this "proverb" evokes the entire unit about the necessity to "remember."

Deut 6:16 presents an argument from the contrary based on comparison as a means of clarifying the Shema with its elaboration and restatement: "Do not put the Lord your God to the test, as you tested him at Massah" (6:16). Early Christian wisdom rhetorolect shortens the statement to a proverbial form by reciting only the first part of the verse: "Do not put the Lord your God to the test." What, then, about Deut 8:2? Why does Jesus recite this verse? If a person reads all of Deut 6–8, the message becomes clear: When you reach a state of being blessed by abundant food, family, cattle, and riches, do not make the mistake of thinking you did it "on your own." In other words, remember that the Lord your God has blessed you. One of the key words is "remember." Deut 8:2–3 elaborates this as an exhortation that leads off the chapter that concludes this part of Deuteronomy:

[74] Luke 4:4 is shorter, not containing "but by every word that comes from the mouth of God."

> Remember the long way that the LORD your God has led you these forty years in the wilderness, in order to humble you, testing you to know what was in your heart, whether or not you would keep his commandments.
> [3] He humbled you by letting you hunger, then by feeding you with manna, with which neither you nor your ancestors were acquainted, in order to make you understand that one does not live by bread alone, but by every word that comes from the mouth of the LORD.

Early Christian wisdom rhetorolect shortens this to the last verse: "One does not live by bread alone, [but by every word that comes from the mouth of the Lord]." Early Christian wisdom rhetorolect reconfigures the emphasis on being humbled by God (Deut 6:2-3) to a principle that "The one who humbles himself will be exalted."[75] The longest list of blessings early Christian rhetorolect contains, spelling out blessings that come when people live Torah wisdom to "completion," is present at the beginning of the Sermon on the Mount in Matt 5:3-11:

> [Jesus said,] [3] "Blessed are the poor in spirit, for theirs is the kingdom of heaven.
> [4] Blessed are those who mourn, for they will be comforted.
> [5] Blessed are the meek, for they will inherit the earth.
> [6] Blessed are those who hunger and thirst for righteousness, for they will be filled.
> [7] Blessed are the merciful, for they will receive mercy.
> [8] Blessed are the pure in heart, for they will see God.
> [9] Blessed are the peacemakers, for they will be called children of God.
> [10] Blessed are those who are persecuted for righteousness' sake, for theirs is the kingdom of heaven.
> [11] Blessed are you when people revile you and persecute you and utter all kinds of evil against you falsely on my account."

In Matthew Jesus emphasizes, like Deut 28:1, that blessedness (*makarios*) comes from doing "all" the commandments (Matt 5:17-20). These are described in relation to the concepts of poor in spirit, mourning, restraint or meekness, hungering and thirsting for righteousness, being merciful, being pure in heart, being a peacemaker, and accepting persecution and being reviled by others when one is living according to righteousness. For early Christian wisdom rhetorolect, then, the focus moves significantly away from the land and productivity of food and abundant livelihood to relationships within community. Again the relation to one's neighbor becomes paramount.

After Moses presents the blessings, he presents to Israel curses that will come upon them if they do not do all the commandments. In Deut 28:15-20 he presents them as follows:

[75] Jas 1:9-11; Matt 23:12; Luke 14:18; 18:14; 1 Pet 5:6.

> [Moses said,] "But if you will not obey the LORD your God by diligently observing all his commandments and decrees, which I am commanding you today, then all these curses shall come upon you and overtake you:
> [16] Cursed shall you be in the city, and cursed shall you be in the field.
> [17] Cursed shall be your basket and your kneading bowl.
> [18] Cursed shall be the fruit of your womb, the fruit of your ground, the increase of your cattle and the issue of your flock.
> [19] Cursed shall you be when you come in, and cursed shall you be when you go out.
> [20] The LORD will send upon you disaster, panic, and frustration in everything you attempt to do, until you are destroyed and perish quickly, on account of the evil of your deeds, because you have forsaken me."

God's blessings come by living the wisdom from God. Curses come when people live in disobedience. Deut 28:15-19 formulates this in terms of direct opposites, asserting "cursedness" (*epikataratos*) for every item that was identified in Deut 28:3-6 as a part of "blessedness" (*eulogēmenos*). We will see in the next chapter that, for the most part, when early Christian discourse addresses cursedness, it moves into prophetic rhetorolect. The reason is that the topic of cursedness usually occurs in a context where the discourse is confronting someone about their wrongdoing. This confrontational mode regularly invites the prophetic pronouncement "Woe" (*ouai*), rather than focusing on a description and explanation of "cursedness" (*epikataratos*), like one finds in Gal 3:10, 13.[76] The directive in early Christian wisdom rhetorolect is "Bless and do not curse" (Luke 6:28; Rom 12:14; Jas 3:9-10). One of the few wisdom statements about being cursed is found on the lips of Jesus in Luke 17:1: "Occasions for stumbling are bound to come, but woe to anyone by whom they come!" A basic condition of blessedness in contrast to cursedness is presupposed in early Christian wisdom rhetorolect, but the ambiguities of living in God's world in a state of blessedness or cursedness move the focus more toward living in a state where fruit of the Spirit is enacted in one's relationships with others in the world of the neighbor.

Proverbial Torah Wisdom in Pseudo-Phocylides 3-8

It was common in the Mediterranean world for Torah wisdom to become proverbial wisdom.[77] We have already seen evidence of this in early Christian wisdom rhetorolect. It is important for us to see at least a glimpse of this outside early Christianity, before moving into a discussion of Solomon and the role of proverbial wisdom in the Hebrew

[76] Cf. Heb 6:8; 2 Pet 2:14.

[77] See *Letter of Aristeas*; Sirach; Wisdom of Solomon; Mishnah, *Pirke Aboth* 1; Walter T. Wilson, *The Sentences of Pseudo-Phocylides* (CEJL; Berlin/New York: Walter de Gruyter, 2005) 4-39, 73-83.

Bible and the OT Apocrypha. The writing regularly called "The Sentences of Pseudo-Phocylides"[78] exhibits well how Torah wisdom was moving into proverbial wisdom prior to and alongside early Christian discourse. Ps-Phoc 3-8 presents six of the commandments of the Decalogue in the form of proverbial wisdom:

> 3 Neither commit adultery nor arouse male passion.
> 4 Neither contrive deceptions nor defile your hands with blood.
> 5 Be not unjustly rich but earn a living from licit means.
> 6 Be content with what you have and refrain from what belongs to others.
> 7 Do not tell lies, but always say things that are true.
> 8 First of all honor God, and thereafter your parents.[79]

If one abbreviates the corresponding commandments as they exist in Deut 5:16-21 (cf. Exod 20:12-17) by omitting the statements after the first clause in the first and last commandment recited in Ps-Phoc 3-8, they appear in the following form:

> 16 Honor your father and your mother (cf. Ps-Phoc 8).
> 17 You shall not murder (cf. Ps-Phoc 4).
> 18 Neither shall you commit adultery (cf. Ps-Phoc 3).
> 19 Neither shall you steal (cf. Ps-Phoc 5).
> 20 Neither shall you bear false witness against your neighbor (cf. Ps-Phoc 7).
> 21 Neither shall you desire[80] your neighbor's wife (cf. Ps-Phoc 6).

Ps-Phoc 3-4 shares a pattern with Luke 18:18 and Rom 13:9 at the beginning of the list. Rather than listing the commandments in the order of murder first and adultery second, like one finds in Deut 5:17-18/Exod 20:13-14; Mark 10:19/Matt 19:18, the list begins with an injunction against adultery first and murder second.[81] This also coheres with the appearance of "first purity" in the list of "wisdom from above" in Jas 3:17, followed by peaceable, gentle, willing to yield, and full of mercy and good fruits, which would appear to be contraries to murdering someone. In addition, the placing of adultery before murder coheres with the beginning of Paul's "deeds" (*erga*) of the flesh in Gal 5:19, which begins with fornication and impurity, and only later in the list refers to anger, quarrels, dissensions, and factions.[82] Ps-Phoc 3-4,

[78] See James H. Charlesworth, *The Old Testament Pseudepigrapha* (2 vols.; Garden City, NY: Doubleday, 1983, 1985) 2:563-82; cf. P.W. van der Horst, *The Sentences of Pseudo-Phocylides: With Introduction and Commentary* (Leiden: Brill, 1978).

[79] Unless otherwise indicated, the translation is from Wilson, *The Sentences of Pseudo-Phocylides*, 73.

[80] Regularly translated "covet."

[81] Cf. Wilson, *The Sentences of Pseudo-Phocylides*, 78-80.

[82] For the relation of murder to anger, see Matt 5:21-22; cf. Loader, *The Septuagint, Sexuality, and the New Testament*, 22.

then, by emphasizing adultery over murder, shows a relationship to early Christian wisdom rhetorolect as it appears in Luke 18:18, Rom 13:9; Jas 3:17; and Gal 5:19.

Ps-Phoc 8 shares a pattern with Mark 10:19/Luke 18:18 by ending with "Honor your father and mother." This contrasts with Deut 5:22/Exod 20:17, which ends with "Do not desire (covet)."[83] Thus, there is a significant pattern also at the ending of the list in Ps-Phoc 3-8 that coheres with early Christian wisdom rhetorolect, namely an emphasis on honoring one's father and mother. There is still another pattern of importance in Ps-Phoc 8, namely an emphasis on honoring God first of all (*prōta*).[84] Thus, in a context of emphasizing that one must honor one's father and mother, Ps-Phoc 8 places a priority on loving God even more than one's parents. This coheres with the emphasis in early Christian wisdom rhetorolect on "loving God" as the commandment which is "first of all" (Mark 12:28-29/Matt 22:38). One begins to see, therefore, highly complex "levels" and "regions" of relationships between a text like Pseudo-Phocylides and early Christian discourse. There is rarely a "simple" relationship. Early Christian discourse is related in multiple ways to Mediterranean literature, whether it is biblical literature or another kind of literature.

Also the middle of the list in Ps-Phoc 3-8 has a relation to early Christian discourse. Ps-Phoc 5-6 present injunctions against becoming rich unjustly and desiring (coveting) something that belongs to another person. These two verses have a relation to the inclusion of "Do not defraud" in Mark 10:19 and Jas 5:4 (cf. Deut 24:14)[85] and the emphasis on "desire" (coveting) in early Christian wisdom rhetorolect. In addition, the inclusion of "Do not tell lies, but always say things that are true" in Ps-Phoc 7 seems to be related to "Do not bear false witness," which is present in Mark 10:19/Matt 19:18/Luke 18:18. Overall in Ps-Phoc 3-8, therefore, one sees ways in which Torah wisdom was blending with proverbial wisdom in the Mediterranean world. In this context, one also sees that the movement from Torah wisdom to proverbial wisdom in various texts exhibits multiple kinds of relationships to emphases that are present in early Christian discourse. In highly dynamic ways, then, early Christian discourse was participating in various kinds of conversations and emphases in Mediterranean society, culture, and religion.

A common phenomenon when Torah wisdom becomes proverbial wisdom is for various topics to blend with one another in various kinds

[83] Matt 19:18 and Rom 13:9 end with "Love your neighbor as yourself."

[84] The Greek of Ps-Phoc is based on Wilson, *The Sentences of Pseudo Phocylides*, 217-22; cf. P.W. van der Horst, *The Sentences of Pseudo Phocylides: With Introduction and Commentary* (Leiden: Brill, 1978) 88-102.

[85] Cf. Jas 5:4.

of "argumentative" ways. This is the nature of social, cultural, and ideological networks of topoi blending together as people explain who they are, clarify who they are over against other people, and develop systems of thought and action they perceive to be new ways of living life in the Mediterranean world.[86] Networks of reasoning and argumentation blend together in distinct ways among different groups of people at different times and in different places. A major challenge for socio-rhetorical interpretation is to uncover particular networks of reasoning and to identify particular modes of argumentation in particular different writings and "cultures" of discourse in the Mediterranean world.

Another way to see "argumentative" features in various kinds of Mediterranean literature that is somehow related to early Christian discourse is to observe the presence of both positive and negative injunctions about life. The first two proverbial sentences in Ps-Phoc 3-8 build another negative injunction as they reconfigure the negative injunction in the Decalogue. Ps-Phoc 3 adds "Do not arouse male passion" to "Do not commit adultery"[87] and Ps-Phoc 4 adds "Do not contrive deceptions" to the biblical injunction "Do not murder," which it transforms into "Do not defile your hands with blood." Thus, one way to reconfigure and elaborate Torah wisdom is to multiply negative injunctions.

Yet another way to reconfigure and elaborate is to create positive injunctions. Three of the proverbial sentences in Ps-Phoc 3-8 introduce a positive injunction that stands as a contrary to the reconfigured negative injunction in the Decalogue. Ps-Phoc 5 introduces a positive injunction "Earn a living from licit means" as the contrary to "Do not be unjustly rich," which is a reconfiguration either of "Do not steal" or "Do not defraud."[88] Ps-Phoc 6 introduces a positive injunction "Be content with what you have" as the contrary to "Refrain from what belongs to others," which is a reconfiguration of "Do not desire (covet)." Ps-Phoc 7 introduces a positive injunction "Always say things that are true" as the contrary of "Do not tell lies," which is a reconfiguration of "Do not bear false witness." Again the relationships are complex. Not only is there reconfiguration of Torah wisdom to proverbial wisdom. In the context of this reconfiguration, there is elaboration in the form of the addition of positive injunctions in contexts of negative injunctions.

Ps-Phoc 8 uses the occasion of the one positive commandment in the Decalogue, "Honor your father and mother," to introduce a hierarchy of

[86] Johan C. Thom, "'The Mind Is Its Own Place': Defining the *Topos*," in *Early Christianity and Classical Culture: Comparative Studies in Honor of Abraham J. Malherbe* (ed. J.T. Fitzgerald, T.H. Olbricht, and L.M. White; NovTSup 110; Leiden: Brill) 555-73; Abraham J. Malherbe, "The Christianization of a *Topos* (Luke 12:13-34)," *NovT* 38 (1996) 123-35.

[87] See Wilson, *The Sentences of Pseudo-Phocylides*, 79-80, for other texts that present adultery as inclusive of other sexual infractions like male-male sex.

[88] Wilson, *The Sentences of Pseudo-Phocylides*, 80-81; see Mark 10:19.

honoring God and honoring one's parents. This creates two positive injunctions in the form of "First of all honor God," which is a reconfiguration of "Love the Lord your God with all you heart, soul, and mind," and the additional positive injunction "and thereafter (honor) your parents."

The end result in Ps-Phoc 3-8 is the creation of five positive injunctions in the context of seven negative injunctions. It is noticeable that the positive injunctions emerge progressively out of negative injunctions:

Negative Injunctions	Positive Injunctions
Do not commit adultery (3). Do not arouse male passion (3). Do not contrive deceptions (4). Do not defile your hands with blood (4).	
Be not unjustly rich (5).	Earn a living from licit means (5).
Refrain from what belongs to others (6).	Be content with what you have (6).
Do not tell lies (7).	Always say things that are true (7).
	First of all honor God (8).
	Honor your parents after honoring God (8).

Ps-Phoc 3-8 shows a noticeable progression from negative to positive injunctions. Ps-Phoc 3-4 contain only negative injunctions. Ps-Phoc 5-7 contain a positive injunction alongside a negative. Ps-Phoc 8 contains only positive injunctions. Sometimes, then, as Torah wisdom is being transformed into proverbial wisdom there is a noticeable creation of new positive proverbial injunctions.

The presence of positive injunctions in Ps-Phoc 3-8 is especially noticeable, perhaps, at the end of the list. The Decalogue contains four negative commands in its emphasis on honoring God:

1. (Because) I am the LORD your God, who brought you out of the land of Egypt, out of the house of slavery, you shall have no other gods before me (5:7).
2. You shall not make for yourself an idol, whether in the form of anything that is in heaven above, or that is on the earth beneath, or that is in the water under the earth (5:8).
3. You shall not bow down to them or worship them, for I the LORD your God am a jealous God, punishing children for the iniquity of parents, to the third and fourth generation of those who reject me, but showing steadfast love to the thousandth generation of those who love me and keep my commandments.
4. You shall not make wrongful use of the name of the LORD your God, for the LORD will not acquit anyone who misuses his name.

Ps-Phoc 8 does not include any negative injunction as it emphasizes the importance of honoring God. Rather the list ends with two positive injunctions: (1) First of all honor God; and (2) thereafter your parents. A similar positive emphasis on honoring God and honoring parents also exists in early Christian discourse. It will be important to see how often early Christian discourse also has a tendency to move beyond negative injunctions into positive injunctions about living one's life in the world.

There are two special points of relation between Ps-Phoc 3-8 and early Christian discourse that may help us to see yet one more aspect of the general movement of Torah wisdom into proverbial wisdom. It is noticeable that the New Testament does not contain a book of laws, like Leviticus or Deuteronomy, or a book of Proverbs. Rather, various reconfigurations of laws and proverbs are present in multiple kinds of argumentative discourse that elaborate, amplify, and reconstrue previous and contemporary traditions in the Mediterranean world. Two points of contact between Ps-Phoc 3-8 and writings in the NT can serve as examples.

The positive injunction at the beginning of Ps-Phoc 6, "Be content with what you have" (*arkeisthai pareousi*) has a fascinating relation to the injunction at the ending of Heb 13:5, which also can be translated, "Be content with what you have" (*arkoumenoi tois parousin*). Heb 13:1-5 has an interesting blend of negative and positive injunctions.

Positive Injunctions	Negative Injunctions
Let mutual love continue (13:1).	Do not neglect to show hospitality to strangers (13:2).
Remember those who are in prison (13:3).	
(Remember) those who are being tortured (13:3).	
Let marriage be held in honor by all (13:4).	Let the marriage bed be kept undefiled (13:4).
	Keep your lives free from the love of money (13:5).
Be content with what you have (13:5).	

Heb 13:1-5 begins and ends with positive injunctions. In this overall context there are three negative injunctions embedded in five positive injunctions. There is, in addition, another very noticeable feature. In this short span of verses, there are three rationale clauses, and two clauses that argue from analogy or comparison. The rationales are:

(1) for by doing that some have entertained angels without knowing it (13:2).
(2) for God will judge fornicators and adulterers (13:4).
(3) for he has said, "I will never leave you or forsake you (13:5).

The arguments from analogy or comparison are:

(1) as though you were in prison with them (13:3).
(2) as though you yourselves were being tortured (13:3).

The presence of these clauses moves Torah wisdom beyond proverbial wisdom into "argumentative wisdom." Beginning with the positive injunction to "Let mutual love continue," Heb 13:1-6 moves through a series of negative and positive injunctions toward a positive injunction at the end, "Be content with what you have," supported by authoritative written testimony that leads to a conclusion that recites yet more authoritative written testimony. In other words, the sequence is not simply a list of proverbial sentences. Rather, it is a progression of positive and negative injunctions, supported by various kinds of argumentative clauses, which reaches a conclusion in a statement that itself is amplified by recitation of authoritative written testimony.

In contrast to being a list of proverbial statements, Heb 13:1-5 is argumentative discourse containing proverbial statements. There is a positive injunction at the beginning that has the nature of a thesis about the importance of mutual love ("Let mutual love continue"). Next there is an argument from the opposite ("Do not …") supported by a rationale ("for …": 13:2). Then there are two positive injunctions supported by an argument from analogy or comparison ("Remember … as though you …" 13:3). Then there are both positive and negative injunctions about marriage (mutual love) supported by a rationale referring to God that reconfigures a commandment in the Decalogue ("Do not commit adultery") (13:4). After these statements, there are generalized negative and positive injunctions about the relation of life to money and possessions, supported by a rationale that refers to God and reconfigures the commandment "Do not desire (covet)" (13:5). Then there is a conclusion that focuses on the Lord who, as helper, creates a confidence within the believer to do what should be done, no matter the criticism or opposition (13:6). Herein lies another clue to the nature of early Christian discourse. As early Christians contributed to an overall movement in the Mediterranean world to transform Torah wisdom into proverbial discourse, they created argumentative discourse that not only uses Torah wisdom but also uses argument from rationales, analogies, comparisons, and appeals to authoritative written testimony to support their reasoning.

Early Christian discourse, then, moves Torah wisdom into various kinds of argumentative proverbial wisdom that are significantly complex in structure and function. Yet one more example, this time focusing on only one verse, may help to illustrate the inner workings of this process. Ps-Phoc 7 ("Do not tell lies, but always say things that are true") has a fascinating relation to words in Eph 4:25 that may be translated "Putting away falsehood, let all of us speak the truth to our neighbors." Both Ps-Phoc 7 and these words in Eph 4:25 are a reconfiguration of "Do not bear false witness against your neighbor" (Deut

5:20/Exod 20:16).[89] Eph 4:25 is not, however, a proverbial statement. Rather, it is a sentence containing proverbial words that introduces a portion of text (Eph 4:25-5:2) that concludes a preceding argument (4:17–4:24). For this reason, the sentence begins with "So then" or "Therefore" (*dio*). In addition, the sentence contains a rationale at the end that moves the statement decisively beyond Torah wisdom into characteristic Christian discourse ("for we are members of one another"). In this form, the statement can function as the introduction of an argument that moves through a statement not to grieve the Holy Spirit of God (4:30) and to forgive one another "as God in Christ has forgiven you" (4:32) to a concluding exhortation:

> Therefore be imitators of God, as beloved children, and live in love, as Christ loved us and gave himself up for us, a fragrant offering and sacrifice for God. (Eph 5:1-2)

This conclusion is deeply grounded in Torah wisdom, which includes an injunction to love the Lord God with all one's heart, soul, and mind. This Torah wisdom, however, has been reconfigured into argumentative discourse containing proverbial speech that envisions a relation between God and Christ that enacts sacrificial rituals described in Leviticus. The inner processes by which Torah wisdom has been reconfigured into this argumentative discourse are so highly complex that we must not try to discuss them further at this point. We have, however, seen a few of the processes. One is the movement of Torah wisdom into proverbial wisdom. Another is the creation of positive injunctions in the midst of negative injunctions. Still another is the addition of rationales and arguments from opposition, analogy, comparison, and recitation from authoritative written testimony. Yet another is the construction of argumentative units that move from an introduction to an amplified exhortative conclusion. Little by little, we can begin to see inner processes by which Torah wisdom becomes not only proverbial wisdom but highly complex argumentative wisdom discourse.

The Complete Argument in Hellenistic-Roman Discourse: Epictetus, *Discourses* 2.26.1-7

At this point it is important to introduce a basic feature of the inner argumentative texture of Hellenistic-Roman wisdom discourse to exhibit yet a broader aspect of the Mediterranean environment in which early Christian discourse emerged. As we begin this section, we must recall the emergence of assertions, rationales, opposites, contraries, and analogies in the biblical creation story, and the presence of opposites and negatives in a writing like Pseudo-Phocylides. Also, we must recall how Torah wis-

[89] Wilson, *The Sentences of Pseudo-Phocylides*, 81-82.

dom moves not only into proverbial wisdom but into modes of highly complex argumentative wisdom discourse in the New Testament. In rhetorical manuals from the *Rhetorica ad Herrenium* in the 80s BCE through the *Progymnasmata* of Hermogenes in the second century CE, rhetoricians observed a basic pattern of wisdom argumentation among Hellenistic-Roman speakers and writers. These rhetoricians, of course, did not identify this pattern as wisdom discourse. Rather, they considered it to be a procedure of speaking on the same theme with variations. A synopsis of their presentations reveals nine aspects of argumentation that one could expect to appear. These aspects are: (1) introduction; (2) theme, thesis, or chreia; (3) reason or rationale; (4) restatement of the theme, thesis or chreia, with or without reasons or rationales; (5) contrary or opposite; (6) example or comparison; (7) analogy; (8) citation of authoritative testimony; (9) exhortative conclusion.[90] It is important to emphasize that this progressive pattern is internal to "basic wisdom" argumentation in Mediterranean society and culture, and it is likely to be basic in many other societies also. Epictetus's *Discourses*, which is an excellent example of Hellenistic-Roman wisdom literature, is an excellent place to find illustrations of the pattern. Epict. *Disc* 2.26.1-7 shows the basic pattern of wisdom argumentation well:

Epictetus, *Discourses* 2.26.1-7 (trans. George Long)

General thesis: Every error comprehends contradiction:

Rationale containing negatives: for since the one who errs does not wish to err, but to be right, it is plain that he does not do what he wishes.

Example: For what does the thief wish to do? That which is for his own interest.

Contraries, adversatives, and opposites: If, then, the theft is not for his interest, he does not do that which he wishes. But every rational soul is by nature offended at contradiction, and so long as it does not understand this contradiction, it is not hindered from doing contradictory things: but when it does understand the contradiction, it must of necessity avoid the contradiction and avoid it as much as a man must dissent from the false when he sees that a thing is false; but so long as this falsehood does not appear to him, he assents to it as to truth.

Restatement of thesis for personal life: He, then, is strong in argument and has the faculty of exhorting and confuting, who is able to show to each man the contradiction through which he errs and clearly to prove how he does not do that which he wishes and does that which he does not wish.

[90] Cf. *Rhet ad Her* 2.18.28-19.30; 4.43.56-44.57; Hermogenes, *Progymnasmata* 1.10–8.14. See Vernon K. Robbins, "Progymnastic Rhetorical Composition and Pre-Gospel Traditions: A New Approach," in *The Synoptic Gospels: Source Criticism and the New Literary Criticism* (ed. C. Focant; BETL 110; Leuven: Leuven University Press, 1993) 111-47; idem, *Exploring the Texture of Texts*, 21-22, 53-58.

Rationale with adversatives, contraries, and opposites: For if any one shall show this, a man will himself withdraw from that which he does; but so long as you do not show this, do not be surprised if a man persists in his practice; for having the appearance of doing right, he does what he does.

Recitation of authoritative testimony: For this reason Socrates, also trusting to this power, used to say, "I am accustomed to call no other witness of what I say, but I am always content with him with whom I am discussing, and I ask him to give his opinion and call him as a witness, and though he is only one, he is sufficient in the place of all."

Analogy: For Socrates knew by what the rational soul is moved, just like a pair of scales, and that it must incline, whether it chooses or not.

Concluding exhortation: Show the rational governing faculty a contradiction, and it will withdraw from it; but if you do not show it, rather blame yourself than him who is not persuaded.[91]

One sees the underlying argumentative texture of wisdom discourse in Hellenistic-Roman literature in this short portion of Epictetus. Beginning with a statement of a thesis, Epictetus immediately presents a rationale to support the thesis. After presenting the rationale, he presents an example of the thesis in the well known social personage of a thief. This example creates the context for a series of statements using five negatives (not), two adversatives (but),[92] and the word "non-interest" (*asympheron*) to clarify the thesis by means of opposites and contraries. After presenting the argument from opposites, contraries, and adversatives, he restates the thesis in terms of personal action and supports it with further rationales, adversatives, contraries, and opposites. Then he recites an authoritative testimony attributed to Socrates. After this he invokes an analogy between the rational soul and a pair of scales: the rational soul is moved by personal witness just as a pair of scales is moved by a weight. Then he concludes with an exhortation to show the rational governing faculty a contradiction and it will withdraw from it (an imperative about the abstract thesis); and if you do not show it, blame yourself rather than him who is not persuaded (an imperative about the personal thesis).

The basic features of this argumentative texture, characteristic of wisdom discourse in Mediterranean society and culture, are widespread throughout the writings in the New Testament. A basic difference, we will see below, is that early Christian wisdom rhetorolect blends other modes of discourse, like prophetic, apocalyptic, and priestly discourse into this pattern. The passage from Epictetus above illustrates how much Hellenistic-Roman discourse stays in the domain of wisdom argumentation, without blending other modes of discourse with it.

[91] Trans. George Long, edited and revised by Vernon K. Robbins. Downloaded on March 29, 2006, from http://www.constitution.org/rom/epicdisc.htm.

[92] *ouk ... asympheron ... de ...mē ... ouden ... de ... mē ....*

Conclusion

This chapter has explored the story-line of early Christian wisdom rhetorolect from its beginnings in the story of creation through Moses. It has also explored the manner in which Torah wisdom became proverbial wisdom in the Mediterranean world outside the boundaries of Jewish writings perpetuated in the name of biblical personages. The next chapter will explore the story-line of early Christian rhetorolect from Solomon through the OT Apocrypha. Then it will present examples of the manner in which wisdom rhetorolect blends with prophetic, apocalyptic, precreation, miracle, and priestly rhetorolect in early Christian discourse.

5

Christian Wisdom Rhetorolect Part II: Solomon, Wisdom in Divine History, and the New Testament

Wisdom and Solomon

Solomon: 1 Kings 3–4 as an Understanding Network

Now that we have gotten a glimpse of some of the complexity of early Christian wisdom discourse, the natural movement of Torah wisdom into proverbial wisdom in the Mediterranean world, and some basic aspects of the argumentative texture of wisdom discourse in the Mediterranean world, let us return to the story-line of early Christian wisdom rhetorolect as it moves from Moses to King Solomon. When Solomon became king, he prayed to God for wisdom:

> [Solomon said,] "Give your servant therefore an understanding mind to govern your people, able to discern between good and evil; for who can govern this your great people?"...
> 12 [God said to him,] "I now do according to your word. Indeed I give you a wise and discerning mind; no one like you has been before you and no one like you shall arise after you." (1 Kgs 3:9, 12)

The clear evidence that King Solomon received this wisdom from God emerged when two women came to him with a newborn child, each claiming that the child was theirs (1 Kgs 3:16-22). Solomon exhibited this wisdom by asking for a sword and giving a direction to cut the living boy in half, giving half to one and half to the other (3:24-25). When one of the women expressed compassion for the child and asked the king to give the child to the other woman, Solomon decided she was the mother of the child and directed that the child be given to her (3:26-28). As a result of this decision, the reputation of King Solomon for his wisdom spread to many nations (1 Kgs 4:34). Finally this caused the Queen of Sheba to visit him, bearing luxurious gifts (1 Kgs 10:1-2). When the king could answer all her questions, she blessed Solomon's God saying: "Blessed be the LORD your God, who has delighted in you and set you on the throne of Israel! Because the LORD loved Israel forever, he has made you king to execute justice and righteousness." Part of the wisdom story-line in early Christianity is a statement that Jesus has wisdom that is even greater than the wisdom of Solomon (Matt 12:42/Luke 11:31)...[1] Also, Solomon is known for receiving from God riches and honor as a result of his wisdom (1 Kgs 3:13; 10:23-25). Early Christian wisdom rhetorolect remembers this, again in the form of comparison with Jesus, whose wisdom is greater than Solomon. The reasoning about Solomon blends with reasoning about the productivity of vegetation in God's created world:

> Consider the lilies, how they grow: they neither toil nor spin; yet I tell you, even Solomon in all his glory was not clothed like one of these.
> 28 But if God so clothes the grass of the field, which is alive today and tomorrow is thrown into the oven, how much more will he clothe you – you of little faith! (Luke 12:27-28; cf. Matt 6:29-30)

Solomon's Wisdom, the Household, and Nature: Proverbs as a Tree of Life Network

The Hebrew Bible perpetuates the story of King Solomon in the form of proverbial wisdom. This proverbial tradition presents the household as the primary location for the transmission of God's wisdom into human bodies. Biblical wisdom discourse presupposes that life begins, grows, and attains its primary nature in a household under the care of a father and mother. The goal in the household is to raise a child who produces good, righteous action and thought. Words spoken by the father and mother are the primary agent of the nurturing, growth, and maturation. Prov 6:20-22 says:

> 20 My child, keep your father's commandment,
> and do not forsake your mother's teaching.
> 21 Bind them upon your heart always;
> tie them around your neck.
> 22 When you walk, they will lead you;
> when you lie down, they will watch over you;
> and when you awake, they will talk with you.[2]

In the household, children's parents teach them God's wisdom in the form of commandments and other teachings. Primary conceptual blending with the creation of the world occurs in the reasoning about the teachings and commandments to the child. Prov 6:20-23 introduces an enthymeme containing an exhortative thesis supported by a rationale that presupposes that the words of the parents are light. Thus Prov 6:20-

[1] This appears in apocalyptic rhetorolect that envisions her rising at the end of time and judging "this generation" for its wickedness.

[2] The three occurrences of "they" occur in the form "it" in the Hebrew.

22, an expanded exhortative thesis, continues with: "For the commandment is a lamp and the teaching a light, and the reproofs of discipline are the way of life" (6:23). This rationale exhibits conceptual blending of a lamp in a household with light in the created order. Light enables the entire world to be productive. When commandment and teaching are a lamp and a light, they enable the household to be a created order that produces good things. The speech of parents is a light that functions like a lamp in the house and a light in the world. This light nurtures children in the ways of God while they are in the household, and it leads them to the way of life when they walk out in the world. This light watches over them when they lie down and talks with them when they are awake.

Wisdom discourse not only speaks of commandments and teachings as light, but it speaks of people who themselves produce righteousness through their thoughts, speech, and actions as people who produce light: "The light of the righteous shines brightly, but the lamp of the wicked goes out" (Prov 13:9). Here we see for the first time in our discussion the appearance of "those who are wicked." While the righteous are like the lights that God created and placed in various locations in the universe to give light to the earth, the wicked are like the darkness where a lamp goes out. The wicked do not create light in darkness. Rather, they themselves are part of the darkness. Indeed, the righteous are like the light of the day: "But the path of the righteous is like the light of dawn, that shines brighter and brighter until the full day" (Prov 4:18). This evokes the path of the wicked, which is like a night when even the moon and the stars give no light. The transmission of light from God to people of all kinds, and the invitation and responsibility of humans to transmit this in their speech and actions is summarized in Prov 29:13–17:

> 13 The poor and the oppressor have this in common:
> the LORD gives light to the eyes of both.
> 14 If a king judges the poor with equity,
> his throne will be established forever.
> 15 The rod and reproof give wisdom,
> but a mother is disgraced by a neglected child.
> 16 When the wicked are in authority, transgression increases,
> but the righteous will look upon their downfall.
> 17 Discipline your children, and they will give you rest;
> they will give delight to your heart.

The sequence in Prov 29:13–17 begins with God's giving of "light to the eyes" of both the poor and the oppressor. This light is to guide the king in understanding that the poor need equity. In turn, parents are to act and speak toward their children in a manner that enables the children to see the path of light and walk upon it.

Psalm 119:130 says, "The unfolding of your words gives light; it imparts understanding to the simple." God's light does not only allow people to see, but it allows people to understand. Once they are able to understand, they are able to speak this wisdom to other humans. The medium for this light of wisdom is God's words. The commands and reproofs of God, working together, light a path and direct a person toward a path that leads to life. God's light, then, is life, and a primary medium for this light to people is God's words.

Expanding on the picture of the Garden of Eden, wisdom discourse presents wisdom itself as a tree of life: "[Wisdom] is a tree of life to those who take hold of her, and happy are all who hold her fast" (Prov 3:18). Soothing speech is also a tree of life: "A soothing tongue is a tree of life, but perversion in it crushes the spirit" (Prov 15:4). Also, the actions of the righteous are a tree of life: "The fruit of the righteous is a tree of life, and he who is wise wins souls" (Prov 11:30). Thus, "Be fruitful and multiply" in Gen 1:28 does not simply reach its goal in giving biological life to more human beings. Rather, since humans are able to create light in the world through their speech and action, which is speech and action "in the image of God," they are able to create light which enables other people to see "what is good," to walk a path that creates light, and, indeed, to be so fruitful that they are a tree of life to others.

Wisdom discourse elaborates God's creation of humans in the image of God by presenting humans with the ability to create light in their own households, in God's "public" world, and in people's bodies, including their own. Humans are to be creators of light both inside and outside their bodies and their households. The light humans create – inside their own bodies, inside the bodies of others, and out in the world – enables bodies to grow and mature in the productivity of goodness and righteousness. This light shines in the form of commandments, teachings, thoughts, and actions.

Following the guidance about reasoning and picturing in biblical discourse, a full-bodied mode of interpretation is attentive to the manner in which a particular kind of discourse, like wisdom discourse, focuses on parts of the body in addition to the eye. It is conventional knowledge that wisdom discourse focuses on the ears and the heart. Prov 1:8 asserts: "Hear, my child, your father's instruction, and do not reject your mother's teaching." Some form of the verb *akouein*, to listen, occurs eighteen times in the LXX of Proverbs.[3] This presupposes attention to ears. Some form of the word *ous*, ear, occurs twelve times in the LXX of

[3] Prov 1:5, 8, 33; 4:1, 10; 5:7, 13; 7:24; 8:32, 33; 16:21; 18:13; 19:20; 20:12; 22:17; 23:19, 22; 29:24.

Proverbs.[4] Reasoning about the ears and hearing in wisdom discourse presupposes that wisdom comes through the ears into the heart. People reason and think about things by "saying in their heart."[5] People have "thoughts of the heart" (Gen 6:5; Deut 15:9), and people remember by "laying it to one's heart" or "laying it up in one's heart."[6] There is also "keeping it in one's heart" (Prov 4:21; Luke 2:19, 51).[7] Thus, wisdom discourse conventionally focuses on ears as receivers of wisdom and heart as a place where wisdom is stored, remembered, and used for reasoning about life.

The book of Proverbs nurtures the picture of wisdom as God's light with explicit statements about God's eyes. Prov 5:21 says, "For human ways are under the eyes of the Lord, and he examines all their paths." Also, Prov 15:3 says, "The eyes of the Lord are in every place, keeping watch on the evil and the good." In addition, Prov 22:12 says, "The eyes of the Lord keep watch over knowledge, but he overthrows the words of the faithless." These statements extend God's seeing beyond seeing light to seeing knowledge. This creates a context that invites people to take the imagery further. Not only do the eyes of God see and oversee wisdom, the eyes of humans see wisdom. Prov 17:24 says, "The discerning person looks to wisdom, but the eyes of a fool to the ends of the earth."

Wisdom discourse in the NT continues this conventional reasoning, and it develops the function of the eye in a special way.[8] A clue to the special function of the eye in early Christian wisdom discourse lies in Ps 19:8, which says: "the commandment of the Lord is clear, enlightening the eyes." Early Christian wisdom discourse presents the following statements about the eye in Luke 11:34-36:[9]

> Your eye is the lamp of your body. If your eye is healthy, your whole body is full of light; but if it is not healthy, your body is full of darkness. Therefore consider whether the light in you is not darkness. If then your whole body is full of light, with no part of it in darkness, it will be as full of light as when a lamp gives you light with its rays."

[4] Prov 2:2; 4:20; 5:1, 13; 18:15; 20:12; 21:13; 22:17; 23:9,12; 25:12; 28:9.

[5] Gen 24:45; Deut 7:17; 8:17; 9:4; 18:21; 29:19; Pss 10:13; 14:1; 53:1; Isa 47:8; 49:21; Jer 13:22; Obad 1:3; Mark 2:8; Luke 5:22; Rom 10:6; Rev 18:7; see John J. Pilch and Bruce J. Malina (eds.), *Handbook of Biblical Social Values* (Peabody, MA: Hendrickson, 1993) 69.

[6] Exod 7:23; Deut 4:39; 11:18; 32:46; 1 Kgs 8:47; 2 Chr 6:37; Job 22:22; Ps 119:11; Isa 47:7; 57:1; Jer 12:11; Mal 2:2; see idem, *Handbook*, 69.

[7] Pilch and Malina, *Handbook*, 69.

[8] The eye is a body zone associated with emotion-fused thought: Bruce J. Malina, *The New Testament World: Insights from Cultural Anthropology* (rev. ed.; Louisville: Westminster/John Knox, 1993) 74; Robbins, *Exploring the Texture of Texts*, 30-31.

[9] Par. Matt 6:22-23.

The presupposition in antiquity was that the eye produces light.[10] A healthy eye is able to see when the light it produces meets light from the outside. In biblical tradition, "The Lord gives light to the eyes" (Prov 29:13) and "The light of the eyes rejoices the heart" (Prov 15:30). In addition, "The precepts of the Lord are right, rejoicing the heart; the commandment of the Lord is clear, enlightening the eyes" (Ps 19:8). Thus, the heart and the eyes, informed by the light of God's wisdom, work together to produce light in the body.[11] The natural state of the inner body is darkness, and only if the eye "shines light into the heart" will the body be full of light. Here the intersubjective body is a microcosm of the cosmos. When it is illumined with God's light, it becomes a well-ordered body, doing God's will and following God's ways. This light creates the possibility for a human to become a tree of life that produces fruit that nurtures life.

Humans have the power from God to create light; darkness exists as an environment for the creation of light. When the image of light emerges in the context of Jesus' transmission of God's wisdom, pictorial reasoning emerges that Christ is the light of the world.[12] Elaboration of this pictorial thesis includes an analogy between God's creation of the world with light and Jesus' creation of a well-ordered intersubjective body with the light of wisdom.

Wisdom in God's World

Sirach and Bodies: The Righteous People in the History of God's World

In a context where we see Torah wisdom moving into proverbial wisdom and proverbial wisdom moving into programmatic argumentative discourse in the Mediterranean world, it is important to see an overall story-line of personages that "deutero-biblical" wisdom literature was presenting in the context of Mediterranean literature. By the time of the emergence of Christianity, Sirach had named thirty people, the judges, and the twelve prophets for their productivity of righteousness and goodness.

[10] See *Test. Job* 18:4: "My eyes, acting as lamps, looked about"; Dale C. Allison, Jr., "The Eye Is the Lamp of the Body (Matthew 6.22-23=Luke 11.34-36)," *NTS* 33 (1987) 70.

[11] John J. Pilch and Bruce J. Malina (eds.), *Handbook of Biblical Social Values* (Peabody, MA: Hendrickson, 1993) 68-72.

[12] John 1:9; 3:19; 8:12; 9:5; 12:46.

The Righteous People in God's World		
From the Beginning of Time to the Flood	From the Patriarchs to Joseph in Egypt	From the Exodus through the Conquest of Canaan
Adam [13] Seth [14] Enoch [15] Shem [16] and Noah [17]	Abraham [18] Lot [19] Isaac [20] Jacob [21] Joseph [22]	Moses [23] Aaron [24] Phinehas [25] Joshua [26] Caleb [27] the judges [28]
From the Beginning of the Kingship through Elisha	During the Latter Part of the Kingship	The Return and Restoration of Jerusalem
Samuel [29] Nathan [30] David [31] Solomon [32] Elijah [33] Elisha [34]	Hezekiah [35] Isaiah [36] Josiah [37] Jeremiah [38] Ezekiel [39] Job [40]	Zerubabel [41] Jeshua [42] Nehemiah [43] The twelve prophets," who "comforted the people of Jacob and delivered them with confident hope." [44]

[13] Sir 49:16; Wis 10:1-2; NT 9 times.
[14] Sir 49:16; Luke 3:38.
[15] Sir 44:16; 49:14; Luke 3:37; Heb 11:5; Jude 14.
[16] Sir 49:16; Luke 3:36.
[17] Sir 44:17-18; Wis 10:4; NT 8 times.
[18] Sir 44:19-21; Wis 10:5; NT 71 times.
[19] Sir 16:8; Wis 10:6-8; Luke 17:28-29, 32; 2 Pet 2:7.
[20] Sir 44:22; NT 20 times.
[21] Sir 44:23; Wis 10:10-12; NT 17 times.
[22] Sir 49:15; Wis 10:13-14; NT 9 times.
[23] Sir 45:1-5; Wis 10:16-21; NT 79 times.
[24] Sir 45:6-17; NT 5 times.
[25] Sir 45:23-24.
[26] Sir 46:1-8; Acts 7:45; Heb 4:8.
[27] Sir 46:7-10.
[28] Sir 46:11-12; Acts 13:20.
[29] Sir 46:13-20; Acts 3:24; 13:20; Heb 11:32.
[30] Sir 47:1.
[31] Sir 45:25-26; 47:2-11; NT 60 times.
[32] Sir 47:12-23; NT 12 times.
[33] Sir 48:1-12; NT 29 times.
[34] Sir 48:12-14; Luke 4:27.
[35] Sir 48:17-25; Matt 1:9.
[36] Sir 48:22-25; NT 22 times.
[37] Sir 49:1-3; Matt 1:10-11.
[38] Sir 49:4-7; Matt 2:17; 16:14; 27:9.
[39] Sir 49:8.

In Sirach, then, thirty named people, the judges, and the twelve prophets emerge as the righteous people in biblical wisdom tradition who filled God's history with good things until the time of the priests who lead in righteousness at the time of the writing of Sirach.

These people and groups are juxtaposed to certain individuals and groups who produced wickedness and evil. According to Sirach, God did not forgive the Nephilim of Gen 6:1-4 (16:7); the neighbors of Lot (16:8); Dathan, Abiram, and their followers, and the company of Korah who conspired against Aaron (45:18-22; 16:6);[45] the 600,000 rebellious Israelites who died in the wilderness (16:10; 46:8);[46] and the Canaanites destroyed during the conquest (16:9). In addition, Rehoboam, son of Solomon, caused the people to revolt and Jeroboam led Israel and Ephraim into sin (47:23-27).

In relation to the unrighteous people in the history of God's world, Sir 16 presents a special meditation on the production and multiplication of "worthless children." As Sir 16:1-2 says: "Do not desire a multitude of worthless children, and do not rejoice in ungodly offspring. If they multiply, do not rejoice in them, unless the fear of the Lord is in them." The inner nature of God's created world is "to be fruitful and multiply." But it is goodness and righteousness that God desires to multiply, not wickedness and evil. Sir 16:3 goes so far as to say: "... to die childless is better than to have ungodly children." Then there is discussion of the ancient giants (16:7), the neighbors of Lot (16:8), the doomed nation (16:9), and the 600,000 stubborn foot soldiers (16:10), who all acted unrighteously. To deepen the reader's understanding of the wisdom that guides righteous people, Sir 16:26-30 summarizes how the Lord created the world, arranged his works in an eternal order, and filled it with his good things.

Sirach 17 contrasts the multiplication of wickedness of evil with the good things God gave to human beings. God granted humans "authority over everything on earth" (17:2), "made them in his own image" (17:3), gave them "discretion and tongue and eyes, ears and a mind for thinking" (17:6), "filled them with knowledge and understanding, and showed them good and evil" (17:7). God "bestowed knowledge upon them, and allotted to them the law of life" (17:11), and "established with them an eternal covenant, and revealed to them his decrees" (17:12).

[40] Sir 49:9.

[41] Sir 49:11; Matt 1:12-13; Luke 3:27. Sir 49:12 also names Jeshua, son of Jozadak, as righteous.

[42] Sir 49:12.

[43] Sir 49:13.

[44] Sir 49:10.

[45] Cf. Sir 45:18-22; Jude 11.

[46] Cf. Exod 12:37.

"Their eyes saw his glorious majesty, and their ears heard the glory of his voice. He said to them, 'Beware of all evil.' And he gave commandment to each of them concerning the neighbor" (17:13-14).

It is remarkable how close the NT writings replicate the list of people and groups in wisdom tradition who either produced goodness and righteousness or multiplied wickedness and evil. Only six of the people Sirach names as producing righteousness are absent from the NT: Phinehas, Caleb, Nathan, Ezekiel, Jeshua, and Nehemiah. The NT makes specific reference to three of the twelve prophets Sirach mentions as a group: Hosea,[47] Joel,[48] and Jonah.[49] In addition, NT writings recite verses or portions of verses from eleven of these twelve prophets,[50] omitting recitation only of Obadiah. The NT specifically mentions three groups of people who were unrighteous: the "angels" (Nephilim) in Gen 6,[51] the neighbors of Lot,[52] and the people associated with Korah.[53] In addition, the NT refers to the disobedient people during the time of Noah.[54] Early Christian discourse, then, has a close relation to the history of the righteous and unrighteous people in the world as recounted in Sirach.

The Incontestable Nature of God's Wisdom

In the context of the growing number of personages associated with wisdom discourse in the biblical story, it is important to look more closely into the nature of wisdom in relation to some other forms of discourse in the Hebrew Bible and the Mediterranean world more broadly. In biblical wisdom discourse, it is possible to have conversation with God, but this conversation is not usually "argumentative dialogue with God." The exception to this is the book of Job, which we will discuss in the next volume. Wisdom dialogue with God regularly holds humans accountable to God's wisdom. In wisdom discourse, there is a presupposition that it is not possible to have a truly argumentative conversation with God – conversation that might "hold God accountable."

[47] Rom 9:25.

[48] Acts 2:16.

[49] Matt 12:39-41; 16:4, 17; Luke 11:29-30, 32.

[50] (1) Hosea: 1 Pet 2:10; Rom 9:25-27; Matt 2:15; 9:13; 12:7; 1 Cor 15:55; Rev 6:16; (2) Joel: Acts 2:17-21; Rom 10:13; (3) Amos: Acts 7:42-43; 15:16-17; Rev 4:8; 15:3; (4) Jonah: Matt 12:40; (5) Micah: Matt 2:6; 10:35-36; Luke 12:53; (6) Nahum: Rom 10:15; (7) Habakkuk: Acts 13:41; Rom 1:17; Gal 3:11; Heb 10:37-38; (8) Zephaniah: Rev 14:5; (9) Haggai: Heb 12:26; (10) Zechariah: Matt 21:5; 26:31; 27:9; Mark 14:27; John 12:15; 19:37; Eph 4:25; Jude 9, 23; Rev 1:7; (11) Malachi: Matt 11:10; 17:10-11; Mark 1:2; 7:27; 9:11; Rom 9:13.

[51] 2 Pet 2:4.

[52] Luke 17:28-29; 2 Pet 2:7-8.

[53] Jude 11.

[54] 1 Pet 3:20.

God's wisdom is meant to be good, beyond question. It is good, from above. When God speaks wisdom, it is a "good reality" that cannot be countered. Only some other "counterfactual" mode of discourse is able truly to establish argumentative dialogue with God.[55]

Wisdom discourse features pronouncements of God that are, for all intents and purposes, not challengeable. What God pronounces happens, and what God commands is the way things will be done. Either people will live according to God's precepts and be blessed, or people will follow their own precepts and be cursed. In wisdom discourse, the focus is upon that which is good. God sees that which is good, explains that which is good, and instructs people to follow that which is good. The goal is for people to see that which is good, bring the light of this wisdom into their bodies, be productive through the nurturing that comes from this light, and enjoy life in the world God has created.

There is some conversation between people and God in wisdom discourse, but the dialogue features exchanges of information rather than argumentation. When God makes statements, people may ask questions to get clarification. People cannot, however, argue with God about the application of the commands. God may provide rationales, but people may not ask God for a rationale or argue with God about the rationale. God may ask questions of people, and people may ask questions of God. The purpose and goal of this dialogue must be to exchange information in a context where God knows what is good, does what is good, sees what it good, shows what is good, and expects people to do what is good.

Wisdom assertions regularly are considered definitive. There is no successful way to argue against them. They are grounded in the nature of God's created world. Thus, they are "self-evident." Wisdom statements that correlate trees, vines, and fruit with human thought and activity are an example. As we have seen above, these sayings build on the conceptuality of productivity that lies at the center of the creation story in Gen 1–3. Luke 6:43-45 exhibits the inner nature of wisdom reasoning very well:

Thesis: [43] No good tree bears bad fruit, nor again does a bad tree bear good fruit;
Rationale: [44] for each tree is known by its own fruit.
Opposites and contraries: Figs are not gathered from thorns, nor are grapes picked from a bramble bush.
Example: [45] The good person out of the good treasure of the heart produces good, and the evil person out of evil treasure produces evil;
Rationale: for it is out of the abundance of the heart that the mouth speaks.

[55] See prophetic discourse in the next chapter.

When wisdom discourse from the cosmos is taken into the intersubjective body, the realm of vegetation moves beyond the concept of "that which is good" to the realm of good versus evil or that which is bad. This sequence shows the direct blending of the realm of vegetation with the heart, action, and speech. In the realm of vegetation, everything produces "of its kind," whether it is a fig tree, a thorn bush, a grape vine, or a bramble bush. In Gen 1–3, this "order" in God's creation is "good." If, however, fruit is for "food" (Gen 1:29; 2:9, 16), then all fruit trees are not the same. It begins with the thesis, then, that "No good tree bears bad fruit, nor again does a bad tree bear good fruit." The indisputable rationale, from the realm of reasoning about vegetation is that "each tree is known by its own fruit." Wisdom argumentation regularly uses opposites and contraries to clarify the reasoning: "Figs are not gathered from thorns, nor are grapes picked from a bramble bush." At this point, the reasoning from vegetation is applied to the human realm through general example: "The good person out of the good treasure of the heart produces good, and the evil person out of evil treasure produces evil." This is supported by the rationale: "For it is out of the abundance of the heart that the mouth speaks."

Luke 6:43-45 par. blends the realm of fruit-bearing trees in God's created world with the production of good and evil by humans. When it does this, the heart, the body in action, and the mouth are ready at hand. Blending the concept of a man's treasure chest with the heart in the body, Jesus states the thesis that "the good man out of the good treasure of his heart produces good, and the evil man out of his evil treasure produces evil." Then Jesus supports this with the rationale that "out of the abundance of the heart his mouth speaks." In other words, the mouth speaks "whatever kind" is present and overflowing from the heart.

Here one sees the "natural" progressive texture of thesis, rationale. opposites and contraries, and general example. This may be taken into the realm of human action, where it functions by analogy. Luke 6:46-49 does this:

> *Question:* [46] "Why do you call me 'Lord, Lord', and do not do what I tell you?
>
> *Analogy:* [47] I will show you what someone is like who comes to me, hears my words, and acts on them. [48] That one is like a man building a house, who dug deeply and laid the foundation on rock; when a flood arose, the river burst against that house but could not shake it, because it had been well built.
>
> *Opposite analogy:* [49] But the one who hears and does not act is like a man who built a house on the ground without a foundation. When the river burst against it, immediately it fell, and great was the ruin of that house."

Here the reasoning has been brought from the realm of vegetation into the realm of human action. Again, however, the reasoning is "indisputable." There is an inner logic that people "know to be true."

Wisdom from God: James 3:13-18

We can see further aspects of early Christian wisdom rhetorolect through analysis of Jas 3:13-18. The topos of wisdom emerges fully in the question in 3:13: "Who is wise and understanding among you?" A question designed to stimulate thinking is characteristic of teaching and learning, discourse regularly characterized as didactic or instructive. A teacher asks a question for the purpose of leading a hearer into inquiry about the nature of life and the means by which people produce goodness and righteousness in the world. In this instance, specific topoi of wisdom rhetorolect emerge in the terminology of "wise" (*sophos*) and "understanding" (*epistēmēn*) in the opening question.

After the question comes an elaboration ([*ex*]*ergasia*) that "works (out)" an extended answer to the question. The first part of the elaboration is a thesis in the form of an exhortation: "Show by your good life that your works are done with gentleness born of wisdom" (3:13b). As is customary in the discourse in Mediterranean moral philosophy, a speaker regularly moves beyond a "philosophical" thesis to a thesis in the form of a command or directive. For example, to set the stage for the argumentation in Epictetus, *Discourses* 1.25.1, the discourse moves beyond the thesis, "It is difficulties that show what men are" to the exhortative thesis, "When a difficulty befalls, remember that God, like a physical trainer, has matched you with a rugged young man." An exhortation to "Remember" or "Show by your good life" regularly is embedded in the theses early Christian discourse presents. In other words, early Christian wisdom rhetorolect is not simply philosophical reflection on a thesis. Rather, it is discourse designed to move a person into purposeful action through emotion-fused thought that motivates a person toward the production of good and righteous deeds. The focus is on the intersubjective body, namely a body living among other bodies in God's created world, and its subject matter is "wisdom" that people should have learned from their parents in the household where they grew up. The exhortative thesis explicitly refers to a good (*kalē*) manner of life that produces special deeds (*erga*) because they are informed by wisdom (*sophia*). In this instance, the attribute of gentleness or restraint (*praütēs*) is an inner part of the wisdom.

After the exhortative thesis comes an argument from contraries and opposites supported by a rationale:

(a) But if you have bitter envy and selfish ambition in your hearts, do not be boastful and false to the truth (3:14).

(b) Such wisdom does not come down from above, but is earthly, unspiritual, demonic (3:15).
(c) For where there is envy and selfish ambition, there will also be disorder and wickedness of every kind (3:16).

The initial statement (3:14) explores a conditional possibility that people may have bad things rather than good things in their hearts. Instead of rejoicing in one's heart about another's good fortune and benefit, people may desire to have what other people have and may strive simply for personal benefit at the expense of other people. The protasis ("if" clause: *ei* ...) in the conditional statement explores emotion-fused thoughts in one's heart that are contraries to "good thoughts" that fill the heart of a wise person. They are contraries rather than opposites, since there can be so many of them. We must recall that an opposite is a direct contradiction, expressed with a direct negative formulation: wise/unwise; wise/foolish; good/evil; righteous/unrighteous; love/hate. In a context of opposites, there may be many contraries: jealously, anger, intimidation, harassment, abuse, disrespect, disloyalty, unconcern, selfishness, etc. The conditional statement begins with two possessions in the heart that are contrary to the emotion-fused thoughts that fill the heart of a wise person: bitter envy and selfish ambition. After the protasis comes a negative apodosis (presupposing an implied "then" ...) containing two prohibitions: "do not be boastful and (do not be) false to the truth."

If people's hearts are filled with "unwise" emotion-fused thoughts, they will boast of wrong things. The content of the protasis indicates that such people will boast about themselves: the things they have, in a context of wanting what other people have (envy); and their own achievements, in a context of seeking success only for themselves (selfish ambition). In addition, such people will say things that are not true. Since their hearts are filled with thoughts and desires that focus only on themselves, their thinking and acting processes are not true to the interdependent relation they have to other people and to God's created world. Therefore, their thoughts and actions are not only bad but are also not "true." If they speak, they will say things that only boast about themselves and are "untrue." One should only speak, according to this wisdom, if one's heart is filled with wise thoughts that keep a person from making exaggerated and untrue statements. If people have wisdom in their hearts, they will describe all things, including themselves, without exaggeration and, thus, will speak truth rather than falsehood.

After the conditional statement that explores thoughts and speech that are contrary to wisdom (3:14), the next statement (3:15) defines wisdom through a statement that causes the hearer to supply opposites for all the concepts in verses 13-15. There is wisdom from above and there is an "opposite wisdom" that is earthly, unspiritual, and demonic. The introduction of opposites creates an emergent structure[56] in the mind of the hearer that invites an opposite for every concept in the context: (3:13) wise and understanding/foolish and without understanding; good life/evil life; gentleness/violence; born of wisdom/born of evil; (3:14) bitter envy/joyous giving; selfish ambition/generous encouragement of others; boastful/non-boastful; false/truthful; (3:15) from above/(from) below; earthly/heavenly; unspiritual/spiritual; demonic/godly.

The purpose of contraries and opposites is to clarify a thesis by giving it more extended definition. Once the process begins, the mind virtually automatically begins to create additional contraries and opposites. A good life is guided by wisdom from above (3:13). A life guided by earthly, unspiritual, and demonic things is naturally an evil life. Jas 3:16 supports this emergent structure of contraries and opposites with a rationale that explains the effect of the "envy" and "selfish ambition" named in 3:14 as disorder (*akatastasia*) and social wickedness of every kind (*pan phaulon pragma*). All of the dynamics of God's creation of the "good" world support this rationale. As it says in Sir 16:27, 28-29: "[the Lord] arranged his works (*erga*) in an eternal order (*eis aiōna*).... They do not crowd one another, and they never disobey his word. Then the Lord looked upon the earth and filled it with his good things (*tōn agathōn autou*)."[57] Gentleness born of wisdom (3:13), being guided by words from God's wisdom, creates a context of order that has the potential to fill the entire human realm with God's goodness. This order creates peacefulness, rather than discord and conflict. Bitter envy and selfish ambition (3:14) produce disorder and wickedness of every kind. The purpose of wise action is to produce "order" and "goodness of every kind."

After the rationale in 3:16 focuses on envy and selfish ambition, 3:17 "runs" or "elaborates"[58] the contraries and opposites by presenting a list of attributes that are contrary or opposite to wisdom that is earthly, unspiritual, and demonic. At this point, some new contraries emerge. Wisdom from above is "first pure" (*hagnē*).[59] At this point, a touch of priestly rhetorolect blends into the wisdom rhetorolect in Jas 3:13-18. The blending of wisdom and priestly rhetorolect is dynamically present in the story of King Solomon whose "wisdom from above" included instructions for building the temple (1 Kgs 5–7). The blending of wisdom with

[56] Fauconnier and Turner, *The Way We Think*, 42-46, 48-49, 85-86.

[57] Cf. Gen 1:1-31; Ps 104.

[58] Fauconnier and Turner, *The Way We Think*, 44, 48-49.

[59] Cf. the "pure manner of life" (*hagnēn anastrophēn*) in 1 Pet 3:2 with Jas 3:13b, 17a. For the purity of God's wisdom or precepts (*logia*), see Pss 12:6 (LXX: 11:7); 19:9 (LXX: 18:10); Prov 15:26; 19:13 (LXX); 21:8. For the priestly nature of this purity, cf. Prov 20:9 with Ps 51.

priestly discourse is exceptionally strong in Sirach (see esp. 45:6-25; 47:13; 49:1-3; 50:1-29[60] and noticeably present in Wisdom of Solomon.[61] Prov 20:9 says: "Who can boast (*kauchēsetai*) of having a pure (*hagnēn*) heart?" Jas 3:17 is an elaboration of Jas 3:14, which argues that a person whose heart is filled with bitter envy and selfish ambition must not be boastful (*katakauchasthe*). Only a person who speaks pure words could dare be boastful, since "The words (*logia*) of the Lord are pure words (*logia hagna*)" (Ps 12:6 [LXX 11:7])."[62]

In addition to purity, wisdom from above is "peaceable, gentle, willing to yield, full of mercy and good fruits, without a trace of partiality or hypocrisy."[63] The priority of "peaceable" after "then" (*epeita*), and the embedding of "good fruits" in the middle between "gentle, open to persuasion, full of mercy" and "without partiality or hypocrisy" creates a repetitive texture that dominates the conclusion of the elaboration (3:17-18: peaceable ... good fruits ... fruit of righteousness ... in peace ... make peace).[64] This early Christian wisdom focuses on "sowing fruit of righteousness" in a context of peace that "makes peace." The elaboration presupposes an argument from analogy with God's good creation. When God created the "good" world in which humans live, God made fruit trees of every kind that were good (Gen 1:11-12) and gave every tree with fruit in its seed to humans for food (Gen 1:29). When the man and woman ate of the "tree of the knowledge of good and evil" (Gen 2:16-17; 3:6), they became like God (or gods), who knows good and evil (Gen 3:22). Early Christian wisdom rhetorolect presupposes that humans can only "eat from the tree of life and live forever" (Gen 3:22) if they take "wisdom from above" into their hearts. They must "take hold of" wisdom, because it is a tree of life (Prov 3:18). When they do this, they are in a position to produce "righteous fruit" which is a "tree of life" that is the opposite of violence. As Prov 11:30 says, "The fruit of the righteous is a tree of life, but violence takes lives away." Prov 7:13 (LXX) adds the priestly dimension of this peace that takes violence away through sacrificial ritual when it says: "Sacrifices are peaceable (*eirēnikē*) for me; today I have paid my vows." As Jas 3:17 says, "This wisdom from above is first pure; then it is peaceable" (*eirēnikēi*).

[60] C.V. Camp, "Storied Space, or, Ben Sira 'Tells' a Temple," in Gunn and McNutt, *"Imagining" Biblical Worlds*, 64-80.

[61] Cf. Wisdom 3:5-6, 14; 4:2; 7:22, 24-25; 8:20; 9:8; 10:20; 11:15-16; 12:3-5; 14:11-31; 15:6, 15-19; 18:9, 24.

[62] Cf. Ps 19:7-9 (LXX 18:8-10); Prov 15:26; 21:8.

[63] L.T. Johnson, *The Letter of James* (AB 37A; New York: Doubleday, 1995) 274-75, thinks the words translated "without a trace of partiality or hypocrisy" mean "it is simple and not insincere."

[64] *eirēnikē ... karpēn agathēn ... karpos dikaiosunēs ... en eirēnē ...poiousin eirēnēn.*

Jas 3:18 presents the conclusion of the elaboration on wisdom from above: "And the fruit of righteousness is sown in peace by those who make peace." At this point, the imagery from God's productive creation reaches its fullness in the topics of righteousness and peace. This is one instance of a statement of "finalization" in early Christian wisdom rhetorolect.[65] The result of wise emotion-fused thought and conduct, produced by wisdom from above, is the "fruit of righteousness." This fruit is then "sown" by people who "make peace" by "sowing in peace." This conclusion is a remarkable reconfiguration of the LXX account of the creation story in Gen 1–3. Instead of sowing grain, wise humans sow fruit of righteousness. This sowing produces peace. For the epistle of James, then, those who "believe in our glorious Jesus Christ" (2:1) do not engage in acts of partiality (2:9) and other acts that produce "disorder and wickedness of every kind" (3:16), but their acts are "peaceable, gentle, willing to yield, and full of mercy," producing good fruits that yield a harvest of righteousness (3:17-18).

Wisdom Blends in the New Testament

Wisdom Blends with Prophetic, Apocalyptic, Priestly, and Miracle Rhetorolect: James 2; 4–5

The concept of completion or finalization of Torah wisdom in the adult world of one's neighbors is clearly present in Jas 2:8-13. The wisdom argumentation here begins with "You shall love your neighbor as yourself," which it calls the "kingly" law according to the scripture (2:8). The "kingdom" orientation, which is openly stated in 2:5, introduces the vistas of early Christian prophetic rhetorolect. In other words, here wisdom rhetorolect is not only taken into the adult world of "neighbors," but into the adult realm of leadership in a large realm of land with political boundaries. The language of "choosing" is part of the dynamics of prophetic rhetorolect, where God selects a group of people to be "his people" (the kingdom of God), chooses a "king" to rule over them, and has to choose and call prophets to challenge the leaders to live according to Torah wisdom. The hearers are being asked to bring the dynamics of the divine kingdom into their community life with their "brothers and sisters" (2:5).[66]

[65] For "finalization," see M.M. Bakhtin/P.N. Medvedev, *The Formal Method in Literary Scholarship: A Critical Introduction to Sociological Poetics* (trans. A.J. Wehrle; Baltimore and London: Johns Hopkins University Press, 1978) 129-41, esp. 130: "Every genre represents a special way of constructing and finalizing a whole, finalizing it essentially and thematically (we repeat), and not just conditionally or compositionally"; cf. Bakhtin, *The Dialogic Imagination*, 426.

[66] Wesley H. Wachob, *The Voice of Jesus in the Social Rhetoric of James* (SNTSMS 106; Cambridge, UK: Cambridge University Press, 2000) 85-104, 121-22, 138-53.

Early Christian wisdom rhetorolect merges naturally not only with priestly and apocalyptic rhetorolect but also with prophetic and miracle rhetorolect. The manner in which early Christian miracle rhetorolect emerges out of Hebrew Bible prophetic discourse will be explained in some detail in Chapters 5 and 6. At present, the issue is the blending of wisdom, prophetic, apocalyptic, priestly, and miracle rhetorolect together in early Christian discourse. Throughout the first three chapters of James, wisdom rhetorolect dominates. Beginning with Jas 4:1, the tone shifts to a confrontational mode characteristic of prophetic rhetorolect. It is not appropriate here to analyze the dynamic blending of rhetorolects throughout all the verses in the last two chapters of James. Therefore, the analysis will select certain portions of Jas 4–5 to illustrate how early Christian wisdom rhetorolect may invite prophetic, apocalyptic, priestly, and miracle rhetorolect into its discourse.

Let us recall, from analysis earlier in this chapter, that Jas 3:13-18 contains what one might call "vintage wisdom rhetorolect" in early Christian discourse. Speaking directly about wisdom and understanding, it presents "gentleness born of wisdom" as a resource within the human body that produces a fruit of righteousness that makes peace. When "purity" heads the list of characteristics of "the wisdom from above" (3:17), an interpreter sees how early Christian wisdom rhetorolect blends naturally with priestly rhetorolect. The analysis of 1 Cor 3 below exhibits how Pauline discourse dynamically blends wisdom rhetorolect both with priestly and apocalyptic rhetorolect. The first task here will be to show how the tone and mode shifts when wisdom rhetorolect modulates into prophetic rhetorolect. This occurs when the theses, rationales, questions, answers, contraries and opposites, analogies, and conclusions move beyond exhortation, which is a natural, internal aspect of wisdom rhetorolect, into confrontation that indicts the hearers for doing things wrong.

James 4:1-3 exhibits a modulation from wisdom to prophetic rhetorolect in its opening questions: "Those conflicts and disputes among you, where do they come from? Do they not come from your cravings that are at war within you?" These are not the more gentle questions of wisdom rhetorolect, which "explore" topics for the purpose of instruction and exhortation. Rather, this is a sequence of two questions that accuse the hearers of engaging in conflicts and disputes because they have cravings (*hēdonōn*) at war in their bodies. In other words, the thesis (4:1a: there are conflicts and disputes among you) and the rationale (4:1b: because you have cravings at war within you) are confrontational and accusatory, rather than instructive, exploratory, and explanatory. James 4:2-3 then presents a series of statements related to a list of vices common to wisdom rhetorolect. This list, however, is presented in a confrontational rather than explanatory mode:

> [2]You want something and do not have it; so you commit murder.
> And you covet something and cannot obtain it; so you engage in disputes and conflicts.
> You do not have, because you do not ask.
> [3]You ask and do not receive, because you ask wrongly, in order to spend what you get on your pleasures.

Rather than being a list that explores and explains the nature of envy that leads to murder, coveting that leads to disputes and conflicts, asking that leads to receiving, and asking wrongly that does not lead to receiving, this list accuses its hearers of doing the terrible things it talks about. This is the nature of prophetic rhetorolect. The presupposition is that the speaker understands him/herself to be called and designated by God to confront people who are not doing the will of God. The mode of speech is second person plural direct address that tells the hearers what they are doing wrong.

James 4:4-6 continues by calling the hearers "adulterers." Here one notices the dramatic contrast between wisdom rhetorolect, which regularly addresses its hearers as "brothers," "friends," or some similar term designed to produce an experience of kinship or friendship between the speaker and the hearers. This speech creates sharp opposition between the speaker and the hearers. The speaker is on the side of God; the hearers are acting against God and God's ways. After calling the hearers adulterers, the speaker presents a thesis using the common "you know" (*oidate*) feature of wisdom rhetorolect: You know that friendship with the world is enmity with God. But the mode in which it is presented is not the mode of wisdom rhetorolect. The thesis is formulated as a confrontational question characteristic of prophetic rhetorolect: "Do you not know ("you adulterers!") that friendship with the world is enmity with God?" Then the speaker presents a conclusion introduced with "therefore" (*oun*). Again, however, the tone is prophetic: "Therefore whoever wishes to be a friend of the world ("like you do!") becomes an enemy of God." The conclusion acquires its prophetic bite by presenting a negative example with the implication that the hearers are the kind of person being described. Again, argument from example (even negative example) is highly characteristic of wisdom rhetorolect. But the discourse in Jas 4:4 makes it accusatory rather than explanatory and instructive. The tone is prophetic rather than didactic, namely an instruction in wisdom. James 4:5-6 continues with two arguments from authoritative testimony. This is a conventional move in the elaboration of an argument in early Christian wisdom rhetorolect. Here, however, the speaker does not simply "appeal" to written authority. Rather, in a manner characteristic of prophetic rhetorolect, the speaker makes it confrontational and oppositional: "Or do you suppose that it is for nothing (*dokeite hoti kenōs*) that the scripture says, 'God yearns jealously for the spirit that he has made to dwell in us'?" In and of themselves, the recitation of the "sentence" in 4:5[67] and the parallelismus membrorum in 4:6[68] could function naturally as an aspect of wisdom rhetorolect. In fact, the question and answer in 4:4, the recitations of authoritative testimony in 4:5-6, and the exhortations in 4:7-10 could be straightforward wisdom rhetorolect if the name-calling (4:4: you adulterers; 4:8: you sinners, you double-minded people), the haranguing phrases (4:4: Do you not know?; 4:5: Or do you suppose that it is for nothing that the scripture says?), and the opening of 4:9 ("Lament and mourn and weep!") were omitted. The overall content is fully at home in wisdom rhetorolect:

> [4] Friendship with the world is enmity with God.
> Whoever wishes to be a friend of the world becomes an enemy of God.
> [5] God yearns jealously for the spirit that he has made to dwell in us.
> [6] God opposes the proud, but gives grace to the humble.
> [7] Submit yourselves therefore to God.
> Resist the devil, and he will flee from you.
> [8] Draw near to God, and he will draw near to you.
> Cleanse your hands and purify your hearts.
> [9] Let your laughter be turned into mourning and your joy into dejection.
> [10] Humble yourselves before the Lord, and he will exalt you.

All of these statements could occur in the progressive texture of these verses as wisdom rhetorolect. The blending of wisdom and prophetic rhetorolect is obvious in 4:4-9. James 4:10, however, ends the sequence with a statement fully at home in wisdom rhetorolect, without any blending of another rhetorolect. The overall sequence of Jas 4:1-10, then, exhibits a blending of prophetic rhetorolect into wisdom rhetorolect. The sequence of the rhetorical elaboration is conventional for wisdom rhetorolect. The tone, however, has been programmatically transformed into prophetic rhetorolect until it modulates back into wisdom rhetorolect in the final statement in 4:10.

James 4:11–5:6 continues with prophetic rhetorolect dynamically blended into wisdom rhetorolect. Then in 5:7-11 prophetic rhetorolect blends with apocalyptic rhetorolect,[69] and 5:12 appears to be a blend of wisdom, prophetic, and apocalyptic rhetorolect. Since the analysis of 1 Cor 3 below will present an example of wisdom rhetorolect blending

[67] The source for the recitation is unknown.

[68] Prov 3:34 (LXX); cf. 1 Pet 5:5.

[69] See Todd C. Penner, *The Epistle of James and Eschatology: Re-reading an Ancient Christian Letter* (JSNTSup 121; Sheffield: Sheffield Academic Press, 1996).

with apocalyptic rhetorolect, there will not be an analysis of Jas 4:11–5:12 in the present context.

A new phenomenon emerges in Jas 5:12-20, namely a dynamic blend of wisdom, priestly, and miracle rhetorolect. For this reason, we will spend some time with analysis and interpretation of these final verses of the epistle of James. In the context of a blending of wisdom, prophetic, and apocalyptic rhetorolect, the discourse turns to people who are suffering: Are any among you suffering? They should pray. Are any cheerful? They should sing songs of praise (5:13). On the one hand, the approach is to instruct the hearers. Thus, the underlying mode remains wisdom rhetorolect. On the other hand, the concern about suffering invites priestly rhetorolect into the discourse. The priestly rhetorolect, in turn, invites miracle rhetorolect into the context of the blend of wisdom and priestly rhetorolect. In the midst of this, Elijah emerges from the storyline of Israel as an example for members of the believing community. It will be important for us to look carefully at the manner in which Elijah functions in the context of the blended discourse we are interpreting.

James 5:13-14 introduces three questions followed by three answers. First, if anyone is suffering (*kakopathei*), they should pray. Second, if anyone is cheerful (*euthumei*), they should sing songs of praise. Third, if anyone is sick (*asthenei*), they should call for elders of the church. These three topoi are common in wisdom rhetorolect. Often wisdom rhetoro–lect invites discussions of patience, endurance, and perhaps anticipation of better times in a context of suffering or illness. Instead, these three topoi create a context for blending priestly and wisdom rhetorolect in early Christian discourse.

One can imagine quite another way of discussing the three topoi present in Jas 5:13-14. For example, if one is suffering, perhaps this person should ask him/herself if he/she should change some daily habits. In other words, the person might be asked to engage in philosophical introspection or examination of their style of life. In addition, if a person is cheerful, perhaps they should use the opportunity to cheer up someone who is mourning the death of a loved one or who is suffering from an illness. If a person is sick, surely they should go to a physician. Instead, the discourse blends all three topoi with a context of worship. The person who is suffering should pray; the person who is cheerful should sing songs of praise (*psalletō*); and the person who is sick should call elders of the church. In other words, the question and answer style here, so common in wisdom rhetorolect, provides a means to discuss rituals of worship.

The third topos holds special interest for us here, since the blend of wisdom and priestly rhetorolect invites miracle rhetorolect into its discourse. The topos of prayer occurs eight times in verbs and nouns throughout verses 13-18,[70] establishing a repetitive texture in the discourse that focuses on priestly actions toward God that energize an exchange of benefits between God and humans. In addition, there is a ritual of anointing the sick person with oil in the name of the Lord (5:14). As humans give benefits to God, often by giving special attention to other human beings "in the name of God," God gives special benefits to humans. James 5:13-14 functions as wisdom rhetorolect that instructs the community concerning certain daily priestly activities. In the context of this focus of wisdom instruction on priestly rituals, the argumentative mode shifts to a progressive texture that alternates theses, cases, results, and conclusions designed to convince a hearer that God does miraculous things in response to prayer.

The unit continues with an account of the anticipated result: "and the prayer of faith will save the sick man, and the Lord will raise him up; if he has committed sins, he will be forgiven" (Jas 5:15). Instead of productivity of goodness and righteousness, as in wisdom rhetorolect, the emphasis is on restoration. With miracle rhetorolect, it is not a matter of initial creation of ordered goodness. Rather, in a context where order has fallen into disorder, strength has fallen into weakness, health has disintegrated into illness, the action of a community of believing people restores a person to health. The dynamics of wisdom rhetorolect are nearby, however, since the restoration is not just physical. Just as wisdom rhetorolect can feature forgiveness through mercy, so miracle rhetorolect emphasizes the integration of the sick man back into the community through forgiveness.

The instructions in Jas 5:13-15 are guidelines for the wise. But the instructions are aimed at "saving the sick man," a result whereby "the Lord will raise him." This is the reasoning of Christian miracle rhetorolect. Thus, pictorial narration (rhetography) of a healing moves toward pictorial narration of a successful conclusion that combines miracle rhetology (the sick man will be saved) and rhetography (the Lord will raise him). The conditional construction at the end about committing sins and being forgiven is a special feature of Christian miracle rhetorolect, which we will see in a later chapter. While the topic under discussion is a person who is sick, the internal logic of the progression in 5:15-16 is a combination of wisdom and miracle reasoning.

The first column of the table below presents the progressive texture of the wisdom reasoning in Jas 5:14-16. This is reasoning that presents a thesis, a rationale for the thesis, and a conclusion. James 5:14 presents the question and the instruction. James 5:15-16 supports the instruction with

[70] Let him pray (13) ... let them pray (14) … the prayer of faith (15) …pray for one another … the petition of the righteous … (16) … Elijah prayed with prayer (17) … again he prayed (18).

a thesis that the prayer of faith will save the sick, and the Lord will raise them up; and anyone who has committed sins will be forgiven. This thesis is the deductive result of observing a series of healings. Healing stories in the cultural setting, then, are the (inductive) basis for believing the thesis in Jas 5:15. Once it is true that the prayer of faith will produce such results, then the rationale for the thesis is obvious: the prayer of the

Wisdom Reasoning	Miracle Reasoning
Question and Answer Instruction: Are any among you suffering? They should call for the elders of the church and have them pray over them, anointing them with oil in the name of the Lord (5:14).	*Question:* Are any among you suffering? *Case:* They should call for the elders of the church and have them pray over them, anointing them with oil in the name of the Lord (5:14).
Thesis: The prayer of faith will save the sick, and the Lord will raise them up; and anyone who has committed sins will be forgiven (5:15).	*Result/Case:* The prayer of faith will save the sick, and the Lord will raise them up; and anyone who has committed sins will be forgiven (5:15).
Rationale: The prayer of the righteous is powerful and effective (5:16b).	*Result:* Therefore confess your sins to one another, and pray for one another, so that you may be healed (5:16a).
Conclusion: Therefore confess your sins to one another, and pray for one another, so that you may be healed (5:16a).	*Rule:* The prayer of the righteous is powerful and effective (5:16b).

righteous is powerful and effective (5:16b). The conclusion to be drawn from the thesis and the rationale is that people should confess their sins to one another, and pray for one another, so they may be healed (5:16a). From the perspective of wisdom argumentation, then, the reasoning moves from a thesis through a rationale to an exhortative conclusion. The second column presents Jas 5:14-16 from the perspective of reasoning in miracle rhetorolect. Miracle rhetorolect presents inductive reasoning that moves through a series of cases to a deductive rule that God's power through the prayer of the righteous performs miraculous deeds.[71] From this perspective, Jas 5:14 focuses on the action of elders as a potential narrative that will produce healing. Miracle rhetorolect regularly presents a story, where the initial statements recount actions by a healer on the malfunctioning body of a person. James 5:14 pictures such actions as a scene that presupposes previous stories that make each action in the scene plausible. The hearer is to envision the calling together of the elders, the praying of the elders over the sick person, and the anointing of

[71] Robbins, "Miracle Discourse in the Synoptic Gospels," in *The Role of Miracle Discourse in the Argumentation of the New Testament* (ed. D.F. Watson; Symposium; Atlanta: SBL, 2009)

the sick person with oil. James 5:15 presents the customary results of miracle stories when elders take this action: after the elders do these things, the sick are saved, the Lord raises them up, and the person's sins are forgiven. James 5:16a presupposes that the next natural result will be collective action by the community to be healed: they confess their sins to one another and pray for one another, so all may be healed. From the perspective of miracle rhetorolect, Jas 5:16b presents the deduction each member should make from the series of actions and results in 5:14-16a: the prayer of the righteous is powerful and effective, which is the natural manner in which the conclusion of a miracle story regularly produces a thesis about how the miracle occurred. In other words, this is the moment in the progressive texture of a miracle story when the narrator presents "wisdom" about the miracle that is a deduction on the basis of the action in a story. James 5:14-16, then, contains progressive texture characteristic of reasoning and exhortation characteristic of instructive wisdom rhetorolect dynamically blended with miracle rhetorolect.

James 5:17-18 also blends wisdom and miracle rhetorolect. The elaboration moves to an argument from example embedded in a syllogistic sequence characteristic of wisdom rhetorolect, but its subject matter is miracle rhetorolect:

> *Rule:* The prayer of a righteous man has great power in its effects.
> *Case:* 17 Elijah was a man of like nature with ourselves and he prayed fervently that it might not rain,
> *Result:* and for three years and six months it did not rain on the earth.
> *Case:* 18 Then he prayed again and the heaven gave rain,
> *Result:* and the earth brought forth its fruit.

As is characteristic of wisdom rhetorolect, the unit begins with a "wisdom rule." When wisdom rhetorolect invites miracle rhetorolect into itself, accounts of individual healers naturally evoke general premises on the basis of their attributes and actions. But then it presents summarizing pictorial narration of actions of Elijah, a prophet who produced a series of miracles in biblical tradition. The narration does not refer to his healing of a person, however, which is the topic of the passage. Rather, it moves into the arena of wisdom rhetorolect with its focus on productivity in God's creation. Functioning as a prophet who brings God's will to people who are to enact the attributes of God's kingdom, Elijah prays for rain to cease as a form of punishment of the people. After the rain ceased for three years and six months, Elijah prayed again and restored the creation to its ordered processes of productivity. Thus, the argument from example reaches deeply into the dynamics of both wisdom and prophetic rhetorolect in support of miracle rhetorolect. Miracle rhetorolect, then, has a close affiliation both with wisdom and prophetic rhetorolect during the Hellenistic period. One can see this in Sirach 45:3

(Moses); 45:19; 48:4-5 (Elijah); 48:12-13 (Elisha). The emphasis is that God either grants certain individuals the ability to perform miracles "by their word" (Sirach 45:3) or God's word performs the miracles (48:5). By the end, Jas 5:14-18 blends an array of topics central to wisdom, prophetic, and miracle rhetorolect: sickness, prayer, anointing with oil, name of the Lord, faith, being saved (healed), being raised up, sin, forgiveness, righteousness, power, rain, and fruit. The miracle rhetorolect has a narrational texture of "narrative summary" characteristic of wisdom rhetorolect. Jas 5:17-18 presents no detailed contextual description and no dramatic sequence of personal action or confrontation. Rather, the two events attributed to Elijah are told as "information" that guides a person toward "prayer action" in a context of crisis based on need. James 5:17-18, then, exhibits a dynamic blend of wisdom and miracle rhetorolect fully related to the blending in 5:14-16.

James 5:19-20 concludes the epistle of James with a sequence of statements that blend wisdom, priestly, and miracle rhetorolect. James 5:19 begins with the characteristic address of wisdom rhetorolect, "brothers," which is appropriately translated inclusively as "brothers and sisters" in the NRSV. In other words, in contrast to the confrontational prophetic mode present in 4:1-10; 1:13–5:6, the last two verses return to the kinship and friendship mode present in 1:2; 2:1, 14; 3:1, 10, 12; 4:11.[72] Then it presents an "if (*ean*) … (then) you should know (*ginōskete*) …" statement characteristic of conditional reasoning in wisdom rhetorolect. The purpose of didactic wisdom is to give a person information that will guide them toward right action in the future. The final two verses address a situation where a member of the community has wandered away from the wisdom of God (5:19: the truth [*alētheia*]) and another member has brought the person back. James 5:20 talks about this action from a perspective of miracle rhetorolect. The person who brought the wandering person back to the community has "saved" the sinner's soul from death (*sōsei psychēn* [*autou*] *ek thanatou*). And then another comment blends priestly rhetorolect with the blend of wisdom and miracle rhetorolect in the verse: "and he will cover a multitude of sins." The priestly dynamics of 5:13-16,[73] then, remain nearby to the very end of the epistle.

[72] Notice also the shift to "beloved" in the apocalyptic rhetorolect in Jas 5:7-12.

[73] It is likely that 5:12, which we have not discussed here, already introduced priestly rhetorolect into the discourse of chapter five.

Wisdom Blends with Priestly and Apocalyptic Rhetorolect in Households: 1 Corinthians 3

We saw above how priestly rhetorolect blends with wisdom rhetorolect in the concept of purity (*hagnē*) that stands first in the list of attributes of "wisdom from above" in Jas 3:17. We also mentioned that wisdom and prophetic rhetorolect blend with apocalyptic rhetorolect in Jas 5:7-12. 1 Corinthians 3 shows an even more dramatic way in which a blending of wisdom and priestly rhetorolect may invite apocalyptic rhetorolect into its domain. As Paul uses basic argumentative techniques of wisdom discourse to address the Corinthians in 1 Cor 3, he introduces an analogy between the Christians at Corinth and a "house of God" (3:9-11) that creates a bridge to apocalyptic rhetorolect blended with priestly rhetorolect in 3:12-17.

Paul begins 1 Cor 3 by addressing the Corinthians as brothers,[74] which evokes a relationship to them as members of the same family. From the position of an older brother relation to them, he refers to a past time when it was necessary for him to speak to them as infants (3:1). Using food imagery that is naturally internal to wisdom rhetorolect, Paul recalls how he fed them milk rather than solid food, acting as a parent/nurse to them (3:2). The manner in which Paul refers to their lack of readiness for solid food in the past, and even in the present, introduces the concept of growth to maturity that lies at the base of wisdom rhetorolect (3:2-3). The goal is that the Corinthians grow into mature adults who are able to produce the good fruits of God's goodness and righteousness, which includes not quarreling with one another and not behaving according to human inclinations (3:3).

As Paul's discourse continues, it moves outside the household into the vegetational world of God, where plants grow into a fullness where they produce a harvest. Paul achieves this transition by referring to Apollos and himself as servants (*diakonoi*). This term is a natural extension of the household language of brothers in 3:1, since a household in antiquity contained not only people who had a "blood-relation" to one another, but also to people who prepared and served the food (servants), attendants who performed manual labor or other service (*hypēretēs*: 1 Cor 4:1), and stewards who managed the household (*oikonomoi*: 1 Cor 4:2). Planting and growing food is integral to the activities of a household, and it moves naturally into a blend with God's created world, where God gives the plants their growth (3:6-7). Here one sees the natural blending of household and God's vegetational world that lies at the base of Christian wisdom rhetorolect. Even if Paul planted, and Apollos wa-

[74] The NRSV appropriately translates this "brothers and sisters" to indicate the inclusive from of address this would have been to the men and women in the Christian households in Corinth.

tered, God is the one who gives the plants their growth (3:6). As Paul asserts in 3:9, they are fellow workers *(synergoi)* with God, and the Corinthians are God's field (*geōrgion*) and God's building (*oikodomē*). The households of God in Corinth blend with God's created world, where Paul and Apollos work cooperatively with God among the Corinthian believers, who are God's field. Thus, eating and growing from infancy to adulthood in God's household (3:1-3) blends with planting, watering, and growing in God's field (3:6-9) in Paul's wisdom rhetorolect at the beginning of 1 Cor 3.

The overall nature of Paul's discourse in 1 Cor 3 as wisdom rhetorolect is clear from the ending of the chapter in 3:18-23. Paul's topic concerns the challenge to become wise, rather than to become fools (3:18). The overall goal must be to understand the unusual nature of God's wisdom, rather than to follow the wisdom of this world (3:18-19). A beginning place for the Corinthians to attain this knowledge is a proper understanding of their relation to all things in the world. They do not simply have a relationship to their human leaders, like Paul and Apollos. Rather, as infants in Christ (3:1), all things belong to them. This means that their leaders Paul, Apollos, and Cephas; the world, life, death, the present, and the future belong to them (3:21-22). In turn, they belong to Christ and Christ belongs to God (3:23). Paul's wisdom rhetorolect in 1 Cor 3, then, is designed to establish an understanding of a believer's relationship to all things in the world, including human leaders with whom they may have a close personal bond.

The relationship of the believer to Christ, and its results, makes this wisdom discourse distinctive in the Mediterranean world. Many forms of wisdom discourse in the Mediterranean world evoked complex systems of relationships among humans, the cosmos, life, death, the present, and the future. The unusual feature of Paul's discourse is the assertion that the Corinthians are "infants in Christ" (3:1) who should grow, with God's help, into full adulthood "in Christ." The Corinthians are infants in a household. They do not, however, belong to adults who run this household, nor do they belong directly to God in the manner in which other people in the Mediterranean world might consider themselves to be "owned by God." The Corinthian believers live in a "family network" in which they are infants who have a responsibility to grow into responsible adults. While certain human leaders have responsibilities over them, these leaders are not the ones who give them their identity or "own" them. These leaders have been assigned by the master (*kyrios*) of the household to function as "servants" (*diakonoi*) to lead them into belief (3:5). Therefore, no one should boast about their leaders (3:5) or identify themselves on the basis of the names of those leaders (1:12; 3:4). Rather, these infants are to be identified on the basis of "the Lord Jesus

Christ" (1:2), to whom "they belong." Their relationship to God occurs through their relation to Christ as "the Lord" of this distinctive family network. As a result of the relation of Christ to God, all things in the world belong to the believers (3:21-22). Their identity in the "family network" of Christ and God makes them "fellow owners" of everything in the world: their leaders (who are servants), the world itself, life, death, and time from the present to the future (3:21-23).

Paul is able to formulate the remarkable "wisdom" he communicates in 1 Cor 3 only by blending multiple Christian rhetorolects into his wisdom discourse. In this chapter, he vividly blends imagery internal to early Christian priestly and apocalyptic rhetorolect. Priestly rhetorolect, with all the imagery associated with temples in antiquity, blends dynamically with the "extended household imagery"[75] when the progressive texture of 3:9 ends with "God's building you are." Paul's use of the term *oikodomē* creates a vivid blend of God's house (*theou oikos* = temple) with family household (*domos*).[76] The household to which the Corinthians belong is God's building. This creates a transition to Paul's discourse about his own activity as a master builder (3:10: *architechtōn*) who laid the foundation, who is Jesus Christ (3:11). This "mixing" of imagery, which includes both inanimate objects and people ("infants in Christ" who need to be fed, servants who plant and water, God's fellow workers, God's field, God's building, Paul as master builder, Christ as the foundation), becomes central to Christian discourse as a result of dynamic blending of multiple rhetorolects together. Multiple modes of conceptualization map over one another like a series of pictures that blend together on a visual screen. Successive mapping highlights certain things and overshadows certain other things. This brings certain things into the foreground and causes other things to move into the background. The imagery of believers in Christ as God's building moves momentarily into the foreground in 3:16: "Do you not know that you are God's temple and that God's Spirit dwells in you?" Not only is Christ the foundation! The Corinthians are God's temple! Through his blending of wisdom and priestly rhetorolect, Paul creates an image of the Corinthians (who are infants in Christ) as God's temple in whom God's spirit dwells. It will be necessary for us to return to God's spirit in a moment. But first we must turn to the other rhetorolect Paul blends with wisdom and priestly rhetorolect.

[75] By "extended" I am referring to the extension of the activities of the household out into the fields, where food is produced for the household. This extension makes stewards, servants, attendants, and laborers all part of the household.

[76] John R. Lanci, *A New Temple for Corinth: Rhetorical and Archaeological Approaches to Pauline Imagery* (New York: Peter Lang, 1997).

In the midst of Paul's discussion of the Corinthians as God's building, himself as the master builder, and Christ as the foundation of the building, Paul introduces apocalyptic rhetorolect in 3:12-15. The emergence of apocalyptic rhetorolect coincides with a decisive shift in the argumentative texture of 1 Cor 3. Prior to 3:12, Paul's discourse contains the common features of wisdom rhetorolect. This includes assertions that function as theses (3:1), adversative qualifications of statements (but: 3:1, 6, 7); negatives that introduce contraries, opposites, or negative examples that clarify (3:1, 2, 3, 4, 7, 11); reasons, rationales, and explanations (3:2, 3, 4, 9, 11), and conclusions (3:5, 7). The argumentative texture of Paul's discourse shifts in 3:12, where a pattern of "if … (then) …" constructions continues through 3:18. In 3:12, Paul shifts into future conditional statements that contain vivid apocalyptic imagery. If anyone builds on Christ the foundation with gold, silver, precious stones, wood, hay, straw, then the work of each builder will become visible, for the Day will disclose it, because it will be revealed with fire, and the fire will test what sort of work each has done (3:12-13). The introduction of this vivid imagery into the blend of wisdom and priestly rhetorolect Paul has created in 3:1-11 adds a decisively distinctive dimension to early Christian wisdom discourse. One of the aspects of "mature" Christian wisdom is an apocalyptic understanding of the way God will function at the end of time, namely "knowledge" about the Day of the Lord.[77] Early Christian wisdom, then, not only concerned relationships of people to one another, to Christ, to God, and to the world. It also concerned, as we recall, productive-reproductive time, which has a seasonal nature. Since seasonal time began in the story of creation that started the story of wisdom, issues could easily emerge concerning "endings of seasons" of times in God's created world. Paul's focus in 1 Cor 3 includes the present and the future. Believers who know God's wisdom will know that their "family" identification "in Christ" puts them in a relationship where both the present and the future "belong to them" (3:22). They know this, because, in turn, they know that they belong to Christ and Christ belongs to God (3:23). In 1 Cor 3, Paul's focus on the future invites apocalyptic rhetorolect into wisdom rhetorolect.

The apocalyptic rhetorolect in 1 Cor 3 does not stand alone. Rather, at all points it blends with the other rhetorolects in the context. Its emergence in 3:12-13 works with the topoi of foundation and builder

[77] As we will see in the chapters on apocalyptic, when apocalyptic functions as the host for wisdom, wisdom includes "knowledge that will be disclosed at the end of time." Matthew Goff has discussed this "mystery that is to be" in apocalypticized wisdom exceptionally well in "Wisdom, Apocalypticism, and the Pedagogical Ethos of 4QInstruction," in Wright and Wills, *Conflicted Boundaries*, 57-67; idem, *Discerning Wisdom: The Sapiential Literature of the Dead Sea Scrolls* (VTS 116; Leiden and Boston: Brill, 2007) 9-68.

Paul introduced in 3:10-11, and it introduces a new topos of "testing" in 3:13. This means that the apocalyptic imagery maps both over the household, which extends into the feeding, planting, watering, and growing in God's field, and over God's house with its foundation, gold, silver, and precious stones. "The Day" will not simply inspect this household/house of God. It will test it with fire. In other words, there will be "a season of fire." Only that which resists being burned up by the fire and that that which is "refined" by fire will survive. The imagery of Paul's wisdom discourse shifts decisively, then, from feeding, nurturing, and upbuilding (3:1-11) to a season of testing that has the potential to destroy it all (3:13). In the midst of this, the focus is on "the work of each builder." Continually, then, Paul personifies the inanimate objects in the chapter. The Corinthians are God's field, God's building (3:9); the foundation of the building is Jesus Christ (3:11); and the Corinthians are God's temple (3:17). This leads to a focus on the people, rather than the inanimate objects, in the progressive texture of the discourse. And in the process, Paul's wisdom rhetorolect blends with apocalyptic and priestly rhetorolect. In 3:12-17, the buildings are only the agency by which "people" are tested and possibly destroyed. The nature of the work of each builder will be disclosed by the fire. This introduces a shift to apocalyptic rhetorolect. If what is built on the foundation survives, the builder will receive a reward; but if it burns up; the builder suffers loss and will be saved, but only through fire (3:14-15). The discourse builds on the concept of "wages" that a laborer receives for work (3:9). Builders will receive a wage, or suffer loss, on the basis of how they build on the foundation. But God will not destroy people who build on the foundation. Rather, these builders will suffer loss and be saved, but only through fire. But God may actually destroy some people. At this point Paul returns to a personification of an inanimate object. God will destroy anyone who destroys God's temple. Believers are that temple, and that temple is holy (3:17). This dynamically invites priestly rhetorolect into the blended wisdom-apocalyptic discourse. The internal purpose of God's wisdom is to nurture and "upbuild" things and people to full maturity, completion, and holiness. The conceptualization of holiness invites priestly rhetorolect into the discussion. Internal to the wisdom Paul describes is a "testing" of the builder. If the test shows a failure to upbuild, the result is a loss that leads to refinement through fire (3:14-15). Paul's focus on an ending that reveals bad or evil actions integrates apocalyptic rhetorolect into his wisdom rhetorolect. Since the imagery concerns the building of a temple, his assertions also blend priestly rhetorolect with the blended wisdom and apocalyptic rhetorolect. Every person must know (wisdom) that a person who destroys God's temple (priestly), rather than builds on it (whether in the best way or in a less than best way), will be destroyed (apocalyptic: 3:17).

The "if ... (then) ..." argumentative pattern of the apocalyptic rhetorolect in 3:12–17 reaches its conclusion in 3:18, where Paul returns to the topic of wisdom. The exhortative blend of wisdom and apocalyptic rhetorolect in 3:18 puts Paul in a confrontative role characteristic of prophetic rhetorolect. The opening part of 3:18 is fully characteristic of both apocalyptic and prophetic rhetorolect: "Do not deceive yourselves." But Paul then shifts immediately into exhortative wisdom rhetorolect containing an "if ... (then) ..." thesis followed by a rationale:

> *Thesis:* If you think you are wise in this age, you should become fools so you may become wise.
> *Rationale:* For the wisdom of this world is foolishness with God. (3:18b–19a)

It is noticeable that Paul does not attack the Corinthians in the mode of either a prophetic or apocalyptic indictment. In other words, he does not say: If you think you will escape the testing of God, you will be destroyed. For your dissensions are destroying God's temple. Instead of returning to a discussion of the dissensions among them for the purpose of indicting them, he modulates the confrontation into an exhortation supported by a rationale. This mode of exhortation is characteristic of wisdom rhetorolect. Even when Paul confronts the Corinthians, he continues to teach them. If they would like to be wise in this age (and he hopes they would like to do this), they should become fools so they can become wise (3:18b–c). Why? Because the wisdom of this world is foolishness to God (3:19a). This is vintage Pauline wisdom rhetorolect, filled with paradox but always trying to give reasons. Having achieved an apocalyptic distinction between being wise "in this age" (3:18) and being wise "for the Day" (3:13), which he has defined as "foolishness with God" (3:19), Paul recites two portions of scripture that function as written authority that confirms the rationale that the wisdom of this world is foolishness with God.

The first recitation of written authority is present in Job 5:13. The entire parallelismus membrorum is:

> He catches the wise in their craftiness;
> And the schemes of the wily are brought to a quick end.

Paul omits the second part of the verse, making it a proverbial sentence dominated by the presence of the letter "s" (sigma) in the first half: he catches the wise ... (*ho drassomenos tous sophous* ...). Then Paul recites Ps 94:11, adding a reference to the wise:

> The Lord knows the thoughts of the wise (*tōn sophōn*),
> that they are futile.

Both of these authoritative statements contain the word "the wise." In the mode of wisdom rhetorolect, they confirm that God has asserted in written scripture that the craftiness of the wise causes God to "catch" them and the "reasonings" (*dialogismous*) of the wise produces a context where God knows the futility of their purposes. These two statements lead to Paul's conclusion: So let no one boast about human leaders (3:21). Paul's focus is still on people who, in "their wisdom," build up or destroy. Again, however, Paul does not simply end with an exhortation. In the mode of wisdom rhetorolect, he provides a rationale that summarizes the entire chapter:

> For all things are yours, whether Paul or Apollos or Cephas or the world of life or death or the present or the future – all belong to you, and you belong to Christ and Christ belongs to God. (3:21b-23)

In this final statement, Paul presents a long declarative assertion that describes the relationship of the Corinthian believers to their leaders, to the world, to life and death, to the present and the future, and to Christ and God. The one thing Paul does not speak about in 3:18-23 is the Spirit. Thus, we must now turn to this topic.

When Paul refers to the Corinthians as infants in Christ in 3:1, he describes their status as "fleshly" (*sarkinos*) rather than "spiritual" (*pneumatikos*). What is the nature of being "spiritual" in this context? In 3:16, Paul says: "Do you not know that you are God's temple and God's Spirit dwells in you?" Does this mean that the background for Paul's concept of spirituality in 3:1 is priestly rhetorolect? Is Paul's concept of the spirituality of a person guided by the imagery of a temple where people bring sacrifices, offer up praise to God, pray to God, sing to God, and in return receive blessings, forgiveness, and redemption? Is it the case, then, that Paul was already introducing a priestly concept of belief and benefit from God in 3:1? Or are there other possibilities?

Is it possible that Paul's belief in God's miraculous work in believers while they are on earth lies behind his understanding of a spiritual person? In other words, does miracle rhetorolect lie in the background, perhaps blended with priestly rhetorolect? Perhaps an interpreter should give special attention to Paul's emphasis that the speech and proclamation he brought to the Corinthians came "with a demonstration of the Spirit and of power, so that your faith might rest not on human wisdom but on the power of God" (2:4-5). Perhaps the miraculous power of God works cooperatively with the Spirit precisely toward the goal of transforming fleshly beings into spiritual beings.

Or is the background for Paul's concept of the spiritual person primarily apocalyptic rhetorolect? One thinks immediately of Paul's concept in 1 Cor 15:44 that the body is sown a physical (*psychikon*) body and raised a spiritual body. Paul asserts in 15:50 that "flesh and blood cannot inherit the kingdom of God." Is Paul's concept of a person's transformation from a person of flesh to a person of spirit (3:1) an issue of "belonging" not only to the present but also to the future (3:22)? Even then, this would take us back to priestly rhetorolect, now in a context of baptism, where a person enters into the temporal sequence of the death and resurrection of Jesus (cf. Rom 6:3-5). Therefore, either a focus on miracle or apocalyptic rhetorolect appears to include a blending with priestly rhetorolect related to Paul's assertion in 1 Cor 3:16. Paul's concept of "a spiritual person" appears to hold close at hand some aspect of the holiness of God's temple. In this context, then, Paul's discourse appears to be a multiple blend of wisdom, miracle, priestly and apocalyptic discourse.

The imagery at the beginning of 1 Cor 3 is wisdom rhetorolect. Beginning with the growth of children to adults, the discourse moves into the productivity of plants in fields, where God makes everything grow. From this point, the discourse moves into the activities of building a house that feature yet a third way in which humans may be co-creators with God in the production of something that grows, or is built up, into completion or maturity. When that which is built up is conceptualized as "God's building" (3:9), the stage is set for Paul's wisdom rhetorolect to blend with priestly rhetorolect concerning God's temple. When the goodness and righteousness of the work of building is tested by fire, apocalyptic rhetorolect blends with wisdom rhetorolect. At this point, the imagery moves to "the Day" when the nature of the work is "revealed with fire" (3:13). Wisdom rhetorolect invites apocalyptic rhetorolect as a way to negotiate whether the work has followed a way of righteousness or a way of evil or discord. In this passage, God is the one who, through grace, gives the skillful worker the ability to do fine craftsmanship for God (3:10). In turn, Jesus Christ is the foundation of the house (3:11).

When apocalyptic rhetorolect speaks of the Day when the nature of the craftsmanship will be revealed, it is negotiating the relation of the Corinthians and their human leaders, including Paul, to God who gives growth (3:6, 8) and to whom all things belong. This issue is theological, focusing on the relation of God to people and things in God's created world. Paul's discourse also negotiates the relation of the Corinthians to Christ, who is the Lord (3:5) of the house in which the Corinthians belong as "infants" (3:1). This issue is Christological, focusing on the relation of Christ both to God's work and to people and their works in God's created world. When Paul's discourse moves even further to Christ as the foundation of the Corinthians, who are God's and are God's temple (3:11, 16-17, 23), the issue becomes decisively ecclesiological. This means it is focused on the nature of the church (*ekklēsia*) in the world. Wisdom, priestly, and apocalyptic rhetorolect blend together, then, in a remarkable kind of "Christ" oriented wisdom discourse that emerges during the 50s CE. A result of this blending is the creation of tightly interwoven theological, Christological, and ecclesiological emphases in a distinctive kind of "wisdom" discourse in the Mediterranean world.

Theology, Christology, and Ecclesiology become Prominent as Wisdom Blends with Apocalyptic and Precreation Rhetorolect: 1 Cor 2:6-10

In the context of a blend of early Christian wisdom and apocalyptic rhetorolect, 1 Cor 2:6-10 contains a glimpse of precreation, namely non-time before the creation of the world. In this context we will see still another way the discourse in 1 Cor brings theology, Christology, and ecclesiology into prominence through the blending of multiple rhetorolects together:

> [6] Yet among the mature we do speak wisdom, though it is not a wisdom of this age or of the rulers of this age, who are doomed to perish. [7] But we speak God's wisdom, secret and hidden, which God predefined (*pro-ōrisen*) before the ages for our glory. [8] None of the rulers of this age understood this; for if they had, they would not have crucified the Lord of glory. [9] But, as it is written, "What no eye has seen, nor ear heard, nor the human heart conceived, what God has prepared (*hētoimasen*) for those who love him" – [10] these things God has revealed to us through the Spirit; for the Spirit searches everything, even the depths of God.

The initial issue in 1 Cor 2:6-10 concerns the relation of human wisdom and power in the believing community (ecclesiology) to God's wisdom and power (theology). The problem is the story of Jesus Christ as God's Messiah (Christology). God's wisdom and power should have been present and active in God's Messiah in such a manner that he would be able to destroy the enemies of Israel and establish a kingdom of peace and justice that people could easily recognize as God's kingdom on earth. Instead, earthly rulers arrested Jesus and killed him. No matter what the conclusion of this story might be, belief that Jesus was God's Messiah appears to be folly rather than wisdom and weakness rather than a manifestation of God's power. The answer among early followers that was most successful after Jesus' death came from thinking about Jesus in relation to the end of time. Focusing on the end of time, they reasoned that Jesus had been resurrected into "the coming age" and would return again soon to exhibit decisively his manifestation of the power and glory of God. Thus, early Christians developed extensive apocalyptic rhetorolect to talk about Jesus, and this is the topic of Chapters 8-9 in this volume. The apostle Paul, however, presented the story about Jesus' death and resurrection in the mode of an "argumentative wisdom" that was significantly successful in certain regions and cities of Asia Minor,

Macedonia, and Greece. Through his letters and his speech, therefore, he was building a special kind of early Christian rhetorolect that interpreters regularly refer to as "Pauline," since it has many distinctive qualities in relation to other traditions of early Christian discourse. As Paul faced the challenge of explaining to early Christians in Corinth how the "gospel" story presented God's "wisdom and power," 1 Cor 2:6-10 exhibits how Paul could move towards "pre-time with God," rather than to "end-time with God." The movement of Paul's thought in 1 Cor 2:6-10 invites precreation rhetorolect into an early Christian blend of wisdom and apocalyptic rhetorolect.

The motivation for Paul's move towards God's pre-time is, in the first instance, ecclesiological. How, Paul asks, can people who are part of the "believing community" understand their proclamation about Jesus to be God's wisdom? In 1 Cor 2:7, Paul asserts that the answer lies in the realm of God's activity "before the ages" (*pro tōn aiōnōn*). Both wisdom and apocalyptic discourse speak of God's wisdom as "secret and hidden," and this is where Paul begins in 2:7. Instead of emphasizing that everything that is hidden will be revealed, as is characteristic of apocalyptic rhetorolect, Paul asserts that the secrecy and hiddenness of God's wisdom is a result of God's "pre-definition" of divine wisdom "before the ages for our glory." We must notice that there is no assertion here that God created the ages through Christ. In other words, Paul does not assert a "precreation Christology." Rather, Paul's answer is a "theological" answer. Prior to the ages, God pre-defined divine wisdom and power in the manner that Jesus Christ manifested in his death on the cross. The Christology here is a "Christology of crucifixion," which creates an ecclesiological challenge, since it is such a puzzling kind of wisdom to proclaim. Paul gives the answer in a manner that moves toward "precreation theology," namely something that God did prior to creating the world. Paul's assertion is that, prior to God's "pronouncement" of the world into being, God pre-defined "divine wisdom" in the manner in which it has been revealed in the crucifixion of "the Lord of glory" (2:8). The divine wisdom Paul is attempting to explain, therefore, is a wisdom that God revealed through the life, death, and resurrection of Jesus. Since God was "behind it all," so to speak, it seems obvious that God had "pre-defined" divine wisdom in this manner sometime in God's eternity prior to God's creation of the ages.

Paul asserts in 2:9 that he finds evidence of God's "pre-definition" of divine wisdom in scripture, which he recites as: "What no eye has seen, nor ear heard, nor the human heart conceived, what God has prepared (*hētoimasen*) for those who love him." Scholars have been unable to identify a verse that functions as the intertext for 1 Cor 2:9.[78] It is noticeable that the final part of the verse features the central command of Jewish wisdom tradition that understands the Torah to be God's wisdom, namely to love God. Central to this tradition is the Jewish Shema, where the people of Israel are commanded to "love (*agapēseis*) the Lord your God with all your heart (*kardias*), and with all your soul (*psychēs*) and with all your might (*dynameōs*)" (Deut 6:5). In 1 Cor 1–2, Paul is attempting to understand "what did not go up onto the human heart" (1 Cor 2:9)[79] but what it is now possible to see in the crucifixion and to hear in Paul's proclamation (1 Cor 2:1-2). The key for "precreation" conceptualization of "Christian" wisdom, then, is Paul's quest to understand "what God has prepared for those who love him."[80] Paul places God's preparation of the "grace" God bestows on people who love God in "God's non-time" that existed before God's creation of the world.

In the context of early Christian wisdom rhetorolect, the Christian precreation story-line begins with movement in the mind of God prior to God's actions of creating the world. As we have seen earlier in this chapter, God's creation of the world establishes the horizons for early Christian "wisdom" rhetorolect. In the context of this wisdom rhetorolect, the "secret and hidden" nature of God's wisdom in the proclamation of the crucifixion of God's Messiah can be understood with a perspective that focuses on God's "predefinition" of divine wisdom "before the ages." In eternity prior to God's creation of the world, God "established a horizon of thought" for "divine wisdom" that functioned later as a "scandal" to the Jews and "foolishness" to the nations (1 Cor 1:23). One cannot properly speak of God's establishing of the "scandalous foolishness" of divine wisdom as an "event," since there is no "time" in eternity in which an event can occur. The horizon exists eternally, which means "before creation," but this also means it exists in the present and the future. Human minds regularly comprehend this movement in the mind of God by establishing a temporal horizon of "before the ages" to approach its "mystery." In the mind of God, which means before all "time," and therefore "throughout all time and after all time," God's "predefined" wisdom chooses "what is foolish in the world to shame the wise" and "what is weak in the world to shame the strong"

[78] Hans Conzelmann, *1 Corinthians: A Commentary on the First Epistle to the Corinthians* (Hermeneia; Philadelphia: Fortress, 1975) 63. He indicates, however, that Origen considered Paul to be reciting a verse from the Elijah apocalypse (Orig., *Comm. in Matt.* 5.29, on Matt 27:9). In the Bible, Isa 64:3; Ps 31:20 in particular are related to Paul's recitation.

[79] Anthony C. Thiselton, *The First Epistle to the Corinthians: A Commentary on the Greek Text* (NIGTC; Grand Rapids, MI: Eerdmans, 2000) 249.

[80] Cf. Rom 8:28-30.

(1 Cor 1:27). Thus, the early Christian precreation story-line "begins" sometime during eternity prior to God's creation of the world.

To understand the manner in which 1 Cor 2:6-10 represents a blending of wisdom rhetorolect with precreation rhetorolect, we must see how Genesis 1 lies in the background of certain statements in 1 Cor 1–2. As Paul explains the nature of God's wisdom, he exhibits an understanding that somehow Christ transcends being strictly "human" (*anthrōpos*). Paul refers to that which is "human" (*anthrōpos*) nine times in 1 Cor 1:25 (2); 2:5, 9, 11 (3), 13, 14.[81] 1 Cor 1:25 refers to human "wisdom" and human "strength," 2:5 contrasts "human" wisdom with the power of God, and 2:9 refers to what the human "heart" can conceptualize. In 1 Cor 2:11 Paul introduces the problem: "For what human knows the things of the human except the spirit of the human which is in him?" In 1 Corinthians, the answer for Paul lies in the relation of the human spirit to the spirit of God, which is bestowed on humans by God (1 Cor 2:12). The spirit of God, Paul asserts, is able to reveal "what God has prepared for those who love him" (2:9), because the spirit searches even "the depths (*bathē*)" of God (2:10).

The focus in 1 Cor 1–2 on the nature of that which is "human" (*anthrōpos*) and on the activity of the spirit of God (*pneuma tou theou*) exhibits the presence of Gen 1 in the background. When God began to create the world, the spirit of God (LXX: *pneuma tou theou*) was bearing itself (*epephereto*) above (*epanō*) the waters (Gen 1:2). In other words, both God and the spirit of God were present when God created the world. This would mean that the spirit of God was also present when God created those who were "human" (*anthrōpos*: Gen 1:26-27).[82] In 1 Cor 1–2, Paul's answer for how humans can understand the things of God lies in the role of the "spirit of God." The spirit of God understands what is truly God's (2:11), and "we," as Paul says, can understand the things of God because the spirit of God has taught these things to "us" (2:13). Paul ends the chapter with: "'For who has known the mind of the Lord so as to instruct him?' But we have the mind of Christ." Is it the case that the spirit of God taught Christ, just as the spirit of God teaches those who believe in Christ? The answer in Christian discourse seems to be, "No," since the Father, rather than the spirit of God, "handed over" the wisdom of God to the Son (Matt 11:25-27; Luke 10:21-22). Or are there better ways to understand the transmission of God's wisdom to Christ? Early Christian precreation rhetorolect finds remarkable ways to talk about Christ's relation to God. Usually Paul turned to the end of

[81] All the occurrences use the Greek noun *anthrōpos* except 1 Cor 2:13, which uses the adjective *anthrōpinēs* in relation to the genitive of "wisdom" (*sophias*).

[82] The "us" in "Let us make" (Gen 1:26), then, could be understood as God and the spirit of God.

time when he focused on the secret and hidden nature of God's wisdom, as we will see in chapter eight and nine on apocalyptic rhetorolect. At times, however, he turned to the period of non-time before God created the world. This interplay between God's precreation wisdom and the hidden wisdom that is revealed during the ending of time proved to be highly generative for early Christian thought. Thus, it will be necessary to return to this interplay in a number of contexts in these two volumes on the invention of Christian discourse.

Wisdom becomes Theological-Christological-Ecclesiological Doctrine as it Blends with Prophetic, Priestly, Apocalyptic, and Precreation Rhetorolect: 1 Timothy 6:2b-16

The deuteropauline discourse of 1 Tim 6:2b-16 also is blended wisdom discourse. This discourse, however, places the productivity of God's vegetative world in the background to foreground a realm of truth grounded in "the sound (*hygiainousin*) words of our Lord Jesus Christ, and the teaching (*didaskaliāi*) that is in accordance with godliness (*eusebeian*)" (6:3). The basis of the reasoning, then, is a blending of theology and Christology that emphasizes the teachings of Jesus Christ. Prophetic rhetorolect qualifies the teachings of Christ as authoritative. The narrator claims that the "sound teaching" was "entrusted" (*episteuthēn*) to him in the form of "the glorious gospel of our blessed God" (1:11). This means that the narrator was appointed by God to be a "herald (*kēryx*) and apostle" (2:7) to proclaim a "knowledge (*epignōsin*) of truth" (2:3) with the following content:

> there is one God,
> there is also one mediator between God and humankind, Christ Jesus, himself human, who gave himself a ransom for all. (1 Tim 2:5)

Emphasis on God's creation of the world recedes into the background as wisdom and priestly rhetorolect (Christ's function as a ransom: *antilytron*) moves into the foreground. God as creator of the world is not absent from this early Christian wisdom rhetorolect. According to the narrator, God "gives life to all things" (6:13) and "everything created by God is good" (4:4). This wisdom orientation is qualified, however, with priestly rhetorolect when the narrator adds that nothing in God's created world is to be rejected "provided it is received with thanksgiving (*eucharistias*), for it is sanctified (*hagiazetai*) by God's word and by prayer (*enteuxeōs*)." This wisdom discourse presupposes that certain things present in God's created world are not clearly good. Perhaps humans or some other powers regularly turn God's good things into things that either are not good or are clearly evil. In any case, priestly activity by leaders and believers are essential to assure the goodness of God's created things. Both believers and leaders are exhorted to make things in God's world good through ritual actions. The term the narrator uses for the attribute that guides all activities toward goodness is "godliness" (*eusebeia*). Thus, priestly rhetorolect blends dynamically with wisdom rhetorolect as instruction begins in 1 Tim 6:2b-5:

> *Exhortative Rule:* Teach and urge these things.
> *Case:* [3] Whoever teaches otherwise and does not agree with the sound words of our Lord Jesus Christ and the teaching that is in accordance with godliness, [4] is conceited, understanding nothing, and has a morbid craving for controversy and for disputes about words.
> *Result:* From these come envy, dissension, slander, base suspicions, [5] and wrangling among those who are depraved in mind and bereft of the truth, imagining that godliness is a means of gain.

There is no dominant imagery of trees, vines, fields, and fruitfulness in the discourse in 1 Tim 6:2b-16. Rather, there is a repetitive appeal to godliness (6:3, 5, 6, 11) that is representative of the overall texture of 1 Tim (2:2; 3:16; 4:7-8; 5:4). In the context of this emphasis on godliness, the list of vices does not begin with wrong actions associated with productivity and reproductivity like adultery or fornication but with wrong thinking that produces and reproduces conflictual uses of words. Thus, being conceited (*tetyphōtai*), understanding nothing (*mēden epistamenos*), and having a craving for controversy and word wars (*logomachias*) stand at the top of the list of vices (6:4a). Then the list presents the social results of this wrong thinking: envy, dissension, slander, base suspicions, wrangling among those depraved in mind and bereft of truth, and imagining that godliness is a means of gain (6:4b-5). This means that this doctrinal wisdom rhetorolect overmaps wisdom rhetorolect that blends language about the heart and mouth with reasoning about good and bad fruit[83] with a new map. This new map blends language about sound teaching from the Lord Jesus Christ with reasoning about inner modes of the mind that pollute understanding, produce misdirected and abusive use of words, and create disorder and conflict in the community. An earlier focus on God's created world is overmapped by a blended theological and Christological focus that emphasizes the sound words of the Lord Jesus Christ. Rather than emphasizing an opposition between light and darkness, therefore, it emphasizes an opposition between the sound words of the Lord Jesus Christ and words that disrupt community life and create conflict and dispute. The goal in sight is not the processes by which an individual person becomes a tree of life, but the processes by which a community becomes a group that uses words to create order and praise of God and the Lord Jesus Christ. The focus is ecclesiological, oriented toward creating an assembly of people who not only live peace-

[83] Matt 7:15-20; 12:33-35; Luke 6:43-45; Jas 3:10-12.

fully with one another but who live on the basis of sound words of the Lord Jesus Christ that create good words among God's assembled people on earth.

After a focus on the vices that emerge from wrong understanding that produces destructive uses of words, 1 Tim 6:6–12 turns toward the virtues that emerge from "godliness combined with contentment":

> *General thesis:* [6] Of course, there is great gain in godliness combined with contentment;
> *Rationale:* [7] for we brought nothing into the world, so that we can take nothing out of it; [8] but if we have food and clothing, we will be content with these.
> *Opposite:* [9] But those who want to be rich fall into temptation and are trapped by many senseless and harmful desires that plunge people into ruin and destruction.
> *Rationale for the opposite:* [10] For the love of money is a root of all kinds of evil, and in their eagerness to be rich some have wandered away from the faith and pierced themselves with many pains.
> *Exhortation:* [11] But as for you, man of God, shun all this; pursue righteousness, godliness, faithfulness, love, endurance, gentleness. [12] Fight the good fight of the faith; take hold of the eternal life, to which you were called and for which you made the good confession in the presence of many witnesses.

1 Tim 6:6 moves from exhortation into a mode of reasoning containing similarities with the moral philosophy we briefly saw in the previous chapter with the discussion of both Pseudo-Phocylides 3-8 and Epictetus, *Discourses* 2.26:1-7. 1 Tim 6:5 begins with a general thesis that reconfigures the vice of "imagining that godliness is a means of gain (*porismon*)" (6:5) into the "great gain (*porismos megas*) of godliness with contentment (*autarkeias*)" (6:6).[84] Then it provides a rationale about being content (6:7 8) that focuses on one's possessions. On the one hand this focus is a configuration of "Do not desire (covet)" that has a deep relation to Ps. Phoc. 6: "Be content (*arkeisthai*) with what you have and refrain from what belongs to others." On the other hand it has a significant relation to the words exhibited in Epictetus 2.26.6 about contentment: "I am always content (*arkoumai*) with him with whom I am discussing, and I ask him to give his opinion and call him as a witness." Contentment both with possessions and with words helps to create good community.

The repetitiveness of "godliness" in 1 Tim adds a special feature in relation to "contentment" with one's possessions.[85] Contentment in 1 Tim

[84] Cf. 1 Tim 4:8; Phil 4:11–13; Martin Dibelius and Hans Conzelmann, *The Pastoral Epistles* (Hermeneia; Fortress Press, 1972) 84; *TDNT* 1:466–67.
[85] 1 Tim 6:6, 8.

not only focuses on an absence of desire to accumulate more possessions, which causes people to fall into temptation, but on a presence of desire that plunges people into "ruin (*olethron*) and destruction (*apōleian*)" (6:8-9). Nearby in the discourse of 1 Tim is language that blends precreation and apocalyptic rhetorolect dynamically together. One must be ever mindful of God, who is the "King of the ages" (1:17) and of the presence of God, Christ Jesus, and the elect angels (5:21). The discourse overmaps a directly apocalyptic emphasis on "the end time" with a precreation emphasis on God's eternal time, within which God makes the Lord Jesus Christ manifest in the world. In other words, a potentially apocalyptic emphasis on the "revelation" (*apokalypsis*) and "coming near" (*parousia*) of the Lord Jesus Christ is overmapped with an emphasis on God's action of producing a "manifestation" or epiphany (*epiphaneia*) of the Lord Jesus Christ (6:14) in the world.[86] Apocalyptic is not a dominant rhetorolect in this doctrinal wisdom discourse. Both the beginning of time in God's creation of the world and the end of time in the Day of the Lord move into the background in this doctrinal discourse. This discourse replaces an emphasis on time with an emphasis on God's "non-time" sovereignty. Ruling eternally means, of course, that God works energetically with time, when it exists from the creation of the world to the end of the world. But God exists and works eternally, even when there is no "time." Therefore, the issue is the "manifestation" of the Lord Jesus Christ in the sphere of time God created when God created the world, rather than a particular time in the future when God will "reveal" the powerful and glorious Lord Jesus Christ in a particular coming to earth in the future. Nevertheless, reverberations of apocalyptic rhetorolect are ever near, easy to pull into the discourse when it seems beneficial. People must not "fall into the snare of the Devil" (3:6; 5:15; cf. 1:20), or they will experience "ruin and destruction" (6:9).

A remnant of the emphasis on God's vegetative world in wisdom rhetorolect emerges in the view of money as "the root" (*hriza*) of all kinds of evil (6:10).[87] From this root could spring up a tree of death. But this narrator does not go there. Again, the vegetative imagery of early Christian wisdom rhetorolect lies in a far distant background. People who love money have wandered away from "the faith" (6:10), which is focused on the sound teachings of our Lord Jesus Christ. If the "man of God" stays focused on "the faith" which is taught and proclaimed, he will naturally pursue righteousness, godliness, faithfulness, love, endur-

[86] Cf. 2 Tim 1:10; 4:1, 8; Tit 2:11, 13; 3:4.

[87] For root in wisdom rhetorolect in the NT, see Matt 13:6-7; Mark 4:16-17; Luke 8:13; Eph 3:17; Col 2:7; cf. Heb 12:15.

ance, and gentleness (6:11).[88] These are not "fruit (*karpos*) of the spirit" (Gal 5:22) but attributes of "godliness" (*eusebeia*).

As this wisdom discourse continues, it reconfigures the vice of fighting over words (*logomachia*) in 1 Tim 6:4-5 into the virtue of "fighting the good fight of the faith" (*agōnizou ton kalon agōna tē pisteōs*) in 6:12. In the mode of prophetic rhetorolect, acceptance of this fight is put in terms of something the hearer is called to do. The task is to "take hold of the eternal life" (6:12). God's concern that the man might "reach out his hand and take also from the tree of life, and eat, and live forever" (Gen 3:22) has moved completely into the background. In the foreground is the image of an athlete or soldier who, victoriously running a good race or fighting a good fight (6:12; cf. 1:18), grasps "the eternal life" as though it were the prize at the end of a contest or spoils at the end of a battle. Life is a struggle and a fight. Priestly rhetorolect emerges as this man of God is reminded that he "made the good confession in the presence of many witnesses" for the purpose of taking hold of the eternal life.

The passage ends with the blending of apocalyptic and precreation rhetorolect observed above. God is "the blessed and only Sovereign, the King of kings and Lord of lords" who "has immortality and dwells in unapproachable light, whom no one has ever seen or can see" (6:15-16). The story of the Lord Jesus Christ exists in the context of this overall story of the eternal God:

> *Exhortation:* [13] In the presence of God, who gives life to all things, and of Christ Jesus, who in his testimony before Pontius Pilate made the good confession, I charge you [14] to keep the commandment without spot or blame until the manifestation of our Lord Jesus Christ, [15] which he will bring about at the right time – he who is the blessed and only Sovereign, the King of kings and Lord of lords.
>
> *Rule:* [16] It is he alone who has immortality and dwells in unapproachable light, whom no one has ever seen or can see;
>
> *Priestly Conclusion:* to him be honor and eternal dominion. Amen.

Recalling God's giving of life to all things in the story of creation, the final exhortation moves to an injunction "to keep the commandment without spot or blame until the manifestation of our Lord Jesus Christ"

[88] Cf. 1QS 4:1-6: These are the ways in the world for the enlightenment of the heart of man ... : a spirit of humility, patience, abundant charity, unending goodness, understanding, and intelligence; (a spirit of) mighty wisdom which trusts in all the deeds of God and leans on His great loving-kindness; a spirit of discernment in every purpose, of zeal for just laws, of holy intent with steadfastness of heart, of great charity towards all the sons of truth, of admirable purity which detests all unclean idols, of humble conduct sprung from an understanding of all things, and of faithful concealment of the mysteries of truth. (Vermes)

(6:14). "Purity," which is an internal dimension of Torah and proverbial wisdom rhetorolect that focuses on the commandments of God, now receives a new focus. The hearer is exhorted to keep "the commandment" without spot or blame. It is possible that "the commandment" refers to a public charge that had become traditional in the context of calling people to be leaders and teachers in the early Christian community.[89] This focus is not oriented toward commandments that emerged in the story of God's creation of the world and God's establishment of holy people through Torah. Rather, the focus is on "the knowledge of the truth" found in the sound words of our Lord Jesus Christ (6:3). The focus has become Christological. In addition, as the narrator was entrusted with the glorious gospel of the blessed God (1:11) and now teaches it to the hearers, so the narrator reminds the hearers that they were called and commanded to confess their knowledge in the context of their gathered worship (6:12-14). Thus the focus is also ecclesiological. The knowledge the hearer has about God and about the Lord Jesus Christ must be enacted ritually among gathered believers for the purpose of creating words that produce the goodness of God on earth.

Rather than teaching wisdom that emerges from God's creation of the world, then, 1 Tim 6:2b-16 teaches "the mystery of our godliness" (3:16), which is a story about Christ that weaves precreation, prophetic, and apocalyptic rhetorolect into creedal rhetorolect:[90] "He was revealed in flesh, vindicated in spirit, seen by angels, proclaimed among Gentiles, believed in throughout the world, taken up in glory" (1 Tim 3:16). The imagery of God the creator, God "who gives life to all things" (6:13), lies in the background of the claims in 1 Timothy. But they lie very far in the background. The story of the Lord Jesus Christ as true doctrine lies in the foreground, making God as creator of the world only a faint echo in the din of a battle related to God's action as King of kings and Lord of lords, who is in the realm of an unapproachable light whom no one has ever seen or can see (1 Tim 6:12-16). The light in the discourse is unapproachable, in the mode of primordial light in precreation rhetorolect. There is not even an emphasis in 1 Tim on the Lord Jesus Christ as light. The emphasis is not on light, which God made visible in the world. God's light is unapproachable! The emphasis is on the Lord Jesus Christ, whom God has made manifest through the sound teachings of the Lord Jesus Christ.

Priestly rhetorolect blends with precreation and apocalyptic rhetorolect as this doctrinal wisdom discourse reaches a momentary con-

[89] Dibelius and Conzelman, *The Pastoral Epistles*, 89; Jouette M. Bassler, *1 Timothy; 2 Timothy; Titus* (ANTC; Nashville: Abingdon, 1996) 114.

[90] Creedal rhetorolect, which reached its fully-developed form during the fourth century CE, will be a significant topic of discussion in the next volume.

clusion in "Amen" (6:16). The narrator recites a doxology to God, pronouncing upon God "honor and eternal dominion" (6:15-16). Dwelling in unapproachable light, God is "the blessed and only Sovereign, the King of kings and Lord of lords." The narrator is grateful to be a member of "the household of God, which is the church of the living God, the pillar and bulwark of the truth" (1 Tim 3:15). The truth that guides this household is not simply the knowledge of good and evil from the story of God's creation of the world or Torah wisdom that comes from God's creation of a holy people on earth. Rather, this household is guided by the knowledge of the truth that there is one God and there is one mediator between God and humankind, Christ Jesus, himself human, who gave himself a ransom for all (2:5-6). Theology and Christology blend together in this wisdom discourse to bring a distinctly "Christian" creedal rhetorolect into the foreground. This wisdom overmaps knowledge about creation and about Torah with creedal knowledge about the Lord Jesus Christ. The self-evident and incontestable nature of knowledge about the creation of the world and about the commandments God gave to Moses now shifts to the self-evident and incontestable nature of knowledge about the Lord Jesus Christ.

Conclusion

As we will see in the next two chapters, a primary difference between wisdom and prophetic discourse lies in the mode of communication between God and humans. As we have seen above, the inner nature of wisdom discourse is to be unchallengeable, because it is "self-evident" in the realm of God's created world. God's incontestable and unstoppable speech brought light into the world, and this light is the source of all productivity in the world. Darkness is the negative counterpart to wisdom in God's world. Sometimes darkness is quite neutral, simply the place where God and humans create light through wisdom. At other times darkness is aggressive, attempting to overcome wisdom and light. On earth, the household is a primary place where God's wisdom is transmitted by parents to children. Through conceptual blending, household and God's created world blend with the intersubjective body of humans to cultivate light, in the form of wisdom, in the world. Through this blending, humans become productive agents who multiply goodness and righteousness in God's world. As the story continues, God's wisdom comes to Moses in the form of Torah and to Solomon in the form of proverbs. Thus, God's incontestable wisdom takes the form both of commandments and of proverbs as it informs early Christian wisdom rhetorolect.

As wisdom rhetorolect develops in early Christianity, it moves beyond the story of God's creation of the world, God's giving of commandments to Moses, and God's giving of proverbs to Solomon toward the story of Jesus' appearance, life, death, and resurrection on the earth. This creates a context where the story of the Lord Jesus Christ as incontestable is embedded in the incontestable story of God's creation of the world and God's giving of commandments and proverbs as light to direct God's people in the production of goodness on earth. Early Christian wisdom rhetorolect, then, moves energetically toward "Jesus story" wisdom that becomes doctrine and creed. There is to be "no doubting" of the story of Jesus, just as there is no doubt that God created the world, gave commandments to Moses, and gave proverbs to Solomon.

In the next two chapters we turn to early Christian prophetic rhetorolect. The inner nature of biblical prophetic rhetorolect concerns the relation of particular decisions by God to the will of humans. In the reasoning of prophetic rhetorolect, God finds it necessary again and again to confront "select" humans and groups with "unusual words from God" that demand actions that are not only challenging and difficult but filled with discomfort and/or danger. A primary focus in prophetic rhetorolect is on the creation of "God's kingdom." God's kingdom is to be a place where humans live together in a manner that exhibits the special nature of God's goodness and righteousness. In other words, prophetic rhetorolect presupposes that the natural will of humans rebels against the will of God. Humans, following their own will, produce kingdoms based on self-pride, envy, and greed. God's will, in contrast, is based on goodness and righteousness. Prophetic rhetorolect presents God's selection of special individuals and groups to embody God's goodness and righteousness in a manner that exhibits the special nature of God in the world. In other words, prophetic rhetorolect focuses on the creation of God's kingdom, rather than the creation of the entire world.

6

Christian Prophetic Rhetorolect Part I: Kingdom, Confrontation, Abraham, Moses, and Samuel

Introduction

The primary internal dynamic of early Christian prophetic rhetorolect is confrontation with a purpose of holding people responsible to God's will. Biblical prophetic rhetorolect emerges when God decides to create a kingdom of people on earth who have special responsibility to live according to God's will. To initiate a special kingdom, God confronts various people with directions concerning actions God wants them to take to create this kingdom. The actions they must undertake include confrontation of various people to communicate to them the will of God concerning their actions, speech, and beliefs. Thus, prophetic rhetorolect moves beyond God's wisdom to particular decisions God makes to select a particular group of people who will enact God's righteousness and justice on earth.[1] In order to fulfill this responsibility, special people must have more information than basic knowledge about God available through God's created world and the wisdom parents hand on to their children. Rather than focusing on people from childhood to adulthood, prophetic rhetorolect focuses on the responsibilities of adult leaders to fulfill God's will to have a special kingdom of righteous people on earth.

Early Christian prophetic rhetorolect moves toward its goals by blending together human experiences of a region of land ruled by a king, God's heavenly world where God rules as king, and the intersubjective bodies of leaders, prophets, and members of the earthly kingdom to which God has a special relation. This conceptualization

[1] Yehoshua Gitay, *Prophecy and Persuasion* (Bonn: Linguistica Biblica, 1981); idem, "Rhetorical Criticism and the Prophetic Discourse," in *Persuasive Artistry* (ed. D.F. Watson; Sheffield: JSOT Press, 1991) 13-24; idem, "The Realm of Prophetic Rhetoric," in *Rhetoric, Scripture & Theology: Essays from the 1994 Pretoria Conference* (ed. S.E. Porter & T.H. Olbricht; JSNTSup 131; Sheffield: Sheffield Academic Press, 1996) 218-29.

emphasizes how God authorizes certain people to be kings, calls specific people to be prophets, and chooses special groups to be recipients of special blessings in a context of special responsibilities on earth. As early Christianity broadened its mission beyond the boundaries of Judaism to Gentiles, its prophetic rhetorolect emphasized the beginnings and endings of earthly kingdoms rather than the specific geographical boundaries of God's kingdom on earth. This created a special emphasis on time: the beginning and continuation of God's kingdom on earth. In other words, in contrast to a focus on the beginnings and continuation of God's created world, as in wisdom rhetorolect, the focus in early Christian prophetic rhetorolect is on the beginnings and continuation of God's kingdom of earth. This focus implies, or directly asserts, the end of the rule of other kings over God's people on earth, wherever their geographical location may be. On the one hand, this creates an awareness and acceptance, in early Christian prophetic rhetorolect, that rulers of various kinds govern specific regions of God's created world, and God's prophets and people must find ways to live as God's chosen people in those regions. On the other hand, this creates natural movement toward apocalyptic rhetorolect, where the emphasis is on the end of all earthly kings when God's Messiah in heaven becomes ruler of all of God's created world. In early Christian apocalyptic rhetorolect, God is conceptualized as Almighty Emperor not only over all the earth but over the entire universe, which is perceived to be God's empire. Along with God's rule as an emperor, Christ rules from heaven as king over all of God's kingdom until the end of time, when Christ turns the kingdom over to God. In contrast to apocalyptic rhetorolect, early Christian prophetic rhetorolect conceptualizes God as king rather than emperor and Jesus as earthly Messiah rather than heavenly king.

In early Christian prophetic rhetorolect, God functions as King of the heavens and focuses in a special way on people God has chosen and called to enact and exhibit righteousness and justice on earth. When Jesus functions as God's Messiah on earth, his rule as earthly king blends with the fate of God's prophets. This creates a curious blend of earthly king and earthly prophet, where God authorizes an earthly prophetic king to die a kingly prophetic death. The first century Christian focus on Jesus as an earthly Messiah therefore blends three spaces – God's kingship in heaven, God's kingdom on earth where God's Messiah was killed, and God's special people who believe in Jesus as God's Messiah. This blend presents a goal of enacting righteousness and justice on earth through the medium of "special words and deeds of God" that God makes known through prophets who accept Jesus' role as a rejected king. In this way, prophetic rhetorolect blends the roles of the prophet into the roles of the king. The effect is that prophetic confrontation becomes "kingly" (messianic) confrontation and rejection of the prophet becomes rejection of the king. This means that the person whom God chose and anointed as king over God's kingdom on earth fulfills the role of a prophet who is rejected and killed by people who do not like his "kingly" message. In first century Christian prophetic rhetorolect, then, a person who is prophetic is "anointed like a king" and a person who is "kingly" is rejected like a prophet. This ironic prophetic rhetorolect introduces the image of a group of people on earth who live in a paradoxical "kingdom of God" as a result of God's calling of a special "prophet-king" to be his Messiah.

The effect of prophetic rhetorolect in early Christian discourse was not only the production of distinctively authorized confrontational modes in the Mediterranean world but also the production of story-lines that validated the authorization. Building on the tradition of Hebrew Bible prophetic discourse, Christianity produced story-lines that validated Jesus and his followers as people specially authorized by God to confront large groups of people with special messages and actions that communicated God's will for their present time. Both the actions and the speech were perceived to be ways to communicate special actions God was taking in their present context, special directions for what people must do in the face of God's actions, and the consequences if people did not take the necessary actions. As Christianity spread throughout the Mediterranean world, leaders of the movement regularly spoke in strongly confrontational ways in public settings. Their speech regularly included a rehearsal of special actions God had taken in the past, stories about people God had chosen in the past to communicate special messages about God's actions, assertions about the rejection, suffering, and sometimes death of people who carried out God's directions, and assertions about actions God will take in the future. This mode of speech in public settings was often considered foolish, unreasonable, or politically rebellious. As a result, various early Christian leaders were censured, whipped, beaten, imprisoned, and in some instances killed for their public actions. In a context, then, where Christianity was nurturing a new *paideia* in the Mediterranean world, various leaders of this messianite movement continually confronted groups of people publicly with words they asserted were given to them by God to speak to them. These "words" were a medium both for telling stories of people in the past who confronted leaders and large groups of people with God's will and for rehearsing difficulties these people faced when they confronted people in this manner. These words also announced what God would do in the future in relation to the things the prophet was saying to them.

There are three basic rhetorical resources for early Christian prophetic rhetorolect: (1) the story of Abraham; (2) the story of Moses; and (3) stories and oracles of prophets and kings during the time of kings over Israel. The resource for the story of Abraham is in Genesis, the resource for Moses is in Exodus through Deuteronomy, and the resources for the prophets of Israel are in the historical accounts of the kings of Israel (1–2 Kings; 1–2 Samuel; 1–2 Chronicles) and the books containing the stories, sayings, and speeches of the Hebrew prophets. Early Christianity could also conceptualize David as a prophet who produced Psalms that told special stories of suffering and joy, and contained sayings that spoke of the past, the present, and the future in terms of God's will. The Hebrew Bible, therefore, is a rich resource for stories about prophets and sayings by prophets. In Mediterranean literature, various "mediums" in sanctuaries and various types of philosophers, like the Cynics, adopted modes of speech, and either enacted stories or told stories, that confronted people with "special truth" about their lives in the world. Thus there were various places, people, and traditions that supported the mode of speech and action advanced by early Christian prophetic rhetorolect.

One of the basic characteristics of early Christian prophetic rhetorolect is to turn wisdom discourse into confrontational speech. This often occurs by adding terms and phrases that define the hearers as foolish, ignorant, unrighteous, hateful, disobedient, etc. and by accusing people of not doing what they have been told to do or doing something they know they should not do. Thus, it is natural for negative assertions and examples in wisdom rhetorolect to be changed into negative assertions and examples to attack the hearer as someone who has enacted this negative thing. Thus, prophetic rhetorolect often has a natural "judicial" tone at its base that indicts the hearer as guilty of wrongdoing. But early Christian prophetic rhetorolect also features blessings. One of its distinctive features is a focus on the Kingdom of God, which is the inheritance of those who believe that Jesus is the Messiah (*Christos*: the anointed one). When early Christian conceptualization blends the status of Jesus as God's son with the status of the adult Jesus as God's anointed one, Jesus becomes "the Messiah" who brings both authoritative blessings and authoritative curses. Early Christian prophetic rhetorolect focuses on the adult Jesus both holding other adults responsible for their actions and speech in God's earthly kingdom and blessing those who, ironically, have a special place in God's kingdom. This means that early Christian prophetic rhetorolect both adopted and adapted previous biblical prophetic traditions as it focused on ironic blindness, deafness, and hardheartedness in contexts of ironic blessedness. On the one hand, this created a special opening for early Christian miracle rhetorolect to feature special healings of blindness, deafness, paralysis, and death. On the other hand, in early Christian prophetic rhetorolect itself ironic blindness and ironic deafness continually occur in contexts where specially chosen people experience the blessings of God's kingdom. In many ways, then, early Christian prophetic rhetorolect extends the ironies of Israelite blessings and curses into its story of Jesus and Jesus' followers. There are, however, special ways of blending the concept of God as heavenly king and Jesus as God's prophet-king Messiah on earth that create special paradoxes and ironies. In this context, both the story of Jesus and the stories of "believers" in God's Messiah contain special, authoritative dynamics that emerge from God's special will for God's chosen people on earth.

Prophetic Speech Genres, Typical and Atypical Biblical Prophetic Literature, Prophetic Discourse, and Early Christian Prophetic Rhetorolect

As we begin to discuss first century CE Christian prophetic discourse, it is important to distinguish between prophetic speech genres (both oral and written), typical and atypical biblical prophetic literature, prophetic discourse, and early Christian prophetic rhetorolect.

The primary biblical prophetic speech genres (oral and written) emerge from contexts of confrontation that presuppose that God's cosmic will stands in significant opposition to adult leadership and activity in God's kingdom on earth. In Israel, the primary prophetic speech genres were lawsuit speech, appeal for repentance, and oracles of promise.[2] Internal to the lawsuit speech was "reproach and threat" containing the ideal form: "Because you have done this evil, therefore, thus says the Lord, disaster will come upon you."[3] The appeal for repentance modifies the lawsuit speech by adding an utterance that "leaves Israel a chance to alter its course and reengage Yahweh in dutiful obedience."[4] An example is: "But as for you, return to your God, hold fast to love and justice, and wait continually for your God" (Hos 12:6).[5] Oracles of promise, in contrast to the other two, regularly contain a reference to "in that day" or "behold the days are coming." In these oracles, "prophetic utterance breaks completely beyond the limits

[2] Walter Brueggemann, *Theology of the Old Testament: Testimony, Dispute, Advocacy* (Minneapolis: Fortress Press, 1997) 635-39.

[3] John J. Schmitt, "Preexilic Hebrew Prophecy," *ABD* 5:484, explaining that "One finds many other terms to describe the two parts of the form: 'invective,' 'reason,' 'accusation' for the 'reproach,' and 'judgment,' 'sentence,' 'verdict' for the 'threat'."

[4] Brueggemann, *Theology*, 636.

[5] See other examples ibid., 637.

of the conditional covenant of Moses in order to assert the unconditionally positive resolve of Yahweh."[6]

Centripetal movement in Israelite culture produced biblical prophetic literature, sometimes called "prophetic anthologies,"[7] that contain large amounts of these prophetic speech genres. Interpreters regularly identify this "typical" biblical prophetic literature with the "latter prophets," which Christians call the major and minor prophets. If a person would exclude Jonah and Daniel as "atypical" because of their large amount of narrative and unusual content, this would leave a list of fifteen typical prophetic books: Isaiah, Jeremiah, Ezekiel, Hosea, Joel, Amos, Obadiah, Jonah, Micah, Nahum, Habakkuk, Zephaniah, Haggai, Zechariah, and Malachi. Among these it is possible that one could view Joel, Amos, Obadiah, Micah, Nahum, and Zephaniah in particular as examples of primary rather than secondary biblical prophetic literary genre, since they contain a series of primary Israelite prophetic speech genres in what might be considered a "simple" rather than "complex" generic manner.[8] All the rest are clearly "secondary" prophetic literary genre, because they contain a significant variety of primary speech genres.

This means that the "former prophets," which are narrative literature regularly called deuteronomic writings (Joshua, Judges, 1–2 Samuel, and 1–2 Kings), are "atypical" biblical prophetic literature. They are atypical, because they place primary prophetic speech genres in the context of elaborated prophetic narrative, rather than prophetic narrative in the context of elaborated prophetic oracles. This raises a very important issue in relation to early Christian prophetic discourse. There is no book in the NT that is organized around elaborate prophetic oracles, though the organization of Matthew in relation to five major discourses is a very interesting issue in this regard. The Gospels of Matthew, Mark, and Luke, the Acts of the Apostles, and Galatians 1–2 in particular have an important relation to elaborated prophetic narrative in the Hebrew Bible. This calls attention to an important aspect of "typical" Hebrew Bible prophetic literature, namely that most of it contains a combination of prophetic oracles and prophetic narrative. Isaiah and Jeremiah are perhaps most notable for containing extended prophetic narratives,[9] but Ezekiel also contains significant amounts of prophetic narrative, and Jonah and Daniel, as noticed above, foreground narrative as a context for the prophetic transmission of God's word and will. This relation of prophetic narrative to pro-

[6] Ibid., 637-38.
[7] Ibid., 483.
[8] Bakhtin, *Speech Genres*, 61-62, 72-76, 98-99.
[9] Isa 7–8; 20; 36–39; Jer 1; 19–22; 24–29; 32–35; 52.

phetic oracle is highly significant for understanding the nature of early Christian prophetic rhetorolect.

It is important in relation to the presence of both prophetic oracle and prophetic narrative in the Hebrew Bible to know about a shift that occurred when the fourth century CE Christian codex presented the Jewish Hebrew Bible as a collection of "Old Testament" writings that preceded the New Testament. In the Jewish Hebrew Bible, all the prophetic books except Daniel (Joshua through Kings, Isaiah, Jeremiah, Ezekiel and the Twelve minor prophets) stand in the center of the collection, framed by the Torah at the beginning and the Writings at the end. This means that immediately after the Torah, the Hebrew Bible contains extended prophetic narratives followed by extended prophetic oracles, all designed to hold Israel accountable to the Torah.[10] When Christians made the Hebrew Bible into the "Old Testament," they rearranged the books so the "latter prophets" (Isaiah through Malachi), plus Lamentations, Baruch, and Daniel, stand at the end.[11] With this arrangement, biblical prophetic writings dominated by elaborate prophetic oracles create a transition from the prophets of Israel to Christianity. But this is only part of the story. In the context of this shift in arrangement of the books in the Hebrew Bible, early Christian prophetic rhetorolect referred to, recited from, imitated, adapted, and reconfigured narrative portrayals not only of Elijah and Elisha in the deuteronomic writings but also Abraham and Moses, whose stories are in the Torah. In addition, NT writings contain recitations of many portions of the Psalms as prophetic discourse. Thus, in addition to approaching Torah, prophecies, "discourse of notable men," parables, and proverbs as "wisdom discourse" (Sir 39:1-3), early Christians were interpreting major portions of the Torah and the Psalms, as well as the narrative and oracular prophetic writings, as "prophetic" discourse.

But there is still another important part of the story. By the sixth and fifth centuries BCE, biblical prophetic writings began to contain sections that interpreters consider "proto-apocalyptic" discourse. Paul D. Hanson identifies Isaiah 56–66, Haggai, the Chronicler, and Zechariah 9–14 as important in this transition.[12] Stephen L. Cook, in turn, considers Ezekiel 38–39, Zechariah 1–8, and Joel as important transitions to apocalyptic literature.[13] The "apocalypticization" of prophetic biblical discourse is so strong in Daniel that it is regularly considered an apocalyptic book, and it is strong enough in Ezekiel that some inter-

[10] James A. Sanders, "Canon," *ABD* I:844-45.

[11] For an excellent display and discussion of the shift, see Jack Miles, *Christ: A Crisis in the Life of God* (New York: Vintage Books, 2001) 318-23.

[12] Paul D. Hanson, *The Dawn of Apocalyptic* (Philadelphia: Fortress Press, 1975).

[13] Stephen L. Cook, *Prophecy & Apocalypticism: The Postexilic Social Setting* (Minneapolis: Fortress Press, 1995).

preters talk about it as apocalyptic literature. This is a topic that is explored in detail in Chapters 8 and 9 in this volume. The important issue here is the relation of prophets to apocalyptic seers. Why was there literature that "indexed" the prophet, and what happened that shifted the indexing to the apocalyptic seer? Hanson describes the context as follows:

> After 587 the picture changes. Israel's political identity as a nation comes to an end. The office of kingship ends. The prophets no longer have the events of a nation's history into which they can translate the terms of Yahweh's cosmic will. Hence the successors of the prophets, the visionaries, continue to have visions, but they increasingly abdicate the other dimension of the prophetic office, the translation into historical events. At that point we enter the period of the transition from prophetic into apocalyptic eschatology.[14]

Here we notice the importance for prophets of having "the events of a nation's history into which they can translate the terms of Yahweh's cosmic will." If we adapt the wording to refer to "the events of a kingdom's history," we can understand the inner workings of early Christian prophetic rhetorolect. By the end of the first century CE, Christians thought that "events of God's kingdom on earth" had "restarted" with the births of John the Baptist and Jesus and had continued in the events of the followers of Jesus. This "prophetic" view dominates the underlying story-line of the Gospels of Matthew, Mark, and Luke, the Acts of the Apostles, and Paul's story of his life in Gal 1–2. In Chapters eight and nine we will discuss how apocalyptic rhetorolect blends with these prophetic events, and in the next volume we will discuss how precreation rhetorolect reconfigures these events in the Gospel of John.

In the context where first century Christians valued "prophets" who could give special meanings to events in God's earthly kingdom, early Christian prophetic rhetorolect emerged as an idealized cognitive model (ICM). As we recall, in sociorhetorical terms, an ICM contains argumentative-enthymematic structuring, image-description structuring, metaphoric mapping, and metonymic mapping. The argumentative-enthymematic structuring in early Christian prophetic rhetorolect produces confrontation first and foremost through theses of accusation and theses of blessing, both accompanied by reasons. Often, but not always, these theses and reasons are elaborated through techniques of the complete argument characteristic of early Christian wisdom rhetorolect. The image-description structuring emphasizes the relation of events in God's renewed kingdom on earth to God's initial inauguration of and commu-

[14] Hanson, *The Dawn of Apocalyptic*, 16.

nication with a chosen kingdom of Israel. This structuring produces a sequential history that begins with Israel in the past, restarts with the story of Jesus after the kingdom of Israel came to an end, and continues after the death and resurrection of Jesus in the lives of Jesus' followers. The metaphoric mapping focuses on God's "earthly kingdom" over which God is heavenly king, in which Jesus is God's prophet-king Messiah, and in which followers of Jesus are authoritative prophets "anointed" for confrontation of people that leads to their rejection and perhaps even their death. In the metonymic mapping, being "called," "chosen," or "anointed" may evoke the entire prophetic system of understanding, but also referring to God as king, Jesus as prophet or Messiah, life on earth as life in God's kingdom, or receiving an "inheritance" from God may evoke the entire language-world of early Christian prophetic rhetorolect. The key for these terms to evoke prophetic, rather than apocalyptic, rhetorolect is a focus on the ongoing life of humans on earth. When there is an emphasis on transformation that transfers humans from earthly life to heavenly life, the system is apocalyptic rather than prophetic. Early Christian prophetic rhetorolect, in contrast, features confrontation for the purpose of moving people toward responsible action in God's kingdom on earth.

The time-space (chronotope) of first century Christian prophetic rhetorolect is "continued" time in the context of the beginning and ending of kingdoms. This continuation provides the occasion for various people to extend the manner of life into the present and future that certain people lived in the past. Since kingdoms have a beginning, middle, and end in the history of God's world, different challenges exist in relation to responsibilities during the beginnings, highpoint, and final days of a kingdom. In order for a kingdom to come into existence, there must be "a call" of a prophet to take unusual actions that provide a context for God to bring a "special" kingdom into existence on earth. Once the kingdom has come into existence, God calls prophets to confront leaders of that kingdom with their violations of agreements God has made with them to establish their special blessings as they live on earth. During a nation's downfall and end, and immediately after these tragic events, prophets turn more and more to visions as a medium of God's communication with them.

Prophetic discourse focuses on the beginnings and endings of kingdoms in the history of God's people in the world. The traditional view, regularly called "Deuteronomic" or "Deuteronomistic" in relation to the prophetic history in Deuteronomy, 1-2 Samuel and 1-2 Kings, is that people, and especially leaders, are responsible for evil and injustice in the world. Because the fault lies in the domain of actions of people, God confronts people to correct the situation. When God has dealt decisively with the evil that people have created by selecting individual people and groups to confront them with the will of God, then God oversees the renewal of people and their groups on earth. These processes of confrontation often lead to suffering, rejection, death, and destruction. The perception is that people have created the contexts that cause the death and destruction, rather than that God has simply lost patience with all humans and decided to destroy them. If God does inflict death and destruction, God's action is limited to specific people in contexts where these people have created special evil in the world. After the destruction, or even in the midst of it, God renews his kingdom through newly "anointed" leadership. Early Christianity uses this mode of understanding dynamically to talk about Jesus as "the Christ" who came to bring the Kingdom of God to those who are in a position to hear and respond.

In contrast to early Christian wisdom rhetorolect, which nurtured a new *paideia* in the Mediterranean world, early Christian prophetic rhetorolect nurtured multiple implicit and explicit story-lines that explained not only the role and responsibilities of every believer in the history of God's world, but also the role and responsibilities of people like John the Baptist, Jesus, Peter, Stephen, Paul, and others in the history of God's world. Sometimes the story-lines simply created a picture for believers of who they were and how and why they and other people in the history of God's world were authorized to confront people not only in their "inner" community but also in public. Sometimes the story-lines are explicitly argumentative, in rhetorical terms "enthymematic." In other words, instead of simply creating a picture, the story-lines function as emergent structures for assertions, arguments, and stories based on: (1) a person (including the speech of "personified scripture"); (2) an "event-picture";[15] (3) a story; or (4) a series of events. Assertions emerged on the basis of persons, like "Jesus was the prophet like Moses about whom Moses spoke," "Jesus is the seed of Abraham," or "Jesus is Son of David." Arguments emerged on the basis of event-pictures, like "Just as Abraham believed God and it was reckoned to him as righteousness, so, you see, those who believe are descendants of Abraham" (Gal 3:6-7) and "Jesus replied, '... I tell you that Elijah has already come, and they did not recognize him, but they did to him whatever they pleased. So also the Son of Man is about to suffer at their hands.' Then the disciples understood that he was speaking to them about John the Baptist" (Matt 17:12-13). Early Christian stories emerged on the basis of biblical stories, like Herod's killing of all

[15] An event-picture evokes a situation that implies a specific action or set of actions. Therefore, rather than simply picturing a "situation" like a household, it pictures a context in which an event took place but does not present a story of the event.

children two years old or under (Matt 2:13-18), which reconfigures an event in the story of Moses (Exod 1:16) and blends it with a prophetic oracle in Jer 31:15. And sometimes early Christian prophetic rhetorolect was based on a generalized picture of a series of events, like: "Rejoice and be glad, for your reward is great in heaven, for in the same way they persecuted the prophets who were before you" (Matt 5:12/Luke 6:23). Multiple prophetic story-lines supported multiple modes of understanding and action that created "new stories" in the Mediterranean world. It was not stories about Zeus, Hera, and Apollo, or Achilles, Hector, King Priam, and Helen that were the important stories. Rather the stories of Abraham, Moses, Samuel, David, Amos, Isaiah, and Jeremiah were the focus for understanding the nature of God's world and one's responsibilities in it.

To see how wisdom rhetorolect can easily be changed to prophetic rhetorolect, let us look at Luke 12:13-21, which is an excellent example of wisdom rhetorolect. When someone in the crowd calls Jesus "Teacher" and requests Jesus to tell his brother to divide the family inheritance with him, Jesus responds as a teacher rather than a judge with: "Take care! Be on your guard against all kinds of greed; for one's life does not consist in the abundance of possessions" (12:15). This is classic early Christian wisdom rhetorolect. This mode continues in Luke 12:16-21, where Jesus' response moves into argument from analogy (*parabolē*: 12:16). The analogy is a context where the land of a rich man produced abundantly. This is precisely the environment of productivity one expects in early Christian wisdom rhetorolect. When the man has so much grain from his crops that he has no place for them, instead of giving the grain to the poor he builds larger grain houses to store it and tells his soul he will relax, eat, drink and be merry (12:16-19). At this point God tells the man he is a fool and demands his life from him (12:20). Then Jesus pronounces the wisdom statement: "So it is with those who store up treasures for themselves but are not rich toward God" (12:21). This is one of the highpoints of early Christian wisdom rhetorolect in the synoptic Gospels. God confronts the man with language that has the tone of prophetic confrontation, "You fool!" (12:19). Since God is not calling the man to change his point of view, realize what he is doing wrong, and then confront others with the new understanding he has about God, this is not prophetic rhetorolect. Rather, this is simply the moment in wisdom rhetorolect where a person finds out how important it is not to forget God when they become rich.

Speech about the rich becomes prophetic in early Christian discourse when a person, regularly Jesus or one of his followers, accuses the rich of wrongdoing or makes a pronouncement that curses them. Thus, Jesus' statement in Luke 6:24, "But woe to you who are rich, for you have received your condemnation," is early Christian prophetic rhetorolect. Likewise Jas 5:1-6 is classic early Christian prophetic rhetorolect:

> Come now, you rich people, weep and wail for the miseries that are coming to you. [2] Your riches have rotted, and your clothes are moth-eaten. [3] Your gold and silver have rusted, and their rust will be evidence against you, and it will eat your flesh like fire. You have laid up treasure for the last days. [4] Listen! The wages of the laborers who mowed your fields, which you kept back by fraud, cry out, and the cries of the harvesters have reached the ears of the Lord of hosts. [5] You have lived on the earth in luxury and in pleasure; you have fattened your hearts on a day of slaughter. [6] You have condemned and murdered the righteous one, who does not resist you.

These five verses are excellent examples of early Christian prophetic rhetorolect. The narrator uses topoi that are central to wisdom rhetorolect with a tone of confrontation that implies that the narrator is speaking authoritative words of God. Of special importance in our present context is to observe the emergence of the topos of "fire" in 5:3. We will notice below how early Christian prophetic rhetorolect moves beyond the emphasis on light in wisdom to the negotiation of both light and fire from God in prophetic rhetorolect. In Jas 5:3, the rust of the gold and silver the rich have stored away will eat their flesh "like fire." It is noticeable that this prophetic rhetorolect does not speak of "the fire of God" that will come and burn them up, which is characteristic of early Christian apocalyptic rhetorolect.[16] Rather, the analogy of rust to fire that eats one's flesh exhibits a natural progression from early Christian wisdom rhetorolect, which focuses on light in relation to darkness, to early Christian prophetic rhetorolect, which regularly negotiates the relation of light to fire.

The other side of early Christian prophetic rhetorolect is its "positive" confrontational dimension.[17] Not only Jesus, but also early Christian leaders, emphasize the special blessings that come upon those faithful people whom God chooses to live in the special responsibilities of God's righteousness and justice on earth. This positive confrontational mode is on Jesus' lips in Luke 6:20-23:

> [20] Then he looked up at his disciples and said:
> "Blessed are you who are poor,
> for yours is the kingdom of God.
> [21] "Blessed are you who are hungry now,

[16] Prophetic in rhetorolect in Numbers, Deuteronomy, and Amos, in particular, feature the fire of God that burns people up.

[17] I am grateful to Bart Bruehler for emphasizing this, with special reference to Walter Brueggemann, *The Prophetic Imagination* (Philadelphia: Fortress Press, 1978) and *Hopeful Imagination: Prophetic Voices in Exile* (Philadelphia: Fortress Press, 1986).

for you will be filled.
"Blessed are you who weep now,
for you will laugh.
22 "Blessed are you when people hate you, and when they exclude you,
revile you, and defame you on account of the Son of Man.
23 "Rejoice on that day and leap for joy, for surely your reward is great
in heaven; for that is what their ancestors did to the prophets."[18]

In contrast to the beatitudes in Matt 5:3-10, which are early Christian wisdom rhetorolect that uses third person narration to define the blessed as the poor in spirit, those who mourn, the meek, etc., Luke 6:20-23 presents early Christian prophetic rhetorolect. Jesus confronts people who look like they are being cursed by God with the nature of their blessedness. In other words, Jesus' speech acquits the hearers of any wrongdoing that is causing their circumstances. Jesus does not pronounce them guilty but acquitted. Though their poverty could be interpreted as a curse for not fulfilling the commandments of God, they are participants in the kingdom of God (6:20). Though their hunger and weeping could be interpreted as God's punishment of them for wrongdoing, Jesus confronts them with future blessings that come to those who live faithfully as God's people under extremely difficult circumstances (6:21). Living in the mode of prophetic life, people will hate, exclude, revile, and defame them on account of the Son of Man (6:22). Indeed, they need to rejoice that God's reward lies in the future, just as the prophets understood, rejoiced, and were faithful to God's calling (6:23).

Centripetal forces in first century Christian culture produced Gospels and Acts in which prophetic rhetorolect functions as the host for other first century Christian rhetorolects. In this context, prophetic rhetorolect had a basic effect of creating "Christian story." This role of prophetic Christian story functions strongly in Paul's letter to the Galatians, where Paul tells "his own prophetic story," in certain "speeches" in Acts (Peter, Stephen, Philip, Paul), and in prophetic curses and blessings in Gospels. Centrifugal forces in first century Christian culture produced a presence of some prophetic rhetorolect in virtually all the NT writings. One of the symptoms of its centrifugal presence is the occurrence of some form of the Greek stem *prophēt-* ("pre-assert" or "pro-claim") in 17 of the 27 books in the NT.[19] Prophetic discourse was widespread throughout the Mediterranean world, especially through the presence of prophetic oracles from the sanctuaries of Del-

[18] For detailed analysis of the beatitudes, see Vernon K. Robbins, "Pragmatic Relations as a Criterion for Authentic Sayings," *Forum* 1.3 (1985) 35-63. Online: http://www.religion.emory.edu/faculty/robbins/Pdfs/Pragmatic.pdf

[19] Matthew, Mark, Luke, John, Acts, Romans, 1 Corinthians, Ephesians, 1 Thessalonians, 1 Timothy, Titus, Hebrews, James, 1-2 Peter, Jude, and Revelation.

phi and Dadonis. Both prophetic literature and prophetic discourse functioned as resources whereby the earliest Christians created prestigious story-lines from authoritative people in the world of the biblical past into the story-lines of the predecessors of Jesus, the story-line of Jesus himself, and the story-line of the followers of Jesus.

The Early Christian Story-Line of Biblical Prophets

The writings of the New Testament exhibit selectivity from the Hebrew Bible that emphasizes three key periods of time in which God gave prophetic messages to people in the world:

1. God's calling of Abraham to special tasks that would create blessed nations (Gentiles) in God's created world;
2. God's calling of Moses to liberate Hebrews from enslavement in Egypt by identifying them as a people who would become a kingdom of priests and a holy nation in the world.
3. God's calling of prophets to confront kings and other leaders of Israel during the times when portions of "the land of Canaan" were ruled over by kings.

The beginning of the Christian prophetic story occurs in God's speech to Abraham.[20] Early Christian discourse presupposes that special adult people are called to special prophetic tasks by God's direct confrontation of them with speech. When these adults hear the words of God, they regularly engage in dialogue with God to clarify the message that is being communicated to them. The effect of the dialogue is to create a relation of the adult to God whereby the prophet can hold God responsible for certain things God has said in relation to God's holding the prophet responsible for certain things God has communicated to the prophet.

For the Christian prophetic story, God's call to certain adults is the beginning of God's kingdom on earth as well as the special orientation of God to righteousness and justice on earth. The people who hear the words of the prophet, and see his actions, must take these words and actions seriously, since God has authorized them through special events of calling and sending the prophet. Special difficulties arise, because the words of the prophet concern special actions in the context of special criticisms and indictments of actions that leaders consider to be "the way God wants people to be faithful" in God's kingdom. In other words, the message of the prophet is not simply traditional wisdom. It is "special wisdom of the will of God" that leaders see simply as criticism of their leadership. The special insights into the will of God that prophets claim to have is not only perceived to be an annoyance.

[20] For the Qur'an, the prophetic story-line begins with God's speech to Adam and continues through God's speech to Noah before the time of Abraham.

Regularly it is perceived by leaders to be rebellion against God's holy ways by people who simply want to cause trouble and disorder.

Early Christian prophetic rhetorolect blends stories about the call and actions of prophets with confrontational statements prophets made during various periods of human history. This is a blending of the geography of particular kingdoms on earth with the biblical geography of the heavens where God dwells. With this move, prophetic discourse makes assertions about the nature of God's speech in the world, moving beyond images of creation to images of confrontation that create new kingdoms on earth in a context that regularly leads to serious consequences for, if not the discontinuation of, an existing kingdom.

In order for the biblical story of God's calling of prophets to function as an authoritative mode of confrontation of leaders and groups in the world, there had to be a place where humans experienced the power and effect of such speech in the history of God's people on earth. In the biblical tradition, and in early Christian tradition, the Firstspace of prophetic discourse is a kingdom, a geographical region ruled over by a king. Christian speakers and writers built early Christian prophetic rhetorolect by blending together Firstspace images and reasoning related to kingdoms with Secondspace in the heavens, where they perceived God to reign as a king with special interest and focus on a particular kingdom of people on earth. When biblical tradition blended kingdom with God's dwelling place in the heavens, it pictured God as king and God's kingdom on earth as ruled by an earthly king who was specially anointed for the task, responsible for pursuing righteousness and justice rather than self-gain, and vulnerable to prophets who confronted them with special insights about God's will for their activities. Activities and relationships in kingdoms throughout the Mediterranean world provided social, cultural, and ideological geography for early Christian prophetic discourse. Activities and relationships in kingdoms blended naturally with geographical regions ruled over by people who had been "authorized" by various events to rule over the people and resources of the people in that region. In turn, this knowledge about kingdoms blended with conceptualization about how God relates to "his special people on earth." Naturally, God relates to them as a king who rules over them. God, of course, is a benevolent king, championing righteousness and justice. But God also must be an active ruler. God must intervene when earthly leaders are not leading properly to send "decrees" through prophets concerning the will of God as king over the earthly king and all leaders and people in his region. All of the activities people experienced in actual kingdoms on earth functioned by analogy with God's ruling of a particular group of people in a particular geographical region on earth. God sat on a royal throne in heaven and made decrees that emissaries carried to various places in the region over which God ruled. God sent these decrees out through people whom God called and appointed to this task. People, in turn, had responsibilities like those well-known in kingdoms that actually existed during their lifetime, or had existed in the past.

Once kingdom reasoning merged comfortably with reasoning about God's ruling over a specific group of people from the heavens, this blended reasoning traveled naturally into reasoning about the intersubjective bodies of prophets as Thirdspace. Specially selected adults become authorized agents to pronounce God's will in the world. They have a special responsibility to state what God requires of people, no matter the consequences. In addition, people who are understood to be God's king have a special relation to God. They are anointed by God as agents of righteousness and justice throughout God's kingdom. Certain adult humans, therefore, are the special focus of early Christian prophetic rhetorolect. Not everyone can be a prophet and not everyone can be a king. God selects only certain very special adults to fulfill these roles in the world. Early Christian prophetic rhetorolect, therefore, is a network of reasoning that focuses on the establishment of righteousness and justice in God's world. Enactment of righteousness and justice occurs through specially selected people, some of whom function as prophets and kings in the story-line of God's activities, and some who are simply part of the group God has selected to establish, maintain, renew, or begin anew the special kingdom God has planned for the world.

Kingdoms and Prophets as Spaces and Places for Prophetic Rhetorolect

Religious Blending	Prophetic Rhetorolect
Social, Cultural, & Physical Realia (1st Space)	Region ruled by a King, its Leaders, its People
Visualization, Conceptualization, & Imagination of God's World (2nd Space)	God as King, God on kingly throne in heavenly court, Selected humans as prophets, Selected people as God's kingdom, Jesus as Prophet-Messiah selected and sent by God
Ongoing Bodily Effects and Enactments: Blending in Religious Life (3rd Space)	Leaders and Members of a Kingdom as enactors and receivers of God's righteousness and justice on earth

The Hebrew Bible begins its prophetic story about God's creation of a special kingdom on earth with Abraham. This story represented an account of the beginning of the kingdom of God's special people on earth. At its beginning point, the conceptualization of God as king was not fully enacted. Nor was Abraham fully developed as a prophet who received special messages from God that he systematically transmitted to certain leaders and groups of people in contexts of confrontation.[21] In the Hebrew Bible Abraham engages God, rather than leaders on earth, in dialogue. Nevertheless, early Christians considered the nature of God's selection of Abraham, the nature of the messages God gave to Abraham, and the actions of Abraham to be resources for early Christian prophetic rhetorolect. The story of Abraham, then, moves toward the story of Moses as the next major resource for early Christian prophetic rhetorolect. God's calling of Moses and Moses' special way of carrying out the tasks God gave to him make him, from the perspective of early Christian discourse, a model prophet. Beyond the story of Moses, early Christian prophetic rhetorolect selectively uses portions of the accounts of Elijah and Elisha and the prophetic oracles of Amos, Hosea, Isaiah, Jeremiah, and other prophetic writings as resources.

As mentioned earlier, prophetic rhetorolect negotiates God's relation to light and fire, rather than God's primary relation to light, as we have seen in early Christian wisdom rhetorolect. For early Christian prophetic rhetorolect, people in the world live in a dynamic sphere characterized by light from God and fire from both humans and God. Perhaps the imagery of fire emerges from the use of fire by one kingdom against another, where they may burn villages, cities, crops, and even people as they confront one another. In any case, fire often is present in prophetic contexts where people both receive God's word and violate God's word. Early Christian prophetic rhetorolect uses its reasoning about political kingdoms and God's ruling as king from the heavens to formulate authoritative speech that accuses people of wrongdoing and sometimes warns them that the consequences of continuing with evil ways of life in the world may lead to a fiery result. Thus, as early Christian prophetic rhetorolect sanctions certain people with authoritative speech about God's will and with the necessity to use their speech in confrontational ways to fulfill God's wishes for the world, this discourse sometimes presents speakers negotiating God as light with fire that either comes from God or that exists in a place where people may go at the end of a life that has followed evil ways.

Abraham as a Beginning for the Prophetic Story-Line: Genesis 12–25

Even though no New Testament writing refers to Abraham as a prophet, Genesis 12–25 presents the beginnings of the early Christian prophetic story-line. Why does the Christian prophetic story-line begin with Abraham? There are at least four reasons. First, Abraham is "called" by God to be a person who fulfills a sequence of tasks in the

[21] Both rabbinic literature and the Qur'an develop the image and function of Abraham as a confrontational prophet in his hometown and in the places where he travels.

context of promises by God about blessings and curses. Second, God's call to Abraham concerns a specific area of land, where people will live as "God's people," "God's nation," or "God's kingdom." Third, God speaks to Abraham a number of times, either directly or through a messenger/angel, to give him specific directions and promises. Fourth, Abraham's acceptance of God's tasks creates significant difficulties with which Abraham struggles obediently and faithfully.

The relation between God and Abraham in Gen 12–25 exhibits how confrontation lies both at the base and the center of prophetic discourse. At the base of prophetic discourse lies God's confrontation of an individual with a message about responsibilities, promises, and possible punishments. This confrontation occurs as a result of a decision by God to act in a special way toward a specific group of people in the course of God's history with the world. A prophet's confrontation of people is perceived in the discourse to occur as a result of God's "calling" of that individual to perform a specific set of tasks that involves both words and actions. At the center of prophetic discourse, then, a prophet is considered to be authorized by God to confront certain individuals and groups on the basis of guidelines God has communicated to the prophet. Thus, both God's action and speech and the prophet's action and speech involve confrontation. The discourse presupposes that God takes action in special ways as events occur in the history of the world. It also presupposes that God expects prophets, leaders, and others to take special action to change the way things are occurring. Both God's action towards the prophet and the prophet's action toward other people involve speech as part of the action. Prophetic discourse, then, concerns words and actions both by God and by humans. Both God and humans confront certain people and groups for the purpose of communicating special decisions God makes about specific individuals and groups during the course of God's history with humans in the world.

We will see in the next chapter that the focus of prophetic discourse on specific individuals and groups on earth differentiates it from apocalyptic discourse. At the base of apocalyptic discourse lies God's concern with all that lies in the heavens, on earth, under the earth, and outside the realms of the ordered world God created at the beginning of time. In contrast, prophetic discourse focuses on specific individuals and groups God chooses to exhibit the nature of God's righteousness and justice on earth. As the history of Israel unfolded, prophetic discourse broadened in scope to include the relation of the heavens to multiple nations in the regions of the Mediterranean Sea and the Tigris and Euphrates Rivers. There is, then, a somewhat natural, gradual movement in biblical literature from prophetic toward apocalyptic discourse, which contains a broader focus.[22]

[22] Hanson, *The Dawn of Apocalyptic*; Cook, *Prophecy & Apocalypticism*.

Since the focus in prophetic literature was on a particular region of land, the earliest apocalyptic literature also exhibited this more limited focus. Early Christian apocalyptic rhetorolect, as we will see in the next chapter, participated in a movement of apocalyptic discourse beyond a focus on people in power over one specific area of land toward a focus on all powers, human and spiritual, throughout the entire cosmos.

What, then, is the nature of God's initial call to Abraham? First, God chooses and calls Abraham to, "Go." Second, God sends Abraham to "a particular land." These two aspects of God's call to Abraham are evident in Gen 12:1-3: "Now the LORD said to Abram, 'Go from your country and your kindred and your father's house to the land that I will show you.'" Third, God confronts Abraham for the purpose of making his descendants into a special group of people on earth: either into one "great nation" (Gen 12:2) or into "a multitude of nations" (Gen 17:4-5).[23] Fourth, God's promise to Abraham contains blessings and curses when God says:

> 2 "... I will bless you, and make your name great, so that you will be a blessing. 3 I will bless those who bless you, and the one who curses you I will curse" (Gen 12:2-3).

Fifth, God's focus on Abraham and a specific area of land is a result of God's focus on humans who live in God's created world. This is evident in God's assertion to Abraham that "in you all the families of the earth shall be blessed" (Gen 12:3). The primary focus of prophetic discourse is on people. God confronts specific people for the purpose of creating a special group of people in a particular region of God's created world for the purpose of making God's righteousness and justice a blessing to all people on earth.

Early Christian prophetic rhetorolect confronts people with God's call and promise to Abraham for the purpose of reminding them of their identity as "descendants of the prophets and of the covenant." Acts 3:24-25 feature Peter asserting:

> 24 And all the prophets, as many as have spoken, from Samuel and those after him, also predicted these days. 25 You are the descendants of the prophets and of the covenant that God gave to your ancestors, saying to Abraham, "And in your descendants all the families of the earth shall be blessed." [24]

[23] There is agreement in Genesis that Abraham will have as many descendants as there are stars in the sky and sand in the sea. There is tension, however, over whether these descendants well be one great nation (Gen 12:2) or a multitude of nations (17:4-5).

[24] See Gen 17:3, 5 for God's promise to Abraham that he would have "many nations" as his descendants; cf. Gen 15:4-5; 22:16-17.

In early Christian discourse, Abraham is the starting point in the prophetic story-line. God's promises to Abraham, from the perspective of early Christians, were a means by which a particular group of people whom God selected for special attention could transmit God's blessings from generation to generation in the history of God's people on earth. These special people are descendants of Abraham, and they become descendants through the promises God made to him and to the prophets who came after him. The goal of God, from the Christian perspective, was to bring a blessing to all people on earth by selecting and confronting specific individuals and groups of people in a specific region of God's creation, namely the region of the Mediterranean Sea and the Tigris and Euphrates Rivers. This "nation of people," from the perspective of prophetic rhetorolect, would transmit God's blessing to all people on earth.

Early Christian prophetic rhetorolect presupposes that a prophetic relation to God begins with God's confrontation of a person with a command to take action to fulfill a special task God has for them. In Acts 7:2-3, Stephen replies to the high priest with a summary of the beginning point of the Christian prophetic story-line:

> 2 "Brothers and fathers, listen to me. The God of glory appeared to our ancestor Abraham when he was in Mesopotamia, before he lived in Haran, 3 and said to him, 'Leave your country and your relatives and go to the land that I will show you'" (Acts 7:2-3).

As Stephen continues the story of Abraham, he emphasizes both that Abraham responded obediently to God's directions (7:4) and that a result of Abraham's obedience was a group of descendants with an identity of "resident aliens" and a life of enslavement and mistreatment (Acts 7:6; cf. Gen 15:13-14). Internal to the early Christian prophetic story-line, therefore, is an emphasis on the necessity both for obedience to God's call to special tasks in the world and for acceptance of a life of displacement, vulnerability to other people's power, and abuse as a result of one's identity. There is, however, always a promise standing in the background of early Christian prophetic rhetorolect that God will remain true to a vision of a place on earth where God will enact righteousness and justice on earth. Thus, Stephen continues his account of Abraham with:

> "But I will judge the nation [Egypt] that they serve," said God, "and after that they shall come out and worship me in this place" (Acts 7:7).

God's action of judging (*krinō*) people who rule over the people God has chosen is an internal aspect of early Christian prophetic rhetorolect. The important thing for this rhetorolect is that God works continually with particular people in special ways and in specific circumstances to create a place on earth where people enact God's righteousness and justice. This leads to an extended story-line featuring many people whom God has summoned throughout history to perform special tasks that participate in God's promises to bring special blessing to all people on earth.

As early Christians recount their version of the prophetic story-line, they emphasize special inner attributes of Abraham that enabled him to respond obediently to God. In Rom 4:18, Paul interprets Abraham's response to God as an action of belief based on hope:

> Hoping against hope, he believed that he would become "the father of many nations," according to what was said, "So numerous shall your descendants be." (Rom 4:18)

Through hope and belief, according to Paul, Abraham became the father of many nations. Paul's particular way of interpreting the results of Abraham's hope and belief, of course, is to focus on many nations rather that one great nation. This focus allows him to move the prophetic promises of God beyond the nation of Israel toward "the nations" (*ta ethnē*), which NT interpreters regularly translate into English as "Gentiles." In Pauline discourse, the focus on "many nations" essentially means non-Jewish nations in the region of the Mediterranean Sea and the Tigris and Euphrates Rivers. In the NT, "Gentiles" means people in the Mediterranean world who worship gods and goddesses like Zeus, Isis, Hermes, etc. In other words, this discourse does not have people like Hindus or Buddhists in view, even though these people existed at the time of the writing of the NT. Muslims also are not in view, since they did not have an identity in the historiography of the world until the 7th century CE.[25]

First, it is important for us to notice an aspect of the focus on Abraham as the father of many nations that is not clearly evident in Paul's interpretation but may play a role in a more subtle manner in first century Christian discourse. Gen 17:5 features God changing Abram's name to Abraham when God makes him "the father of a multitude of nations," implying that "*raham*," which means exceedingly fruitful or exceedingly numerous in Hebrew, would mean more than one nation. This kind of focus on the name of a person in the context of God's confrontation of them may be an aspect of early Christian prophetic rhetorolect. One notices an emphasis on names, which includes multiple names, special names, and a change of names, in prophetic contexts in the NT writings. The opening chapter of Matthew features a message from the angel of the Lord to Joseph that the son born to Mary

[25] From the perspective of Muslims, of course, many people beginning with Adam were "muslim," namely people totally obedient to God.

will be named Jesus, "for he will save his people from their sins" (Matt 1:21). In the same context, the word "spoken by the Lord through the prophet" says that the son born to Mary will be named Emmanuel, "which means, 'God with us'" (Matt 1:22). Then the second chapter of Matthew ends with a statement "spoken through the prophets" that Jesus will be called a "Nazorean" (Matt 2:23). Multiple names for Jesus clearly are a part of early Christian prophetic rhetorolect.

It is possible that the special focus on names in early Christian prophetic rhetorolect extends to followers of Jesus. Mark 3:13 features prophetic phrases when Jesus goes up the mountain and calls to him those whom he wanted, and they come to him. Mark 3:14 emphasizes that Jesus "names them apostles" when he appoints them to their tasks. Then Mark 3:16-17 feature Jesus giving certain apostles special names, the name Peter to Simon and the name Boanerges, meaning Sons of Thunder, to James and John, sons of Zebedee. In turn, Simon Peter identifies Jesus as "the Messiah, the Son of the living God" in Matt 16:13-16 when the issue of Jesus' relation to Elijah, Jeremiah, and other prophets has emerged in the context of Jesus' activity. When Simon Peter is able to identify Jesus in this manner, Jesus praises him as son of the prophet Jonah, because this was not ordinary knowledge but "prophetic" information revealed to Simon by Jesus' father in heaven (16:17). The source of Simon's knowledge of the identity of Jesus, then, is perceived to be the source from which all prophets receive their knowledge. When Jesus continues, he gives a special prophetic name and task to Simon, namely "the rock [Peter] on which I will build my church" (Matt 16:18).[26] Peter's prophetic task is embedded in his special name, just like the name Jesus means that he will save his people from their sins (Matt 1:21). Thus, wherever a prophetic name is present, there also is a prophetic task and identity assigned to that person by God.

Second, we must notice that both Pauline discourse and the epistle to the Hebrews focus on Abraham's response to God with the Christian topos of faith. Heb 11:8 asserts: "By faith Abraham obeyed when he was called to set out for a place that he was to receive as an inheritance; and he set out, not knowing where he was going." According to Hebrews, Abraham was able to respond unconditionally to God's call to action, because he possessed the personal attribute of "faith." This topos functions in Hebrews as an emergent structure for blending pro-

[26] The change of Saul's name to Paul in Acts 13:9 appears simply to be a matter of using his Roman rather than Jewish name. An important feature of the accounts of the confrontation of Paul with his prophetic task, however, is the voice's calling of Paul by name, "Saul, Saul" (Acts 9:4; 22:7; 26:14), and identification of itself as Jesus (Acts 9:5; 26:15) or Jesus of Nazareth (Acts 22:8).

phetic rhetorolect with miracle discourse as it emphasizes renewal of powers of the body and with apocalyptic discourse as it emphasizes resurrection of the dead. Hebrews 11:11-12 states:

> By faith he [Abraham] received power of procreation, even though he was too old – and Sarah herself was barren – because he considered him faithful who had promised. 12 Therefore from one person, and this one as good as dead, descendants were born, "as many as the stars of heaven and as the innumerable grains of sand by the seashore."

Faith was the means by which God transformed Abraham's aged body into a fully functioning agent of new life and also the means by which God resurrected Abraham from "one as good as dead" to a "fully living being."[27] Early Christian prophetic rhetorolect that talked about Abraham, then, functioned as an emergent structure for both miracle and apocalyptic discourse through its focus on the topos of faith.

When Paul's letters interpret Abraham's belief as faith, the emphasis is that uncircumcised people of the nations ("Gentiles") may enter into God's "righteousness" by having faith similar to Abraham's. Romans 4:3, 9, 11 contain the following statements:

> 3 For what does the scripture say? "Abraham believed God, and it was reckoned to him as righteousness." ... 9 Is this blessedness, then, pronounced only on the circumcised, or also on the uncircumcised? We say, "Faith was reckoned to Abraham as righteousness." ... 11 The purpose was to make him the ancestor of all who believe without being circumcised and who thus have righteousness reckoned to them.[28]

In Gal 3:6-9, Paul's discourse about Abraham's "faith" calls this message to the Gentiles "the gospel":

> Just as Abraham "believed God, and it was reckoned to him as righteousness," 7 so, you see, those who believe are the descendants of Abraham. 8 And the scripture, foreseeing that God would justify the nations (Gentiles) by faith, declared the gospel beforehand to Abraham, saying, "All the nations (Gentiles) shall be blessed in you." 9 For this reason, those who believe are blessed with Abraham who believed. (Gal 3:6-9)

Abraham functions in early Christian discourse as an important beginning for prophetic rhetorolect, because this story is a major beginning point for "the gospel." When God called Abraham, confronting him with speech that commands him to go to a particular land that he will show him and to perform duties God will give him to perform, God was presenting the beginning of the gospel story.

[27] See Gen 17:1; 18:11-14; 21:2-3 for emphasis on the old age of Abraham and Sarah.
[28] See Gen 15:6; 18:19 for righteousness in relation to Abraham's faith; cf. Gen 17:9.

We will see below how Galatians 3 and Romans 4 reconfigure the story of God's promise of descendants and land to Abraham into the promise of an inheritance through Christ. We will also see how Abraham functions as a beginning point for the Gospel story in Matthew. The story of Abram is a beginning for the Christian prophetic story-line because Abram was "called" by God to fulfill a sequence of tasks in the context of promises by God about blessings and curses. Abram's name was changed to Abraham by God when God made him the ancestor of many nations and formed a special covenant with him. The New Testament reconfigures Abraham's hope as an enduring faith in God. Due to this enduring faith, Abraham and Sarah "received power of procreation" (Heb 11:11-12). God promises Abraham both descendents and land, but early Christian rhetorolect focuses on the descendants. In Christian prophetic rhetorolect, Abraham's belief in the power of God is faith through which God reckoned to him righteousness for many nations (Gentiles).

Moses as a Continuation of the Prophetic Story-Line: Exodus

The story-line of early Christian prophetic rhetorolect continues beyond Abraham with Moses. New Testament writings speak of Moses as a prophet whom God raised up from his own people (Acts 7:37), in fulfillment of Moses' statements in Deut 18:15-22. In what ways is Moses perceived to be a prophet in NT writings? First, God directly confronts Moses and tells him specific things he must do to fulfill a decision God has made. Second, both actions and words are central to God's message and to the tasks Moses must perform. Third, God's actions and words concern both blessings and curses. Fourth, the actions and words are focused on a particular group of people whom God identifies as "God's people," "God's nation," or "God's kingdom." Fifth, God identifies not only a special group of people but also a specific area of land as an environment where God's righteousness and justice are to be enacted on earth. Sixth, Moses' acceptance of God's tasks creates a covenant between God and Moses, to which God promises to be faithful. Seventh, the tasks God gives to Moses are difficult to fulfill, causing Moses significant difficulties and even causing him to fall short of perfect fulfillment of the tasks.

God calls Moses to his prophetic task in Exodus 3. While Moses is tending his father-in-law Jethro's sheep in the wilderness of Midian, an angel of the Lord appears to him "in a flame of fire out of a bush" at the mountain of God called Horeb (Exod 3:1-2). As noted earlier, God's association with fire in prophetic rhetorolect is a feature different from wisdom rhetorolect, where God's relation to light is so dominant that fire plays no role in it. In contrast to wisdom rhetorolect, where

God's word creates light, in God's prophetic call to Moses, God's word comes out of fire (Exod 3:4). Fire creates a context where God's voice initiates dialogue by speaking names. When God calls out the name of Moses, a dialogue begins whereby Moses acknowledges his identity before God and God names the identity of the divine voice: "I am the God of your father, the God of Abraham, the God of Isaac, and the God of Jacob" (Exod 3:4-6). Prophetic discourse, then, is an environment where names already exist for things both on earth and in heaven. God's words use identities and reveal identities to create contexts for specific actions and speech. In addition, rather than simply asking questions, which is a central characteristic of wisdom rhetorolect, God tells stories. God's story to Moses in Exod 3:7-8 is about people the Lord identifies as "my people" and about a specific region of land:

> Then the LORD said, "I have observed the misery of my people who are in Egypt; I have heard their cry on account of their taskmasters. Indeed, I know their sufferings, [8] and I have come down to deliver them from the Egyptians, and to bring them up out of that land to a good and broad land, a land flowing with milk and honey, to the country of the Canaanites, the Hittites, the Amorites, the Perizzites, the Hivites, and the Jebusites. [9] The cry of the Israelites has now come to me; I have also seen how the Egyptians oppress them. (Exod 3:7-8)

The Lord's story to Moses concerns injustice in the world. In contrast to the creation story, where "God saw that it was good," the Lord sees "how the Egyptians oppress them." God describes the injustice as something being done by the Egyptians to "my people." Then the Lord explains to Moses the plan for correcting the situation, which requires that Moses undertake special actions to fulfill what the Lord has decided should be done: "So come, I will send you to Pharaoh to bring my people, the Israelites, out of Egypt" (Exod 3:10).

The opening scene of the Moses story, then, has a number of things in common with the opening scene of the Abraham story, with some notable differences. Major differences emerge in the presence of fire,[29] of a story about past and present actions that are producing injustice in the world, and of extended dialogue.[30] After the Lord tells the story about the oppression by the Egyptians and what Moses must do to remove it, Moses engages in dialogue with God throughout Exod 3:11–4:17. The dialogue clarifies how Moses will have the power to

[29] See the presence of fire in God's covenant with Abraham in Gen 15:7-21 and God's command that Isaac be a "burnt offering" on the mountain (Gen 22:1-14).

[30] Dialogue between God and Abram/Abraham begins in Gen 15 and, as is well known, is especially dynamic in the scene prior to the Lord's destruction of Sodom (Gen 18:22-33).

do what he must do, reveals the specific name of God Moses is to use in communication with the Israelites, and gives Moses specific statements he is to say both to the Israelites and to the pharaoh/king of Egypt. Moses nurtures the dialogue along with a series of questions and statements designed to get further information from the Lord: "Who am I to do this?" (3:11); "If I say and they say, what shall I say?" (3:13); "But suppose they do not believe me or listen to me" (4:1); "O my Lord, … I am slow of speech and slow of tongue" (4:10); "O my Lord, please send someone else" (4:13). When Moses shifts from questions to statements, the Lord introduces a question followed by a series of commands: "What is that in your hand?" (4:2); "Throw it on the ground" (4:3); "Reach out your hand and seize it by the tail" (4:4); "Put your hand inside your cloak" (4:6); "Put your hand back into your cloak" (4:7). After this, God presents two "if … then …" statements to Moses:

> If they will not believe you or heed the first sign, they may believe the second sign. [9] If they will not believe even these two signs or heed you, you shall take some water from the Nile and pour it on the dry ground; and the water that you shall take from the Nile will become blood on the dry ground. (Exod 4:8–9)

One of the special characteristics of the story is the conclusion to Moses's dialogue with the Lord. When Moses insists that he is not eloquent, God shifts into "rhetorical questions," namely questions that simply are occasions for God to give further information and commands:

> "Who gives speech to mortals? Who makes them mute or deaf, seeing or blind? Is it not I, the LORD? [12] Now go, and I will be with your mouth and teach you what you are to speak." (Exod 4:11-12)

God as creator of the world and all people in it, which is central to wisdom discourse, underlies prophetic discourse. But prophetic discourse emphasizes the necessity to go and use one's mouth in a context where God has told the person what to speak. When Moses says, "O my Lord, please send someone else" (4:13), the Lord becomes angry with Moses, tells him to speak to Aaron about "serving as a mouth for him," and commands him to take his staff in his hand to perform the signs (4:14–17). It seems remarkable that the scene ends with anger between the Lord and Moses rather than amiable agreement. But this is an important feature of prophetic discourse. There is no presupposition that prophetic discourse has an amiable, winning tone. Rather, it regularly alternates positive, promising statements with negative, judgmental assertions. In contrast to wisdom discourse, which creates light that nurtures goodness, prophetic discourse comes out of the fire of

God in a manner that calls for action in contexts of unrighteousness and injustice. Prophetic discourse negotiates both anger and mercy within God. Anger and mercy intermingle in God's attributes as God devises plans to correct unrighteousness and injustice in the world. Rather than attempting to deal with "all" of the world, God selects particular individuals, commands them to perform certain tasks, gives them speech to say to people in the context of their actions, engages in dialogue with the people he selects, accepts anger as a natural dynamic between God and the prophet, and refuses to take "No" as an answer from the prophet.

Early Christian prophetic rhetorolect in Stephen's speech in Acts 7 interprets God's call of Moses as "the fulfillment of the promise that God had made to Abraham" (7:17). The Christian story starts with a king of Egypt who had not known Joseph and "forced our ancestors to abandon their infants so they would die" (7:19). Moses was born "beautiful before God," abandoned after three months in his father's house, and adopted by Pharaoh's daughter (7:20-21). Moses was instructed in all the wisdom of the Egyptians and was powerful in word and deeds (7:22). Thus, the early Christian Moses story begins with wisdom rhetorolect blended with miracle rhetorolect.

The Christian story moves next to Moses at forty years of age, when he saw one of his relatives among the Israelites being wronged (*adikoumenon*: 7:23). The topos here, of course, is injustice, which lies at the base of prophetic rhetorolect. As an adult, Moses moves beyond a life guided by wisdom into a life that confronts injustice with decisive action. According to this early Christian prophetic rhetorolect, Moses "made justice" (*epoiēsen ekdikēsen*) by striking down the Egyptian, supposing "that his kinsfolk would understand that God through him was rescuing them, but they did not understand" (7:24-25). Here are three additional early Christian prophetic topoi: (1) special action by God through a wise and powerful adult to enact righteousness and justice among certain humans God has chosen to be "God's people" on earth; (2) rejection of the prophet by his own kinsfolk, who also are God's specially chosen people; and (3) an inability of those among whom the prophet lives to understand God's will from the speech and action of the prophet. The prophetic emphasis continues as Stephen recounts how, on the next day, Moses attempted to establish peace (*synēllassen … eis eirēnēn*) among two men who were treating each other unjustly (*adikeite allēlous*: 7:26). Again the attempt by Moses to establish justice in the world is rejected when the man who was treating his neighbor unjustly (*adikōn*) questions Moses' right to be a ruler and judge (*archōn kai dikastēn*) over them and asserts that Moses probably wishes to kill him, like he killed the Egyptian the day before (7:27-28). From the perspective of this early Christian account, Moses possessed the attributes of a prophet and experienced the rejection of a prophet already at forty years of age, before God had called him to his specific task of freeing Israel from the Egyptians.

According to the Christian account, forty years later, namely when Moses was eighty, God called Moses to his special task. The Christian account emphasizes that "the voice of the Lord" (*phōnē kyriou*) out of "the flame of a burning bush" (*phlogi pyros batou*) identified itself as "the God of your fathers, the God of Abraham, Isaac, and Jacob" (7:30-32). The voice explains that the Lord also has seen "the wickedness (*kakōsin*) to my people" and emphasizes the relation of the action of God and the prophet when it says: "I have come down to rescue them. Come now, I will send you to Egypt" (7:34).[31]

In the midst of the Moses story, Moses tells the Israelites: "The Lord your God will raise up for you a prophet like me from among your own people; you shall heed such a prophet" (Deut 18:15). This statement by Moses provides the link in early Christian prophetic rhetorolect to the story of Jesus as "the prophet like Moses" who rose up from among God's own people. As mentioned above, early Christian discourse uses many verses from "the writings" to present a prophetic story-line that begins with Abraham and continues through Jesus and his followers to the present. The special link Paul found between Abraham and Jesus concerned God's statement that "the offspring" of Abraham would receive the promises to Abraham (Gal 3:16-18). Rather than focusing on promises, the relation of Moses to Jesus focuses on the prophets themselves.

While the Abraham story features God making a statement that provides a link to the identity of Jesus, namely, an assertion about Abraham's "offspring," early Christian prophetic rhetorolect observes that Moses himself, with God's instruction, referred to himself as a prophet and referred to another prophet "like him" who would come after him. Early Christian prophetic rhetorolect places words from Deut 18:15-18 on the lips of Peter in Acts 3 that introduce a story-line that moves from Moses through all the prophets to Jesus through a prophecy of Moses himself:

> Moses said, "The Lord your God will raise up for you from your own people a prophet like me. You must listen to whatever he tells you.
> 23 And it will be that everyone who does not listen to that prophet will be utterly rooted out of the people." 24 And all the prophets, as many as have spoken, from Samuel and those after him, also predicted these days. (Acts 3:22-24)

[31] Cf. Exod 3:9-10.

Later in Acts 7, Stephen repeats the story-line recounted by Peter:

> And Stephen replied, "... [37] This is the Moses who said to the Israelites, 'God will raise up a prophet for you from your own people as he raised me up.' [38] He is the one who was in the congregation in the wilderness with the angel who spoke to him at Mount Sinai, and with our ancestors; and he received living oracles to give to us." (Acts 7:2, 37-38)

In addition to emphasizing that Moses was a prophet whom God raised up from the Israelites themselves (7:37), this early Christian story emphasized that Moses received "living oracles" (*logia zōnta*) to give to people after the time of Jesus (7:38). These oracles, in their view, lead to the story of Jesus as God's Messiah.

Exact words from God's call of Moses function as another resource for early Christian prophetic rhetorolect. When Sadducees confront Jesus about resurrection from the dead, Jesus recites the words God used as a special identity when he called Moses:

> Jesus answered them, "... [31] And as for the resurrection of the dead, have you not read what was said to you by God, [32] 'I am the God of Abraham, the God of Isaac, and the God of Jacob'? He is God not of the dead, but of the living." (Matt 22:29, 31-32)

God's words of identification to Moses also are present in Peter's speech to the people in Jerusalem in Acts 3:

> When Peter saw it, he addressed the people, "... [13] The God of Abraham, the God of Isaac, and the God of Jacob, the God of our ancestors has glorified his servant Jesus, whom you handed over and rejected in the presence of Pilate, though he had decided to release him." (Acts 3:12-13)

The story of Moses flows directly down to and through the story of Jesus in early Christian prophetic rhetorolect. The God of Abraham, Isaac, and Jacob called Moses to a prophetic task that leads to Jesus, the prophet like him, who was rejected by the people but glorified by God.

Thus, early Christian prophetic rhetorolect weaves Moses's promise of a prophet like him into the story-line of Jesus son of Joseph on the lips of Jesus himself, Jesus' disciples, and Stephen. In addition, this rhetorolect presents Jesus using the statement of identification God made to Moses, "I am the God of your father, the God of Abraham, the God of Isaac, and the God of Jacob," as a way of identifying God as a God of resurrection. Early Christian prophetic rhetorolect uses particular items in the story of Abraham and the story of Moses as "prophetic links" in a story-line from Abraham to Moses and all the prophets of Israel down to Jesus himself.

The Gospel of John makes Moses' promise of a prophet like himself into an internal part of the story of Jesus. In John, after Jesus calls Philip to follow him (1:43), Philip finds Nathanael and says to him: "We have found him about whom Moses in the law and also the prophets wrote, Jesus son of Joseph from Nazareth" (John 1:45). In John, Moses' promise of a prophet like himself who would rise up is the beginning of a prophetic story-line that moves down to "Jesus son of Joseph from Nazareth." This is a fascinating addition to the story-lines in the genealogies of Jesus in Matt 1:2-16 and Luke 3:23-38, which follow Jesus' ancestry through Joseph. Abraham is a key personage in both genealogies (Matt 1:2; Luke 3:14), but Moses is not. Thus, Jesus is Abraham's "seed" through Joseph in the genealogies, but Jesus is a "prophet like Moses" on the basis of words of God to Moses that Moses told to the people. In contrast to the story-lines in the genealogies in Matthew and Luke, the Gospel of John emphasizes that "Jesus son of Joseph" is promised both in the writings of Moses and in the prophets after him.

Christian prophetic rhetorolect in John 5 features Jesus using Moses' promise of a prophet like him to challenge "the Judeans" who had started to persecute Jesus for healing on the Sabbath (John 5:16). Jesus asserts to them, "If you believed Moses, you would believe me. But if you do not believe what he wrote, how will you believe what I say?" (John 5:46-47). In John, Jesus uses the writings of Moses as prophetic rhetorolect that undergirds his own identify as the prophet like Moses who would arise after him.[32] Jesus confronts the Judeans with prophetic speech designed to authorize his own identity as "the prophet" after Moses.

The Moses story is very important for the prophetic rhetorolect in Acts, the Gospel of Matthew, and the Gospel of John in particular. Building upon an understanding that God's call of Moses is "the fulfillment of the promise that God had made to Abraham" (Acts 7:17), some early Christian prophetic rhetorolect focuses on the prophet Moses himself. In other words, some early Christian prophetic rhetorolect not only appeals to the prophetic nature of the law of Moses, but it also appeals to "the prophet like Moses" about whom Moses spoke and understands this prophecy to refer to Jesus.

Samuel as a Prophetic Beginning of Kingship in Israel: 1 Samuel 3–16

The early Christian prophetic story-line continues beyond Abraham and Moses to Samuel, the prophetic priest who anointed David King of Israel. The story of Abraham, the story of Moses, and the story of

[32] See Wayne A. Meeks, *The Prophet-King: Moses Traditions and the Johannine Christology* (NovTSup 14; Leiden: E.J. Brill, 1967).

Samuel each has its own way of blending prophetic discourse with priestly discourse. This will be an important discussion in the chapter on priestly discourse in the next volume. For this chapter, it is important to see how Samuel is the next key personage in the early Christian prophetic story-line from Abraham and Moses to Jesus.

Acts 3 places Samuel at the beginning of the prophetic story-line that leads from Abraham to the story of Jesus when it features Peter saying:

> [24]And all the prophets, as many as have spoken, from Samuel and those after him, also predicted these days. [25] You are the descendants of the prophets and of the covenant that God gave to your ancestors, saying to Abraham, "And in your descendants all the families of the earth shall be blessed." [26] When God raised up his servant, he sent him first to you, to bless you by turning each of you from your wicked ways.' (Acts 3:24-26)

In this account, Samuel is featured as the beginning of a story-line of "all the prophets who predicted 'the days' after the death and resurrection of Jesus." The story-line from Samuel through Jesus to the present informs the hearers that they are descendants of prophets and of the covenant God gave to the patriarchs through Abraham. In addition, Peter adds a prophetic interpretation of the story-line when he describes God's "sending" of Jesus to them for the purpose of "blessing" them by "turning" each of them from their wicked ways. This interpretation presents Jesus in the mode of a prophet sent by God for the purpose of confronting people for the purpose of turning them from their wicked ways so they can receive the blessings awaiting them in God's kingdom.

When Acts 13 presents Paul telling the story of Israel to Israelites and God-fearers in the synagogue at Antioch in Pisidia, it features Paul including Samuel at a key turning point in the story. As Paul tells the account of God's choosing of Israel, making them great in Egypt, leading them out into the wilderness for forty years, and then destroying seven nations in the land of Canaan so they received an inheritance for about four hundred fifty years, he tells about God's transfer of their leadership from judges to prophets at the time of Samuel (Acts 13:17-20). The shift to Samuel introduces the topic of Israel's asking God for a king, and this topic introduces a story-line that leads from Saul (13:21) to David, son of Jesse (13:22) to "a Savior, Jesus" who came after John "proclaimed a baptism of repentance to all the people of Israel" (13:23-24). This prophetic story-line leads to the Baptist's prophetic function of announcing the one who was coming after him (13:25). In early Christian discourse, Samuel is the beginning of the line of prophets that brings God's promises to Israel and God's leading of Israel through King David to Jesus, whose coming was predicted by John who baptized. After focusing on "the prophet Samuel" (13:20), "David, son of Jesse" (13:22), "a Savior, Jesus" (13:23), and John (13:24-25), Paul refers to the hearers as "descendants of Abraham's family and others who fear God" (13:26). This early Christian prophetic story-line features the prophet Samuel as the link between the time of Abraham and Moses and the time of the kingship that led to Jesus the Savior of Israel.

One of the key functions of Samuel internally in the prophetic tradition is a prophetic critique of sacrifice. This occurs in the words of Samuel to King Saul in 1 Sam 15:

> Has the LORD as great delight in burnt offerings and sacrifices, as in obeying the voice of the LORD? Surely, to obey is better than sacrifice, and to heed than the fat of rams. [23] For rebellion is no less a sin than divination, and stubbornness is like iniquity and idolatry. Because you have rejected the word of the LORD, he has also rejected you from being king. (1 Sam 15:22-23)

This prophetic language is reconfigured in Amos 5 into:

> I hate, I despise your festivals, and I take no delight in your solemn assemblies.
> [22] Even though you offer me your burnt offerings and grain offerings, I will not accept them;
> and the offerings of well-being of your fatted animals I will not look upon.
> [23] Take away from me the noise of your songs; I will not listen to the melody of your harps.
> [24] But let justice roll down like waters, and righteousness like an ever-flowing stream. (Amos 5:21-24)

Hosea 6 contains a closely related prophetic critique of sacrifice:

> For I desire mercy (*eleos*) and not sacrifice, the knowledge (*epignōsin*) of God rather than burnt offerings. (Hos 6:6)

In turn, Isaiah 1 presents these words:

> Hear the word of the LORD, you rulers of Sodom!
> Listen to the teaching of our God, you people of Gomorrah!
> [11] What to me is the multitude of your sacrifices? says the LORD;
> I have had enough of burnt offerings of rams and the fat of fed beasts;
> I do not delight in the blood of bulls, or of lambs, or of goats ... [17] learn to do good; seek justice, rescue the oppressed, defend the orphan, plead for the widow. (Isa 1:10-11, 17)

Micah 6 features the following:

> "With what shall I come before the LORD, and bow myself before God on high?

> Shall I come before him with burnt offerings, with calves a year old?
> 7 Will the LORD be pleased with thousands of rams, with ten thousands of rivers of oil?
> Shall I give my firstborn for my transgression, the fruit of my body for the sin of my soul?"
> 8 He has told you, O mortal, what is good; and what does the LORD require of you but to do justice, and to love kindness, and to walk humbly with your God? (Mic 6:6-8)[33]

From Samuel through Amos, Hosea, Isaiah, and Micah, God spoke out for mercy and justice in the context of sacrifice. In the eyes of God, sacrifice without mercy and justice is unacceptable.

Early Christian discourse transmits the tradition of a critique of sacrifice as a blend of wisdom and prophetic rhetorolect. On the one hand, in Mark 12:33 a scribe produces a critique of sacrifice as part of Torah wisdom. The scribe, coming to Jesus while Jesus is teaching in the Jerusalem temple, asks Jesus which commandment is first of all (12:28). When Jesus responds with the early Christian blend of the Shema and Lev 19:18 discussed in Chapter 5, the scribe commends Jesus for his correct understanding (12:32). As the scribe summarizes what Jesus has said about loving God and loving one's neighbor, he adds that loving one's neighbor as oneself "is much more than all whole burnt offerings and sacrifices" (12:33). The phrase "whole burnt offerings and sacrifices" occurs more than one hundred times in the LXX.[34] Thus it exists as "cultural intertexture" related to many verses in biblical tradition rather than particular "oral-scribal intertexture" related to a specific passage.[35] In 1 Sam 15:22, Samuel emphasized to King Saul the importance of "obedience (*to akousai*) to the voice of the Lord" in the context of burnt offerings and sacrifices. Indeed, obedience (*akoē*) to God "is better than sacrifice, and to hearken than the fat of rams." In Hos 6:6, the prophetic oracle explains that God desires "knowledge (*epignōsin*) of God rather than burnt offerings." In early Christian discourse, the scribe is presenting Torah wisdom close in content to Prov 21:2-3:

> 2 All deeds are right in the sight of the doer,
> but the LORD weighs the heart (*kardias*).
> 3 To do righteousness and justice
> is more acceptable to the LORD than blood sacrifices.

[33] Cf. Prov 21:3; Jer 6:20; Pss 40:6; 51:16.

[34] Craig A. Evans, *Mark 8:27–16:20* (WBC 34B; Nashville: Thomas Nelson, 2001) 264.

[35] Vernon K. Robbins, *The Tapestry of Early Christian Discourse: Rhetoric, Society and Ideology* (London: Routledge, 1996) 108-14, 129-42; idem, *Exploring the Texture of Texts: A Guide to Socio-Rhetorical Interpretation* (Valley Forge, PA: Trinity Press International, 1996) 58-62.

Loving God with one's whole heart and loving one's neighbor, in early Christian wisdom rhetorolect, "is much more than all whole burnt offerings and sacrifices" (Mark 12:33).

Matthew 9:13 continues the emphasis that prophetic critique of sacrifice is a matter of knowing the wisdom of God. When Pharisees question Jesus' disciples why their teacher eats with tax collectors and sinners, Jesus overhears and answers that they should "Go and learn (*mathete*) what this means, 'I desire mercy, not sacrifice'" (Matt 9:13). Jesus' response selects wording from Hos 6:6 in a manner that implies that this is Torah wisdom that the Pharisees should learn from reading scripture. Indeed, the emphasis in the context is on Jesus as a teacher. In the mode of early Christian wisdom rhetorolect, Jesus responds to the Pharisees in terms of knowledge they need to learn.

Matthew 12:7 features a response by Jesus to Pharisees with a critique of sacrifice that blends prophetic, wisdom, and priestly rhetorolect. In a context where Jesus' disciples pluck grain on the Sabbath and eat it, because they are hungry, the Pharisees confront Jesus with the unlawfulness of what his disciples are doing (Matt 12:1-2). The action of the Pharisees is prophetic, confronting Jesus with Torah in a context of wrong action. Jesus confronts them in turn in a prophetic manner, telling them a story with priestly content about the bread of Presence in the house of God (12:3-4) and then emphasizing that Torah allows priests to do all kinds of things on the Sabbath without being guilty of violating the laws of God (12:5). Then Jesus responds with a blend of wisdom and prophetic rhetorolect: "I tell you, something greater than the temple is here. But if you had known what this means, 'I desire mercy and not sacrifice,' you would not have condemned the guiltless, for the Son of Man is lord of the Sabbath" (12:6-8). Again, Jesus emphasizes that God's prophetic critique of sacrifice is something the Pharisees should know. But the confrontation moves beyond teaching into prophetic confrontation as Jesus' tell them that "if they had known" this aspect of God's wisdom they "would not have condemned the guiltless." Jesus' language indicts the Pharisees as having done something wrong with their speech. In this context, then, Torah wisdom about God's critique of sacrifice becomes early Christian prophetic rhetorolect on the lips of Jesus.

After Samuel, a significantly long list of biblical prophets function as a resource for early Christian prophetic rhetorolect. Nathan, Elijah, Elisha, Amos, Hosea, Isaiah, Jeremiah, Ezekiel, and Malachi are some but not all of the names. Attempting to summarize the use of all of prophet literature in the NT would lead to a book itself, rather than two chapters on prophetic rhetorolect in earliest Christianity. This chapter will now turn from the prophets of Israel to prophets and prophetic speech in Greek and Roman literature. Once this discussion has brought this chapter to an end, the next chapter will feature an analysis and interpretation of selected portions of prophetic rhetorolect in the writings in the New Testament.

Prophetic Discourse in Greek and Roman Literature as an Environment for Christian Prophetic Rhetorolect in the Mediterranean World

Prophetic discourse was widespread and well-known throughout the Mediterranean world, as David E. Aune's masterful study, *Prophecy in Early Christianity and the Ancient Mediterranean World*, has shown.[36] Prophetic speech was associated with oracles given by a "*mantis*, which is usually translated 'diviner,' 'soothsayer,' 'seer,' or, less appropriately, 'prophet,'" at "sacred places which had venerable histories supported by a variety of foundation myths."[37] These sacred places flourished during the time of the Greek city-states, when delegations with political issues consulted the gods. They became less central to Greek history during the mid-fourth to mid-first centuries BCE when the political power of the Greek city-states had a more complex relation to broader regions of power and influence. During this later time, individuals with more private problems, rather than representatives of groups with political issues, consulted the gods.[38]

People in the ancient Mediterranean world knew about oracles from many sources. "Thousands of oracles and oracle fragments" are available to us through publications documenting inscriptions and writings from ancient sanctuaries, and oracles gleaned from a wide variety of literary sources.[39] The writings of Plato and Aristotle alongside the writings of Aristophanes are important early sources. The histories, from Herodotus through Thucydides, Xenophon, Polybius, and Livy have even more abundant information. Plutarch's three essays on oracles exhibit an informative philosophical view of prophetic discourse at the beginning of the second century CE.[40] Aune's collection and analysis of oracle questions and responses, types of one-part and two-part response oracles, special types of oracles distinguished by their content,

[36] David E. Aune, *Prophecy in Early Christianity and the Ancient Mediterranean World* (Grand Rapids: Eerdmans, 1983) 23-79.

[37] Ibid., 23-24.

[38] Ibid., 24.

[39] See, e.g., ibid., 361, n. 1.

[40] *Plutarch's Moralia* V (ed. F.C. Babbit; LCL; Cambridge, MA: Harvard University Press, 1984) 194-501. These three essays discuss oracles from a second century CE philosophical perspective: "The E at Delphi" (*De E apud Delphos*), "The Oracles at Delphi no Longer Given in Verse" (*De Pythiae oraculis*), and "The Obsolescence of Oracles" (*De defectu oraculorum*).

and types of unsolicited oracles is a rich treasure chest of information for anyone interested in the broader environment of prophetic discourse in which early Christian prophetic rhetorolect functioned and flourished.[41] Prophetic discourse was present in Mediterranean antiquity as poetry, question and response interchange, riddle, sapiential sentence, beatitude, and letter. When early Christians moved out into the Mediterranean world with prophetic rhetorolect nurtured especially in relation to biblical prophecy, they entered environments where prophetic discourse was alive with many forms and functions.

For our study, an important aspect of ancient Greek and Roman oracles is their relation to stories and story-lines in Mediterranean antiquity. By the first century CE, a large number of oracles were known to people either as a statement that gave rise to a philosophical discussion or as part of a story or story-line. When a prophetic oracle evoked a philosophical discussion, the discussion could be about the nature of oracles themselves: whether the voice of a god actually produced the oracle, whether a god wrote the oracle, whether the god supplied "the origin of incitement" and the prophetic priestess then produced the oracle from her natural faculties, etc.[42] When a prophetic oracle was part of a story or story-line, it functioned somewhere on a spectrum from a dispensation of wisdom or directions for action to a statement that implied or confirmed a person's status or authority, an impending victory, an impending defeat, a need to be careful, a cause for rejoicing, or an expectation of doom. Many times the implication of the oracle was perceived to be clear only after a particular event or series of events occurred. In other words, the story about a person, group, city, or "nation" in which the oracle played a role is as important as the oracle itself.

As aspect of prophetic oracle that Aune's work did not explore is the degree to which prophetic oracles are presupposed to be "confrontational." One of the reasons is that so much of Greco-Roman prophetic speech emerges from contexts of "consultation" rather than confrontation. Through the cultural influence of philosophy, there is a strong emphasis in the Greco-Roman world on a person's receiving of a prophetic oracle in a context where the person was "seeking" knowledge. In early Christian discourse, when people sought knowledge, they received wisdom statements. They received "prophetic" statements, in contrast, when they were "confronted" either by God or a God-informed and God-inspired communicator of the message. In other words, early Christian prophetic rhetorolect is virtually all "unsolicited," to use a term Aune introduced to describe legitimation oracles (recognition, commendation, and self-commendation), the oracular

[41] Ibid., 52–77.
[42] See e.g., Plutarch, Oracles at Delphi 397B–D.

letter, and oracles of doom (unconditional oracles and oracles of ultimate deliverance).[43] Rather than seeking prophetic oracles, early Christians either perceived themselves to be confronted by them, either through God or through Jesus, or they confronted other people with them. In early Christian prophetic rhetorolect, therefore, prophetic oracles are most often uninvited, and they are regularly startling to the hearer, whether the prophetic speech is positive or negative.

The rhetorical nature of a large amount of early Christian prophetic rhetorolect is like the prophetic discourse in historical and biographical writings in Mediterranean antiquity. Herodotus's *History*,[44] for example, has many sections with prophetic dynamics close to early Christian prophetic rhetorolect. There is room here for analysis of only one short section from Herodotus, and even this section is quite long for our purposes here. Herodotus 5.92 contains a long speech attributed to Socles, a Corinthian, to Lacedaemonians, in other words the people of the city-state of Sparta. This speech contains a blend of prophetic and wisdom rhetoric that contains fascinating similarities with portions of early Christian prophetic rhetorolect.[45] Socles, speaking for the city-state of Athens, presents his speech as a response to Hippias who spoke officially for the Spartans in 5.91. Herodotus 5.92 continues in response:[46]

> Thus spoke the Lacedaemonians, but their words were ill received by the greater part of their allies. The rest then keeping silence, Socles, a Corinthian said:
>
> *Result:* "Verily the heaven shall be beneath the earth and the earth aloft above the heaven, and men shall dwell in the sea and fishes where men did dwell before,
>
> *Case:* now that you, Lacedaemonians! are destroying the rule of equals (*isokratias*) and making ready to bring back despotism (*tyrranidas*) into the cities –
>
> *Rule:* despotism, a thing as unrighteous (*adikōteron*) and bloodthirsty as anything on earth." (5.92, p. 103)

Socles begins by confronting the Spartans with the topos of justice (*dikē*) in the city-state. The topoi are despotism (*tyrranidas*) versus "the rule of equals" (*isokratias*), which are central topoi for Greco-Roman prophetic discourse. Confronting the Spartans with direct address, Socles asserts that the establishment of despotism in the city-states would overturn the order of the created world, making the heaven below the earth, the earth above the heaven, the sea the place where humans dwell, and

[43] Aune, *Prophecy*, 66–77.

[44] Herodotus completed his *History* and died sometime between 430 and 420 BCE.. His writing was well-known during the first centuries CE.

[45] For Aune's references to and discussion of Herodotus 5.92, see *Prophecy*, 64, 78, 364, 368.

[46] Herodotus 5.92 (LCL; trans. A.D. Godley; Cambridge, MA/London: Harvard University Press, 1922) 103–15, with some revisions by the author).

the earth the place where fishes dwell. Socles's speech opens with a sequence of prophetic reasoning in the form of an enthymematic syllogism containing Result, Case, and Rule. The reasoning works through a blending of the social realm with the realm of the created world, with the result that it is a blend of prophetic and wisdom discourse. The social realm of the world is meant to have a harmonious relation to the order in the created world (wisdom discourse). The order in the social realm is understood to be justice (*dikē*) based on the rule of equals (*isokratias*). When leaders establish despotism (*tyrranidas*), they bring disorder in the form of injustice (*adikōteron*) into the world (prophetic discourse). Disorder in the social realm throws the created world into upheaval, making the heavens dwell below the earth, the earth dwell above the heavens, humans dwell in the sea, and fish dwell on earth.

Socles continues with blended prophetic and wisdom reasoning, presenting yet another enthymeme based on something the Spartans could do in the future. Socles proposes that the Spartans set up a despot in their own city-state before forcing despotism on their allies:

> *Result:* For if indeed this seems to you to be a good thing (*chrēston*), that the cities be ruled by despots (*tyranneuesthai*),
> *Rule:* you yourselves should first set up a despot (*tyrannon*) among yourselves and then seek to set up such for the rest.
> *Case:* but now, having never made trial of despots (*tyrannōn*), and taking most careful heed that none shall arise at Sparta, you deal wrongfully (*parachrōsthe*) with your allies. (5.92, pp. 103-105)

Socles confronts the Spartans prophetically about dealing improperly with their friends. They have never tried despotism themselves; therefore they do not know what damage it does. If they think it is such a good thing, they should try it first at Sparta, and if it works well there they will have a basis for recommending it to their allies.

After his opening arguments, Socles introduces conditional reasoning that leads to a story about a daughter named Labda who becomes the mother of a son, and this son begins a story-line that has serious consequences for Corinth. When an interpreter is thinking about early Christian prophetic rhetorolect, similarities with Stephen's speech in Acts 7 hover naturally in the background. Socles's speech moves into a long story-line much like Stephen's argumentation before the temple leaders in Jerusalem. While Stephen's speech tells a story about Abraham, Joseph, Egypt, a daughter of Pharaoh, Moses, David, and Solomon, Socles's speech tells a story of the Corinthian State, the Bacchiadae, Amphion, the lame daughter of Amphion named Labda, Eetion, Cypselus, Thrasybulus, and Periander. The story-line begins with the rule of the Bacchiadae and moves to the oracle of the priestess at Delphi to Eetion, husband of Labda, the lame daughter of Amphion:

Rule: But had you such experience of that thing as we have, you would be sager advisers concerning it than you are now.

Case: For the Corinthian State was ordered in such manner as I will show. The Few ruled; these few, called Bacchiadae, held sway in the city, marrying and giving in marriage among themselves. Now Amphion, one of these men, had a lame daughter, whose name was Labda. Seeing that none of the Bacchiadae would marry her, she was married to Eetion son of Echecrates, of the township of Petra, a Lapith by lineage, of the posterity of Caeneus. No sons being born to Eetion by this wife or any other, he set out to Delphi to enquire concerning issue; and straightway as he entered the Pythian priestess spoke these verses to him:

> Eetion, yet high honor is thine, though honor'd thou art not.
> Labda conceiveth anon; and a rolling rock she shall bear thee,
> Fated on princes to fall, and execute justice (*dikaiōsei*) on Corinth.
> (5.92, p. 105)

Socles introduces the conditional reasoning that if the Spartans had the experiences of despotism with which the Corinthians have had to deal, they would not recommend despotism to their allies. He then supports the Rule (thesis) he introduces with a story-line beginning with the rule of the Bacchiadae to the promise of a son to Eetion, husband of Amphion's lame daughter Labda. As the story unfolds, it has rhetorical similarities to the opening chapters of the Gospel of Matthew. The oracle of the priestess at Delphi prophesies that though Eetion is not an honored man, yet he is highly honored among divine powers, since his wife Labda will conceive and bear a son who will execute justice on Corinth.

After reciting the oracle of the Delphic priestess, Socles continues by correlating the Delphic oracle to Eetion with an oracle that had been given earlier to the Bacchiadae:

> This oracle given to Eetion was in some way made known (*exangelletai*) to the Bacchiadae, by whom the former oracle sent to Corinth was not understood, although its meaning was the same as the meaning of the oracle to Eetion; it was this:
>
> Lo, where the eagle's mate conceives in the rocks, and a lion
> Mighty and fierce shall be born; full many a knee shall he loosen.
> Wherefore I bid you beware, ye Corinthian folk, that inhabit
> Nigh Pirene fair and the heights o'erhanging of Corinth.
>
> This oracle, formerly given to the Bacchiadae, was past their interpretation; but now, when they learned of that one what was given to Eetion, straightway they understood that the former accorded with the oracle of Eetion; and understanding this prophecy too they sat still, purposing to destroy whatever should be born to Eetion. (5.92, pp. 105–107)

Socles asserts that when the Delphic oracle to Eetion became known to the Bacchiadae who were ruling at Corinth, they were able for the first time to understand the meaning of an oracle that have been given earlier to them. Both oracles, it was now clear to them, predicted the end of their rule through a child to be born to Labda, the lame daughter of Amphion. In other words, the eagle is Eetion, his mate is Labda, and the fierce and mighty lion will be the son of Labda. They know at this time, then, that they must destroy whatever child is born to Labda.

The story Socles tells next shows how the attempt of the Bacchiadae to kill the newborn son of Labda was thwarted. In other words, similarities with the opening chapters of the Gospel of Matthew continue (Matt 2). The ten men whom the Bacchiadae sent to Petra to kill the child agreed to a plan that whoever first had the child in their hands would kill it by throwing it to the ground. When Labda brought the child to them, "by heaven's providence it smiled (*theiēi tychēi prosegelase*) at the man who took it" (5.92, p. 107), and the compassion that filled the man prevented him from killing it. When the first man handed the child to the second man, he could not kill it either. One by one, all ten men are unable to kill the child. After the tenth man gave the child back to the mother and they have left the house, immediately after the door is shut they begin criticizing one another for not being able to do what they had agreed to do. After discussing the matter for some time, they decide that they must go back into the house and do what they had told the Bacchiadae they would do. But, Socles says, "it was necessary (*edei*) that Eetion's offspring should be the source of ills for Corinth" (5.92, pp. 108-10). Therefore, Labda's son must somehow escape being killed. Since Labda could hear the men's conversation by standing close to the door after she shut it, she feared on the basis of what she heard that they would return and kill her child. Therefore, she hid the child in a chest (*kypselē*). When the men returned, they looked everywhere but were unable to find the child. Finally, they decided to return to the Bacchiadae and simply say that they had done what they agreed to do. After this incident, Eetion's son was named Cypselus (*Kypselos*) after the chest in which his mother had hidden him.[47]

After recounting the failure of the Bacchiadae to kill Cypselus while he was a newborn child, Socles moves immediately to Cypselus as an adult:

> When Cypselus had become a man, and was seeking a divination, there was given him at Delphi an oracle (*chrēstērion*) of double meaning (*amphidexion*), and when he trusted in it, he grasped at Corinth and won it. This was the oracle (*chrēsmos*):

[47] Recall the discussion of the importance of names and naming in prophetic discourse in the Hebrew Bible and the New Testament.

> Happy (*olbios*) is the man who comes down to my temple,
> Cypselus Eetides, great king of Corinth renowned,
> Happy himself and his sons; yet his son's sons shall not be happy.
>
> Such was the oracle (*chrēstērion*)... (5.92, p. 109)

Cypselus, son of Eetion, became despot over Corinth and treated the people of Corinth extremely badly. He banished many of them, and robbed many others, creating a bad life for most of the people. He reigned thirty years, died a natural death, and his son Periander succeeded him with despotic power. Soon Periander began to communicate with Thrasybulus, despot of Miletus, who was even more bloodthirsty than Cypselus had been. Periander accepted Thrasybulus not only as his model but also as his counselor, slaying many of the prominent people of Corinth, banishing others, and stripping all the women of Corinth naked in the temple of Here in response to an oracle of the dead his wife Melissa had been given in Thesprotia on the river Acheron. Socles ends his speech with:

> *Rule:* Know then, ye Lacedaemonians, that such a thing is despotism (*tyrannis*), and such are its deeds (*ergōn*).
> *Case:* We of Corinth did greatly marvel when we saw that you were sending for Hippias; and now we marvel yet more at your speaking thus; and we entreat (*epimartyrometha*) you earnestly in the name of the gods (*theous*) of Hellas not to establish despotism (*tyrannidas*) in the cities. But if you will not cease from doing this, and will unrighteously attempt to bring Hippias back,
> *Result:* then be it known to you that the Corinthians for their part do not consent to it. (5.92, pp. 113-15)

Socles ends with enthymematic prophetic reasoning that focuses on despotism, the gods of Hellas, righteous and unrighteous action, and an unwillingness on their part to participate in an action that would create hardship, humiliation, injustice, and death. His prophetic story-line moves to a conclusion that confronts the Spartans with the violation of justice their intended action would perform. In the name of the gods of Hellas, he appeals to them to change their minds and asserts that the Corinthians will not agree to what they intend to do.[48]

Conclusion

Prophetic speech both in the Hebrew Bible and in Greco-Roman literature is a dynamic force for the creation of stories and story-lines.

[48] Hippias, representing Sparta, responds back to Socles in Herodotus 5.93, arguing that he has more exact knowledge of the oracles than any man. Nevertheless, the opinion of the Corinthians prevails, with an entreaty to the Spartans to do no hurt to a Greek city. As a result of the majority consensus against the wishes of the Spartans, Hippias stops trying to persuade them and departs.

Biblical prophecy is regularly unsolicited. God confronts individuals and groups either directly or through intermediaries, without any request for information from the people whom the speakers confront. Greco-Roman prophecy, in contrast to biblical prophecy, regularly is solicited by people from a god at an oracle sanctuary.

Both biblical and Greco-Roman prophetic discourse have a close relation to wisdom discourse, containing prophetic oracles in the form of wisdom or directions for action as well as severe judgment of previous or present actions. In addition, prophetic speech in both biblical and Greco-Roman literature becomes confrontational speech from a god that functions in highly complex ways in stories and story-lines. Sometimes prophetic speech brings blessings. These blessings regularly are unexpected or even unwanted, since not only great expectations but also hardship and sometimes even death are required as a result of the blessings. Prophetic speech brings severe criticism and even curses at least as often as it brings blessings, with the result that much prophetic discourse features negative judgments about previous actions or ongoing actions in the present.

Most of the functions of prophetic discourse in the Hebrew Bible and in Greco-Roman literature are present in early Christian prophetic rhetorolect. These functions occur in the biographical-historical narration in the Gospels and Acts, in prophetic story-lines in the Epistles, and even in prophetic moments in the Revelation to John. The next chapter will analyze some of the functions of prophetic discourse in the Gospels and Acts, and in some letters attributed to Paul. There will be no analysis and interpretation of early Christian prophetic rhetorolect in the Revelation to John in the next chapter, since all of the early Christian prophetic rhetorolect in Revelation is hosted by apocalyptic rhetorolect. Since the cultural frame of apocalyptic discourse stands in the foreground in Revelation, we will not analyze prophetic rhetorolect in Revelation until Chapters 8 and 9, which discuss early Christian apocalyptic rhetorolect. This will give us an opportunity to analyze early Christian prophetic rhetorolect in various contexts where it is dominated by early Christian apocalyptic rhetorolect.

7

Christian Prophetic Rhetorolect Part II: Story-Lines in the New Testament

Prophetic Rhetorolect as Internal Emergent Structure for Early Christian Story-Lines

A primary effect of prophetic rhetorolect in early Christian discourse was the creation of argumentative story-lines from the past to the present. The basic structure of the enthymematic argumentation was:

> *Thesis:* You are blessed but suffering,
> *Rationale:* because you are participating in a story-line that began with the prophets and continues into your present action.

This prophetic rhetorolect came into Christian discourse by the 50s, creating a story-line from the prophets of Israel through Jesus to the followers of Jesus. Throughout the last half of the first century, Christian prophetic rhetorolect functioned as an emergent structure for detailed story-lines featuring specific personages. John the Baptist, Jesus, Stephen, Peter, Paul, and Paul's associates are the primary personages during the first century.

1 Thessalonians: Prophetic Story-Line of Persecution Blends with Priestly, Wisdom, and Apocalyptic Rhetorolect

In 1 Thess, which most interpreters consider the earliest writing in the NT and date 49-50 CE, Pauline discourse introduces early Christian prophetic rhetorolect that evokes a story-line from the prophets of Israel through Jesus, the earliest followers of Jesus in Judea, Paul and his associates, and members of the Christian community in Thessalonica. Paul's statements in 1 Thess 1–2 evoke the following sequence of events from the time of the prophets of Israel to the time of the writing of the letter:

1. The Judeans killed the prophets (2:14-15)
2. The Judeans killed the Lord Jesus (2:14-15)
3. The churches of God in Christ Jesus in Judea suffered under Judeans (2:14)
4. Paul and his associates were approved by God to be entrusted with the message of the gospel of God (2:4) and appointed

(*keimetha*) for persecutions (3:3-4, 7)
5. Judean Christians persecuted (*ekdiōxantōn*) Paul and his associates by hindering them from speaking to Gentiles so they may be saved (2:15-16)
6. Paul and his associates suffered (*propathontes*) and were shamefully mistreated (*hybristhentes*) in Philippi (2:2)
7. Paul and his associates faced much conflict (*pollōi agōni*) in Thessalonica as they transmitted God's word to them (2:2, 13)
8. The Thessalonians were chosen (*eklogēn*) and called (*kalountos*) by God (1:4; 2:12)
9. The Thessalonians have suffered (*epathete*) under much tribulation (*thlipsei pollōi*) from other Thessalonians (1:6; 2:14)

In this context, Paul asserts a prophetic indictment against those who are causing suffering by persecution: "But wrath has come upon them until the end" (1 Thess 2:16).[1] 1 Thess 1–3 presents this prophetic story-line in the context of a blend of priestly, wisdom, prophetic, and apocalyptic rhetorolect. Priestly rhetorolect in 1 Thess features blessing,[2] thanksgiving and prayer to God,[3] and pure, upright, and blameless activity.[4] Wisdom rhetorolect is present throughout the three chapters as Paul refers to what is known[5] and remembered,[6] commends the Thessalonians for becoming examples by imitating people who are models of right behavior,[7] and relates to them as family.[8] Apocalyptic rhetorolect is vividly present in 1:10; 2:19; 3:13 as Paul refers to the resurrection of the Lord Jesus Christ and his return from heaven,[9] and then it becomes dominant in 1 Thess 4–5. As this early Christian blend of rhetorolects unfolds, a prophetic story-line interprets the activities of Paul, Paul's associates, and the Thessalonians as being guided by God. This kind of guidance began with the prophets of Israel, continued through the death of the Lord Jesus, and continues through the followers of Jesus to the time of the writing of the letter.

The discourse in 1 Thess 1–3 evokes a particular prophetic story-line through its rhetography, namely its evocation of pictures of persecution in various situations. Intertwining with this rhetography is a prophetic rhetology that explains why Paul, his associates, and the

[1] For translation and discussion of this verse in its context, see Abraham J. Malherbe, *The Letters to the Thessalonians* (AB 32B; New York: Doubleday, 2000) 164-79.
[2] 1 Thess 1:1; 3:11-13.
[3] 1 Thess 1:2-3; 2:13; 3:9-10; cf. 1 Thess 5:16-18.
[4] 1 Thess 2:10; 3:13; cf. 1 Thess 5:23.
[5] 1 Thess 1:4, 5, 8; 2:1, 2, 5; 3:3, 4.
[6] 1 Thess 1:3; 2:9; 3:6.
[7] 1 Thess 1:7; 2:14.
[8] 1 Thess 2:7-8, 9, 11, 14, 17; 3:2, 7.
[9] Cf. 1Thess 5:23.

Thessalonians all experience suffering and persecution. The reasoning in the rhetology is easily displayed as an enthymeme:

> *Thesis:* We and you are being persecuted,
> *Rationale:* because we and you were destined and chosen to continue the story-line of persecution that began with the prophets.

This is "prophetic" reasoning, where the "lot" of those who are called by God to be persecuted is explained by a story-line that begins with the prophets and continues through the story of Jesus and his followers. In Paul's terms, the life of the Thessalonians is a "prophetic" life. God has chosen and appointed them to live a "prophetic" life, which means a life that will include suffering and persecution for the things they believe, say, and do.

Q Sayings

It is informative that various sayings in the Q strata of Gospel tradition exhibit a similar prophetic story-line. Perhaps the clearest place where this story-line is evoked is in the beatitudes shared by Matthew and Luke:

Matt 5:11-12	Luke 6:22-23
[11] Blessed are you when people revile you and persecute you and utter all kinds of evil against you falsely on my account. [12]Rejoice and be glad, for your reward is great in heaven, for in the same way they persecuted the prophets who were before you.	[22] Blessed are you when people hate you, and when they exclude you, revile you, and defame you on account of the Son of Man. [23]Rejoice on that day and leap for joy, for surely your reward is great in heaven; for that is what their ancestors did to the prophets.

The rationale evokes a story-line of persecution from the prophets to the followers of Jesus: You are being reviled and abused, because your mode of life is a continuation of the story of persecution from the prophets of Israel through the Son of Man to your present mode of life.[10]

Galatians: Paul's Isaiah-Jeremiah Story-Line and the Believer's Abrahamic Story-Line

Paul's letter to the Galatians evokes two interrelated prophetic story-lines. First is Paul's own prophetic story-line, which emphasizes divine appointment of him to confront the Galatians with a message God has transmitted recently to humans. Second is a story-line from Abraham through Jesus to Paul and other believers that explains how God offers salvation to humans after the crucifixion and resurrection of Jesus Christ. Paul's own story-line does not emphasize persecution, though Paul does refer to himself as "still being persecuted (*diōkomai*)" in Gal

[10] See Aune's more lengthy discussion of the Q material in *Prophecy*, 157-58.

5:11. Rather, Paul introduces his own prophetic story-line to establish an authoritative framework for confronting wrong beliefs and actions he believes to be widespread among the Galatian Christians.

Paul begins his letter with strong early Christian prophetic rhetoro–lect: "Paul an apostle – sent neither by human commission nor from human authorities, but through Jesus Christ and God the Father, who raised him from the dead" (Gal 1:1). This opening verse evokes an image of Paul being confronted, called, and sent sometime in the past by Jesus Christ and God the Father. The rhetography of this verse evokes three implicit events in the story-line: (1) the death of Jesus Christ: (2) God's raising of Jesus Christ from death; and (3) appointment of Paul as an apostle "through" both Jesus Christ and God the Father. But the rhetography does not stand alone. The verse also contains rhetology, an argument from contraries. Paul was not sent either "from" a human or "through" a human. There could be other alternatives: (a) through an angel (see Gal 1:8); (b) through a high priest; (c) from a king, etc. Perhaps Paul's full meaning appears to be: "neither from a human nor through a human, but through our Lord (Jesus Christ)[11] and the one God (the Father)." The combined rhetography and rhetology introduces an argumentative "dialect," rhetorical speech that focuses on two particular "personages," a Lord named Jesus who has a surname "Christ" and "God the Father" who raised Jesus Christ from the dead.

After the long opening in Gal 1:1-5, the letter begins with strong confrontational, prophetic rhetorolect. Authorized as a spokesperson for Jesus Christ and God the Father, Paul confronts the Galatian Christians directly ("I" and "you") on the basis of the "prophetic" summons of them by "the one who called them in grace [or "the grace of Christ"] (1:6) through "the gospel of Christ" (1:7). Again the argument has the nature of a rhetorical dialect, rather than standard rhetorical argumentation when it contains the unusual words "in grace," "in the grace of Christ,"[12] and "the gospel of Christ." This is certainly not widespread Greco-Roman argumentation, and it is not conventional Jewish argumentation. Rather, it is a particular rhetorical dialect in the Mediterranean world that claims prophetic validity related to the authority of prophets in biblical tradition but focused on a special relation between Jesus Christ and God the Father.

Paul continues with argumentation that evokes a somewhat sharper pictorial image of the event through which Paul received the authoritative message he is handing on to the Galatian Christians. The gospel that Paul proclaimed was not "according to a human" ("of human origin": 1:11), because he did not receive it from a human, nor was he

[11] Cf. Gal 1:3, 19; 5:10; 6:14, 18.

[12] See the textual variants.

taught it, but he received it through an "apocalypsis" (a "revelation") of Jesus Christ (1:12). The rhetography of this discourse, which implicitly evokes a specific event in which Jesus Christ became visible to Paul from the heavens, was "narrativized" in early Christian literature in Acts 9:1-9; 22:4-11; 26:9-18. The overall story-line that unfolds in Gal 1:12-14 contains the following events:

1. God set Paul apart before he was born and called him through his grace (1:15)
2. Paul violently persecuted the church of God and was trying to destroy it (1:13)
3. Paul advanced in Judaism beyond many of his people of the same age (1:14)
4. God revealed his Son to Paul, so that he might proclaim his Son among the Gentiles (1:16)
5. Paul went away to Arabia, and afterwards returned to Damascus (1:17)
6. After three years Paul went up to Jerusalem to visit Cephas and stayed with him fifteen days (1:18)
7. Paul saw James the Lord's brother while he was visiting Cephas (1:19)
8. Paul went into the regions of Syria and Cilicia (1:21)
9. After fourteen years Paul went up again to Jerusalem with Barnabas, in response to a revelation, taking Titus along with him (2:1-2)
10. Paul had a private meeting with the recognized leaders of the churches in Christ movement (2:2)
11. The leaders did not compel Paul to circumcise Titus, though he was Greek (2:3)
12. False believers slipped in to spy on the freedom Paul and his followers have in Christ Jesus to enslave them, but Paul and Titus did not submit to them (2:4-5)
13. James, Cephas (Peter), and John (acknowledged "pillars") gave Barnabas and Paul the right hand of fellowship to go to the Gentiles, while they would go to the circumcised, asking only that Paul and Barnabas remember the poor (in Jerusalem through a collection of money from the Gentile churches) (2:7-10)
14. Cephas, present with Paul in Antioch, ate with the Gentiles in the church (2:12)
15. When certain people came from James to Antioch, Cephas drew back from the Gentiles and kept himself separate for fear of the circumcision faction (2:12)
16. The other Jews in the church at Antioch joined Cephas in this hypocrisy, including Barnabas (2:13)
17. Paul opposed Cephas to his face, because he saw that Cephas and all of the Jews including Barnabas were not acting consistently with the truth of the gospel (2:11, 14)
18. Paul said to Cephas before all of the people gathered, "If you, though a Judean, live like a Gentile and not like a Judean, how can you compel the Gentiles to live like Judeans?" (2:16)

This is an eighteen event story-line of Paul's "prophetic" life. Internal to the story, embedded in a manner that only people who know biblical prophetic literature would recognize, are words in Gal 1:15 that evoke both Isaiah's and Jeremiah's call to their prophetic life. Paul does not appeal openly to the call either of Isaiah or Jeremiah and argue for a relation between their prophetic life and his own. Rather, Paul's discourse simply uses wording from both Isaiah's and Jeremiah's call.

Gal 1:15-16	Isa 49:1c (LXX)	Jer 1:4-5
[15]But when God, who had set me apart from my mother's womb (*ek koilias mētros mou*) and called (*kalesas*) me through his grace,	... from my mother's womb (*ek koilias mētros mou*) he called (*ekalesen*) my name.	Now the word of the LORD came to me saying, [5] "Before I formed you in the womb (*en koiliāi*) I knew you, and before you came out from the womb (*ek mētras*) I consecrated (*hēgiaka*) you;
was pleased [16]to reveal his Son to me, so that I might proclaim him among the nations (*en tois ethnesin*), I did not confer with any human being		I appointed you a prophet to the nations (*eis ethnē*)."

Paul's narrative refers to God's calling of him from his mother's womb with verbatim language from Isa 49:1 (LXX) and to God's sending of him to the nations (Gentiles) with language closely related to Jer 1:5. This scriptural language functions internally in Paul's own wording, reflecting oral usage of well-known biblical phrasing, rather than functioning externally to Paul's wording through explicit recitation that would give authoritative support to his wording. This is a natural function of biblical wording in a context where people hear scripture read regularly and use biblical phrasing in appropriate contexts. Certain people would readily recognize the writings that function as a resource for the wording, while others would not. For those who would recognize the wording, Paul's discourse would evoke a story-line from the prophets Isaiah and Jeremiah to Paul and his special mission to the nations (Gentiles).

Once Paul establishes the prophetic dynamic of his discourse, the succeeding events unfold like the autobiographical accounts of events in biblical prophetic literature. Using careful detail and coherent repetition, Paul sets forth a narrative that authorizes him prophetically to confront Cephas in Antioch "to his face" when he withdraws from eating with the Gentile members of the community (2:11). As Paul's language unfolds, he uses wording of "self-condemnation" (*kategnōsmenos*: 2:11), "hypocrisy" (2:13), "led astray," and acting consistently with "the truth of the gospel" (2:14), which are ready at hand in early Christian prophetic rhetorolect. The events in Paul's account of his "prophetic" life reach their conclusion in a prophetic rhetorical question to Cephas in front of the entire assembly: "If you, though a Judean, live like a Gentile (*ethnikōs*) and not like a Judean, how can you compel the Gentiles (*ta ethnē*) to live like Judeans?" (2:14).

After Paul has completed his prophetic story-line, he moves into wisdom rhetorolect to explain the dynamics and responsibilities of being a Jew by birth who is entrusted with a special message from God to the nations (2:15-21). In 3:1-5, he shifts back into prophetic rhetorolect with accusations of foolishness ("You foolish Galatians": 3:1; "Are you so foolish": 3:3) and a series of rhetorical questions characteristic of prophetic argumentation (3:1-5).

When Paul returns to wisdom rhetorolect in Gal 3:6, he introduces a series of event-pictures that evoke a prophetic story-line that begins with Abraham, continues through God's giving of the Torah to Israel, and reaches its conclusion in Jesus and people who believe in Jesus as God's Messiah. This story-line explains God's giving of salvation to the nations (Gentiles) through Abraham. Paul's discourse presents blended wisdom rhetorolect to the end of the epistle, with a significant shift into prophetic rhetorolect in Gal 5:7-12. The story-line which the wisdom rhetorolect presents, however, is prophetic, with its beginning point in Abraham.

Paul's presentation of the Abraham story-line in Galatians begins with the "event-picture" of Abraham believing God and God reckoning Abraham's belief to him as righteousness (Gal 3:6). On the basis of this event-picture, Paul argues from analogy that just as Abraham believed God and it was reckoned to him as righteousness, so those who believe are sons (the descendants) of Abraham (3:7). It is noticeable that Paul does not assert that God reckons as righteous all who believe in God. The reason is that he presents prophetic reasoning focused on a double promise to Abraham, namely an initial promise that he would have many descendants and a later promise that he and Sarah would have a son after the time when childbirth was natural for them. Prophetic reasoning, then, is produced through people and events, rather than simply through the nature of God and God's created world, which is the manner in which wisdom reasoning is produced.

After the initial assertions in Gal 3:6-7, Gal 3:8 personifies "the writings" (scripture) as proclaiming the gospel beforehand to Abraham, because they foresaw that God would justify the nations (Gentiles) by faith in the future. Early Christian prophetic rhetorolect, then, even personifies scripture! The writings themselves "preach the gospel" before the coming of Christ, because they know what God's decisions and actions will be in the future. Early Christian personification of scripture in this manner gives us one of the clearest insights into the inner workings of early Christian prophetic rhetorolect. Not only all people and events in the history of God's created world can become the agency for prophetic reasoning, but anything written in "the writings" (scripture) can become the agency for early Christian prophetic reasoning! Moreover, this reasoning implicitly creates a story-line from the past to the present and the future. All the biblical writings function as a prophetic voice in the past that starts somewhere in a story-line of God's "pre-Christ" actions with Israel through the story of Jesus as God's Messiah into the future.

The gospel that scripture proclaimed to Abraham beforehand was that "All the nations (Gentiles) will be blessed in you" (Gen 22:18; Gal 3:8). Paul's discourse regularly, but certainly not always, makes biblical discourse into proverbial discourse. The speech of scripture to Abraham in Gal 3:8 is prophetic proverbial speech, which is a natural rhetorical form of speech that blesses. In short, the statement of scripture in Gal 3:8 is a prophetic beatitude: "All the nations will be blessed in you." Early Christian prophetic rhetorolect not only confronts its hearers with indictments of wrongdoing. It also confronts people with the blessings they are experiencing as a result of God's actions in the world. In Gal 3:9, Paul moves the event of scripture's preaching of the gospel beforehand into enthymematic reasoning:

> *Rule (Rationale):* The scripture foresaw that God would justify the nations by faith.
> *Result/Case:* The scripture declared beforehand to Abraham, "All the nations shall be blessed in you."
> *Result:* For this reason, those who believe are blessed with Abraham who believed. (Gal 3:9)

Paul's prophetic reasoning works with the domains of God, scripture, people, and events in Gal 3:8-9. In this framework, it presents what can appropriately be called enthymematic "prophetic reasoning." Because scripture foresaw that God would justify the nations by faith in the future, it proclaimed the gospel beforehand to Abraham: "All the nations (Gentiles) will be blessed in you." Therefore, those who believe are blessed with Abraham who believed.

Without indicating to the hearer/reader that he has moved to the next event-picture in his prophetic story-line, Paul blends his argumentation about Abraham with argumentation about God's giving of the Torah (law: *nomos*) to Israel (Gal 3:10). Paul clarifies his understanding of the relation of the two event-pictures in Gal 3:17: "My point is this: the law, which came four hundred thirty years later, does not annul a covenant previously ratified by God, so as to nullify the promise." The key to the story-line is the interpretation of scripture's preaching of the gospel beforehand (*proeuēngelisato*) as God's "promise" (*epangelian*) to Abraham (3:14, 17-18). Paul reasons that a promise God made at an earlier time in the history of Israel, God cannot annul at a later time, using the human analogy of a will that cannot be changed or annulled once it has been certified (Gal 3:15).

The promise to Abraham introduces the next event-picture in Paul's argument: "Now the promises were made to Abraham and to his offspring; it does not say, "And to offsprings," as of many; but it says, "And to your offspring," that is, to one person, who is Christ (Gen 12:7; 17:8; Gal 3:16; cf. 3:19). After this, the next event-picture in Paul's argument is: "Christ redeemed us from the curse of the law by becoming a curse for us – for it is written, 'Cursed is everyone who hangs on a tree'" (Deut 21:23; Gal 3:13). The key to the next event in the prophetic story-line is the interpretation of Christ's crucifixion as a curse. Paul introduced the concept of curse in Gal 3:10: "All who rely on the works of the law are under a curse (*kataran*); for it is written, 'Cursed is everyone who does not observe and obey all the things written in the book of the law'" (Deut 27:26; Gal 3:10).

Abraham Story-Line	Argumentation
(1) Event-Picture: Abraham "believed God and it was reckoned to him as righteousness" (Gen 15:6: Gal 3:6).	(1) Just as Abraham, so those who believe are the descendants of Abraham (Gal 3:6-7).
(2) Personified Scripture: The scripture, foreseeing that God would justify the nations (Gentiles) by faith, declared the gospel beforehand to Abraham, saying, "All the nations (Gentiles) shall be blessed in you" (Gen 22:18; Gal 3:8).	(2) For this reason, those who believe are blessed with Abraham who believed (Gal 3:9). God granted the inheritance to Abraham through the promise (3:18).
(3) My point is this: the law, which came four hundred thirty years later than Abraham, does not annul a covenant previously ratified by God, so as to nullify the promise (Gal 3:17).	(3) For if the inheritance comes from the law, it no longer comes from the promise (Gal 3:18).
(4) Now the promises were made to Abraham and to his offspring; it does not say, "And to offsprings," as of many; but it says, "And to your offspring," that is, to one person, who is Christ (Gen 12:7; 17:8; Gal 3:16; cf. 3:19).	(4) And if you belong to Christ, then you are Abraham's offspring, heirs according to the promise (Gal 3:29).
(5) Christ redeemed us from the curse of the law by becoming a curse for us – for it is written, "Cursed is everyone who hangs on a tree" – in order that in Christ Jesus the blessing of Abraham might come to the Gentiles, so that we might receive the promise of the Spirit through faith (Gal 3:13-14).	(5) All who rely on the works of the law are under a curse; for it is written, "Cursed is everyone who does not observe and obey all the things written in the book of the law" (Deut 27:26; Gal 3:10).

This prophetic story-line is an emergent structure that invites further elaboration. In Gal 4:21-27, Paul introduces two sons to Abraham and their mothers, a slave woman named Hagar and a free woman who corresponds to the Jerusalem above and whom Paul calls "our mother" (Gal 4:26). This leads to Isaac, about whom Paul says: "Now you, my friends are children of the promise, like Isaac" (Gal 4:28). Then in Rom 4:10 Paul observes that Abraham's faith was reckoned to him as righteousness before, rather than after, he was circumcised. In addition, Paul reasons that the promise came to Abraham when his body "was already as good as dead" (Rom 4:19). This leads to reasoning that God's reckoning of people as righteous comes when people "believe in him who raised Jesus our Lord from the dead" (Rom 4:24). In turn, it is possible to take this reasoning to Isaac, arguing that Abraham was willing to offer up his son, since "He had considered the fact that God is able even to raise someone from the dead – and figuratively speaking, Abraham did receive him back" (Heb 11:19-20). We will see further below that the Gospel of Matthew expands the prophetic story-line from Abraham through three sets of fourteen generations, which include King David and his son Solomon, down to Joseph the husband of Mary, who gave birth to Jesus, who is called the Messiah (Matt 1:2-17).

At this point, it is important to notice that the Gospel of Matthew begins its account of the genealogy of Jesus the Messiah, the son of David, with Abraham (Matt 1:2). Abraham, whose name means "father of a multitude of nations" according to Gen 17:5, is the beginning of Matthew's gospel story. This prophetic genealogy highlights King David (1:6, 17) and the deportation to Babylon when the kingdom of Israel came to an end (1:11-12, 17) in the prophetic story-line to Jesus the Messiah (1:16-17). Here one sees again the importance of the focus on God's kingdom in the world. One also sees how the title Messiah or Christ is a prophetic title, focused on the renewal of God's kingdom on earth. This prophetic dimension continues, as most readers will know, with a sequence of stories in Matt 1:18–3:6 in which major events in the gospel story from the birth of Jesus to the coming of John the Baptist fulfill "what had been spoken by the Lord through the prophet[s]" (1:22; 2:15, 17, 23; 3:3) or "what has been written by the prophet" (2:5). These chapters, which the canonical arrangement places at the beginning of the New Testament, present a special dimension of prophetic rhetorolect that reverberates throughout Christian discourse. From the perspective of Christian prophetic rhetorolect, all events surrounding the story of Jesus are in some way "prophetic" in nature. By this, Christian discourse means that God was the initiator of all of the events and thus all the participants in the events were somehow participating in God's way of working in the world to bring a blessing to all people in it through specific people God selected in a particular region on which God focused.

In a context where we are discussing the overall nature of Christian discourse, it is important to see even a broader implication of the opening chapters of the Gospel of Matthew for Christian discourse. Early Christian prophetic rhetorolect introduced a perspective that any event in the history of Israel had the potential to be part of "the gospel story," because God was somehow involved in it. Therefore, early Christian prophetic rhetorolect created gospel story through a dynamic use of a large number of verses in "the writings."[13] These passages, from the perspective of prophetic rhetorolect, were "God's statements" to humans about promises, goals, and judgments for the history of people on earth. The first phase of this gospel story concerned the story of Israel and, as we have just seen, the second phase concerned all the events that brought about the life, death, and resurrection of Jesus of Nazareth. But, from the perspective of Christian prophetic rhetorolect, the gospel story does not stop here.

Since, in the view of early Christians, God continued to be active in relation to "his people" on earth after Jesus' death and resurrection, the third phase for the gospel story concerns any situation or story that somehow exhibits the relation of God to God's people throughout all the history of people on earth. This means that prophetic rhetorolect introduced dynamics into Christian discourse that started the gospel story with Abraham, continued it through the story of Jesus, and eventually has extended it into events that occur around Jesus' followers to the present day. For Christian discourse, prophetic story is first and foremost gospel story, a story about the good news of God's activity in the world. Christian prophetic rhetorolect and, as a result gospel story, intermingles God's speech to specific people with stories about God's people and the contexts in which they live. In the midst of these stories, God's prophets confront other people with "God's words," with which they themselves have also been confronted.

As one sees in the wording of the opening chapters of Matthew, statements from God may come directly from God, or they may come from "the writings," namely scripture. In the context of the four centuries after the life of Jesus, during which Christians considered more and more "writings" about Jesus and his followers to be "authoritative," stories not only about Jesus but also about Jesus' followers began to function in the mode of Christian prophetic rhetorolect. Within time, therefore, prophetic rhetorolect began to function as a mode of thinking and argumentation that extended the gospel story throughout all history to

[13] The word early Christians used for the books that are commonly called the Old Testament or the Hebrew Bible was simply "the writings" (*hai graphai*).

the end of time. Indeed, since anyone at any point in the history of the world may be confronted to be obedient to God's will, any person at any time and place may, from the perspective of Christian prophetic rhetorolect, become a descendant of Abraham through faith.

In the Hebrew Bible, God promised to give a particular land to the offspring of Abraham.[14] Through the writings of Paul in particular, early Christian prophetic rhetorolect reconfigured the promise of "land" to the promise of an "inheritance" (*klēronomia*) through Christ, who was "the offspring" of Abraham. While Pauline discourse emphasizes God's promise through Abraham to "many nations," it focuses on the singular form of "offspring" to interpret Christ as "the offspring of Abraham." This means that prophetic rhetorolect that focuses on Abraham becomes Christological in a special way through Paul's letter to the Galatians. This Christological focus capitalizes on the emphasis in the Abraham story on God's promise to Abraham of many descendants through "an offspring." This is different from the Moses story, which emphasizes the receiving of a particular region of land as a promise. Christian prophetic rhetorolect presents a decisive shift from an emphasis on inheriting land to inheriting "promises" in Paul's letters. It is natural for this shift to focus in some special way on Jesus. In Galatians, Paul shifts the emphasis by focusing on "the offspring" of Abraham. In overall Christian prophetic rhetorolect that emerged from the first century, Abraham became the beginning of the gospel story for all people in the world without this special focus by Paul. Nevertheless, when Galatians became a part of the NT canon of literature, this unusual argument by Paul became part of overall Christian prophetic argumentation.

The Isaiah Prophetic Story-Line in the Gospel of Mark

After letters attributed to Paul generated various prophetic story-lines during the 50s and 60s, Gospels and the Acts of the Apostles generated additional prophetic story-lines from 70 to100 CE. The prophetic book of Isaiah played a major role in these new story-lines, making Isaiah perhaps the most frequently recited Hebrew Bible book in the New Testament.[15] Verses in Isaiah function as resources for many events in the Christian story.

The Gospel of Mark, regularly dated ca. 69-71 CE, opens by attributing the beginning of the Gospel of Jesus Christ to the prophet Isaiah. This brings to mind Paul's assertion in Gal 3:8 that scripture preached the gospel beforehand (*proeuēngelisato*) to Abraham. The Gospel of

[14] Gen 13:14-15; 17:8; 24:7.

[15] If Isaiah is the most frequently recited biblical book in the NT, Psalms is unquestionably second in frequency.

Mark does not present an argument that the gospel began with Abraham. Rather, according to Mark, the prophet Isaiah preached the beginning of the Gospel of Jesus Christ when he talked about a voice crying out in the wilderness (Isa 40:3). The irony, of course, is that the content of "what is written in Isaiah the prophet" is a blend of Exod 23:30; Mal 3:1; and Isa 40:3. While interpreters have clarified various aspects of these opening verses of Mark, they regularly have not clearly described the rhetography of the verses.

Mark 1:2-3 opens the gospel story with God speaking to Jesus Christ. God tells Jesus: "Behold I am sending my messenger before your face, who will prepare your way, a voice of one crying out in the wilderness, 'Prepare[16] the way of the Lord, make straight his paths." Mark achieves this rhetography by blending words from Exod 23:20 and Mal 3:1 with Isa 40:3. The words from Exod 23:20 come from a section of Torah where God spoke to Moses:

> The Lord said to Moses: "Thus you shall say to the Israelites: 'You have seen for yourselves that I spoke with you from heaven. (20:22) ...' ... These are the ordinances that you shall set before them: (21:1) ... Behold I am sending my angel/messenger (*angelon*) before your face, to guard you on the way (*en tēi hodōi*) and to bring you to the place that I have prepared (*hētoimasa*) for you. Be attentive to him and listen to his voice; do not rebel against him, for he will not pardon your transgression; for my name is upon him" (23:20-21).

In the mode of early Christian prophetic rhetorolect, Mark begins with God speaking from heaven, but the one to whom God is speaking is God's Messiah Jesus, rather than Moses. To rephrase Paul's words in Gal 3:8, since scripture knew beforehand that John the Baptizer would prepare the way for Jesus, it preached the gospel beforehand to Moses about a messenger who would lead the way for Jesus.

As God speaks to Jesus through the words of Exod 23:20 attributed to the prophet Isaiah, God's words emphasize the person "who (*hos*) will prepare the way" (Mark 1:2), rather than the place "which (*hēn*) God has prepared" (Exod 23:20). This shift reveals the rhetorical effect of LXX Mal 3:1, 22-23[17] which reconfigures Exod 23:20 in terms of the coming of Elijah, "who (*hos*) will turn the heart of a father to his son and the heart of a man to his neighbor" (LXX Mal 3:23). The shift of emphasis onto the person who will prepare the way provides the bridge to Isa 40:3 and the means for early Christian rhetorolect to reconfigure its meaning. In the Hebrew Bible and the Dead Sea Com-

[16] All the synoptic writers contain *kataskeuasei* rather than *hētoimasa*, which Stendahl considers to exhibit clear proof that it is based on the massoretic *piel* reading: Krister Stendahl, *The School of Saint Matthew* (Philadelphia: Fortress, 1968) 51.

[17] HB Mal 3:1; 4:5-6.

munity, Isa 40:3 focuses on the location of the way "in the wilderness" (*en tēi erēmōi*). Thus, Isa 40:3 reads: "A voice cries out, "In the wilderness prepare the way of the Lord, make straight in the desert a highway for our God." By focusing on the person rather than the way, early Christian prophetic rhetorolect reconfigures the meaning of Isa 40:3 to mean: "A voice of one crying out in the wilderness, "Prepare the way of the Lord" (Mark 1:3; Matt 3:3; Luke 3:4; John 1:23). Then the focus on the person who will lead the way, rather than God's preparation of the way, produces a change in the final line of Isa 40:3. Rather than using the wording, "make straight in the desert a highway for our God," early Christian prophetic rhetorolect modifies the wording to "make his paths straight" (Mark 1:3/Matt 3:6/Luke 3:4). Since early Christians "knew" that scripture was talking about John the Baptizer and Jesus, they produced prophetic rhetorolect containing scriptural wording that identified the one preparing the way as "a voice crying in the wilderness" and the way as "the way of the Lord Jesus."

It is important to notice that Markan narration produces the beginning of the gospel out of what is written in Isaiah the prophet in such a way that it causes a "run-on" narrational string from Mark 1:3 through 1:8.[18] In other words, Markan narration of the beginning of the Gospel of Jesus Christ through Isaiah the prophet does not end with Isa 40:3 in Mark 1:3. Rather, Markan narration unfolds a story-line from Isaiah to John the Baptizer's promise that "one stronger than him" was coming after him. We saw above how Paul's autobiographical prophetic story line in Galatians used wording from Isaiah and Jeremiah internally to produce narration that carried his own personal story-line forward to a point where he confronts Cephas prophetically before the people assembled in the church at Antioch. In Mark, the prophetic beginning of the story-line in Isaiah moves up to the prophetic words of John the Baptizer:

> He who is stronger than me is coming after me,
> of whom I am not worthy
> stooping down to loosen the thongs of his sandals.
> I baptized you with water;
> but he himself will baptize you with holy spirit. (Mark 1:7-8)

On the one hand it is noticeable how the prophetic focus is on people rather than on "the way." On the other hand, it is noticeable how the narration focuses on promise rather than indictment. In Matt 3:7-10, 12 and Luke 3:7-14, 17, John the Baptizer comes with scathing judgments of people's actions. But not so in Mark. The story-line in

[18] Vernon K. Robbins, "Interfaces of Orality and Literature in the Gospel of Mark," in *Performing the Gospel: Orality, Memory, and Mark* (ed. R.A. Horsley, J.A. Draper, and J.M. Foley; Minneapolis: Fortress Press, 2006) 132 [125-46].

Mark emphasizes promises that come from God through Isaiah, and, for those who recognize it, through Moses and Malachi to John the Baptizer, who promises the coming of Jesus after him.

Recitation from Isaiah plays a further role in Mark 4:11-12, when Jesus teaches beside the sea in parables. In this context, the recitation emerges as wisdom rhetorolect that explains the nature of the kingdom of God as a mystery that has been given to Jesus' disciples to understand. For people outside the circle of Jesus' disciples, everything occurs in analogies they are not able to understand. This means that:

> looking they may indeed look, but not perceive,
> and listening they may indeed listen, but not understand;
> so that they may not turn again and be forgiven. (Isa 6:9–10; Mark 4:12)

This prophetic speech has been made into early Christian wisdom rhetorolect by changing it from second person address to third person explanation. Isaiah 6:9–10 presents words that the voice of the Lord spoke to Isaiah, which Isaiah in turn is to speak to Israel.

> 9 And he [the voice of the Lord] said, "Go and say to this people:
> 'Keep listening, but do not understand;
> keep looking, but do not perceive.'
> 10 Make the heart of this people dull,
> and stop their ears,
> and shut their eyes,
> so that they may not look with their eyes,
> and listen with their ears,
> and comprehend with their heart,
> and turn and be healed." (Isa 6:9-10)

Since the kingdom of God is a central topos of this early Christian prophetic rhetorolect, Jesus' discussion with his disciples is a blend of wisdom and prophetic rhetorolect. Markan discourse makes the recitation of this prophetic discourse from Isaiah into early Christian wisdom rhetorolect by abbreviating and reconfiguring wording in the mode of the instructions to Isaiah in 6:10 rather than in the mode in which Isaiah is to confront them in 6:9. Mark 4:12 does not confront the people who are listening to the parables with prophetic speech that tells them to keep looking and not perceiving and listening but not understanding. Rather, it is wisdom rhetorolect addressed to Jesus' disciples about people "outside" who will not be able to understand the mystery of the kingdom like the "insider" disciples are able to understand.

A key topos in prophetic discourse is "heart" (*hē kardia*), regularly translated either as "mind" or as "hearts" in English versions. The question in early Christian prophetic rhetorolect is whether people's seeing and hearing enables "their heart" (*hē kardia autōn*) to respond, or if their heart becomes "hardened" (*pōroō*), distant (*porrō*), or filled with "evil

The heart connects wisdom and prophetic the

reasonings" (*dialogismoi kakoi*). The heart, then, is a "bridge topos" between wisdom and prophetic rhetorolect. We saw in the previous chapters how "loving the Lord your God with all your heart" and having Torah wisdom in one's "heart" is central to early Christian wisdom rhetorolect. In early Christian prophetic rhetorolect, the issue is the hardness or dullness of the heart, or its distance from God. In a context where the heart is obviously a problem, early Christian discourse shifts from instructional wisdom to confrontational prophetic rhetorolect.

It is important to notice that the recitation of Isaiah in Mark 4:12 is not attributed to Isaiah but to Jesus. An important rhetorical characteristic of the Gospel of Mark is that after the attribution of wording to Isaiah the prophet in Mark 1:2-3, Markan narration itself never attributes wording to Isaiah, Jeremiah, Moses, David, or any other prophet in the manner in which Matthew, Luke, and John assert in a statement like: "This occurred to fulfill what is written in …" Part of the "prophetic register" in the Gospel of Mark is the function of scriptural wording "internally" in the story itself, rather than "externally" to the story, like it often functions in Matthew, Luke, and John.[19] After the initial recitation of "Isaiah" by Markan narration in Mark 1:2-3, only people in the story itself, rather than Markan narration, attributes wording to scripture. This means that scripture becomes an internal part of the narration of Gospel story itself in Mark, rather than wording that functions as external testimony to it.

In Mark 4:12, reconfigured wording from Isa 6:9-10 is attributed to Jesus through an inner dynamic of early Christian prophetic rhetorolect related to the attribution of wording from Exod 23:20 and Mal 3:1 to Isaiah in Mark 1:2-3. Mark 4:12 reconfigures words that God spoke to Isaiah in Isaiah 6:9-10 into words of Jesus to his disciples. This reconfiguration places seeing first and hearing second, like Isa 6:10, but it uses participles and verbs about seeing and hearing in a manner related to Isa 6:9. The participles and verbs do not evoke second person confrontation, the natural mode for prophetic rhetorolect, but third person explanation, the natural mode for wisdom rhetorolect. In Mark 4:1-20, then, wisdom rhetorolect is the host for topoi of prophetic rhetorolect.

The topoi of prophetic rhetorolect in this context cause the reader to anticipate a story line with three steps in it:

1. People outside the circle of Jesus' disciples will see and hear Jesus but not be able to understand what they see and hear;
2. Jesus' disciples will understand what they see Jesus do and say;
3. On the basis of what they see and hear, Jesus' disciples will become faithful disciples who carry the gospel story forward after their time with Jesus.

[19] Robbins, "Interfaces," 131.

The primary rhetorical effect of prophetic rhetorolect in early Christian discourse, then, is not reasoning by analogy but reasoning by story-line. The hearer/reader of Mark anticipates that the gospel story-line will show a sequence where people outside the circle of Jesus' disciples will not be able to understand Jesus' actions and teachings, but Jesus' disciples will understand it. The narrator sets the stage for this story-line in Mark 3:5 when Jesus grieved at "the hardness of the heart" of the Pharisees who would not accept Jesus' reasoning about curing the man with the withered hand on the Sabbath (3:4) and the Pharisees immediately conspired with the Herodians how to destroy him after he restored the man's hand (3:6).

Most readers know that the irony of Isaiah's rhetoric becomes an internal part of the story of the disciples themselves in the Gospel of Mark. While they should, on the basis of Jesus' assertion in Mark 4:12, be able to understand the meaning of what Jesus does and says as the story unfolds, in fact they do not. The first instance where Markan narration uses wording from Isa 6:9-10 to explain to the reader the disciples' inability to understand is Mark 6:52. Having seen Jesus feed 5,000 people with five loaves and two fish (6:30-44), they were utterly astonished when Jesus walked on water to them while they were in a boat (6:45-51). The Markan narrator, using wording from Isa 6:9-10, explains to the reader that they were astonished, "because they did not understand (*synēkan*) about the loaves, but their heart (*autōn hē kardia*) was hardened (*pepōrōmenē*)" (Mark 6:52). This is a shocking indictment of the disciples who, according to Mark 4:11-12, have been given the mystery of the kingdom of God. Still, however, the primary rhetorolect of Mark 6:52 is wisdom, namely explanation to the hearer/reader that the disciples could not comprehend Jesus' ability to walk on water to them, because their hearts had become hardened so they had not understood how Jesus had been able to feed 5,000 people with five loaves and two fish. Rikki Watts's thesis that Mark presents a framework of understanding that is deeply embedded in Isaiah is correct.[20] Mark's wisdom rhetorolect blends with the understanding of the story of Israel in Isaiah, which presents the people of Israel themselves, those whom God has specially chosen, as unable to understand the workings of God in their present context. In like manner, Mark presents the disciples whom Jesus has specially chosen (3:13-19), and to whom he has explained everything in private (3:34), as unable to understand God's workings in the ongoing events of the story of Jesus.

Soon after the narrator's characterization of Jesus' disciples as unable to understand because of the hardness of their heart (6:52), Jesus uses

[20] Rikki E. Watts, *Isaiah's New Exodus in Mark* (WUNT, 2nd ser. 88; Tübingen: J.C.B. Mohr [Paul Siebeck], 1997).

words from LXX Isa 29:13 which sharpen the issue of understanding. The issue, in Mark, is the disciples' eating without washing their hands (7:2). When Pharisees and scribes from Jerusalem ask Jesus why his disciples do not live according to the tradition of the elders, but eat with defiled hands (7:5), Jesus confronts them with prophetic rhetorolect that recites words from Isaiah (Mark 7:6-7). With words from LXX Isa 29:13, Jesus confronts the Pharisees and scribes on the basis of "their heart." Jesus uses second person confrontation of the Pharisees and scribes throughout Mark 7:6-13 as he says:

> 6 "Isaiah prophesied rightly about you hypocrites, as it is written,
> 'This people honors me with their lips,
> but their heart (*hē kardia autōn*) is far from me;
> 7 in vain do they worship me;
> teaching human precepts as doctrines.'
> 8 You abandon the commandment of God and hold to human tradition."
> 9 Then he said to them, "You have a fine way of rejecting the commandments of God in order to keep your tradition! 10: For Moses said, 'Honor your father and your mother'; and, 'Whoever speaks evil of father or mother must surely die.' 11 But you say that if anyone tells father or mother, 'Whatever support you might have had from me is Corban' (that is, an offering to God) – 12 then you no longer permit doing anything for a father or mother, 13 thus making void the word of God through your tradition that you have handed on. And you do many things like this."

In these verses, prophetic rhetorolect has become primary. Wisdom rhetorolect now functions as a guest in the context of confrontational prophetic rhetorolect. Reciting authoritative words of Isaiah, Jesus argues that Isaiah prophesied that Pharisees and scribes, as primary leaders of the people of Israel, would honor God with their lips, but their heart would be far from God. Jesus frames his recitation of Isaiah with direct address to the Pharisees and scribes, beginning with an accusation of hypocrisy (7:6) and ending with the accusation: "You abandon the commandment of God and hold to human tradition" (7:8). As Jesus continues with an accusation that they reject the commandment of God in order to follow their own tradition, he argues that they violate Torah wisdom by having people tell their father or mother that support they think they should receive has been dedicated to the Jerusalem temple as an offering to God, "Corban." Jesus ends with the prophetic accusation: "And you do many things like this" (7:13).

After Jesus has confronted the Pharisees and scribes with prophetic rhetorolect in Mark 7:6-13, in the mode of wisdom rhetorolect he explains to the crowd that nothing that goes into a person defiles them, but only what comes out of a person (7:14-15). But the story continues. The Markan narrator tells the hearer/reader that Jesus went with his disciples into the house, and Jesus' disciples showed that they did not understand "the parable" Jesus had spoken when they asked him what it meant (7:17). Jesus' disciples, who should be able to understand all of Jesus' parables, could not understand either Jesus' prophetic confrontation of the Pharisees and scribes or his wisdom teaching to the crowd! At this point, Jesus confronts his own disciples with prophetic rhetorolect:

> 18 "Then do you also fail to understand?
> Do you not see that whatever goes into a person from outside cannot defile,
> 19 since it enters, not the heart but the stomach, and goes out into the sewer?" (7:18-19)

The issue is "the heart," and the disciples fail to understand the nature of the heart in relation to defilement. The story-line the hearer/reader anticipated near the beginning of the story changes decisively at this point. The narrator has prepared the hearer/reader in Mark 6:52; 7:17 for the inability of the disciples to understand Jesus' actions and teachings. But only in Mark 7:18 does Jesus use prophetic rhetorolect directed against the disciples, accusing them also of not understanding the nature of the heart. Just as Israel could not understand, so Jesus' own specially chosen disciples are unable to understand!

Jesus shifts back to wisdom rhetorolect as he teaches the disciples in even more detail about the nature of the human heart:

> 20 And he said, "It is what comes out of a person that defiles.
> 21 For it is from within, from the human heart (*kardias*), that evil reasonings (*dialogismoi*) come:
> fornication, theft, murder, 22 adultery, avarice, wickedness, deceit, licentiousness, envy, slander, pride, folly.
> 23 All these evil things come from within, and they defile a person." (Mark 7:20-23)

Again, the topos of this wisdom rhetorolect is a central topos of prophetic rhetorolect, namely the human heart. In the context of prophetic rhetorolect, early Christian wisdom rhetorolect contains more detailed explanation of the nature of the human heart. Pauline discourse presents a related set of details in Gal 5:13-26. In the context of wisdom rhetorolect focused on "You shall love your neighbor as your self" in Gal 5:13-15, Paul's discourse never mentions "the heart" (cf. Gal 5:16-25). Dominated by imagery from wisdom rhetorolect, the goal in Gal 5:13-23 is "fruit" (*karpos*) of the Spirit rather than deeds of the flesh. The issue is deeds of "the flesh (*sarx*) with its passions (*pathēmasin*) and desires (*epithymiais*)" (Gal 5:24) rather than "evil reasonings" (*kakoi dialogismoi*) that come out of "the heart" (*kardia*) that is hardened, dull, or far from God (Mark 7:6-23). Issues concerning the heart, then, vary depending on the dominance of wisdom or prophetic rhetorolect in the context.

While Jesus' prophetic confrontation of his disciples in Mark 7:18-19 initiates a substantive shift in the mode in which Jesus speaks to his disciples in the Markan story-line, Jesus' discussion with them in Mark 8:17-21 is even more decisive. In Mark 8:1-10 Jesus once again feeds a large group of people with a small amount of food, this time 4,000 people with seven loaves and a few small fish. Then the Pharisees ask Jesus, in order to test him, for a sign from heaven, and he refuses to give them a sign (Mark 8:11-12). After this, Jesus travels to the other side of the sea and has an extensive interchange with his disciples. The narrator tells the hearer/reader that the disciples had forgotten to bring bread, so they had only one loaf with them in the boat (Mark 8:14). After Jesus tells them to beware of the yeast of the Pharisees and Herod, they speak their concern to Jesus that they have no bread (8:15-16). At this point, Jesus shifts into dramatic prophetic confrontation of them, using words from Isa 6:9-10:

> 17 Why are you talking about having no bread?
> Do you still not perceive or understand?
> Is your heart (*tēn kardian hymōn*) hardened?
> 18 Do you have eyes, and fail to see?
> Do you have ears, and fail to hear?
> And do you not remember?
> 19 When I broke the five loaves for the five thousand, how many baskets full of broken pieces did you collect?" They said to him, "Twelve."
> 20 "And the seven for the four thousand, how many baskets full of broken pieces did you collect?" And they said to him, "Seven."
> 21 Then he said to them, "Do you not yet understand?" (Mark 8:17-21)

Jesus maintains direct confrontation of his disciples throughout these verses, addressing them repetitively in second person. Rather than appealing authoritatively to Isaiah, as he did with the Pharisees in 7:6, Jesus configures words of Isaiah into his own speech. Jesus now confronts his disciples prophetically with the voice of Isaiah functioning internally in his own words. This action by Jesus leaves no doubt that the story-line of the disciples has changed from the story-line set forth in Mark 4:11-12. Functioning internally in early Christian prophetic rhetorolect, Isa 6:9-10; 29:13 change the story-line anticipated in a context of wisdom rhetorolect into a story-line where the disciples themselves are on the "outside" of understanding Jesus' actions and words. A wisdom story-line has become a prophetic story-line in which Jesus' confrontation of his disciples stands in the foreground.

Anticipated Wisdom Story-Line	Unfolding Prophetic Story-Line
(1) people outside the circle of Jesus' disciples will see and hear Jesus but not be able to understand what they see and hear;	(1) people outside the circle of Jesus' disciples will see and hear Jesus but not be able to understand what they see and hear;
(2) Jesus' disciples will understand what they see Jesus do and say;	(2) Jesus' disciples see and hear Jesus but also are not able to understand what they see and hear;
(3) on the basis of what they see and hear, Jesus' disciples will become faithful disciples who carry the gospel story forward after their time with Jesus.	(3) Will Jesus' disciples be able to become faithful disciples who carry the gospel story forward after their time with Jesus?

Prophetic rhetorolect regularly leaves a significant question about the story-line of God's chosen people: Will they or will they not ever understand the nature of God's will for his people in the world. In Mark, this story-line raises a question about Jesus' disciples. After being introduced to the secret of the kingdom of God (Mark 4:12), they become unable to understand Jesus' activity and message. Will they ever be able to understand? This question remains with the hearer/reader at the end of the Gospel of Mark.

The Isaiah Prophetic Story-Line of the Gospel of Matthew

Isaiah functions as a substantive resource for expanding and interpreting the story-line of the life of Jesus in the Gospel of Matthew. Written approximately fifty years after the death of Jesus, thirty years after the prophetic persecution story-line in 1 Thessalonians, and probably ten years after the Isaianic story-line in Mark, Matthew contains an even more highly blended and complex early Christian prophetic story-line. The opening verses in Matt 1:1-17 introduce a story-line from Abraham through David to Joseph, the husband of Mary, as mentioned above. Matt 1:18–2:13[21] introduces dream-visions reminiscent of the story of Joseph in the Hebrew Bible. Matt 2:13-23 introduces childhood escape from a ruler's brutal killing of young children reminiscent of the story Moses.[22] In the context of these multiple story-lines, Matthean narration uses words from Isaiah, Micah, Hosea, Jeremiah,[23] and unknown "prophets" (Matt 2:23) to present detailed episodes at the beginning of the story of Jesus. In contrast to the gospel in Mark, the narration does not flow naturally and directly out the words of the prophets. Rather, Matthew repetitively interrupts the narration of the story of Jesus to present authoritative external words from prophets in the past to interpret and configure the story of Jesus. In Matthew, then,

[21] Matt 1:20, 24; 2:12-13, 19, 22.

[22] See the similarities with the story of Cypselus in Herodotus 5.92 above.

[23] Isa 7:14 (Matt 1:23); Mic 5:2 (Matt 2:6); Hos 11:1 (Matt 2:15); Jer 31:15 (Matt 2:18).

the narrator programmatically steps out of the gospel story-line to present an argument from ancient prophetic testimony for the meaning of this phase of the gospel story line.

Matt 1:23 presents LXX wording of Isa 7:14; 8:8, 10 to support the identity of Mary as a "virgin" and provide a second naming of Jesus as Emmanuel, "God with us." This second name appears nowhere else in the NT, but in Matthew it expands the use of Isaiah to present the beginnings of the gospel story without referring to the prophet Isaiah as the resource for the wording. Isaiah's name appears for the first time in Matt 3:3 to interpret the activity of John the Baptist with Isa 40:3. This is, of course, the context in which the prophet Isaiah appears in the Gospel of Mark. In contrast to Mark 1:2, however, Isa 40:3 is not part of an unfolding scene of God's speech to Jesus that is "the beginning of the gospel" (Mark 1:1). Rather, Isa 40:3 is "a second voice" outside the narration that identifies John as "the one who was spoken about through Isaiah the prophet." Isaiah and his words are external to the narration of the gospel story, rather than internal to it. Isaiah is part of a "line up" of prophets in Matthew who stand outside the gospel story and either spoke or wrote words that pointed forward to an episode in the story of Jesus. The rhetorical effect in early Christian discourse is an expansion of the number of people in whom the gospel story has its "beginnings." Matthew precedes the gospel of the adult Jesus with an extended introduction of "the beginnings" of the gospel in more than fifty people from the story of Israel. This introduction begins with Abraham, continues through King David, and comes to fruition through three unnamed prophets who spoke or wrote words that interpret the meaning of Jesus' birth (1:22; 2:5, 15), a group of prophets who spoke about Jesus' home in Nazareth (2:23), and the prophet Jeremiah who spoke about the weeping and lamentation over the death of children two years and younger after the birth of Jesus (2:17). Jeremiah, then, is the only named prophet in Matthew's account of the beginnings of the gospel story. All the other prophets who played a role are unnamed in Matthean narration. In other words, the prophetic rhetorolect that presents the beginnings of the gospel in Matt 1 simply refers to "prophets" except for Jeremiah in 1:17.

After the beginnings of the gospel in stories about Jesus' birth and reference to Jesus' boyhood home in Nazareth, the Gospel of Matthew presents the story of the adult Jesus beginning with John the Baptist. The prophet Isaiah appears as a named personage for the first time in Matt 3:3 as his voice interprets John the Baptist as "the voice of one crying in the wilderness, 'Prepare the way of the Lord, make his paths straight.'" Isaiah's name first appears in Mark, as mentioned above, in relation to the coming of John the Baptizer. But there is a major difference in Isaiah's function at the beginning of the Markan and Matthean accounts. In Mark 1:2, Isaiah functions as a "writing" containing the beginning of the gospel. In Matt 3:3 Isaiah functions as "a voice" who spoke about John the Baptist as "the voice of one crying out in the wilderness." Indeed, in Matthew Isaiah is always someone who speaks, and never "words that are written." In Luke, in contrast, Isaiah is always "a book" (3:4; 4:17). For Matthew, John the Baptist presents the voice of "the gospel itself," and Isaiah's voice speaks of his voice. Isaiah is not a writing in which a person finds "the beginnings of the gospel" (Mark 1:2), nor is it a book of the sayings of Isaiah (Luke 3:4). In Matthew, Isaiah is a voice who speaks of events in the gospel story itself, beginning with John's words, "Repent, for the kingdom of heaven has come near" (Matt 3:2).[24] As soon as Matthean narration of the gospel story itself starts, then, Isaiah appears as a named prophet who spoke words that pointed to the opening event in the story.

Isaiah appears a total of seven times during the gospel story in Matthew,[25] always functioning as a speaking voice and never as words that "are written." He appears the second time in Matt 4:14 with words that point to the region where Jesus repeats the gospel message of John the Baptist, "Repent, for the kingdom of heaven has come near" (Matt 4:17). This region is:

> Land of Zebulun, land of Naphtali,
> on the road by the sea, across the Jordan, Galilee of the Gentiles –
> [16] the people who sat in darkness
> have seen a great light,
> and for those who sat in the region and shadow of death
> light has dawned. (Matt 4:15-16; cf. Isa 9:1-2)

Isaiah interprets the place where Jesus will preach the gospel as "Galilee of the nations (Gentiles)." This is an important interpretation, of course, in relation to Paul's emphasis about Abraham and the nations (Gentiles) twenty or more years before this presence of Isaiah in Matthew's story of Jesus. For the Matthean account Jesus, whose heritage begins with Abraham, moved to "Capernaum by the sea" when he became an adult, so he could proclaim the gospel to "Galilee of the nations (Gentiles)." Isaiah testified that this would happen, and Jesus fulfilled it by moving away from Nazareth to Capernaum, making it his home as he began his adult ministry (4:13).

The third time Isaiah appears in the story-line of Matthew's gospel is 8:17, where Jesus heals Peter's mother-in-law who was lying sick in bed with a fever. The Matthean prophetic story-line, then, moves

[24] Cf. Mark 1:14-15.

[25] Matt 3:3; 4:14; 8:17; 12:17; 13:14, 35; 15:7.

from John the Baptist in the wilderness through Capernaum on the sea to the house of Peter's mother-in-law in Capernaum (Matt 8:5). Just as Isaiah predicted, Jesus would not only preach the coming of the kingdom of heaven to Galilee of the nations (Matt 4:15-17), but also, "He took our sicknesses (*astheneias*)[26] and bore our diseases (*nosous*)"[27] (Matt 8:17; Isa 53:4).

Isaiah appears the fourth time in the story-line of Matthew's Gospel in Matt 12:17, immediately after Pharisees began to conspire against him, how to destroy him (12:14), when he had healed a man with a withered hand on the Sabbath. Isaiah, speaking words from God, has a long speech that interprets this development in the story-line of Jesus:

> 18 Here is my servant, whom I have chosen,
> my beloved, with whom my soul is well pleased.
> I will put my Spirit upon him,
> and he will proclaim justice to the nations (Gentiles).
> 19 He will not wrangle or cry aloud,
> nor will anyone hear his voice in the streets.
> 20 He will not break a bruised reed
> or quench a smouldering wick
> until he brings justice to victory.
> 21 And in his name the nations (Gentiles) will hope. (Matt 12:18-21; cf. Isa 42:1-4, 9)

There is an embryonic story-line in this speech by Isaiah: (1) God chose Jesus for a particular task, since God was pleased with him; (2) God put God's Spirit upon Jesus to empower him for his difficult task; (3) Jesus will proclaim justice to the nations (Gentiles); (4) Jesus will not wrangle or cry aloud, nor will anyone hear his voice in the streets; (5) he will not break a bruised reed or quench a bruised reed until he brings justice to victory; and (6) in his name the nations (Gentiles) will hope. Again the nations (Gentiles) appear as an audience for Jesus' activity through the agency of the prophet Isaiah in Matthew.

The fifth time Isaiah appears in the Matthean story-line is 13:14, where Jesus interprets his teaching to the crowd in parables with words of Isaiah. Again Isaiah gives a long speech:

> You will indeed listen, but never understand,
> and you will indeed look, but never perceive.
> 15 For this people's heart (*kardia*) has grown dull,
> and their ears are hard of hearing,
> and they have shut their eyes;

[26] Cf. Matt 10:8; 25:36, 39.

[27] Cf. Matt 4:23, 24; 9:35; 10:1. The chapter on miracle rhetorolect in the next volume will discuss at some length the relation of early Christian prophetic rhetorolect to early Christian miracle rhetorolect.

> so that they might not look with their eyes,
> and listen with their ears,
> and understand with their heart (*kardiāi*) and turn –
> and I would heal them. (Matt 13:14-15)

In contrast to Mark 4:12; 8:18 and Luke 8:10, which present abbreviated and reconfigured portions of Isa 6:9-10,[28] Matt 13:14-15 recites all of LXX Isa 6:9-10. The irony is that Isaiah's "voice" in Matt 13:14-15 is the only context in the NT gospels that presents verbatim, lengthy wording of "written" Isaiah. In other words, attributing words of written Isaiah to the "speaking" Isaiah does not lead to an abbreviated *chreia*[29] but an expanded chreia.[30] The expanded form features the presence of "the heart" in the rationale at the beginning and the conclusion (Matt 13:15a, 15f). A central topos, as discussed above, in early Christian Isaianic prophetic rhetorolect is the heart, and Matthew's reference to it through Isaiah places the heart at the center of the challenge that lies before people who are confronted with the story-line of the Gospel in Matthew.

Matt 13:14-15 represent a new stage in the Matthean prophetic story-line, since the speech of Isaiah does not occur in Matthean narration but on the lips of Jesus. When Isaiah's voice is an internal part of Jesus' voice, Jesus is able to continue the prophetic rhetorolect in Matt 13:16-17. Since Jesus is talking to his disciples rather than the crowds, he does not turn the prophetic speech of Isaiah into judgmental indictment but uses the occasion as an opportunity for prophetic blessing:

> [16] But blessed are your eyes, for they see, and your ears, for they hear. [17] Truly I tell you, many prophets and righteous people longed to see what you see, but did not see it, and to hear what you hear, but did not hear it. (Matt 13:16-17)

Early Christian prophetic rhetorolect in Matthew features Jesus transforming the ironic, negative speech of Isaiah into a blessing on those in his inner circle. In Matthew, Jesus' disciples are not plagued overall with an inability to understand. Rather, Jesus uses Isaiah's voice as an opportunity to contrast the inability of the crowds to understand Jesus with the special blessings that come upon the disciples, because

[28] Also John 9:38; 12:40, which will be discussed below.

[29] Namely memorable speech or action attributed to a specific person.

[30] See Theon, *Progymnasmata* 213.10 (Walz); Ronald F. Hock and Edward N. O'Neil (eds.), *The Chreia in Ancient Rhetoric. Volume I. The Progymnasmata* (Atlanta: Scholars Press, 1986) 100-103; George A. Kennedy, *Progymnasmata: Greek Textbooks of Prose Composition and Rhetoric* (Writings from the Greco-Roman World 10; Atlanta: SBL, 2003) 21-22; Vernon K. Robbins, "Chreia & Pronouncement Story Synoptic Studies," in B.L. Mack and V.K. Robbins, *Patterns of Persuasion in the Gospels* (Sonoma, CA: Polebridge Press, 1989) 17-19; online: http://www.religion.emory.edu/faculty/robbins/patterns/Ch1Chreia.pdf.

they are able to hear, to understand, and to become faithful "scribes" of Jesus' words and deeds. Thus, in Matthew Jesus completes his teaching in parables with a special discussion with his disciples, asking them:

> [51] "Have you understood all this?"
> They answered, "Yes."
> [52] And he said to them, "Therefore every scribe who has been trained for the kingdom of heaven is like the master of a household who brings out of his treasure what is new and what is old." (Matt 13:51-52)

In the context of Jesus' teaching of parables in Matthew, then, prophetic speech of Isaiah creates an opportunity both for pronouncing a special blessing on the disciples and for blending wisdom rhetorolect that compares "every scribe trained for the kingdom of heaven" to "the master of a household who brings out of his treasure what is new and what is old" (Matt 13:52). The truest disciple of Jesus is a "scribe trained for the kingdom of heaven," like the person writing the Gospel of Matthew! The irony of written and oral word deepens even further, then, in this context of Isaiah's words. First, Jesus takes lengthy verbatim words of written Isaiah internally into his own speech. Second, Jesus refers to the words of written Isaiah as words Isaiah spoke prophetically. Third, Jesus' recitation of the words of Isaiah creates a context not only for blessing his disciples but also for praising those disciples who become writers, namely "scribes trained for the kingdom" like the writer of the Gospel of Matthew.

In the sixth and final appearance of Isaiah in the Matthean storyline,[31] Jesus recites Isaiah's words to Pharisees and scribes from Jerusalem, whom he calls "hypocrites." According to Jesus, Isaiah prophesied:

> This people honors me with their lips,
> but their heart is far from me;
> [9] in vain do they worship me,
> teaching human precepts as doctrines. (Matt 15:8-9; cf. LXX Isa 29:13)

After Jesus has praised "every scribe trained for the kingdom" in Matt 13:52, then, he confronts Pharisees and scribes who criticize Jesus' disciples for not washing their hands before they eat (Matt 15:2).[32]

[31] Textual variation adds Isaiah in Matt 13:35, where the narrator recites Ps 78:2, but this appears to be added as a result of the other appearances of Isaiah in Matthew.

[32] Jesus criticizes the Pharisees and scribes by accusing them of following and appealing to "the tradition of the elders" (*hē paradosis tōn presbyterōn*: Matt 15:2, 3, 6) rather than the "word," "law," or "commandment" of God, depending on which variant reading of 15:6 is to be accepted. If "the word of God" (*ton logon tou theou*) is to be accepted, Jesus may be challenging written traditions produced by Pharisees and scribes which are perceived to be contrary to words spoken by God. Later in the story (Matt 23:2) Jesus asserts

Proceeding consistently with his view that the disciples have truly heard and understood his teaching to them (Matt 13:16–17), Jesus defends the action of his disciples by arguing that "it is not what goes into the mouth that defiles a person, but it is what comes out of the mouth that defiles" (Matt 15:11). Problems arise even in Matthew, however, when the disciples ask Jesus if he is aware that the Pharisees took offense (*eskandalisthēsan*) at what he had said to them (Matt 15:13). Jesus answers his disciples by telling them:

> [13] Every plant that my heavenly Father has not planted will be uprooted. [14]Let them alone; they are blind guides of the blind. And if one blind person guides another, both will fall into a pit. (Matt 15:13–14)

When Peter asks Jesus to "explain this parable to us" (Matt 15:15), the tide turns on the disciples. Instead of displaying that they are able to hear and understand Jesus' parables, they display an inability to understand that should not be present in them. At this point, Jesus turns what should have been wisdom rhetorolect into prophetic rhetorolect by confronting the disciples with teaching blended with biting words of Isaiah:

> Are you also still without understanding? [17] Do you not perceive that whatever goes into the mouth enters the stomach, and goes out into the sewer? [18] But what comes out of the mouth proceeds from the heart (*kardias*), and this is what defiles. [19] For out of the heart (*kardias*) come evil intentions, murder, adultery, fornication, theft, false witness, slander. [20] These are what defile a person, but to eat with unwashed hands does not defile. (Matt 15:16–20)

The words, "Are you still without understanding? Do you not see …," are, of course, a reconfiguration of words from Isa 6:9–10. The topos of being without understanding (*asynetoi*) reverberates with the first and last lines of Jesus' recitation of Isa 6:9 in Matt 13:14–15 (*ou mē synēte; tēi kardiāi synōsin*). The topos of perceiving (*noeō*) regularly is a variation in the tradition of Isa 6:10.[33] The disciples are now in a position where "seeing and hearing they do not see and understand." In Matthew, when Jesus lists to the disciples the evil reasonings that come out of the heart, he lists murder (*phonoi*: Matt 15:19) first, rather than fornications (*porneiai*: Mark 7:21). The reason would seem to be related to the story-line of Matthew, which places the Pharisees' conspiring to destroy Jesus (Matt 12:14) and Herod's murder of John the Baptist (Matt 14:5) in a sequence that leads to this story in Matt 15:1–20. Mark, in contrast, places the Pharisees' decision to try to kill Jesus early in the story (Mark

that the "spoken" words of the scribes and Pharisees must be accepted as authoritative interpretations of the Torah of Moses.

[33] See John 12:40 (*noēsōsin tēi kardiai*); cf. Matt 16:9, 11; 24:15.

3:6), and Mark 6:30–8:21 is a context that develops the topos of the lack of understanding by the disciples. Again, for the Matthean story the issue is what comes out of the heart. Therefore, Jesus concludes his confrontation of his disciples with, "These [what come out of the heart] are what defile a person, but to eat with unwashed hands does not defile" (Matt 15:20).

In Matthew, then, the prophetic story-line features Jesus blessing his disciples but then facing a lack of understanding among them, which he confronts. But the real target of confrontational prophetic rhetorolect in Matthew remains the scribes and Pharisees. This builds to Jesus' long prophetic speech of woe to "scribes and Pharisees, hypocrites" in Matt 23:13-39. Chosen by God to proclaim judgment (Matt 12:18-21), Jesus confronts the scribes and Pharisees with neglecting the weightier matters of the law: justice, mercy, and faith (Matt 23:23). In Matthew, the story-line of Isaiah's speech moves from prophetic rhetorolect of promise to prophetic rhetorolect of indictment and woe. As Bernard Combrink has indicated, Matt 23:13-39 contains seven Woes.[34] Each Woe begins with a statement of the Result of a certain action, which is a Case against them. The argumentation is enthymematic: a statement supported by a reason, with either an unexpressed or expressed Rule hovering nearby. The opening Woe signals the topos of kingdom that is at stake in prophetic rhetorolect:

> *Result:* But woe to you, scribes and Pharisees, hypocrites!
> Case: For you lock people out of the kingdom of heaven. For you do not go in yourselves, and when others are going in, you stop them. (Matt 23:13-14)

As mentioned above, early Christian prophetic rhetorolect moves beyond the focus on a region of land with a particular boundary. Rather, the focus is on God's relation to believers who have received Torah wisdom from their ruler, imaged as a king, who promises blessings if the guidelines are followed and woes if they are violated. Jesus begins with a general indictment of scribes and Pharisees for stopping people from going into the kingdom of heaven, indeed "locking people out" and not even going in themselves. This is a severe judgment by Jesus, since in Matt 23:2 he has identified the scribes and Pharisees as the official, authoritative interpreters of Torah wisdom. Jesus' prophetic discourse in Matt 23:13-39 presupposes the wisdom with which the chapter begins, where Jesus teaches the crowds and disciples that the scribes and Pharisees teach authoritatively but do not practice what

[34] H.J. Bernard Combrink, "Shame on the Hypocritical Leaders in the Church: A Socio-Rhetorical Interpretation of the Reproaches in Matthew 23," in *Fabrics of Discourse: Essays in Honor of Vernon K. Robbins* (ed. D.B. Gowler, L.G. Bloomquist, and D.F. Watson; Harrisburg: Trinity Press International, 2003) 1-35.

they teach. Doing what one teaches is a fundamental requirement of teacher-philosophers in the Mediterranean world,[35] and the ideological texture of Matt 23:1-7[36] features Jesus teaching that the scribes and Pharisees violate this principle. As is characteristic of early Christian prophetic rhetorolect, the "location" for thinking about this is God's kingdom. The issue in this context is leaders who either allow people or prevent people from entering into God's kingdom and who either enter it or do not enter it themselves. One sees, then, that while the focus is not on a region of land with specific boundaries, this early Christian prophetic rhetorolect presupposes that God's kingdom has boundaries that people either can or cannot cross to enter it. The conceptualization still focuses on a particular region with specific boundaries. It is as though the kingdom of heaven has a boundary with a gate or door which people either are or are not allowed to enter.

The second Woe focuses on mission activity to gain members for the kingdom of heaven:

> *Result:* Woe to you, scribes and Pharisees, hypocrites!
> *Case:* For you cross sea and land to make a single convert, and you make the new convert twice as much a child of hell as yourselves. (Matt 23:15)

This Woe identifies the boundaries of the kingdom through a juxtaposition of "the kingdom of the heavens" (23:13) and Gehenna. There are, then, two alternative spaces: "the eschatological space of God's salvation that is promised through Jesus to Israel"[37] and "the place of fiery judgment."[38] This Woe accuses the scribes and Pharisees of traveling in mission across sea and land to make a proselyte, namely to find a Gentile who will accept immersion and circumcision to become a full member of the chosen people of Israel.[39] The Woe introduces an identity for the convert on the basis of the spatial imagery. Instead of making the person a child of the kingdom of the heavens, they make the person a child of Gehenna. Again, the spatial conceptualization of prophetic rhetorolect is strong. The goal is to have an identity in relation to a kingdom over which God rules; the alternative is to have an identity with a space of fiery punishment.

[35] Wayne H. Merritt, *In Word and Deed: Moral Integrity in Paul* (ESEC 2; New York: Peter Lang, 1993).

[36] Combrink, "Shame," 34-35.

[37] Ulrich Luz, *Matthew 21–28* (Hermeneia; Minneapolis: Fortress Press, 2005) 117.

[38] Duane F. Watson, "Gehenna," ABD 2:927.

[39] Luz, *Matthew 21–28*, 118; for the debate whether Jews actively recruited converts during the 1st century, see the references in Luz, 117, n. 45.

The third Woe begins with a repetitive texture focused on blindness and ends with the imagery of the throne of God and the one seated on the throne:

> *Result:* Woe to you, blind guides,
> *Case:* you who say, "Whoever swears by the sanctuary is bound by nothing, but whoever swears by the gold of the sanctuary is bound by the oath."
> *Result:* 17 You blind fools!
> *Rule:* For which is greater, the gold or the sanctuary that has made the gold sacred?
> *Case:* 18 And you say, "Whoever swears by the altar is bound by nothing, but whoever swears by the gift that is on the altar is bound by the oath."
> *Result:* 19 How blind you are!
> *Rule:* For which is greater, the gift or the altar that makes the gift sacred?
> *Rule:* 20 So whoever swears by the altar, swears by it and by everything on it; 21 and whoever swears by the sanctuary, swears by it and by the one who dwells in it; 22 and whoever swears by heaven, swears by the throne of God and by the one who is seated upon it. (Matt 23:16-22)

This Woe begins with the prophetic topos of blindness. Jesus does not accuse the scribes and Pharisees of not hearing properly or of having a heart that is hardened. Rather, his accusation builds on the lines the Matthean narrator recited in Matt 13:14-15 from Isa 6:9-10: "you will indeed look, but never perceive ... and they have indeed shut their eyes; so that they might not look with their eyes ..." The Matthean story intensified this "not seeing" by featuring Jesus defining the Pharisees and scribes as "blind guides of the blind" after reciting LXX Isa 29:13 against them in Matt 15:8-9. The third Woe, then, continues the topos of being "blind guides." This is a focus on leaders characteristic of early Christian prophetic rhetorolect. Leaders have special responsibilities within God's kingdom.[40] Being blind is an illness to be healed, so Jesus heals many blind people in Matthew.[41] Being a blind guide of people is the exact opposite of prophets of Israel. Prophets are "seeing" guides (seers) who confront people so they may see, understand, repent, and live according to the light of God's wisdom.

After Jesus confronts the scribes and Pharisees about their role as blind guides, he addresses them as blind "fools" (Matt 25:17). Being a fool, of course, is a central topos of wisdom rhetorolect, opposite of being wise. Immediately after this accusation, Jesus introduces a pro-

[40] Combrink, "Shame," 21.
[41] Matt 9:27-31; 11:5; 12:22; 15:30-31; 20:29-34; 21:14.

verbial Rule in the form of a question: "For which is greater, the gold or the sanctuary that has made the gold sacred?" (Matt 25:17). The addition of a Rule to the Result and the Case gives the enthymematic reasoning a full syllogistic form, blending reasoning characteristic of wisdom rhetorolect with confrontation characteristic of prophetic rhetorolect. The third Woe ends with a series of Rules in Matt 23:19-22 characteristic of wisdom reasoning as it begins with a question and ends with a series of informative statements. The reasoning moves dramatically to a central topos of prophetic rhetorolect at the end, when it focuses on heaven, the throne of God, and the one seated on the throne (Matt 23:22). God seated on his throne in heaven is a central image of kingship associated with early Christian prophetic rhetorolect and God's kingdom. As the Woe addresses the making of oaths by the sanctuary, the gold of the sanctuary, and the altar, it gradually progresses to the issue of making an oath "by heaven" and "by the throne of God and by the one seated upon it." Thus, the wisdom reasoning blends with prophetic reasoning, moving the focus beyond sanctuary, gold of the sanctuary, and altar to God's kingship in heaven and the necessity of remaining true to that kingship.

The fourth Woe stays with the problem of blind leadership as it moves to specific matters of Torah practice:

> *Result:* [23] Woe to you, scribes and Pharisees, hypocrites!
> *Case:* For you tithe mint, dill, and cummin, and have neglected the weightier matters of the law: justice and mercy and faith.
> *Rule:* It is these you ought to have practiced without neglecting the others.
> *Result:* [24] You blind guides!
> *Case:* You strain out a gnat but swallow a camel! (Matt 23:23-24)

The accusation is that the scribes and Pharisees focus so intently on tithing the smallest herbs, not to mention grain or other larger items, that they neglect the greater requirements of Torah, which are justice, mercy, and faith. This interpretation is, of course, central to prophetic discourse, "as can be seen in Isa 1:17; Jer 22:3; Hos 6:6; Zech 7:9-10; and Mic 6:8,"[42] which we have discussed earlier. The emphasis here is on the deeds of the scribes and Pharisees themselves, as well as the way their actions are guides to others. Leaders must lead by example as well as by specific teaching. As the prophetic accusation indicts the scribes and Pharisees for neglecting central features of Torah wisdom, it reaches its conclusion in one more identification of them as "blind guides" (Matt 23:24). Blind leadership is the issue throughout the third and fourth Woes as they progress through the issue of making oaths to the tithing practices of the scribes and Pharisees themselves.

[42] Combrink, "Shame," 22.

The fifth Woe contains the final accusation of blindness, "You blind Pharisee!", as it addresses purity rituals concerning cups and plates:

> *Result:* 25 Woe to you, scribes and Pharisees, hypocrites!
> *Case:* For you clean the outside of the cup and of the plate, but inside they are full of greed and self-indulgence.
> *Result:* 26 You blind Pharisee!
> *Rule:* First clean the inside of the cup, so that the outside also may become clean. (Matt 23:25-26)

This Woe moves from the Result to the Case in a manner that introduces a Result of blindness that invites a proverbial Rule that is to be considered a proper guide to action and understanding.[43] The key for understanding the Rule at the end of the Woe lies in the argument about washing in Matt 15:17-20. Neither defilement nor cleanness can result from what goes inside a person. Rather, what proceeds out from the heart in speech and action defiles or makes clean. The problem, Jesus says in the fifth Woe, is that the scribes and Pharisees are filled inside with greed and self-indulgence (cf. Matt 15:19). If, instead, they were filled with justice, mercy, and faith (Matt 23:23), then the outside would become clean!

The sixth Woe continues the topic of inside and outside:

> *Result:* 27 Woe to you, scribes and Pharisees, hypocrites!
> *Case:* For you are like whitewashed tombs, which on the outside look beautiful, but inside they are full of the bones of the dead and of all kinds of filth.
> *Result:* 28 So you also on the outside look righteous to others, but inside you are full of hypocrisy and lawlessness. (Matt 23:27-28)

In this instance, the argument is by analogy. The accusation is that scribes and Pharisees are like whitewashed tombs that look beautiful on the outside but are full of dead bones and filth on the inside. It is possible that this Woe refers especially to the whitewashing of tombs during Passover to help people from inadvertently making themselves impure by stepping on graves. There is, however, no word or phrase that implies a reference to activity during Passover.[44] The argument juxtaposes "righteousness" with "hypocrisy and lawlessness." Thus, again it high-

[43] In contrast to the display of Matt 23:26 in Combrink, "Shame," 22, I think the display should be:

> *Result:* You blind Pharisee!
> [*Unexpressed Case:* For you try to clean the inside by cleaning the outside of the cup and the plate.]
> *Rule:* First clean the inside of the cup, so that the outside also may become clean.

[44] Combrink, "Shame," 23; W.D. Davies and D.C. Allison, *A Critical and Exegetical Commentary on the Gospel according to Matthew* (3 vols.; ICC; Edinburgh: T. & T. Chark, 1988-97) 3:302.

lights central topoi of prophetic rhetorolect, the necessity to do whatever one does in a manner that enacts righteousness, which is perceived in prophetic discourse to be the key to living a life according to Torah.

The seventh Woe introduces a progression from a discussion of tombs to the topos of the deaths of prophets, coordinating a reference to the prophets with a reference to "the righteous":

> *Result:* [29] Woe to you, scribes and Pharisees, hypocrites!
> *Case:* For you build the tombs of the prophets and decorate the graves of the righteous, [30] and you say, "If we had lived in the days of our ancestors, we would not have taken part with them in shedding the blood of the prophets."
> *Rule:* [31] Thus you testify against yourselves that you are descendants of those who murdered the prophets.
> *Result:* [32] Fill up, then, the measure of your ancestors. [33] You snakes, you brood of vipers!
> *Rule:* How can you escape being sentenced to hell?
> *Result/Rule:* [34] Therefore, "Behold, I send you prophets, sages, and scribes,
> *Case:* some of whom you will kill and crucify, and some you will flog in your synagogues and pursue from town to town,
> *Result:* [35] so that upon you may come all the righteous blood shed on earth, from the blood of righteous Abel to the blood of Zechariah son of Barachiah, whom you murdered between the sanctuary and the altar." [36] Truly I tell you, all this will come upon this generation. (Matt 23:29-36)

In the seventh Woe, Jesus' confrontational speech speaks specifically of prophets, and when it does it evokes an implicit story-line that reaches into activities people are performing in the context of Jesus' lifetime. The story-line begins "in the days of our ancestors" when people shed the blood of the prophets (Matt 23:30). This beginning continues into the present and future as God continually sends "prophets, sages, and scribes" and the scribes and Pharisees will continue to kill and crucify some of them, and flog some of them in their synagogues and pursue them from town to town (Matt 23:34). As Jesus' discourse evokes this general prophetic story-line, it evokes a specific story-line from the shedding of "the blood of righteous Abel to the blood of Zechariah son of Barachiah, whom [they] murdered between the sanctuary and the altar" (Matt 23:35). Again we see how a major effect of early Christian prophetic rhetorolect is the evocation of story-lines that move from the past through the story of Jesus into the present and the future. It is impossible to reach an accurate decision about the identity of "Zechariah son of Barachiah."[45] Rather, as Ulrich Luz proposes:

> Abel is the first murdered righteous person in the canon of the Old Testament (Gen 4:8-10), Zechariah ben Jehoiada (2 Chr 24:20-22) the last. Defining the temporal limits thus serves to encompass the entire biblical time.[46]

The *Protevangelium of James*, written during the 2nd century CE, ends by narrating the death of Zechariah, father of John the Baptist. The final words of Zechariah accuse the agents of Herod who kill him while he is "serving at the altar" (23:1) with "shedding the innocent blood at the entrance to the temple of the Lord" (23:8).[47] Whatever the exact history of variant readings and/or errors may be, early Christian prophetic rhetorolect focusing on suffering, persecution, and death of God's prophets continued to have a rhetorical effect of nurturing new stories and story-lines beyond the first century CE.

The absence of a rhetorical awareness of prophetic rhetorolect in NT writings is nowhere more evident than in commentary on Matt 23:34 and the final unit of Jesus' speech in 23:35-39. Focusing on literary-historical issues concerning the origin of the saying and the possibility of a *Sophia* Christology in Matthew, most modern commentators do not even raise the possibility that the prophetic speech attributed to Jesus in these units will be perceived by the hearer/reader as Jesus reciting words of God to the scribes and Pharisees.[48] One of the rhetorical characteristics of prophetic literature, and perhaps nowhere more than in Isaiah and Jeremiah, is the difficulty of identifying the "voice" of the prophet in relation to the voice of God as the oracles unfold.[49] Luke 11:49, which is the Q parallel to Matt 23:34, attributes the saying to the wisdom of God and identifies those sent as "prophets and apostles." Matthew has revised the saying so it focuses on "prophets, sages, and scribes." When the speech attributed to Jesus says, "Therefore" (*dia touto*), the Matthean hearer/reader would understand the following words to be prophetic speech attributed to God, "Behold, I myself send to you prophets and sages and scribes, some of whom you will kill and crucify, and some of whom you will flog in your synagogues and

[45] See Luz, *Matthew 21–28*, 154-55.

[46] Ibid., 155.

[47] Ronald F. Hock, *The Infancy Gospels of James and Thomas* (The Scholars Bible 2; Santa Rosa, CA: Polebridge Press, 1995) 75.

[48] Cf. Luz, *Matthew 21–28*, 152-54.

[49] Klaus Baltzer, *Deutero-Isaiah: A Commentary on Isaiah 40–55* (trans. Margaret Kohl; ed. P. Machinist; Hermeneia; Minneapolis; Fortress Press, 2001); William L. Holladay, *Jeremiah 1* (2 vols.; ed. P.D. Hanson; Hermeneia; Philadelphia/Minneapolis: Fortress Press, 1986, 1989).

pursue from city to city" (23:34). Rather than simply assigning 23:34 to the voice of Jesus,[50] interpreters should be debating whether only 23:34 or all of 23:34-35 would be perceived as the voice of God in Matthew's narration. It is noticeable that many modern translations omit the "Behold" (*idou*) at the beginning, which is characteristic of the speech of God or a messenger of God, from the saying.[51] There is a possibility that the hearer/reader would perceive "so that" (*hopōs*) at the beginning of 23:35 to make a transition back to Jesus' own voice with a threat of judgment before the confirmation of the judgment that begins with "Truly, I say to you" (23:36). This would give the *hopōs* a function parallel to the *hōste* at the beginning of Matt 23:31. It is likely, following the evidence of Migaku Sato,[52] that the hearer/reader would perceive the voice of God to continue through the threat of judgment in Matt 23:35. Jesus' prophetic voice, then, reasserts itself on its own terms in 23:36 with an authoritative confirmation of God's speech.

Prior to Jesus' introduction of the prophetic voice of God in Matt 23:34-35, Jesus' prophetic speech launches an accusation that the scribes and Pharisees "testify against themselves that [they] are descendants of those who murdered the prophets" (Matt 23:31). Again this is Matthean revision of tradition, this time in a manner that attributes speech to the voice of the scribes and Pharisees. This leads to Jesus' naming of scribes and Pharisees as a "brood of vipers" in Matt 23:33, which is reminiscent of John the Baptist's opening confrontation of Pharisees and Sadducees in Matt 3:7. In Matthew, then, prophetic rhetorolect produces a blending of John's and Jesus' prophetic announcement of the kingdom of heaven (Matt 3:2; 4:7), confrontation of the Pharisees as a brood of vipers (3:7; 23:33), and arrest, death, and burial (14:3-12; 26:47–27:66) accompanied by reports of their being raised from the dead (14:2; 28:1-10). In addition, the language Jesus uses to condemn the scribes and Pharisees for "filling up the measure of [their] ancestors" who shed "righteous blood" on the earth (23:32-33) blends into the Matthean story-line as Judas says, "I have sinned by betraying innocent blood" (27:4), as Pilate publicly announces that he is "innocent of [Jesus'] blood" and as all the people say, "His blood be on us and on our children!" (27:24-25). Early Christian prophetic rhetorolect in Matthew blends the story-line of suffering-dying prophets deeply into the Gospel story of John the Baptist and Jesus in a manner that has introduced serious problems of anti-Judaism throughout

[50] Cf. Luz, *Matthew 21–28*, 152-54.

[51] Cf. NRSV, RSV, NIV, ESV; contrast NASV, ASV, KJV.

[52] Migaku Sato, "Q und Prophetie" (diss., Berne, 1984) 147-48, 154, n. 132; see Luz, *Matthew 21–28*, 150.

the centuries.[53] In Matthew, the dynamic creation of early Christian prophetic stories and story-lines produces the devastating pronouncement by Jesus: "Fill up, then, the measure of your ancestors, you snakes, you brood of vipers! How can you escape being sentenced to hell?" (Matt 23:32-33). Perhaps nowhere is the rhetorical nature of early Christian prophetic rhetorolect more evident than in the speech attributed to Jesus. As the story-lines of John the Baptist, Judas, Pilate, the people of Jerusalem, the righteous Abel, the righteous Zechariah, and Jesus blend together, early Christian prophetic rhetorolect attributes speech to Jesus that condemns the scribes and Pharisees with the voice of God and his own voice in the powerful tradition of God's judgmental voice to Israel in the Hebrew prophets. "Truly I tell you," Jesus says, "all this will come upon this generation" (Matt 23:36). Jesus' argumentative prophetic rhetorolect reaches its penultimate conclusion in Jesus' authoritative confirmation of God's pronouncement of judgment on the scribes and Pharisees, again in a manner that creates anti-Jewish ideology that remains alive in a significant amount of Christian discourse at the beginning of the twenty-first century.

The final unit in Jesus' speech confronts Jerusalem as a city that kills the prophets and ends up with a desolate house:

> *Case:* [37]Jerusalem, Jerusalem, the city that kills the prophets and stones those who are sent to it!
> *Rule:* "How often have I desired to gather your children together as a hen gathers her brood under her wings,
> *Case:* and you were not willing!"
> *Result:* [38]Behold, your house is left to you, desolate.
> *Case:* [39]For I tell you, you will not see me again until you say, "Blessed is the one who comes in the name of the Lord." (Matt 23:37-39)

In the final unit, Jesus personifies Jerusalem as the one who kills the prophets and confronts her in the style of a classic prophetic lament.[54] Again the voice of God is present in: "How often have I desired to gather your children together as a hen gathers her brood under her wings, and you were not willing!" (23:37). In the tradition of God's first person voice throughout Israel's history (cf. Exod 19:4; Jer 9:11; 13:27; 15:5-9, 11-14, 19-21),[55] Jesus speaks God's voice against Jerusalem in Matt 23:37. God yearns to gather those who have been chosen under God's wings, but stubbornness prevails. The final Matthean unit exhibits the dynamic development of the early Christian prophetic story-line that existed in embryonic form in 1 Thessalonians. A story of

[53] See Luz, *Matthew 21–28*, 156-57, 164-65.

[54] Craig S. Keener, *A Commentary on the Gospel of Matthew* (Grand Rapids/Cambridge, UK: Eerdmans, 1999) 557.

[55] Also cf. Jer 25:4; 26:4-6, 15.

the prophets of Israel being killed by the people to whom they were sent now reverberates through a story that extends all the way from the righteous Abel to Jesus' death in Jerusalem. Again in the great tradition of Israel's prophets, Jesus' voice personifies the city of Jerusalem. As the voice of Jesus accuses Jerusalem of killing all the prophets, this early Christian prophetic rhetorolect presents Jesus evoking his own story-line as he speaks prophetically to scribes, Pharisees, and Jerusalem itself. In Matthew, Jesus himself is killed as a prophet in Jerusalem. In this instance, we see how early Christian prophetic rhetorolect not only creates new story-lines but it also blends these story-lines into the inner fabric of its newly created judgmental pronouncements. In Matthew, the traditional story-line of Jerusalem and the prophets of Israel blends with the story-line of the prophet Jesus and his fate in Jerusalem in a manner that blends the prophetic voice of God with the prophetic voice of Jesus. After reciting words of God to Jerusalem in a prophetic mode, Jesus says, "See, your house is left to you, desolate. For I tell you, you will not see me again until you say, "Blessed is the one who comes in the name of the Lord" (Matt 23:39). Again, willingness or stubbornness is the issue. Only with willingness to welcome its prophets can Jerusalem become a house filled with its children, namely the children of Israel. Jesus ends by confronting Jerusalem with seeing rather than being blind. "Look! Your house is left to you like a desert (*erēmos*)," an image echoing Tob 14:4.[56] A house filled with the children of Israel will include a house containing prophets who call the people to be filled with justice, mercy, faith (Matt 23:23), purity (23:26); righteousness; and lawfulness (23:28, 29, 35) on the inside. When this happens, words of blessing and praise of God will come out of the mouths of the people in Jerusalem (cf. Matt 15:18–19), and they will welcome the one who comes in the name of the Lord (23:39).

In Matthew, then, early Christian prophetic rhetorolect becomes a highly detailed mode of story-telling and argumentation. On the one hand, it produces multiple, dynamically blended story-lines that extend from the death of Abel at the beginning of the story-line of Israel to the death of Jesus in Jerusalem. On the other hand, it creates judgmental argumentation on the lips of Jesus that moves beyond modes of wisdom argumentation into authoritative modes of testimony and pronouncement that reverberate with the voice of God and God's prophets throughout the history of Israel. Direct address and name calling drive the argumentation forward, creating ever new contexts and stories for God's ongoing challenge to people who strive to live the ways of God. With early Christian prophetic rhetorolect, the story of Jesus begins to become the story of all people on earth. The story begins

[56] Scholars also regularly refer to 1 Kgs 9:7–8; Jer 12:7; 22:5.

with the death of Abel, after God's creation of the world and the expulsion of Adam and Eve from the Garden of Eden. The story continues throughout all the time of Israel into minute details about people in the story of Jesus from the time of Herod the king (Matt 2:1) to chief priests, Pharisees, and Pilate who secure the tomb of Jesus until the third day after his death (Matt 27:62-63). Prophetic rhetorolect, then, is not simply argumentative. It creates story-lines that repeatedly interrupt themselves with external voices that verify their inner divine authority. In Matthew, the story of Jesus not only fulfills the statements by God's prophets in the past. Rather, the fullness of the prophets dwells in multiple stories and story-lines that keep Jesus with the hearer/reader "always, to the end of the age" (Matt 23:20).

The Prophetic Story-Line of the Gospel of Luke 4:14–19:27

Prophetic rhetorolect played a dynamic role in the creation of yet additional early Christian story-lines in the Gospel of Luke.[57] There is not space here to rehearse or rework the dynamic role of prophetic rhetorolect in Luke 1–4:13,[58] beyond calling attention to the explicit references to prophecy in the narrational introduction to the speech of John the Baptist's father Zechariah (1:70) and his reference to his son as "prophet of the Most High" in 1:76. Nor will we add to our earlier comments on the presentation of John the Baptist in Luke 3:1-20 above or analyze the particular nuances of the Lukan account of the devil's testing of Jesus in the wilderness (4:1-13).[59] Rather, we will begin with Jesus' return to Galilee after the devil "departed from him until an opportune time" (4:13).

Luke 4:16–7:35: Enacting a Story-Line Announced by Isaiah

When Jesus comes to his home synagogue in Nazareth after his encounter with the devil, his recitation of Old Testament scripture confronts God's people with special responsibilities for the poor, the captive, the blind, and the oppressed (Isa 61:1-2; 58:6). This introduces Isaianic prophetic topoi into Luke's story-line in a manner that differs from the Isaianic prophetic topoi in Matt 12:

[57] See Aune, *Prophecy*, 155-59.

[58] See analysis of priestly rhetorolect in Vernon K. Robbins, "Bodies and Politics in Luke 1–2 and Sirach 44–50: Men, Women, and Boys," *Scriptura* 90 (2005) 724-838.

[59] See V.K. Robbins, "The Socio-Rhetorical Role of Old Testament Scripture in Luke 4–19," in *Z Noveho Zakona / From the New Testament: Sbornik k narozeninam Prof. ThDr. Zdenka Sazavy* (ed. Hana Tonzarova and Petr Melmuk; Prague: Vydala Cirkev ceskoslovenska husitska, 2001) 81-85 [81-93]. Online: http://www.religion.emory.edu/faculty/robbins/pdfs/SazavaLukePubPgs.pdf

Luke 4:16-19	Matthew 12:18-21
(1) God anointed Jesus for a particular set of tasks;	(1) God chose Jesus for a particular task, since God was pleased with him;
(2) *God anointed Jesus with the Spirit of the Lord;*	(2) *God put God's Spirit upon Jesus* to empower him for his difficult task;
(3) Jesus will bring good news to the *poor*;	(3) Jesus will proclaim *justice* to the *nations (Gentiles)*;
(3) Jesus has been sent to proclaim release to the captives;	(4) Jesus will not wrangle or cry aloud, nor will anyone hear his voice in the streets;
(4) Jesus has been sent to proclaim *recovery of sight to the blind*;	(5) he will not break a bruised reed or quench a bruised reed until he brings *justice* to victory;
(5) Jesus has been sent to let the oppressed go free;	(6) in his name the *nations (Gentiles)* will hope.
(6) Jesus has been sent to proclaim the year of the Lord's favor.	

The Lukan story amplifies some, but not all, of the prophetic topoi in 4:16-30 either in Luke or Acts. The Sermon on the Plain begins with prophetic blessing upon the poor (6:20-23). Then Jesus confronts the rich with prophetic woes (6:20-25).[60] This prophetic rhetorolect sets the stage for wisdom rhetorolect about lending without expecting anything in return (6:34-35) and about giving that brings abundance (6:38). Later, Jesus presents highly developed wisdom argumentation about wealth, possessions, and unfailing treasure in heaven (12:13-34).[61] This wisdom rhetorolect continues as Jesus tells a parable and presents an argument about managing wealth (16:1-13), but immediately after it Luke contains a prophetic exchange between Jesus and Pharisees:

> The Pharisees, who were lovers of money, heard all this, and they ridiculed him. [15] So he said to them,
> *Case:* "You are those who justify yourselves (*hoi dikaiountes heautous*) in the sight of others;
> *Rule:* but God knows your hearts (*tas kardias hymōn*);
> *Result:* for what is prized by human beings is an abomination (*bdelygma*) in the sight of God. (Luke 16:14-15)

Prophetic topoi are evident as Jesus accuses the Pharisees of justifying themselves, rather than living a life according to justice; informs them that God "knows" their "hearts," and describes what is prized by human beings as "an abomination in the sight of God."

Wisdom rhetorolect continues with a parable about a rich man who refuses to respond to the hunger and misery of a poor man covered

[60] For the nature of the enthymematic argumentation in the Lukan beatitudes and woes, see V.K. Robbins, "Pragmatic Relations as a Criterion for Authentic Sayings," *Forum* 1.3 (1985) 35-63; http://www.religion.emory.edu/faculty/robbins/Pdfs/Pragmatic.pdf

[61] Abraham J. Malherbe, "The Christianization of a *Topos* (Luke 12:13-34)," *NovT* 38 (1996) 123-35.

with sores (16:19-31). Jesus ends the parable with reference to listening to Moses and the prophets, and asserts that people who do not listen to them will never be convinced to repent, even if someone rises from the dead (16:31). Later, Lukan narration presents a story in the mode of wisdom rhetorolect of a rich ruler who comes to Jesus wanting to inherit eternal life (18:18-25). Afterwards, Jesus discusses possessions and "following" with his disciples, again in a mode of wisdom rhetorolect (18:26-30). Then the topos of wealth is developed further in a mode of early Christian wisdom rhetorolect in the story of Zaccheus (19:1-10), the parable of the ten pounds (19:11-27), a discussion of taxes (20:20-26), and the widow's offering (21:1-4). Thus, as is widely known, the Gospel of Luke develops the topos of poverty and wealth both with narrative description and with argumentative discourse. The regular procedure is for Lukan narration to develop the topic in a mode of wisdom rhetorolect, with only occasional progressions into prophetic confrontation.

The Greek Septuagint adds "regaining of sight to the blind" to the Hebrew of Isa 61:1, and Luke 4:18 and 7:22 include this topos.[62] Blindness, as we have seen above, is a natural bridge topos from prophetic to miracle rhetorolect, since there is a longing and sometimes a promise in prophetic rhetorolect for blindness to be healed so people will repent and participate fully in God's kingdom. It will be necessary to develop the healing of blindness further in the chapter on miracle rhetorolect, but at the moment we must notice that the narrator gives a summary that includes Jesus' giving of sight to the blind in 7:21, a blind person receives his sight in a narrative account in 18:35-41, and there is an emphasis on Paul's being healed of blindness in Acts 9:17-18; 22:11-13. Thus, among the topoi in Luke 4:18-19, only "bringing good news to the poor" is fully developed both in prophetic and wisdom narration and argumentation. In addition, there is a movement from prophetic to miracle rhetorolect as Jesus gives sight to blind people in accordance with the emphasis in LXX Isa 61:1, as well as in Isa 35:5.

It is not clear who all the "oppressed" may be who are "set free" (Luke 4:18) in the Lukan story. Surprisingly, the Gospel of Luke shows no development of the topos of release of captives, except Barabbas who is released rather than Jesus (22:18-25). However in Acts, the second volume of the Lukan account, release from prison becomes a prominent feature in the narrative (Acts 12:6-10, 17; 16:23-27).[63]

[62] Both the Hebrew and the Greek Septuagint of Isa 35:5 refer to "the eyes of the blind" being opened in a context of healing the deaf, lame and dumb.

[63] John B. Weaver, *Plots of Epiphany: Prison-Escape in Acts of the Apostles* (BZNW 131; Berlin/New York: Walter de Gruyter, 2004).

After Jesus' recitation of Isa 61:1-2; 58:6, some people respond critically to Jesus and Jesus confronts the people of Nazareth by reciting an abbreviated account of Elijah's beneficial visit to the widow of Zarephath in Sidon (Luke 4:25-26; cf. 1 Kgs 17:1-16) and Elisha's cleansing of the leprosy of Naaman the Syrian (Luke 4:27; cf. 2 Kgs 5:1-14). Again we see how prophetic rhetorolect evokes story-lines in early Christian discourse. Jesus' reference to Elijah in Luke 4:25-26 implicitly evokes Elijah's bringing of unlimited food to the widow's household, and this topos may be enacted in Jesus' feeding of 5,000 in 9:10-17.[64] Elijah's raising of the son of the widow from death to life in 1 Kgs 17:17-24 is not only enacted in the narrative of the raising of a twelve year old girl (8:40-42, 49-56),[65] but more explicitly in the raising of the son of the widow of Nain earlier in the story (7:11-16). Jesus' reference to Elisha's cleansing of a leper in Luke 4:27 is embellished in Luke not only with the cleansing of the leper in 5:12-14, but also with the cleansing of ten lepers, one of whom is a Samaritan, in 17:11-19. Thus, in Luke many new story-lines not in Mark or Matthew emerge in early Christian discourse.

In Luke 7:22, Jesus restates the program of activity that Luke 4:16-30 introduced to the story. Jesus' restatement places the receiving of sight by the blind in a place of emphasis at the beginning and the poor having the good news preached to them at a place of emphasis at the end of the list.[66] In between, the Lukan Jesus lists: (a) the lame walk; (b) the lepers are cleansed; (c) the deaf hear; and (d) the dead are raised (7:22). This evokes a story-line of healing in Luke that, again, bridges from prophetic rhetorolect to wisdom rhetorolect focused on the poor to miracle rhetorolect focused on healing in early Christian discourse. Throughout both Luke and Acts there is no narrative of a deaf person receiving hearing. In turn, there is no story in Luke about a lame man being healed so he can walk, but Acts contains two such stories (3:1-10; 14:8-10) and a summary referring to many lame who were cured (8:7).

It is clear, then, that the Lukan story develops many of the prophetic topoi of Luke 4:16-30 in narrative enactment and in wisdom and prophetic argumentation. Preaching good news to the poor, giving sight to the blind, healing lepers, and raising the dead become a programmatic part of Jesus' activity as the story unfolds. Release from prison and healing the lame are developed in Acts rather than the Gospel of Luke. Healing the deaf so they may hear is not enacted explicitly in a story or in an argument in Luke or Acts. Rather, at the end of Acts

[64] Notice Jesus' healing of people also in the context (Luke 9:11), similar to the range of benefits Elijah brought to the widow.

[65] Present also in Mark 5:21-24, 35-43//Matt 9:18-19, 23-26.

[66] Regularly, the emphatic positions are at the beginning and the end.

Paul asserts that "this people" "will never understand," because "their ears are hard of hearing" (Acts 28:27). It will be necessary to discuss this further in the section on Acts below.

Luke 7:36–14:24: Eating with Pharisees

After Jesus' restatement of his activity in Luke 7:22, he dines three times in a house of a Pharisee (7:36-50; 11:35-54; 14:1-24). At these dinners, Jesus introduces topoi either from Deuteronomy or from Isaiah in a manner that transforms traditional religious issues into prophetic confrontation that focuses on social responsibility. Jesus' activity in these settings reconfigures emphases at the beginning of the prophetic book of Isaiah. In Isa 1:16-17, the prophet summarizes what the LORD says to the people with an emphasis on social responsibility:

> [16] Wash yourselves; make yourselves clean, [17] learn to do good; seek justice, rescue the oppressed, defend the orphan, plead for the widow.

Characteristic of his speech at the three dinners in a house of a Pharisee in Luke 7:36–14:35, Jesus confronts people in 7:36-50 in a manner similar to Isaiah's confrontation of the people of Israel. In each instance, Jesus criticizes a focus on traditional religious issues that bypasses social responsibilities. In the house of Simon the Pharisee, Simon raises a traditional religious issue concerning the association of a holy prophet with a sinner. In 7:41-43, Jesus transforms the religious issue into an issue of "forgiving a financial debt" (7:41). Jesus' conversation with Simon blends mild prophetic confrontation with wisdom rhetorolect as Jesus confronts him about forgiveness:

> Then turning towards the woman, he said to Simon, "Do you see this woman?
> *Case:* I entered your house; you gave me no water for my feet, but she has bathed my feet with her tears and dried them with her hair. [45] You gave me no kiss, but from the time I came in she has not stopped kissing my feet. [46] You did not anoint my head with oil, but she has anointed my feet with ointment.
> *Result:* [47] Therefore, I tell you, her sins, which were many, have been forgiven; hence she has shown great love.
> *Rule:* But the one to whom little is forgiven, loves little." (Luke 7:44-47)

From the perspective of the Lukan presentation of Jesus, forgiveness concerns wealth, which is an issue that goes back to Deut 6, which Jesus recited to the devil in response to two of the tests (Luke 4:5-12). When Jesus asks Simon which debtor loves the creditor more (Luke 7:42), he has evoked the topos of "love" central to Deut 6–7 and early Christian wisdom rhetorolect. The topos of love is not only present in Deut 6:5 (the Shema) but continues into Deut 7, where the assertion is made that the Lord brought Israel out of Egypt, "because the Lord loved you" (7:8) and the Lord is "the faithful God who maintains covenant loyalty with those who love him" (7:9). In Deut 7:13, the assertion is made that if you heed the Lord's ordinances, "he will love you, bless you, and multiply you." He will bless the fruit of your womb, ground, grain, wine, oil, cattle, and flock. Indeed, "you shall be the most blessed of people" (7:14), including the removal of illness and disease (7:15). When Jesus responds to Simon, he is developing a topos that the testing of Jesus by the devil implicitly introduced into Lukan discourse. When Jesus' response to Simon turns Simon's concerns about "sinfulness" into the topic of "love," which concerns God's giving of abundant wealth, the woman's willingness to anoint Jesus' feet with expensive ointment (Luke 7:37-38, 46) emerges as a paradigmatic instance of "love" (7:47). The woman, Jesus asserts, knows how to enact love by multiple acts of generosity with oil, an item which is actually mentioned as one of God's "blessings" in abundance to Israel in Deut 7:13. Forgiveness of debts and generosity with one's possessions must have priority as one begins to discuss sinfulness and forgiveness. Thus, wisdom rhetorolect dominates at the first dinner, with only a mild blending of prophetic rhetorolect in Jesus' confrontation of Simon about his absence of actions of hospitality.

At the second dinner (Luke 11:37-52), where the Pharisee who invited Jesus is amazed that Jesus did not wash his hands before he ate (11:38), Jesus embeds Torah wisdom topoi in woes that progress toward accusations that evoke the story-line of the death of prophets. Jesus' initial response to the Pharisee's amazement focuses on washing cups and dishes (11:39-41). In the context of an emphasis on the inside in relation to the outside, Jesus accuses Pharisees of being "full of greed and wickedness" on the inside and presents a solution of "giving for alms those things that are within." As Jesus speaks, he confronts Pharisees in the plural as "fools (*aphrones*)!" (11:40), which is first and foremost a topos of wisdom rhetorolect. The next step in Jesus' confrontation of the Pharisee contains three woes, two introduced with "Woe to you Pharisees!" (11:42-43) and a final one simply with "Woe to you!" (11:44). In the first woe, Jesus embeds the topoi of judgment (*krisis*) and love (*agapē*) of God in an accusation that their preoccupation with tithing mint, rue, and herbs of all kinds leads to their neglect of the truly important things (11:42). The important things Jesus is talking about stand at the center of Torah wisdom. In the second woe, Jesus accuses them of loving (*agapate*) the highest seat of honor in the synagogues and greetings in the marketplaces (11:43). Again, the topos of "love" reverberates with requirements characteristic of Torah wisdom. Jesus' accusation is that their love is misplaced; it should be focused on God first and then on loving one's neighbor as oneself. In the third woe, Jesus says they are like unmarked graves over which people walk without realizing it (11:44). Again the issue concerns Torah wisdom, in this instance becoming unclean through contact with something associated with corpses. The first three woes, then, confront Pharisees with Torah wisdom without bringing central topoi of early Christian prophetic rhetorolect into the foreground.

After the first three woes, a lawyer (*nomikos*) addresses Jesus as "Teacher" and tells Jesus that he is insulting (*hybrizeis*) them as well as the Pharisees. Again, the focus of attention is on Torah wisdom, which Lukan narration perceives to be the domain of lawyers. At this point, Jesus confronts the lawyer with three woes in which an elaborated woe in the middle introduces the story-line focused on the death of prophets. In this instance the opening and closing woes begin with "Woe to you lawyers!" and the middle woe begins simply with "Woe to you!"

In the opening woe, Jesus accuses lawyers of loading people down with burdens too heavy to bear and not lifting a finger to ease the burden (11:46). This topic moves beyond Torah wisdom toward prophetic rhetorolect, because it concerns the social responsibilities of lawyers. Jesus does not accuse lawyers of not following Torah wisdom themselves, like he accuses the Pharisees in the first three woes (11:42-44), but he accuses them of working with Torah wisdom in a manner that creates an unacceptable burden for other people in society. This is a central issue in prophetic rhetorolect, which concerns the responsibilities of leaders to make society work in a just manner.

In the middle woe, Jesus accuses lawyers of building the tombs of prophets their ancestors killed (11:47). This leads to an elaborate prophetic argument that recites a statement of "the Wisdom of God" as authoritative testimony:

> *Result:* Woe to you!
> *Case:* For you build the tombs of the prophets whom your ancestors killed.
> *Result:* 48 So you are witnesses and approve of the deeds of your ancestors;
> *Case:* for they killed them, and you build their tombs.
> *Rule:* 49 Therefore also the Wisdom of God said, "I will send them prophets and apostles, some of whom they will kill and persecute",
> *Result:* 50 so that this generation may be charged with the blood of all the prophets shed since the foundation of the world, 51 from the blood of Abel to the blood of Zechariah, who perished between the altar and the sanctuary.
> *Result:* Yes, I tell you, it will be charged against this generation. (Luke 11:47-51)

In this unit, the opening woe and the closing assertion that "this generation" will be held accountable for its actions provide a clear prophetic dynamic for the reasoning internal to it. Beginning with direct address characteristic of prophetic confrontation, Jesus first pronounces woe on lawyers. Continuing with language of direct confrontation, Jesus supports his statement of condemnation with a story-line from their ancestors who killed the prophets to lawyers who currently honor the prophets of the past by building tombs for them. One would think such activity should be praised. The implication evidently is that "The only prophet you honor is a dead prophet."[67] When Jesus recites words of the Wisdom of God as authoritative testimony for his accusation, he names "prophets and apostles" as those who are sent and subsequently killed or persecuted.[68] This evokes a story-line from the prophets of the past through Jesus and his apostles after him. In other words, the story-lines of both early Christian wisdom and early Christian prophetic rhetolect blend to introduce a story-line that will continue beyond the Gospel of Luke through the Acts of the Apostles. The Lukan wording of Jesus' appeal to the story-line from Abel to Zechariah does not contain "son of Barachiah" (Matt 23:35). This leaves the possibility open for a story-line that reaches beyond the OT canon to the death of Zechariah the father of John the Baptist "between the altar and the sanctuary," of which a version can be found in *Prot. Jas.* 23:1. In addition, Jesus' statement describes the story-line reaching back into "the foundation of the world." In this statement, one gets a fleeting glimpse of that sphere of "non-time" that will come into the foreground in early Christian precreation rhetorolect. Is it possible that the killing of prophets and apostles is part of the inner fabric of the world itself? Early Christian prophetic rhetorolect provides a bridge to precreation rhetorolect as its story-line reaches back into God's predefinition of God's wisdom. Could it be possible that the wisdom and power of God actually looks to "worldly wisdom" like something foolish, weak, and shameful?[69] Could this not be a reasonable explanation of why people have killed God's prophets and apostles since the foundation of the world? Jesus ends his confrontation of the lawyers with a prophetic assertion that this generation truly will be held accountable for the way it responds to the prophets and apostles the Wisdom of God sends to them.

The third and final woe in Jesus' speech is very short:

> *Result:* Woe to you lawyers!
> *Case:* For you have taken away the key of knowledge; you did not enter yourselves, and you hindered those who were entering.' (Luke 11:52)

[67] T.W. Manson, *The Sayings of Jesus: As Recorded in the Gospels according to St. Matthew and St. Luke* (London: SCM, 1949) 101; cf. Darrell L. Bock, *Luke 9:51–24:53* (BECNT; Grand Rapids, MI: Baker Books, 1996) 1120.

[68] Contrast "prophets, sages, and scribes" in Matt 23:34.

[69] See the discussion of 1 Cor 2:6-10 above, pp. 206-10.

Jesus' speech ends with an accusation related to the beginning of Jesus' prophetic confrontation of scribes and Pharisees in Matt 23:13-39. Instead of asserting that the lawyers "lock people out of the kingdom of the heavens" (Matt 23:13), the Lukan version presents Jesus accusing lawyers of "taking away the key of knowledge (*gnōseō*)." In this final assertion by Jesus to the lawyers, we recognize the topos of "knowing, remembering, and doing" that lies in Deut 8:2-5. Jesus' reference to the key of knowledge builds upon and expands topoi central to Deut 6–8. This means that Jesus' speech at the second dinner in the house of a Pharisee returns to wisdom rhetorolect at its conclusion. It is noticeable, indeed, that the Lukan speech never mentions "the kingdom of the heavens," like Matt 23:13, nor does it mention "the throne of God and the one who is seated on it" (Matt 23:22). In fact, throughout the Gospel of Luke prophetic rhetorolect regularly blends with wisdom rhetorolect, moving a prophetic confrontation into didactic sayings and parables. This contrasts significantly with Matthean prophetic rhetorolect, which regularly strengthens its accusations by referring to the fiery region of Gehenna[70] and the weeping and gnashing of teeth.[71] Instead of ending with an assertion that "their house is left to them desolate" (Matt 23:38), the Lukan Jesus ends with an assertion that the lawyers have not only taken away the key of knowledge that could open the Wisdom of God to the people of their time, but they have not entered into the Wisdom of God themselves and have hindered others from entering into it (Luke 11:49).

At Jesus' third and final dinner in the house of a ruling Pharisee, his actions begin with healing (14:2-4) in a manner that reconfigures Deut 7:15: "The LORD will turn away from you every illness." In Luke 14, the illness of dropsy is a symbol of greed, which is based on the insatiable thirst and hunger of a man with this disease.[72] When Jesus heals the dropsy, he is symbolically healing the illness of greed in the presence of people of wealth. As Jesus interprets the significance of what he has done, he addresses the topos of "honor," which is a widespread Mediterranean value, and introduces the well-known argumentative topos: "All who exalt themselves will be humbled, and those who humble themselves will be exalted" (Luke 14:11). Since the topos of humbling oneself and being exalted is central to Deut 8:3, 14-19, Jesus' speech is remaining in the domain of wisdom rhetorolect. Once the people of Israel receive all their wealth, they must not "exalt themselves" but "humble

[70] Cf. Matt 5:22, 29, 30; 10:28; 18:9; 23:15, 33; the only reference to Gehenna in Luke is 12:5.

[71] Cf. Matt 8:12; 13:42, 50; 22:13; 24:51; 25:30; the only reference to weeping and gnashing of teeth in Luke is 13:28.

[72] Willi Braun, *Feasting and Social Rhetoric in Luke 14* (SNTSMS 85; Cambridge: Cambridge University Press, 1995).

themselves" before God. This leads into the specific topoi of Isaiah concerning "the poor, the maimed, the lame, the blind" (Luke 14:13), which is a Lukan reconfiguration of Isa 61 and 35. Instead of confronting his host prophetically, however, Jesus explains "blessing" to him in a mode of wisdom rhetorolect: "And you will be blessed, because they cannot repay you, for you will be repaid at the resurrection of the righteous" (Luke 14:14). This is a reconfiguration and blending of assertions about blessing in Deut 7:13-14 and Isa 61:5-9. After this, Jesus responds to a man who says, "Blessed is he who shall eat bread in the kingdom of God!", with a parable that enacts the Lukan reconfiguration of Isaianic prophetic discourse that focuses on "the poor and maimed and blind and lame" (14:21). Jesus' speech ends with the master telling his slave, "Go out into the roads and lanes, and compel people to come in, so that my house will be filled. For I tell you, none of those who were invited will taste my dinner" (Luke 14:24). As Willi Braun has written, "the host appears to have become convinced, in the words of Marcus Aurelius, 'of need for reform and treatment of (his own) character.'[73] He has undergone a Lukan kind of conversion, notwithstanding the absence of technical conversion language (*metanoia, epistrophē* and derivatives) in the narrative."[74] Instead of prophetic confrontation that polarizes the relation between Jesus and his interlocutor, then, Jesus' prophetic rhetorolect blends so fully with wisdom rhetorolect that it persuades his host, a leader of the Pharisees, to enact the principles with which Jesus has confronted him.

Luke 14:1-24 presents the highpoint of Jesus' encounter of Pharisees with the Deuteronomic-Isaiah program of redemption that provides primary inner dynamics for the story-line of the Gospel of Luke. Jesus' statements at the third and final dinner in a Pharisee's house make it clear that "household" activity is "public" activity that must meet the test of justice and love, which combines emphases in Deuteronomy with emphases in Isaiah. Once again, then, we see a blending of wisdom and prophetic rhetorolect. In this instance, the blending produces severe reprimand but ends with a house full of people gathered from "the roads and lanes" (Luke 14:23), rather than a house that has been "left to you, desolate" (Matt 23:38). Lukan prophetic rhetorolect persistently blends prophetic topoi from Isaiah with Torah wisdom from Deuteronomy to produce a story-line designed to bring blessing rather than eternal judgment on the people of Israel and the followers of Jesus.

[73] *Meditations* 1:7.

[74] Braun, *Feasting and Social Rhetoric in Luke 14*, 127-28.

Luke 15: Seeking and Saving the Lost

When the Lukan story reaches Luke 15, another topos moves into the center: seeking and saving the lost. The sociorhetorical resource for this topos is Ezek 34, where God's word comes to the prophet in a context after the destruction of Jerusalem and its temple. After Jerusalem and the temple were destroyed, God's people were scattered throughout the world. In this context, one must not only heal, but one must seek, find, and save the lost who are scattered hither and yon across the face of the earth. The words of Ezek 34:11-12, 16, responding to the abuse of the people by the leaders of Israel (Ezek 34:3-10), present a challenge to Israel that moves one step beyond the program of Isaiah:

> [11] For thus says the LORD God: I myself will search for my sheep, and will seek them out. [12] As shepherds seek out their flocks when they are among their scattered sheep, so I will seek out my sheep. I will rescue them, from all the places to which they have been scattered on a day of clouds and thick darkness.... [16] I will seek the lost, and I will bring back the strayed, and I will bind up the injured, and I will strengthen the weak, but the fat and the strong I will destroy. I will feed them with justice.

Rather than reciting some portion of Ezek 34 to the Pharisees and scribes who were "grumbling" at Jesus' welcoming and eating with tax collectors and sinners (Luke 15:1-2), Jesus recites a parable that enacts the central topoi of Ezek 34. In a context where even one sheep is lost, a shepherd will leave the flock and seek it until he finds it (Luke 15:4). When he finds it, he will rejoice, because he has found the one who was lost (Luke 15:6). The setting for the parable (Luke 15:2) and the ending statement by Jesus (15:7) renew the topos of "sinfulness" in Jesus' first dinner in the house of a Pharisee (7:37, 39, 47-49). Still concerned with "sinfulness," the Pharisees and scribes grumble at Jesus' activity, this time at his acceptance of tax collectors and sinners rather than with one specific sinful woman. Occurring immediately after Luke 14, Jesus' description of the "one sinner who repents" evokes an image of a person who is "humble" rather than "exalted" (14:11). With the image of the "shepherd" seeking the lost one, a new topos emerges in the midst of the Deuteronomy-Isaiah program, and the primary sociorhetorical resource for this topos is Ezek 34.

After telling the parable of the shepherd with a hundred sheep, Jesus turns to a woman with only ten silver coins. Losing one of them, she lights a lamp, sweeps the house, and searches carefully until she finds it (15:8). At this point, she calls her friends and neighbors together to rejoice, since she has found the coin that was lost. Once again, then, Jesus introduces wealth, or the meagerness of wealth, as a topos. The woman exemplifies a person to whom wealth is not abundant. As she rejoices with others over the coin that was lost, she moves the topos of sinfulness (15:10) one step toward the issue of wealth, or the lack of it.

Luke 15:1-32 begins with the topos of property and the dividing of property among sons. In a context where the younger son "sins against heaven and his earthly father" (15:18, 21) by wasting all his possessions (15:13-14), he returns to his father. The result of the repentant return is the bestowal of gifts of wealth and celebration by the father. This story reconfigures the commands to Israel in Deut 6–8 through the topos of seeking and saving the lost in Ezek 34. The father embodies the attributes of a shepherd who will "rescue" (Ezek 34:12) and "feed" (34:13-14) the lost, "bring back the strayed and bind up the injured" (34:16) rather than simply "clothe himself" (34:3), while failing to "bring back the strayed" (34:4). The parable of the prodigal son, then, exhibits a father who embodies the attributes of the shepherd that God asks people to be in Ezek 34, rather than the attributes of the shepherds who abuse their people and fail to seek them out when they are lost. Once again, then, prophetic discourse gives rise to Lukan prophetic rhetorolect that blends dynamically with wisdom rhetorolect to present a story-line of redemptive confrontation.

Luke 16–19:27

Luke 16–18 elaborate, amplify, and integrate the topoi of Deuteronomy 6–8 and Isaiah in a context oriented toward the seeking and saving of the lost. Luke 16:1-8 focuses on a manager of money and follows with an elaboration that ends with the assertion that one cannot serve God and wealth (16:13). The topos of "serving God," we recall, is central to Deut 6 (cf. 6:13). The chapter continues with a description of the Pharisees as "lovers of money" (16:14), and when Jesus tells them that "God knows their hearts" (16:15), the story is developing a blend of topoi central to Deut 6–8 and prophetic discourse. The parable of the Rich man and Lazarus (16:19-31) ends with an appeal to "listen to Moses and the prophets" (16:31), the parable of the Widow and the Unjust judge features a God who will "grant justice to his chosen ones who cry out" (cf. Isa 1:17), and the parable of the Pharisee and the Tax Collector paradigmatically exhibits, as mentioned above, the principle from Deut 8:2-3 about the necessity to humble oneself (Luke 18:14). The story of the Rich ruler who came to Jesus, knowing the commandments (Luke 18:20; cf. Deut 6, 8), yet being unwilling to sell his possessions and give the money to the poor (Luke 18:22), sets the stage for a discussion of the relation of Jesus' followers to possessions (18:28-30). Throughout all of this, the Lukan story explores a blend of prophetic and wisdom topoi that focuses on how "those who are lost may be found" and how "those who have wealth" may learn to "seek and save the lost."

Luke 19:1-10 presents the climax of the section on seeking and saving the lost (15:1–19:10). Zaccheus, who is both rich (blessed by the standards of Israel) and a chief tax collector (lost to the house of Israel), welcomes Jesus into his house and explains that he gives half of his possessions to the poor and, if he defrauds anyone, he pays it back fourfold (19:8). When Jesus sees how this person, who is "lost" in the eyes of the Pharisees, embodies the attributes of a rich man who gives generously to the poor and corrects any injustice that occurs, Jesus pronounces him "a son of Abraham." In Jewish tradition, Abraham is the model of a wealthy man who remained generous all his life.[75] The story ends with Jesus' assertion that "the Son of man came to seek out and to save the lost" (19:10), recalling the topos he had introduced in the parable of the shepherd who, having lost one sheep, sought it until he found it (15:4). At this point in the story, the prophetic topos of seeking, finding, and saving the lost from Ezek 34 reaches its highpoint and conclusion before the transitional parable of the ten pounds that introduces the violent dynamics of the passion narrative in Luke 19:28–23:56.

Lukan narration continually blends prophetic rhetorolect with wisdom rhetorolect as its story-line unfolds. Prophetic discourse does not remain external to the narration of the story-line of the Gospel. Rather, prophetic topoi provide dynamics and principles that stories and speeches enact as the story-line unfolds. As the stories occur, wisdom topoi blend with prophetic topoi to create a story of redemptive confrontation. Only some of the stories end with bitter division between Jesus and his interlocutors. Instead, many of the stories and scenes depict reconciliation or even conversion to Jesus' point of view. All does not go well, since the story-line takes Jesus to his death and burial. At the end of the story, however, Jesus has risen from the dead, has spent forty days with his followers, and is taken into heaven while he is blessing those who worship him and return to Jerusalem with great joy (24:51-52). The prophetic story-line ends, then, in a manner related to Elijah's ascent into heaven at the end of his life. Early Christian prophetic rhetorolect generates its own specific emphases in its own way. In the process, however, biblical prophetic discourse plays a central role in helping to create a story-line that has the ability to function powerfully in the broader Mediterranean world.

[75] See, for instance, the *Testament of Abraham*.

The Prophetic Story-Line in the Acts of the Apostles

The rhetorical nature of the story-line in Acts is so complex that it is possible to address only a few aspects of its dynamics in this context.[76] Since we have given special attention to Isaianic prophetic rhetorolect in Mark, Matthew, and Luke, we will continue to follow the nature of Isaianic rhetoric in Acts. It is important to start, however, with a few basic observations about Acts in relation to prophets and prophecy. Acts refers to singular or plural prophets thirty-one times.[77] In addition, a form of the verb "to prophesy" occurs four times.[78] One of the occurrences of the plural noun for prophets occurs in a programmatic statement by Peter to Israelites at Solomon's Portico in the Jerusalem temple in Acts 3:17-18:

> [14] "But you rejected the Holy and Righteous One and asked to have a murderer given to you, [15] and you killed the Author of life, whom God raised from the dead... [17] And now, brothers, I know that you acted in ignorance, as did also your rulers. [18] In this way God fulfilled what he had foretold through the mouth of all the prophets, that his Messiah would suffer."

This statement by Peter evokes a suffering-dying story-line from the prophecies of the Israelite prophets to the Messiah Jesus. Rather than highlighting only the deaths of the prophets of Israel, as we have seen in certain contexts above, it blends both the prophecies and the deaths of the prophets. In addition, it moves the status of Jesus beyond the role of God's anointed prophet (Luke 4:18) to "the Anointed of God," namely God's Messiah (Acts 3:18).

We have seen above the centrality of the heart in early Christian prophetic rhetorolect. In Acts, an emphasis on "the mouth of the prophets" blends with the emphasis on the heart. Thus, in a context of twenty references to "the heart" in Acts,[79] there are twelve references to "the mouth"[80] that concern hearing and understanding messages from God. One of the important references to the mouth occurs in the passage just presented above: "In this way God fulfilled what he had

[76] See Todd C. Penner, *Praise of Christian Origins: Stephen and the Hellenists in Lukan Apologetic Historiography* (ESEC 10; Edinburgh: T. & T. Clark, 2004).

[77] Singular (14 times): Acts 2:16, 30; 3:22, 23; 7:37, 48, 52; 8:28, 30, 34; 13:6, 20; 21:10; 18:25; plural (17 times): Acts 3:18, 21, 24, 25; 7:42; 10:43; 11:27; 13:1, 15, 27, 40; 15:15, 32; 24:14; 26:22, 27; 28:23.

[78] Acts 2:17, 18; 19:6; 21:9.

[79] Acts 2:26, 37, 46; 4:32; 5:3, 4; 7:23, 39, 51, 54; 8:21, 22, 37; 11:23; 13:22; 14:17; 15:9; 16:14; 21:13; 28:27. In a number of these verses, modern translations use phrasing that omits "the heart" from the wording.

[80] Acts 1:16; 3:18, 21; 4:25; 8:32, 35; 10:34; 15:7; 18:14; 22:14; 23:2 (also 11:8, in which Peter says nothing profane or unclean has ever entered his mouth). It is remarkable how many modern translations use phrasing that omits "the mouth" from the wording.

foretold through the mouth of all the prophets..." (Acts 3:18). In turn, emphasis on the heart and the mouth is related to twenty-one references to "the word of the Lord/God" in Acts.[81] Most of these references participate in the early Christian prophetic rhetorolect in Acts. We will not, however, be able to discuss each instance in the context of this chapter.

As the opening chapters of Acts unfold, Peter and John are arrested, imprisoned (4:3), and put on trial for their preaching (4:3-12); but they are released when the temple hierarchy see the man whom they had cured standing beside them with nothing to say in opposition (4:14) and they are given an order to stop speaking or teaching in the name of Jesus (4:18). This is prophetic narration configured in terms of early Christian prophetic rhetorolect. After they are released, they report what had happened to their friends (4:23) and raise their voices to God in prayer (4:24-30). Then the narrator presents the following account:

> When they had prayed, the place in which they were gathered together was shaken; and they were all filled with the Holy Spirit and spoke the word of God with boldness. (Acts 4:31)

This is early Christian prophetic rhetorolect. It presents the story of the calling and empowering of Peter and the apostles by reconfiguring antecedent prophetic tradition. Peter and the apostles pray that the Lord, looking at the threats of the chief priests and elders, will give them the ability to speak the word of the Lord with all boldness (4:29). After their prayer, tremors in the earth exhibit the presence of the power of God,[82] they are filled with the Holy Spirit, and they speak the word of God with all boldness (4:31). Prophetic calling and empowerment by the Holy Spirit, then, continues beyond the story-line of John the Baptist (Luke 1:15) and Jesus (Luke 3:22; 4:18) to the story-line of Peter and the apostles in Acts. This is the beginning of twenty-one repetitive occurrences of "the word of God/the Lord" in Acts 4—19.[83] As the early Christian prophetic story-line moves from the Israelite prophets through John the Baptist and Jesus to Peter and the apostles, the apostles must be willing to speak the word of the Lord with all boldness. As they do, "the word of the Lord/God" becomes a dynamic presence among the followers of Jesus.[84]

After a series of events in Acts including the death of Ananias and Sapphira (5:1-11), the performance of many signs and wonders

[81] Word of God: Acts 4:31; 6:2, 7; 8:14; 11:1; 12:24; 13:5, 7, 46; 17:13; 18:11; word of the Lord: Acts 4:29; 8:25; 13:44, 48, 49; 15:35, 36; 16:32; 19:10, 20.

[82] Cf. Isa 6:4.

[83] See n. 81 above.

[84] Yun Lak Chung, "'The Word of God' in Luke-Acts: A Study in Lukan Theology," Ph.D. dissertation, Emory University, 1995.

through the apostles (5:12), and the bringing of many sick people to the apostles to be cured (5:15-16), the high priest arrests the apostles and puts them in public prison (5:17-18). After an angel of the Lord opens the prison doors and tells the apostles to go into the temple and tell "the whole message about this life," they do this (5:19-21). When the temple hierarchy have the apostles brought before the council the next day for their preaching in the temple, Peter and the apostles tell them, "We must obey God rather than any human authority" (5:29). Here we see inner reasoning central to early Christian prophetic rhetorolect on the lips of Peter and the early apostles. The apostles must do what God has told them to do. When the apostles tell their prophetic story, the temple hierarchy become so angry with their interpretation of the death of Jesus that they want to kill them (5:30-33). A Pharisee named Gamaliel, whom the narrator calls "a teacher of the law" (5:34), advises against it, using reasoning in accord with early Christian prophetic rhetorolect:

> So in the present case, I tell you, keep away from these men and let them alone; because if this plan or this undertaking is of human origin, it will fail; [39] but if it is of God, you will not be able to overthrow them – in that case you may even be found fighting against God! (Acts 5:38-39)

In Acts, the story of early Christianity is told as a story of God's actions through apostles. This conceptualization moves beyond the concept of the twelve being sent out "to proclaim the kingdom of God and to heal" (Luke 9:1-6) to a prophetic story of the early Christian apostles that continues the story-line of God and the prophets of Israel.[85] If God is guiding the speech and action of the apostles, then resisting the apostles is an act of resisting God!

In Acts 6–7 this Christianized prophetic story takes an additional step. In a context where the apostles appoint deacons to make the daily distribution of food to widows (6:1-6) so they themselves do not "neglect the word of God" (6:2), the number of disciples increases in Jerusalem as "the word of God continues to spread" (6:7). But conflict grows as well as the number of disciples. When members of some of the synagogues stir up "the people as well as the elders and the scribes" (6:12) against the deacon named Stephen, saying he speaks "blasphemous words against Moses and God" (6:11), Stephen is brought to trial before the high priest and the temple council. Stephen's defense to the high priest takes the form of retelling the story-line of Israel from Abraham (7:2) through David and Solomon (7:45-47) to the context

[85] Jacob Jervell, *Luke and the People of God: A New Look at Luke-Acts* (Minneapolis: Augsburg, 1972).

in which he is being tried in the context of the temple at Jerusalem. When Stephen's story reaches David and Solomon, he interrupts the story-line by reciting a portion of the prophet Isaiah:

> 46 David found favor with God and asked that he might find a dwelling-place for the house of Jacob. 47 But it was Solomon who built a house for him. 48 Yet the Most High does not dwell in houses made by human hands; as the prophet says,
> 49 "Heaven is my throne,
> and the earth is my footstool.
> What kind of house will you build for me, says the Lord,
> or what is the place of my rest?
> 50 Did not my hand make all these things?" (Isa 66:1-2)
> 51 You stiff-necked people, uncircumcised in heart and ears, you are for ever opposing the Holy Spirit, just as your ancestors used to do. 52 Which of the prophets did your ancestors not persecute? They killed those who foretold the coming of the Righteous One, and now you have become his betrayers and murderers. 53 You are the ones that received the law as ordained by angels, and yet you have not kept it. (Acts 7:46-53)

Stephen's recitation of Isa 66:1-2 does not simply assert that God will leave the city of Jerusalem desolate (Matt 23:38) or that a time will come when people of Jerusalem with "say to the mountains 'Fall on us'; and to the hills, 'Cover us'" (Luke 23:30). Rather, through Isaiah Stephen asserts that God's kingdom moves beyond a kingship focused on the human made temple of Jerusalem itself to God's kingship in heaven. This happens through the "reconfigured prophetic story" of the death of God's earthly Messiah-King, which is the means by which God makes Jesus "Lord and Messiah" in heaven (Acts 2:34-36). Once the voice of "the prophet" interrupts the story-line Stephen is telling (Acts 7:49-50), Stephen's voice flows directly into prophetic confrontation of the chief priest and temple council as "stiff-necked people, uncircumcised in heart and ears" (7:51). Stephen's prophetic voice evokes the story-line of early Christian prophetic rhetorolect from the prophets of Israel, whom "their ancestors" persecuted, and brings it up to date with recent events that brought Jesus' life to an end. According to Stephen's story-line, the high priest and council of the temple, to whom he is speaking, themselves became betrayers and murderers of "the Righteous One" whose coming the prophets had foretold (Acts 7:51-52). The situation is especially serious, Stephen asserts, since the high priest and the council are "the ones that received the law as ordained by angels" but did not keep it (Acts 7:53). This, we recognize, is central reasoning and accusation in prophetic discourse. By having Stephen tell this story in a manner that moves directly into prophetic confrontation, Acts 7 makes this prophetic reasoning and confrontational argumentation internal to the early Christian story-line of Jesus' followers after Jesus' death, burial, resurrection, and ascension into heaven.

It is noticeable that Stephen's prophetic rhetorolect claims that both the heart and the ears of the high priest and the council need to be circumcised (7:51). We have seen the centrality of the heart in our discussions of prophetic rhetorolect in Mark, Matthew, and Luke. In Acts, the necessity for hearing the word of God from "the mouth" of the prophets and apostles becomes a central topos in relation to the heart. The problem with the heart of the chief priest and council is clearly stated in Acts 7:54, although it is not evident from many modern English translations. According to the narrator, "When [the chief priest and council] heard these things, they became enraged in their hearts and ground their teeth at Stephen" (7:54). The special prophetic aspect of narration in Acts regularly emerges from what happens in the hearts of people who hear "the word of God/the Lord" from the apostles. When the chief priest and council become enraged in their hearts against Stephen, according to early Christian prophetic rhetorolect their hearts stand in a long tradition of resistance to the word of God that has produced suffering, persecution, and even death of God's prophets. When the people hear Stephen, "filled with the Holy Spirit," say that he sees "the heavens opened and the Son of man standing at the right hand of God," they cover their ears, rush against him, drag him out of the city, and stone him (7:56-58). In the internal logic of the narration, this occurs because their "hearts and ears" are not circumcised (7:51). The absence of circumcision of their hearts and ears causes them to be "stiff-necked" (*sklērotrachēloi*). This is a continuation of the tradition in Jer 7:25-26:[86]

> [25] From the day that your ancestors came out of the land of Egypt until this day, I have persistently sent all my servants the prophets to them, day after day; [26] yet they did not listen to me, or pay attention, but they stiffened their necks (*esklērynan ton trachēlon*). They did worse than their ancestors did. (Jer 7:25-26)

It is also closely related to Isa 48:3-4:

> The former things I declared long ago, they went out from my mouth (*stomatos*) and I have made them known … I know that you are hard (*sklēros*) and your neck (*trachēlos*) is an iron sinew…. (Isa 48:3-4)

In the story of Stephen's death, early Christian prophetic rhetorolect moves decisively beyond the story of Jesus' death in Jerusalem to the followers of Jesus. When Stephen's prophetic speech accuses the people of being in need of circumcision of their "heart and ears" (7:51), and this

[86] Cf. Jer 17:23; 19:15; Isa 48:3-4; Exod 33:3, 5; 34:9; Deut 9:6, 13; Prov 29:1.

speech brings his death at the hands of his hearers, early Christian prophetic rhetorolect becomes internal not only to the preaching of the followers of Jesus in Acts but also to their actions in relation to other people and the potential end of their lives in the service of God's word.

As the prophetic story-line continues in Acts, the word of God spreads to Samaria. When the people of Samaria "accept the word of God," the apostles at Jerusalem send Peter and John to them and the people in Samaria "receive the Holy Spirit" (Acts 8:14-17). Here we see the other side of early Christian prophetic rhetorolect in Acts, namely the ability to accept God's word in one's heart and the gift of the Holy Spirit as an indication of this openness. When Simon wants to buy the power to have the Holy Spirit come on anyone upon whom he lays his hands, Peter identifies his monetary approach to the Holy Spirit as a problem with "his heart." Since Simon's "heart is not right before God" (8:21), Peter asserts, he must pray to the Lord and have, if possible, the intent of his heart be forgiven (8:22: *aphethēsetai*). This is a recontextualization and reconfiguration of Isa 6:9-10 as it is recited in Mark 4:12. The issue is if Simon can "turn and it may be forgiven (*aphethēi*)" to him (Isa 6:10; Mark 4:12). Early Christian prophetic rhetorolect in Acts presents a story-line in which certain people's hearts are unable to be forgiven and set right with God. Others, in contrast, are able to respond, which leads to the next story in Acts.

After Peter and John speak the word of the Lord in Samaria, they return to Jerusalem (8:25). An angel of the Lord tells Philip, however, to go down from Jerusalem to Gaza (8:26). There Philip comes upon an Ethiopian eunuch sitting in his chariot, reading from the prophet Isaiah (8:28). In a prophetic mode of proclaiming the word of God, Philip "opens his mouth" and proclaims to the eunuch how the story in Isa 53:7-8 applies to the story of Jesus. The eunuch immediately accepts the message and asks Philip what is to prevent him from being baptized (8:35-36). Some manuscripts add an assertion by Philip that if the eunuch believes with his whole heart he may be baptized (8:37).[87] After the Holy Spirit snatches Philip away, like the spirit transports prophets of Israel to new places,[88] the eunuch goes on his way rejoicing (8:39). Instead of resisting in his heart or not having his heart right with God, the heart of the eunuch is moved to belief and rejoicing.

Luke features people explicitly reading from scripture in Luke 4 and in Acts 8. Jesus read from Isaiah at the beginning of his adult ministry, interpreting how God had anointed him to preach good news to the

[87] The addition is clearly later, containing language characteristic of the Gospel of John; but the addition is a natural expansion of the inner presupposition of the story from the perspective of early Christian prophetic rhetorolect.

[88] Cf. 1 Kgs 18:12; 2 Kgs 2:11, 16; Ezek 3:14; 11:1; Bel 1:34-36.

poor, proclaim recovering of sight to the blind, and proclaim the acceptable year of the Lord. We have discussed above how the Gospel of Luke creates a story-line in which Jesus enacts the topoi in the passage from Isaiah. In Acts 8, an Ethiopian eunuch reads a passage from Isaiah that interprets the end of Jesus' life. The passage evokes the story-line of God's prophets who suffer and die, interpreting his death as a humiliation that denied him justice as it took his life away from the earth.

After people in Samaria accept the word of God and the Ethiopian eunuch goes his way rejoicing, people of the nations (Gentiles) accept the word of God (10:34–11:1). The word of God continues to advance and gain adherents through the activity of Barnabas and Saul (12:24-25). When the Holy Spirit sends Barnabas and Saul to Seleucia, Cyprus, and Salamis, they "proclaim the word of God in the synagogues of the Jews" (13:5), and on the island of Paphos the proconsul requests to hear the word of God and believes as a result of the teaching about the Lord (13:7, 12).[89] When Paul and Barnabas preach in Antioch of Pisidia (13:16-41), and many Jews and devout converts to Judaism follow Paul and Barnabas (13:43), Paul and Barnabas encounter opposition from Jews in the synagogue on the next sabbath. In response, Paul and Barnabas boldly tell them:

> It was necessary that the word of God should be spoken first to you. Since you reject it and judge yourselves to be unworthy of eternal life, we are now turning to the Gentiles. [47]For so the Lord has commanded us, saying,
> "I have set you to be a light for the Gentiles,
> so that you may bring salvation to the ends of the earth." (Isa 49:6)
> [48] When the Gentiles heard this, they were glad and praised the word of the Lord; and as many as had been destined for eternal life became believers. [49] Thus the word of the Lord spread throughout the region. [50]But the Jews incited the devout women of high standing and the leading men of the city, and stirred up persecution against Paul and Barnabas, and drove them out of their region. [51] So they shook the dust off their feet in protest against them, and went to Iconium. [52] And the disciples were filled with joy and with the Holy Spirit. (Acts 13:46-52)

Early Christian prophetic rhetorolect in Acts presents the Isaiah passage about being "a light for the nations (Gentiles)" at a point where Jews in Antioch of Pisidia contradict what Paul and Barnabas preach. This is a continuation of the early Christian prophetic story-line from Simeon's words in Luke 2:32, and it is related to the Matthean recita-

[89] This story, as many in Acts, contains dynamic blending of miracle and prophetic rhetorolect, which will be the subject of a later chapter.

tion of Isa 9:1-2 in Matt 4:15-16.[90] As the word of the Lord spreads further, then, it spreads to the nations (Gentiles).

When disagreement emerges between "certain individuals from Judea" and Barnabas and Paul concerning the necessity for believers from the nations (Gentiles) to be circumcised according to the custom of Moses in order to be saved (Acts 15:1), Peter, Barnabas, and Paul meet with elders in Jerusalem to discuss the matter (15:6). When Peter makes an argument about God making no distinction between Jews and Gentile believers, he makes it on the following terms:

> [8] And God, who knows the human heart, testified to them by giving them the Holy Spirit, just as he did to us; [9] and in cleansing their hearts by faith he has made no distinction between them and us. (Acts 15:8-9)

The issue is the hearts of people which, as we have seen above, is a central topos of prophetic discourse. Acts moves the Christian prophetic reasoning in the Gospels about that which comes out of the heart into the center of the discussion about salvation coming to Gentile believers without being ritually circumcised according to the custom of Moses. If the inside is clean, then the outside also will become clean (Luke 11:40-41; Matt 23:26). The reasoning in Acts is developed in the discussion of clean and unclean in the story of Peter's acceptance of the conversion of Cornelius (Acts 10). When Peter is confronted with eating "all kinds of four-footed creatures and reptiles and birds of the air" (10:12), he asserts, "I have never eaten anything that is profane or unclean" (10:14). The voice from heaven, in turn, asserts, "What God has made clean, you must not call profane." Peter later explains to the people in Cornelius's household the procedure by which God cleanses people:

> All the prophets testify about him that everyone who believes in him receives forgiveness (*aphesin*) of sins through his name. (Acts 10:43)

One may wonder where this reasoning is "in all the prophets." The reasoning is closely related to the discussion of "unclean" (*akatharta*) and "sins" (*hamartiai*) in God's calling of Isaiah in Isa 6:1-10. The issue about being clean in prophetic discourse is not a matter of what one eats with one's mouth, but it is what God and humans do with the mouth (Isa 6:7), ears, eyes, and heart (Isa 6:10). God is the one who cleanses (Isa 6:7), and God cleanses through forgiveness (*aphethēi*: Isa 6:10 in the wording of Mark 4:12). Here, then, is a bridging between prophetic and priestly rhetorolect, which will be the subject of a later chapter. Nearby also is the topos of *pistis*, regularly translated "truth" in OT literature and "faith" in the NT. For example, Jer 5:3 asks: "O

[90] Cf. Luke 1:78-79.

Lord, do your eyes not look for *pistis*?"[91] Prophetic reasoning in Acts presupposes that the "cleansing of their hearts by faith (*tēi pistei*)" (Acts 15:9) is a sign that God has "circumcised their hearts." Accordingly, in Acts *pistis* is present with the Holy Spirit in people whose hearts have accepted the word of God (6:5; 11:24). Paul explains God's action further as he tells King Agrippa what the Lord Jesus told him when he confronted him on the road to Damascus:

> [17] I [Lord Jesus] will rescue you from your people and from the nations (Gentiles) – to whom I am sending you [18] to open their eyes so that they may turn (*epistrephai*) from darkness to light and from the power of Satan to God, so that they may receive forgiveness of sins [through God's action] and a place [which God has prepared] among those who are sanctified (*hēgiasmenois*) by faith (*pistis*) in me." (Acts 26:17-18)

The Lord Jesus will open the eyes of the nations (Gentiles) so their hearts are able to turn from darkness to light. This turning enables God to forgive their sins (cleanse their hearts) so they are able to enter the place God has prepared for those who have been sanctified by faith in the Lord Jesus (namely, by faith in his name). As Peter says in Acts 10:43: "All the prophets testify about him that everyone who believes in him receives forgiveness of sins through his name." Again, the topoi of "unclean," "sin," and "forgiveness" bridge to priestly rhetorolect and create a blend that will be discussed in more detail in the chapter on priestly rhetorolect.

Prophetic rhetorolect focused on the heart extends throughout Acts to the final scene, where Paul meets with Jews in Rome. The issue, as Acts formulates it, is if the Jews in Rome are able to hear, see, and understand:

> [23] After they [the Jews] had fixed a day to meet him [Paul], they came to him at his lodgings in great numbers. From morning until evening he explained the matter to them, testifying to the kingdom of God and trying to convince them about Jesus both from the law of Moses and from the prophets. [24] Some were convinced by what he had said, while others refused to believe. [25] So they disagreed with each other; and as they were leaving, Paul made one further statement: "The Holy Spirit was right in saying to your ancestors through the prophet Isaiah,
>
> [26] 'Go to this people and say,
> You will indeed listen, but never understand,
> and you will indeed look, but never perceive.
> [27] For this people's heart has grown dull,
> and their ears are hard of hearing,
> and they have shut their eyes;
> so that they might not look with their eyes,

[91] Cf. LXX Jer 7:28; 9:3; 39:40-41.

and listen with their ears,
and understand with their heart and turn –
and I would heal them.' (Isa 6:9-10)

28 Let it be known to you then that this salvation of God has been sent to the Gentiles; they will listen." (Acts 28:23-28)

Reciting Isa 6:9-10 in its complete form,[92] Paul speaks to Jews in Rome with a directness that imitates Jesus' way of speaking to Pharisees and scribes in Matt 15:7-9/Mark 7:6-7. The prophetic story-line in Acts ends with Paul reciting the same Isaiah passage to Jews in Rome that Mark presents Jesus as reciting to his disciples in the context of his teaching in parables (4:12) and as reconfiguring in response to his own disciples when they lack understanding (7:18; 8:17-18, 21). In turn, Matthew initially presents Jesus reciting this Isaiah passage at length to explain to his disciples how blessed they are (Matt 13:13-17) and to place a special blessing on disciples who become "scribes trained for the kingdom of heaven" (13:51-52). Later, however, Jesus uses speech that evokes the Isaiah passage when his disciples do not understand Jesus' teaching that what comes out of the heart defiles a person rather than that which goes into the mouth (Matt 15:16-20). The Gospel of Luke presents Jesus reciting an abbreviated version of Isa 6:9-10 only once, namely to his disciples to explain to them how people who are not disciples are unable to understand the nature of God's kingdom. Throughout the rest of Luke, there is no context in which disciples have such difficulty understanding things that Jesus speaks to them with words that evoke Isa 6:9-10. Rather, the full recitation of Isa 6:9-10 occurs in Luke's second volume, the Acts of the Apostles, and it occurs on the lips of Paul to Jews in Rome. Early Christian prophetic rhetorolect, then, extends the story-line of those who "looking do not perceive and hearing do not understand" (Luke 8:10) beyond the story of Jesus and his disciples to the story of Paul and Jews in far off Rome. Along the way, of course, Isa 49:6 plays a key role in authorizing Paul's turning to the nations (Gentiles) in a context of rejection by Jews (Acts 13:47). In Acts, Paul's mission to the nations (Gentiles) brings a full recitation of Isa 6:9-10 against Jews at the very end of the story-line. This means that early Christian literature presents an Isaianic prophetic story-line that spans all the way from "the beginnings of the Gospel" (Mark 1:2-3) to the final scene of the mission of followers of Jesus in Rome (Acts 28:24-28).

92 Cf. Matt 13:14-15.

The Isaiah Prophetic Story-Line in the Gospel of John: Prophetic Rhetorolect Blends with Precreation Rhetorolect

Early Christian prophetic rhetorolect receives new dimensions in the Gospel of John, because it functions in a context where precreation rhetorolect is dominant. In other words, precreation rhetorolect is the host and prophetic rhetorolect is the guest, in contrast to Matthew, Mark, and Luke, where prophetic rhetorolect is a prominent host rhetorolect in many sections of the story.[93] A later chapter will present detailed information about early Christian precreation rhetorolect,[94] but it is important in this present chapter to make a few observations about the nature of early Christian prophetic rhetorolect in the context of Johannine precreation rhetorolect.

When the Christian gospel story-line begins with "the Word of God" before the creation of the world (John 1:1-2), rather than with a word of God to Isaiah (Mark 1:1-3), things change concerning the way the word of God comes into the human realm. In John, God's prophet *par excellence* is Jesus, rather than Isaiah or any other prophet, since Jesus is "the" word of God to the world. One of the characteristics of Johannine vocabulary in a context where Jesus himself is the full, prophetic word of God to people on earth, is the occurrence of the verb "to prophesy" only once, when the narrator refers to the speech of the high priest Caiaphas, who "prophesied that Jesus was about to die for the nation, and not for the nation only, but to gather into one the dispersed children of God" (John 11:51-52). In John, the high priest, rather than the voice of Moses, David, or Isaiah introduces a prophetic story-line about the effect of Jesus' death that moves the high priest, Pharisees, and the temple council into action: they plan from that day on to put Jesus to death (11:53). If, in the context of precreation rhetorolect only the high priest prophesies, what about other people in the Johannine gospel story?

In contrast to an emphasis that John the Baptist is a prophet, the opening chapter of the Gospel of John presents the Baptist repetitively denying that he is "the prophet," along with other names or titles associated with prophetic rhetorolect. The progressive texture of his statements moves through assertions that he is "not the Messiah," "not Elijah," and "not the prophet" to an assertion that he is "the voice of one crying in the wilderness ... as the prophet Isaiah said" (John 1:20-23). In other words, the Baptist is "the voice" rather than "a prophet." Interestingly enough, Isaiah has the status of the prophet who said the Baptist would be "the voice," but there is no statement suggesting that the Baptist is a prophet in a line of prophets from Isaiah to the time of

[93] I am indebted to Priscilla Geisterfer for the language of host and guest rhetorolect.

[94] See the basic discussion of precreation rhetorolect in Chapter 3, p. 111.

Jesus. What is the significance of the Baptist's strong negative assertions about himself in terms of early Christian rhetorolects?

It is very important to notice that Johannine narration begins the unit about the Baptist with the following statements:

> This is the testimony (*martyria*) given by John when the Jews sent priests and Levites from Jerusalem to ask him, "Who are you?" [20] He confessed (*hōmologēsen*) and did not deny (*ērnēsato*) it, but confessed (*hōmologēsen*), "I am not the Messiah." (John 1:19-20)

The narration that creates the context for the Baptist's speech introduces topoi that are central to precreation rhetorolect: testimony, confession, and denial. One might think that the Baptist's statements are an act of denial. The narrator clarifies that they were not an act of denial (*ērnēsato*) but a "testimony" (*martyria*), an act of "confession" (*hōmologēsen*). The presence of these words in the story of John the Baptist exhibit the function of people in the Gospel of John who would ordinarily be considered participants in an ongoing prophetic story-line. Instead of functioning as prophets, people who function positively alongside the Johannine Jesus "witness," "testify," or "give testimony" to Jesus as the light of the world.

The pervasiveness of the language of witness and testimony throughout the Gospel of John is more difficult to see in English translations that in Greek, since the root *martyr-* is present in all the words translated either as testimony or witness. Forms of the verb to testify, to give testimony, to witness, or to give witness (*martyreō*) occur forty-two times,[95] and forms of the noun testimony or witness (*martyria*) occur fourteen times.[96] The first verses that speak of John the Baptist in the Gospel of John (1:6-9) introduce the language and function of the Baptist in relation to Jesus, who existed with God before the creation of the world:

> There was a man sent from God, whose name was John. [7] He came as a witness (*martyrian*) to testify (*martyrēsēi*) to the light, so that all might believe through him. [8] He himself was not the light, but he came to testify (*martyrēsēi*) to the light. [9] The true light, which enlightens everyone, was coming into the world. (John 1:6-9)

Instead of asserting that "The one who is more powerful than me is coming after me; I am not worthy to stoop down and untie the thong of his sandals. I have baptized you with water; but he will baptize you

[95] John 1:7, 8, 15, 32, 34; 2:25; 3:11, 26, 28, 32; 4:39, 44; 5:31, 32, 33, 36, 37, 39; 7:7; 8:13, 14, 18; 10:25; 12:17; 13:21; 15:16, 27; 18:23, 37; 19:35; 21:24.

[96] John 1:7, 19; 3:11, 32, 33; 5:31, 32, 34, 36; 8:13, 14, 17; 19:35; 21:24. Forms of the verb to confess occur three times in John 1:20; 9:22; 12:42, and forms of the verb to deny occur four times in John 1:20; 13:38; 18:25, 27.

with the Holy Spirit" (Mark 1:7-8), the Johannine narrator says, "The true light, which enlightens everyone, was coming into the world" (John 1:9). This is a shift from prophetic rhetorolect to precreation rhetorolect. Jesus is not "the coming one" in a prophetic story-line but the Word of God who will come into flesh after being with God before creation. John 1:3-4 narrates this precreation story-line as it tells how the word was "light" (cf. Gen 1:3) who caused all things to come into being in the world, and what came into being through him as word/light was life (cf. Gen 1:11-30). In a context where "the one who is coming" is word/life/light, the "prophetic" role of the Baptist is to witness or give testimony to the light, not to be a prophet who brings a word of God to humans. In early Christian discourse, then, prophetic rhetorolect becomes "testimony" rhetorolect in a context of precreation rhetorolect. People who would ordinarily speak in the tradition of the prophets now speak in an early Christian tradition of people who give testimony or witness that should lead others "to believe"[97] in the story-line that begins with Jesus as "the Word" with God before the time of creation. Only some time after the beginning of the world, then, did "God's Word" come to humans through the man Jesus who came and dwelt in flesh on earth (John 1:14).

As we have seen above, the precreation rhetorolect in the Gospel of John does not completely suppress language about the prophets. Indeed, the term prophet occurs fourteen times in singular or plural in John.[98] The first three occurrences are in the account of the Baptist's testimony that he is not "the prophet" (1:21, 23, 25). The fourth occurrence is on the lips of Philip when he tells Nathanael:

> We have found him about whom Moses in the law and also the prophets wrote, Jesus son of Joseph from Nazareth. (John 1:45)

The narrator nowhere tells where the law or the prophets give a description that Philip considers to apply to Jesus. Scholars regularly consider the passage about "the prophet like Moses" described in Deut 18:15-18 to be the description in the law.[99] This may also be the understanding when the people respond after they see Jesus' feeding of

[97] Forms of the verb "to believe" (*pisteuō*) occur 86 times in John: 1:7, 12, 51; 2:11, 22, 23, 24; 3:12, 15, 16, 18, 36; 4:21, 39, 41, 42, 48, 50, 53; 5:24, 38, 44, 46, 47; 6:29, 30, 35, 36, 40, 47, 64, 69; 7:5, 31, 38, 39, 48; 8:24, 30, 31, 45, 46; 9:18, 35, 36, 38; 10:25, 26, 37, 38, 42; 11:15, 25, 26, 27, 40, 42, 45, 48; 12:11, 36, 37, 38, 39, 42, 44, 46; 13:19; 14:1, 10, 11(2), 12, 29; 16:9, 27, 30, 31; 17:8, 20, 21; 19:35; 20:8, 25, 29, 31. There are no occurrences of the noun "faith" (*pistis*) in John. This will be a topic of discussion in the chapter on precreation rhetorolect.

[98] John 1:21, 23, 25, 46; 4:19, 44; 6:14, 45; 7:40, 52; 8:52, 53; 9:17; 12:38.

[99] Wayne A. Meeks, *The Prophet-King: Moses Traditions and the Johannine Christology* (NovTSup 14; Leiden: E.J. Brill, 1967); Raymond E. Brown, *The Gospel according to John I–XII* (AB 29; New York: Doubleday, 1966) 86.

5,000 people with "This is indeed the prophet who is to come into the world" (6:14).[100] It is not clear from Johannine narration where the prophets wrote about Jesus son of Joseph from Nazareth.[101]

It is not possible to discuss here all the references to the prophets or "the prophet" in the Gospel of John, because they are significantly disparate in character and have a complex relation to Johannine topoi and emphases. The reason for this complexity is the subservient role prophetic rhetorolect plays to precreation rhetorolect in the Gospel of John. Since precreation rhetorolect is the cultural frame that provides the dynamic emergent structures for the discourse in the Gospel of John, the other rhetorolects play various roles, which in many instances are new roles in early Christian discourse.

In relation to Isaianic prophetic rhetorolect in early Christian discourse, there is a very interesting feature in the Gospel of John. After Jesus raises Lazarus from death (John 11), enters Jerusalem for the Passover Festival (John 12:12-15), and tells Philip, Andrew, and some Greeks attending the festival that "The hour has come for the Son of Man to be glorified" (12:20-23), Johaninne narration recites two passages from the prophet Isaiah to interpret the problem that:

> Although he had performed so many signs in their presence, they did not believe (*episteuon*) in him. (John 12:37)

The two passages from the prophet Isaiah unfold as follows:

> 38 This was to fulfil the word spoken by the prophet Isaiah:
> "Lord, who has believed (*episteusen*) our message,
> and to whom has the arm of the Lord been revealed?" (Isa 53:1)[102]
> 39 And so they could not believe (*pisteuein*), because Isaiah also said,
> 40 "He has blinded their eyes
> and hardened their heart (*kardian*),
> so that they might not look with their eyes,
> and understand with their heart (*kardiāi*) and turn –
> and I would heal them." (Isa 6:10)
> 41 Isaiah said this because he saw his glory (*doxan*) and spoke about him.
> 42 Nevertheless many, even of the authorities, believed (*episteusan*) in him. But because of the Pharisees they did not confess (*hōmologoun*) it, for fear that they would be put out of the synagogue; 43 for they loved human glory (*tēn doxan tōn anthrōpōn*) more than the glory that comes from God (*tēn doxan tou theou*).

[100] Brown, *John I–XIII*, 234; D. Moody Smith, Jr., *John* (ANTC; Nashville: Abingdon Press, 1999) 149.

[101] Brown wonders, in ibid., 86, if this could be a reference to Malachi's prediction of the coming of Elijah.

[102] Cf. Rom 10:16.

Placed in the context of a story-line informed by early Christian precreation rhetorolect, there are new aspects to the ears, eyes, hearts, and mouths of people. The issue in the Gospel of John is hearing the message, seeing the signs, believing, and confessing the glory of God. The topos of the heart, so central to prophetic rhetorolect, does not appear in John until the narrator's recitation of Isa 6:9-10 in John 12:40. After this, some new functions for the heart appear in Gospel discourse.[103] Not only does the devil "put it into the heart of Judas son of Simon Iscariot to betray him" (John 13:2), a concept close at hand in Luke 22:3, but Jesus "nurtures" the hearts of his disciples in special ways. First, Jesus tells them, "Do not let your hearts be troubled (*tarassethō*). Believe (*pisteuete*) in God, believe (*pisteuete*) also in me" (John 14:1). Belief in both God and Jesus will remove "troubledness" from their heart. Second, Jesus teaches his disciples:

> [27] Peace (*eirēnē*) I leave with you; my peace (*eirēnēn*) I give to you. I do not give to you as the world gives. Do not let your hearts be troubled (*tarassethō*), and do not let them be afraid (*deilatō*). (John 14:27)

Instead of giving "grace," "justification," food, clothing, shelter, or something else, Jesus gives "peace" to his disciples.[104] Peace is a gift designed to remove fear that is cowardly or timid. Third, Jesus is willing to bring sorrow (*lypē*) to the hearts of his disciples when the source of that sorrow is truth (*alētheia*; John 16:6-7). Truth is a special topos of precreation rhetorolect,[105] designed to clarify the difference between darkness,[106] which is the nature of the world, and light,[107] which is the nature of God and Jesus. Fourth, Jesus promises a future when joy will fill their hearts:

> So you have pain (*lypēn*) now; but I will see you again, and your heart (*kardia*) will rejoice, and no one will take your joy from you. (John 16:22)

Through Jesus' speech, precreation rhetorolect reconfigures the prophetic topos of "blessedness" into the precreation topos of "peace" that removes "troubledness" from the heart and brings joy. The issue is not simply stubbornness, hard-heartedness, or being stiff-necked versus

[103] There are six references to the heart (*kardia*) in John: 12:40; 13:2; 14:1, 27; 16:6, 22.

[104] Cf. Rom 14:17: For the kingdom of God is not food and drink but righteousness and peace and joy in the Holy Spirit.

[105] Truth (*alētheia*) occurs 21 times in John: 1:14, 17; 2:21; 4:23, 24; 5:33; 8:32, 40, 44(2), 45, 46; 14:6, 17; 15:26; 16:7, 13; 17:17, 19; 18:37, 38.

[106] Darkness (*skotia*) occurs in John 1:5; 6:17; 8:12; 12:35, 46; 20:1; also see 3:19. See also 1 Jn 1:5; 2:8, 9, 11.

[107] Light (*phōs*): John 1:4, 5, 7, 8, 9; 3:19, 20, 21; 5:35; 8:12; 9:5; 11:9, 10; 12:35, 36, 46. Enlighten (*phōtizō*): 1:9.

accepting and being blessed. Rather, the issue is being troubled and sorrowful about Jesus' death and removal from the earth. In this context, Jesus gives the gift of "peace" to the hearts of his disciples for the purpose of removing their troubledness and their grief through the gift of peace that brings joy to their hearts.[108] Believing is an important mode of activity for this nurturing of the heart.[109] The first issue is believing in the glory of God[110] rather than the glory of man (John 12:43). The second issue is confessing it. In the context of precreation rhetorolect, prophetic belief, which enables the heart to turn and repent, is reconfigured into belief in the glory of God, which becomes flesh as light in the Son of God. Precreation belief fills the heart with love for the glory that comes from God to earth, and out of this love in the heart comes confession of belief that removes troubledness, grief, and fear from the heart and fills the heart with joy.

Conclusion

Early Christian prophetic rhetorolect takes the form of confrontational speech, story-line, and story. From a tradition of the beginning and ending of kingdoms in the Hebrew Bible, early Christian prophetic rhetorolect selects an emphasis on the beginning of the kingdom of God in the midst of God's people in the world. In the context of the beginning of God's kingdom, early Christian prophetic rhetorolect emphasizes a story-line from the prophets of Israel through Jesus to Jesus' followers that features suffering, rejection, persecution, and even death. The earliest appearances of this story-line are in 1 Thessalonians and the Q material, which suggests its presence during the 50s. In the letter to the Galatians, Paul presents his own story-line in a manner that evokes the call and responsibilities of Isaiah and Jeremiah in the Hebrew Bible. The end-point of his story-line is prophetic confrontation of Peter and Barnabas about full inclusion of people of the nations (Gentiles) in the Christian community on the basis of faith rather than circumcision. Paul develops this prophetic story-line to believer's through Abraham's acceptance of God's promises to him through faith. An end result of Paul's multiple prophetic story-lines is a blending of a story-line of suffering and rejection with a story-line of promise of salvation to the nations without the ritual of circumcision.

[108] Cf. Eph 1:2; 2:14, 15, 17; 4:3; 6:15, 23. Also see Rom 5:1; 8:6; 14:17, 19; 15:13, 33; 16:20 and notes 95 and 100.

[109] Cf. Rom 15:13: May the God of hope fill you with all joy and peace in believing (*eirēnēs en tōi pisteuein*), so that you may abound in hope by the power of the Holy Spirit.

[110] There are fifteen references to glory in John 1:14; 2:11; 5:41, 44; 7:18; 8:50, 54; 9:24; 11:4, 40; 12:41, 43; 17:5, 22, 24. In addition, there are fifteen occurrences of a form of the verb "to glorify": 7:39; 8:54(2); 11:4; 12:16, 23, 28(2); 13:31, 32; 14:13; 15:8; 16:14; 17:1, 4, 5, 10; 21:29.

The Gospels of Mark, Matthew, and Luke develop complex story-lines by prefixing a story of Jesus' death and resurrection with, among other things, rhetoric from prophetic verses in Isaiah. Mark presents what is written in Isaiah as "the beginning of the Gospel" (Mark 1:1-3). Then throughout the story, the disciples grow in their lack of understanding, embodying Isa 6:9-10 which talks about the people of Israel to whom Isaiah went as people who seeing did not see, hearing did not hear, and were not able to turn and be forgiven because they did not understand.

Early Christian prophetic rhetorolect acquires additional dimensions in the Gospel of Matthew. In the beginning chapters, Matthew interrupts the story-line of his Gospel to interject the voice of prophets who interpret the events that occur as fulfillment of statements by prophets of Israel. Extended portions of Isaiah function in this external role to interpret Jesus' adult activity in "Galilee of the nations" (Matt 4:15)" and Jesus' healings as a way of bringing hope to the nations (Gentiles) "in his name" (Matt 8:17; 12:21). After this, Jesus himself recites portions of Isaiah as a way of bringing special blessings on disciples who are scribes "trained for the kingdom" (Matt 13:16-17, 53) in a context where "outsiders" do not understand the nature of the kingdom. Later, however, when Jesus recites Isa 29:13 to Pharisees and scribes to criticize their purity rituals (Matt 15:8-9), Jesus applies the topos of "not understanding" to his own disciples when they do not understand the importance of what comes out of the heart in contrast to what goes into the mouth (Matt 15:16-20). Jesus enacts the full force of his prophetic statements about people not understanding the kingdom, however, in the seven Woes addressed to scribes and Pharisees in Matt 23. The implications of these Woes extend all the way to the story of the crucifixion of Jesus through the topos of being innocent or guilty of someone's blood (Matt 23:29-36; 27:4, 24-25).

In the Gospel of Luke, Jesus' reading from Isaiah in his hometown synagogue at Nazareth establishes basic topoi for the unfolding story-line. Jesus pronounces blessings on the poor, heals the blind, raises the dead, and cleanses lepers as a fulfillment of prophetic statements of Isaiah blended with actions of Elijah and Elisha. When Jesus is invited to dinner on three different occasions by Pharisees, he confronts his hosts and those in attendance with topoi that emerge both from Isaiah and from Ezekiel 34, which emphasizes seeking and saving the lost. Regularly in Luke, in contrast to Matthew, Jesus is presented as using prophetic discourse as a way to move into wisdom discourse. Instead of building prophetic confrontation to conclusions of anger and division, like the Gospel of Matthew often presents Jesus' speeches, the Gospel of Luke regularly moves toward conclusions that many people accept, praise, or even respond to by changing their ways.

The Acts of the Apostles builds on the prophetic rhetorolect in the Gospel of Luke by featuring Jesus as "the prophet like Moses" whom Moses himself predicted and by presenting an extended story-line of suffering, persecution, and even death by followers of Jesus. In Acts, then, Jesus' death on the cross is an event in an ongoing story-line that continues with the imprisonment of Peter and John, the death of Stephen, and the rejection of apostles who preach the word of God where they go. This rejection is offset, however, by an interwoven story-line of acceptance by many people including people of the nations (Gentiles). One of the highpoints is an Ethiopian eunuch's acceptance of Philip's interpretation of Isa 53 as applying to the life and death of Jesus (Acts 8:26-39). Another highpoint is Paul's and Barnabas's special mission to people of the nations (Gentiles) on the basis of Isa 49:6, which they accept as the Lord's command to "be a light for the nations (Gentiles)" (Acts 13:47). The mission to the nations (Gentiles) continues all the way to Rome, where the final scene features Paul reciting Isa 6:9-10 to Jews in Rome to confront them with the result of their refusal to believe his message. In this context, he says, the Holy Spirit through Isaiah has sent the salvation of God to the nations (Gentiles) who will listen (Acts 28:23-28).

In the context of precreation rhetorolect in the Gospel of John, the topoi of early Christian prophetic rhetorolect are reconfigured into topoi that serve the purpose of belief in Jesus as the Word who became flesh as God's light and truth in the world. This emphasis changes the role of John the Baptist from a prophet to a voice that testifies to the light. In addition, Jesus alone is "the prophet" who has come into the world. With precreation as the host rhetorolect, the emphasis on the heart changes to a focus on believing and confessing that Jesus is God's light to the world. In addition, instead of criticizing his disciples for not understanding, Jesus nurtures the hearts of his disciples by giving them peace that removes sorrow and fear and produces joy in their hearts.

Now that we have seen how early Christian prophetic rhetorolect creates stories and story-lines through confrontation and blessing, we will turn to early Christian apocalyptic rhetorolect in the next chapter. There we will see how early Christians moved beyond a mode of conceptualization focused on God's kingdom on earth to a mode of conceptualization dominated by the role of Jesus as God's Messiah enthroned in heaven. We will see that this is a conceptual move beyond kingdom to empire. In early Christian apocalyptic rhetorolect, God is conceptualized as an All Powerful emperor with various powerful people in heaven, including his Messiah, to assist him with activities of judgment and redemption when evil spiritual forces have invaded the ordered world God created at the beginning of time.

8

Christian Apocalyptic Rhetorolect Part I: Empire, Destruction, and Transformation

Introduction

The primary internal dynamic of early Christian apocalyptic rhetorolect is God's dramatic transformation of the created world into a totally righteous and holy space with the assistance of heavenly beings who perform various tasks for God. Some Mediterranean discourse presented a range of processes that would cause the universe eventually to become a fiery mass where all created things would be destroyed.[1] Biblical (Jewish) apocalyptic discourse emerged in the form of information that existed in heaven that God made available in various ways to humans on earth. A basic message of the information was that God would ultimately change the nature of the created world through divine actions from heaven.

Biblically-oriented apocalyptic focuses on evil in the world that results from actions that violate divinely established boundaries throughout the entire universe. In other words, apocalyptists believe that evil is not something that exists in certain limited regions of God's universe. Rather, there is evil in the universe that is so aggressive and comprehensive that it corrupts God's entire world. As apocalyptists attempt to understand how such widespread evil could exist in a world that God intended to be good and righteous, most of them focus on the activities of one or more of the following: (1) the angel-spirits God created in heaven; (2) the first human God created on earth; (3) humans who tried to build a tower into the heavens; (4) nations that have tried, or are currently trying, to rule over all humans on earth. Apocalyptists are not unified in their account of how the incredible, horrendous evil that exists in the world came into existence. They do agree, however, that evil has somehow aggressively pervaded and corrupted God's good universe, that the way this happened is so complex that the answers lie

[1] John J. Collins (ed.), *The Encyclopedia of Apocalypticism. Volume 1: The Origins of Apocalypticism in Judaism and Christianity* (New York: Continuum, 1998) 58, 74-76, 111-12, 115-17.

outside the realm of the usual human means and capacities for understanding, and that these answers exist in the heavens, where they are mysteriously hidden.

For apocalyptists, then, there is no way that even the most intelligent, perceptive human can understand the nature of evil in the universe by careful observation, meditation, and reflection on things that are visible to the eye and audible to the ear in God's created world. The only possibility for understanding lies outside God's visible, created world. Fortunately, apocalyptists believe, there have been very special people whom God has allowed on certain unusual occasions to see dreams or visions, or to hear picturesque pronouncements by angels, that reveal heavenly mysteries. These people were shown the origins, internal nature, and pandemic proportions of evil, and they were shown God's plans for redemptive transformation. Perhaps the most fortunate thing, however, is that, at the time these special people saw and heard what they did, either God or an angel told them to write everything down so other people could learn about these things by having someone read to them what they wrote.

In the context of the multiple answers apocalyptists give for the origins and proportions of evil in God's universe, two major streams of apocalyptic emerge by the first century CE that are important for understanding apocalyptic conceptuality in early Christian literature. The first stream can be called angel-spirit apocalyptic and the second can be called earth-material apocalyptic. Angel-spirit apocalyptic focuses on the ministering spirits God created to oversee all things in God's universe and how specific actions of these heavenly angel-spirits with human blood and flesh produced evil, unclean spirits on earth led by a master rebel against God. Major topics in this tradition are blood desire and decay that leads to death. The emergence of evil, unclean spirits creates counter-spheres of actions by good, holy, and eternal angel-spirits and evil, corrupt demon-spirits that raise difficult questions about the relation of beings in the realm of human life to beings in the realm of heaven. Earth-material apocalyptic, which represents a shift in focus in the context of spirit-angel apocalyptic, focuses on the manner in which both heavenly and earthly beings take on characteristics of earthly substances as they carry out their roles in the heavens and earth that God created. Major topics in this tradition are political power and wealth. The "earthly" characteristics focus both on the earthly "materials" of clay, metal, and stone and on earthly kinds of "flesh," both wild and domesticated. Just as clay, metal, and stone cover a span from "ordinary" forms to sculpted, refined, and "precious" forms, so flesh covers a span from "wild" animals to domesticated animals of value in the agricultural-city domain of human society. Major topics in the earthly "material-flesh" tradition are power and wealth. The presence of beings both in heaven and on earth whose earth-material bodies, instruments, and possessions exhibit their power to build and destroy raises perplexing questions about the nature of both heavenly and earthly realms. As this stream of tradition develops within spirit-angel apocalyptic, it focuses on cities, both in the heavens and on earth, as spaces where either that which is good, holy, and eternal or that which is evil, unholy, and temporary exists. In other words, the earth-material apocalyptic stream, in particular, exhibits a focus on "urban" worlds which rulers use as bases for local power and far-reaching destruction of others, and where people accumulate wealth in a manner that causes large numbers of people to live in poverty and starvation. The "answer" from the heavens is the creation of an "alternative city" with everlasting protection, eternal health and food, and wealth characterized by "refined" and "precious" earth materials which are pure and holy.

Both the angel-spirit tradition and the earth-material tradition embedded in it make visible to humans, who are a blend of spirit-blood-flesh and earth material, the complexity of "embodiments" of both good and evil throughout the entire universe. Embodiments both in heaven and on earth reveal the nature of blood desire and political power, which preserve and protect their own sphere and devour and destroy other spheres. The relation of the spirit-body nature to the earth material nature of both heavenly and earthly beings in apocalyptic literature reveals that God's "created" world, whether it be the heavens God created or the earth God created, has ironies, paradoxes, and conflicting forces internal to its inner fabric. God's world is, then, truly puzzling. Why would God create a world that is so problematic? One basic answer apocalyptists give is God's love of creating order. Another is God's desire to be praised through worship and song. Apocalyptists wrestle with these questions in the midst of many other related questions and provide answers of various kinds on the basis of what they have seen and heard in the heavens. As this present chapter unfolds, we will see how the book of Daniel in the Hebrew Bible contains a blend of traditions that becomes especially important for understanding apocalyptic in first century Christian writings. In the language of cognitive scientists, the book of Daniel becomes an "emergent structure" of great importance for the blends that occur during the first century CE. Our approach will focus on what happens to angel-spirit and earth-material apocalyptic when first century Christians present God's Messiah Jesus as a major personage in the apocalyptic story of the world.

Apocalyptic Speech Genres, "Biblical" Apocalypses, "Biblical" Apocalyptic Literature, Apocalyptic Discourse, and Early Christian Apocalyptic Rhetorolect

As we continue this discussion of early Christian apocalyptic, it is important to distinguish, in a manner slightly different from previous chapters, among apocalyptic speech genres (oral and written), "biblical" apocalypses, "biblical" apocalyptic literature, apocalyptic discourse, and early Christian apocalyptic rhetorolect. The placement of the term biblical in quotation marks points to literature and streams of tradition related to the Hebrew Bible and the Christian Bible that are not actually in either biblical canon. Much of this literature, then, exists in what is regularly called "the Old Testament Pseudepigrapha."[2]

In contrast to wisdom and prophetic literature, multiple instances of "typical" apocalyptic literature do not exist in the Hebrew Bible. When John J. Collins described in 1979 what he considered to be "a general consensus among modern scholars" about "a phenomenon which may be called 'apocalyptic'," he presented "an ill-defined list" that included "the Jewish works Daniel (chs. 7–12), *1 Enoch, 4 Ezra* and *2 Baruch* and the Christian book of Revelation."[3] One notices immediately that there is reference to six chapters of one book in the Hebrew Bible (Daniel), one deuterocanonical or apocryphal book (*4 Ezra*), two pseudepigraphical writings (*1 Enoch, 2 Baruch*), and one NT writing (Revelation). Here we see that apocalyptic was an emerging phenomenon after the fall of the nation of Israel, rather than a centripetal "form-shaping ideology" in Israelite culture that produced multiple instances of apocalyptic writings in the Hebrew Bible. Here we recall Paul D. Hanson's distinction between prophetic and apocalyptic literature, and his explanation for it:

> After 587 the picture changes. Israel's political identity as a nation comes to an end. The office of kingship ends. The prophets no longer have the events of a nation's history into which they can translate the terms of Yahweh's cosmic will. Hence the successors of the prophets, the visionaries, continue to have visions, but they increasingly abdicate the other dimension of the prophetic office, the translation into historical events. At that point we enter the period of the transition from prophetic into apocalyptic eschatology.[4]

Apocalyptic literature emerged when the people of Israel were ruled over by "nations of the world." As "Ezra" states in *4 Ezra* 4:22-23: "I

[2] James H. Charlesworth, *The Old Testament Pseudepigrapha* (2 vols.; Garden City, NY: Doubleday, 1983, 1985). Hereafter abbreviated *OTP*.

[3] John J. Collins, "Introduction: Toward the Morphology of a Genre," in *Apocalypse: The Morphology of a Genre* (ed. John J. Collins; Semeia 14; Missoula, MT: SBL, 1979) 3.

[4] Hanson, *The Dawn of Apocalyptic*, 16.

do not wish to inquire about the ways above, but about those things that we daily experience: why Israel has been given over to the nations in disgrace; why the people whom you loved has been given over to godless tribes, and the law of our ancestors has been brought to destruction and the written covenants no longer exist." In this context, apocalyptic visionaries envisioned God's reign as rule over the entire world as a cosmic empire. God's focus is not simply on a particular "kingdom" on earth, but on ruling over all the nations and empires in the world. But there is also another dimension. When apocalyptic visionaries have their special experiences of receiving knowledge that has been mysteriously hidden in the heavens, either an angel or a voice from heaven tells them to write down what they have seen and heard. In the words of Jonathan Z. Smith, building on Paul D. Hanson's insights:

> In the Near Eastern context, two elements are crucial: scribalism and kingship. The *situation* of apocalypticism seems to me to be the cessation of native kingship; the *literature* of apocalypticism appears to me to be the expression of archaic, scribal wisdom as it comes to lack a royal patron.[5]

As apocalyptic literature expanded the Israelite prophetic focus on God's cosmic will for God's kingdom on earth to a focus on God's status as eternal emperor over the entire cosmic world as God's empire, it also emphasized the role of the seer as a writer. This produced a view of apocalyptic literature as authoritative writing that communicated new, previously hidden, heavenly knowledge in a direct manner that not only supplemented, but in important ways superseded, all other "scripture," including the Torah, the Prophets, and the Writings. Apocalyptic literature, and along with it apocalyptic discourse, functioned as an "all-consuming" mode of writing and conceptualization. Apocalyptists brought all the authoritative dimensions of wisdom, Torah, and prophecy into the service of a "totalistic" way of viewing all the actions of God in every time and space in the universe.[6]

In *The Apocalyptic Imagination*, which was published five years after the *Semeia* volume that reported the results of the SBL Literary Genres Project on apocalyptic, John J. Collins reiterated the definition of an apocalypse advanced by the members of the Project:

> Specifically, an apocalypse is defined as: "*a genre of revelatory literature with a narrative framework, in which a revelation is mediated by an otherworldly being to a human recipient, disclosing a transcendent reality which is both temporal, insofar as it envisages eschatological salvation, and spatial insofar*

[5] Jonathan Z. Smith, *Imagining Religion: From Babylon to Jonestown* (Chicago and London: University of Chicago Press, 1982) 94.

[6] Cf. William A. Beardslee, *Literary Criticism of the New Testament* (Philadelphia: Fortress Press, 1970) 53-56.

as it involves another, supernatural world."[7]

Then he asserted that "this definition can be shown to apply to various sections of *1 Enoch,* Daniel, *4 Ezra, 2 Baruch, Apocalypse of Abraham, 3 Baruch, 2 Enoch, Testament of Levi* 2–5, the fragmentary *Apocalypse of Zephaniah,* and with some qualification to *Jubilees* and the *Testament of Abraham* (both of which also have strong affinities with other genres)" and "to a fairly wide body of Christian and Gnostic literature and to some Persian and Greco-Roman material."[8] One notices five important shifts in the list as he applies the definition of apocalypse "to various sections" of writings. First, the Hebrew Bible book of Daniel is placed after *1 Enoch.* Whether this positioning was conscious or unconscious, this ordering reflects the manner in which *1 Enoch* in the Pseudepigrapha, of which major 2nd century BCE fragments were found at Qumran, was emerging as a model for apocalyptic literature that was either as important as or more important than Daniel in the Hebrew Bible. Second, the list of Pseudepigraphic writings is expanded beyond *2 Baruch* to include *Apocalypse of Abraham, 3 Baruch, 2 Enoch, Testament of Levi* 2–5, and the fragmentary *Apocalypse of Zephaniah.* This expansion exhibits an awareness of how apocalyptic literature proliferated in Jewish culture outside of Christian circles. Third, the inclusion of *Jubilees* and *Testament of Abraham* indicates a growing awareness that some apocalyptic literature rewrites and reconfigures biblical tradition in a manner designed to exhibit "the real cosmic story" that was occurring during the time of biblical history, which sheds light on "the real significance of contemporary persons and events in history."[9] Fourth, the list adds Christian apocalypses, including Revelation in the NT, and Gnostic literature. This addition exhibits an awareness that there is an extensive Christian history of apocalyptic literature from the first through the fifth centuries CE and that a significant amount of Gnostic literature participates in this history. Fifth, the list adds Persian and Greco-Roman literature. This addition shows how apocalyptic literature was a widespread cultural phenomenon in the Mediterranean world. It was not limited to Jewish and Christian tradition, but for various reasons it was produced, valued, and promulgated in many regions of the world of late antiquity.

In the context of this wide range of apocalyptic literature, interpreters regularly do not present a taxonomy of apocalyptic speech genres,

[7] John J. Collins, *The Apocalyptic Imagination: An Introduction to Jewish Apocalyptic Literature* (2nd ed.; Grand Rapids, MI and Cambridge, UK: Eerdmans, 1998, [c1984]) 5; cf. Collins, "Introduction: Toward the Morphology of a Genre," 9.

[8] Ibid.

[9] Christopher Rowland, *The Open Heaven: A Study of Apocalyptic in Judaism and Early Christianity* (New York: Crossroad, 1982) 2.

like they do for wisdom and prophetic discourse. Christopher Rowland, however, uses three primary apocalyptic speech genres whereby "knowledge of God and secrets of the world above, [are] revealed in a direct way": (1) dreams; (2) visions; or (3) angelic pronouncements.[10] These three speech genres, he proposes, regularly occur in a literary form that can be called "an apocalypse," which contains a narrative introduction (sometimes called a "legend") that establishes a context for the dream, vision, or angelic pronouncement. Often the seer who receives the communication engages in dialogue with the intermediary, asking questions and sometimes offering an interpretation that the intermediary evaluates as significantly lacking in understanding. Many times the intermediary presents an explicit interpretation of the dream, vision, or pronouncement to the seer. Sometimes there are admonitions after the visionary disclosure.[11]

By the first century CE, apocalyptic had emerged as a cultural system of belief within Judaism. In other words, in the language of cognitive science it had become an idealized cognitive model (ICM).[12] As we recall, an ICM contains argumentative-enthymematic structuring, image-descriptive structuring, metaphoric mapping, and metonymic mapping.

In the case of apocalyptic, it is important to discuss the image-descriptive structuring before the argumentative-enthymematic structuring. In apocalyptic, the discourse introduces theses, rationales, and conclusions to the hearer/reader through exceptionally picturesque scenes. The specificity and concreteness of apocalyptic discourse lies in revelation to specific people, display of very detailed descriptions of beings (God, beasts, evil personages, good personages), display of spaces (bountiful gardens, beautiful cities, spaces of punishment, spaces of worship, altars, temples, walls), and display of procedures (programmatic destruction of portions of the earth, specific procedures of torture, specific processes of journey of a righteous soul into heaven and then into the paradise of jubilation, specific processes of journeys through the heavens and throughout the cosmos).[13] Through these

[10] Rowland, *The Open Heaven*, 9-10.

[11] Ibid., 49-52.

[12] George Lakoff, *Women, Fire, and Dangerous Things: What Categories Reveal about the Mind* (Chicago and London: University of Chicago Press, 1987) 68-90.

[13] John J. Collins, ed., *Apocalypse: The Morphology of a Genre* (Semeia 14; Chico, CA: Scholars Press, 1979); idem, *Jewish Wisdom in the Hellenistic Age* (Louisville: Westminster John Knox, 1997); idem, *The Apocalyptic Imagination: An Introduction to Jewish Apocalyptic Literature* (2nd ed.; Grand Rapids: Eerdmans, 1998); idem, ed., *The Encyclopedia of Apocalypticism* (vol. 1 of *The Origins of Apocalypticism in Judaism and Christianity;* New York: Continuum, 1998); Adela Yarbro Collins, "Early Christian Apocalyptic Literature," *ANRW* 25.6:4666-4711; Greg Cary and L. Gregory Bloomquist, *Vision and Persuasion: Rhetorical Dimensions of Apocalyptic Discourse* (St. Louis, MO: Chalice, 1999); Greg Carey,

visual descriptions, apocalyptic discourse creates vivid pictures of personified desire, evil, sin, death, etc. Evil is not simply hardness of heart; it is personified in "the devil." Desire is not simply something in the heart; it is personified as "angels of God impregnating beautiful maidens on earth." Sin is not simply a state of disobedience; it is pictured as estrangement from the glory of God, which produces nakedness that requires people to cover their bodies with clothes. In turn, death is personified as something fierce, violent, and evil, and it can be destroyed and thrown into a burning fire in the depths of the earth.

In the context of the image-descriptive structuring, argumentative-enthymematic structuring configures all time (past, present, and future) and all space (cosmic, earthly, and bodily) in terms of good and holy or evil and corrupt. This argumentative structuring occurs through a combination of theses and rationales that summarize attributes and actions of God in the past, present, and future in relation to the actions of humans and good and evil spirits both on earth and in the heavens in the past, present, and future. The effect of these theses and rationales is to make God's actions in all time (past, present, and future) and all space (heaven, earth, Sheol, etc.) into the Rule that governs Cases and Results. In other words, the rule is not limited to God's giving of Torah (wisdom discourse), God's choosing of particular individuals or groups (prophetic discourse), God's intervention in particular unusual circumstances (miracle discourse), or God's removal of sin through sacrificial offerings (priestly discourse). Rather, the Rule in apocalyptic discourse evokes all of God's actions at all times and in all spaces. All past, present, and future events (human and divine) are "God's story" that creates a universe where righteousness is preserved and unrighteousness is destroyed. The Cases feature "the identification" of those who are righteous and those who are evil. The Results feature the manner in which the righteous will be preserved and the unrighteous will be destroyed.

In the context of this argumentative-enthymematic structuring, regularly there is an explicit command to the seer to write down what he has seen and heard. Sometimes there also are commands that what is written down must be read to others, and occasionally there are prohibitions against anyone changing any of the wording of what is written down. This has caused Jonathan Z. Smith and others to emphasize that one of the major effects of apocalyptic as a speech genre is its "scribalization" (making into written "letters" [*grammata*]) or "scripturalization"

Ultimate Things: An Introduction to Jewish and Christian Apocalyptic Literature (St. Louis, MO: Chalice Press, 2005) 2-17.

(making into "writings" [*graphai*]) of God's relation to the world.[14] The overall result of apocalyptic discourse, then, is that "the entire biblical story" becomes "scripture": God's written "Word" that produces the Rules for being preserved or being destroyed. This means that the story of God in the Hebrew Bible is simply the beginning of God's story. God's story continues into the present and into the future as a promise of transformation of evil into destruction and good into redemption. Thus, apocalyptic discourse authorizes not only its own interpretation of the past biblical story but also its interpretation of post-biblical events as "scripture," since all of God's ongoing story is "Rule" that enacts "Results" on "Cases."

The experience of Jews, and then of Christians, of imperial rule over them created a new metaphoric mapping, namely a mapping of eternal emperor onto God and eternal empire onto the cosmos. God was not simply the cosmic king in the heavens. Apocalyptic visionaries pictured God as an eternal emperor who ruled over "God's empire," which was the entire universe. Apocalyptists do not regularly refer to God as "King" either of the heavens or of the earth, as is often present in prophetic literature.[15] Rather, God is "the Most High" (*ho hypsistos*), the one who is above everyone and everything, including time. Various apocalyptic writings list a series of titles for God in their attempt to communicate this "highest" status. Daniel 2:47, for example, refers to God as "God of gods, Lord of kings, and a revealer of mysteries." *1 Enoch* 1:3 refers to "the God of the Universe, the Holy Great One"; *1 Enoch* 37–71 refers regularly to "the Lord of the Spirits" and "the Antecedent of Time"; *1 Enoch* 63:2 refers to "the Lord of the Spirits, the Lord of kings, the Lord of rulers, the Master of the rich, the Lord of glory, and the Lord of wisdom." *1 Enoch* 63:4 adds: "Now we have come to know that we should glorify and bless the Lord of kings – him who rules over all kings."

In the place of the sage or the prophet, then, came the visionary, the seer who had seen, heard, and written down what is mysteriously hidden in the heavens. The primary social-cultural-ideological location and institution that produced a valuing of the apocalyptic seer was the experience of an empire, which made multiple nations subservient to it. The conceptuality in apocalyptic moves beyond "kingdom," which has limited boundaries on earth, to "eternal empire," which includes all time and all space. In a context, then, where all of scripture was being "sapi-

[14] Jonathan Z. Smith, *Imagining Religion: From Babylon to Jonestown* (Chicago and London: University of Chicago Press, 1982) 94.

[15] The "Commander-in-chief" (*archistratēgos*) Michael, is being elusive with Abraham when, in Test. Abraham 2:6 (Rec. A), he tells Abraham that he has come from "the great city," sent by "the great king."

entialized" and selected portions of scripture were being made into "prophetic story," apocalyptic literature introduced "scribalization" or "scripturalization" that made writings into authoritative communications directly from God.[16] These writings presented a "totalistic" view of God's power in a context where God had created a world that introduced "visible" time and space into the universe. The earthly institution of "imperial government," namely a form of rule that potentially extended over all nations, people, and regions of the earth, provided the metaphoric mapping. God's eternal empire is the context for visible, bodily, earthly, experience-based images for communicating knowledge about God in apocalyptic literature and discourse.

Metonymic mapping in apocalyptic discourse occurs in the form of assertions, words, or phrases that invite people to recruit totalistic, picturesque scenes in their mind. Apocalyptic literature features scenes that contain explicit action, imply action, or are the result of action. Some of the prominent metonymic assertions for these scenes are: (1) the heavens "opened" or "split apart"; (2) a fiery throne became visible (perhaps with the Lord God sitting on it); (3) "the dead were raised" or "the earth gave back those who sleep in it"; (4) the righteous were victorious over death; (5) this age gave way to the coming age; (6) tribulations were worse than at any time since God created the earth; (7) a new earth or paradise came into view; (8) a new city came down to earth from heaven; (9) the Lord sat on the throne of judgment and books in heaven were opened. Any one of these assertions may invite a hearer or reader to recruit the entire conceptual system in their mind. Over time, many of these assertions were abbreviated into single metonymic words. Some of these words are: revelation, resurrection, tribulations, paradise, judgment, and end-time.

The time-space (chronotope) of early Christian apocalyptic rhetorolect is "partitioned" time in a context of "eternal empire" time. This partitioning creates at least the following "parts" of time: (1) before creation; (2) creation; (3) Adam; (4) Noah; (5) Abraham; (6) Moses; (7) David, Solomon, and the kings of Israel; (8) the time of the nations; and (9) "that time" (the end of times or the end of "time").[17] The great sea, the heavens, mountains, cities, and spaces of sleep have special importance in the context of these parts of time. For humans, this means that "the time" in which one lives is important, and the space in which one lives is important in relation to the time. Since time exists in "parts," it is important for humans to know the part of time in which they are living in a certain space. If a person misunder-

[16] Cf. Rowland, *The Open Heaven*, 13-22.

[17] See the twelve parts of "that time" or "the end of times" in *4 Ezra* 14:11-12 and *2 Bar* 27; 53–70. Also, see *4 Ezra* 14:10-18 for the concept that time grows old and weak.

stands the part of time in which they are living in a certain space, they may quite unknowingly do wrong things. One of the problems can be taking for granted there will be more time, when in fact time has "run out." Another problem can be thinking time has run out in this space, when in fact there is a considerable amount of time left. Knowing the part of time in which one is living in a certain space is a way of knowing if there is a significant amount of time left, even if one does not know exactly how much time there may be. This concept of time and space requires, first and foremost, that a person be "alert to time" in their specific space. Earthly time and space are not something that simply last forever. Therefore, a person must "use" time in a particular space carefully and faithfully, because both time and space are limited. This makes time and space "precious" possessions, something to be valued highly and to be lived in wisely. To understand how precious they are, one must have help from people who have had the special opportunity to see into the special mysteries of time and space and to hear special interpretations of them. Simply looking at God's created world might give a person the impression that in God's world there is always plenty of time and space. If a person knows the insights of those who have seen into the special nature of God's time in the context of all space in the universe, one will know there is a limited amount of time and space on earth and one must use them wisely in order for there to be any chance of receiving as an inheritance "the kind of time and space that never ends."

Apocalyptic discourse functioned centrifugally in first century Christian writings, producing Gospels and Letters that contain many different kinds of apocalyptic features and dimensions. Sometimes there are only a few "conceptual" dimensions that appear here and there in a NT writing. At other times, there are assertions, word patterns, or phrases that foreground apocalyptic reasoning, if only for a moment in the discourse. In still other instances, one or more primary apocalyptic speech genres appear.

There are two NT letters in which apocalyptic words, phrases, and conceptuality are so prominent that they can appropriately be called apocalyptic letters: 2 Thessalonians and Jude. In addition, there are seven apocalyptic letters in Rev 2:1–3:22. Beyond this, there are important apocalyptic "moments" or "highpoints" in other letters: 1 Corinthians 15; 2 Corinthians 5, 12; 1 Thessalonians 4–5; 2 Peter 2–3; 1 John 2–4. Among the Gospels, Matthew contains the most explicit, sustained apocalyptic phrases and images, even though many interpreters consider Mark, with its ending in 16:1-8, to present a more "radical" apocalyptic view of the life of Jesus than Matthew.

Apocalyptic discourse was such an important aspect of first century Christian culture that centripetal forces nurtured it into a "form-shaping ideology" in the "Apocalypse to John" which, within four centuries, was placed in a position of "the final word" in the NT. Unlike any other known apocalypse prior to it, this writing uses the Greek word *apokalypsis* (revelation) like a title in the first verse:

> [1] Revelation of Jesus Messiah, which God gave him to show to his servants what must soon take place; and he made it known by sending his angel to his servant John, [2] who bore witness to the word of God and the testimony of Jesus Messiah, even to all that he saw. (Rev 1:1-2)

The apocalyptic discourse that follows this opening is earth-material apocalyptic embedded in angel-spirit apocalyptic. In the context of God as "the Alpha and the Omega," "the Lord God, who is and who was and who is to come, the Almighty (*pantokratōr*)" (1:8), Jesus Messiah (1:1-2, 5) is:

> one like the Son of Man, clothed with a long robe and with a golden sash across his chest. [14] His head and his hair were white as white wool, white as snow; his eyes were like a flame of fire, [15] his feet were like burnished bronze, refined as in a furnace, and his voice was like the sound of many waters. [16] In his right hand he held seven stars, and from his mouth came a sharp, two-edged sword, and his face was like the sun shining with full force. (Rev 1:13-16)

This is Jesus Messiah in the mode of earth-material apocalyptic. Jesus Messiah, who is a heavenly being, has characteristics of earthly substances. These characteristics portray Jesus Messiah in an apocalyptic tradition that focuses on political power and wealth, in which cities regularly play a major role. In this context, the earth-material is a blend of descriptions of "the Ancient of Days" in Daniel 7 and the angel Gabriel in Daniel 10. It will be necessary for us to explore this in detail in the next chapter. In this present chapter, it is necessary for us to set the stage for understanding the highly complex combination of apocalyptic images, concepts, arguments, and forms in NT writings. In the context of first century Christian literature, the Lord's Messiah Jesus rules from heaven over Christ's kingdom, until the end when everything is turned over to God. Apocalyptic literature expanded the Israelite prophetic focus on God's cosmic will for God's kingdom on earth to a focus on God's status as eternal emperor over the entire cosmic world as God's empire. First century Christian apocalyptic rhetorolect used both the angel-spirit and earth-material streams of Jewish apocalyptic as it added Jesus as God's Messiah to the conceptual system. The use of the two streams of tradition adds a complexity to first century Christian apocalyptic that presents a special challenge to NT interpreters. Since most interpreters do not approach the presence of apocalyptic in the NT from the perspective of these two related, interactive streams of tradition, a significant amount of new analysis and interpretation needs yet to be pursued. This chapter and the following one will start this new approach.

The Early Christian Apocalyptic Story-Line

In early Christian apocalyptic rhetorolect, special issues arise over the nature and times of God's transformation of Jesus Christ when he is in various spaces in God's universe. Since a primary emphasis of apocalyptic discourse is on time in particular spaces, early Christian apocalyptic rhetorolect focused on the nature of Christ from the time of his birth through the time when be became a heavenly being until the time when he will end all time in the future. We will see in the next volume that precreation discourse reconfigured apocalyptic discourse into an emphasis on Christ as a person who comes from non-time prior to the creation of the world, lives temporarily within human time and space, and then returns to the realm of non-time with God the Father. Early Christian apocalyptic rhetorolect, in contrast, focuses on Jesus Christ within human time and space. When human time and space is the realm of focus, the issue is the apocalyptic conception and birth of Jesus and successive transformations of Jesus into various forms as a personified agent of God's holiness and power until the time when he will come to earth in the future to overcome all evil in the world.

Writings in the New Testament focus especially on six moments in the Hebrew Bible as they create an apocalyptic story of God's world:

- The successful tempting of Adam and Eve by Satan, who is understood to be an evil angel cast out of heaven by God. Satan, working through Eve, caused God to cast Adam and Eve out of the Garden of Eden, and Satan continually causes people to go astray in the present;
- God's taking of Enoch into heaven, where he oversaw God's destruction of the world through a flood and the rescue of Noah by means of an ark that floated on the water;
- God's destruction of Sodom and Gomorrah with fire from heaven;
- God's sending of ten plagues against the Egyptians;
- God's empowerment of "one like a son of man" in the heavens to have authority and power over kingdoms on earth;
- God's development of a process of resurrection of the dead as a way to transport faithful people who have died away from an environment of divine destruction into an environment of eternal well-being.

One of the goals of early Christian apocalyptic rhetorolect is to answer the question: "How was evil able to invade the fabric of God's good world with such force and power that God could decide at a future time to destroy everything he created, except some righteous people?" The schemes of Satan become one resource for answering this question. Sexual activity by heavenly beings and by humans becomes another resource for answering this question. The creation of idols for worship becomes yet another resource for answering this question.

For the Christian apocalyptic story, a series of moments within time became important for God's apocalyptic transformations of Jesus. Mary's conception of Jesus was an apocalyptic moment of transformation in which God created a heavenly being to be born into the world to oppose all personifications of evil both in the earthly realm of human life and in the realms of the heavens above and the abyss below. The baptism of Jesus was a special apocalyptic moment of transformation, when Jesus became a personification of God's holy spirit who could withstand all testing by Satan and drive demons out of people who were possessed by evil spirits. The moment when God transformed Jesus into a brightly shining being while he was on top of a mountain with three of his disciples was a decisive apocalyptic moment that previewed his resurrection into heaven. One of the most important apocalyptic moments in Jesus' life was his death, when God raised him from burial into eternal life and power. Another really decisive apocalyptic moment in Jesus' activity, of course, will happen in the future when he subdues all evil powers and reigns victoriously over everything in God's world, before turning it over to God. Any combination of these views work together in first century Christian discourse to present Jesus from an apocalyptic perspective. One of the focuses of transformation in early Christian apocalyptic rhetorolect, then, is on Jesus himself. Within this reasoning, one of the issues can be the combination of events that present God's transformation of Jesus Christ into a personification of God's holiness and power while he was on earth and when he is in the heavens after his death.

Not only Christ but also believers were a focus of God's transformation in early Christian apocalyptic rhetorolect. Here various questions emerged. Does God transform believers into people who live in the benefits of an apocalyptically transformed world already at baptism? Does participation in the Lord's Supper continually renew a believer's participation in the benefits of an apocalyptic sphere of the world transformed by God? Does a believer enter the benefits of an apocalyptically transformed world at death or does a believer receive all the benefits of God's transformed world only at a later time when all the dead will be resurrected? Thus, believers also are a focus of God's powers of transformation in early Christian apocalyptic rhetorolect.

In addition to Jesus Christ and believers, the world is a focus of God's activities of transformation in early Christian apocalyptic rhetorolect. Did God begin to transform the world apocalyptically with the appearance of the angel Gabriel to Zechariah to announce to him the birth of John the Baptizer who would prepare the way for Jesus? Was the dramatic beginning of God's apocalyptic transformation of the world the conception of Jesus in the womb of Mary while she was still a virgin? Did God's apocalyptic transformation of the world begin with John the Baptist's preaching of the coming judgment of God? Did God's apocalyptic transformation of the world begin with Jesus casting demons out of possessed people? Did God's apocalyptic transformation of the world begin with Jesus' crucifixion? Did God's apocalyptic transformation of the world begin with Jesus' resurrection from the dead? Will God's apocalyptic transformation of the world begin only when Jesus comes from heaven to earth in the future? Will God apocalyptically transform the world only after Jesus returns to earth and rules over it 1,000 years? Thus, the world itself is a focus of God's powers of transformation in early Christian apocalyptic rhetorolect, and points of view varied among early Christians concerning exactly how God's powers worked to effect these changes.

Early Christian apocalyptic rhetorolect is dramatically focused on God's transformation of special people like Jesus, believers and unbelievers, the world, and even time itself. This means that God's activities of transformation are not limited to the abilities or efforts of humans to transform themselves through repentance and obedience, nor are they limited to the abilities or efforts of humans to transform themselves during their time of life on earth. Rather, early Christian apocalyptic rhetorolect focuses on powers of transformation that lie outside the realm of human life and outside the realm of time itself. The processes of transformation come from the realm of God and concern God's transformation of humans, the world, and time itself into "heaven-like" personages and spaces, and into eternal "non-time." Time is transformed beyond the cycle of conception, birth, life, and death into eternity.

Early Christian apocalyptic rhetorolect moves toward its goals by blending human experiences of living in an empire, which inhabitants of the empire perceive to extend over the entire inhabited world and to be ruled by an emperor who lives far away in an imperial household, with God's heavenly world, where God rules as emperor over the heavens, the earth, the seas, the abyss, and personified agents of good and evil in the cosmos. This conceptualization emphasizes that God is ultimately in control of all things everywhere. Nothing visible or invisible to humans escapes God's power of righteousness and holiness.

Emperor, Empire, and Imperial Agents as Spaces for Apocalyptic Rhetorolect

Religious Blending	Apocalyptic Rhetorolect
Social, Cultural, & Physical Realia (1st Space)	Political Empire, Imperial Temple, Imperial Army
Visualization, Conceptualization, & Imagination of God's World (2nd Space)	God as Almighty (*Pantokratōr*), Jesus as King of King and Lord of Lords Emergence of a new age in God's world
Ongoing Bodily Effects and Enactments: Blending in Religious Life (3rd Space)	Human body as Receiver of resurrection & eternal life in a "new" realm of well-being

As early Christianity extended its presence throughout the Roman empire, its apocalyptic rhetorolect emphasized the eternal nature of God's rule over everything, in a context where kingdoms rise and fall through war, famine, earthquake, disease, and other disasters. This created a special emphasis on eternal time, which apocalyptic rhetorolect refers to as ages, epochs, or eras. These ages, epochs, and eras transcend the time periods of various kingdoms on earth. This focus gives new meaning to references to God as Almighty or Most High, now emphasizing the nature of God as a divine being who transcends concepts of kingship. In early Christian apocalyptic rhetorolect, God is not simply King of kings and Lord of lords. In Revelation, God is the Almighty, the one who was, is, and ever will be.[18] In turn, the heavenly Jesus Christ is the King of kings and Lord of lords.[19] Jesus Christ is the highest personified agent who will assist God with the establishment of divine rule over everything that exists. In the view of early Christians, God is the powerful one beyond all kingly powers, including the powers of Jesus Christ. For them, God has authorized and empowered the heavenly Jesus Christ to rule over all earthly kings and powers, until they are entirely under his control. When Jesus Christ has established this control over all earthly powers, he will turn "his kingdom" over to God, the Almighty (*Pantokratōr*), who rules over all things eternally.

In early Christian apocalyptic rhetorolect, God transforms Jesus into different bodily and heavenly forms as he functions as the highest personified agent in God's establishment of divine rule over all that exists. When Jesus is an earthly being, God transforms him into a human personage with the ability to drive evil spirits out of humans, and at certain moments God transforms Jesus into a shining angel-like being or a being who can walk on water while he is on earth. After Jesus

[18] Rev 1:8; 4:8; 11:17; 15:3; 16:7, 14; 19:6, 15; 21:22.
[19] Rev 17:14; 19:16.

dies, God transforms Jesus into a heavenly being. Once Jesus becomes a heavenly being, he is able to take various personified forms like an angel, a heavenly blend of God and angels, a judge who sits on a throne, a lion, a ram, or a warrior. Indeed, through various processes of transformation, the heavenly Christ becomes a being whose powers are greater than all the eternal ministering angel-spirits God created on the first day of the creation of the world. In other words, early Christians "Christianize" Mediterranean apocalyptic discourse by placing Jesus Christ in various roles where God has transformed him into a personage who embodies the transformative powers that God puts into play at the end of time. Through multiple transformative processes, God gradually but faithfully overcomes all forms of evil power in the universe to create a realm where righteous and holy people can be eternally in the presence of God, the heavenly Jesus Christ, and angels and saints who continually praise and worship God.

As a result of its emphases, early Christian apocalyptic rhetorolect does not allow a localization of focus on "the heart," as in prophetic rhetorolect, but focuses on the heart as part of the holiness or unholiness of the entire human body. This will bring us to a discussion of priestly rhetorolect in the next volume. The transformation of the body includes the entire human body, and apocalyptic rhetorolect entertains the possibility of the transformation of the entire body through destruction as well as redemption. This focus produces two central topoi of apocalyptic discourse: "flesh" and "blood." Entire flesh and blood bodies may be destroyed through fire and disintegration, or they may be redeemed through ritual or other physical processes that destroy physical, temporal, or sinful aspects of flesh and blood bodies. From the perspective of the reasoning internal to apocalyptic discourse, these processes are related to "refinement by fire," an image that regularly hovers nearby in apocalyptic discourse. A primary result of apocalyptic processes is movement either toward the transformation of a human body into a heavenly-like being or into destruction. There may be a stage in which a human body is transformed into a new creation while it is still on earth. Or a human body may only be partially transformed, with complete transformation only occurring at the time of death. In fact, apocalyptic discourse itself is a rhetorical ritual. Through its assertions and argumentation, it recreates all regions of time and space in the body and in the world on the basis of their relation to the sacred or the profane.[20]

[20] Vernon K. Robbins, "Rhetorical Ritual: Apocalyptic Discourse in Mark 13," in *Vision and Persuasion: Rhetorical Dimensions of Apocalyptic Discourse* (ed. G. Carey and L.G. Bloomquist; St. Louis, MO: Chalice Press, 1999) 97.

Apocalyptic discourse sometimes transforms humans into heavenly beings without any special process of destruction. Especially as a result of God's destruction of evil through the story of Noah and the flood, believers may perceive rituals with water to be a special means for people to experience transformation from flesh and blood beings into beings living in an apocalyptically transformed sphere in the world. At other times, apocalyptic discourse transforms people through processes of destruction. God is the one, of course, who decides such things. Apocalyptic discourse simply reports them. Humans are the recipients of God's decisions, in a context where everything God decides was preordained before the ages. The discourse reports the effects of God's actions through its assertions and argumentation.

The focus on the eye in early Christian apocalyptic rhetorolect emphasizes seeing beyond the earthly realm into the mysteries of the heavens. In contrast to wisdom rhetorolect, which focuses on what is visible to the eye in the realm of earthly life, apocalyptic rhetorolect considers it not very helpful to look at the created world to understand the mysterious ways of God. Since the created world is so filled with evil, the primary things the eye may see are chaos, destruction, hatred, and division. To understand the nature of God, therefore, a person must gain vision into the heavens. Only by seeing what is happening in the heavens can one see the ways in which God is transforming the world and its people at present, and will more dramatically transform the world and its people in the future.

The effect of apocalyptic rhetorolect in early Christian discourse was primarily threefold. First, early Christians produced scenes focused on processes initiated by God from the heavens that had produced in the past, were producing in the present, or would produce in the future dramatic transformations of the created world. Second, early Christians revised biblical story-lines into eras in which personified agents of evil continually and aggressively invaded God's created order since the time of creation to produce disorder, suffering, violence, destruction, and death. Third, they created new story-lines that presented the actions of personified agents of God's holiness and power who played a role in the past, play a role in the present, and will play a role in the future to create well-being for believers.

Extra-Biblical Apocalyptic Reconfiguration of Biblical Stories and Story-Lines

For the story-line of apocalyptic discourse, it is necessary to put writings outside the biblical canon in a primary position for interpretation. The reason is that a major rhetorical effect of apocalyptic discourse is a rewriting of the biblical story in a manner that sets good, holy, righteous spirits in opposition to evil, polluted, unrighteous spirits from the beginning of creation until the end of the ages. An interpreter can see how this rewriting worked only by including a wide range of Jewish literature that began to play a significant role in Jewish life during the second century BCE and continued to be written throughout the time of the emergence of Christianity. For reasons that will be explained below, it is important for us to begin with the pseudepigraphical writings entitled *Jubilees* and *1 Enoch*.[21]

Jubilees could be called "The Revelation to Moses," except that the writing does not feature the kinds of "heavenly events" throughout that interpreters regularly expect in an apocalyptic writing. The apocalyptic dimensions of the writing emerge from the reconfiguration of Moses' forty days and forty nights on Mount Sinai. Instead of the Lord giving to Moses only the "two stone tablets of the Law and the commandment,"[22] "the Lord revealed to him what (was) in the beginning and what will occur (in the future), the account of the division of all the days of the Law and the testimony" (*Jub.* 1:4). In other words, the Lord revealed to Moses an apocalyptic account of the beginning of time until the end of time. Since time began with God's creation of the world, the story-line God tells Moses begins with this event. As the story unfolds, the "earthly" end point in view is Israel's conquest of the land of Canaan. The story is an angel-spirit apocalyptic story. Every event in the story-line stands under the "Day of Judgment" that will come at the end of time, after events in history in which good and evil spirits have played a major role.

Since *Jubilees* reconfigures only certain events in the biblical story into events that are properly interpreted as apocalyptic, it is important to start with its story-line and to correlate various events in its story-line with accounts in *1 Enoch* as the story-line unfolds. Overall, stories in which good and evil spirits are actors can appropriately be identified as stories the writer has reconfigured into apocalyptic events. The inability of good spirits to rule decisively over evil spirits is a result of complications built into God's decision to include flesh and blood living creatures who communicate through language in the created world, both through internal processes in their "flesh" and "blood," and through their vulnerability to influence by evil spirits.[23] Flesh and

[21] Since major portions of both *1 Enoch* and *Jubilees* were found among the manuscripts of the Qumran writings, it is clear that they were composed by 100 BCE; see George W.E. Nickelsburg, *1 Enoch 1* (Hermeneia: Minneapolis: Fortress Press, 2001); James C. VanderKam, *The Book of Jubilees* (Guides to Apocrypha and Pseudepigrapha; Sheffield: Sheffield Academic Press, 2001); Carey, *Ultimate Things*, 69-76.

[22] Exod 31:18; 32:15; Deut 9:11; *Jub.* 1:1;

[23] According to *1 En.* 3:28, all living creatures spoke "with one another with one speech and language" until the serpent led Eve astray. After that, God stopped all the animals from speaking.

blood living beings continually are agents of evil in God's created world.[24] One of the rhetorical effects of the reconfigured story is a confidence that God's good spirits really do have the upper hand, even though they regularly function under conditions in which their powers are limited by the activities of evil spirits in God's created world.

1 Enoch is a highly complex apocalyptic writing, containing a large number of scenes and discussions that provide information about apocalyptic writings prior to and during the second century BCE. *1 Enoch* 1–36 is important for helping us understand how angel-spirit apocalyptic discourse reconfigured biblical story-lines both in and beyond the story-line of the Torah. While it would be good to have the space to work with apocalyptic sections in Isaiah and many other prophetic writings,[25] it will be necessary for us to limit our discussion to writings that shed light on specific developments in early Christian apocalyptic discourse. For this, Daniel is especially important, and we will include portions of a few other writings in addition. The goal of this section is to provide a basic account of Jewish apocalyptic reconfigurations of the biblical story-line of God's world by the first century CE, when Christianity emerged in the Mediterranean world.

God's Creation of Good Angels on the First Day of Creation

One of the keys for understanding the inner workings of angel-spirit apocalyptic rewriting of the biblical story is God's creation of good angels on the first day of creation. In *Jub.* 2:2-3, the angel of presence rehearses to Moses the decisive reconfiguration of Genesis 1 in the following manner:

> 2:2 For on the first day he created the heavens, which are above, and the earth, and the waters and all of the spirits which minister before him:
> the angels of the presence,
> and the angels of sanctification,
> and the angels of the spirit of fire,
> and the angels of the spirit of the winds,
> and the angels of the spirit of the clouds and darkness and snow and hail and frost,
> and the angels of resoundings and thunder and lightning,
> and the angels of the spirits of cold and heat and winter and springtime and harvest and summer,
> and all of the spirits of his creatures which are in heaven and on earth.

[24] The chapter on early Christian priestly rhetorolect in the next volume will discuss how flesh and blood living beings can, through sacrificial activities, become agencies for redemption. This creates a context where even humans, as flesh and blood living beings, have the potential to be agencies for redemption.

[25] See Paul D. Hanson, *The Dawn of Apocalyptic* (Philadelphia: Fortress Press, 1975); Collins (ed.), *Encyclopedia of Apocalyptic*; Carey, *Ultimate Things*, 50-68.

> And (he created) the abysses and darkness – both evening and night – and light – both dawn and daylight – which he prepared in the knowledge of his heart. [3] Then we saw his works and we blessed him and offered praise before him on account of all his works because he made seven great works on the first day. (*Jub.* 2:2-3 *OTP* II: Wintermute)

On the first day, God created seven things: the heavens, the earth, the waters, all the spirits that minister to him, the abysses, the darkness, and light. At the end of the day, the spirits that minister to the Lord God, rather than the Lord God himself, saw all the works God had created. When they saw all of it, they "blessed him and offered praise before him on account of all his works because he had made seven great works on the first day" (*Jub.* 2:3). Apocalyptic reconfiguration of the biblical story features God's creation not only of all things including the waters and the abysses, but it also features God's creation of "angel-spirits" on the first day of creation. This creates a context where, from the beginning, angel-spirits "see" God's creation and worship God for what God has created. It is important to notice that the apocalyptic account of creation in *Jubilees* does not feature God as seeing everything that was created and calling it good. This leads to the next observation.

One of the characteristics of apocalyptic discourse is an awareness that not all of the created order is, in fact, good. There is no question that it is "great"; but the reader soon begins to see that goodness does not hold sway throughout all of it. It is not clear, for example, that the waters, the abysses, and the darkness are good. It also becomes apparent that not all of the ministering angel-spirits God creates are good. On the first day of creation, then, the judgment is that the creation God made was "great." It is a symbol of God's remarkable power, a truly remarkable feat of making things out of nothing. But is it good? The unfolding story-line shows how the great creation God made had internal complications in it that provided multiple opportunities for evil to begin, grow, and aggressively invade the wonderful world God had made. On the first day, God created "great things," which includes not only the "good" things featured in Genesis 1, but also the waters, all of the spirits that minister to him, the abysses, and the darkness (*Jub.* 2:2). The important thing, from the perspective of *Jub.* 2, is that all these things God "prepared in the knowledge of his heart" (*Jub.*2:2), and the angel-spirits saw God's works, blessed God, and offered praise before God for these great works (*Jub.* 2:3). In other words, an apocalyptic account begins with created beings worshipping God. These activities by the angel-spirits evoke inner workings of priestly discourse focused on the holiness of God, rather than with God's seeing of goodness, which evokes inner workings of wisdom discourse focused on the production of goodness and righteousness in the world.

In apocalyptic discourse, actions that exhibit the greatness of God lead to a "sanctification" of the creation which finally makes everything "holy." It will be necessary for us to pursue this in detail in the chapter on early Christian priestly rhetorolect in the next volume. In this chapter and the next on early Christian apocalyptic rhetorolect, it is important for us to see how difficult it is for God to work with flesh and blood living beings in the created world. In other words, the writers of apocalyptic literature perceive the most difficult problems within God's creation to be a result of dealing with flesh and blood living beings in the world. But the problems do not simply "reside" in these flesh and blood beings. The overall problem resides in the relation of ministering angel-spirits, all of whom have certain powers, to flesh and blood beings. When certain good angel-spirits become evil in the context where they are carrying out their responsibilities of overseeing flesh and blood beings in the world, an interaction among evil spirits, good spirits, and flesh and blood beings sets the stage for all of the terrible things that cause God's great creation to be an environment of evil spirits pitted against good spirits.

Ministering spirits are able to cause trouble within flesh and blood living beings, since there are so many ministering spirits and each one has a different role and different powers. In *Jubilees*, there are eight kinds of ministering spirits: (1) angels of presence; (2) angels of sanctification; (3) angels of the spirit of fire; (4) angels of the spirit of the winds; (5) angels of the spirit of the clouds and darkness and snow and hail and frost; (6) angels of resoundings and thunder and lightning; (7) angels of the spirits of cold and heat and winter and springtime and harvest and summer; and (8) all the spirits of his creatures which are in heaven and earth (*Jub.* 2:2). All of these ministering spirits should continually focus on the greatness of God. But what if they begin to use some of their powers to satisfy desires of their own, rather than simply to fulfill God's work in the created world? What if their desires begin to focus more on things in God's created world over which they are watching than on God who gave them the responsibility and power to watch over those things? This leads to the next important event in the reconfigured biblical story.

Sexual Violation of the Boundaries of Heaven and Earth by Sons of God

Angel-spirit apocalyptic contains a "cosmological" story that blames heaven for the aggressive evil that pervaded the entire world that God created.[26] Angel-spirit apocalyptic discourse reconfigures Gen 6:1-5 into the major event when evil powers engaged in actions that began to create evil, disorder, unrighteousness, violence, destruction, and death in the world God had created to produce life. This apocalyptic reconfiguration is recounted or referred to in many places in Jewish literature after the second century BCE. First, let us look at the biblical account of the event in Gen 6:1-5 that apocalyptic discourse reconfigured:

> 1 When people began to multiply on the face of the ground, and daughters were born to them,
> 2 the sons of God saw that they were fair; and they took wives for themselves of all that they chose.
> 3 Then the LORD said, "My spirit shall not abide in mortals forever, for they are flesh; their days shall be one hundred twenty years."
> 4 The Nephilim were on the earth in those days – and also afterward – when the sons of God went in to the daughters of humans, who bore children to them. These were the heroes that were of old, warriors of renown.
> 5 The LORD saw that the wickedness of humankind was great in the earth, and that every inclination of the thoughts of their hearts was only evil continually. (Gen 6:1-5 NRSV)

This strange story in the Hebrew Bible presents sons of God, who are divine beings in heaven, violating boundaries between heaven and earth by developing sexual desire for beautiful daughters of men on earth, giving in to that desire, and bearing children with these human women. Angel-spirit apocalyptic discourse reconfigures this story on the basis of God's creation of eight types of angel-spirits on the first day of creation. *Jub.* 5:1-2 describes it this way:

> 5:1 And when the children of men began to multiply on the surface of the earth and daughters were born to them, the angels of the Lord saw in a certain year of that jubilee that they were good to look at. And they took wives from themselves from all of those whom they chose. And they bore children for them; and they were the giants. 5:2 And injustice increased upon the earth, and all flesh corrupted its way; man and cattle and beasts and birds and everything which walks on the earth. And they corrupted their way and their ordinances, and they be-

[26] Martinus C. de Boer refers to this story as foundational for the "stream" of Jewish "cosmological" apocalyptic eschatology that existed alongside the stream of Jewish "forensic" apocalyptic eschatology during the 1st century CE, particularly in *4 Ezra* and *2 Baruch.* See M.C. de Boer, "Paul and Apocalyptic Eschatology," in Collins, *The Encyclopedia of Apocalypticism*, 345-83; idem, "Paul and Jewish Apocalyptic Eschatology," in *Apocalyptic and the New Testament: Essays in Honor of J. Louis Martyn* (ed. Joel Marcus and Marion L. Soards; JSNTS 24; Sheffield: JSOT Press, 1989) 169-90; idem, *The Defeat of Death: Apocalyptic Eschatology in 1 Corinthians 15 and Romans 5* (JSNTS 22; Sheffield: JSOT Press, 1988).

> gan to eat one another. And injustice grew upon the earth and every imagination of the thoughts of all mankind was thus continually evil.

There are six points of reconfiguration of the biblical story in *Jub.* 5:1-2 that are important for our understanding of apocalyptic discourse in this chapter and the next.

First, instead of referring to the heavenly beings as "sons of God," *Jub.* 5:1 refers to them as "the angels of the Lord." This exhibits a change from widespread Ancient Near Eastern mythology that recognizes the existence of many gods and children of gods. Apocalyptic discourse replaces the concept of many gods with the concept of many spirit beings. Within time, some of these spirit beings either become "false gods" or themselves help people to create false gods in the form of idols. Apocalyptic discourse reconfigures the concept of the existence of many gods in the world by having God create many ministering angel-spirits of all kinds on the first day of creation.[27] From the perspective of apocalyptic discourse, any beings that humans consider to be a god, other than the God who created all things, is a "false god." Indeed, it is likely to be a demon, namely an "evil spirit being" that has somehow become an object of false worship.

Second, apocalyptic discourse presupposes that the birth of the giants to the children of men corrupted "all flesh," which included "man, cattle, beasts, birds, and everything which walks on the earth" (*Jub.* 5:2). In apocalyptic discourse, humans are simply one of the many kinds of flesh and blood living creatures on earth. According to *Jub.* 3:28, all flesh and blood living creatures on earth shared two basic relationships at the beginning of creation. On the one hand, all had bodies of flesh and blood, unlike God's ministering angel-spirits, who had spirit bodies and did not procreate, because they possessed eternal life. On the other hand, all flesh and blood earthly creatures spoke "with one another with one speech and language" (*Jub.* 3:28). This changed after the serpent led Eve astray, which we will discuss below. After the serpent led Eve astray, God stopped all the flesh and blood living creatures except humans from speaking. This meant that after humans were cast out of the Garden of Eden, they still shared with animals "living flesh and blood on earth," but animals could no longer converse with one another using one language, nor could they have conversation with humans.[28]

[27] In apocalyptic discourse, it was necessary for God to create all the ministering angel-spirits on the first day of creation, because angels were created as eternal beings and not beings that procreated (see *1 En.* 15:6-7). This creates a context were the angel of the Lord's use of "we" throughout *Jubilees* means "we ministering angel-spirits" who help God by performing all kinds of tasks for God.

[28] This conflicts, of course, with the view that certain animals, like Balaam's ass, could talk to certain humans!

Third, the violation of the boundaries of heaven and earth by the ministering angel-spirits produced "corruption of all flesh." In a context where humans and creatures already were separated from one another by not being able to speak to one another with one speech and language, they became further separated from one another by special desires that developed "within all flesh." As God says to the ministering angel-spirits who had become evil:

> "You [used to be] holy, spiritual, the living ones, [possessing] eternal life; but now you have defiled yourselves with women, with the blood of the flesh begotten children, you have lusted with the blood of the people, like them producing blood and flesh, (which) die and perish." (*1 En.* 15:4)

God explains that wives had not been created among the ministering angel-spirits, because, being "spiritual, (having) eternal life, and immortal in all the generations of the world," they did not need to procreate. Indeed, God had created the ministering angel-spirits to dwell as eternal beings in heaven and not to dwell on earth (*1 En.* 15:6-7). All earthly living creatures, in contrast to them, were created as procreating flesh and blood creatures. They need to procreate, because flesh and blood lose their "living properties" and "perish," that is, they disintegrate into "stuff like the earth" after a certain period of time when they have life.

Fourth, the reasoning about "all flesh" corrupting its way after the heavenly angels procreated with the earthly women appears to be based on a presupposition about the nature of spirit and spirit beings. In *1 En.* 15:8-9, God explains that the giants born from the union of the angel-spirits and the women are "evil spirits upon the earth." The nature of these earthly evil spirits is that "evil spirits come out of their bodies" and travel around, doing evil both "on the earth and inside the earth." The reasoning appears to be that "spirit," in contrast to "flesh," can travel anywhere and penetrate through anything and everything in God's world. "Spirit breath" is necessary for all flesh and blood beings on earth to live. When angel-spirit entered into blood and flesh beings, angel-spirit mixed with blood inside flesh. Since "spirit" is not limited to the confines of a blood and flesh body, it can travel around anywhere on the earth or inside the earth. But now the "spirit" of these beings born to women are "eternal spirit" corrupted with blood, which dies. In other words, what was previously spirit-breath in humans had become "eternal spirit-blood" in flesh and blood beings on earth. This created earthly beings who possessed "eternal spirit that breathed with blood." Prior to their existence on earth, these spirit beings had breathed with praise and worship of God (*Jub.* 2:3). The mixture of this heavenly spirit-breath with blood created "evil spirits on the earth," because the breath of these beings sought the presence of blood and flesh rather than the presence of God. These evil spirits started pursuing flesh and blood beings rather than pursuing the tasks God had assigned for them in the world. As God explains:

> 11 The spirits of the giants oppress each other; they will corrupt, fall, be excited, and fall upon the earth, and cause sorrow. They eat no food, nor become thirsty, nor find obstacles. 12 And these spirits shall rise up against the children of the people and against the women, because they have proceeded forth (from them). (*1 En.* 15:11-12)

The nature of these evil spirits is that "they will corrupt until the day of the great conclusion, until the great age is consummated, until everything is concluded (upon) the Watchers and the wicked ones" (*1 En.* 16:1). These spirits do not die "a natural death," because they are impregnated with eternal spirit. The only way they will die, then, is if God destroys them. From the perspective of apocalyptic discourse, the birth of these giants brought "eternal evil" both onto the earth and inside the earth. The only way this eternal evil can be destroyed is if God at some time destroys it. In the meantime, this evil continually spreads into "all flesh" on the earth.

Fifth, a primary symptom of the corruption of "all flesh" was that all flesh and blood creatures began to eat one another. This means that flesh and blood animals began to eat other flesh and blood animals including humans, and humans began to eat flesh and blood animals including other humans.[29] This was a violation of Gen. 1:29-30, where "every green plant" was given to flesh and blood creatures to eat and "every plant yielding seed" and "every tree with seed in its fruit" was given to flesh and blood humans to eat. This is important information since, according to apocalyptic discourse, evil spirits themselves do not eat food or become thirsty.[30] Once God's angel-spirits entered into the flesh and blood of female flesh, however, "all flesh" on earth began to desire the pleasure of eating flesh and blood living beings (humans and all creatures became carnivorous, and humans even became cannibals). In other words, sexual desire within eternal spirits for flesh and blood spread into unrestrained desire within all flesh on earth to eat flesh and drink blood (*1 En.* 7:5). But the desire did not stop with eating and drinking. People began to kill each other simply to make the blood of other humans flow out onto the ground. In other words, "injustice grew upon the earth and every imagination of the thoughts of all mankind was thus continually evil" (*Jub.* 5:2). Respect among flesh and

[29] See *1 En.* 7:4-5: So the giants turned against (the people) in order to eat them. 5 And they began to sin against birds, wild beasts, reptiles, and fish. And their flesh was devoured the one by the other, and they drank blood.

[30] See *1 En.* 15:11.

blood living beings, both among humans and between humans and other creatures, disappeared. All flesh and blood earthly beings began to eat one another and to drink each other's blood. This disrespect grew into killing one another simply as a way of life. According to *1 En.* 8:1, the ministering angel-spirit named Azazel helped this process along by teaching "the people (the art of) making swords and knives, and shields, and breastplates." This created a situation where Michael, Surafel, and Gabriel "saw much blood being shed upon the earth" and great "oppression being wrought upon the earth" (*1 En.* 9:1). In other words, sexual desire within heavenly beings caused the birth of earthly beings who not only desired to eat flesh and drink blood but also desired simply to cause the blood of other flesh and blood beings to run out on the ground.

Sixth, apocalyptic discourse embeds a statement by God about a short length of life by humans in Gen 6:3 into this overall story. As a result of the corruption of "all flesh" in the realm of God's created world, God made a decision in the following words: "My spirit will not dwell upon humans forever; for they are flesh, and their days will be one hundred and ten years" (*Jub.* 5:8; Gen 6:3).[31] This, of course, is a disastrous result and circumstance. It means that humans will not be blessed with long life, like they are promised in wisdom discourse, but will have short lives that end after one hundred and ten years.

In the apocalyptic story of the world, God regularly reveals another plan through another command, and in this instance God does two things. On the one hand, God commanded that all of his corrupted angels on earth "be uprooted from all their dominion" and bound by the good angels "in the depth of the earth" (*Jub.* 5:6). Second, God "sent his sword" among his corrupted angels, with the result that "they began to kill one another until they all fell on the sword and were wiped out from the earth" (*Jub.* 5:9). Then *Jubilees* adds:

> [10] And their parents also watched. And subsequently they were bound in the depths of the earth forever, until the day of great judgment in order for judgment to be executed upon all of those who corrupted their ways and their deeds before the Lord. [11] And he wiped out every one of them from their places and not one of them remained whom he did not judge according to all his wickedness. (*Jub.* 5:10-11)

This event is recounted in early Christian apocalyptic rhetorolect in two places. Most interpreters consider Jude 6 to be the earlier statement:

> And the angels that did not keep their own position but left their proper dwelling have been kept by him in eternal chains in the nether gloom until the judgment of the great day. (Jude 6)

[31] Gen 6:3 gives the number as 120 years.

Then 2 Pet 2:4 presents the event as follows:

> God did not spare the angels when they sinned, but cast them into hell and committed them to chains of deepest darkness to be kept until the judgment. (2 Pet 2:4)

According to the apocalyptic story, God cast those ministering angel-spirits who had become evil into a pit in the darkness in depths of the earth. God's answer to the action of those ministering angel-spirits who turned evil was to uproot, destroy, bind, and imprison them in the depths of the earth.

Human Violations of Boundaries of Knowledge and Power between Heaven and Earth

As apocalyptic versions of biblical stories emerged from the second century BCE onward, a new emphasis was placed on boundaries God ordained for humans at the time of Noah. These boundaries existed in a context where God created a new and righteous nature in humans. This new and righteous nature was a gift that God gave. The people who received this new and righteous nature did not earn it through good actions, but they were simply given this nature as part of God's ordaining of all things in the world. *Jub.* 5:12–13 explains it as follows:

> [12] And he made for all his works a new and righteous nature so that they might not sin in all their nature forever, and so that they might all be righteous, each in his kind, always. 13a And the judgment of all of them has been ordained and written in the heavenly tablets without injustice. (*Jub.* 5:12–13a)

Along with this new and righteous nature came God's ordaining "without injustice" of judgment on all beings. These judgments are kept eternally in written tablets that are in heaven.

This ordaining of all things in the world changes the context for belief and action by humans. Once a person has a new and righteous nature, the emphasis is not on receiving a long life as a result of producing righteousness but on a necessity not to violate boundaries that God ordained for all things in the universe. Sins that bring about doom, therefore, are sins that violate boundaries God has ordained. *Jubilees* 5:13b–15 continues with this emphasis on boundaries:

> [13b] And (if) any of them transgress from their way with respect to what was ordained for them to walk in, or if they do not walk in it, the judgment for every (sort of) nature and every kind has been written. [14] And there is nothing excluded which is in heaven or on earth or in the light or in the darkness or in Sheol or in the depths or in the place of darkness. [15] And all their judgments are ordained, written, and engraved. (*Jub.* 5:12–15)

From the side of heaven, the ministering angels violated boundaries between heaven and earth through sexual activity with blood and flesh humans on earth. How do the boundaries function from the side of the earth? It is important first to go to the story of Noah to see how it works there.

From the perspective of apocalyptic discourse, God saved Noah from the flood because God showed partiality to him for the sake of his sons. Once God shows partiality by creating a new and righteous nature in Noah, Noah's "heart was righteous in all of his ways just as it was commanded concerning him. And he did not transgress anything which was ordained to him" (*Jub.* 5:19). Most of the time, that is! Throughout the centuries, the stories of Noah alternate between accounts that emphasize his generosity to accounts that emphasize his focus on material things for himself. In a framework where interpreters struggled with Noah's righteousness in relation to his transgressions, like his drunkenness (Gen 9:21), they agreed that God simply decided to change things through Noah.[32] In contrast to the prophetic story-line where God chooses Abraham and Abraham demonstrates his righteousness by believing God's promises, the apocalyptic story-line pays special attention to an emphasis that Noah simply "found favor in the sight of the Lord" (Gen 6:8). As apocalyptic writers struggled with how this could be, they solved the problem by reasoning that God had already at the time of Noah, prior to the time of Abraham, ordained that certain people of Israel would be righteous in all their ways. The people ordained by God to be righteous, however, continually faced the responsibility not to transgress the boundaries God had established throughout the universe. If they violated these boundaries, even they themselves would face doom.

In the context of the boundaries God established throughout the universe at the time of Noah, *1 Enoch* 65 emphasizes that instead of God calling out to Noah, like he did to Abraham, Noah "went to the extreme ends of the earth" and cried out to his great grandfather Enoch in bitterness, "Hear me! Hear me! Hear me! ... Tell me what this thing is which is being done upon the earth ... perhaps I will perish with her in the impact" (*1 En.* 65:2-3). Immediately after a "tremendous turbulence upon the earth" and a "voice from heaven," Enoch came to Noah and asked him why he was crying out "so sorrowfully and with bitter tears" (*1 En.* 65:4-5). Instead of a story-line like prophetic discourse, where God speaks to Abraham, Moses, or Elijah, in the apocalyptic story-line a heavenly personage regularly speaks to the human on earth. In this instance the heavenly person is

[32] See Louis Ginzberg, *The Legends of the Jews* (trans. H. Szold; Philadelphia: Jewish Publication Society of America, 1968) I:145-47, 159-60, *et passim*.

Noah's great grandfather Enoch, whom God took into heaven at the end of his life (Gen 5:24). When Enoch comes to Noah and talks with him, the conversation again is characteristic of apocalyptic discourse. They talk about what has gone wrong with the entire earth and how God will judge all who dwell on earth to correct the situation. Enoch explains that an order of doom has been issued from heaven on all who dwell on earth (*1 En.* 65:6), because humans have acquired and are using a long list of secrets and powers they should not be using:

> they have acquired the knowledge of all the secrets of the angels, all the oppressive deeds of the Satans, as well as their most occult powers, all the powers of those who practice sorcery, all the powers of (those who mix) many colors, all the powers of those who make molten images, how silver is produced from the dust of the earth, and how bronze is made upon the earth – for lead and tin are produced from the earth like silver – their source is a fountain inside (which) stands an angel, and he is a running angel. (*1 En.* 65:6-8)

Here we see how a major boundary between heaven and earth in apocalyptic discourse works from the side of humans on earth. In this account, humans have acquired heavenly knowledge and power that God ordained to remain secret from humans on earth. The personages who have taught these forms of knowledge and power to humans, naturally, are the evil angels, who, according to the apocalyptic story are also under an order of doom from God for violating this boundary of knowledge and power, as well as the sexual boundary of blood and flesh (*1 En.* 65:11). Noah will be spared from the doom that other humans face, Enoch tells him, because he is "pure and kindhearted" and "detests the secret things" (65:11). It is not, then, that Noah has righteously performed deeds according to Torah, since God has not yet given Torah to Moses.[33] Rather, Noah did not transgress the boundaries between heaven and earth by desiring the secret knowledge of the angels.

Here, then, we see another side of the boundaries between heaven and earth. Angels are not to desire things that are particular to living beings on the earth, namely blood and flesh. In turn, humans are not to desire knowledge that is the particular wisdom of the angel-spirits in charge of overseeing the entire universe. The irony, of course, is that apocalyptic discourse reveals secret knowledge in the heavens and tells stories about the ways in which a long list of humans acquire this knowledge through heavenly beings whom God gives the task of transmitting the knowledge. But the knowledge these good heavenly beings transmit to humans is secret knowledge God wants humans to have, rather than the secret knowledge that angel-spirits have about the

[33] Rabbis had various opinions concerning how Noah did or did not fulfill certain stipulations of the Torah of Moses: see Ginzberg I:145-70.

inner workings of the created world. As we will see below, there are two problems here. First, since angel-spirits are ordained to oversee every aspect of the universe, there is a boundary between the knowledge God ordained them to have and the knowledge God ordained humans to have. Second, when some angel-spirits became evil, they had the knowledge and power to do special things like sorcery, magic, mass rebellion against God, etc. In apocalyptic discourse, then, God is perceived to have ordained a boundary between heaven and earth concerning not only blood and flesh but also multiple kinds of knowledge and power. The story of the world, therefore, is an account of multiple kinds of violations of God's boundaries both from the side of heaven and from the side of the earth.

The Flood and Reappearance of Evil Spirits in the Apocalyptic Story-Line

As apocalyptic discourse reconfigures the biblical story of the flood itself, certain angels are put in charge of releasing the waters of punishment underground (*1 En.* 66:1). Other angels make the ark out of wood for Noah (*1 En.* 67:2). Meanwhile, evil angels are imprisoned underground and tortured in water that becomes a fire that burns forever (*1 En.* 67:13). After the Flood occurs, all of the "purified" earth is assigned to the three sons of Noah. Shem was assigned to the middle of the earth (*Jub.* 8:12-16), Ham was assigned all the portion to the south and west (*Jub.* 8:22-24), and Japheth was assigned all the portion toward the north and east (*Jub.* 8:25-29). Here the difference between the "kingdom" in view in prophetic discourse and the "world" in view in apocalyptic discourse is clearly evident. The perception is that the three sons of Noah are assigned to "all the land in the world," since God is ruler of all the world. Our proposal above has been that this is a move beyond the concept of a kingdom like Canaan, namely a particular area of land ruled by a king, to an "empire" that people perceive to be all the region of the earth that is occupied by humans.

After all the purified earth has been assigned to the three sons of Noah, each of the sons has children, which leads to subdivisions of all the land to them (*Jub.* 9:1-13). A signal of problems in the future emerges when Noah asks his sons to swear an oath of curse:

> 14 And Noah made them all [the sons of Noah and their children] swear an oath to curse each and every one who desired to seize a portion which had not come in his lot. 15 And they all said, "So be it and so let it be to them and to their sons forever in their generations until the day of judgment in which the Lord God will judge them with a sword and with fire on account of all the evil of the pollution of their errors which have filled the earth with sin and pollution and fornication and transgression." (*Jub.* 9:14-15)

Again one sees the centrality of boundaries in apocalyptic discourse. So long as the sons of Noah and their sons do not transgress the boundaries of the particular area of land "ordained" to them, all will be well. When any one of them "desires" a portion outside his lot, on the day of judgment "the Lord God will judge them with a sword and with fire," because what they have done causes "all the evil of the pollution of their errors" to fill "the earth with sin and pollution and fornication and transgression." Here one sees yet one more means by which the earth becomes filled with sin, pollution, fornication, and transgression, rather than with all the good things God intended to fill the earth at the time of creation. This means that at least three kinds of "coveting" cause the earth to be filled with sin, pollution, fornication, and transgression. The first is the coveting of blood and flesh sex on earth by the sons of God; the second is coveting by humans of secret knowledge and power that God ordained only for the ministering angel-spirits; and the third of coveting by humans for land that is ordained by God to be possessed by other humans. Coveting (desire for), then, is the source of sin, pollution, fornication, and transgression both in heaven and on earth. Apocalyptic discourse perceives actions of coveting to emerge both from heaven and from earth. The result of this universe-wide coveting is the filling of the entire universe with sin, pollution, fornication, and transgression.

According to the story-line of apocalyptic discourse, all of God's attempts to disable the power of the evil spirits through imprisonment in the depths of the earth do not prevent the evil spirits from once again creating havoc on the earth. Just when one should expect that all the evil spirits were absent from the earth, they reappear in the affairs of humans:

> [1] In the third week of that jubilee the polluted demons began to lead astray the children of Noah's sons and to lead them to folly and to destroy them. [2] And the sons of Noah came to Noah, their father, and they told him about the demons who were leading astray and blinding and killing his grandchildren. (*Jub.* 10:1-2)

In the context of the oath of a curse that Noah made his sons make, the reader could expect an implication near at hand that the demons would be able to reappear when the sons of Noah began to seize each other's land. The problem becomes so severe that the Lord God finally directs his good angels to bind all the evil spirits on the earth (*Jub.* 10:7). At this point, the chief of the evil spirits, Mastema (Satan), enters the story-line. He requests that God allow one-tenth of the evil spirits to remain on the earth under his control and place nine-tenths of them down in "the place of judgment" (*Jub.* 10:8-9). The reasoning of Mastema is that the ordained task of evil spirits is "to corrupt and lead astray" humans according to the judgment of Mastema. They have been ordained to do this "because the evil of the sons of men is great" (*Jub.* 10:8). In other words, even the task of the evil spirits has been ordained in the context of the evil inclination in humans, so some of the evil spirits should be allowed to continue their work under the guidance of Mastema! God agrees to this, and the good angels bind nine-tenths of the evil spirits in the place of judgment and leave the other one-tenth on earth "subject to Satan upon the earth" (*Jub.* 10:11). Here we see the remarkable turn in the apocalyptic story-line. The incredible evil that exists throughout the centuries of the world is a result of God's willingness after the flood to leave one-tenth of all the evil spirits on earth under the command of Satan. God did this, according to the story, because Satan and evil spirits were ordained to perform a task of corrupting and leading humans astray in the context of the evil inclination in humans.

Once apocalyptic discourse introduces the conceptual framework that God ordained demons to corrupt and lead astray humans in the context of the evil inclination of humans, the stage is set for apocalyptic reconfiguration of all parts of the biblical story-line both before and after the flood. In other words, a major rhetorical effect of the apocalyptic concept of God's ordaining of all events throughout history is the potential reconfiguration of all biblical stories from the beginning to the end into stories of conflict between God's good spirits and the evil spirit-demons on earth led by Satan. The only question is which stories will be reconfigured by whom once the process of reconfiguration begins in the second century BCE.

Apocalyptic Reconfigurations of the Garden of Eden

Christian readers in particular might imagine that the story of Eve and the serpent in the Garden of Eden would be one of the first stories to be reconfigured into an apocalyptic story that features the serpent as Satan. This is not the case, however. In the earliest apocalyptic versions of the Garden of Eden, the serpent remains "the wisest of all creatures" in a context where good angel-spirits play a key role in overseeing the Garden. In *Jubilees*, the story of the Garden of Eden is reconfigured on the terms of apocalyptic discourse only by including actions by good ministering angel-spirits of God. Forty days after Adam was created by God, the good angel-spirits brought him to the Garden of Eden from 'Elda, the land where God had created him (*Jub.* 3:32), and then eighty days after Eve had been created, they took her also to the Garden of Eden (*Jub.* 3:9, 12). Then later the good angel-spirits taught Adam how to till the land in the Garden of Eden (*Jub.* 3:15). When the serpent comes one day to the woman in the Garden and begins to talk with her (*Jub.* 3:17-19), he is simply the wisest of all the earthly creatures God created on the sixth day of creation. The serpent is not, according to the story in *Jub.* 3, the leader of the evil spirits on earth (Satan) who tricks the mother of all humans on earth, nor is he himself an evil spirit. Rather, he is simply the creature among all other creatures who is wise enough to know that if Adam and Eve eat the fruit of the tree in the midst of the garden, their "eyes will become opened" and they "will become like gods" and "will know good and evil" (*Jub.* 3:19). Thus, even though good ministering angel-spirits are in charge of the Garden, the serpent is neither an evil ministering angel-spirit nor a creature who has been influenced by an evil angel-spirit.

Angel-spirit apocalyptic reconfiguration of the story of Eve in the Garden so that evil angel-spirits play a role, however, is close at hand. *1 En.* 69:6 mentions, simply as an off-hand remark, that the angel Gader'el misled Eve. In addition, Gader'el showed humans how to kill people by hitting them and how to make instruments of death like "the shield, the breastplate, the sword for warfare, and all (the other) instruments of death to the children of the people" (*1 En.* 69:6). It is noticeable once again that there is no reference to Satan, the leader of the evil spirits on earth, as the one who persuaded Eve to eat from the tree. Rather, in this instance the evil angel-spirit who had detailed knowledge about warfare misled Eve.

Apocalyptic reconfiguration of the story of the Garden of Eden in a manner that is closer to the Christian story that emerged is present in *The Life of Adam and Eve* (Latin) and *The Apocalypse of Moses* (Greek), which were probably written sometime between 100 BCE and 200 CE.[34] Both writings feature good angel-spirits and the devil, who sometimes takes the form of an angel.[35] According to this version of the story, when Eve tells her children and her children's children what happened in the Garden, she starts by saying that God divided the Garden between Adam and herself to guard over different parts of it. All the male animals were in Adam's part, and all the female animals were in Eve's part. Satan went into Adam's part and tempted the serpent to participate in a plan that would allow him to eat of the fruit of Paradise rather than the weeds that all the other animals ate. The primary thing the serpent would have to do was allow Satan to speak through his mouth at the proper time (*ApMos* 15:1—16:5). The serpent finally agreed to cooperate. When the angels of God went up to worship, Satan came in the form of an angel and sang hymns to God. Satan bent over the wall, like an angel, and asked Eve what she was doing in Paradise. When she told him God had placed her and Adam

[34] *OTP* 2:252.
[35] *OTP* 2:258-95.

in Paradise to guard it and eat from it, the devil answered her through the mouth of the serpent. When the serpent tells her he knows they do not eat from every plant, she tells him about God's command not to eat from the tree in the midst of the Garden (*ApMos* 17:1-5). Satan tells her there is no need for them simply to eat the food that the animals eat. In fact, when they eat of the tree, their eyes will be opened and they will be like gods, knowing good and evil, and this is why God had told them not to eat of it. Eve is still afraid to take of the fruit, even though she sees how beautiful it is (18:1-6). But after the serpent convinces her to open the gate and the serpent comes into Paradise, Satan, through the mouth of the serpent, tells her he has changed his mind and will not let her eat of the fruit. Then he makes her swear an oath that she will not eat of the fruit unless she also gives some to her husband. After she makes the oath, the serpent climbs the tree, sprinkles "his evil poison" of "covetousness" (desire) on the fruit, bends the branch down, and Eve takes it and eats it. At this point, Eve explains to her children that covetousness (desire) is the origin of every sin (19:1-3).

As Eve continues her story, she says that when her eyes were opened and she saw her nakedness, she realized she was "estranged from her glory," and she wept about the oath she had taken. Meanwhile, the serpent comes down from the tree and vanishes (20:1-5). After covering herself with leaves from the tree from which she has eaten, Eve calls to Adam, "shows" him the "great mystery" of the tree, and quickly persuades him to eat. After he eats and sees what happens to him, he says, "O evil woman! Why have you wrought destruction among us? You have estranged me from the glory of God" (21:1-6). In the same hour they hear the archangel Michael sound his trumpet, calling the angels who watch the Lord God pronounce sentence on Adam. God came to Paradise seated on a chariot of cherubim, with angels praising him. All the plants of the Garden bloomed forth when God came, and "the throne of God was made ready where the tree of life was" (22:1-4). After God interrogates Adam at some length (23:1-5), God pronounces three sentences. Adam's sentence is hardship tilling the earth and having the animals rising up in disorder against him (24:1-4), Eve's sentence is birth pangs when bearing children and being ruled over by her husband (25:1-4), and the serpent's sentence is eating dust every day, crawling on his belly, having no hands, feet, ear, wing, or limb, and being hated by humans "until the day of judgment" (26:1-4).

This apocalyptic version of the story of the Garden of Eden retains many features of the biblical version in Genesis 3. There are six things, however, we should observe about reconfiguration of the story. First, in a context where good angels primarily spend their time worshipping God, Satan, the "angel of evil," spends his time devising ways to convince humans to disobey commandments of God. Second, the greatest sin is "desire" (covetousness), a compulsion to have something that is on the other side of a boundary one is not supposed to transgress. Third, covetousness (desire) is called the "evil poison of Satan" and considered to be the origin of every sin. Fourth, God names Eve's giving in to desire (covetousness) "the sin of the flesh" (25:3). Fifth, the results of the sin of desire (covetousness) are many. Humans are not only estranged from the glory of God, but men and women are put in difficult relationships to one another. Men must suffer great hardship to get food and women must suffer great pain to give birth to children. In addition, a hierarchy is established between men and women, with men ruling over women. And still more, animals rise up in disorder against humans, and there is hatred between certain humans and animals. Sixth, God's punishment of Adam, Eve, and the serpent is told in the form of an official judgment scene in the presence of God's throne and angels worshipping God.

It is not clear that this fully apocalyptic configuration of the story of the Garden of Eden had occurred by the first century CE when Christianity was first emerging. Virtually all of the topoi were present in first century Christian discourse, but sometimes they played a role in discourses other than apocalyptic discourse. Jas 1:13-16 is a prime example of the topoi in early Christian wisdom rhetorolect:

> 13 No one, when tempted, should say, "I am being tempted by God"; for God cannot be tempted by evil and he himself tempts no one. 14 But one is tempted by one's own desire, being lured and enticed by it; 15 then, when that desire has conceived, it gives birth to sin, and that sin, when it is fully grown, gives birth to death. 16 Do not be deceived, my beloved. (Jas 1:13-16)

When Jas 1:13-16 speaks of being tempted by evil, it names the primary evil as one's own desire, and it asserts that desire gives birth to sin and sin to death. But there is no mention of Satan and no mention of a day of judgment. As a result, Jas 1:13-16 is early Christian wisdom rhetorolect, rather than early Christian apocalyptic rhetorolect. This rhetorolect, however, personifies one's own desire, sin, and death, making all of them subjects or objects of verbs of action. One's own desire not only tempts, lures, and entices a person, but, like a woman, it is able to conceive and give birth. Sin, which is the offspring of one's own desire, grows up, and gives birth to death. Death, in turn, is the offspring of sin. This is the kind of personification that provides a bridge from wisdom discourse to apocalyptic discourse. If this were early Christian apocalyptic discourse, evil would be personified as Satan, one's own desire would be called the poison of Satan, sin would be called the sin of flesh, and death would be something that could "lose" the contest between life and death, so that something could be "victorious" over it. As wisdom rhetorolect that personifies desire, sin, and death, Jas 1:13-16 is ready to "be completed," as it were, by "filling in the blanks" with early Christian apocalyptic conceptuality and language.[36]

A similar situation exists in Rom 7:7-25, which is an even more complex passage. Sin seizes an opportunity in the commandment, "You shall not covet," and produces all kinds of covetousness in a person (7:7-8). Sin can die, since "Apart from the law sin lay dead" (7:8). Sin can come back to life (7:9). Sin can deceive and kill (7:11). Sin works death until it becomes sinful beyond measure (7:13). It is natural that many interpreters will consider this personification of sin to be apocalyptic discourse. Perhaps, however, it is more informative to talk about it as a type of early Christian priestly rhetorolect. There is a restraint in the mode of personification in these verses that keeps them from being full-blown apocalyptic discourse. In priestly discourse, sin is something that can be removed and perhaps even "sent somewhere else." This kind of personification, like the kind we saw above in Jas 1, creates a natural bridge to apocalyptic discourse. One might appropriately call Rom 7:7-25 early Christian wisdom rhetorolect that has been energized both by priestly and apocalyptic discourse.

Paul's letter to the Corinthians asserts, in one of only two references to Eve[37] in the NT:

> But I am afraid that as the serpent (*ophis*) deceived Eve by its cunning, your thoughts will be led astray from a sincere and pure devotion to Christ. (2 Cor 11:3)

Here there is no reference to Satan. Rather, it is the serpent who deceives Eve, not Satan. Paul could be presupposing, of course, that Satan spoke through the mouth of the serpent, but he does not say so. One can argue that Paul is following the biblical version of the story, rather than an apocalyptic version. In 2 Cor 11:14, however, Paul asserts that "even Satan disguises himself as an angel of light." The close proximity of this statement to Paul's assertion about Eve's deception easily raises the question if Paul is thinking of a version of the story of the Garden of Eden close to the version in *The Apocalypse of Moses*, where Satan takes the form of an angel and sings hymns to God (*ApMos* 17:1).

[36] See "completion" in Gilles Fauconnier and Mark Turner, *The Way We Think: Conceptual Blending and the Mind's Hidden Complexities* (New York: Basic Books, 2002) 42-44, 48.

[37] The other reference is 1 Tim 2:13-15: "For Adam was formed first, then Eve; 14 and Adam was not deceived, but the womas was deceived and became a transgressor. 15 Yet she will be saved through childbearing, provided they continue in faith and love and holiness, with modesty."

Apocalyptic Dream Visions of History featuring Animal Creatures

In the context of the angel-spirit apocalyptic reconfigurations of biblical stories in extra-biblical Jewish literature from the second century BCE onwards, earth-material apocalyptic dream vision accounts emerged that depicted eras of history through animal creature imagery. This mode of apocalyptic discourse moved beyond imagery of good and evil angel-spirits into imagery of good and evil animal creatures. In other words, while the angel-spirit apocalyptic discourse discussed above reconfigured biblical stories by introducing imagery from the conceptual domain of heavenly bodies, which were perceived to be spirit bodies, the apocalyptic discourse we will now discuss presented eras of history through stories of animals, namely "earth-material" creature bodies. The most famous account is the Animal Apocalypse in *1 Enoch* 85–90. This apocalypse presents an earth-material version of the "cosmological" account of the origin of evil in God's created world[38] that provides a rhetorical bridge from apocalyptic angel-spirit stories focused on flesh and blood to apocalyptic earth-material stories focused on "earthly-substance" beings, both heavenly and earthly, who wield political and material power and possess wealth of great value. The Animal Apocalypse account is part of a sequence of two dream visions by Enoch. The sequence and their relationship are important for understanding the nature of dream vision accounts and the earth-material creature symbolism in them.

In *1 Enoch* 83–90, the heavenly Enoch recounts to his son Methuselah two dream visions he had while he lived on earth, the first when he was learning to write and the second before he was married to Methuselah's mother Edna (*1 En.* 83:2). The first dream revealed to Enoch the nature of the end time: Enoch saw heaven thrown down on earth and the earth swallowed up in the great abyss, along with mountains, hills, and trees (83:3-4). When Enoch told his grandfather Mahalalel the dream vision (83:6-7), his grandfather told him to "make supplication to the Lord of glory" that a remnant may remain upon the earth and that God may not obliterate the whole earth (83:8). In response to his grandfather's instruction, Enoch first blesses God at length for his magnificent creation (83:11–84:2), acknowledges God's unlimited rule, power, and wisdom (84:3), and admits that the angels of God's heaven are doing wrong and that God has wrath upon human flesh until the

[38] Martinus C. de Boer does not discuss the earth-material apocalyptic version of cosmological apocalyptic eschatology, which attributes pervasive evil in the cosmos to angels who descended to earth as stars and became big and dark cows who impregnated the heifers of the cows descended from the first bull and cow (Adam and Eve): "Paul and Apocalyptic Eschatology" and "Paul and Jewish Apocalyptic Eschatology."

day of judgment (84:4). Then Enoch requests that God "not obliterate all human flesh and devastate the earth," but that God remove from the earth the flesh that has aroused His wrath and "raise up as a seed-bearing plant forever" the righteous and true flesh (84:5-6). There is no response from heaven to Enoch's supplication at the end of the first dream vision. Rather, later in life when Enoch was soon to be married he had a second dream vision that provided God's answer to his supplication.

Enoch's second dream reveals to him the nature of the world from creation to the end time and God's judgment, which would occur in the context of the Maccabean Revolt and rule (167-161 BCE). It is important to notice that the first dream vision ended with Enoch's use of an image internal to wisdom discourse when he asked God to raise up righteous and true flesh "as a seed-bearing plant forever" (84:6). In the second vision, God answers Enoch's supplication with animal creature imagery rather than vegetation imagery. In other words, the goal for humans in the Animal Apocalypse is to become snow-white cows, rather than eternal seed-bearing plants or trees of life. This answer is unusual in biblical tradition, since it does not feature the vegetational metaphorical sphere to picture goodness and righteousness, which is so prominent in biblical wisdom discourse. Rather, it features the metaphorical sphere of animal creatures who come forth from the earth.

The animal creature metaphorical sphere is not unknown, by any means, in biblical discourse, since Israel often is referred to as God's sheep, rather than God's vineyard. But it comes as a surprise when the Animal Apocalypse presupposes that Israel's nature as sheep is a lesser mode of human being than Israel's nature as cattle. According to the Animal Apocalypse, humans came forth from the earth as cows, but later through Jacob they became sheep! The challenge for God is to restore humans to their original nature as cows. In other words, the Animal Apocalypse presupposes that humans are part of God's animal creature world that emerged out of the earth, rather than God's world of vegetation. This point of view seems reasonable enough from the perspective of Genesis 2 in the biblical story of creation. But the dominance of vegetation imagery in wisdom discourse put imagery of fruit-bearing plants in the foreground for picturing human thoughts and actions of goodness and righteousness, rather than pure white cows. The Animal Apocalypse puts the metaphorical sphere of animal creatures created from the earth in the foreground to depict pure, righteous humans, rather than the metaphorical sphere of bountiful vegetation. God first created humans from the earth as pure white cows. After they became sheep, the challenge for God was to transform them back into pure white cows. The drama of the Animal Apocalypse unfolds as cows become not only sheep but other kinds of animals before God uses special means to transform them back into cows at the end time. While this may sound very strange, as the plot unfolds various aspects of the account begin to resonate closely with portions of Daniel in the Hebrew Bible, and with the Revelation to John in particular in the New Testament.

Enoch's second dream vision (*1 Enoch* 85–90), "the Animal Apocalypse," does not simply focus on the end of time. Rather, it presents an apocalyptic account from Adam to God's judgment of the world and God's transformation of all humans (who exist in the form of all kinds of animals) into snow-white cows (the pure, righteous "earth-material" animals God intended them to be). The first era in the Animal Apocalypse extends from Adam to the flood (*1 En.* 85:3–89:9).[39] In this first era, good people from Adam onward are depicted as animals that are beneficial to humans (cows, sheep, etc.) and evil people are depicted as wild animals, birds, or beasts. The story unfolds as the heavenly Enoch, the great grandfather of Noah, tells this second dream vision to his son Methuselah (the grandfather of Noah). George W. Nickelsburg divides this first era into four segments:

1. Adam and Eve and their Children (85:3-9)
2. The Fall of the Watchers and the Violence of the Giants (86:1-6)
3. Divine Judgment (87:1–88:3)
4. Noah and the Flood (89:1-8)

In the initial segment of the first era, a white bull (Adam) comes forth from the earth, and then a young heifer (Eve) comes forth (*1 En.* 85:3; Gen 2) with a black calf (Cain) and a red calf (Abel: *1 En.* 85:3; Gen 4:1-2). The black calf strikes the red calf and pursues it over the earth, causing it to disappear, and the black calf grows big, mates with a heifer calf that comes to it and produces many cattle (*1 En.* 85:4-5; Gen 4:3-24). After the first heifer (Eve) searches for the red calf and mourns when she cannot find it, the first bull (Adam) comforts her, and together they produce many cows including a white bull (Seth) and many black bulls and cows (*1 En.* 85:5-10; Gen 4:17-26).

There are four observations about these initial events that are important for our discussion. The account begins with Genesis 2:7, omitting God's creation of the world, which includes God's creation of vegetation in Genesis 1. This means that the account begins with God's creation of living animal creatures out of the earth. As the account continues, it moves directly to Genesis 4, omitting the story of the Garden of Eden. In other words, the story again omits the account of the abundant vegetation in God's world and moves directly on to the

[39] Nickelsburg, *1 Enoch 1*, 354.

story of the living animal creatures God formed from the earth, which include humans. There are two observations about this that are important for our discussion. First, apocalyptic story-lines are highly selective, with one account omitting events that another account may feature as important for the apocalyptic story of the world. Second, Enoch's second dream vision focuses on God's animal creature world to tell its apocalyptic version of the relation of humans to God, rather than on God's world of abundant vegetation. This mode of storytelling moves away from the focus on vegetation in wisdom discourse to a focus on earth-made animal creatures in the world, which often is present in prophetic discourse. In this context, a third observation provides a key to understanding the account. Where the creatures remain the same, their color regularly is symbolic of an important aspect of their meaning. In the words of Nickelsburg:

> Adam's whiteness suggests his purity, and hereafter it will be an identifying characteristic of the line that continues through Seth (vv 8-10), Shem (89:9), Abraham (89:10), Isaac (89:11), and Jacob (a white ram, 89:12) and that will reappear in the eschaton (90:37-38). Abel's red color is symbolic of his blood (cf. 89:9, "red as blood"), or perhaps his bloody sacrifice. At the very least, the black or dark color attributed to Cain foreshadows his murder of Abel (cf. Job 6:16, of the treachery of Job's enemies); it also allows the reader to identify the non-Sethite progeny of Adam. The image might possibly reflect the haggadic notion later attested in Jewish, Christian, and Gnostic literature that Cain was begotten by Satan.[40]

In other words, when the account presents a number of people in the same earth-made animal species (e.g., cow), the color of the animal regularly is an important indicator of its meaning in the story. Fourth, it is important to remember that this account is dream vision apocalyptic discourse. To put this another way, the portrayal of persons in the form of earth-made animal creatures does not occur regularly in accounts that claim to be straightforward information from a heavenly figure to a person on earth, like one sees in *Jubilees*, but in accounts of dream visions by a person on earth. This does not mean that all dream visions contain animal creature imagery, since even Enoch's first dream vision does not contain animal creature imagery. But when animal creature imagery occurs in apocalyptic discourse, it regularly occurs in dream visions. Let us now continue with the next portion of the first era.

The second segment of the first era in the Animal Apocalypse continues beyond its account of the birth of many white cattle (*1 En.* 85:10) to the story of the sons of God who impregnated the daughters

[40] Nickelsburg, *1 Enoch 1*, 371.

of humans in Gen 6:1-4. The account in the Animal Apocalypse depicts the sons of God as stars that fell from heaven (*1 En.* 86:1-6). After a number of the stars fall from heaven, they become cattle among the cows (86:1-3), impregnate the cows with their "sexual organs like horses," and cause the cattle to produce "elephants, camels, and asses" who bite the cattle, gore them with their horns, and begin to eat them (86:4-6). In this segment it is important to see the transformation of heavenly bodies into earth-material animal creature bodies, and to see the transformation of good animal creatures (cows) into animal creatures that begin to fight, destroy, and eat one another. These transformations are part of the internal nature of apocalyptic discourse. A major focus in much apocalyptic discourse is the transformation of earth-material human bodies into heavenly bodies. In the Animal Apocalypse, in contrast, God transforms heavenly bodies into earth-material animal creature bodies (which will include human-like bodies) and then transforms one kind of animal creature body into other kinds of animal creature bodies as the story unfolds.

The third segment features seven white men coming down from heaven and three of these men taking Enoch[41] "from the generations of the earth," lifting him up to a high place, and telling him to stay there until he sees everything that will happen to the elephants, camels, asses, stars, and cattle – all of them (87:4). While Enoch watches, one of the four other beings from heaven seizes the first star that fell, binds its hands and feet, and throws it into an abyss (88:1).[42] One of the other beings draws a sword and gives it to the elephants, camels, and asses, and they begin to attack one another, causing the entire earth to quake (88:2). Still another of the beings throws stones from the sky on the fallen stars, gathers and takes away all the stars with sexual organs like horses, binds them hand and foot, and casts them into the pits of the earth (88:3). This, of course, is an earth-material dream vision account of the apocalyptic version of Gen 6:1-4,[43] which tells how certain evil angels called the Watchers (of humans) impregnated the daughters of earth-material humans, gave birth to evil demons on the earth, and were subsequently bound and cast into a pit in the bowels of the earth by good angels. It is important to observe the introduction of heavenly beings into the animal creature account not only as stars who transform into cows but also as earth-material humans, or human-like beings. In addition, Enoch himself becomes a human actor in the account, watching the events that occur. In other words, animal creatures, heavenly bodies like "stars," heavenly "human-like" beings, and real earth-

[41] "Me," the narrator of the story.
[42] See Nickelsburg's comment on this in *1 Enoch 1*, 374-75.
[43] Cf. *Jub.* 5:10-11; *1 En.* 10:11-14; 14:3-5; 18:11; 19:1; 21:6-10.

material humans participate in the story and either become transformed or are participants in transformations that occur in some way in the story (like stars who become cows causing other cows to produce elephants, camels, and asses).

The fourth and final segment of the first era (89:1-9) presents a dream vision version of the flood. One of the four beings from heaven goes to the white bull (Noah) and teaches it a secret (89:1). Though this being was born a bull, it becomes a human who builds himself a boat and lives on the boat with three bulls (Noah's sons Shem, Ham, and Japheth). Enoch watches while water cascades down in seven streams from heaven and rises from underground fountains until "water, darkness, and mist" cover the whole earth (89:4). All the cattle, elephants, camels, and asses sink to the bottom and drown (89:6). After a while, the water descends, the ground becomes visible, the boat settles onto the earth, the darkness vanishes, all becomes light, and the white bull (Noah) with the three bulls (Noah's sons) come out of the boat (89:8-9). In this segment, we see the first animal creature (a white bull) in the account become a human. We will see a few (but very few) other transformations of animal creatures into humans as the story continues.

In this final segment of the first era, one notices once again the remarkable selectivity of the account. There is no mention of animals of every species on the ark, birds that are sent out to see if there is land somewhere, sacrifices that Noah and his sons offer, a rainbow, or other details of the story of the flood. Rather, the dream vision condenses the story-line into an account of earth-material animal creatures, of an earth-creature who is transformed into a man (Noah), of heavenly beings who come to earth in the form of earth-material men to perform various tasks, and of fallen stars who become earth-material cattle who cause other cattle to give birth to elephants, camels, and asses and then are bound hand and foot and cast into pits in the earth.

The second era in the Animal Apocalypse account extends from the renewal of creation after the flood to the great judgment after the Maccabean Revolt (89:9–90:27).[44] Nickelsburg has divided this into seven segments:

1. From the Disembarkation to the Exodus (89:9-27)
2. From the Exodus to Moses' Death (89:28-38)
3. From the Entrance into the Land to the Building of the Temple (89:39-50)
4. The Apostasy of the Two Kingdoms (89:51-58)
5. The Commissioning of the Seventy Shepherds and the Angelic Scribe (89:59-64)

[44] Nickelsburg, *1 Enoch 1*, 354-55.

6. The First Period: The Twelve Shepherds until the Exile (89:65-72a)
7. The Second Period: The Twenty-Three Shepherds from the Return to Alexander (89:72b–90:1)
8. The Third Period: The Twenty-Three Shepherds from Alexander into the Second Century (90:2-5)
9. The Fourth Period: The Twelve Shepherds until the End Time (90:6-19)

The second era is so long, and has so many details, that it is not feasible to give a full account of it here. Instead, a few special characteristics of this era will be highlighted to exhibit the nature of the earth-material animal creatures, the heavenly beings, and the occasional humans (!) in this earth-material animal creature apocalyptic account.

In the first segment of the second era (89:9-27), the three bulls (sons of Noah) with the white bull who had become a man (Noah) beget wild beasts and birds. In turn, the beasts and birds beget "lions, leopards, wolves, dogs, hyenas, wild boars, foxes, squirrels, pigs, falcons, vultures, kites, eagles, and ravens" (89:10: Gentiles). But also a white bull is born (89:10: Abraham), who begets a wild ass (89:11: Ishmael) and a white bull (Isaac). The bull then bears a black wild boar (89:12: Esau) and a white ram[45] (89:12: Jacob). The boar begets many boars and the ram begets twelve sheep (89:12: the twelve sons of Jacob). When the twelve sheep grow up, they give one of their members (Joseph) to the wild asses (Ishmaelites[46]), who give him away to the wolves[47] (Egyptians), with whom he then lives (89:13). The ram[48] brings the eleven sheep to dwell with and pasture in the midst of the wolves, and they multiply and become many flocks of sheep (89:14: Israelite slaves).

At this point "the Lord" becomes a personage in the story. In *1 En.* 89:15–90:40, "the Lord of the sheep" occurs twenty-six times; "the Lord" five times; "their Lord" four times; "our Lord" once; and "the Lord of righteousness" once.[49] Sometimes the Lord is clearly the Lord God, as when the sheep "complain unto their Lord" (89:15); at other times the Lord is clearly Moses, as when "the Lord of the sheep" goes with them as their leader, with a face that is "glorious, adorable, and marvelous to behold" (89:22). At other times, it is not entirely clear if

[45] All occurrences of "ram" in *1 Enoch* follow Nickelsburg, *1 Enoch 1*, 365, 368, n. 89:12b. In some instances there is a different translation in E. Isaac, "1 (Ethiopic Apocalypse of) Enoch," *OTP* 1:5-89.

[46] For Ishmaelites rather than Midianites, see Nickelsburg, *1 Enoch 1*, 378.

[47] Possibly hyenas: Nickelsburg, *1 Enoch 1*, 378.

[48] See note 45 on "ram."

[49] Following Nickelsburg, *1 Enoch 1*, 364-67, 387-88, 402: "the Lord of the sheep": 89:16, 22, 26, 29, 30, 33, 36, 42, 50 (twice), 51, 52, 54, 57, 70, 71, 75, 76; 90:14, 15, 17, 18, 20 (twice), 29, 33, 38; "the Lord": 89:18, 54; 90:17, 21, 34; "their Lord": 89:15, 16, 20, 24; "our Lord": 89:31; and "the Lord of righteousness": 90:40.

"the Lord of the sheep" is the Lord God or Moses. The uncertainty of reference has an intriguing relation to the uncertainty at times whether "the Lord" refers to the Lord God or to the Lord Jesus Christ in some of the writings of Paul in the NT.

The following account gives only a few highlights of a very detailed story. When the sheep "complain unto their Lord (God)" (89:15) and "pray to their Lord (God)" (89:16), the Lord of the sheep (Moses?) descends to them from a lofty chamber (89:16). The sheep go to the wolves and speak to them "in accordance to the word of the Lord (God?)" (89:18). Then the Lord (God) came to the sheep and began to strike the wolves (the plagues: 89:20). Once the sheep arrive in the desert, they begin to open their eyes and see while the Lord of the sheep (Moses?) "was pasturing them and giving them water and grass, and that sheep was going and leading them" (89:28). After the sheep become afraid and can no longer "stand before our Lord (God or Moses?) or look at him" (89:31), "the Lord of the sheep (God) was filled with great wrath against them, and that sheep (Moses) discovered it and went down from the summit of that rock and came to the sheep and found most of them blinded and straying" (89:33). Finally, "that sheep that had led them, that had become a man (Moses), was separated from them and fell asleep" (89:38; cf. 89:36). Once the sheep enter the land (Canaan) under the leadership of other sheep, "the dogs, foxes, and the wild boars began to devour those sheep" until the Lord of the sheep (God) raised up three rams in succession. The first ram (89:42: Saul) "began to butt and pursue with its horns" until it forsook its path (89:44). The Lord of the sheep (God) send a sheep (Samuel) to another sheep (David) to appoint it to be "ram and ruler and leader of the sheep" (89:45). This ram begat many sheep until it fell asleep. Then the third ram (Solomon), who was a little sheep, became a ram (89:48b). Then the house became large and broad, with a large and high tower built upon it for the Lord of the sheep (God: 89:50).

After the building of the house, the sheep began to abandon "that house of theirs" (89:51). When the Lord of the sheep (God) summoned some from among the sheep (prophets) and sent them to the sheep, the sheep began to kill them, but one of them (Elijah) escaped safely (89:51-52). Then Enoch says: "the Lord of the sheep saved it (Elijah) from the hands of the sheep and brought it up to me and made it dwell there" (89:52). At this point, language of "abandonment" begins.[50] The sheep "abandoned the house of the Lord and his tower, they went astray in everything, and their eyes were blinded" (89:54). In turn, the Lord of the sheep (God) works "much slaughter on them" and abandons them into the hands of the lions, leopards, wolves, hye-

[50] See Nickelsburg on "abandonment," *1 Enoch*, 393.

nas, foxes, and all the beasts, "and those wild beasts began to tear those sheep in pieces" (89:55). Although Enoch cried out (89:57), the Lord of the sheep (God) was silent and "rejoiced because they were devoured and swallowed up and carried off, and he abandoned them into the hands of all the beasts as fodder" (89:58).

After this, the Lord of the sheep (God) summoned seventy shepherds and an angelic scribe: twelve until the exile (89:65-72a); twenty-three shepherds from the return to Alexander (89:72b–90:1); twenty-three shepherds from Alexander into the second century BCE (90:2-5); and twelve shepherds until the end time (90:6-19). There is a debate in scholarship concerning the identity of the seventy shepherds and the scribe.[51] Ezekiel 34 features shepherds who are in charge of Israel and abuse their power by making Israel suffer. This is a major theme in *1 En.* 89–90.[52] The twelve shepherds during the fourth period are worse than any who have come before them. As *1 En.* 90:17-19 presents it:

> [17] And I looked at that man who wrote the book at the word of the Lord, until he opened the book of the destruction that those last twelve shepherds worked, and he showed before the Lord of the sheep that they had destroyed more than those before them. [18] And I saw until the Lord of the sheep came to them and took in his hand the staff of his wrath and struck the earth, and the earth was split, and all the beasts and all the birds of heaven fell (away) from among those sheep and sank in the earth, and it covered over them. [19] And I saw until a large sword (Judas Maccabeus?)[53] was given to those sheep, and the sheep went out against all the wild beasts to kill them, and all the beasts and the birds of heaven (Hellenistic rulers?) fled before them. (*1 En.* 90:17-19)

The time of Maccabean rule appears to be the context for the final era, when God judges the world and establishes a new world. God's striking of the earth, the splitting of the earth, and the sinking of the beasts and birds into the earth is a returning of destructive earth-material beings back into the earth from which they came.

The third era in the Animal Apocalypse features the Judgment and the New Age (90:20-42).[54] Nickelsburg divides it into three segments:

1. The Judgment (90:20-27)
2. A New Beginning (90:28-38)
3. The Conclusion to the Vision (90:39-42)

The final portion of the Animal Apocalypse begins:

[51] Nickelsburg, *1 Enoch 1*, 388-401.

[52] Nickelsburg, *1 Enoch 1*, 389-94.

[53] Cf. 2 Macc 15:15-16, when Jeremiah appears in a vision to Judas Maccabeus and gives him a sword; see Jonathan A. Goldstein, *II Maccabees* (AB 41A; Garden City, NY: Doubleday, 1983) 499.

[54] Nickelsburg, *1 Enoch 1*, 355.

> And I saw until a throne was constructed in the pleasant land and the Lord of the sheep sat upon it, and he took all the sealed books and opened those books before the Lord of the sheep. (*1 En.* 90:20)

The similarity of this scene with Daniel 7:9-10 is striking. The differences also are striking. Instead of "thrones" being set in place in the heavenly throne room (Dan 7:9), "a throne" is constructed "in the pleasant land" (*1 En.* 90:20). The focus on the land coheres with the account of Israel and the nations as an "earth-material" account. Similarities and differences are of equal interest in the description of God. Dan 7:9 describes God as "an Ancient One" who "took his throne, his clothing was white as snow, and the hair of his head like pure wool … The courts sat in judgment, and the books were opened." In turn, *1 En.* 90:20 says "the Lord of the sheep sat upon it (the throne), and he (the one the Lord summoned to be a scribe in *1 En.* 89:61-64) took all the sealed books and opened those books before the Lord of the sheep." *1 Enoch* 85–90 never describes the Lord of the sheep in the judgment scene as being clothed in white or having hair like pure wool. Rather, "the three" who come and take Enoch's hand are "clothed in white" (*1 En.* 90:31), and "all those sheep" who are "gathered into that house" in the new age "were white, and their wool was thick and pure" (*1 En.* 90:32-34). It appears, however, that the "Ancient One" in Dan 7 has features that would be natural for "the Lord of the sheep" who is described in the Animal Apocalypse. When Moses is described as the Lord of the sheep leading Israel out of Egypt, "his face was dazzling and glorious and fearful to behold" (*1 En.* 89:22). After the Lord of the sheep goes up to the summit of a high rock" (89:29), "his appearance was majestic and fearful and mighty" 89:30). Then that sheep became a man (89:36, 38). After the Lord of the sheep causes rams (kings) to arise to lead the sheep (89:42-50), there are no descriptions of the appearance of the Lord of the sheep. It is noticeable that the Lord of the sheep took the book from the hand of the scribe, read it, and set it down in 89:71 (cf. 89:77). When the Lord of the sheep "came upon them in wrath" (90:15), he "took in his hand the staff of his wrath and struck the earth, and the earth was split, and all the beasts and all the birds of heaven fell (away) from among those sheep and sank in the earth, and it covered over them" (90:18). In contrast, Dan 7 describes the action of the "Ancient One" with "the hair of his head like pure wool" with passive verbs:

> [11] And as I watched, the beast was put to death, and its body destroyed and given over to be burned by fire. [12] As for the rest of the beasts, their dominion was taken away, but their lives were prolonged for a season and a time. (Dan 7:11-12)

We will discuss below the shift that occurs when political power and wealth, rather than earthly progeny, becomes the focus. The dramatic finish during the final era in the Animal Apocalypse occurs when, in the context of the judgment of the sheep, a white bull is born with large horns. After the wild beasts and all the birds of heaven are afraid of it and petition it continually, all their species are changed and they become white cattle (90:37-38). As Nickelsburg states:

> the birth of this extraordinary human being triggers the transformation of the whole human race, Israelites and Gentiles, into primordial righteousness and perfection…. [T]he present text … juxtaposes the transformation with the birth of a figure, into whose image, so to speak, the human race is transformed. The closest analogy is in the two-Adams theology of the apostle Paul.[55]

In the Animal Apocalypse, once all the sheep including Enoch (90:31) are gathered into the new house brought by the Lord of the sheep (90:28-29), the end time messiah comes in the form of a white bull with large horns (90:37). All the wild beasts and birds of heaven are afraid of it and petition it continually (90:37) until, finally, all their species are changed into white cattle (90:38). Among the cattle is a large animal leader with large black horns on its head, and the Lord of the sheep rejoices over it and over all the cattle (90:38). At this point, Enoch awakes from his dream, blesses the Lord of righteousness and gives him glory, and weeps bitterly for everything that will come to pass on the basis of what he saw in his second dream and what he remembers about his first dream (90:39-42).

The importance of this dream vision mode of apocalyptic discourse will become more and more evident as we proceed through apocalyptic discourse in Daniel and in the New Testament. The account in this volume and the next will be incomplete in many ways. The goal is to introduce strategies of analysis and interpretation that exhibit and analyze modes of blending that occurred during the Hellenistic-Roman era in which Christianity emerged. These strategies of analysis and interpretation have the potential to shed light on multiple aspects of biblical, Jewish, and Christian discourse that readers and interpreters know well in certain ways but do not understand well in other ways. The next step to help us understand some of the new challenges that lie before analysis and interpretation emerge as we turn to the book of Daniel in the Hebrew Bible.

[55] Nickelsburg, *1 Enoch 1*, 407.

Apocalyptic Discourse in Daniel

The book of Daniel in the Hebrew Bible helps to set the stage for understanding the nature of apocalyptic in the writings in the New Testament.[56] The first six chapters of Daniel present angel-spirit apocalyptic narrative containing wisdom-story legends in contexts of powerful cities, kings, and kingdoms. These chapters share many emphases and themes with the three Synoptic Gospels and the Acts of the Apostles at the beginning of the New Testament. The last six chapters of Daniel (7–12) present earth-material apocalyptic visions, which share many emphases and themes with the Revelation to John at the end of the New Testament. In basic ways, then, the first and last parts of the book of Daniel have a deep and substantive relation to the writings that open and close the NT canon. It will be important to discuss this further below.

For a reader who approaches the book of Daniel in the Hebrew Bible as a prophetic book, it can be a surprise to discover that the first six chapters do not contain the word "prophet" (*prophētēs*) or any other formulations from the Greek stem *prophēt-*, which might mean "to prophesy" or might characterize someone's activity as "prophesying." There are four occurrences of the noun "prophet" in chapter nine of Daniel (9:2, 6, 10, 24), but none of them refers to Daniel or any other person in the Daniel narrative.[57] Instead of words for prophet or prophesying, Dan 1–6 contains eight occurrences of the word "wisdom" (*sophia*),[58] and fourteen occurrences of the word "wise man" (*sophos*).[59] This means that Dan 1–6 contains apocalyptically configured wisdom stories in a context of cities, kings, and kingdoms. The focus on wisdom in these stories creates angel-spirit apocalyptic rather than earth-material apocalyptic. In other words, in the first six chapters,

[56] Carey, *Ultimate Things*, 37-49.

[57] All the references to prophets in Daniel refer specifically or generally to prophets in the history of Israel with no specific reference to Daniel. Daniel 9:2 refers to the number of years (seventy) that Daniel perceived to be the length of time before the devastation of Jerusalem "according to the word of the Lord to the prophet Jeremiah." Then in Dan 9:6, Daniel confesses to God in prayer: "We have not listened to your servants the prophets…." After this, Daniel confesses to God that "our kings, our officials, and our ancestors … have not obeyed the voice of the Lord our God by following his laws, which he set before us by his servants the prophets" (9:9-10). Lastly, in Dan 9:24 "the man Gabriel" (9:21) tells Daniel that a period of seventy weeks (of years: 9:2) has been decreed to bring things to completion with both his people and his holy city in six ways: (1) to finish the transgression; (2) to put an end to sin; (3) to atone for iniquity; (4) to bring in everlasting righteousness; (5) to seal both vision and prophet; and (6) to anoint a most holy place. The reference to sealing "both vision and prophet" naturally holds great interest for anyone interpreting the opening of the seals in Rev 5–8.

[58] Dan 1:4, 17, 20; 2:20, 21, 23, 30; 5:14.

[59] Dan 2:12, 13, 14, 18, 21, 24(2), 27, 48; 4:3, 15; 5:7, 8, 15.

angels have no earth-material form,[60] and God communicates with the spirit of Daniel and kings through dreams and visions.[61] Angels are spirit-beings who perform certain tasks for God to fulfill God's plans for faithful human beings. Since dialogue with kings who rule over kingdoms is a central feature of prophetic discourse, Dan 1–6 is a blend of wisdom and prophetic discourse that functioned as an especially dynamic emergent structure for early Christian discourse. But there is more, since there is an emphasis on faithful prayer, worship, fasting, holiness, and purity that blends wisdom and prophetic discourse with priestly discourse in Dan 1–6. In the end, Dan 1–6 is a dynamic blend of wisdom, prophetic, priestly, and apocalyptic discourse in an angel-spirit apocalyptic mode of narration.

From the perspective of the two streams of apocalyptic in Judaism we have described above, Dan 1–6 presents angel-spirit apocalyptic events with some earth-material topoi blended into some of the activities of the kings. In other words, the dreams and events with statues to be worshipped in the angel-spirit apocalyptic stories in the first six chapters set the stage for Daniel's earth-material dream-visions in Dan 7–12. One of the important differences between the first six chapters and the last six is that the angel-spirit apocalyptic dimensions in Dan 1–6 originate with dreams and actions of kings, while the dream-visions in Dan 7–12 originate with Daniel. A major topos in Dan 1–6 is each king's interest in becoming the ruler of all nations and peoples on earth, and a major means toward this "total rule" is worship of some foreign god or idol. In the context of Jewish apocalyptic, of course, this worship is a violation of the daily practice of blessing and praising "the Most High" who created everything in the universe, which the angels established on the first day of God's creation of the world (*Jub.* 2). When various kings in Babylon take actions to become the ruler of all nations and peoples on earth, Daniel emerges as a very special "wise man" who communicates the mistakes of these kings by interpreting dreams and other unusual things that happen to the kings. Daniel is able to interpret these things as a result of "revelations" from the God of heaven.[62] This is communicated to the reader by verses like Dan 2:22, where Daniel praises and blesses the God of heaven, because "He reveals (*anakalyptōn*) deep and hidden things." Then Daniel tells the king that "there is a God in heaven who reveals mysteries, and he has disclosed to King Nebuchadnezzar what will happen at the end of days" (2:28).

[60] Dan 3:25, 28; 6:22.

[61] Dan 2:1, 3, 35; 4:8, 9, 18; 5: 11, 12, 14, 20; 6:3; 7:15 (cf. 10:17).

[62] *Apokalyptō* terminology is used to talk about these "revelations" in Dan 2:19, 22, 28, 29, 30, 47(2), 10:1; 11:35.

The content of both dreams and actions by kings in the angel-spirit apocalyptic stories in Dan 1–6 set the stage for the earth-material apocalyptic visions of Daniel in Dan 7–12. King Nebuchadnezzar's dream in Dan 2 features a great statue made of gold, silver, bronze, iron, and clay, and in Daniel 3 the king builds a golden statue, which everyone should fall down and worship. These "earth-materials," namely metals and clay, are the "substance" of political power and wealth in earth-material apocalyptic. The events themselves remain in the domain of angel-spirit apocalyptic narrative, since no heavenly being appears in the form of these earth-materials and no creature-like or beast-like beings emerge from the sea or are present on the earth.

Earth-material apocalyptic imagery continues to hover over the angel-spirit apocalyptic accounts in Dan 3–6 when Daniel and his companions are protected from the raging flames in the fiery furnace by God's angel (3:28). The implicit imagery is that they are not made of metals that would be refined by blazing fire but by pure and holy bodies that fire does not destroy. When King Nebuchadnezzar's mind is changed into the mind of an animal as he lives among animals (4:15-16) and his hair becomes as long as eagles' feathers and his nails become like birds' claws (4:32-33), one is seeing imagery close to inner dimensions of the Animal Apocalypse in *1 Enoch* 85–90. Likewise, the imagery of the political power of King Darius in lions who can "overpower" and "break all bones of people in pieces" (6:24) is imagery at home in earth-material apocalyptic. Daniel and his companions, however, are nurtured by angel-spirit modes of beings. No heavenly being comes in an "earth-material" form to destroy the king or any representatives of the king. Also, while King Nebuchadnezzar's hair becomes as long as eagles' feathers and his hair becomes like birds' claws (4:33), which are images of political power in earth-material apocalyptic, he is not able in this "earthly-substance" form to rule over people like an eagle or destroy nations with his claws. The earth-material imagery in Dan 2–6, then, presents topics of political power and wealth in a mode of angel-spirit apocalyptic. Daniel's spirit is repeatedly informed by God's direct revelations to him in contexts where an angel may come from heaven to protect him from a devouring fire (3:28) or shut the mouths of hungry lions (6:22). Nowhere does Daniel or any king contend with or see vicious beasts like dragons, many-headed serpents, or beasts with bodies composed of clay, metals, and body-parts of animals. Likewise, no angel that comes to Daniel's aid displays a visibility that looks like earth materials. Rather, Dan 1–6 contains wisdom-legends that have been configured into angel-spirit apocalyptic events dealing with political power and wealth. In the context of these angel-spirit events, iron, bronze, silver, and gold mixed with clay (2:31-35), as well as eagle feathers and bird claws, exhibit the nature of political power and wealth in all its glory and in all its vulnerability. In this mode, the story awaits earth-material apocalyptic visions to bring the plot to a dramatic apocalyptic conclusion.

Earth-material apocalyptic visions emerge suddenly in Dan 7 and continue to the end of Daniel. In this portion of Daniel, dream visions appear directly to Daniel when he is sleeping, without any preceding dream, action, or experience of a king. These chapters contain earth-material apocalypses that function as a precedent for the earth-material apocalyptic scenes in the Revelation to John at the end of the NT. After King Darius[63] has written "to all peoples and nations of every language throughout the world," telling them they must "tremble and fear before the God of Daniel" (Dan 6:25-28), Daniel has "a dream and visions of his head as he lay in bed" (7:1). In a quintessential apocalyptic gesture, Daniel writes the dream down (7:1). The dream vision recounts the rule of various kingdoms in an earth-material apocalyptic mode until heaven intervenes. Daniel saw "the four winds of heaven" creating a hurricane in the great sea (7:2). As a result of the hurricane, four great beasts came up out of the sea, different from one another (7:3). The first animal creature is like a lion with eagles' wings, and its wings are plucked off and it is lifted up from the ground and made to stand on two feet like a human being, and it is given a human mind (7:4). Here we see a variation on the angel-spirit dream vision in Dan 4:13-16, where a tree (who is a non-Israelite ruler) is destroyed and made into a human with an animal mind. The second animal creature from the sea looks like a bear with three tusks among its teeth, and it is told to arise and devour many bodies (7:5). The third animal creature is like a leopard with four wings and four heads, and it is given power to rule (7:6). Then a fourth animal creature, "terrifying and dreadful and exceedingly strong" (7:7) comes out of the sea. It has iron teeth, feet that destroy everything on which they stamp, and ten horns with a little horn, containing human eyes and an arrogant mouth, that comes up and plucks up three of the ten horns (7:7-8).

There are three observations about these powerful animal creatures that call for comment here. First, these beasts have a strong relation both to the lions, leopards, eagles, and other animals (Gentiles) who come forth from the sons of Noah (*1 En.* 89:10) and the lions, leopard, and other animals whom God allows to "tear the sheep in pieces" just prior to the exile in the Animal Apocalypse (*1 En.* 89:55). Second, the animal creatures in Daniel are not pictured as populations of people but

[63] For identification of King Darius, see, e.g., Stephen R. Miller, *Daniel* (NAC 18; Broadman & Holman Publishers, 1994) 171-77; Norman W. Porteous, *Daniel: A Commentary* (Philadelphia: Westminster Press, 1965) 83-84.

as powerful rulers and kingdoms. Third, human characteristics emerge in relation to two of the animal creatures: (a) the lion-eagle that is made into a human with a human mind (Dan 7:4), and (b) the beast with iron teeth and ten horns in which a little horn emerges with human eyes and a mouth that speaks arrogantly (Dan 7:8). Again, the earth-material mode of apocalyptic storytelling in Dan 7 focuses on non-Israelite rulers and kingdoms rather than on populations of people that emerge from Adam and Eve and their descendants, as in the Animal Apocalypse in *1 En.* 85–90. In other words, the focus is on political power and wealth, rather than on demographic or ethnic identity.

The sequence of political beasts in Daniel leads to a scene in heaven, where thrones are placed, the Ancient One takes his throne, fire streams out from the presence of the throne, thousands and thousands serve and attend the Ancient One, the court sits in judgment, and the books are opened (7:9-10). We have observed above how the Ancient of Days has hair like pure wool (7:9), which would be a natural characteristic of the Lord of the sheep in the Animal Apocalypse in *1 En.* 85–90. After the destruction and burning of the fourth beast (Dan 7:11) and the disempowerment of the other beasts (Dan 7:12), "one like a human being" comes with clouds to the Ancient One, and he is given dominion, glory, and kingship over all peoples, nations, and languages, and his kingship will never be destroyed (7:13-14). This dream vision puzzles and terrifies Daniel so thoroughly that he asks one of the heavenly attendants to interpret it, which he does (7:15-17). Instead of everyone becoming white cows who will gather forever in the house of God (*1 En.* 90:32-38), "the holy ones of the Most High" will receive an everlasting kingdom "and all dominions shall serve and obey them" (Dan 7:27; cf. 7:18). This focus on political power remains through Daniel 11. Therefore, "redemption" until Daniel 12 takes the form of receiving an eternal kingdom to which all people on earth are subservient, rather than on an eternal gathering of all people in the house of God. The focus, then, is on political rule rather than on faithful worship. The narrative has shifted its focus from faithful worship and praise of God (Dan 1–6) to God's superiority over all political power and wealth on earth.

The fourth dream vision in Dan 8 is of special interest in relation to the Animal Apocalypse in *1 En.* 85–90. In the third year of the reign of King Belshazzar, Daniel saw a vision in which he saw himself in Susa, the capitol of Persia (Dan 8:1-2). Looking up, he saw a ram with two horns, one longer than the other, standing by the river Ulai and then charging westward and northward and southward (8:3-4). Everything is powerless against the ram until a male goat with a horn between its eyes appears from the west, strikes the ram breaking its two horns, throws the ram to the ground, and tramples it (8:5-7). At the height of the power of this great goat, the great horn is broken and in its place rises up "four prominent horns toward the four winds of heaven" (8:8). Then a little horn comes out of one of the four and grows exceedingly great "toward the south, toward the east and toward the beautiful land" (cf. *1 En.* 90:20). When this little horn grew as high as heaven and "threw down to the earth some of the host and some of the stars, and trampled on them," it even acted arrogantly against "the prince of the host" (God) and "took the regular burnt offering away from him and overthrew the place of his sanctuary" (Dan 8:10-11). Then Daniel heard two holy ones in conversation about how long this transgression could continue, and the answer is given of two thousand three hundred days before the sanctuary will be restored to its rightful state (8:13-14).

Here it is important for us to observe four things. First, Dan 8 depicts a non-Israelite king, rather than an Israelite king, as a ram. Second, Dan 8 identifies a non-Israelite ruler as a goat, an animal that surprisingly is not present in the Animal Apocalypse in *1 Enoch* 85–90. Third, an animal (the goat) grows so high it is able to overpower even some of the heavenly powers (some of the host and the stars). Fourth, specific earthly events, namely an overtaking of the Jerusalem temple and a disruption of its regular burnt offering, are blended into the animal creature imagery, namely the growth, throwing down, and trampling activity of the goat.

After Daniel's vision in Dan 8:1-14 a personage like a man, whom a human voice identifies as the angel Gabriel, appears to Daniel and interprets the vision for him. For our discussion here, the descriptions of Gabriel in Dan 8:15-18 and 10:4-6 are especially important. The issue is the potential for a heavenly being to be described not only in terms of earthly animal creature bodies, including human bodies, but also in terms of earthly substances, like metals, clay, and stone. In Dan 8:15 Gabriel appears "standing" before Daniel, "having the appearance of a man." Gabriel's appearance, however, is frightening, causing Daniel to fall prostrate before him (8:17). As the scene continues, Gabriel speaks to Daniel, causing him to fall into a trance with his face to the ground. Then Gabriel touches Daniel and sets him on his feet (8:18). The experience causes Daniel to be "overcome" and "sick for many days" before he can return to the king's business (8:27). When Daniel sees Gabriel a second time, Gabriel looks like

> a man clothed in linen, with a belt of gold from Uphaz around his waist. [6] His body was like beryl, his face like lightning, his eyes like flaming torches, his arms and legs like the gleam of burnished bronze, and the sound of his words like the roar of a multitude. (Dan 10:5-6)

In this description, earthly substances characteristic of the statue in Dan 2:31-35 and the rulers and kingdoms in Dan 2:37-45; 4:15; and 7:2-7 are present in the body of the angel Gabriel. In other words, while on earth interpreting issues of political power, a characteristic of Gabriel's body may be earthly substances characteristic of the "technological" nature of powerful kingdoms. In other words, when apocalyptic discourse in the book of Daniel describes heavenly beings from a political point of view, the "substance" of their "bodies" may be a blend of human characteristics and earthly substances like metals, clay (probably "ceramic clay"), and/or stone. In the context where Gabriel is described as "a man" with clothing and body parts that are described in relation to earthly substances, lightning, and flaming torches, and he speaks words that roar (Dan 10:5-6), he talks to Daniel about "the prince of Persia" opposing him and Michael helping him before he comes to explain to Daniel what is to happen to his people at the end of days (10:13-14). He tells Daniel there will be another vision for those final days (10:14) and that he must return "to fight against the prince of Persia, and when I am through with him, the prince of Greece will come" (10:20). Then he explains that only he (Gabriel) and "Michael, your prince" contend "against these princes" (10:21). In Dan 10, then, the reader sees what one might call "the fully political" Gabriel. When Gabriel is engaged in political battle on earth, his "body" is a blend of human features, heavenly powers (like lightning), and earthly substances characteristic of powerful rulers and kingdoms.

In the final chapter of the book of Daniel (Dan 12), the emphasis on the political power of heaven and heavenly beings changes into an emphasis on the ability of heavenly powers to transform earthly human bodies into bodies with heavenly characteristics. At the end of time, according to Dan 12, Michael the great prince will arise and all of Daniel's people who are "found written in the book" shall be delivered (12:1-2). When many who sleep in the dust of the earth awaken, those who are wise "shall shine like the brightness of the sky" and those who lead many to righteousness will be "like the stars forever and ever" (12:3). In other words, the final goal of the book of Daniel lies beyond political victory in a transformation of wise and righteous people into heavenly-like beings. As we proceed, it will be important for us to keep in view the relation of the "politically" redemptive powers of heavenly beings to the "final" redemptive powers of heavenly beings in apocalyptic discourse.

Apocalyptic Discourse in the Mediterranean World as an Environment for First Century Christian Apocalyptic Rhetorolect

When Christianity emerged during the first century CE, apocalypticism was a widespread and growing phenomenon in the Mediterranean world. As is clear from Volume 1 of *The Encyclopedia of Apocalypticism*,[64] the widespread origins, the historical, social, cultural, and ideological dynamics, the number and nature of the streams of tradition, and the boundaries of apocalyptic with wisdom, prophetic, priestly, mystical, and astronomical or astrological traditions are highly contested in modern scholarship. It is obvious also, however, that any discussion of the emergence of Christian discourse in the Mediterranean world cannot avoid serious discussion of apocalyptic speech forms, literature, and discourse. Our argument is that a focus on inner sociorhetorical dynamics that attend to a combination of image-descriptive and argumentative-enthymematic structuring and of metaphorical and metonymical mapping in a context of sapientialization, scribalization, scripturalization, and canonization can help us to address certain issues concerning apocalyptic discourse in new and beneficial ways.

Since the arena of non-Jewish and non-Christian Mediterranean apocalyptic literature and discourse is so vast, it is more difficult than ever to decide what text or combination of texts to bring before a reader at the end of this chapter to help the reader move yet one step further toward a sociorhetorical understanding of the function of apocalyptic in first century Christian discourse. As a result of viewing first century Christian discourse in a context that reaches from hymns to Zeus and Isis and the rabbinic story-line of *Pirke Aboth* 1 to the Nicene Creed in the fourth century CE, the decision has been made to end this chapter with a focus on the Egyptian apocalypse of "The Oracle of the Potter." The overall rhetorical movement of this text, its structuring of images and argumentation, and its metaphorical and metonymic mapping help to exhibit the remarkable challenges, and yet the inescapable necessity, of discussing the elusive nature of apocalyptic discourse in the Mediterranean world during the time of the emergence of Christianity during the first century CE.

An Egyptian Apocalypse: The Oracle of the Potter

The Oracle of the Potter is an account by "the Potter" of an epiphany that reveals a sequence of actions by gods in the context of evil and disorder in the world. The apocalyptic dimensions of the text are related to Jewish and Christian angel-spirit apocalyptic rather than earth-material apocalyptic, since there is no imaging either of gods or of political kingdoms in terms of clay, metal, stone, and/or animal. Instead of angel-spirits, however, there are gods who move from one place to another. In this way the text exhibits a world of Mediterra-

[64] John J. Collins (ed.), *The Encyclopedia of Apocalypticism. Volume 1: The Origins of Apocalypticism in Judaism and Christianity* (New York: Continuum, 1998).

nean gods and goddesses, rather than the angel-spirit tradition of Jewish apocalyptic.

When Jonathan Z. Smith presented a brief interpretation of this oracle as an apocalyptic text in 1975, he argued that a major reason one could see its apocalyptic nature was its existence in multiple versions.[65] Because apocalyptic was such a scribal tradition, writing, rewriting, supplementing, reconfiguring, and reimagining the situation and meanings related to the text is central to its nature as apocalyptic discourse. Of special importance for Smith's interpretation was the existence of a 2nd century CE narrative frame for the story, which is extant only in P. Graf 29787:[66]

> During the reign of king Amenhotep (18th Dynasty), a potter, at the command of Hermes-Thot, goes to the island of Helios-Re where he practices his art. But the people are upset by this sacrilegious action. They pull the pottery out of the oven, break it and drag the potter before the king. The potter defends himself by interpreting this action as a prophetic sign. Just as the pottery has been destroyed, so Egypt, and finally the city of the followers of the evil god Typhon-Set will be destroyed.[67]

Smith explains that this text is "an epiphany of the ancient ram-headed deity Chnum who created the sun, the gods and man on his potter's wheel."[68] This allows the interpreter to understand that "For Chnum to have his pots broken is to plunge the world into total decreation and chaos.... The island of Helios-Re (in Egyptian, the Island of Flames) is the traditional birthplace of the solar deity and the scene of his defeat of the powers of chaos and darkness."[69]

Attempting to read this text with understanding from beginning to end exhibits well the highly challenging nature of interpreting apocalyptic during the time of the emergence of first century Christianity. The text moves beyond the boundaries of wisdom and prophetic tradition into the mysterious, esoteric realm of apocalyptic discourse. The hearer/reader knows the text is somehow working with boundaries of "historical" meanings and understandings. Yet the meanings always lie beyond clear and definitive interpretation, because they present "cosmic" explanations for the events and actions. This is the realm of apoca-

[65] Jonathan Z. Smith, "Wisdom and Apocalyptic," in *Religious Syncretism in Antiquity: Essays in Conversation with Geo Widengren* (ed. Birger A. Pearson; Missoula, MT: Scholars Press, 1975), 131-56 = idem, *Map is Not Territory*, 67-87.

[66] Smith, *Map is Not Territory*, 81.

[67] L. Koenen, "The Prophecies of a Potter: A Prophecy of World Renewal Becomes an Apocalypse," in D.H. Samuel (ed.), *Proceedings of the Twelfth International Congress of Papyrology* (1970) 249 [249-54]; Smith, ibid.

[68] Ibid., 82.

[69] Ibid.

lyptic texts. They continually push beyond that which can be clearly understood into the inner, mysterious, cosmic nature of events in the world. One of the keys to its mode of understanding is the ordering of its assertions into sequences that give certain meanings to its images, arguments, metaphors, and metonymies. The meanings of the assertions, however, are continually elusive, moving interpreters into controversies that can never be resolved. From this perspective, let us approach the four sections and conclusion of the Oracle of the Potter as an example of apocalyptic discourse outside the realm of Judaism and/or Christianity in the Mediterranean world. The first section unfolds as follows:

Earthly and Cosmic Evils during the Time of the Typhonians

> [1] The river, [2] [since it will not have] sufficient water, [will flood] but (only) a little so that scorched will be [3] [the land –] but unnaturally. [For] in the [time] of the Typhonians [4] [people will say] "Wretched Egypt, [you have been] maltreated [5] by the [terrible] malefactors who have committed evil against you." [6] And the sun will darken as it will not be willing to observe the evils (*ta kaka*) in Egypt. [7] The earth will not respond to seeds. These will be part of its [8] blight. [The] farmer will be <du>nned for taxes <for> wh<at> he did not plant. [9] There will be fighting in Egypt because people will be in need of food. [10] What one plants, [another] will reap and carry off. When this happens, [11] there will be [war and slaughter] which [will kill] brothers and wives. [12] For [these things will happen] when the great god Hephaistos will desire [13] to return to the [city], and the Girdlewearers will kill each other as they [14] [are Typhonians. –] evil will be done (*kakōthēsetai*). And he will pursue (them) on foot [15] [to the] sea [in] wrath and destroy many of them [16] because [they are] impious.

In the mode of apocalyptic partitioning of time, this initial section of the oracle describes the time of the Typhonians (1-16a). The image-descriptive structuring presents a sequence from insufficient irrigation of the land by the Nile river to darkening of the sun, absence of sprouts from seeds, unjust taxation by rulers, fighting and murder as a result of starvation, and flight to the sea in an attempt to avoid death and destruction. As the sequence unfolds, the text presents rationales that embed argumentative-enthymematic structuring in the narrative sequence. The lack of sufficient irrigation is not simply an ordinary phenomenon of nature, but it happens because "terrible malefactors" are committing evil (4-5) and because the great god Hephaistos wishes to return to the city (12-13). Who are the evildoers, that they can disrupt even the sun, earth, and ordinary family relationships (6-11)? Why can the great god not return to the city? Metaphoric mapping in the text transfers the domain of historical events to the domain of cosmic struggle between evil "Typhonians" and the great god Hephaistos. According to Stanley M.

Burstein, the Typhonians are followers of Typhon (Seth), "the Egyptian god of the desert, storm and foreigners, and brother and mortal enemy of Osiris."[70] This cosmic struggle emerges in a repetitive texture of evil-doing (*kakourgeō*) in the text. Lines 4 and 5 use three present or perfect tense participles referring to "evil-doing" to describe the maltreatment by the terrible evildoers during this time.[71] Line 6 characterizes the things happening during this time as "the evils in Egypt."[72] Then line 14 summarizes the terrible actions during this time as "evil that will be done."[73] While the metaphoric mapping makes the text highly challenging to interpret, the metonymic mapping of the evils in the text provide a pattern of understanding for the hearer/reader. These are the beginnings of a time of "tribulation," a period of time that will eventually move into some kind of dramatic transformation. But how long will the tribulations last, and what will happen next? This leads to the next section of the Oracle:

Social Tribulations during the Time of Foreign Kings

> <The king> will come from Syria, he who will be hateful to all [17] men, [–] ... and from Aithiopia [18] there will come ... He (together with some) of the unholy ones (will come) to Egypt, and he will [19] settle [in the city which] later will be deserted (*erēmōthēsetai*). [– [20] –]. [21] Their children will be made weak, and the country will be in confusion, [22] and many of the inhabitants of Egypt will abandon (*kataleipsousin*) [23] their homes (and) travel to foreign places. <Then there will be slaughter among friends>; and people will lament [24] their own problems although they are less than those of others. [25] Men will die at the hands of each other; two of them [26] will come to the same place to aid one. Among women [27] who are pregnant death will also be common. The Girdlewearers will kill themselves [28] as they also are Typhonians.

The image-descriptive structuring during this second era begins with a focus on hatred (16b) and continues with reference to death (25, 27), murder (23), and leaders destroying themselves (27-28). Unholy people come to Egypt (18); young and unborn children and their mothers experience evil and death (21, 27-28); friends not only destroy bonds of friendship but friends themselves (23, 26); and leaders do violence to other leaders (28a). Children will be made weak and the countryside will be in confusion (21); people will abandon their homes and travel to foreign places (22-23); friends will murder friends (23); people will

[70] Stanley M. Burstein, *The Hellenistic Age from the battle of Ipsos to the death of Kleopatra VII* (Cambridge: Cambridge University Press, 1985) 138.

[71] *talaina Aigyptos, kekakourgōmen hyparcheis deinois kata sou kekakourgōmenois kakourgēmasin* ("Wretched Egypt, you have been maltreated by the terrible malefactors who have committed evil against you").

[72] *ta en Aigyptai kaka.*

[73] *kakōthēsetai.*

lament their own problems even if they are less than those of others (24); men will die at each other's hands (25); and pregnant women will die (27). The argumentative-enthymematic structuring in this section occurs in the form of a "when ... then ..." sequence in which the coming of the hateful and unholy people to the city are the rationale for the disruption of social relationships. All of these things happened, because hateful and unholy people came to the city. But who are these people? Metaphoric mapping is present in the repetition of the statement at the end of the previous section that the Girdlewearers (Greek and Macedonian rulers) will kill themselves, since they also are Typhonians, namely people who worship the evil god who is the mortal enemy of Osiris (13, 28). The "real" problem, according to the discourse, concerns worship of the right god. Again the discourse is on the boundaries of historical events and actions. Interpreters can always justifiably enter into debate concerning the historical context for this discourse. But again the metonymic mapping provides a cross-mapping of domains for the hearer/reader. This is the second period within the time of tribulations the text is describing. This is a time when foreign kings come from Syria and Ethiopia (16b-28a), and their coming produces violence that extends from households and friends to rulers and the entire countryside. Occupied by confusion, disorder, and self-interest, people destroy even their own friends and allies. Disorder and destruction are present from the bottom of the social order to the top, with abandonment of homes (22-23), killing of friends as though they were enemies, and rising up to destroy one's own political allies (23-28). While the meanings of many of the details are elusive, they cause the hearer/reader to recruit the conceptual system of the partitioning of time within apocalyptic reasoning. While the first period of tribulation was caused by conflict between gods and allegiance to gods, the second period was caused by the arrival of hateful and unholy foreign rulers who continued to worship the wrong god. So what will happen next? Will things get still worse? Probably so. This takes us to the next section of the Oracle:

Desolation of the All-Nurturing City

> Then Agathos Daimon will [29] abandon (*kataleipsei*) the city that had been founded and enter Memphis, and [30] the city of foreigners, which had been founded, will be deserted (*exerēmōthēsetai*). This will happen [31] at the end of the evils (*epi telei tōn kakōn*) (of the time) when there came to Egypt a cr<owd> [32] of foreigners. The city of the Girdlewearers will be abandoned (*erēmōthēsetai*) like [33] my kiln because of the crimes which they committed against Egypt. [34] The cult images, which had been transported there, will be brought back again to [35] Egypt; and the city by the sea will be a refuge for fishermen because [36] Agathos Daimon and

> Knephis will have gone to Memphis, [37] so that passersby will say "All-nurturing was this city [38] in which every race of men settled."

The image-descriptive structuring during the third era (28b-38a) describes the desertion of "the city that had been founded" in the context of the transporting of the cult images to Memphis and asserts that the city by the sea will become a refuge for fishermen. The argumentative-enthymematic structuring asserts that these things will happen as a result of the movement of the god Agathos Daimon away from the city to Memphis. Also, the reason that the city by the sea becomes a refuge for fishermen is that the gods Agathos Daimon and Knephis move to Memphis. But exactly what meanings are associated with all the assertions? Metaphoric mapping is transferring historical events to the domain of movements of the gods from one city to another. "The city that had been founded" is Alexandria by the sea. When the god Agathos Daimon abandons Alexandria and moves to Memphis along with the god Knephis, Alexandria, the city of Girdlewearers, becomes a deserted place that becomes a refuge for fishermen. Memphis then becomes a city praised by passersby as "all-nurturing" for people who settle there from everywhere. The metaphorical mapping associates the movements of the gods to Memphis as the cause for the destruction of Alexandria, rather than as the result of Alexandria being conquered and Memphis being made the new capital. Moreover, the movement of the gods is related to the people's destruction of the kiln of the potter whose work imitates the god Chnum, who is the "potter" creator. Again, metonymic mapping allows the hearer/reader to "know" that the destruction of Alexandria is the climactic part of the time of tribulations. This is "the end" of the evils (*epi telei tōn kakōn*) which occurred with the coming of foreigners to Egypt (30-32). Shifting from predictions of death and murder to abandonment and desolation, the oracle asserts that the All-nurturing city (Alexandria) will become a wasteland when Agathos Daimon, the patron god of Alexandria, leaves it and goes to Memphis (28-29). What, then, will happen next?

Prosperity when the King descended from Helios appears

> Then will Egypt [39] flourish when the generous fifty-five year [40] ruler appears, the king descended from Helios, the giver of good things (*agathōn*), the one [41] installed by the greatest goddess [Isis], so that the living will pray [42] that the dead (*proteteleutēkotas*) might arise (*anastēnai*) to share th(e) [43] prosperity (*agathōn*). Finally the leaves will fall. The Nile, which had lacked water, [44] will be full and winter, which had changed its orderly ways, [45] will run its proper course and then summer will resume its own [46] track, and normal will be the wind's breezes which previously [47] had been weak. For in the <time> of the Typho-

> nians the sun will [48] darken to highlight the character of the evils <and> to reveal the greed of the [49] Girdlewearers. And Egypt [–].

The image-descriptive structuring of the final era (38b-49a) describes the leaves falling at their proper time, the Nile functioning properly during winter and summer because it is full of water, and the breezes of the wind being strong enough to do their work (43-48). The argumentative-enthymematic structuring presents the prosperity caused by the king descended from Helios (40) as the opposite of the "time of the Typhonians," when nothing ran its proper course or was strong enough to do its proper work (43-49). The time of evils was caused by the Typhonians and Girdleweavers, and the time of prosperity is caused by the new king. The metaphoric mapping associates the experience of prosperity and cosmic order with the appointment of the king by the god Helios and the installation of the king to the goddess Isis. As David E. Aune describes it:

> This vivid prediction of the collapse of the political, economic, and social order of Ptolemaic Egypt, followed by its reestablishment under the leadership of a savior-king, is based on the myth and ritual of the Egyptian enthronement ideology. The prophecies of the potter are patterned after the myth of Osiris: when the followers of Seth-Typhon revolt, Osiris kills Seth and a new king is installed as Horus by his mother Isis. This archaic native Egyptian tradition has been transformed into an apocalyptic scheme for the renovation of the cosmos.[74]

This metaphoric mapping creates the context for metonymic mapping, where the readers "know" the fourth era is the time of reversal after the times of tribulation, which brought natural and social disorders. When the king descended from Helios, the sun god Re, is installed by the goddess Isis, the natural order of both the heavens and earth will be restored. This is the era of transformation into a renewed cosmic order, which even brings forth hopes of resurrection from the dead. The words and phrases work metonymically as they invite the hearer/reader to invite the entire conceptual system, in which times of tribulation move to a time of transformation into blessing and hope. When the new ruler appears, the living will pray that those who have already died may arise to share in the prosperity of this fifty-five year era (39–43). This is the end of the Oracle, but what will be in the conclusion of the text? Could one anticipate that there will be provision for the text to be written down?

[74] See David E. Aune, *Prophecy in Early Christianity and the Ancient Mediterranean World* (Grand Rapids, MI: Eerdmans, 1983) 77.

Conclusion

> Having spoken clearly up to this point, he fell [50] silent. King Amenophis, who was grieved by the many disasters [51] he had recounted, buried the potter in Heliopolis [52] and placed the book in the sacred archives there and [53] unselfishly revealed it to all men. [54] Speech of the potter [55] to King Amenophis, <translated> as accurately as [56] possible, concerning what will happen in Egypt.

King Amenophis oversees the burial of the potter in the city that honors the god Helios and the placement of the book that records the oracle in the sacred archives, where these things can be revealed to all people. The internal sociorhetorical dynamics of this apocalyptic discourse exhibit structuring of images and argumentation, and mappings of metaphor and metonymy that persuade through pictorial narration in which metaphor communicates the cosmic nature of local events and metonymy invites the hearer-reader to recruit a cosmic drama of gods at work in the "ordinary," daily events of humans.

Conclusion

Two modes of Jewish apocalyptic discourse emerged during the second century BCE and continued on through the succeeding centuries. This means that both modes were present during the emergence of Christianity and continued to be produced as Christianity continued. The Jewish angel-spirit apocalyptic mode features reconfigurations of biblical stories by introducing good angel-spirits and evil angel-spirits or demons into them. This mode of apocalyptic discourse is present in the first six chapters of Daniel in Hebrew Bible, without the presence of any evil, demonic spirits in the account. In extra-biblical Jewish literature from the second century BCE onwards, angel-spirit apocalyptic discourse is well-developed, with detailed accounts about evil, demonic angel-spirits as well as good, holy angel-spirits. A second mode of Jewish apocalyptic discourse, which we call earth-material apocalyptic, features dream visions in which good and evil forces are pictured in relation to earthly substances. When angels, and indeed God, appear in the accounts, there are descriptions of their visual form in relation to precious or ordinary stone, highly valued or less valued metals, domesticated or wild creatures, and/or clay. This earth-material mode of apocalyptic discourse, embedded in angel-spirit apocalyptic discourse, occurs in Daniel 7–12 in the Hebrew Bible and in the Revelation to John in the New Testament.

The Jewish angel-spirit mode of apocalyptic discourse, which is in Daniel 1–6, is the primary apocalyptic mode in Matthew, Mark, Luke, Acts, and the letters in the New Testament. The Jewish earth-material mode of apocalyptic that personifies good and evil personages in "earth-material" form becomes a Christian mode of discourse only in the Revelation to John at the end of the New Testament. But things are never truly simple, of course. Many details and controversies await us as we move to the next chapter, which focuses on the nature of first century Christian apocalyptic rhetorolect as it functions throughout the NT writings.

9

Christian Apocalyptic Rhetorolect Part II: Periodization, Angel-Spirits, and Earth-Material Beings

Introduction

The NT begins with three prophetic narrative Gospels that configure certain events in the life of Jesus according to angel-spirit apocalyptic, which features angels, Satan, demons, unclean spirits, and holy spirit. After the Gospel of John, which foregrounds early Christian precreation rhetorolect as a context for the story of Jesus, the Acts of the Apostles contains prophetic narrative that configures the "witness mission" of Jesus' followers to the Gentiles in terms of angel-spirit apocalyptic. In the middle of the NT stands twenty-one letters attributed to Paul, James, John, Peter, and Jude, which embed angel-spirit apocalyptic in various ways in the time of Jesus and his followers. At the end of the NT stands an apocalypse that embeds an earth-material apocalyptic message focused on cities, military power, and wealth in an angel-spirit apocalyptic message.

First century Christians transferred the practice of angel-spirit apocalyptic "rewriting" of past biblical events, like one sees in *Jubilees*, to angel-spirit apocalyptic "telling" of the story of Jesus and his followers. Just as the practice of angel-spirit apocalyptic rewriting in Judaism was selective with regard to the events it reconfigured, so it is with first century Christian story-telling. In other words, as Jewish apocalyptists rewrote selective biblical events by highlighting the role of good and/or evil spirit beings in the stories, they recounted other events in a quite "biblically straightforward" manner. By biblically straightforward, we mean in the manner in which the story is told in the biblical account. A similar kind of selectivity exists in the NT writings that tell the story of Jesus and his followers. Many of the "Christian" events are told in a manner that can appropriately be called a quite straightforward "biblical" manner. In many instances in the NT, this is a "prophetic" manner, namely a manner characteristic of prophetic biblical narrative or speech. In the midst of prophetic stories and prophetic speech, however, first century Christian apocalyptic storytelling features angels, Satan, and evil, demonic spirits who play significant roles, or are considerable topics of discussion.

One of the things that is "new" in the NT, therefore, is the recounting of events about Jesus and his followers in the extracanonical mode of apocalyptic "rewriting" of the Bible. This means that the Gospels, Acts, and Letters in the NT contain apocalyptic features much like they are present in extracanonical rewritten Bible, rather than like they occur in Daniel in the Hebrew Bible. As we said in the previous chapter, there is an uncanny relation between the first half and last half of the book of Daniel and the opening and closing of the NT canon. In many ways the book of Daniel in the Hebrew Bible is a Jewish "proto-configuration" of the overall framework of the NT, whereby narratives containing angel-spirit apocalyptic events at the beginning set the stage for earth-material apocalyptic visions of God's judgment of the world at the end. In comparison to the book of Daniel, there are three Gospels and the Acts of the Apostles at the beginning of the NT that present prophetic narratives blended with wisdom stories and sayings, miracle stories, and angel-spirit apocalyptic events. As with Daniel, this blend creates a context for a focus on priestly issues of prayer, fasting, purity, holiness, and praise and worship of God. The NT enriches the apocalyptically configured prophetic narratives in the Synoptic Gospels and Acts with the Gospel of John and twenty-one letters as it moves toward its dramatic conclusion in an earth-material Apocalypse to John.

The Gospel of John and the twenty-one letters blend first century Christian wisdom, prophetic, precreation, miracle, and priestly rhetorolect in a variety of ways with angel-spirit apocalyptic. The large corpus of letters plus seven apocalyptic letters at the beginning of Revelation function as a bridge from the apocalyptically configured narratives at the beginning of the NT to the earth-material apocalypse at the end. The Revelation to John at the end presents God's heavenly Messiah Jesus as a blend of metals, head and hair like white wool, fire, sun, and voice with the roar of mighty waters who, as "one like the Son of man," dictates seven letters for John to write down and send to seven churches in Asia Minor (Rev 1–3). After dictating the letters, this "one like the Son of man" appears as the Lion of Judah who is the Little Ram who was slain (Rev 5), and then as King of kings and Lord of lords who destroys evil nations with the two-edged sword that comes out of his mouth (Rev 17; 19). This change in form of God's Messiah Jesus is startling, but as we have noted above, it has a deep relation to the apocalyptic dream-visions in the last six chapters of the book of Daniel in the Hebrew Bible. The dramatic differences between apocalyptic in most of the NT and in the Revelation to John has been, and still is, a topic of much concern and discussion among biblical scholars, theologians, clergy, lay people, and perhaps others. Rarely, however, is there an awareness of the real internal issue, namely the existence of two noticeably alternative streams of apocalyptic tradition both before and during the emergence of Christianity in the Mediterranean world, one focused on angel-spirit beings and their relation to flesh, blood, and desire, and another that embeds earth-material beings and their relation to clay, precious metals and stones, cities, military power, and wealth in the angel-spirit stream of tradition.

The centrifugal effect of apocalyptic discourse in first century Christianity was so pervasive that virtually every writing in the NT contains some dimension of apocalyptic conceptuality. Earth-material apocalyptic, however, is in the foreground only in the Revelation to John. All the other NT writings, to the extent that they contain apocalyptic conceptuality, present aspects of angel-spirit apocalyptic with very few events that qualify as "apocalypses."[1] This raises issues for interpreting "apocalyptic" in first century Christian writings with which many interpreters have grappled over many decades. During the last part of the twentieth century, the SBL Literature Genres Project on apocalyptic confronted interpreters with the issue of whether or not it was appropriate to refer to Mark 13 as a "little apocalypse," and, as a consequence, Matthew 24–25 and Luke 22 as modifications that either strengthen or weaken the apocalyptic emphases in Mark 13.[2] The issue is that there is no angelic mediator to Jesus of the content in Mark 13 and parallels. Our approach is somewhat different. One of the characteristics of the angel-spirit stream of apocalyptic was "rewriting" biblical history in a manner that makes angels and demonic spirits (including their satanic leader) participants in the events of history. In other words, apocalyptists considered most biblical accounts of events to be told in a manner that did not reveal the true mysterious powers at work in the events.[3] Apocalyptically informed writers knew how "unseen" powers were at work, because scenes in the heavens had revealed these dimensions of the events either to them or to previous apocalyptic writers. The "unknown dimensions" of the events regu-

[1] Christopher Rowland, *The Open Heaven: A Study of Apocalyptic in Judaism and Early Christianity* (New York: Crossroad, 1982) 351-441; John J. Collins, *The Apocalyptic Imagination: An Introduction to Jewish Apocalyptic Literature* (2nd ed.; Grand Rapids, MI: Eerdmans, 1998) 256-79.

[2] John J. Collins, ed., *Apocalypse: The Morphology of a Genre* (Semeia 14; Chico, CA: Scholars Press, 1979) 9; Adela Yarbro Collins, "Early Christian Apocalyptic Literature," *ANRW* 25.6 (1988) 4691; idem, *Cosmology and Eschatology in Jewish and Christian Apocalypticism* (JSJSup 50; Leiden: Brill, 1996) 7; Rowland, *The Open Heaven*, 43-48.

[3] Rowland, *The Open Heaven*, 2.

larly involved the actions of good angel-spirits in relation to the actions either of evil humans or of rebellious angel-spirits who had become demonic, evil spirits on earth. Thus, a number of apocalyptists specialized in rewriting well-known biblical stories in a manner that revealed how various angel-spirit beings had been "invisibly" at work in the events.

As we observed in the previous chapter, apocalyptists divided the history of the world into parts. During the first century CE, both newly emerging Jewish apocalyptic literature and emerging Christian literature were presenting "special" apocalyptic understanding of various parts of this world history.[4] In other words, each "part" of world history was a potential emergent structure for apocalyptic interpretation of the nature of this age, the end, and eternal time after the end. The best way for us to set the stage for understanding which parts of time emergent Christian literature configured apocalyptically and how they configured it is to begin with periodization of world history in The Animal Apocalypse (*1 En.* 85–90), The Apocalypse of Weeks (*1 En.* 93:1-10; 91:11-17), *4 Ezra* 14, and *2 Baruch* 53–70. As the chapter unfolds, it will not be possible to discuss all the literature in the New Testament. Rather, we will illustrate the points of view of this book by focusing on the undisputed letters of Paul, the Sayings Gospel Q, the Synoptic Gospels and Acts, 2 Thessalonians, Jude, 2 Peter, and the Revelation to John.

Apocalyptic Periodization in *1 Enoch* 85–93, *4 Ezra*, and *2 Baruch*

We will begin with periodization in portions of two Jewish apocalypses that emerged between 70 and 120 CE, *4 Ezra* and *2 Baruch*,[5] since scholars already have observed important relationships between these two texts and the undisputed letters of Paul. As the discussion develops, we also will include *1 Enoch* 85–93. In *4 Ezra* 14, a voice out of a bush, identifying itself by saying, "I revealed myself in a bush and spoke to Moses…" (14:3), tells Ezra that "the age of the world" (i.e., "this age") has twelve parts. Without explaining the nature of each part, the voice asserts that nine and one-half of the parts already have passed, leaving two and one-half parts remaining (14:11-12). This sets the context for exhortations to Ezra about his own life (14:13-18) and instructions to Ezra about writing the visions in tablets, making some of the writings available to the general public, and giving some of the writings only "to the wise among your people" (14:19-48). *2 Baruch* 53–70 subsequently presents the twelve parts of this history of the world (this age) as a series of six dark (evil) and six bright (righteous)

[4] Ibid., 136-46; Collins, *The Apocalyptic Imagination*, 63-65, 155-57, 225, 229, 239-40.
[5] Carey, *Ultimate Things*, 147-68.

waters between God's creation of the world (53:1-2 [Gen 1]) and the end, which itself contains dark waters (70:1–71:2) and bright waters (72:1–74:4). A brief look at the twelve parts of this age and the evil and good parts of the end time can help us to understand, by comparison, how early Christian literature configured certain parts of time apocalyptically as it emerged during the first century CE.

For *2 Baruch*, God's creation of the world takes place through the word going out from God in the form of a great cloud coming up from the sea and covering the earth (53:1; 56:3). Through this process the length of the world "was established in accordance with the abundance of the intelligence of him who let it go forth" (56:4). As the angel Ramael (55:3) explains to Baruch, the length of the time of the world can be understood as twelve parts, with dark waters (evil parts) and bright waters (righteous parts) alternating with each other in a sequence. The following table displays the twelve parts:

Periodization of This Age in 2 Baruch

(1) Adam, sinful angels, and the flood	dark waters	56:5-16
(2) Abraham and his family	bright waters	57:1-3
(3) Egypt	dark waters	58:1-2
(4) Moses through Caleb and Law	bright waters	59:1-12
(5) Judges/Amorites	dark waters	60:1-2
(6) David, Solomon, and Zion	bright waters	61:1-8
(7) Jeroboam, Jezebel, and Salmanassar, king of Assyrians	dark waters	62:1-8
(8) Hezekiah vs Sennacherib, king of Assyrians	bright waters	63:1-11
(9) Manasseh, son of Hezekiah	dark waters	64:1–65:2
(10) Josiah, king of Judah, and Law	bright waters	66:1-8
(11) Destruction of Zion/Jerusalem and Babylonian exile	dark waters	67:1-9
(12) Rebuilt Zion/fall of nations	bright waters	68:1-8

A few brief observations can help us as we make a transition to the nature of parts of time in first century Christian apocalyptic rhetorolect. In *2 Baruch*, the history of "this age" begins with a dark (evil) time that includes Adam, Enoch, the sinful angels, Noah, and the flood (56:1-16). The first part of time, therefore, includes the biblical events in Genesis 2–9. It is noticeable that there is no reference to Enoch or Noah, since this is a dark time and they are "bright" forces. Rather, there is reference to "the transgression which Adam, the first man, committed" (56:5), which brought "untimely death" and a long list of subsequent evils into being. The evils include mourning, affliction, illness, labor, and pride. In addition, "the realm of death began to ask to be renewed with blood, the conception of children came about, the passion of parents was produced, the loftiness of men was humiliated, and goodness vanished" (56:6). This began a process whereby "from these black waters again black was born, and very dark darkness originated" (56:10). This leads to a reference to angels who "came down and mingled themselves with women," while other angels "restrained themselves," in a context where "those living on earth perished together through the waters of the flood" (56:10-15). We will see below that this grouping of evils around the transgression of Adam is characteristic of Paul's apocalyptic view of world history in the NT. Paul also does not mention Enoch or Noah during the first part of the history of the world, or in any of his letters. Rather, Adam is the focus of Paul's attention for the emergence of death and all kinds of evil associated with blood, flesh, and desire in the history of the world.

In *2 Baruch*, the second part of time is a bright (righteous) time that includes "the fountain of Abraham and his generation, and the coming of his son [Isaac], and the son of his son [Jacob], and of those who are like them" (57:1).[6] During this time, the unwritten law was in force, the works of the commandments were accomplished, belief in the coming judgment was brought about, hope of the world which will be renewed was built, and the promise of the life that will come later was planted (57:2). Again we will see below that Paul's writings in the NT present the time of Abraham apocalyptically as a time of righteousness, belief, hope, and promise, as well as a time that defined the nature of the coming judgment.

After the time of Abraham in *2 Baruch*, there are five dark parts of time interwoven with five bright parts of time. The dark parts of time are Egypt, the judges, Jeroboam, Manasseh, and the destruction of Jerusalem, which results in the Babylonian exile. The bright parts of time are Moses, David, Hezekiah, Josiah, and the rebuilding of Zion. The dark parts of time are characterized by sins (58:1; 60:2; 62:2), death (58:1-2; 64:2), wickedness (58:1; 60:1; 62:7; 64:2), oppression (58:1), pollutions (60:1-2; 64:2), idolatry (62:1-3; 64:3-8; 67:2, 6), famine (62:4), exile (62:5-6; 64:5), killing (64:2), and abolishing priests and offerings (64:2; 67:6). In contrast, the bright parts of time focus on the Law, righteousness, promise, faith, removing idolatry, and trusting and hoping in God.

The bright parts of time are as important as the dark parts of time for understanding the manner in which early Christian literature presented its apocalyptic account of the time of Jesus and his followers until the end of time. For *2 Baruch*, in the time from Moses through Caleb "the lamp of the eternal law which exists forever" and "the promise" and "the fire" were present,[7] and Moses showed the people detailed aspects

[6] Cf. *Jub.* 23:10.

[7] Cf. the fire for Manasseh in 2 *Bar.* 64:7.

of the end of time, the place of faith, the orders of the archangels, and many other things (59:1-12). We will see below that Paul viewed the time of Moses as a significant mixture of dark and bright features. During the time of David and Solomon in *2 Baruch*, appropriate activities occurred in the sanctuary of Zion, rest and peace reigned, and "the righteousness of the commandments of the Mighty One was accomplished in truth" (61:1-8). Later Hezekiah, trusting upon the works of God and hoping upon God's righteousness, prayed to God and received the power to save Zion from the attack of the Assyrian king Sennacherib (63:1-11). Josiah, "who was the only one in his time who subjected himself to the Mighty One with his whole heart and his whole soul," purified the country from idols, restored priests and offerings, and destroyed evil ones throughout his kingdom (66:1-5). As a result, "he will receive reward forever and ever and be honored with the Mighty One more than many in the last time" (66:6). During the sixth bright time, Zion will be rebuilt and priests and offerings will be restored (68:5).

After describing the twelve parts of world history, namely "this age," the angel Ramael describes to Baruch the contents of the dark waters and bright waters of the end time. The contents of the dark and bright waters of the end time are as follows:

The Dark and Bright Waters of the End Time in 2 Baruch

The Coming of the Harvest: Dark Waters
(13) 70:2 Coming of the harvest of the seed of evil ones and good ones after the time of the world has ripened
(14) 70:3 Hatred, fighting, despised rule the honorable
(15) 70:4 Poor delivered to the rich
(16) 70:5 Wise silent, foolish speak
(17) 70:6 Tribulations
(18) 70:7 Most High gives sign: prepared nations war against remaining rulers
(19) 70:8 Earthquake, fire, famine
(20) 70:9 People delivered into the hands of "my Servant, the Messiah"
(21) 70:10 Whole earth devours its inhabitants
(22) 71:1-2 Holy land protects its inhabitants

The Coming of the Anointed One: Bright Waters
(23) 72:2a Coming of time of the Anointed One after the signs and the moving of the nations
(24) 72:2b-6 The Anointed One will call the nations, sparing some and killing others
(25) 73:1 The Anointed One will sit down in eternal peace on the throne of the kingdom: joy will be revealed and rest will appear
(26) 73:2 Health, no illness, fear, tribulation, or lamentation; joy will encompass the earth
(27) 73:3 No untimely death, no sudden adversity

(28) 73:4 Uprooting of judgment, condemnations, contentions, revenges, blood, passions, zeal, hate, and all such things
(29) 73:6 Wild beasts serve men; asps and dragons subject themselves to children
(30) 73:7 Women have no birth pangs
(31) 74:1 Reapers will not become tired; farmers will not wear themselves out, since the products will shout out speedily
(32) 74:2 End of that which is corruptible; beginning of that which is incorruptible

In *2 Baruch*, the angel Ramael describes the dark waters of the end time (70–71) before describing the bright waters (73–74). Overall, the dark waters are "the time of the coming of the harvest" (70:2) while the bright waters are "the time of the coming of the Anointed One" (72:2). It is noticeable that the time of the harvest identifies various evils on the earth (70:3-5) that reach a highpoint in tribulations (70:6) before the Most High gives a sign that puts good nations into action against evil nations; there is earthquake, fire, and famine; and then all people are delivered into the hands of God's Servant, the Messiah (70:7-9). After this, the whole earth devours its inhabitants, but the holy land protects its inhabitants (71:1). In contrast to the time of the harvest, the time of the Messiah moves quickly through judgment of the nations (72:2-6) to the Messiah's sitting on the throne of eternal peace (73:1), after which there is a list of evil things that will no longer exist and good things that will exist (73:2-7). The description ends with the earth generating its produce without tiring labor (74:1), with the end of that which is corruptible, and with the beginning of that which is incorruptible (74:2). The coming of the Messiah to judge the nations, then, is the means by which the final "bright waters" come into being.

When a person puts *2 Baruch* 56–74 alongside The Animal Apocalypse in *1 Enoch* 85–90, which we discussed in the previous chapter, and The Apocalypse of Weeks in *1 Enoch* 93:1-10; 91:11-17, a person gets the following display:

Apocalyptic Times and Spaces in 1 Enoch *85–93;* 2 Baruch *56–74*

1 Enoch 85–90	*1 Enoch* 93:1-10; 91:11-17	*2 Baruch* 56–74
(1) 85:3-9 Adam and Eve and their Children	(1) 93:3 First Week: Adam to Enoch; righteousness (good)	(1) 56:5-16 Adam, sinful angels, and the flood (dark)
(2) 86:1-6 The Fall of the Watchers and the Violence of the Giants	(2) 93:4 Second Week: deceit and violence; Noah saved (good); Conclusion: iniquity and law for sinners afterwards (evil)	
(3) 87:1–88:3 Divine Judgment of the Watchers		

(4) 89:1-8 Noah and the Flood		
(5) 89:9-27 Noah's Descendants; Abraham and his Descendants; Egypt; Moses to the Red Sea	(3) 93:5 Third Week: Conclusion: Abraham, plant of righteous judgment; Abraham's son [Isaac], eternal plant of righteousness (good)	(2) 57:1-3 Abraham and his family (bright)
		(3) Egypt 58:1-2 (dark)
(6) 89:28-38 From the Wilderness to Moses' Death	(4) 93:6 Fourth week: [Moses]; Conclusion: visions of angels, eternal covenant; tabernacle (good)	(4) 59:1-12 Moses through Caleb and Law (bright)
		(5) 60:1-2 Judges/Amorites (dark)
(7) 89:39-50 From Entrance into the Land to the Building of the Temple	(5) 93:7 Fifth week: [Solomon]; Conclusion: Kingdom; Temple (good)	(6) 61:1-8 David, Solomon, and Zion (bright)
(8) 89:51-58 The Apostasy of the Two Kingdoms	(6) 93:8 Sixth week: [Kings of Israel]; blindness; straying hearts; Elijah ascends (good); Conclusion: Temple Destruction; Exile (evil)	(7) 62:1-8 Jeroboam, Jezebel, and Salmanassar, king of Assyrians (dark)
(9) 89:59-64 The Commissioning of the Seventy Shepherds and the Angelic Scribe		(8) 63:1-11 Hezekiah vs Sennacherib, king of Assyrians (bright)
(10) 89:65-72a The First Period: The Twelve Shepherds; Temple Destruction; Exile		(9) 64.1–65.2 Manasseh, son of Hezekiah (dark)
		(10) 66:1-8 Josiah, king of Judah, and Law (bright)
		(11) 67:1-9 Destruction of Zion/Jerusalem and Babylonian exile (dark)
(11) 89:72b–90:1 The Second Period: The Twenty-Three Shepherds from the Return (Rebuilding) to Alexander	(7) 93:9-10; 91:11 Seventh week: Perverse generation; wicked deeds (evil); Conclusion: Elect ones of righteousness chosen from the eternal plant of righteousness (Abraham's progeny); given sevenfold wisdom and knowledge to execute judgment on violence and deceit (good)	(12) 68:1-8 Rebuilt Zion/fall of nations (bright)
(12) 90:2-5 The Third Period: The Twenty-Three Shepherds from Alexander into the Second Century bce		
(13) 90:6-19 The Fourth Period: The Twelve Shepherds until the End Time		

(14) 90:20-27 Judgment in the pleasant Land (of Israel)	(8) 91:12-13 Eighth week: Week of righteousness; wicked delivered into hand of the righteous	
(15) 90:28-29 New Beginning: A New House	Conclusion: Building of Temple for Great King in glory for eternity (good)	
	(9) 91:14 Ninth week: Great Righteous Judgment over the whole earth	(13) 70:2 Coming of the harvest of the seed of evil and good ones of the whole world after the time of the world has ripened (dark)
		(14) 70:3 Hatred, fighting, despised rule the honorable (dark)
		(15) 70:4 Poor delivered to the rich (dark)
		(16) 70:5 Wise silent, foolish speak (dark)
		(17) 70:6 Tribulations (dark)
		(18) 70:7 Most High gives sign: prepared nations war against remaining rulers (dark)
		(19) 70:8 Earthquake, fire, famine (dark)
		(20) 70:9 People delivered into the hands of "my Servant, the Messiah" (dark)
		(21) 70:10 Whole earth devours its inhabitants (dark)
		(22) 71:1-2 Holy land protects its inhabitants (dark)
		(23) 72:2a Coming of time of the Anointed One after the signs and the moving of the nations (bright)
	(10) 91:15-16 Eternal judgment executed by angels of eternal heaven	(24) 72: 2b-6 The Anointed One will call the nations, sparing some and killing others (bright)
(16) 90:30-39 All gathered in the New House	(11) 91:17 Eternal age of goodness and righteousness. Many weeks without number forever; a time of goodness and righteousness; sin shall no more be heard of forever	(25) 73:1 The Anointed One will sit down in eternal peace on the throne of the kingdom: joy will be revealed and rest will appear (bright)
		(26) 73:2 Health, no illness, fear, tribulation, or lamentation; joy will encompass the earth (bright)
		(27) 73:3 No untimely death, no sudden adversity (bright)
		(28) 73:4 Uprooting of judgment, condemnations, contentions, revenges, blood, passions,

		zeal, hate, and all such things (bright)
		(29) 73:6 Wild beasts serve men; asps and dragons subject themselves to children (bright)
		(30) 73:7 Women have no birth pangs (bright)
		(31) 74:1 Reapers will not become tired; farmers will not wear themselves out, since the products will shoot out speedily (bright)
		(32) 74:2 End of that which is corruptible; beginning of that which is incorruptible (bright)

A person readily sees that *2 Baruch* is noticeable for its detailed description of aspects of the end time (Items 13-32). A person also can observe, however, a noticeable similarity in the scheme of periodization from the time of Adam to the kings of Israel. Once a person comes to the kings of Israel, there is considerable variation in emphases as the periods of time move to the exile and judgment at the end time. As we move to first century Christian literature, it will come as no surprise that its discourse contributed significantly to the apocalyptic focus on a special "Messiah,"[8] "Elect One," "Righteous One," "Son," or "Holy One" as a transition from the time of David (still a part of "this age") to the coming age. It will be especially important in our account to observe how first century Christians told stories, made pronouncements, and developed arguments that presented the events of Jesus and his followers with angel spirits, Satan, demonic spirits, and evil historical forces that created a transition from the time of David and the kings of Israel to the end time. In this process, Christians put such an energetic focus on Jesus as God's Messiah that they acquired the name "Messianites," which emerged in Greek as "Christians" (*christianoi*).[9] Our special task in this chapter is to exhibit the ways in which certain "apocalyptic" parts of time functioned as emergent structures for first century Christians as they presented "their time" as a transitional apocalyptic part of "this age." Various apocalyptic parts of time functioned as dynamic cognitive resources for first century Christians as they used, adopted, adapted, configured, and reconfigured stories and arguments to present their views of God, angelic spirit-beings, demonic spirit-beings, predecessors of Jesus,

[8] The word "messiah" means "anointed with oil": *meshiach* (Hebrew); *christos* (Greek); see Marinus de Jonge, "Messiah," *ABD* IV:777-88.

[9] Acts 11:26; 26:28; 1 Pet 4:16. "Messianites" would be a Hebrew rather than Greek word form.

Jesus himself, followers of Jesus, and people who either competed with or opposed Jesus and his followers.

The Emergence of Forensic Apocalyptic Eschatology in the Context of Cosmological Apocalyptic Eschatology during the First Century CE

Martinus C. de Boer has discussed some of the things we have presented above in terms of a stream of apocalyptic tradition he calls "forensic apocalyptic eschatology," which emerged during the first and second centuries CE in the context of "cosmological apocalyptic eschatology."[10] This emerging stream of apocalyptic eschatology, in his view, presented a special opportunity for Paul to appropriate Jewish apocalyptic discourse in a way that was interactive with emerging Jewish apocalyptic conceptions and writings. A major issue, as he explains, is that cosmological apocalyptic eschatology blames heavenly beings for the pervasive evil throughout God's created world. Forensic apocalyptic eschatology, in contrast, holds humans from Adam to the present responsible for the pervasive evil throughout God's created world. In his analysis, he identifies verses in first-second CE Jewish apocalyptic literature that launch a direct polemic against the idea that angels are to blame for the pervasive evil in the world. The blame lies decisively on Adam. As a result of the sin of Adam, not only are humans heirs of an evil, sinful inclination, but Adam's sin was the act that led the angels astray! A key chapter for his analysis is *2 Baruch* 56, discussed above, where the angel Ramael focuses on Adam. Key verses for de Boer's observations are as follows:

> [9] And from these black waters again black were born, and very dark darkness originated. [10] For he who was a danger to himself [Adam] was also a danger to the angels. [11] For they possessed freedom in that time in which they were created. [12] And some of them came down and mingled themselves with women. [13] At that time they who acted like this were tormented in chains. [14] But the rest of the multitude of angels, who have no number, restrained themselves. [15] And those living on earth perished together through the waters of the flood. [16] Those are the first black waters. (*2 Bar.* 56:9-16)

M.C. de Boer observes that this apocalyptic description of world history creates a situation in *2 Baruch* where humans are entirely re-

[10] Martinus C. de Boer, "Paul and Apocalyptic Eschatology," in Collins, *The Encyclopedia of Apocalypticism*, 345-83; idem, "Paul and Jewish Apocalyptic Eschatology," in *Apocalyptic and the New Testament: Essays in Honor of J. Louis Martyn* (ed. J. Marcus and M.L. Soards; JSNTS 24; Sheffield: JSOT Press, 1989) 169-90; idem, *The Defeat of Death: Apocalyptic Eschatology in 1 Corinthians 15 and Romans 5* (JSNTS 22; Sheffield: JSOT Press, 1988).

sponsible for the evils they perform and for belief that may lead them to glory:

> [15] For, although Adam sinned first and has brought death upon all who were not in his own time, yet each of them who has been born from him has prepared for himself the coming torment. And further, each of them has chosen for himself the coming glory. [16] For truly, the one who believes will receive reward. (*2 Bar.* 54:15-16)

Another verse of support for de Boer's approach lies in the Greek of *1 En.* 98:4: "... sin has not been sent into the world. It is the people who have themselves invented it."[11] He chooses the word "forensic" to describe the special focus on Adam especially because of the contents of *2 Baruch* 49–51. In these chapters, God's act of holding humans accountable for their thoughts and actions produces a time of judgment that "is not a cosmic war against cosmological, angelic powers but a courtroom in which all humanity appears before the bar of the Judge."[12] We will argue below that *2 Baruch* 57–59 are just as important for understanding Paul's arguments, since they juxtapose the emergence of "belief in the coming judgment" during the time of Abraham and his descendants with the emergence of "the lamp of the eternal law which exists forever and ever illuminated all those who sat in darkness" during the time of Moses' family and descendants. Paul presented a reconfigured apocalyptic story-line from Adam, Abraham, Moses, and David to the present and future on the basis of his view of God's action of raising Jesus from the dead in the context of his crucifixion, death, and burial.

Our approach, then, considers M.C. de Boer's analysis and interpretation to be the most helpful one available in present scholarship for understanding the relation of apocalyptic literature to Paul's undisputed letters. The limitations of his work for our purpose are fourfold. First, his analysis and interpretation is limited to the undisputed letters of Paul. Our task implicitly includes all the writings in the NT. Second, his approach is limited by a focus only on time, rather than on both time and space in apocalyptic literature. Third, his focus on time needs to be supplemented by more attention to the "parts" of time in apocalyptic presentations of world history. Fourth, the dominant literary-historical approach in biblical studies perpetuates a limited environment for de Boer's perception of how creatively Paul reconfigures the "sources" for his apocalyptic ideas.[13] A sociorhetorical approach views what de Boer calls "sources" as "resources" that contain "emergent structures" for

[11] De Boer, "Paul and Jewish Apocalyptic Eschatology," 178.
[12] Ibid., 176; idem, "Paul and Apocalyptic Eschatology," 359-66.
[13] De Boer, "Paul and Apocalyptic Eschatology," 366-79.

Paul's view of God's activities and achievements through "the Lord Jesus Messiah." M.C. de Boer leads the way with his following observation: "the crucified Christ whom God raised from the dead is Paul's criterion for the appropriation of Jewish apocalyptic-eschatological categories."[14] In our view, Paul's creative reworking of Jewish apocalyptic-eschatological categories requires that we speak of Paul's "reconfiguration" rather than appropriation of Jewish apocalyptic-eschatological categories. In short, Paul was a more creative thinker than most literary-historical interpreters have been able to articulate. Using strategies of sociorhetorical interpretation, we will be able to build on de Boer's work to show that Paul was not "limited" by first century Jewish apocalyptic-eschatological categories as much as many, perhaps most, interpreters presuppose. In the language of current cognitive scientists, apocalyptic-eschatological frames of understanding and reasoning functioned as "emergent structures"[15] for Paul's points of view and arguments. We will show below that in virtually every context of apocalyptic argument in Paul's undisputed writings he was reconfiguring conventional apocalyptic-eschatological categories in significant ways. In our view, many interpreters have been trying to say this for at least a century, but literary-historical categories have either limited the language available to them to show the nature of Paul's creativity, or the overall scholarly environment of analysis and interpretation has significantly limited or even silenced the insights they have presented.

Cosmological and Forensic Angel-Spirit Apocalyptic Rhetorolect in the Undisputed Letters of Paul

The apostle Paul created a Christian apocalyptic story-line through the earthly humans of Adam, Abraham, Moses, David, Christ, himself, fellow believers, and people of the nations, rather than through the heavenly sons of God who lusted after the daughters of humans. It is important for us to know that Paul selected particular apocalyptic time periods and focused on them in particular ways to achieve his version of the apocalyptic story of the world. We have seen above the twelve parts of world history that emerged in *2 Baruch* by the beginning of the second century CE, as well as the dark and bright contents of the end-time. It is important to be attentive to these parts of time as we interpret Paul's letters. Paul's apocalyptic argumentation in 1 Thessalonians (ca. 50-51 CE)[16] focuses on the end-time, rather than on parts of time

[14] Ibid., 367-68.

[15] Gilles Fauconnier and Mark Turner, *The Way We Think: Conceptual Blending and the Mind's Hidden Complexities* (New York: Basic Books, 2002) 42-50.

[16] For the dating of Paul's letters, see Calvin J. Roetzel, *The Letters of Paul: Conversations in Context* (4th ed.; Louisville: Westminster John Knox Press, 1998) 79-118; for an

in this age. In 1 Corinthians (ca. 53-55 CE), Paul adds an apocalyptic focus on Adam (15:20-58) and makes embryonic apocalyptic statements about Moses (9:8-12; 10:1-22). In 2 Corinthians (ca. 56 CE), Paul presents an apocalyptic view of Moses (3:4-18) in an overall context where he uses language about "a new creation" (2 Cor 5:17) and talks about his own "visions and revelations of the Lord" (2 Cor 12:1). In Galatians (ca. 52-56 CE), Paul focuses on his own revelations (1:12, 16; 2:2; 3:23) and Abraham (2:15–4:7; 4:22–5:1) in the context of an apocalyptic focus on "spirit," which we will propose emerges out of his apocalyptic story-line from Adam to the Messiah. In Romans (ca. 56-57 CE), Paul includes David (1:3-5) in a statement that leads into further apocalyptic elaboration of the importance of the times of Adam (5:12-14, 18-21) and Abraham (4:1-15; 5:19-21) for understanding the relation of the time of Moses (2:12-29; 3:19-31; 5:14, 20-21) to the time of the Messiah, tribulations, and judgment. As our discussion of these letters unfolds, we will propose that an implicit dimension of Paul's discussion is an apocalyptic interpretation of the exile as life in this age "among the nations." Paul's interpretation of the exile requires no reference to Babylon or Persia. Rather, it is a "part of time" in which God makes the gospel of faith, spirit, and righteousness available to all people in the world.

Paul's focus on humans rather than heavenly beings in his apocalyptic story-line had the effect of emphasizing the rebellion of humans in a context of de-emphasizing the rebellion of heavenly beings. Focusing on specific humans, Paul blended multiple story-lines together into a new apocalyptic story-line in the Mediterranean world that focused centrally on God's "Lord Jesus Messiah." Once one sees Paul's selective focus on conventional apocalyptic time periods, perhaps the most difficult limitation to overcome in current analysis and interpretation of the undisputed letters of Paul is the focus on apocalyptic eschatology, rather than on the overall conceptual system of apocalyptic discourse in Jewish tradition. The emphasis on history in 19th and 20th century investigations of the NT naturally led to a delimitation of apocalyptic to apocalyptic eschatology, which focuses on the movement of time from this age to the coming age. To put it another way, the last two centuries of NT interpretation have focused on time in a manner that de-emphasized space. Preoccupation with the nature of time led to a selective approach to apocalyptic literature that devalued the highly sophisticated approaches to spaces in apocalyptic literature. Interpretation of spaces is becoming much more important in 21st century

account of apocalyptic rhetoric in the undisputed Pauline letters, see Carey, *Ultimate Things*, 125-41.

knowledge.[17] Along with it comes the possibility of being much more attentive to spaces throughout God's universe in apocalyptic literature. A way to move forward, we suggest, is to remain attentive to the manner in which Paul's argumentation in a particular context focuses on movement from earthly spaces upwards toward heaven in relation to movement from heavenly spaces downward toward earth.

The work of Martinus C. de Boer exhibits in a majesterial way how the focus on time has guided NT interpretation of apocalyptic in the writings of Paul. The investigations, discussions, and debates have been and are deeply informed, intellectually powerful, and theologically rigorous. In the end, however, the selectivity of the topics under investigation and discussion is truly remarkable. *Topoi* concerning time are continually in the foreground, and *topoi* concerning spaces, which include the human body, as well as all kinds of earthly and cosmic "bodies," have been more difficult to bring into the foreground. With the writings of Rudolf Bultmann, the investigation and discussion of spaces focused heavily on "the personal body" of a human being under the rubric of "anthropology."[18] During the last quarter of the 20th century, many kinds of "social" investigations have drawn attention to interrelated spaces in the world. "Mainline" interpretations, however, have quite successfully kept the focus on human bodies in "time," rather than on human bodies in relation to all other kinds of "bodies," animal and otherwise, in multiple spaces throughout God's universe. We will see below that Christopher Rowland in particular wrestled with the relation of time to space in interpretation of apocalyptic in Jewish and Christian tradition, and a growing number of interpreters are now including many of his insights.[19] It is important to rework these contributions in ways that allow us to see more clearly the creative ways in which first century Christian discourse reoriented Mediterranean apocalyptic traditions both spatially and temporally toward a "messiah-oriented" understanding of God, God's emissaries, believers, and unbelievers throughout the history of God's created world.

Apocalyptic Times and Spaces in 1 Thessalonians: Persecution, Death, and Resurrection

In 1 Thess 4:13–5:11, Paul presents "Christian wisdom" that contains three argumentative apocalyptic story-summaries. First there are two

[17] See Bart B. Bruehler, "The Public, the Political, and the Private: The Literary and Social-Spatial Functions of Luke 18:35–19:48," Ph.D. dissertation, Emory University, 2007.

[18] See de Boer, "Paul and Apocalyptic Eschatology," 361-68 on Rudolf Bultmann, Ernst Käsemann, and Albert Schweitzer.

[19] Rowland, *The Open Heaven*.

apocalyptic story-summaries that present an argument (4: that God has a plan to take believers who are “in Messiah,” whether they have already died or still alive, into heaven “to be with the Lord forever” after “the coming of the Lord.” Second there is an argument (5:1-11) that believers “in Messiah” know about “the day of the Lord,” because they are children of light rather than children of darkness. In each part of the argument, Paul embeds one or more “argumentative apocalyptic story-summaries” (4:14, 16-17; 5:3) in an elaboration of early Christian wisdom rhetorolect. The following table, naming and numbering the items as they appear in *1 Enoch* 90; *1 Enoch* 93:9-10; 91:11-17; *2 Baruch* 70–74, displays the contents of the end-time Paul interprets as he presents his argument:

Apocalyptic Times and Spaces in 1 Enoch *90–93;* 2 Baruch *70–74 and 1 Thessalonians*

1 Enoch 90–93; *2 Baruch* 70–74	1 Thessalonians
World History (This Age)	
(7a) *1 En.* 93:9 Seventh week: Perverse generation; wicked deeds; cf. (12) 90:2-5 (evil);	Judeans killed the Lord Jesus and the prophets, displease God and oppose everyone by hindering us from speaking to the nations so they can be saved, filling up the measure of their sins: 2:15-16; Lord Jesus Christ died: 5:10 (dark)
(7b) *1 En.* 93:10; 91:11 Seventh week Conclusion: Elect ones chosen from the eternal plant of righteousness (Abraham’s progeny); given sevenfold wisdom and knowledge to execute judgment on violence and deceit; cf. (13) 90:6-19 (good)	Jesus rose up from the dead: 1:10; 4:14 (bright)
	Satan (time of the Apostles): Blocked our way: 2:18; 3:5; (dark)
	Believers: Children of light, not darkness: 5:4-5
	Spirit: 4:8
End Time	
	Resurrection of dead: 4:16-17; be

	lievers: 4:16–17
(9) *1 En.* 91:14 Ninth week: Great Righteous Judgment over the whole earth. (13) *2 Bar.* 70:2 Coming of the harvest of the seed of evil ones and good ones after the time of the world has ripened (dark)	Coming of the Wrath: 1:10; 2:16; 4:6; 5:2, 9 (dark) Day of the Lord: 5:1–2 (dark)
(17) *2 Bar.* 70:6 Tribulations (dark)	Tribulations: Destined persecutions: 3:3–4; Persecution, distress: 1:6; 3:7; 5:3 (dark)
(18) *2 Bar.* 70:7 Most High gives sign: prepared nations war against remaining rulers (dark)	Cry of command, archangel's call, sound of God's trumpet: 4:16 (dark)
(21) *2 Bar.* 70:10 Whole earth devours its inhabitants (dark)	Sudden destruction like birth pangs: 5:3 (dark)
(23) *2 Bar.* 72:2a Coming of time of the Anointed One after the signs and the moving of the nations (bright)	Coming of God's Son Jesus: 1:10; Lord Jesus: 2:19; 3:13; 4:14–16; Lord Jesus Christ: 5:23 (bright)
(10) *1 En.* 91:15–16 Eternal judgment executed by angels of eternal heaven. (24) *2 Bar.* 72:2b–6 The Anointed One will call the nations, sparing some and killing others (bright)	God calls into Kingdom: 2:12; 5:24; in holiness, not impurity: 4:7, 14 Jesus rescues: 1:10; 4:14–17; 5:4–5, 9–10 (bright)
(11) *1 En.* 91:17 Eternal age of goodness and righteousness. Many weeks without number forever; a time of goodness and righteousness; sin shall no more be heard of forever; cf. (16) *1 En.* 90:30–39. (25) *2 Bar.* 73:1 The Anointed One will sit down in eternal peace on the throne of the kingdom: joy will be revealed and rest will appear (bright)	Live with the Lord Jesus Christ: 4:17; 5:10 (bright)
(27) *2 Bar.* 73:3 No untimely death, no sudden adversity (bright)	No sudden destruction: 5:4–5 (bright)

As we begin a discussion of the apocalyptic aspects of Paul's undisputed letters, it is important to notice one very special characteristic of Paul's early Christian apocalyptic rhetorolect. When Paul used the word "Messiah" (*christos*), he regularly used it without the article "the." This approach is present in 1 Thessalonians, which probably is the earliest writing in the NT (ca. 50–51 CE).[21] Most English translations

[21] Charles A. Wanamaker, *The Epistles to the Thessalonians: A Commentary on the Greek Text* (NIGTC; Grand Rapids, MI: Eerdmans, 1990) 37–45, presents a carefully formu-

simply transliterate the Greek word *christos* as "Christ." On the one hand, this can help modern hearers/readers understand how the discourse in the NT came to be identified as "Christian" discourse. On the other hand, modern hearers/readers regularly do not think about this as an unusual way of using the word "Messiah" that was highly important in first century Christian discourse. Our interpretations throughout this chapter regularly will exhibit this characteristic of NT discourse by translating the Greek word *christos* without the article as "Messiah" and with the article as "the Messiah."[22]

In 1 Thess 4:13-18, Paul begins with movement from earth up to heaven followed by movement from heaven towards earth that brings humans from earth up to heaven. Paul uses two major steps at the beginning of his argument to achieve this movement through space. First there is an introductory thesis and rationale about wanting the Thessalonians to be informed so they do not grieve like people who have no hope (4:13). This thesis and rationale begins with people on earth. Second there is an enthymematic apocalyptic story-summary thesis (Rule) about Jesus: "For since we believe that Jesus died and rose again, even so, through Jesus, God will bring with him those who have died" (14). This story-summary thesis, which contains repetitive use of the name Jesus and the verb "died," begins on earth with movement into heaven that creates the context for God to act from heaven to move humans from earth to heaven. After his initial statement of the story-summary thesis, Paul restates the story-summary in an argumentative apocalyptic story-summary that presents a Case, Result, and Exhortative Conclusion:

> *Apocalyptic Story (Case):* [16]For the Lord himself, with a cry of command, with the archangel's call and with the sound of God's trumpet, will descend from heaven, and the dead in Messiah will rise first. [17]Then we who are alive, who are left, will be caught up in the clouds together with them to meet the Lord in the air;
> *Apocalyptic Result:* and so we will be with the Lord for ever.
> *Exhortative Conclusion:* [18]Therefore encourage one another with these words.

Instead of using the name "Jesus," this argumentative story-summary uses the name "the Lord" in relation to the archangel's call, God's trumpet, and being "in Messiah" to present its reasoning. In this instance, there is movement from heaven to earth that creates the context for humans to move from earth to heaven. The overall sequence

lated argument with the conclusion that Paul wrote 2 Thessalonians before he wrote 1 Thessalonians.

[22] The NRSV usually translates *christos* without the article as "Christ" and with the article as "the Messiah."

blends early Christian wisdom with apocalyptic rhetorolect as it presents an introduction, an enthymematic Rule, an amplified apocalyptic Case, a Result, and an exhortative conclusion. A major rhetorical effect of the sequence is to replace the repetitive emphasis on "Jesus" in 4:14 with a repetitive emphasis on "the Lord" in 4:16-17. This replacement changes the conventional meaning of "the Lord" from the Lord God to "Lord Jesus Messiah." This meaning for "the Lord" coheres with Paul's use of the name "Lord Jesus Messiah" alongside "God the Father" in the address to the Thessalonians at the beginning of the letter (1:1). Also, it coheres with Paul's use of the name "the Lord" in 1:3, 6, 8; 2:15, 19; 3:8, 11, 12, 13; 4:1, 2 for the Lord Jesus. When Paul explains "the will of God" in 4:1-8, his reference to "the Lord" as "an avenger in all these things" (4:6) reverberates with conventional Jewish usage in a manner that could invite people to understand it either as a reference to the Lord God or to the Lord Jesus. As Abraham J. Malherbe says: "It is not clear whether he [Paul] has in mind God or Christ... The description of the judge as an avenger (*ekdikos*) makes it likely that he is referring to God, who was so described in the Jewish tradition ... but Christ is equally described by him as judge ..."[23] In turn, Charles A. Wanamaker says: "The language is drawn from the OT (see esp. Ps. 94:1, which Paul may be quoting). But he probably has in mind here an apocalyptic image of the Lord Jesus as the coming avenger of God's wrath who will inflict severe punishment on wrongdoers who violate the demands of the gospel."[24] In first century Christian discourse, the phrase "the Lord" acquires "multistability."[25] This means that people could hear the title "the Lord" as referring either to the Lord God or to the Lord Jesus Messiah. This does not mean that reference to "the Lord" was "unstable" for first century Christians, whereby it could refer to any number of different personages. The title had "multistability" between God and Jesus. It could refer either to the Lord God or to the Lord Jesus, but people were to limit the term "the Lord" to these two beings. One of the rich dimensions of early Christian discourse is various kinds of multistability, which allow hearers/readers/interpreters to understand assertions within a range of conceptual systems. In Paul's writings, a significant issue can be if "the Lord" refers to the Lord God or to the Lord Jesus. The rhetorical effect of the multistability is to introduce a close relation between God and Jesus that creates a context for lively discussion, debate, and disagree-

[23] Abraham J. Malherbe, *The Letters to the Thessalonians* (AB 32B; New York/London/Toronto/Sydney/Auckland: Doubleday, 2000) 233.

[24] Wanamaker, *The Epistles to the Thessalonians*, 156.

[25] The source of this term is W.J.T. Mitchell, *Picture Theory: Essays on Verbal and Visual Representation* (Chicago and London: University of Chicago Press, 1994).

ment during the second through the fourth centuries CE concerning the humanity and divinity of Christ, and concerning the "Trinitarian" nature of God.

Most interpreters agree that the multistability concerning "the Lord" as an avenger in 4:6 disappears in Paul's apocalyptic story-summary in 4:15-17. In other words, the rhetorical effect of 4:13-18 is to make "Lord Jesus Messiah" the central actor throughout the scene. There is agreement that "the Lord" in 4:15 is a reference to "a word of the Lord" Jesus, although interpretation varies whether this "word" is an actual statement or transmitted saying of Jesus, a saying of Jesus supplemented by Jewish apocalyptic speculation, a prophetic word from the exalted Lord Jesus, or Paul's own midrash on the tradition.[26] Likewise, there is agreement that the "earliest" written use of "*parousia* in its technical meaning" of "the coming of the Lord" in 4:15 is a reference to the coming of the Lord Jesus.[27] This means that "the Lord himself" who will descend from heaven (16) and "the Lord in the air" (17) also are references to "the Lord Jesus" that "Christianize" Jewish apocalyptic tradition.[28] Thus, Paul's statement that "we shall always be with the Lord" (17) is a reference to living forever with the Messiah, which is a conventional *topos* in Jewish apocalyptic literature.[29]

The manner in which Paul ends with an exhortative conclusion shows how early Christian apocalyptic rhetorolect functions in early Christian wisdom rhetorolect in 1 Thessalonians 4–5. The goal of this apocalyptic argumentation is to convince believers "in Messiah" in Thessalonica to live in "wise," supportive, and "comforting" community with one another. The rhetorical nature of the passage is to embed apocalyptic story-summaries in an argumentative sequence that presents early Christian wisdom that is a basis for exhortation to live supportively with one another. In this instance, then, Paul's early Christian apocalyptic rhetorolect is a blend of wisdom argumentation and argumentative apocalyptic story-summary.

When Paul moves to the second part of his presentation of apocalyptic wisdom in 1 Thess 5:1-11, he moves directly from an introductory statement that they do not need anything written to them (5:1) to a thesis that they "know very well that the day of the Lord will come like a thief in the night" (5:2). This introduction creates the context for

[26] Wanamaker, *The Epistles to the Thessalonians*, 170-71; Malherbe, *The Letters to the Thessalonians*, 267-71.

[27] Malherbe, *The Letters to the Thessalonians*, 271-74.

[28] Wanamaker, *The Epistles to the Thessalonians*, 175-76; Malherbe, *The Letters to the Thessalonians*, 273-77; James D. Hester, "Apocalyptic Discourse in 1 Thessalonians," in Duane F. Watson, *The Intertexture of Apocalyptic Discourse in the New Testament* (Symposium 14; Atlanta: SBL, 2002) 155-56.

[29] Malherbe, *The Letters to the Thessalonians*, 277-78.

Paul's argumentative apocalyptic story-summary in 5:3: "When they say, 'There is peace and security', then sudden destruction will come upon them, as labor pains come upon a pregnant woman, and there will be no escape!" After this, Paul presents "apocalyptic wisdom" in the rhetorical form of a typical elaboration of early Christian wisdom rhetorolect.[30]

At least five points are important for our discussion of first century Christian apocalyptic rhetorolect in 1 Thess 4–5. First, apocalyptic discourse is first and foremost "story-like." Often this "story-like" discourse summarizes events from the past in a manner that moves into events in the future. The story-like nature of the discourse invites hearers/readers to recruit images that create picturesque sequences in the mind. These sequences can appropriately be called "scenario events," namely events that exhibit a "script" of action from the past or a "pre-script" of or for future action. A script is a program that has emerged from past actions or has been designed for future actions. This program may exist as a sequence of instructions both for sequences of actions and for timing of actions in certain places and spaces in the future.[31] Second, apocalyptic discourse presents "the inside story" of

[30] Cf. Wanamaker, *The Epistles to the Thessalonians*, 177-90; Duane F. Watson, "Paul's Appropriation of Apocalyptic Discourse: The Rhetorical Strategy of 1 Thessalonians," in *Rhetorical Dimensions of Apocalyptic Discourse* (ed. G. Carey and L.G. Bloomquist; St. Louis: Chalice Press, 1999) 73-78. One way to characterize Paul's rhetorical elaboration is as follows:

5:1 *Thesis:* Now concerning the times and the seasons, brothers and sisters, you do not need to have anything written to you.

Rationale with Analogy: [2] For you yourselves know very well that the day of the Lord will come like a thief in the night.

Restatement of Thesis: [4] But you, beloved, are not in darkness, for that day to surprise you like a thief;

Rationale with Contrary: [5] for you are all children of light and children of the day; we are not of the night or of darkness.

Exhortative Conclusion: [6] So then, let us not fall asleep as others do, but let us keep awake and be sober;

Rationale with Analogy: [7] for those who sleep sleep at night, and those who are drunk get drunk at night.

Restatement of Exhortative Conclusion: [8] But since we belong to the day, let us be sober, and put on the breastplate of faith and love, and for a helmet the hope of salvation.

Summarizing Conclusion:

Thesis: [9] For God has destined us not for wrath but for obtaining salvation through our Lord Jesus Messiah, [10] who died for us,

Rationale: so that whether we are awake or asleep we may live with him.

Exhortative Conclusion: [11] Therefore encourage one another and build up each other, as indeed you are doing.

[31] These definitions of scenario event, script, and program have emerged during the last half century especially in contexts for producing films and programming computers. Once these models exist for us, they can be beneficially used to understand social, cultural, ideological, and religious processes of cognition in antiquity as well as the present. See Gilles Fauconnier, *Mental Spaces: Aspects of Meaning Construction in Natural Language*

whatever it talks about, whether the subject is something that happened in the past, is happening in the present, or will happen in the future. In other words, the narrator does not simply know "obvious" things about the past, present, and future. The narrator knows the "inner meanings" of things that have happened in the past, are happening in the present, and will happen in the future. Third, apocalyptic discourse works as vigorously with space as with time. The issue is space in time and time in space. Fourth, in Paul's undisputed letters the crucified Messiah who died and rose from the dead is the frame that guides the reconfiguration of conventional Jewish apocalyptic traditions. Fifth, the inside apocalyptic story blends a bright side of God's plans with a dark side. As Wanamaker says, "Christ's coming will be a glorious manifestation of the Lord for his obedient followers, but the day of judgment for unbelievers and the disobedient."[32]

It is not clear exactly what conventional apocalyptic tradition might be most closely related to 1 Thess 4–5.[33] In this letter, the overall governing principle (Rule) for Paul is: "you turned to God from idols to serve the living and true God, and to wait for his son from heaven, whom he raised from the dead, Jesus who delivers us from the wrath to come" (1:9-10).[34] This conceptual movement from earth to heaven with implications for God's movement of humans from earth to heaven presents a picturesque apocalyptic scenario "to make clear to his readers what it is that the *Lord* [Jesus] will do at his coming in which they can take comfort."[35] Interpreters regularly cite a wide range of texts to exhibit the intertextual nature of the descent of "the Lord himself," the command, the voice of an archangel, and the trumpet of God.[36] But exactly what the version of that apocalyptic tradition might be is not clear. As Malherbe says: "His elaboration will make use of apocalyptic imagery, but whether he derived it directly from Judaism or from early Christian apocalyptic tradition is impossible to determine with certainty and fortunately is unimportant. What is important is that Paul presents the apocalyptic scenario as a message from the Lord that he offers in a way designed to address his readers' immediate needs."[37]

(Cambridge: Cambridge University Press, 1994) esp. xxxv-xlv; idem, *Mappings in Thought and Language* (Cambridge: Cambridge University Press, 1997). For emerging definitions of English words during recent decades see "Whatis.com" online at: http://whatis.techtarget.com/.

[32] Wanamaker, *The Epistles to the Thessalonians*, 190.

[33] For the range of literature, see Hester, "Apocalyptic Discourse in 1 Thessalonians," 149-59.

[34] Cf. de Boer, "Apocalyptic Eschatology," 370; Victor Paul Furnish, *1 Thessalonians, 2 Thessalonians* (ANTC; Nashville, KY: Abingdon Press, 2007) 47-50.

[35] Malherbe, *The Letters to the Thessalonians*, 273.

[36] See ibid., 273-75.

[37] Ibid., 273.

For our purposes, the important point is that Paul reconfigured Mediterranean traditions into a series of apocalyptic "Messiah" story-summaries that feature Jesus first as an earthly being who became a heavenly being and second as a heavenly being who would descend from heaven to a place where he would be somehow visible, and at this time people who are dead "in Messiah" will rise, people who are alive "in Messiah" will be "snatched up" (*harpazein*) together with them in the clouds to meet the Lord Jesus in the air, and all of these people "in Messiah" will be with the heavenly Lord Jesus Messiah forever. Apocalyptic traditions make it possible for Paul to conceptualize (1) the transformation of a dead flesh and blood Messiah in earthly space into a heavenly being through "resurrection from the dead"; (2) the transformation of both dead and live humans "in Messiah" into beings that can fly up from earthly space into the air; (3) a command from the heavens, the voice of an archangel, and the trumpet of God as events in heavenly space that start the events; and (4) an unspecified space where all people "in Messiah" can be with heavenly Messiah Jesus forever.[38]

1 Thessalonians has a highly limited apocalyptic focus in relation to the full range of topics and issues in apocalyptic literature. To deal with the issue of death in the community at Thessalonica, Paul addresses their concerns over death as a time of "emotional" tribulation. His assertion is that God would address their tribulation with a sequence of actions by his Messiah, in which these people, who had been directed "to believe," would be delivered from their time of tribulation. "Community" tribulation rather than "cosmic" tribulation is the context for Paul's apocalyptic reasoning in 1 Thessalonians. As a discourse designed to guide and comfort, this early Christian apocalyptic rhetorolect is a special kind of early Christian wisdom rhetorolect. All of the picturesque dimensions of the discourse serve the purpose of instructing and nurturing people into productive relationships and activities. There is no perceived need to refer to any other parts of time than the past death and resurrection of Jesus, the turning of the hearers from idols to the true and living God, the present as it leads into the future, and a series of scenario events in the future. Inasmuch as the present is a time of tribulation, even though it is a "mild" time of tribulation in apocalyptic terms, the tumult it creates for the community is a natural context for a first century "messianic" apocalyptic answer.

[38] Whether that space is somewhere in the heavens or on earth is a matter of debate: ibid., 277-78; Furnish, *1 Thessalonians, 2 Thessalonians*, 103-104.

Apocalyptic Times and Spaces in 1–2 Corinthians: Adam, Moses, Christ, Apostles, and Believers

Paul's letters to the Corinthians expand "Christian" apocalyptic periods of time and space back to an era that begins with Adam. Again there is an apocalyptic story-summary of Christ's crucifixion, death, resurrection, and coming of the future as Paul presents his argumentation. These letters create a context in which Paul presents apocalyptic argumentation that includes more information about past time and space as well as more information about future time and space.

Apocalyptic Times and Spaces in 2 Baruch 56–74 and 1–2 Corinthians

2 Baruch 56–74	1-2 Corinthians
World History (This Age)	
(1) 56:5-16 Adam, sinful angels, and the flood (dark)	Adam: 1 Cor 15:20-58; [2 Cor 1:21-22; 3:17-18; 5:5, 17-21; 6:14–7:1] (dark) Man and Woman: 1 Cor 11:8-9, 12 Serpent deceived Eve: 2 Cor 11:3 (dark)
(4) 59:1-12 Moses through Caleb and Law (bright)	Moses: 1 Cor 9:8-12; 10:1-22; 2 Cor 3:4-18 (dark)
	Lord Jesus betrayed: 1 Cor 11:23
	Cross: 1 Cor 1:17-25; 2:2, 8
	Lord Jesus Christ died: 1 Cor 11:26; 15:3; 2 Cor 5:14-15
	Christ buried: 1 Cor 15:4
First Fruits of End Time (Christ; Apostles; Believers)	
God raised Christ (first fruits of the dead): 1 Cor 15:4, 12-20; 2 Cor 5:15; the Lord: 1 Cor 6:14; Lord Jesus: 2 Cor 4:15	
New Adam: 1 Cor 15:20-58; [2 Cor 1:21-22; 3:17-18; 5:5, 17-21; 6:14–7:1] (bright)	
Christ appeared: 1 Cor 15:5-8	
Revelation to Apostles (*apokalypsis/apkalyptō*): 1 Cor 2:9-10; 14:6, 26, 30; 2 Cor 12:1-7	
Mystery: 1 Cor 2:1, 7; 4:1; 13:2; 14:2; 15:51; of unbeliever's heart: 1 Cor 14:25	
Flesh: 1 Cor 3:3-4	
God chose to reduce to nothing things that are: 1 Cor 1:28-31	
Satan (time of the Apostles): destruction of the flesh: 1 Cor 5:5; tests: 1 Cor 7:5; outwits: 2 Cor 2:11; disguises self as angel of light: 2 Cor 11:14; given a thorn in the flesh to torment: 2 Cor 12:7; Beliar: 2 Cor 6:15 (dark)	
Spirit: 1 Cor 2:10-16; 6:19; 12:3, 11, 13; 2 Cor 1:22; 5:5; 7:1	
Transformation of believers: 2 Cor 3:18; 4:16	
New Creation of humanity: 2 Cor 5:17	
Completion of End Time	
	Resurrection of dead: 1 Cor 15:12-19, 21, 29, 32, 35-57; believers: 1 Cor 6:14; 15:14, 17-19, 23; 2 Cor 4:14

(12) 68:1-8 Rebuilt Zion/fall of nations (bright)	God's temple: 1 Cor 3:16-17; 6:19; 2 Cor 6:16; Eternal, heavenly house: 2 Cor 5:3
(13) 70:2 Coming of the harvest of the seed of evil ones and good ones after the time of the world has ripened (dark)	Coming of the Wrath: 1 Cor 2:6; 15:24-28; 2 Cor 5:10; Day of the Lord: 1 Cor 3:13; 2 Cor 6:2; Appointed Time: 1 Cor 7:29; 2 Cor 6:2; Judgment: 1 Cor 4:4-5; 5:13; 11:31-32; Judgment seat of Christ: 2 Cor 5:10; Wages according to Labor: 1 Cor 3:8; 2 Cor 5:10 (dark)
(17) 70:6 Tribulations (dark)	Tribulations: Christ's sufferings: 2 Cor 1:5 (dark) Persecution, distress, sufferings: 2 Cor 1:3-11; 5:2-4; 2:15; 4:8-12, 17-18; 7:4; 12:10 (dark)
(18) 70:7 Most High gives sign: prepared nations war against remaining rulers (dark)	Cry of command, archangel's call, sound of God's trumpet: 1 Cor 15:52 (dark)
(19) 70:8 Earthquake, fire, famine (dark)	Fire: 1 Cor 3:13-15 (dark)
(23) 72:2a Coming of time of the Anointed One after the signs and the moving of the nations (bright)	Coming of Lord Jesus: 1 Cor 11:26; 2 Cor 1:14; Lord Jesus Christ: 1 Cor 1:7-8; Christ: 1 Cor 15:23 (bright)
(24) 72:2b-6 The Anointed One will call the nations, sparing some and killing others (bright)	Christ rescues: 2 Cor 1:10; Christ destroys rulers, authorities, and powers: 1 Cor 15:24 (bright)
(25) 73:1 The Anointed One will sit down in eternal peace on the throne of the kingdom: joy will be revealed and rest will appear (bright)	Christ will reign: 1 Cor 15:25 (bright) Kingdom of God (for believers): depends on power: 1 Cor 4:16; inherit: 1 Cor 6:9-11; 15:50 (bright) Live with the Lord Jesus Christ: 2 Cor 4:14; 5:8 Face to face: 1 Cor 13:12 (bright)
(27) 73:3 No untimely death, no sudden adversity (bright)	No more death: 1 Cor 15:26, 54-56 (bright)
(32) 74:2 End of that which is corruptible; beginning of that which is incorruptible (bright)	Imperishable begins: 1 Cor 15:50-57; 1 Cor 9:25; 15:42, 53-54; 2 Cor 4:17-18 Complete end comes: 1 Cor 13:10 Christ hands Kingdom to God: 1 Cor 15:24-28 Fullness of earth belongs to God: 1 Cor 10:26 (bright)

Paul's use of the word "Messiah" (*christos*) without the article "the" continues in 1 Corinthians 15. The rhetorical effect of this use of the word results in assertions that "Messiah died" (15:3); "But if Messiah is proclaimed as raised from the dead" (15:12); "If there is no resurrection from the dead, then Messiah has not been raised, and if Messiah has not been raised, then our proclamation has been in vain and your faith has been in vain" (15:13-14); "We testified of God that he raised Messiah" (15:15); "For if dead are not raised, then Messiah has not been raised" (15:16); "If Messiah has not been raised, your faith is futile and you are still in your sins" (15:17); "Then those who have died in Messiah have perished. If for this life only we have hoped in Messiah, we are of all people most to be pitied" (15:18-19); and "But in fact Messiah has been raised" (15:20). The word Messiah is the special name for Jesus, and this name establishes a special relation between "believers" and God's Messiah that creates a context for Christians to participate in apocalyptic formulations of "salvation."

It is noticeable when Paul occasionally uses the article "the" when he refers to "Messiah." In 1 Corinthians 15, Paul uses an article when he refers to Messiah as the second Adam. Thus, Paul asserts: "for as all die in Adam, so all will be made alive in *the* Messiah. But each in his own order: Messiah as first fruits, then at his coming those who belong to *the* Messiah" (15:22-23). Here one sees a clue to Paul's thinking about "God's Messiah" that underlies his arguments about "Lord Jesus Messiah." In 1 Corinthians 15, Paul presents an inversion of the cosmological apocalyptic story whereby eternal angel-spirits "created" eternal demonic spirits on earth by impregnating daughters of humans. How, he asked himself, could God transform breathing flesh and blood humans into beings with a "heavenly-created" nature? The answer for Paul was in a "life-creating" (*zōiopoioun*) spirit (*pneuma*) Messiah (1 Cor 15:22, 45; 2 Cor 3:6; Rom 8:11).[39] God, in Paul's view, transformed a "breathing (*psychikon*)" flesh and blood Messiah into an imperishable heavenly-spirit being. While in the far distant past "sons of god" came down to earth and bore children with daughters of men, creating "undying evil" in the world, in the recent past "Messiah" went from earth up to heaven, creating "undying spirit" in which "fleshly" humans could participate through resurrection. According to the apocalyptic version of the story in the distant past, pervasive, eternal, "demonic" evil entered into God's created realm when heavenly-created, eternal, holy spirit bodies "procreated" with earthly-created flesh and blood bodies. The result was "blood-breathing" demonic eternal-spirit bodies characterized by "lust" (desire, covetousness) for all kinds of "evil things," including eating of blood and spilling of blood through murder. According to Paul's apocalyptic story of the recent past, God created eternal, "holy" spirit in his flesh and blood Messiah through resurrection, and this action by God set in motion the reversal of the perpetuation of eternal evil from Adam by transforming believers into children of God through Spirit of God (Gal 3:2-3, 26; Rom 8:9-17). In 1 Corinthians, belief in Messiah's resurrection is the context in which God works this remarkable mystery (1 Cor 15:42-45, 51-52).

In other words, Paul created a cosmological Messiah-spirit story-line by inverting the conventional cosmological sinful angel-spirit story-line. The resources for this inversion came from Jewish apocalyptic

[39] Cf. 1 Cor 15:36; Rom 4:17; Gal 3:21.

conceptuality. Paul asserted that God transformed an earth-dwelling flesh-Messiah into an eternal, imperishable heavenly spirit-being Messiah when he raised Jesus Messiah from the dead. God's resurrection of Messiah from the dead produced a "new Adam" in the earthly realm who is a "life-creating" (*zōiopoioun*) eternal-spirit (*pneuma*) Messiah. The point is that just as God had created eternal angel-spirit beings in heaven who were able to "procreate" eternal-spirit flesh and blood body with earthly beings, so God created an eternal-spirit Messiah out of a flesh-Messiah who is able to "procreate" eternal-spirit heavenly body with believing flesh and blood humans on earth. What is required for the process to work is that people be "in Messiah." When people are "in Messiah," they are, as Paul states, "a new creation": "So if anyone is in Messiah, there is a new creation: everything old has passed away; see, everything has become new! All this is from God, who reconciled (*katallaxantos*) us to himself through Messiah, and has given us the ministry of reconciliation (*katallassōn*)... For our sake he made him to be sin who knew no sin, so that in him we might become the righteousness of God" (2 Cor 5:17-19, 21).

In Paul's view, God provided "new creation" on earth by inverting the process of the continual procreation of "evil and corruption" on earth that had occurred when the sinful angels violated God's boundaries between heaven and earth. To invert the process, God created a life-creating eternal-spirit Messiah "on earth" who reversed the process for those who become "in Messiah." In other words, as God had created angel-spirits in heaven who possessed "eternal spirit," and they were able to generate eternal, evil demonic spirits "through flesh and blood" on earth, so with Jesus God had created an eternal-spirit Messiah on earth through "resurrection from the dead," and he is able to generate eternal, sanctified "human" bodies "through spirit of holiness." As Anthony C. Thiselton has put it: "For Paul *new creation* and *transformation came from beyond and were constituted by the agency of the Holy Spirit*, not an immanent human spirit."[40]

One of the implicit points of 1 Cor 15:44-47 is that the first man was not made of a combination of clay, metal, and stone. In other words, Paul is not thinking in the stream of earth-material apocalyptic tradition but in the stream of angel-spirit apocalyptic tradition. Paul is not trying to work out issues of military power and wealth, but issues concerning the relation among spirit, flesh, and blood. This becomes clear in 1 Cor 15:50 where Paul asserts that "flesh and blood cannot inherit the kingdom of God," nor does the perishable (breathing

[40] Anthony C. Thiselton, *The First Epistle to the Corinthians: A Commentary on the Greek Text* (Grand Rapids, MI: Eerdmans and Carlisle: Paternoster, 2000) 1283.

earthly-creation flesh and blood body) inherit the imperishable (eternal spirit in a heavenly-creation body).

Paul produces his Messiah-spirit inversion of the sinful angel-spirit story-line with an apocalyptic argument that, once again, embeds apocalyptic story-summaries in the argumentation. In this instance, Paul begins with a story-summary that introduces seven scenario events about "Messiah" to the hearer/reader: Messiah: (1) died; (2) was buried; (3) was raised on the third day; (4) appeared to Cephas, then to the twelve; (5) appeared to more than five hundred brothers and sisters at one time; (6) appeared to James, then to all the apostles; and (7) appeared to Paul last of all (1 Cor 15:3-8).[41] This apocalyptic story-summary introduces a sequence of scenario events about a flesh-Messiah who, through resurrection, became a heavenly being who appeared to a large number of people in an order that begins with Jesus' specially chosen disciples, continues with a large number of believers, moves to the head of the church in Jerusalem and people sent out into mission, and ends with Paul, to whom the heavenly Messiah appeared after a period of time in which Paul had persecuted believers in Jesus as God's Messiah. This apocalyptic story-summary creates the context for an elaborate argument about how this sequence of scenario events produced a "life-creating spirit" who overcame the heritage of death produced by the first human, Adam (1 Cor 15:45). We can discuss only a few parts of Paul's elaborate argument here.[42]

The story-summary Paul introduces in 1 Cor 15:3-8 is an expansion of only the first part of the story-summary he had introduced in 1 Thess 4:14: "we believe that Jesus died and rose again." In the context of the expanded story-summary, Paul presents an argument to counter the opposite argument: "there is no resurrection of the dead" (1 Cor 15:12-19).[43] This argument creates the context for Paul to introduce his interpretation of the relation of the apocalyptic time period of Adam to the apocalyptic time period of Messiah's death, resurrection, and appearances (15:20-28). Paul embeds in this argument, which is based on apocalyptic periodization of world history, an expansion of the second part of

[41] For a rhetorical analysis of 1 Cor 15:3-11 as a *narration*, see Anders Eriksson, *Traditions as Rhetorical Proof: Pauline Argumentation in 1 Corinthians* (CBNTS 29; Stockholm: Almquist & Wiksell, 1998) 253-55.

[42] For a sociorhetorical display of the complete argument, see Vernon K. Robbins, *Exploring the Texture of Texts: A Guide to Socio-Rhetorical Interpretation* (Harrisburg, PA: Trinity Press International, 1996) 56-58; cf. Duane F. Watson, "Paul's Rhetorical Strategy in 1 Cor 15," in *Rhetoric and the NT* (ed. S.E. Porter and T.H. Olbricht; Sheffield: Sheffield Academic Press, 1993) 231-41; Margaret M. Mitchell, *Paul and the Rhetoric of Reconciliation: An Exegetical Investigation of the Language and Composition of 1 Corinthians* (Louisville: Westminster/John Knox Press, 1991) 283-90.

[43] For the enthymematic chain of argumentation in 1 Cor 15:12-19, see Eriksson, *Traditions as Rhetorical Proof*, 255-61.

1 Thess 4:14: "through Jesus, God will bring with him those who have died." Paul's expansion in 1 Cor 15:21-28 is an argumentative story-summary containing ten apocalyptic scenario events: (1) death came through a human being [Adam]; (2) the resurrection of the dead has come through a human being [Messiah]; (3) all die in Adam; (4) all will be made alive in his own order in Messiah; (5) Messiah was made alive as the first fruits; (6) at Messiah's coming those who belong to Messiah will be made alive; (7) when the end comes, Messiah will reign until he has put all his enemies under his feet, because God has put all things in subjection under his feet; (8) Messiah will destroy every ruler and every authority and power; (9) the last enemy Messiah will destroy is death; (10) after destroying all powers opposed to God including death, Messiah will hand over the kingdom to God the Father.[44]

One readily observes that the scenario events in Paul's story-summary in 1 Cor 15:21-28 are not what one would call "ordinary" events. These events are not the kinds of happenings that people can "see" as ordinary observers of human activities. Rather, this is an apocalyptic "inside account" of scenario events of world history from the first man Adam to Messiah's handing of his kingdom over to God in the future. One of the challenges for interpreting this section of 1 Cor 15 is that Paul's argument does not introduce the scenario events of the apocalyptic story in a "historical sequence." The reason is that apocalyptic story-telling regularly uses repetitive, cyclic presentation interspersed with exhortative argumentation, rather than historical sequencing, to produce its rhetorical effects. We have seen the repetitive, exhortative nature of apocalyptic argumentation above in the elaborate recycling of world historical events in different modes in *1 Enoch*, and we will see this again in the Revelation to John at the end of this chapter. In apocalyptic scenario events, inside meanings are as important as observable sequences of actions. A major reason is that the "causes" for apocalyptic scenario events always are a blending of God's preordained plans for the world and "historical" events that produce sequences of activities in God's created world. This means that aspects of God's judgment and redemption have always been present in events that humans regularly have perceived to be "sequences of time" in world history. Indeed, a major point of apocalyptic periodization of world history is to show that God's plans for redemption and judgment in the world have always been present in "historical" events and they always will be. In other words, apocalyptists presuppose that God's time and space has always been present and interactive with time and space in God's created world. This is why, for instance, the writer of *Jubilees* 1 could presuppose that God had "revealed" to Moses "both

[44] For 1 Cor 15:20-34 as the rhetorical amplification of a theme, see ibid., 261-67.

what (was) in the beginning and what will occur (in the future), the account of the division of the all of the days of the Law and the testimony" (1:4). Since ordinary people regularly do not see the presence and interaction of all of God's space and time in every era of time, it is necessary for apocalyptic narrators to explain it. This is what Paul does in 1 Corinthians 15. As a narrator with inside apocalyptic knowledge, he is able to explain the deep and mysterious aspects of time and space from the time of Adam to the time when God's Messiah will hand the kingdom over to God.

After Paul's explanation of the relation of Messiah to the time of Adam, he explains the relation of resurrection to spaces in God's world (15:35-41).[45] To explain this, Paul uses analogies from different spheres of God's created world. The human body on earth is like a seed of grain (15:37), but God gives each kind of seed its own body in relation to its spatial context and function. Animals have flesh that serves them well in contexts were there are no houses, no special clothes to wear, etc. Birds have a special flesh for flying through the air, and fishes for living in water (15:38). Heavenly bodies, in turn, have non-flesh properties appropriate to their particular "glory" (sun, moon, stars: 15:39-40). Of special importance for apocalyptic thought is the relation of spirit and body. As it states in *Testament of Naphtali* 2:2: "the Lord forms the body in correspondence to the spirit, and instills the spirit corresponding to the power of the body." As Paul says, "God gives it a body as he has chosen ... It is sown a physical [breathing] body, it is raised a spiritual body" (1 Cor 15:38, 44). Perhaps even more important, however, is the principle in apocalyptic conceptuality that the human body is changeable. According to *2 Baruch* 21:16-17, the nature of humans is always changeable: "For as we were once, we are no longer, and as we are now, we shall not remain in the future. For if an end of all things had not been prepared, their beginning would have been senseless." In Paul's word's, "We will not all die, but we will all be changed" (1 Cor 15:51). In 1 Corinthians, Paul explains his understanding of the process by presenting yet one more argumentative story-summary. In this instance, the story-summary contains three basic scenario events: (1) the last trumpet will sound; (2) the dead will be raised imperishable; and (3) we will be changed (1 Cor 15:52). These scenario events are the rationale that supports his thesis that "We will not all die, but we will all be changed, in a moment, in the twinkling of an eye, at the last trumpet" (15:51-52).[46] Once again we see how apocalyptic story-summary functions internally in support of

[45] For 1 Cor 15:35-49 as *refutation* and *confirmatio*, see ibid., 267-72.
[46] For rhetorical analysis and interpretation of 1 Cor 15:50-57, see ibid., 272-75.

Paul's reasoning about the nature of earthly life, resurrection, and the imperishable, spiritual body that God has established for believers.

In the overall context of 1 Corinthians, Paul introduces the ironic nature of the time of Moses as a mixture of brightness and darkness, but he does not correlate the time of Moses with the time of the first and last Adam. In Paul's story-summary of the time of Moses (1 Cor 10:1-5), all of the ancestors of believers in God's Messiah first "were baptized into Moses in the cloud and in the sea" (1 Cor 10:3).[47] For Paul, the brightness of this baptism lies in the realm of God's spirit.[48] All the people "ate the same spiritual food, and all drank the same spiritual drink, for they drank from the spiritual rock that followed them, and the rock was Christ" (10:4).[49] This internalization of God's spirit, from Paul's perspective, is a preconfiguration of spirit that "proclaims the Lord's death until he comes" through the Lord's Supper (1 Cor 11:23-32) and unites believers with Christ in death and resurrection through baptism (Rom 6:3-5). But the brightness of the working of the spirit during the time of Christ was not present during the time of Moses. Instead, despite the spiritual baptism, eating, and drinking during the time of Moses, "God was not pleased with most of them, and they were struck down in the wilderness" (1 Cor 10:5). In contrast to Jewish apocalyptic literature like *2 Baruch*, then, Paul does not emphasize the coming of "the lamp of the eternal Law which exists forever and ever illuminated all those who sat in darkness" (*2 Bar* 59:2) during the time of Moses. Rather, Paul's story-summary emphasizes God's striking most of the Israelites down in the wilderness (1 Cor 10:5).

Paul's reasoning in 2 Cor 3 extends his perception of the time of Moses as a dark time by describing the law as a "ministry of death" whereby "the letter kills," in contrast to a "ministry of the Spirit" that "creates life" (2 Cor 3:6).[50] In this context, Paul's argumentative story-summary extends from the time of Moses to the time of Christ, con-

[47] Cf. B.J. Oropeza, "Echoes of Isaiah in the Rhetoric of Paul: New Exodus, Wisdom, and the Humility of the Cross in Utopian-Apocalyptic Expectations," in Duane F. Watson, *The Intertexture of Apocalyptic Discourse in the New Testament* (Symposium 14; Atlanta: SBL, 2002) 92-97.

[48] Ibid., 97-103, 106-12.

[49] Paul's "spiritualization" of the exodus in 1 Cor 10:1-22 probably contains "apocalyptic wisdom" when Paul refers to "sacrificing to demons," being "partners with demons," drinking "the cup of demons," and partaking of "the table of demons" (10:20); Anthony C. Thiselton, *The First Epistle to the Corinthians: A Commentary on the Greek Text* (NIGTC; Grand Rapids, MI/Cambridge, UK: Eerdmans and Carlisle: Paternoster Press, 2000) 775-79; cf. Eriksson, *Traditions as Rhetorical Proof*, 166-73; Mitchell, *Paul and the Rhetoric of Reconciliation*, 250-56.

[50] Cf. Edith M. Humphrey, "Ambivalent Apocalypse: Apocalyptic Rhetoric and Intertextuality in 2 Corinthians," in Duane F. Watson, *The Intertexture of Apocalyptic Discourse in the New Testament* (Symposium 14; Atlanta: SBL, 2002) 117-26.

taining four major scenario events: (1) Moses put a veil over his face to keep the people of Israel from gazing at the end of the glory that was being set aside (3:13); (2) their minds were hardened; (3) to this very day, when they hear the reading of the old covenant, that same veil is still there, since only in Christ is it set aside (3:14); (4) all of us, with unveiled faces, seeing the glory of the Lord as though reflected in a mirror, are being transformed into the same image from one degree of glory to another; for this comes from the Lord, the Spirit (3:18). This argumentative story-summary covers a span of time from Moses to the ongoing present. Once Paul presents this argument, he moves through a focus on the presence of the Spirit among believers (3:17-18; 4:13) gradually to a focus that restates the argumentative story-summaries in 1 Thess 4–5 and 1 Cor 15. This time Paul's story-summary contains three scenario events: (1) the one who raised the Lord Jesus; (2) will raise us also with Jesus; and (3) will bring us with you into his presence (2 Cor 4:14). This argumentative story-summary sets the stage for Paul to discuss the time when "the earthly tent we live in is destroyed" and "we have a building from God, a house not made with hands, eternal in the heavens" (2 Cor 5:1). All of these things are possible, according to Paul, because: "He who has prepared us for this very thing is God, who has given us the Spirit as a guarantee" (5:5). It is noticeable in this instance that Paul's assertions move "we" and "us" into the center of the discussion. This focus causes the "story" part of his argument to move into a supportive role rather than to be at the center of the argument, as it is in 1 Thess 4–5 and 1 Cor 15. Still, however, Paul's understanding of the Spirit in all of this is an inversion of the cosmological story of the sinful angels who introduced eternal spirit of evil into the world through lust, desire, and sin. In Paul's view, God has intercepted this ongoing story of sin and death, which he perceives to be from "the time of Adam," with the cosmological story of God's resurrection of his flesh-Messiah into an eternal-spirit Messiah in the heavens. God's resurrection of his Messiah made him into a life-creating spirit. In all of this, it is the Spirit given by God that is the guarantee.

Apocalyptic Times and Spaces in Galatians and Romans: Adam, Abraham, Moses, Christ, Paul, and Believers

In Paul's letters to the Galatians and Romans, the power of the Spirit in his cosmological eternal-spirit Messiah story takes center stage. In Galatians, Paul moves decisively to an apocalyptic story-line from Abraham to Messiah, developing the eternal-spirit insight of his first Adam/last Adam inversion of the cosmological story of the angel-spirits. Moses is on the horizons as Paul refers to "the law of Messiah" in Gal 6:2, but Paul never refers directly to Moses in Galatians. In Romans, Paul adds the time of David to the "Christian" apocalyptic story-line from Adam to Abraham to Moses that he had developed in 1–2 Corinthians and Galatians. An overview of the scope of Paul's apocalyptic vision in Galatians and Romans is present in the following table:

Apocalyptic Times and Spaces in 1 Enoch *85–93,* 2 Baruch *65–74, Galatians, and Romans*

***1 Enoch* 85–90; 93:1-10; 91:11-17; *2 Baruch* 56–74**	**Galatians/Romans**
	Creation: Rom 1:20, 25; 8:18-23
World History (This Age)	
Adam	
(1) *1 En.* 85:3-9 Adam and Eve and their Children; cf. (2-4) *1 En.* 86:1–89:8 (1) *1 En.* 93:3 First Week: Adam to Enoch; righteousness (good); cf. (2) *1 En.* 93:4 (1) *2 Bar.* 56:5-16 Adam, sinful angels, and the flood (dark)	Adam: [Gal 5:5; 5:16–6:1; 6:7-9]; Rom 5:12-14, 18-21 [1:24-32] Adam to Moses: Rom 5:14 The judgment following one trespass: Rom 5:16 (dark)
(3) *1 En.* 93:5 Third Week: Conclusion: Abraham, plant of righteous judgment; Abraham's son [Isaac], eternal plant of righteousness (good); cf. (5) *1 En.* 89:9-27 (2) *2 Bar.* 57:1-3 Abraham and his family (bright)	Abraham: Gal 2:15–4:7; 4:22–5:1; Rom 4:1-25; 5:18-21; 9:4-18 (bright) Children of promise like Isaac, child born according to the Spirit: Gal 4:28-29; Rom 9:7-13 (bright) Sodom and Gomorrah: Rom 9:29 (dark)
Moses	
(4) *2 Bar.* 59:1-12 Moses through Caleb and Law (bright); cf. (6) *1 En.* 89:28-38; (4) *1 En.* 93:6	Moses: (never mentioned by name in Galatians); Rom 5:14; 9:15-18; 10:5, 19 Law: Gal 2:15–4:5; 5:18, 22; Rom 2:12-29; 3:19-31; 5:14, 20-21; 7:1-25; 8:2-4; 9:4, 30-33; works of: Gal 3:12; through angels: Gal 3:19; as disciplinarian: Gal 3:23; is holy: Rom 7:12 God imprisoned all in disobedience: Rom 10:21; 11:30-32; 15:31 Entire law: Gal 5:3, 14

(6) *2 Bar.* 61:1-8 David, Solomon, and Zion (bright); cf. (7) *1 En.* 89:35-50; (5) *1 En.* 93:7	David: Rom 1:3; cf. 9:5 [4:6; 11:9] (bright)
(7) *1 En.* 93:9-10; 91:11 Seventh week: Perverse generation; wicked deeds (evil); Conclusion: Elect ones of righteousness chosen from the eternal plant of righteousness (Abraham's progeny); given sevenfold wisdom and knowledge to execute judgment on violence and deceit (good); cf. (11-13) *1 En.* 89:72b–90:19	Every kind of wickedness: Rom 1:28-32 Elemental spirits enslaved prior to Christ: Gal 4:3, 8-10 Election/Remnant: Rom 8:28-30, 33; 9:6-18, 24-29; 11:5, 7, 28-29; 16:13
Beginning of End Time: Christ	
Birth of Jesus at fullness of time: Gal 4:4; descended from David according to the flesh: Rom 1:3; 9:5 God's Son born under the law: Gal 4:5; Christ is end of the Law: Rom 10:4 God sent his own Son in the likeness of sinful flesh: Rom 8:3; gave him up for all of us: Rom 8:32	
Christ became a servant of the circumcised on behalf of the truth of God in order that he might confirm the promises given to the patriarchs, and in order that the Gentiles might glorify God for his mercy: Rom 15:8-9	
Cross: Gal 5:11; 6:12, 14	
Lord Jesus Christ died: Rom 4:25; 5:6, 8, 10; 6:3; 8:34; 14:15	
God raised Lord Jesus Christ from the dead: Gal 1:1; Rom 1:4; 4:24-25; 6:4; 7:4; 8:34; 10:7-9	
Christ died and lived again, that he might be Lord of dead and living: Rom 6:10; 14:9, 15	
Fruits of End Time: Apostles	
Revelation to Apostles (*apokalypsis/apokalypto*): Gal 1:12, 16; 2:2; 3:23; Rom 1:17-18; 2:5; 3:21; 8:18-19; 16:25	
Paul crucified with Christ: Gal 2:19; 6:14 Christ lives in Paul: Gal 2:20	
Galatians welcomed Paul as angel of God: Gal 4:14	
Mystery: Rom 11:25; 16:25 Invisible: Rom 1:20 (cf. Col 1:15-16; 1 Tim 1:17)	
Fruits of End Time: Believers	
Spirit: Gal 3:2-5; 4:6; 5:5, 16-26; 6:1, 8; Rom 1:4; 5:5; 7:7; 8:2-17, 23, 26-27 (first fruits); 14:17; 15:13, 19 Reversal of sinful angel myth: Rom 8:1-17 (Rom 8:11: If the Spirit of him who raised Jesus from the dead dwells in you, he who raised Christ from the dead will give life to your mortal bodies also through his spirit that dwells in you.)	
Believers baptized into Christ's death and resurrection, dying to sin and death: Rom 6:1-23; died to the law to bear fruit for God: Rom 7:4-6	
Believers crucified the flesh: Gal 5:24	
New Creation of humanity: Gal 6:15 Newness of life: Rom 6:4; 7:6 Transformation of believers: Rom 12:1-2	
Law of Christ: Gal 6:2; of faith: Rom 3:27; spiritual: Rom 7:14; of God: Rom 7:25; 8:7, 22, 25; of the Spirit of Life in Christ Jesus: Rom 8:2 (bright) Law, sin, death: Rom 7:1-25; 8:2 Obedience of faith: Rom 1:5; 6:16-19; 10:16-17; 16:26 (cf. obedience: 2 Cor 7:15; 10:5-6; Rom 5:19; 15:18; 16:19) (bright)	

End Time	
	Resurrection of dead: Rom 4:17; 11:15
	God of peace will crush Satan: Rom 16:20
(13) *2 Bar.* 70:2 Coming of the harvest of the seed of evil ones and good ones after the time of the world has ripened (dark)	Coming of the Wrath: Rom 1:18; 2:5-11; 3:5-6; 4:15; 5:9; 9:22; 12:19; [13:4-5]; Appointed Time/Day: Rom 13:11-12; Judgment: Rom 2:2; 3:19; 11:21;14:10; Judgment seat of Christ: Rom 2:16; Harvest: Gal 6:8-9 (cf. Rom 1:13); Sudden destruction: Rom 9:28-29 (dark)
(17) *2 Bar.* 70:6 Tribulations (dark)	Tribulations: Persecution, distress, sufferings: Rom 8:19 Birth pangs: in Paul until Christ is formed in believers: Gal 4:19 [4:27]; of creation and ourselves: Rom 8:18-23; sudden destruction: 1 Thess 5:3 (dark)
(23) *2 Bar.* 72:2a Coming of time of the Anointed One after the signs and the moving of the nations (bright)	Coming of Christ: Gal 1:1, 3-4; Rom 5–6 (bright)
(24) *2 Bar.* 72:2b-6 The Anointed One will call the nations, sparing some and killing others (bright); cf, (10) *1 En.* 91:15-16	Lord Jesus Christ set believers free from the present evil age: Gal 1:4 (bright)
(25) *2 Bar.* 73:1 The Anointed One will sit down in eternal peace on the throne of the kingdom: joy will be revealed and rest will appear (bright); cf. (16) *1 En.* 90:30-39; (11) *1 En.* 91:17	Kingdom as inheritance: Gal 3:18, 29; 4:1, 7, 30; 5:21; Rom 4:13-14; 8:17 (bright) Christ Jesus at the right hand of God: Rom 8:34 Peace: Rom 5:1; and joy: Rom 14:17; God of peace will crush Satan: 16:20 (bright) With love of God in Lord Jesus Christ: Rom 8:35-39 (bright)
(26) *2 Bar.* 73:2 Health, no illness, fear, tribulation, or lamentation; joy will encompass the earth (bright)	Riches of his glory: Rom 9:23; 14:17 (bright)
(28) *2 Bar.* 73:4 Uprooting of judgment, condemnations, contentions, revenges, blood, passions, zeal, hate, and all such things (bright)	Spirit (working in Kingdom of God) opposes desires of flesh: Gal 5:16-26
(32) *2 Bar.* 74:2 End of that which is corruptible; beginning of that which is incorruptible (bright)	Imperishable begins: Rom 6:22; 8:23 (bright)

Paul's Letter to the Galatians

Paul's apocalyptic argumentation in Galatians begins with an emphasis that God was pleased "to reveal (*apokalypsai*) his Son" (Gal 1:16) to him (Paul) to equip him to proclaim the gospel of Christ (1:7) among the Gentiles. The issue for Paul is whether the Galatians "received the Spirit" when Paul preached to them (3:2). Having started with the Spirit, it is important that they continue in faith in such a manner that they receive the benefits of God's transformation of his flesh-Messiah into an eternal-spirit Messiah through resurrection. In Galatians, this reasoning takes Paul back to an apocalyptic understanding of the time of Abraham. As one can see in the table above, Paul's apocalyptic view of the time of Abraham has a close relation to the positive view of this era in *1 Enoch* 93:5 and *2 Baruch* 57:1-3. For *1 En.* 93:5, Abraham was chosen by God as "the plant of righteous judgment," and the one "after him will go forth" as "the plant of righteousness forever and ever."[51] The assertions in this passage cohere with the view of the era of Abraham as a bright time in *2 Baruch* 57. This time brought forth "the fountain of Abraham, and the coming of his son, and the son of his son, and of those who are like them" (57:1), and during this time "the unwritten law" was in force among them (57:2). Indeed the time of Abraham, according to *2 Bar.* 57:2, brought forth "belief in the coming judgment," built "hope of the world which will be renewed," and planted "promise of the life that will come later."

It is noticeable that the apocalyptic *topoi* of belief,[52] hope,[53] and promise,[54] which are prominent features of the time of Abraham in *2 Baruch*, also are prominent features of the time of Abraham in Galatians and Romans. Paul's focus on the era of Abraham is part of an overall positive view of the time of Abraham in Jewish apocalyptic literature. In Galatians, Paul produces a story-summary containing four apocalyptic scenario events he had not discussed in 1 Thessalonians and 1-2 Corinthians: (1) Abraham believed God; (2) it was reckoned to him as righteousness; (3) the scripture declared the gospel beforehand to Abraham, saying, "All the Gentiles shall be blessed in you"; and (4) those who believe are descendants of Abraham and are blessed with

[51] Translation in George W.E. Nickelsburg, *1 Enoch 1* (Hermeneia; Minneapolis: Fortress Press, 2001) 434, 445-46.

[52] Belief (*pistis*): Gal 1:23; 2:16, 20; 3:2, 5, 7-9, 11-12, 14, 22-26; 5:5-6, 22; 6:10; Rom 1:5, 8, 12, 17; 3:3, 22, 25-28, 30-31; 4:5, 9, 11-14, 16, 19, 20; 5:1-2; 9:30, 32; 10:6, 8, 17; 11:20; 12:3, 6; 14:1, 22-23; 16:26; (*pisteuō*): Gal 2:7, 16; 3:6, 22; Rom 1:16; 3:2, 22; 4:3, 5, 11, 17-18, 24; 6:8; 9:33; 10:4, 9-11, 14, 16; 13:11; 14:2; 15:13.

[53] Hope (*elpis*): Gal 5:5; Rom 4:18; 5:2, 4-5; 8:20, 24; 12:12; 15:4, 13; (*elpizō*): Rom 8:24-25; 15:12, 24.

[54] Promise (*epangelia*): Gal 3:14, 16-18, 21-22, 29; 4:23-28; Rom 4:13, 14, 16, 20; 9:4, 8-9; 15:8; (*epangellomai*): Gal 3:19; Rom 4:21.

Abraham who believed (3:6-9). To explain the effect of this story-summary, Paul uses language about the Spirit. For Paul, "the blessing of Abraham" that can come to the Gentiles "in Christ Jesus" is "the promise of the Spirit through faith" (Gal 3:14). Paul's presentation of his argument for this promise (3:15-18) brings him to a discussion of "the law" without mentioning Moses (Gal 3:19-29). For Paul, the time of the law is a blend of brightness and darkness. On the one hand, the law is not opposed to the promises of God (3:21). On the other hand, it was simply an addition "until the offspring [of Abraham] would come to whom the promise had been made" (3:19). God's Messiah Jesus is, according to Paul, that offspring. God gave the law through angels by a mediator because of transgressions (3:19). But the law as scripture was imprisoned "under the power of sin" (as a result of the time of Adam) "so that what was promised through faith in Jesus Messiah might be given to those who believe" (3:22).

As Paul explains in Galatians how all "in Messiah Jesus" are "children of God through faith," clothed "with Messiah" through baptism, and "heirs according to the promise" (3:26-27, 29), he comes to another story-summary that leads, once again, to language about the Spirit. This argumentative story-summary has six scenario events: (1) the fullness of time came; (2) God sent his Son; (3) God's son was born of a woman; (4) God's son was born under the law, to redeem those who were under the law, so that believers might receive adoption as children; (5) believing Galatians became children of God; and (6) God sent the Spirit of his Son into the hearts of the Galatians, making them heirs of the promise (4:4-7). This argumentative story-summary gives the time of Abraham full stage without introducing the death and resurrection of Christ. In other words, in this section of Galatians an apocalyptic story-summary from Abraham to the present "overmaps" Paul's usual story-summary about Jesus' death and resurrection. This new story-summary moves from Abraham through the law to Gentiles as children of God through "the Spirit of his Son" whom God sent into the Galatians. The "force" that changes people into children of God is the Spirit that God sent from the heavens into humans through Christ. In this instance, Paul's overmapping of the usual story-summary about Christ's death and resurrection with the effect of the Abraham story-summary produces a story-summary that leaves out all reference to death or resurrection. This new language of "children" of God leads to a special discussion of "the promise" of Abraham in relation to Hagar, a slave woman who produced a child "according to the flesh," and a free woman who produced a child "born through promise" (4:22-23). This creates the context for Paul to identify "children of the promise, like Isaac" (4:28) as children "born according to the Spirit"

(4:29). Again, for Paul the Spirit is the true agency of the promise, able to transform people into children of God. For this reason, Paul returns once again to a reference to the Spirit when he discusses the possibility of returning to circumcision (5:2-6). As Paul explains, circumcision has no potential for producing the transformation of the flesh that is essential for redemption. It is "through the Spirit, by faith" that "we eagerly wait for the hope of righteousness" (5:5).

After referring to circumcision, Paul turns to "faith working through love" (5:6), for the purpose of explaining how the Spirit, which at the end of time will transform people into eternal-spirit beings, already functions in the believing community to "enliven" them with "fruit of the Spirit" (5:22, 25). In this context language of Jesus' death, which was absent from the discussion of the time of Abraham, appears in the form of reference to "the cross." Paul begins with reference to "the offense of the cross" (5:11) and moves to a discussion of having "crucified the flesh with its passions and desires" through "belonging to Messiah" (5:24). The effect of Paul's inversion of the cosmological story of the sinful angels with the story of God's eternal-spirit Messiah is even more evident here than in many places in Paul's writings. In Gal 5:16-17, Paul explicitly opposes "the desires of the flesh," which stand at the center of the conventional cosmological story of the sinful angels, with "living by the Spirit." Living by the Spirit bypasses the law (5:18), because it "fulfills the law of Messiah" (6:2). The issue, then, is not law itself, which helps to define the righteousness of God within God's promise (3:17). The issue is the "enlivening" of the body with the Spirit in a manner that removes "the works of the flesh" (5:19-21) and produces "the fruit of the Spirit" (5:23). In this context, Paul reformulates his previous story-summaries about Messiah's death, resurrection, and transformation of believers through resurrection (1 Thess 4–5; 1 Cor 15; 2 Cor 4–5) in terms of crucifying the flesh with its passions and desires through "belonging to Messiah Jesus" (5:24-25). Through his argument in this section, Paul proposes that already in the present age it is possible for believers to experience an "earthly" form of "spiritual" transformation. "Living" by the spirit and being guided by the Spirit (5:25), Paul asserts, is an action of "sowing to the Spirit" that "reaps eternal life from the Spirit" at "harvest time" (6:8-9). Paul's argument exhibits deep relationships to Jewish apocalyptic literature through its metaphors, its concepts of transformation, its focus on periods of world history, and its concerns with spirit, eternal life, desire, flesh, and righteousness.[55] But Paul creates his own point of view through a special focus on God's Messiah, who died as a flesh-Messiah,

[55] See J.L. Martyn, *Galatians* (AB 33A; New York/London/Toronto/Sydney/Auckland: Doubleday, 1997).

was raised as an eternal-spirit Messiah, and who offers benefits to believers of transformations that the Spirit of God can give to humans both during the present age and in the age to come.

Paul's Letter to the Romans

In contrast to Galatians, which contains no story-summary of God's action through the Lord Jesus Messiah's death and resurrection in the context of world history, Paul's letter to the Romans begins with a story-summary containing four scenario events: (1) Jesus Messiah was descended from David according to the flesh; (2) Jesus Messiah was declared to be Son of God with power according to the spirit of holiness by resurrection from the dead; (3) apostles received grace and apostleship to bring about the obedience of faith among all the Gentiles; and (4) Gentiles, including "God's beloved in Rome," have been "called to belong to Jesus Messiah" (Rom 1:3-7). This apocalyptic story-summary omits any explicit reference to Lord Jesus Messiah's appearance to believers (1 Cor 15:5-8), rescuing of believers from the coming wrath (1 Thess 1:10; 4:14-17; 5:10), or destruction of all enemies including death (1 Cor 15:23-28). Instead, the summary moves directly from the Lord Jesus Messiah's descent from David and his status as a result of resurrection to benefits that result for apostles and believing Gentiles. Paul's "gospel" in this context presents a new revelation-story, namely the revealing (*apokalyptetai*) of the righteousness of God "from faith to faith"[56] that occurs in the context of the revealing (*apokalyptetai*) of the wrath of God from heaven "against all impiety and wrongdoing" (Rom 1:16-17).[57] In other words, in Romans there is a change of focus from some kind of revelation of the Lord Jesus Messiah (1 Cor 1:7; 2 Cor 12:1; Gal 1:12)[58] to a revelation sequence based on new terminology. As the sequence is presented by Paul in Romans 1–8, the sequence contains five blended scenario events:

1. a "revealing" of the righteousness of God from faith to faith (Rom 1:16);
2. a "revealing" of the wrath of God from heaven (1:17);
3. a "revelation" of the righteous judgment of God (2:5);
4. a "revealing" of the future[59] glory (8:18);
5. a "revealing" of the sons of God (8:19) who have "the first fruits of the Spirit" (8:23).

[56] Translation in Robert Jewett, *Romans* (Hermeneia; Minneapolis: Fortress Press, 2007) 135.

[57] Cf. 1 Thess 2:16; 4:6; 5:2, 9-10; 1 Cor 2:6; 3:13; 11:32; Gal 6:8.

[58] Cf. Gal 2:2; 2 Thess 1:7; 1 Pet 1:7, 13; 4:13; Rev 1:1.

[59] Jewett, *Romans*, 510.

In this sequence, we see Paul's more fully developed inversion of the cosmological story of the sinful "sons of God" (angels) who brought eternal desire, sin, and death into human flesh, and thus into God's created world. In Romans, Paul reformulates his 1 Corinthians inversion of the cosmological sinful angel story, which is a story of God's Messiah as the last Adam who became a "life-creating spirit" (1 Cor 15:45), into an inversion of the cosmological sinful angel story that "overmaps" the sinful "sons of God" with "first-fruit Spirit" sons of God (Rom 8:23) who are "revealed" (Rom 8:19) in the context of the "revealing" of the future glory (8:18). This new revelation of sons of God occurs in the context of the "revelation" of God's righteous judgment (2:5), which occurs in the "revealing" of the wrath of God from heaven against all impiety and wrongdoing of humans who are suppressing the truth by unrighteousness (1:18). Paul's shorthand for all of these "revelations" is the revealing of the righteousness of God from faith to faith (1:17). In other words, the apocalyptic center of Paul's argumentation in Romans is the revelation of the righteousness of God from faith to faith, rather than the revelation of the Lord Jesus Messiah in all his glory.

This means that a primary challenge lies in an interpretation of what Paul means by "from faith to faith" (Rom 1:17) when he talks about the righteousness of God. Recent interpreters have presented three somewhat different views. James D.G. Dunn, reading the phrase theologically, has argued that it means "from *God's* faithfulness (to his covenant promises) to man's response of faith."[60] Leander E. Keck, reading it Christologically as "through faith for faith" along with Richard Hays and others, understands it to mean that God's righteousness/rectitude is being revealed through Christ's faithfulness for the purpose of the revelation igniting Christian faith.[61] Robert Jewett, reading it from the perspective of Christian mission, understands it to mean from faith community to faith community. In his view, God's righteousness "is being revealed" through "preaching the gospel to establish faith communities, rather than force of arms or apocalyptic military miracle... In the establishment of faith communities as far as the ends of the known world, God will be restoring arenas where righteousness is accomplished, thus creating salvation."[62] Our view is that the answer lies in the realm of "embodied" reasoning. Paul's argument in Romans is: there is a revealing of the righteousness of God from God's faithfulness, embodied in Christ through death and resurrection, to faith embodied in believers through the Spirit's producing

[60] James D.G. Dunn, *Romans 1–8* (WBC 38A; Dallas, TX: Word Books, 1988) 48.
[61] Leander E. Keck, *Romans* (ANTC; Nashville: Abingdon, 2005) 54.
[62] Jewett, *Romans*, 146–47.

of its fruit through community, mission, and intercession. Dunn is right that faith is grounded in God's faithfulness and righteousness. Keck, following Hays and others, is right that Paul understands God's faithfulness Christologically. Jewett is right that the believer's faith is enacted by the Spirit through community, mission, and intercession that produces reconciliation among God, the world, and believers. In other words, for Paul the source of faith through righteousness is grounded theologically and embodied Christologically, and the action of faith through grace is grounded spiritually and embodied communally. The embodiment of God's faithfulness and righteousness in his Messiah makes the embodiment of faith and righteousness available to humans through the Spirit's enlivening of love through grace in community. The complexity of this is as remarkable as the creativity of it in Paul's thinking and in first century Christian communities. It is difficult to overestimate the importance of this formulation by 60 CE in first century Christian discourse. Let us look at how this argument unfolds in Romans.

As Paul develops his argument in Romans 1, he does not focus on all kinds of enemies, including death, that must be overpowered (1 Cor 15:23-28). Rather, his focus is on people whose mind is "unfit"[63] or "disqualified" (*adokimon*).[64] The issue is how God has created a sequence of scenario events that has overcome the sequence of scenario events from idolatry to lusts, dishonorable passions, and an unfit, disqualified mind. For this reason, Paul first presents a dark story-summary with five major scenario events after he has introduced his thesis about the righteousness of God (Rom 1:16-17) and his thesis about the wrath of God (1:18):[65]

1. God created the world, in which his eternal power and divine nature are invisible but have been understood and seen through the things God made;
2. claiming to be wise, humans became fools, exchanging the glory of the immortal God for images resembling a mortal human being or birds or four-footed animals or reptiles;
3. God handed humans over to the lusts (*epithymiai*) of their hearts (1:24);
4. God handed humans over to dishonorable passions (*pathō-atimia*: 1:26);
5. God handed humans over to an unfit, disqualified mind (*adokimon nous*) (1:28).

[63] Ibid., 181-83; Keck, *Romans*, 71.

[64] Dunn, *Romans 1–8*, 66.

[65] Jewett, *Romans*, 136-53.

The result, as Paul explains, is that humans were filled with every kind of wickedness, evil, covetousness, and malice (1:29-32).[66]

As is readily observable, Rom 1:22-32 is a generalized summary of world history from the creation to the time of Paul, rather than an apocalyptic summary that distinguishes periods of time from one another. In this generalized form, the "story" has an important relation to the attack on idolatry in *Wisdom of Solomon* 13:1-9.[67] Rather than building on usual apocalyptic "eras," the summary presents the ways in which God "handed humans over" (NRSV: gave them up) to lusts, dishonorable passions, and an unfit, disqualified mind once they engaged in idolatry. In apocalyptic terms, the reference to lusts sounds like the time of the sinful angels,[68] and the reference to dishonorable passions sounds like Sodom and Gomorrah.[69] But Paul's formulation in Romans resonates with widespread Mediterranean views of vices and perversions among humans.[70] The story-line presents a sequence of the darkening of wisdom in the world as a result of idolatry. This is certainly an overall part of the Jewish apocalyptic "plot" of world history,[71] but Paul presents it in a generalized manner, rather than as a sequence focused on specific apocalyptic eras of time. In Rom 1:22-32, Paul starts with an assertion that humans "claimed to be wise" and presents a sequence that describes how humans "became fools." An important part of Paul's formulation occurs in the language of being "handed over" or "given up" (*paradothē*). This language is repeated three times as Paul asserts that God "handed humans over" to lusts (1:24), dishonorable passions (1:26), and an unfit, disqualified mind (1:28), reaching a point where: "Though they know the righteous decree of God that those who practice such things deserve to die, they not only do such things but also applaud those who practice such things" (Rom 1:32).

After Paul's presentation of the gradual movement of humans downward through depraved actions into an unfit, disqualified mind, his presentation of God's intervention in world history does not take the form of apocalyptic story-summaries. Instead, his arguments become highly "creedal," focused on benefits to believers in such a manner that the "narrative" embedded in them is in the background rather than the foreground. The movement away from narrative-like statements to belief statements occurs through a focus on the time of Abraham, when (1) Abraham believed God, and (2) it was reckoned to him

[66] For details, see ibid., 183-91.
[67] Ibid., 154.
[68] Cf. *1 En.* 15:4; Jude 6; 2 Pet 2:4.
[69] Cf. Jude 7; 2 Pet 2:6-10.
[70] See Jewett, *Romans*, 163-91.
[71] Nickelsburg, *1 Enoch 1*, 52, 423-24.

as righteousness (Rom 4:3). This two-step story-summary becomes a "belief" story that affects the language of Paul's subsequent story-summaries in Romans. After the story of Abraham in Romans, Jesus' death and resurrection function in the background as support for creedal statements about faith, justification, sin, and death. Rather than functioning in the foreground to present God's transformation of his flesh-Messiah into an eternal-spirit Messiah in the heavens, the death and resurrection of Jesus become background scenario events that bring powers of transformation into the lives of believers substantively in the present and definitively at the end of time. The effect of this shift is so substantive for Paul's discourse that the entire book of Romans contains no statements about Christ's coming again.[72] Rather than emphasizing the Lord Jesus Messiah's coming again, Paul emphasizes the coming of the righteousness of God into the world for the purpose of overcoming sin and death in the lives of believers.

The first formulation of a creedal summary in Romans after Paul's presentation of the "belief-story" of Abraham occurs in Rom 4:24-25. The opening assertion, "It will be reckoned to us who believe in him," signals the emphasis on the "story" as a creedal summary. The summary contains three statements: (1) God raised Jesus our Lord from the dead; (2) Jesus our Lord was handed over (NRSV: given up) for your trespasses; (3) Jesus our Lord was raised for your justification. There are at least four important observations for our discussion. First, the summary begins with God's resurrection of the Lord Jesus, rather than with Jesus' death. Second, there is no actual reference to Jesus' death in the summary, though English translations (e.g., NRSV, RSV, and NIV) regularly give this impression. The Greek says that Jesus was "handed over (*paradothē*) for the sake of our transgressions."[73] Occurring at this point in Romans, the emphasis on "handing over" is a reversal of God's handing over or "giving up" of humans to lusts, dishonorable passions, and an unfit, disqualified mind in Rom 1:24-28. The absence of reference to Jesus' death results from Paul's focus on the effects of God's actions on believers rather than on Jesus. In other words, the focus is not on the transformation of a flesh-Messiah through death and resurrection into an eternal-spirit being with glory, power, and authority, but on the effect of the death and resurrection of the Lord Jesus on believers.[74] Third, the last clause refers a second time to God's raising of the Lord Jesus for the purpose of focusing on righteousness ("rightness"

[72] Keck, *Romans*, 35.

[73] Jewett, *Romans*, 322; Dunn, *Romans 1–8*, 196, 241.

[74] Jewett, *Romans*, 341: "There is certainly no place for allusions to the last judgment or eschatological fulfillment in this discussion of current belief in Christ's resurrection and atonement (4:24-25), which is followed in 5:1 and 9 by references to justification as an accomplished fact."

or "vindication": *dikaiōsin*[75]) for believers (cf. Rom 5:18) as God's goal. The result is a reconfiguration of Paul's usual story-summaries about Jesus' death and resurrection into a summary about belief in relation to transgressions and righteousness.[76]

The effect of Paul's shift to creedal summaries continues in Rom 5:8-10, which contains five statements that describe how "God proves his love for us":

1. while we were still sinners Messiah died for us;
2. we have been justified by his blood;
3. we will be saved through him from the wrath of God;
4. while we were enemies, we were reconciled to God through the death of his Son;
5. we will be saved by his life.

These five statements are elaborations of the thesis: "For while we were still weak, at the right time Messiah died for the ungodly" (5:6). Here it is noticeable that the subject of every statement except "Messiah died for the ungodly" is "we." In other words, the believer is the subject of the belief statements that elaborate the statement about Messiah's death. In this context, "we" become the enemies, rather than the apocalyptic authorities and powers to which the apocalyptic account in 1 Cor 15:25-26 refers. With this shift to "us" as the enemies, the solution to the problem lies in reconciliation (*katallassō*)[77] rather than submission (*hypotassō*). It was not sufficient simply for God to devise a way to overpower and destroy unrighteous humans. As a result of God's love (Rom 5:8), God predefined a means by which his righteousness could become available to believing humans through reconciliation.

As Paul continues, he blends assertions about "sin" and "death" with assertions about Adam, Moses, and the law:

1. sin came into the world through one man;
2. death came through sin;
3. death spread to all because all have sinned (5:12);
4. sin was in the world before the law;
5. sin is not reckoned when there is no law (5:13);
6. death ruled (*ebasileusen*) from Adam to Moses;
7. Adam is a type of the one to come (5:14).

In this context, Paul's assertions have moved away from believers ("we") to sin, death, law, Adam, and Moses. In other words, Paul has blended his apocalyptic understanding of the era from Adam to Moses with the era of God's resurrection of the Lord Jesus Messiah. The disastrous nature of the era from Adam to Moses was death's "rule"

[75] Ibid., 343; Dunn, *Romans 1–8*, 196,
[76] Keck, *Romans*, 34-37, 130-32.
[77] Cf. 2 Cor 5:18-21.

(5:14), which allowed sin also to "rule" (5:21) through Adam. Paul does not argue in Romans that God's response to the "rule" of sin and death was simply the transformation of a flesh-Messiah into a powerful eternal-spirit Messiah who destroyed sin and death as enemies (cf. 1 Cor 15:20-28). Rather, Paul "completes"[78] his earlier frame of understanding by inverting the rule of sin and death with the "rule" of "the grace (*charis*) of God and the free gift (*charisma*) in the grace of the one man Jesus Messiah" (Rom 5:21). This means that Paul creates a reversal of the "rule" of death and sin with a "future glory" story (Rom 8:18) containing the following "unfolding" scenario events about the "rule" of grace and the free gift of righteousness:

1. those who receive the abundance of grace and the free gift of righteousness will rule (*basileusousin*) in life through the one man Jesus Messiah (5:17);
2. grace will rule (*basileusōi*) through justification, leading to eternal life through Jesus Messiah our Lord (5:21).

It is not enough for Paul in Romans, then, to have the Lord Jesus Messiah rule over everything in the world including death until he turns the kingdom over to God (1 Cor 15:20-28). Rather, in Romans Paul presents God and the Lord Jesus Messiah working together to establish the rule of the grace of God and the free gift of righteousness over sin and death.

As one faces the challenge to describe Paul's reformulation of the apocalyptic story of the death, resurrection, and coming of the Lord Jesus Messiah into the story of the coming of the righteousness of God through a blend of the wrath and grace of God, one recalls Rudolf Bultmann's view of Paul's "demythologizing" of Jewish apocalyptic mythology and Ernst Käsemann's criticism of anthropology that resulted from it.[79] The intervening years of scholarship suggest that it is necessary to try to describe Paul's reconfiguration of Jewish apocalyptic mythology in new ways. Our way is to use understandings of conceptual blending (integration) theory based on current cognitive science.[80] Our proposal is that Paul has "overmapped" the apocalyptic cosmological story of the sinful angels with an apocalyptic cosmological story of a resurrected flesh-Messiah. This overmapping "inverts" the "corruption" of blood and flesh that occurred through eternal, lustful spirits with the "redemption" of blood and flesh through eternal, spirit of holiness at work in the resurrection of Lord Jesus Messiah from the dead (Rom 1:4). Paul describes the inversion quite clearly in Rom 8:3-4:

[78] Fauconnier and Turner, *The Way We Think*, 43-44, 48.

[79] See de Boer, "Paul and Apocalyptic Eschatology," 361-68 on Rudolf Bultmann, Ernst Käsemann, and Albert Schweitzer.

[80] Fauconnier and Turner, *The Way We Think*.

"by sending his own Son in the likeness of sinful flesh, and to deal with sin, he condemned sin in the flesh, so that the just requirement of the law might be fulfilled in us, who walk not according to the flesh but according to the Spirit." A key to this argument is that God's resurrection of his flesh-Messiah into an eternal-spirit Lord Messiah inaugurates spirit-transformation of humans already in the present age and will effect full spirit-transformation at the end of time.

The challenge for believers, then, is to have "the Spirit of God" within one's body. As Paul asserts in Rom 8:11: "If the Spirit of him who raised Jesus from the dead dwells in you, he who raised Christ from the dead will give life to your mortal bodies also through his Spirit that dwells in you." As many interpreters currently are saying, through all of Paul's "reformulation" of Jewish apocalyptic conceptuality he never truly "moves away" from apocalyptic thinking, but he dramatically reconfigures Jewish apocalyptic understanding Christologically. This is clear from his statement toward the end of his discussion of "justification" in Rom 4–8. At Rom 8:34, Paul presents a new story-summary containing four scenario events: Messiah Jesus: (1) died; (2) was raised;[81] (3) is at the right hand of God; and (4) intercedes for us. The first three scenario events are Paul's conventional "apocalyptic" story-summary. The last scenario event, which is a new feature in Paul's formulations, emphasizes the effect of the risen Messiah's place in heaven on believers at the present time, rather than emphasizing Jesus Messiah's destruction of all enemies including death when he is in the heavens (1 Cor 15:23-28). The issue is if Paul's reconfiguration of an enemy-destroying heavenly Messiah into a heavenly Messiah who reconciles enemies to God through intercession is a "moving away" from apocalyptic thinking.

The answer, we suggest, lies in Paul's further "completion" of his thinking about the Lord Jesus Messiah at the right hand of God. All interpreters agree that Rom 8:34, which says that "Christ Jesus intercedes for us," has an important relation to Rom 8:26-27, which concludes with the assertion that "the Spirit intercedes for the saints according to the will of God." Dunn has appropriately called attention to the relation of Rom 8:34 to the scenes of heavenly intercession and withholding of intercession in *1 En.* 13:4; 14:4-7.[82] In the midst of the sinful angel story in *1 Enoch* 1–16, which is a part of the early text found at Qumran,[83] the sinful angels beg the heavenly Enoch to inter-

[81] See the importance of the "yes" or "rather" (*mallon*) in Jewett, *Romans*, 541-42.

[82] Cf. the actions of the heavenly Adam in *Testament of Abraham* 11; Dunn, *Romans 1–8*, 504.

[83] In contrast to *1 Enoch* 37–71, the Similitudes, of which no fragments were found at Qumran.

cede for them by offering a memorial prayer for them to the Lord of heaven (*1 En.* 13:4). The problem was that, as sinful beings, they were not able to speak or raise their eyes to heaven (13:5). Enoch wrote a petition of forgiveness and longevity for them and recited it to God until he (Enoch) fell asleep (13:6-7). When visions came in his dreams, a voice from heaven asked him to tell the sinful angels "the words of truth" about their situation (13:8-10). After telling the words of truth and reprimand to the sons of heaven, he explains that the petition will not be successful, because judgment has been consummated against them (14:1-7). His vision then takes him to the great house in heaven built of tongues of fire, with its glory, splendor, and majesty, to the lofty throne on which the Great Glory sat (14:8-23). At this point the Lord calls Enoch forward and instructs him to go and tell the sinful spirits of heaven that they should petition in behalf of humans, rather than to have humans petition in behalf of them (14:24–15:2). After Enoch rehearses to the sinful spirit-sons of heaven an account of their wrongdoing and its results in the world (15:3–16:4), Enoch is taken beyond the edge of earth to the end of heaven, and there he is shown the place beyond the chasm where the sinful angel-spirits will be imprisoned until the time of the consummation of all sins (17:1–19:3).[84]

Careful comparison of this story in *1 Enoch* 13–19 with Romans 8:26-39 exhibits how Paul "completed" his Christological inversion of the sinful angel cosmological story with the story of Messiah Jesus' death, resurrection, seat at the right hand of God, and action of intercession for humans in Rom 8:34. The key for interpreting Paul's argument in Rom 8:26-39 is an apocalyptic understanding of the presence, role, and function of the Spirit within believers. Paul's argument moves from an assertion that "the Spirit intercedes for the saints according to the will of God" (8:27) to Messiah Jesus at the right hand of God who intercedes for "us" (8:34) to an argument that nothing in the universe can "separate us from the love of God in Messiah Jesus our Lord" (8:38-39). Raising a series of questions can help us understand how it works. First, how does the Spirit help "us"? Paul's answer is that it prays petitions of intercession "with sighs too deep for words" when "in our weakness" we do not know how to pray as we ought (8:26-27). Second, how does the interceding of the Spirit do its work? The answer is through what "we know" (8:28). The mind of the believer is not unfit or disqualified (1:28), because it is "set on the things of the Spirit" rather than on the things of the flesh (8:5-11), and this is the means by which believers have been made into "sons of God" and "heirs of God" (rather than sons of sinful angels and heirs of eternal-spirit sin and death) (8:12-17). Third, how are believers transformed

[84] For details, see Nickelsburg, *1 Enoch 1*, 234-93.

into beings for whom the Spirit intercedes? Believers have been "conformed to the image of his Son, in order that he might be the firstborn within a large family" (8:29). In other words, God's resurrection of Jesus Messiah set in motion "procreative" powers for believing humans that overpowered the procreative powers of the sinful angels (through Adam) that created the rule of sin and death within humans in the world. These procreative powers of the Spirit bring not only righteousness into the lives of believers but also glorification (8:30) as elect (8:33) children of God (8:21). As Jewett states: "Believers are in the process of being glorified to the image of Christ, as in 2 Cor 3:18, made radiant with righteousness."[85] The procreative powers set in motion by God's resurrection of Jesus Messiah inaugurate a process of transformation in believing humans that begins during their earthly life and reaches the stage of "full glorification" in the coming age. Fourth, if the Spirit intercedes for the believer, who will be the accuser? Here it is noticeable that Paul does not answer: "Satan."[86] The reason is that Paul's apocalyptic scenario presupposes that the Lord Messiah's position at the right hand of God brings "all" evil powers into submission (1 Cor 15:24-28). In Romans, Paul has extended this reasoning into "positive advocacy" by Messiah Jesus for believers, because the Spirit is at work in them transforming them through the powers of righteousness into "justified" and "glorified" beings (8:30). Fifth, what is the possibility that believers will, after all, be separated from God, like the sinful angels were imprisoned in a place beyond earth and heaven until their condemnation at the end of time? Paul's answer is that believers will never be separated from the love of Messiah Jesus their Lord, and this will keep them from being separated from the love of God (8:35-39). Again, Paul's questions and answers are Christological. Whereas the sinful angels had to depend on the heavenly Enoch to try to intercede for them, believers in Christ have Lord Jesus whom God resurrected from his flesh-Messiah into eternal-spirit Messiah at the right hand of God as their intercessor. In this context nothing – which includes hardship, distress, peril, sword (8:35), death, life, angels, rulers, things present, things to come, powers, height, depth, and anything else in creation (8:38-39) – can separate believers from the love of God in Messiah Jesus their Lord.

After Romans 1–8, Paul enters into a long argument about the place of Israel in God's plan of salvation for Gentiles in Romans 9–11. It is not possible for us even to summarize with some detail the "apocalyptic" nature of Paul's argument in these chapters. But we cannot leave Romans without one suggestion for Rom 9–11. When one reviews

[85] Jewett, *Romans*, 530.
[86] Dunn, *Romans 1–8*, 502.

the Jewish apocalyptic literature available to us at present and approaches it in the manner we have in this chapter and the previous one, the probability lies close at hand that we should think of the argumentation in Romans 9–11 as Paul's way of working out an apocalyptic view of the time of the exile.[87] This would mean that Paul's apocalyptic periodization of time in his undisputed letters focused on the eras of Adam, Abraham, Moses, David, and the exile. While working with and writing to early Christian communities, Paul spent most of his time blending the eras of Adam, Abraham, and Moses with the era of God's Messiah and those who believed in this Messiah. In Romans, Paul also introduces the time of David when he describes God's Son as "descended from David according to the flesh" (Rom 1:3). In the background of all of this reasoning about God's will for "the children of promise" (Rom 9:8), Paul was working out, we suggest, God's view of the era of the exile, which was an era that extended from the time after the kings of Israel (when the kingdom of David was destroyed) down into Paul's time. In the context of the exile, Paul argues that Gentiles are "grafted" as a wild olive shoot onto the root of the olive tree (Rom 11:17). We suggest that this image exhibits Paul's blending of the time of Abraham with the time of the exile in Jewish apocalyptic literature. As Nickelsburg explains, the image of Israel as a plant became especially prominent in Jewish apocalyptic literature.[88] The blending of Israel as a "plant of truth" with the emergence of "an eternal plant of righteousness" in the context of "the plant of righteous judgment" in *1 En.* 93:1-10 is particularly suggestive for the movement of Paul's discussion of the righteousness of God into the Gentiles as a wild olive shoot grafted onto the root (Rom 11:17-18). As Nickelsburg states: "Striking throughout the Apocalypse [of Weeks] is the notion that Israel will endure – according to v. 3, because it is a firmly rooted plant."[89] The endurance of Israel, in Paul's view in Romans, occurs through the "revealing" of the righteousness of God from God's faithfulness, embodied in Christ through death and resurrection, to faith embodied in believers through the Spirit's producing of its fruit through community, mission, and intercession.

Conclusion

The apocalyptic story-summaries in Paul's undisputed letters do not simply produce story-lines from the past into the present for purposes of extending the actions of an important prophet beyond the time of

[87] Cf. *1 En.* 89:72–90:27; 93:9-10; 91:11-13; *2 Bar.* 68:1-8.
[88] Nickelsburg, *1 Enoch 1*, 444-45.
[89] Ibid., 445.

Israel's history into the present and future. The story-summaries in Paul's letters that have been discussed in this chapter are apocalyptic accounts of world history that tell "the inside story" of the relation of various epochs of history to one another. The major challenge in world history, from Paul's perspective, was reversal of the time of Adam, which introduced desire, sin, and death into humans. We accept the view, advanced by M.C. de Boer, that Paul's view of the time of Adam coheres with the view in portions of *1 Enoch*, *4 Ezra*, and *2 Baruch* that the full effect of the sin of Adam became evident in the actions of the sinful angels described in Genesis 6 that necessitated the flood that destroyed the world. The question for Paul, then, is how God could reverse the presence of eternally perpetuating evil-spirit in human flesh that produces desire, sin, and death. For Paul, the answer lay in God's actions through the death and resurrection of his Son, Lord Jesus Messiah. For Paul, the story of God's Messiah is the story of God's transformation of a flesh-Messiah into an eternal-spirit Messiah through resurrection. The creative solution by Paul was to conclude that God reversed the effect of the sin of Adam with a cosmological Messiah story that inverted the cosmological actions of the sinful angels. Once God's action of resurrecting his flesh-Messiah intercepts the eternal perpetuation of death in human flesh, God's redemption of flesh-dwelling humans was set in place. Through belief in the resurrection of Jesus Messiah, humans can acquire a status of being "in Messiah." In the context of this belief, God is able to send the Spirit into them to enliven them to produce fruit of the Spirit while they dwell on earth and to transform them into heavenly spirit-beings at the end of time. Finally in Romans Paul reformulates this into God's righteousness coming into the world.

Paul does not discuss the time of Abraham in 1 Thessalonians and 1-2 Corinthians, but this time period becomes prominent in both Galatians and Romans. While Paul discusses Moses in 1-2 Corinthians and Romans, he talks only about the law and not Moses in Galatians. Only in Romans does Paul refer to the time of David, asserting that God's Son was descended from David according to the flesh (1:3)[90] and that David had important things to say about God's reckoning of people as righteous (4:6-8) and about the hardening of hearts within Israel (11:9). In all of this, Paul avoids the time of Enoch, Noah, and the flood. If Paul had gone there with his reasoning, it would have been difficult for him to avoid a story-line from Enoch to Jesus based on God's taking of Enoch into heaven. As *1 En.* 65:12 argued that "the seed of Enoch" would be saved through the flood, so Christians would be "seed of Enoch." Paul does not go there, because he found, instead, an answer

[90] Cf. 2 Tim 2:8.

to the cosmological story of the origins of desire, sin, and death in his first Adam/last Adam apocalyptic story-line. As he developed the details of this apocalyptic story-line, he blended the eras of God's promises to Abraham and God's sharpening of the consciousness of sin and death through Moses and the law with the era of God's transformation of his Davidic-flesh Messiah into an eternal-spirit Messiah through resurrection from death into heaven. The blending of these eras together, in a context of the era of the exile, where Gentiles needed to be reconciled to God, clarified for Paul that the resurrected Christ was seated at the right hand of God not only for the purpose of bringing all cosmic enemies into submission but also for the purpose of bringing reconciliation among God, the world, and humans through God's faithfulness and righteousness.

Apocalyptic Times and Spaces in the Sayings Gospel Q

After the creative apocalyptic thinking of the Apostle Paul appeared in letters written 50-60 CE, Christian Gospels on the life of Jesus appeared during 70-100 CE. In the intervening period between the death of Paul and the appearance of the Gospels, a Roman military campaign against Jews in Galilee and Judea brought destruction to the Jerusalem temple and its surrounding environs 66-70 CE and the end of a Jewish military outpost at Masada in 73 CE. The military conflict and destruction in Galilee and Judea during 66-73 CE created a context in which Christian writings began to include explicit apocalyptic imagery of war between nations, which had not appeared in the writings of Paul. Christians did not, however, place military imagery in the foreground of their apocalyptic presentation of the life of Jesus. Rather, they gave the story of Jesus' life apocalyptic dimensions by including angels, Satan, demons, the splitting open of the heavens, a voice from heaven, and a focus on resurrection from the dead in certain events and conversations. Perhaps the most dramatic new feature was the introduction of an apocalyptic forerunner, John the Baptizer, to the story of Jesus. All of these apocalyptic dimensions and features had the rhetorical effect of making the apocalyptic time period of Jesus Messiah larger than simply his death, resurrection, and exaltation into heaven. In the Gospels, aspects of apocalyptic conceptuality blend into narrative accounts of Jesus' birth, Jesus' experiences as a young adult, and Jesus' public life prior to his death and resurrection.

Though there is dispute about the exact oral and literary process in which it occurred, it is clear that some first century Christians gave special apocalyptic dimensions to the time of Jesus by placing his life in the context of apocalyptic teaching by a person named John the Baptizer.[91] The presence of extended portions of apocalyptic teaching by John the Baptizer in Matt 3:1-12 and Luke 3:1-17, which are not in the Mark 1:2-8 or John 1:19-34, revealed to scholars that a collection of sayings of John the Baptizer and Jesus was emerging in early Christianity during the period of 40-80 CE. For many scholars, though not all, this teaching by John the Baptizer was the beginning of what is now called "The Sayings Gospel Q."[92] It is obvious from various references by the apostle Paul to "words of the Lord" that an early collection of sayings of Jesus existed during Paul's lifetime.[93] Paul, however, does not refer in his letters to John the Baptizer, nor does he refer to Jesus as "the Son of man," both of which are special characteristics of the Sayings Gospel Q. Paul's declaration "by the word of the Lord" that when the Lord comes believers who are alive will not go up into heaven before believers who have already died (1 Thess 4:15) is not present in any NT Gospel.[94] His assertion that "the Lord will come like a thief in the night" (1 Thess 5:2), however, is possibly an allusion to a saying in Q (Luke 12:39).[95] It seems obvious to many scholars, though again not all, that early Christians were adding explicit apocalyptic dimensions to Jesus' teaching during the time of the Jewish-Roman wars of 66-70 CE and its immediate aftermath. For the purposes of this chapter, it is important to discuss some special aspects of the Q material (special sayings in common in Matthew and Luke) in relation to the letters of Jude and 2 Peter. First, we will look at the apocalyptic use of eras in the special sayings in common between Matthew and Luke. Second, we will look at the relation of apocalyptic *topoi* in the Sayings Gospel Q and the letters of Jude and 2 Peter.

Of special interest for our approach in this chapter is the absence of military imagery from the apocalyptic teaching in the special sayings in common between Matthew and Luke.[96] John the Baptizer pictures "the wrath to come" as "an ax" that will cut the root of every unfruitful tree before it is thrown into the fire (Luke 3:7-9/Matt 3:7-10). Then John describes Jesus as coming with a "winnowing fork in his hand" to gather the wheat into his granary and burn the chaff with

[91] John S. Kloppenborg Verbin, *Excavating Q: The History and Setting of the Sayings Gospel* (Minneapolis: Fortress Press, 2000) 66-67.

[92] For the implications of calling the Q material a Gospel, see Kloppenborg Verbin, *Excavating Q*, 398-408.

[93] Helmut Koester, *Ancient Christian Gospels: Their History and Development* (Philadelphia: Trinity Press International, 1990) 52-55.

[94] Wanamaker, *The Epistles to the Thessalonians*, 170-71; cf. Malherbe, *The Letters to the Thessalonians*, 267-70; Furnish, *1 Thessalonians, 2 Thessalonians*, 104-105.

[95] Koester, *Ancient Christian Gospels*, 53; cf. Malherbe, ibid., 292-93; Furnish, ibid., 107.

[96] For the current critical edition of Q, see James M. Robinson, Paul Hoffmann, John S. Kloppenborg, *The Critical Edition of Q* (Hermeneia; Minneapolis: Fortress Press/Leuven: Peeters, 2000).

unquenchable fire (Luke 3:17/Matt 3:12). This is traditional angel-spirit apocalyptic imagery, which uses fruit-bearing trees and harvest-time to describe the time of judgment.[97] When the special sayings in common between Matthew and Luke feature apocalyptic imagery in sayings of Jesus, eras in apocalyptic world history are present that Paul does not feature in his letters: Noah,[98] Sodom,[99] the Queen of the South (era of Solomon),[100] and Jonah (era of kings of Israel after David and Solomon).[101]

Rather than focusing on the Lord's coming to take people up into heaven, like 1 Thess 4–5, the special sayings in common in Matthew and Luke describe either "the coming (*parousia*)" or "the day(s)" of the Son of Man in relation to Noah and the flood, and to lightning that flashes across the entire sky from east to west.[102] Jesus' saying about the time of Noah and the flood begins with a "comparison thesis": "Just as it was in the days of Noah, so too it will be in the days (coming) of the Son of man."[103] Then there is a story summary containing four scenario events: (1) before the flood they were eating and drinking, marrying, and giving in marriage; (2) Noah entered the ark; (3) the flood came; and (4) the flood swept them all away.[104] Matt 24:38 adds that "they knew nothing until the flood came." Nickelsburg observes that *1 En.* 93:4 presents the flood as "the first end," "which reflects a typology between the flood and the judgment" that "recurs explicitly in Matt 24:36-44 and Luke 17:26-27."[105] A major issue surrounding the story-summaries is the degree to which people knew the "inside" story of the sequence of actions that would occur.

Luke 17:28-30 expands the comparison with the coming of the Son of Man to include "the day that Lot left Sodom," and Luke 17:32 discusses the importance of fleeing in relation to Lot's wife. The story-summary about Lot contains four scenario events: (1) they were eating

[97] For the imagery of judgment in Q, see Jonathan L. Reed, "The Social Map of Q," in *Conflict and Invention: Literary, Rhetorical, and Social Studies on the Sayings Gospel Q* (ed. John S. Kloppenborg; Valley Forge, PA: Trinity Press International, 1995) 24-30; Russell B. Sisson, "The Interaction of Social and Scribal Intertexture in Q's Apocalyptic Discourse," in *The Intertexture of Apocalyptic Discourse in the New Testament* (ed. D.F. Watson; Symposium 14; Atlanta: SBL, 2002) 78-79.

[98] Luke 17:26-27/Matt 24:37-39; Gen 6:8–9:29.

[99] Luke 10:12/Matt 10:15; Gen 18:16–19:28.

[100] Luke 11:31/Matt 12:42; 1 Kgs 10:1-10; 2 Chr 9:1-9.

[101] Luke 11:30/Matt 12:41; Jeroboam II (788-747 BCE); 2 Kgs 14:25.

[102] *parousia*: Matt 24:27, 37, 39; day(s): Luke 17:24, 26, 30; Noah, flood, and lightning: Luke 17:24/Matt 24:27. For the nature of judgment and the coming of the Son of Man in Q, see Sisson, "The Interaction of Social and Scribal Intertexture," 69-85.

[103] Luke 17:26/Matt 24:37.

[104] Luke 17:27/Matt 24:38-39.

[105] Nickelsburg, *1 Enoch 1*, 443-44; cf. also *1 En.* 10:1-3; 10:16–11:2; 93:9-10; and ch. 91.

and drinking, buying and selling, planting and building; (2) on the day that Lot left Sodom, it rained fire and sulfur from heaven; (3) it destroyed all of them; and (4) anyone in the field must not turn back; remember Lot's wife (Luke 17:28-29, 31-32). This is compared in Luke 17:30 to "the day that the Son of man is revealed (*apokalyptetai*)." In this instance, the comparison expands beyond the destruction to an elaboration on circumstances various people may face on that day. The circumstances include being on a housetop, in a field,[106] or grinding meal.[107] Luke 12:39-40/Matt 24:43-44 also add a comparison of the Son of Man's coming to a thief breaking into one's house, and they compare the destruction to a Master of a household who cuts a slave into pieces when he unexpectedly returns and finds the slave beating other slaves and getting drunk (Luke 12:46/Matt 24:51). In these instances, the issue is the nature of the destruction when the Son of Man comes, and there is exhortation to act quickly to escape the destruction by fleeing or by constantly remaining vigilant to one's duties. Also the sayings describe the context of the end as a time when son rises up against father, daughter against mother, and daughter-in-law against mother-in-law (Luke 12:53/Matt 10:35). In addition, the end is a time when more will be given to one who already has, and to those who do not have, even what they have will be taken away from them (Luke 19:26/Matt 25:29). There is also fear of being cast into Gehenna (Luke 12:5/Matt 10:28). Satan plays a role in two contexts in the sayings common to Matthew and Luke. One is the testing of Jesus in the wilderness before he begins his public ministry (Luke 4:1-13/Matt 4:1-11). The other is in Jesus' discussion with people who accuse him of casting out demons by Beelzebul (Luke 11:15-20; Matt 12:24-28). In the special sayings common to Matthew and Luke, there is no reference to Adam's bringing of sin and death into the world, the law of Moses as God's means of bringing a consciousness of sin and death, or of Jesus as God's Messiah descended from David according to the flesh.

As the focus in the special sayings in common in Matthew and Luke moves beyond the sudden destruction in the days of the Son of Man to the circumstances of people during this time, there is an important reference to Abraham, Isaac, Jacob, and all the prophets who will be allowed to enter into the Kingdom of God, while others will be thrown out (Luke 13:28/Matt 8:11-12).[108] There is, however, no special reference to Abraham's faith by which God reckoned him as righteous. Beyond this, there is reference to Sodom (Matt 10:15 also

[106] Luke 17:31/Matt 24:17-18, 40.
[107] Luke 17:35/Matt 24:41.
[108] See Santiago Guijarro, "Cultural Memory and Group Identity in Q," *BTB* 37 (2007) 90-100.

includes Gomorrah), the coming of the Queen of the South to visit Solomon[109] and the repentance of the people of Nineveh[110] during the time of Jonah. All of these are warnings to people in the towns of Chorazin, Bethsaida, and Capernaum[111] in comparison to the positive response of people in Tyre and Sidon.[112] In addition, Jonah becomes a "sign" either of proclamation that brings repentance or of the resurrection of the Son of man after three days and nights.[113] The times of Noah, Abraham, Sodom, Solomon (Queen of the South), Jonah, and all the prophets, then, play a role in the apocalyptic view of world history in the special sayings in common in Matthew and Luke. These traditional apocalyptic eras were emerging during the first century CE as "types" of events of the end time, and the people who focused on Jesus of Nazareth as the Messiah of the end time played a creative role in bringing these past eras into the foreground through scenario events they interpreted in relation to the Messiah Jesus and his return as Son of Man.[114]

Beyond the focus on the days of the Son of Man, there is special focus on the disciples of Jesus in two ways. First, there is reference to Jesus' disciples sitting on twelve thrones in a position of judgment over the twelve tribes of Israel in the Son of Man's kingdom (Luke 22:30/Matt 19:28). While this is imagery of political power, there is no military imagery associated with it. Second, there is a series of scenario events in the life of Jesus' disciples that are interpreted in relation to the destruction of Sodom (and Gomorrah). These scenario events interpret the activities of Jesus' followers as a "harvest story," which creates a special time for mission activity of followers in the apocalyptic history of the world. The story begins in Luke 10:2/Matt 9:37-38 with Jesus defining the activities of his followers as "the harvest": "The harvest is plentiful, but the laborers are few; therefore ask the Lord of the harvest to send out laborers into the harvest."[115] This imagery, as the reader will know, is traditional apocalyptic description of the end time. In Matthew and Luke, the time in which followers of Jesus are involved in mission to others becomes "apocalyptic" through Jesus' use of a conventional image of the end of time as "harvest time" for their activities.[116] This emphasis comes from

[109] Luke 11:31/Matt 12:42.

[110] Luke 11:32/Matt 12:41.

[111] Luke 10:12-15/Matt 10:15; 11:21-24.

[112] Luke 10:13-14/Matt 11:21-22.

[113] Luke 11:29-30, 32/Matt 12:40-41; Richard A. Edwards, *The Sign of Jonah in the Theology of the Evangelists and* Q (Naperville, IL: Allenson, 1971).

[114] Cf. Sisson, "The Interaction of Social and Scribal Intertexture," 79-85.

[115] Luke 10:2/Matt 9:37-38.

[116] Luke 10:1-16 makes this "harvest" a mission time for the seventy; Matt 9:37–10:42 a mission time for the twelve disciples.

the special sayings in common in these two Gospels. After Jesus' definition of the mission of his followers as "the harvest," he presents seven scenario events they are commanded to perform: (1) go on your way as lambs into the midst of wolves; (2) carry no purse, nor bag, nor sandals, nor stick, and greet no one on the road; (3) into whatever house you enter, first say, "Peace to this house!"; (4) if a son of peace be there, let your peace come upon him; but if not, let your peace return to you; (5) remain in the same house, eating and drinking whatever they provide, for the laborer deserves to be paid. Do not move from house to house; (6) cure the sick there, and say to them, "The Kingdom of God has come near to you"; (7) into whatever town you enter and they do not welcome you, on going from that town, shake off the dust from your feet.[117] Two of the scenario events (3, 6) are scripted to the point where they tell the traveler what to say as well as what to do. Luke 10:11 adds scripted speech for the scenario event of rejection at the end: "Even the dust of your town that clings to our feet, we wipe off in protest against you. Yet know this: the kingdom of God has come near." The apocalyptic configuration of these scenario events in the special sayings in common in Matthew and Luke creates a special era of time in the future for any believer who accepts a task of "mission" in the name of Messiah Jesus. Apocalyptic rhetorolect in the Q sayings, then, moves beyond paraenesis for creating peaceful believing communities, like one sees in the letters of Paul. First century CE Gospel literature correlates early apocalyptic eras with the time of Jesus in a manner that creates an apocalyptic era for the disciples themselves. This era exists from the time of Jesus until the end of time. A major apocalyptic effect of the Synoptic Gospels is to create scenario events for "the work" of all followers of Jesus in the future. While various aspects of these events lie implicitly in certain statements in the letters of Paul, the Synoptic Gospels create explicit scenario events spoken by Messiah Jesus that create a future program for followers of Jesus in mission until the coming of the Son of Man.

In the special sayings in common in Matthew and Luke, there is no military imagery in the portrayal of the coming of the Son of Man, the plight of people, or the mission activity of Jesus' followers. The closest the special sayings come to military imagery occurs when Luke 11:22 has Jesus compare the coming of the kingdom of God to a strong man who attacks and overpowers an armored person guarding a house, taking away the guard's armor and dividing the plunder (cf. Matt

[117] Words in common to Luke 10:3-11/Matt 10:7-14 as reconstructed in Robinson, Hoffmann, Kloppenborg, *The Critical Edition of Q*, 162-79.

12:29).[118] While the guard has armor, there is no attack by an army on the man, nor is it clear that the guard is a military soldier. The most prominent imagery in the special sayings concerns fruit-bearing plants, households, fields, and work in which people harvest and grind grain into meal. In one instance there is imagery of political power in the hands of Jesus' disciples, namely when they sit on thrones judging the twelve tribes of Israel. There is, however, no implication that the disciples will either engage in or authorize any military activity to carry out their role of judging. All of the imagery, then, is natural in the stream of angel-spirit apocalyptic as we have defined it in the previous and present chapter. The apocalyptic imagery in the special sayings common to Matthew and Luke does not shift into the earth-material imagery characteristic of Revelation, which focuses on cities, wealth, and military power.

Apocalyptic Times and Spaces in the Synoptic Gospels

The Gospel of Mark

The Synoptic Gospels (Matthew, Mark, Luke) were written ca. 70-90 CE.[119] Most maintain that Mark is the earliest Gospel, written ca. 70 CE. Since the Gospel of Mark does not contain the Q material discussed above, there are no references in it to Noah, Sodom, Lot, Gomorrah, Solomon, Queen of the South, Jonah, or the Ninevites. Also, there is no reference to Adam in it. There is one reference to Abraham, and it is present in an intriguing response by Jesus to Sadducees, who, the narrator says, do not believe in the resurrection. Jesus responds to them by reciting that God said to Moses, "I am the God of Abraham, the God of Isaac, and the God of Jacob." Then Jesus says, "He is God not of the dead, but of the living" (Mark 12:26-27). This is an argument from the Torah for belief in the resurrection. The issue, of course, is that the Sadducees traditionally did not find argument for resurrection in the Torah. This verse (Exod 3:6) is understood apocalyptically by first century Christians to mean that if God "is the God of Abraham, Isaac, and Jacob – as he disclosed himself to Moses the great lawgiver – then life, not death, will surely be the destiny of all those linked to him in faith."[120] Again, there is no reference in Mark to the faith of Abraham through which God reckoned him as righteous, like one finds in

[118] Vernon K. Robbins, "Beelzebul Controversy in Mark and Luke: Rhetorical and Social Analysis," *Forum* 7.3-4 (1991) 261-77.

[119] For a basic discussion of apocalyptic rhetoric in the Synoptic Gospels, see Carey, *Ultimate Things*, 102-16.

[120] Craig A. Evans, *Mark 8:27–16:20* (Word Commentary 34B; Nashville, KY: Thomas Nelson Publishers, 2001) 255-58.

the letters of Paul. There is, however, reference to Abraham among "the living," which presupposes his presence in heaven along with Isaac and Jacob.

In the context of an absence of focus on past eras for its apocalyptic presentation of Jesus, one of the most important contributions of the Gospel of Mark to first century Christian discourse is its formulation of two dramatic apocalyptic events in which a voice speaks from heaven: (1) the baptism of Jesus (1:9-11); and (2) the transfiguration of Jesus (9:2-13). The account of the baptism is very brief, describing three events as Jesus was coming out of the water in which he had been baptized: (1) he saw the heavens splitting apart; (2) he saw the spirit descending like a dove on him; and (3) a voice came from heaven, "You are my Son, the Beloved; with you I am well pleased" (1:10-11). The splitting of the heavens apart is a conventional feature of apocalyptic, which allows the seer to observe things in heaven that reveal special information about God's plans and activities with the world. But there is no view of detail in the heavens in the scene. The spirit descends from heaven into Jesus like a dove, and this has been very difficult for scholars to interpret, since there is no other scene in literature directly like it.[121] In our view, Hans Lohmeyer was right when he indicated that a major issue in the context of Mark's account of Jesus' baptism is the manner in which apocalyptic literature describes the visibility of heavenly manifestations to earthly beings.[122] Leander E. Keck's extensive investigation of the issue caused him to conclude that the phrase "like a dove" (*hōs peristeran*: 1:10) is adverbial, and we agree.[123] Mark describes "the Spirit coming with dove-like descent" into Jesus in an apocalyptic context where the heavens have split apart and a voice from heaven declares to Jesus, "You are my Son, the Beloved; with you I am well pleased."[124] As Keck has indicated, one of the closest similarities can be found in Sir 43:13-14, 17, which asserts that "By his (God's) command ... the storehouses are opened, and the clouds fly out like birds ... The voice of his thunder rebukes the earth ... He scatters the snow like birds flying down ... and its descent is like locusts alighting." It is this kind of description in Jewish wisdom literature that apocalyptic literature reconfigured into vivid depictions of spirit beings of various kinds in the heavens, and Christian discourse is a major participant in this apocalyptic movement during the first cen-

[121] See the discussion in Robert A. Guelich, *Mark 1–8:26* (Word Commentary 34A; Nashville, KY; Thomas Nelson, 1989) 32-33.

[122] Hans Lohmeyer, *Das Evangelium des Markus* (KEK; Göttingen & Ruprecht, 1967) 21-22.

[123] Leander E. Keck, "The Spirit and the Dove," *NTS* 17 (1970-71) 41-67; cf. S. Gero, "The "Spirit as a Dove at the Baptism of Jesus," *NovT* 18 (1976) 17-35.

[124] Keck, ibid., 63.

tury CE. What is so noticeable in the context of our discussion is the *topos* of the Spirit in the foreground of the scene, accompanied by the authoritative voice of God from the heavens. As we have seen above, one of the central issues in apocalyptic cosmology was the manner in which heavenly, eternal spirit enters into human beings on earth. While Paul's letters assert that the procreative, "renewing" spirit of God entered into humans through God's resurrection of his Messiah Jesus from the dead, the Gospel of Mark proposes that the procreative, renewing spirit of God entered into Jesus at his baptism. This movement of the descent of the Spirit into Jesus during his lifetime set in motion a conceptuality that blended with prophetic literature in Matthew and Luke to move the time of the descent of the Spirit into Jesus backwards into the time of Jesus' presence in the womb of Mary (Matt 1:20-25; Luke 1:26-38). Again one can see an overall effect of the stream of angel-spirit apocalyptic on first century Christian discourse. Literary-historical interpreters have contributed in a majesterial way to a description of all the "influences" it is possible to find upon Christian discourse in the literature of the time. The fact is that first century Christians were full participants and contributors to emerging apocalyptic conceptuality during the first century CE. For this reason, it is not possible to find precedents in Jewish or other Mediterranean literature of the time for every phenomenon in early Christian literature and discourse. Early Christians used emergent, blending structures of conceptuality in Mediterranean literature, culture, and society of the time as frames within which to tell their "stories" about Jesus and his followers. Their stories and arguments recontextualized, reconfigured, and blended anew the concepts and convictions of people of their time, including their apocalyptic concepts and convictions.

In Mark, the descent of the spirit into Jesus at his baptism equips him to renew people by casting unclean spirits and demons out of them. After calling four fishermen to be his disciples (1:16-20), Jesus begins his public ministry by casting an unclean spirit out of a man in the synagogue at Capernaum (1:21-28). After this, Jesus performs three additional exorcisms (5:1-20; 7:24-30; 9:14-29)[125] in an overall context where the narrator summarizes scenes of wide-reaching healings and exorcisms by Jesus and his disciples, as well as debate about Jesus' ability to cast them out.[126]

In the middle of an overall "gospel" story that features an apocalyptic splitting of the heavens open at Jesus' baptism to inaugurate the

[125] Vernon K. Robbins, "The Intertexture of Apocalyptic Discourse in the Gospel of Mark," in *The Intertexture of Apocalyptic Discourse in the New Testament* (ed. D.F. Watson; Symposium 14; Atlanta: SBL, 2002) 23.

[126] See Robbins, ibid., 22-29.

testing of Jesus prior to his adult ministry (1:9-11), the Gospel of Mark presents a scene of the transformation of Jesus momentarily into a heavenly form while he is on a mountain (9:2-8). This momentary transformation of Jesus creates a context for blending the apocalyptic descent of the spirit into Jesus at his baptism with Jesus' rejection, death, and resurrection after three days. The scene features Jesus on a high mountain at a dramatic turning point in his adult ministry, talking with the heavenly Moses and Elijah (9:4-5). On the one hand, comparison of the scene with the fully apocalyptic version of the Transfiguration in the *Apocalypse of Peter* 15–17 shows how the Markan version is only an apocalyptic glimpse into the nature of Jesus' body in his future heavenly state.[127] On the other hand, the momentary "metamorphosis" (*metemorphōthē*: Mark 9:2) of Jesus in a context of the appearance (*ōphthē*: 9:4) of the heavenly manifestations of Elijah and Moses is a truly remarkable moment in the story. In the midst of this moment, the heavenly voice speaks again, this time saying to the three disciples (Peter, James, John): "This is my Son, the Beloved; listen to him" (9:7). Thus, in Mark an apocalyptic moment at the beginning of the story features the heavenly voice speaking to Jesus and in the middle of the story features an apocalyptic moment when the heavenly voice speaks to three of Jesus' disciples. This apocalyptic framing of the adult life of Jesus prior to his death and resurrection contributed yet another dimension to the apocalyptic story early Christians were able to tell. Now it was not simply the resurrection and return of Jesus after his crucifixion and burial that were apocalyptic events in the story about God's Messiah, but there was an "inside" story at work even during the adult life of Jesus.

It is remarkable how the Markan account of the transfiguration of Jesus exhibits the process of blending an apocalyptic account of the life of the adult Jesus with the apocalyptic account of his resurrection and glorious return in the future. When Jesus is going down the mountain with his disciples after his momentary transfiguration before them, he tells them they must tell no one about the event "until after the Son of Man has risen from the dead" (9:9). William Wrede emphasized that this exhibits how the Gospel of Mark blended the non-messianic account of Jesus, which existed during Jesus' lifetime, with the messianic account that emerged after Jesus' death.[128] It is important to realize that apocalyptic conceptualization enabled early Christians to make the moves they did in a gradual expansion of the "era" of Jesus back to his adult life and finally even back to his conception. In Mark, there is not yet an apocalyptic configuration of Jesus' birth. Rather, there is an

[127] Robbins, ibid., 34-35.
[128] William Wrede, *The Messianic Secret* (Cambridge: James Clarke, 1971).

apocalyptic configuration of Jesus' adult life through scenario moments at his baptism and his transfiguration prior to his journey to Jerusalem, where he is killed. The Gospel of Mark blends the apocalyptic account of Jesus' adult life with his resurrection and return after his death through Jesus' programmatic teaching to his disciples in Mark 8:31–10:45 that the Son of man "must" be delivered up, beaten, killed, and rise up in three days (8:31; 9:9, 31; 10:32-34). According to Mark, then, there is an "inside, apocalyptic story" about Jesus' life and death, which explains how and why Jesus' life continued after his death in the form of a resurrected heavenly being who would return in the future to gather his elect together "from the ends of the earth to the ends of heaven" (Mark 13:27). This brings us to Mark 13, which in modern times regularly has been called either "the Markan apocalypse" or "the little apocalypse."

In Mark 13, a speech by Jesus to four of his disciples (Peter, James, John, and Andrew: 13:3) explains the sequence of time before the coming of the Son of Man. In the context of our present chapter, this means that the Gospel of Mark creates a scene beyond the baptism (1:9-11) and transfiguration (9:2-13) in which Jesus presents a sequence of events to an inner circle of disciples that includes the destruction of the Jerusalem temple (13:1-2, 14) and the coming of the Son of Man (13:26-27). Again from the perspective on early Christian apocalyptic rhetorolect we are taking in this chapter, Jesus' speech contains ten scenario events. First, Jesus describes four scenario events that he calls "the beginning of the birth pangs" (13:9): (1) many will come in the name of Jesus claiming, "I am he!", leading many astray (13:6); (2) there will be wars and rumors of war (13:7); (3) nation will rise up against nation, and kingdom against kingdom (13:8); (4) there will be earthquakes in various places. Second, there are four scenario events about the disciples' preaching of the gospel to all nations (13:10), in a context where they are exhorted to "endure to the end" so they will be saved (13:13): (5) Jesus' disciples will be handed over to councils, beaten in synagogues, and brought before governors and kings for the sake of Jesus (13:9); (6) Jesus' disciples are not to worry what they will say when they are brought to trial and handed over, because the Holy Spirit will give them speech (13:11); (7) brother will betray brother to death, a father his child, and children will rise against parents and have them put to death (13:12); (8) Jesus' disciples will be hated by all because of Jesus' name (13:13). Third, there are five scenario events that begin with the setting up of "the desolating sacrilege," which is wording from Daniel 9:27; 11:31; 12:11 that refers to the desecration of the Jerusalem temple: (9) Jesus' disciples will see the desolating sacrilege set up where it ought not to be (13:14); (10) those in Judea must flee to the mountains (13:14); (11) there will be suffering such as has not been from the beginning of creation to the present (13:17-19); (12) the Lord will cut short the days of suffering so the elect can be saved (13:20); (13) false messiahs and prophets will appear, producing signs and wonders to attempt to lead the elect astray (13:21-22). Four, there are four scenario events associated with the coming of the Son of Man: (14) after the suffering, the sun and moon will become dark, stars will fall from heaven, and the powers in heaven will be shaken (13:24-25); (15) people will see the Son of Man coming in clouds with great power and glory (13:26); (16) the Son of Man will send out the angels and gather his elect from "the four winds, from the ends of the earth to the ends of heaven" (13:27). In the context of these sixteen scenario events, Jesus teaches his four disciples that "heaven and earth will pass away," but his words will not pass away (13:31). Also, he teaches them that no one except God the Father knows the day or hour when the time will come (13:32-33). At this point, Jesus compares the sequence to a man going on a journey, leaving slaves and a doorkeeper in charge until he returns, and they must stay awake, because no one knows when the master will return (13:34-36). The message to all then is, "Keep awake" (13:37).

In the context of the present chapter, it is not feasible to interpret Mark 13 in any detail.[129] What we must observe is Jesus' presentation of sixteen scenario events about the time of the coming of the Son of Man. This sequence presupposes a context in which his disciples are preaching the gospel to all nations, which overlaps with Paul's insistence that he must preach the gospel to Gentiles. The sequence also presupposes that the disciples will suffer in the context of the mission they are commanded to perform, which overlaps both with teaching by Paul and teaching by Jesus in the special sayings in common in Matthew and Luke. In addition, the sequence presupposes there will be wars, but there is no suggestion that the disciples or the Son of Man participate in any way in military activities. After violence and destruction become so great that homes and nations are destroyed, and even the sun, moon, stars, and powers in heaven lose their ability to run the cosmos in an ordered manner, the Son of Man will come on clouds accompanied by angels. The total focus of the Son of Man when he comes is his gathering of the elect from the ends of the earth to the ends of heaven, which has an important relation to the emphasis in 1 Thess 4–5. In other words, Mark 13 does not refer to any dark activities of judgment or destruction by the Son of Man when he comes.

[129] See Vernon K. Robbins, "Rhetorical Ritual: Apocalyptic Discourse in Mark 13," in *Rhetorical Dimensions of Apocalyptic Discourse* (G. Carey and L.G. Bloomquist; St. Louis, MO: Chalice, 1999) 95-121.

The Gospel of Matthew

In contrast to the Gospel of Mark, since the Gospel of Matthew contains the Q sayings, it places the story of Jesus in an apocalyptic context in which the eras of Noah, Sodom, Lot, Gomorrah, Solomon, Queen of the South, Jonah, and the Ninevites play an important role. Again there is no reference to Adam in the story. Both Abraham and David become more prominent in the early Christian Gospels as Matthew opens with: "An account of the genealogy of Jesus the Messiah, the son of David, the son of Abraham" (1:1). After a genealogy that moves from Abraham to David to the exile to the birth of Jesus (1:2-17), there are only three more references to Abraham in Matthew: (1) John the Baptizer's reference to Abraham as the ancestor of Pharisees and Sadducees (3:9); (2) the reference to Abraham, Isaac, and Jacob eating at the table in the kingdom of heaven from the Q material (8:11); and (3) Jesus' recitation to the Sadducees that God is "the God of Abraham, Isaac, and Jacob" from Mark (22:32). Even though the Gospel of Matthew begins the genealogy of Jesus with Abraham, there is no special development of the time of Abraham as a time that shows special "inside" information about Jesus. There is a significant development of David in relation to Jesus in the Gospel of Matthew.[130] All of the contexts, however, perpetuate prophetic and miracle rhetorolect in early Christian discourse more than they perpetuate apocalyptic discourse.

In the short span available to us in this chapter, we will focus on an apocalyptic sequence during the early ministry of Jesus, Jesus' expansion of the Markan apocalypse about the Son of Man, and the time of Jesus from the crucifixion to his appearance to his disciples after his resurrection. First, we will look at the apocalyptic sequence during the early ministry of Jesus. As Günther Bornkamm has shown,[131] when Jesus gets into the boat the first time in his ministry and his disciples follow him into the boat, the storm that arises at sea is a great earthquake (*seismos megas*: 8:24). The disciples' distress at sea, then, is a glimpse of tremors of the end time that are already beginning in the life of the disciples during the ministry of Jesus.[132] In Matthew's account of the sending out of the twelve later in the story, then, Jesus tells the disciples: "truly I tell you, you will not have gone through all the towns of Israel before the Son of Man comes" (10:23). This verse has, of course, caused considerable debate in discussion among scholars, with Albert Schweitzer playing a key role with his assertion that Jesus

[130] Matt 1:1, 6, 17, 20; 9:27; 12:3, 23; 15:22; 20:30, 31; 21:9, 15; 22:42, 43, 45.

[131] Günther Bornkamm, "The Stilling of the Storm in Matthew," in Günther Bornkamm, Gerhard Barth, and Heinz Joachim Held, *Tradition and Interpretation in Matthew* (trans. Percy Scott; Philadelphia: Westminster Press, 1963) 52-57.

[132] Cf. Mark 13:8; Matt 24:7; Luke 21:11; Matt 27:54; 28:2; Rev 6:12; 8:5; 11:13, 19; 16:18: Bornkamm, ibid., 56.

expected the return of the Son of Man before the end of his ministry, but he was forced to change his mind when the Son of Man did not come.[133] For our purposes in this chapter, the important thing to notice is how the Gospel of Matthew extends the end time back into the ministry of Jesus and the mission of his disciples. As we have seen above, the seeds for this development already existed in the interpretation of the mission of the disciples as "the harvest" in the Sayings Gospel Q. Matthew includes an initial earthquake during the time of Jesus' ministry (8:24) and an expectation that the Son of Man would come before his disciples returned from a mission to all the towns of Israel (10:23), prior to other events that present even more of an "inside" apocalyptic story at work during the time of Jesus.

In Matthew's version of the coming of the Son of Man from Mark 13, Jesus speaks to all of his disciples rather than to only four of them (Matt 24:1-4; cf. Mark 13:3). After presenting the Markan information with some significant variations (Matt 24:4-35), Jesus continues with Q material about Noah (24:37-39), people who will be taken quickly away (24:40-41), and the day of the Lord that is coming like a thief in the night (24:42-44). But this is simply the beginning of the Matthean expansion of Jesus' apocalyptic discourse. Matthew also includes a sequence of parables about the end of time (24:45–25:30) which ends with a worthless slave being thrown "into the outer darkness, where there will be weeping and gnashing of teeth" (25:30).[134] At this point, Jesus tells of the coming of the Son of Man in a manner that is unparalleled in any other Gospel.

Jesus' account of the coming of the Son of Man in Matt 25:31-46 includes both a dark and a bright side. The account features the Son of Man coming and sitting on "the throne of his glory" (Matt 25:31) for the purpose of judging "all the nations" who will be gathered before him (25:32). In this context, the Son of Man tells "the sheep at his right hand" that they inherit the kingdom prepared for them from the foundation of the world (25:34), while the goats on his left hand are sent "away into eternal punishment," rather than "into eternal life" (25:46). In Matthew, then, the function of the Son of Man is both to gather the elect and to send the unrighteous into eternal punishment. Still, however, there is no military imagery in the description of the Son of Man. The Son of Man is concerned to know if people fed the hungry, clothed the naked stranger, and visited those in prison (25:35-45), rather than if anyone became a military ruler over a major city and region, gathered wealth to himself in a manner that caused him to turn

[133] Albert Schweitzer, *The Quest of the Historical Jesus: A Critical Study of Its Progress from Reimarus to Wrede* (Baltimore: Johns Hopkins University Press, 1998) 358-64.

[134] Cf. Matt 8:12; 13:42, 50; 22:13; 24:51.

away from worship of God, and deprived people of food and water in a context of sexual excess and ungodliness. Apocalypticism in the Gospel of Matthew, then, extends the stream of angel-spirit apocalyptic that is so dominant in the New Testament, rather than moving into the stream of earth-material apocalyptic that focuses on military power, cities, and wealth.

When the Gospel of Matthew presents the end of the story about Jesus' time on earth, it contains significant apocalyptic dimensions in the account of Jesus' crucifixion, resurrection from the tomb, and appearance to his disciples. When Jesus dies in Matthew, the curtain of the temple is torn in two and there is an earthquake (*hē gē eseisthē*) that causes the tombs to be opened and many saints who had died to be raised (27:51-52). Then the narrator says that after Jesus was resurrected "they came out of the tombs and entered the holy city and appeared to many" (27:53). Then after Jesus has been buried in a tomb, there is a great earthquake (*seismos megas*: 28:2) and the descent of an angel of the Lord from heaven with the appearance of lightning who rolls back the stone (28:2-3). After the angel tells the women that Jesus has been raised from the dead (28:7), Jesus appears to the eleven disciples on "the mountain to which Jesus had directed them." When Jesus appears in this form, the disciples worship Jesus, though some doubt (28:17). Then, telling them he has been given "all authority in heaven and on earth," he commands them to "make disciples of all nations" through baptism and teaching (28:19). These additional apocalyptic scenes and features in the Gospel of Matthew have the rhetorical effect of making the entire time from Jesus' conception in the womb of Mary until his appearance to eleven disciples on a mountain after his resurrection into a special apocalyptic era in world history.

The Gospel of Luke

The Gospel of Luke also, of course, includes the eras of Noah, Sodom, Lot, Gomorrah, Solomon, Queen of the South, Jonah, and the Ninevites in the apocalyptic dimensions of its account of the life of Jesus. Also, it includes a dramatic appearance of the angel Gabriel to Zechariah the father of John the Baptist (1:11-20) and a dramatic scene with Mary (1:26-38) that describes how the Holy Spirit came into her to cause her to conceive and bear a son named Jesus (1:30-37). There are multiple references both to Abraham[135] and to David[136] in Luke. In a recent sociorhetorical investigation of apocalyptic intertexture in

[135] Luke 1:55, 73; 3:8, 34; 13:16, 28; 16:22-25, 29-30; 19:9; 20:37.
[136] Luke 1:27, 32, 69; 2:4, 11; 3:31; 6:3; 18:38-39; 20:41-42, 44.

Luke,[137] L. Gregory Bloomquist identifies five units with apocalyptic dimensions containing references to Abraham,[138] and one unit containing a reference to David.[139] Traditions of God's promise to Abraham (1:55, 73) and Abraham's righteousness (13:28; 16:22-31; 20:37) certainly are evident in these units, but again there is no specific emphasis that Abraham's faith caused God to reckon him as righteous. The one unit containing reference to David (1:68-79) refers to "a mighty savior" who has been raised up "in the house of his servant David" (1:69). These references play a role in thickening the apocalyptic intertexture of the story of Jesus in early Christian discourse. There is, however, a more specific apocalyptic focus in the Gospel of Luke to which we must turn.

Putting insights together from the study mentioned above and from another investigation focused specifically on Luke 21, Bloomquist concluded that a major focus of apocalyptic discourse in the Gospel of Luke is on Jerusalem, to which Jesus travels in 9:51–19:44 and teaches daily in the temple in 19:45–21:38.[140] One very important observation is that a significant number of apocalyptic sayings from Q, plus other apocalyptic sayings and parables, are present in the long account of Jesus' journey to Jerusalem. According to Bloomquist's count, sixteen sections of text in Luke 9:21–19:44 contain significant apocalyptic emphases.[141] Within these sections, a significant number of verses in chapters 10–14, 17, and 19 are Q tradition[142] in the context of Lukan special tradition or redaction[143] and a few verses of Markan tradition.[144]

From the eras of biblical tradition, one notices within special Lukan tradition or redaction references to Abraham's living in a comfortable

[137] L. Gregory Bloomquist, "The Intertexture of Lukan Apocalyptic Discourse," in *The Intertexture of Apocalyptic Discourse in the New Testament* (ed. D.F. Watson; Symposium 14; Atlanta: SBL, 2002) 45-68.

[138] Luke 1:55 (1:46-55); 1:73 (1:68-79); 13:28 (13:22-30); 16:22-25, 29-30 (16:19-31); 20:37 (20:27-38); ibid., 46-53.

[139] Luke 1:69 (1:68-79): ibid.

[140] Ibid.; L. Gregory Bloomquist, "Rhetorical Argumentation and the Culture of Apocalyptic: A Socio-Rhetorical Analysis of Luke 21," in *The Rhetorical Interpretation of Scripture: Essays from the 1996 Malibu Conference* (ed. S.E. Porter and D.L. Stamps; JSNTS 180; Sheffield: Sheffield Academic Press, 1999) 173-209.

[141] Luke 9:23-27, 52-56; 10:8-24; 11:29-32; 12:1-12, 35-48, 49-53, 54-59; 13:1-9, 22-30, 34-35; 14:15-24; 16:19-31; 17:20-37; 19:11-27, 28-44; Bloomquist, "The Intertexture of Lukan Apocalyptic Discourse," 48-51.

[142] On the basis of Robinson, Hoffmann, Kloppenborg, *The Critical Edition of Q*, the following verses are Q tradition: Luke 10:8-16, 21-24; 11:29-32; 12:2-11, 39-40, 42-46, [49], 51, [54-56], 58-59; 13:24-29, [30], 34-35; 14:16-18, [19-20], 21, 23; [17:20-21], 22-24, 26-27, [28-29], 30, 34-35; 19:12-13, 15-24, 26.

[143] Luke 9:52-56; 10:17-20; 12:35-38, 41, 47-48; 52-53, 57; 13:1-9, 22-23; 14:15, 22, 24; 16:19-31; 17:22, 31-33, 36-37; 19:11, 14, 25, 27, 41-44.

[144] Luke 9:23-27; 12:1, 12, 50; 17:25; 19:28-40.

place in Hades (Luke 16:23-31); Abraham's reference to Moses and the prophets in a context of reference to resurrection from the dead (Luke 16:29-31); reference to Lot's wife as well as to Lot (Luke 17:32); and a request by disciples of Jesus to bring fire down from heaven to destroy people, like Elijah did when he had enemies (Luke 9:54: 2 Kgs 1:9-16). Then from the time of Jesus until the end, one notices in special Lukan tradition or redaction Jesus seeing Satan fall from heaven like a flash of lightning (Luke 10:18); an intensification of emphasis on division in households (Luke 12:52-53); Pilate's spilling of the blood of Galileans (Luke 13:1-3); people dying when the tower of Siloam falls on them (Luke 13:4-5); a king slaughtering citizens of his country who hated him (Luke 19:27); people who expected the kingdom of God to come immediately when they arrived in Jerusalem (Luke 19:11); and coming days when enemies of Jerusalem will set up ramparts, surround the city, hem everyone in, and crush the city and everyone in it, because they did not "recognize the time" of their "visitation from God" (Luke 19:44). As Bloomquist has observed, "Luke seems to regard Jesus' approach to Jerusalem and his time there as the rhetorical forum par excellence for apocalyptic discourse."[145]

The Acts of the Apostles

When Bloomquist turns to a sociorhetorical interpretation of apocalyptic in the Acts of the Apostles, he concludes that in the context of a "pattern of waning apocalyptic intertexture" there is an apocalyptic focus on "mission to the Gentiles."[146] In his view, the apocalyptic moment has not passed in Acts. Rather, "it is taking place as a witness to Jesus and under his authority."[147] Bloomquist's point is that "we can see Lukan apocalyptic not as the short-lived, revolutionist, and liminal cultural moment usually associated with a cataclysmic inbreaking, but as an enduring 'revolutionist' and countercultural overthrow."[148]

Bloomquist's analysis of Acts led him to nine sections of Acts which he considers to contain significant apocalyptic discourse.[149] We can only look briefly at a few of them here. Acts 1:7 reconfigures the apocalyptic *topos* of the day (*hēmera*) or hour (*hōra*) when the Son would come to earth (Mark 13:32 par.) into a "time" (*chronos*) or "period" (*kairos*) when followers of Jesus must be the risen Lord Messiah's "witnesses in Jerusalem, in all Judea and Samaria, and to the ends of the earth" (1:8). In other words, the apocalyptic time-space conceptuality

[145] Bloomquist, "The Intertexture of Lukan Apocalyptic Discourse," 66.
[146] Ibid., 67.
[147] Ibid.
[148] Ibid.
[149] Acts 1:3-11; 2:14-36; 3:18-26; 10:34-43; 13:26-43; 15:15-18; 17:30-31; 26:23; 28:25-28; ibid., 53-56.

(chronotope) in Acts reconfigures "the harvest" mission of the seventy in Luke 10:1-16 (Luke's configuration of Q tradition) into a mission of "witnesses" from Jerusalem to the ends of the earth. As Bloomquist has stated, the movement of mission to the Gentiles in Acts is not a sign that "the apocalyptic moment has passed," but a sign that it has been reconfigured in terms of a new time and space. "The Father has set by his own authority" times and periods in which the Lord Messiah's witnesses will go to the Gentiles at "the ends of the earth" (1:7-8). Exactly how long these times and periods will last it is not for them to know (1:7). The apocalyptic moment now is not the return of the Son of Man, the destruction of the city of Jerusalem, or the restoration of the kingdom to Israel. Rather, the apocalyptic moment is the mission of witness, empowered by the Holy Spirit, to the nations of the world (Gentiles). Only God the Father knows how long these times and periods will last, and when they will come to an end!

There are two additional observations that are especially pertinent for this chapter. First, Bloomquist has drawn his conclusions about apocalyptic discourse in both Luke and Acts on the basis of careful enthymematic analysis of argumentation that regularly takes the form of chreia elaboration.[150] If there were time and space in this chapter, it would be appropriate to identify story-summaries and scenario events in the argumentation he has identified as apocalyptic. His analysis and interpretation richly exhibit "embodied reasoning" in the texts, which is a central focus of sociorhetorical interpretation. For this reason, his approach feeds naturally into the analysis and interpretation of this chapter on apocalyptic. Second, Bloomquist's analysis deftly identifies the intertextual importance of the times of "Noah, Abraham, Lot and Lot's wife, Jonah, the Ninevites, David, the Queen of the South (and, through her, Solomon), Elijah, and Elisha"[151] for the apocalyptic focus on Jerusalem in the Gospel of Luke. It does not, however, fully exhibit the nature of the eras from the past that play an important role in the apocalyptic "witness" mission in Acts. For our purposes in this chapter, it is important to discuss certain important aspects in this "apocalyptic" shift.

In all of Acts, there is no reference to Noah, Lot, Lot's wife, Jonah, the Ninevites, the Queen of the South, Elijah, or Elisha. In the apocalyptic units Bloomquist identifies in Acts, however, Abraham, Moses, and David are present. The time of Abraham is the least defined, but it helps to signal the nature of the previous eras of biblical time in the apocalyptic view of world history in Acts. There are seven references to Abraham in Acts (3:13, 25; 7:2, 16-17, 32; 13:26). Acts 3:13 identi-

[150] Bloomquist, "Rhetorical Argumentation and the Culture of Apocalyptic," 188-95.
[151] Bloomquist, "The Intertexture of Lukan Apocalyptic Discourse," 61.

fies the time of Abraham, Isaac, and Jacob as an era that signaled the "glorification" of God's servant Jesus in apocalyptic world history. When God told Abraham, "And in your descendants all the families of the earth [the Gentiles] shall be blessed" (Acts 3:25), the era of Abraham became a bright time for the Gentiles in God's plans. The dark side is that certain people of Israel (3:12) "rejected the Holy and Righteous one" and "killed the Author of life" (3:14-15). These people are, of course, "descendants of Abraham's family" (13:26). The bright side is that God raised the Author of life from the dead, creating a context for witnesses to show the power of God at work through faith (3:15-16). The key to the "inside apocalyptic story," then, is to know the relation of the dark side to the bright side in the eras of world history, like knowing that Noah was rescued when all other people on earth were destroyed. One might think, on the basis of God's promises to Abraham, that all the descendants of Abraham would be blessed. One of the inner dimensions of apocalyptic knowledge, however, is special insight into the exact way God's plans have worked and are working in history through Abraham.

There are nineteen references to Moses in Acts,[152] and five of them appear either in or near units Bloomquist has identified as containing apocalyptic discourse in Acts: 3:22: 13:39; 15:21; 26:22; 28:23. A similar dark and bright side are present in the time of Moses. The bright side is that Moses said, "The Lord your God will raise up for you from your own people a prophet like me. You must listen to whatever he tells you" (Acts 3:22). This is a blend of prophetic and apocalyptic discourse, since the person who knows the "inside apocalyptic story" knows that God raised up this prophet "from the dead"! The dark side of the era of Moses is, of course, that "the law of Moses" could not set people free from their sins (Acts 13:39). "Everyone who believes" in the one whom "God raised up," however, "is set free from all those sins" (13:37-39). Thus, Paul asserts before King Agrippa: "… I stand here, testifying to both small and great, saying nothing but what the prophets and Moses said would take place: that the Messiah must suffer, and that, by being the first to rise from the dead, he would proclaim light both to our people and to the Gentiles" (26:22-23). The time of Moses, then, was a very important era in apocalyptic world history. Moses knew, from the perspective of the story in Acts, that God would raise Messiah Jesus from the dead. But there is a dark heritage as well as a bright heritage from the time of Moses. The key for early Christian apocalyptic knowledge is to know how the bright side of that era works through the story of God's Messiah Jesus.

[152] Acts 3:22; 6:11, 14; 7:20, 22, 29, 31, 32, 35, 37, 40, 44; 13:39; 15:1, 5, 21; 21:21; 26:22; 28:23.

There are ten references to David in Acts,[153] and six of them occur in units Bloomquist has identified as containing apocalyptic discourse: 2:14-36; 13:26-43; 15:16. Bloomquist interprets only the dark side of the era of David: "Contrasting with the positive light cast on the others – Gentiles or prophets to the Gentiles – David, as king, prophesies only how unlike his fate is to that of the one who is his Son!"[154] Again, however, this is only one side of the story. From the perspective of Acts, David was granted an apocalyptic vision of Messiah Jesus, causing him to say, "I saw the Lord [Messiah] always before me, for he is at my right hand so that I will not be shaken" (Acts 2:25). The dark side, indeed, is that David himself did not ascend into the heavens (2:34). The bright side, however, is that David heard "the Lord" say to the Lord Messiah, "Sit at my right hand, until I make your enemies your footstool" (2:34). In the context of the apocalyptic nature of David's seeing and hearing, it is important to see, first, that Peter's sermon presents a dynamic blend of prophetic and apocalyptic discourse and second, that the era of David has both a dark and bright side. Again, the nature of apocalyptic discourse is that it helps the hearer/reader know the "inside story" about the dark and bright side as one faces the challenges of the time in which one lives.

The nature of apocalyptic discourse in Acts, then, shifts the focus beyond the eras that were important in the Q material and the Gospel of Luke. Attentive readers may already have noticed that the three eras that play such an important role in the apocalyptic construal of the mission to the Gentiles in Acts are highly important eras in the apocalyptic view of the world in Paul's undisputed letters, namely Abraham, Moses, and David. Only the era of Adam is missing from Acts. There is no mention of Adam in Acts,[155] so there is no emphasis that Adam brought sin and death into the world. There are, however, some important statements about sin, like the assertion that everyone who believes in the one whom God raised up is set free from sin (13:37-39), that create an environment of blending apocalyptic emphases in Paul's undisputed letters with apocalyptic emphases in Acts in early Christian discourse.

Apocalyptic Times and Spaces in Jude and 2 Peter

The letters of Jude and 2 Peter, written some time after the middle of the first century CE,[156] are interesting for their relation to the special

[153] Acts 1:16; 2:25, 29, 34; 4:25; 7:45; 13:22, 34, 36; 15:16.

[154] Bloomquist, "The Intertexture of Lukan Apocalyptic Discourse," 61.

[155] The Gospel of Luke has one reference to Adam, namely 3:38, which refers to Jesus as "Adam, son of God."

[156] Jerome H. Neyrey, *2 Peter, Jude* (AB 37C; New York: Doubleday, 1993) refers to the date of Jude as "a mystery, with scholars suggesting a date as early as the late apostolic

sayings in common in Matthew and Luke. For this reason, we will discuss them next in this chapter. For interpretation of apocalyptic in 1 Peter, which emphasizes the suffering of Jesus Messiah without the same relation to the Q sayings, see the detailed investigation by Robert L. Webb.[157] Like Jewish apocalyptic literature of the time, first century Christian apocalyptic literature often has relationships and differences from one another that are very difficult to explain. Apocalyptic attention to Noah, the flood, Sodom, Gomorrah, and Lot was widespread in apocalyptic literature during the first century CE, so it is natural that the Q Sayings, Jude, and 2 Peter which do not emphasize eras of apocalyptic time with a specific Pauline focus or a focus like one sees in Acts would work intertexturally with eras of time readily available in Jewish apocalyptic environments.

Apocalyptic Times and Spaces in Jude

Like the Q sayings, Jude features Sodom and Gomorrah as an era of time with a special relation to the end time (Jude 7).[158] Jude begins the dark eras with the time of Cain (Jude 11), refers specifically to the sinful angels who are "kept in eternal chains in deepest darkness until judgment (Jude 6), and continues with destruction of disbelieving Israelites during the time of the exodus, adding that the Lord "once for all" saved a people out of Egypt (Jude 5). Then Jude adds Korah's rebellion (Jude 11), Balaam's prophecy (Jude 11), and Satan's contending with Michael for the body of Moses (Jude 9).[159] There is reference to Adam and Enoch in the context of a prophecy that the Lord will come with ten thousand holy ones to judge all people (Jude 14-15).[160] In the midst of this, there is no reference to Abraham, Lot, the law, David, Solomon, the Queen of the South, or Jonah. A major focus is on ungodly intruders in the believing community before the end (Jude 4, 8, 10, 16-19).[161] Again, this letter contains no reference to the Son of

age (50-60 CE) and as late as mid-second century" (30), and to the date of 2 Peter as after Jude, with the author using Jude as a source (120-22).

[157] Robert L. Webb, "Intertexture and Rhetorical Strategy in First Peter's Apocalyptic Discourse: A Study in Sociorhetorical Interpretation," in *Reading First Peter with New Eyes: Methodological Reassessments of 1 Peter* (ed. R.L. Webb and Betsy Bauman-Martin; LNTS 364; London: T & T Clark, 2007) 72-110.

[158] Duane F. Watson, "The Oral-Scribal and Cultural Intertexture of Apocalyptic Discourse in Jude and 2 Peter," in *The Intertexture of Apocalyptic Discourse in the New Testament* (ed. D.F. Watson; Symposium 14; Atlanta: SBL, 2002) 188-91.

[159] Ibid., 190-92.

[160] Scholars regularly consider Jude 14-15 to be a reference to *1 Enoch*, and some consider it to contain a recitation of *1 En.* 1:9: Neyrey, *2 Peter, Jude*, 79-82; Watson, ibid., 193-94.

[161] Watson, ibid., 194-97.

Man. There is, however, significant apocalyptic overlap in particular with the Q material which, of course, is in both Matthew and Luke.

Apocalyptic Times and Spaces in 2 Peter

The letter of 2 Peter contains so many similarities to the letter of Jude that modern scholars regularly consider Jude to have been a literary source used by its author.[162] 2 Peter emphasizes the plight of the sinful angels (2 Pet 2:4) and the burning of Sodom and Gomorrah to ashes (2:6), and it expands on the influence of the wrongdoing of Balaam (2:15-16). In addition, it refers to Noah and the flood (2 Pet 2:5) and adds the rescuing of Lot to a story-summary about Sodom and Gomorrah (2:7).[163] 2 Peter does not contain, however, any reference to the way of Cain (Jude 11), God's destruction of disbelieving Israelites (Jude 5), Korah's rebellion (Jude 11), or Satan's contending with Michael over the body of Moses (Jude 9). In fact, there is no reference to Moses in 2 Peter, just as there is no mention of Adam, Enoch, Abraham, Lot, David, Solomon, the Queen of the South, or Jonah. The following table exhibits the eras of world history in common among the Sayings Gospel Q, Jude, and 2 Peter:

World History (This Age) in Q; Jude; 2 Peter

Sayings Gospel Q	Jude	2 Peter
	Way of Cain: Jude 11 (dark: Gen 4:9)	
	Sinful angels kept in eternal chains in deepest darkness until judgment: Jude 6 (dark)	Sinful angels cast into hell until judgment: 2 Pet 2:4 (dark)
Noah entered the ark: Luke 17:27/Matt 24:38 (bright)		God saved Noah and seven others: 2 Pet 2:5 (bright)
Days of Noah like day(s) of Son of Man: Luke 17:26-27/Matt 24:37-39 (dark)		Flood destroyed ancient, ungodly world: 2 Pet 2:5 (dark)
Abraham, Isaac, and Jacob will recline at table in kingdom of God: Luke 13:28/Matt 8:11 [also people from east, west, north, south: Luke 13:29] (bright)		

[162] Neyrey, ibid., 120-22; Watson, ibid., 187.
[163] See Watson, ibid., 197-213.

Sodom: Luke 10:12/Matt 10:15 [Luke 17:29] (dark) [Gomorrah: Matt 10:15] (dark)	Sodom, Gomorrah, and surrounding cities punished with eternal fire for sexual immorality and unnatural lust: Jude 7 (dark)	Sodom and Gomorrah: burned to ashes for being ungodly: 2 Pet 2:6 (dark)
[Lot: Luke 17:28-29] (bright) [Lot's wife: Luke 17:32] (dark)		Lot rescued by God: 2 Pet 2:7 (bright)
	Egypt: the Lord saved a people out of the land of Egypt: Jude 5a (bright)	
	Exodus: the Lord destroyed disbelieving Israelites: Jude 5b (dark: Num 14:20-23) Korah's rebellion: Jude 11 (dark: Num 16)	
	Balaam prophesied for gain: Jude 11 (dark: Num 22)	Balaam rebuked for transgression: 2 Pet 2:15-16 (dark: Num 22)[164]
[Satan tested Jesus, Son of God: Luke 4:1-13/Matt 4:1-11]	Satan contended with archangel Michael for body of Moses: Jude 9 (dark)	
Solomon and Queen of the South: Luke 11:31/Matt 12:42 (bright)		
Jonah and the Ninevites: Luke 11:32/Matt 12:41 (bright); Sign of Jonah: [repentance or resurrection: Luke 11:29-30/Matt 12:39-41] (bright)		

In the context of a significant number of eras of world history in common among Q, Jude, and 2 Peter, the letters of Jude and 2 Peter describe the time in which they are written as the last "time" (Jude 17-19) or "days" (2 Pet 3:3), when ungodly scoffers who indulge their own lusts have come into their community. For both of them, the apostles lived in a special era when they were equipped with knowledge to predict that such people would come into believing communities at the end time (Jude 17-18; 2 Pet 3:2-4). As Jude addresses the situation, there is no reference to the death and resurrection of the Lord Jesus Christ, nor is there reference to his place at the right hand of God. Rather, the letter focuses entirely on the time of judgment

[164] Cf. Rev 2:14.

through a recitation of *1 En.* 1:9 that presents four scenario events: (1) the Lord is coming with ten thousands of his holy ones; (2) to execute judgment on all; (3) to convict everyone of all the deeds of ungodliness that they have committed in such an ungodly way; and (4) to convict everyone of all the harsh things that ungodly sinners have spoken against him (Jude 14-15). In the face of these scenario events in the future, the narrator exhorts the hearers/readers to maintain themselves in community through faith, prayer, love, and mercy as they look forward "to the mercy of our Lord Jesus Christ that leads to eternal life" (20-23).

Although 2 Peter presents many items similar to Jude, it signals at the beginning that the hearers/readers "have received a faith … through the righteousness of our God and Savior Jesus Christ" (1:1). This leads to a focus on the time when the narrator himself, along with others, was a witness of the "majesty" (*megaleiotētos*) of Jesus on the holy mountain, when they heard the voice of "the majestic Glory" from heaven saying, "This is my Son, my Beloved, with whom I am well pleased" (1:17-18). Seeing this, the narrator says, assures "the power and coming (*parousia*) of our Lord Jesus Christ" in the future (1:16). In 2 Peter, then, the transfiguration of Jesus is recounted in an argumentative story-summary that confirms knowledge about "the power and coming" of the Lord Jesus Messiah.[165]

As 2 Peter continues, it moves in the final chapter to two story-summaries of the end time. The variations between them are similar to variations one sees in story-summaries that focus on the death and resurrection of Jesus. The first story-summary has four scenario events: (1) the day of the Lord will come like a thief; (2) the heavens will pass away with a loud noise; (3) the elements will be dissolved with fire; and (4) the earth and everything that is done on it will be disclosed (3:10). After this story-summary of the "day of the Lord," there is a version with some slightly different emphases describing the "day of God" with three scenario events: (1) the heavens will be set ablaze and dissolved; (2) the elements will melt with fire; (3) in accordance with his promise, there will be new heavens and a new earth, where righteousness is at home (3:12-13).[166] Again there is no reference to the death and resurrection of Jesus. There is, however, an account of the transfiguration of Jesus, which is perceived to point to "the power and coming of our Lord Jesus Christ" (1:16). The focus on the end time is supported by significant rehearsal of the time of the sinful angels, Noah, Sodom and Gomorrah, Lot (2:4-10), and by reference to Balaam (2:15). The focus on the end time leads to two story-summary formulations, one using the terminology of the day of the Lord (3:10)

[165] Watson, ibid., 199-201.
[166] Ibid., 203-10.

and one of the day of God (3:12-13), each of which points toward a future time when the heavens will pass away, all the elements will be dissolved with fire, and there will be new heavens and a new earth. Here one can see angel-spirit apocalyptic moving into the arena of earth-material apocalyptic. There is a consciousness of the substances of which the earth are made, and the setting of the heavens ablaze to destroy them appears to presuppose that even the heavens have earthly substances in them that will need to be dissolved. 2 Peter, then, contains features that move beyond angel-spirit apocalyptic toward the kind of earth-material apocalyptic one finds in the Revelation to John.

Apocalyptic Times and Spaces in 2 Thessalonians: Rebellion, Lawless One, Lord Jesus Destroyer

2 Thessalonians, attributed to Paul in the NT canon, has an unusual relation to other writings in the NT. It "presupposes and even reproduces some of the contents of 1 Thessalonians," but "in several places identical or similar wording is not matched by a correspondence of thought." [167] The overlap in highly similar wording is not apocalyptic in nature. Rather, it features blessings on the community (2 Thess 2:16-17) and commands that they not be idle (3:6, 10-12) in the name of Paul. In 2 Thess 2:1, however, there is reference to "the coming of our Lord Jesus Messiah and our being gathered together with him," which sounds like a story-summary of 1 Thess 4:15-17. But the apocalyptic focus of 2 Thessalonians is very different from 1 Thessalonians.

The apocalyptic focus of 2 Thessalonians is on "the righteous judgment of God" (1:5). This will occur "when the Lord Jesus is revealed from heaven with his mighty angels in flaming fire, inflicting vengeance on those who do not know God and on those who do not obey the gospel of our Lord Jesus" (1:7-8). Here the emphasis is not on the Lord's taking of believers up to be with him forever (1 Thess 4:17) but on fiery destruction of unbelievers. This emphasis continues with a description of the "coming of the rebellion," the "revelation of the lawless one" (2 Thess 2:3), and the Lord Jesus' annihilation of the lawless one with the breath of his mouth (2:8) in the context of God's sending of "a powerful delusion" to them (2:11). The description refers to "the working of Satan, who uses all power, signs, lying wonders, and every kind of wicked deception" to lead the ungodly astray (2:10). Here, again, one sees aspects that move beyond angel-spirit apocalyptic toward earth-material apocalyptic. The emphasis on flaming fire that accompanies the Lord Jesus, and the emphasis on his in-

[167] Furnish, *1 Thessalonians, 2 Thessalonians*, 128-29: "In addition to the prescripts and closing benedictions, the most striking of these are between 2 Thess 2:16-17 and 1 Thess 3:11-13; 2 Thess 3:8 and 1 Thess 2:9; and 2 Thess 3:10-12 and 1 Thess 3:4 + 4:1, 10b-12."

flicting of "vengeance," sounds like actions of destruction that may be concerned with political issues of power.

As 2 Thessalonians addresses the situation, it presents a detailed picture of the end time: (1) the rebellion comes first and the lawless one is revealed, the one destined for destruction (2:3); (2) there is a time when the lawless one is restrained, "so that he may be revealed when his time comes" (2:6); (3) then the lawless one will be revealed, whom the Lord Jesus will destroy with the breath of his mouth, annihilating him by the manifestation of his coming (2:8). In this scenario, the breath of the mouth of the Lord Jesus appears to be like the breath of the Man from the Sea in *4 Ezra* 13:10-11, namely "something like a stream of fire" (13:10) so that "suddenly nothing was seen of the innumerable multitude but only the dust of ashes and the smell of smoke" (13:11). There is no actual reference to fire that comes out of the mouth of the Lord in 2 Thess 2:8, but the manner in which his breath annihilates the lawless one again moves toward the imagery one finds in earth-material apocalyptic.

There is not only a dark side to the coming of the Lord Jesus in 2 Thessalonians. In this letter, the righteous judgment of God repays "with affliction those who afflict you" and gives "relief to the afflicted as well as to us" (1:5-7). This occurs "when the Lord Jesus is revealed (*en tēi apokalypsēi*) from heaven with his mighty angels in flaming fire (1:7-8). In this context of "the coming (*parousia*) of our Lord Jesus Christ," believers will be "gathered together (*episynagogēs*) to him" (2:1). The time of God's righteous judgment, then, is a blend of the dark and the bright that is internal to the apocalyptic story of the world, namely a story where God destroys all evil and preserves all goodness and holiness.

Earth-Material Apocalyptic in Revelation: Military Son of Man, Lion of Judah, Slain Little Ram of God

The Revelation to John is, as many have observed during the last few decades, the only true "apocalypse" in the NT.[168] Its most striking aspect, however, is the dramatically different mode of apocalyptic it uses to communicate its message. A major reason is its point of view toward space. Rather than wrestling with the challenges of living on earth from a perspective on earth, which is characteristic of every other book in the NT, Revelation focuses on the earth from the perspective of heaven. When Revelation views humanity from the perspective of heaven, ordinary people living in the daily contexts of agricultural villages, towns, and households throughout the world do not come

[168] Rowland, *The Open Heaven*, 11; Collins, *The Apocalyptic Imagination*, 269; Carey, *Ultimate Things*, 179-92.

into view. Instead, the focus is on stylized contexts in cities, where people horde wealth, where arrogance discourages people from worship and praise of God, and where gluttony and sexual indulgence produce poverty, suffering, and death. Along with these cities come political leaders who use precious metals and weapons of warfare to acquire crowns, thrones, and precious gem-stones. Longing for imperial rule, they create contexts of destruction and suffering accompanied by fire, death, grief, and despair. The focus of Revelation, then, is not on guidelines for people to build up one another into communities of love, peace, and hope, but on replacing forces of arrogance, hatred, and ungodliness in cities that have wealth and power with an ideal environment of abundance of food, water, light, health, purity, and joy (Rev 21:22–22:5).

The shift in apocalyptic focus in Revelation produces a presentation of God, God's Son, and God's emissaries through earthly images of wealth and power that are able to destroy the military might of godless earthly rulers and the luxuries of inhabitants who benefit from and abuse the benefits of the power and wealth. An interesting aspect of this stream of apocalyptic is the manner in which God's own space acquires military power, wealth, and abundance. Instead of using images of households, fields, thieves, servants, and masters to describe the nature of the end time, the imagery shifts to God's throne room in the heavens, where "earth-like" gem-stones and metals, thunder and lightning, and heavenly beings and creatures with bodies of "earth-like" substances threaten to destroy anyone or anything that does not praise and worship the majesty, glory, and power of its domain.

One resource for the shift to God's throne room in Revelation is the book of Ezekiel in the Hebrew Bible. In Ezekiel 1, the heavens open and Ezekiel sees visions of God (1:1). One of the most remarkable aspects of these visions is the presence of "earthly" substances in the heavens. The visions contain "fire flashing forth continually" (1:4) in contexts where some things look like gleaming amber (1:4, 27), the gleaming of beryl (1:16), shining crystal (1:22), and sapphire (1:26). Instead of seeing light, which characterizes the nature of God at the end of Revelation (22:5), one sees fire and precious gem-stones, which have their natural place on earth. In addition, there are creatures with "human form" (1:5), composed of earthly metals and parts of earthly creatures. All have faces and wings (1:6). Their faces are like those of a human, a lion, an ox, and an eagle (1:10). Their legs are a blend of the sole of a calf's foot and burnished bronze (1:7). In their midst is something that looks like burning coals of fire, torches moving to and fro, and lightning, and when the creatures dart around they look like a flash of lightning (1:13-14). These descriptions use the earthly substances of metals, precious gem-stones, and burning coals, and they use parts of earthly creatures and fire and lightning in relation to human form to describe the nature of heavenly beings and spaces. As the description brings the hearer/reader toward the throne of God, there is a touch of military imagery when the thunder of the Almighty sounds like the tumult of an army (1:24). When God speaks to Ezekiel, the subject is Israel as "a nation of rebels who have rebelled against me" (2:3). After God's commissioning of Ezekiel (1:28b–3:27), he instructs him to make "a sign for the house of Israel" (4:3). The sign, which he is to draw on a brick, is as follows:

> On it portray a city, Jerusalem; and put siegeworks against it, and build a siege wall against it, and cast a ramp against it; set camps also against it, and plant battering rams against it all around. Then take an iron plate and place it as an iron wall between you and the city; set your face toward it, and let it be in a state of siege, and press the siege against it. (4:1-3)

One readily sees that the focus is on a city, in this instance the city of Jerusalem, and a military siege is the mode of confronting the city. In Ezekiel, then, the open heavens reveal heavenly beings and heavenly spaces described in relation to earthly materials of metal, gemstone, and coal, human form, and parts of creatures like wings and feet. In this context, "people" on earth are "a rebellious nation," and the means of dealing with them is military siege of the city that is perceived to be at the center of the rebellion.

Imagery from Ezekiel 1 was a substantive resource for the portrayal of God and the throne room in Revelation 4.[169] The effect of this orientation, when it moves into apocalyptic discourse, is to bring imagery into the foreground that focuses on cities, military power, and wealth. We have chosen the phrase "earth-material apocalyptic" to describe this stream of apocalyptic tradition, which embeds an "earth-material" focus on cities, military power, and wealth into angel-spirit apocalyptic, which focuses on "spirit-blood-flesh" desire that disrupts communities through "fornication, impurity, licentiousness, idolatry, sorcery, enmities, strife, jealousy, anger, quarrels, dissensions, factions, envy, drunkenness, carousing and things like these" (Gal 5:19-21). In earth-material apocalyptic, one finds virtually all of the emphases of angel-spirit apocalyptic. The emphases of angel-spirit apocalyptic, however, function as background for the depiction of "earth-like" manifestations of God and God's assistants in the foreground. In other words, earth-material apocalyptic "overmaps" the emphases of angel-spirit apocalyptic

[169] David E. Aune, *Revelation 1–5* (WBC 52A; Dallas: Word Books, 1997) 313-14.

with earth-like manifestations of God, God's assistants, and God's realm in the heavens. In earth-material apocalyptic, God uses "earth-like" materials and powers to destroy earthly cities and military powers that produce suffering and death through their indulgences, unclean-nesses, and hording of wealth. Once these cities and military powers are destroyed, God replaces these cities and military powers with a new "heavenly" city that contains even greater "earth-like" wealth and abundance in a context of the absence of the indulgences and unclean-nesses. The remarkable result is the intimate relation of the "inner nature" of God, God's assistants, and God's space in the heavens to the earth-materials that enable "earthly" nations to acquire imperial military power and might, and to amass hordes of wealth in the form of precious metals and gem-stones. In earth-material apocalyptic, in other words, those substances and forms of power that seemed to be "outside" of God in the realm of "rebellious humanity" in the created world are internalized in a "pure and holy" form "inside" of God, God's assistants, and God's realm in the heavens.

As has been noticed in recent scholarship, the Revelation to John is really a circular letter to seven churches in cities in Asia Minor.[170] While many scholars consider its letter form to be "of very limited help in appreciating the content of the book,"[171] it is important to recognize that its letter form establishes an internal connection between Revelation and twenty-one other writings in the NT! Indeed, seven of those twenty-one writings are addressed to cities in the Mediterranean world, and two of those cities (Ephesus; Colossae) are in Asia Minor. The seven letters at the beginning of Revelation establish an epistolary mode for apocalyptic communication with cities that continues until the apocalyptic destruction of "Babylon" (18:1–19:10) and the descent of "the holy city, the new Jerusalem" (21:1–22:7). In other words, Revelation is focused on cities as a context for belief. Its function as a letter to cities supports the urban orientation of its images, its focus, and its mode of communication.

In the context of the shift to earth-material apocalyptic, Revelation has no reference to Adam, Noah, Abraham, Lot, the Queen of the South, Solomon, or Jonah, and, ironically, no reference to Gomorrah. There are three references to David, identifying God's Messiah as one who "has the key of David" (3:7), is "the Lion of the tribe of Judah, the Root of David" (5:5), and is "the root and descendant of David, the bright and morning star" (22:16). There is one reference to Moses

[170] Collins, *The Apocalyptic Imagination*, 270; M. Karrer, *Die Johannesoffenbarung als Brief* (Göttingen: Vandenhoeck & Ruprecht, 1986); Richard Bauckham, *The Theology of the Book of Revelation* (Cambridge: Cambridge University Press, 1993) 12-17.

[171] Collins, ibid.

in the title of a hymn sung by "those who had conquered the beast and its image and the number of its name" (15:3-4). Also, there is one reference to Sodom, along with Egypt, as a prophetic name for Jerusalem,[172] where the Lord was crucified and prophets were killed (11:8). In relation to our focus on the eras of world history that play an intertextural role in the apocalyptic discourse in a particular Christian writing, then, a question emerges concerning the major relationships of the apocalyptic discourse in the Revelation to John to eras in the past.

Beyond Ezekiel, one of the major resources for Revelation is Daniel in the Hebrew Bible, as we have indicated earlier in this chapter. With the use of Daniel, Babylon becomes the major city of focus, rather than Sodom or Gomorrah. Babylon is the city from which King Nebuchadnezzar came to besiege Jerusalem (Dan 1:1), and Babylon is the city of focus as the drama of Daniel unfolds.[173] In Revelation, Babylon is the city that falls, because "She has made all nations drink of the wine of the wrath of fornication" (14:8). She is the city that God remembered "and gave her the wine-cup of the fury of his wrath" (16:19). "Babylon the great, mother of whores and of earth's abominations" was written on the forehead of the great whore seated on many waters (17:1-5). And, of course, Babylon is the "dwelling place of demons" (18:2), whose judgment comes "in one hour" (18:10) as she is destroyed "like a great millstone and thrown into the sea" (18:21). The shift to earth-material apocalyptic in Revelation brings a shift beyond Sodom, Gomorrah, Nineveh, Tyre, Sidon, Chorazin, Bethsaida, and Capernaum to Babylon, the city that caused the exile of Israel and was the context for the apocalyptic drama in Daniel.

Another result of the relationship of Revelation to Daniel is reference to Jesus as "one like the Son of Man" (1:13; 14:14; cf. Dan 7:13), which is not present in any "other" letter in the NT. After the initial discourse of Revelation, which establishes the chain of communication from Jesus Messiah through his angel to John (1:1-2), who is to write it in a book and send it to the seven churches in Asia Minor (1:11), John sees "one like the Son of Man" in the midst of seven golden lampstands in heaven (1:12-13). In the context of all of the other descriptions of "the Son of Man" in the Gospels and Acts, as well as the descriptions of the coming "Lord (Jesus)" in the letters, the description of the Son of Man in Revelation 1 is truly amazing. The most constant feature of the Son of man and the coming Lord in the other NT writings is a reference to power, glory, clouds, and angels.[174] In Revelation 1, the visibility of the Son of man is "like" a blend of metals, white

[172] See Isa 1:10; Jer 23:14; Ezek 16:46-56.
[173] Dan 2:12, 14, 18, 24, 48, 49; 3:1, 12, 30; 4:6, 29, 30; 5:7; 7:1.
[174] Cf. Mark 13:26-27, etc.

wool, snow, fire, stars, and sun, and his "audibility" is "like the sound of many waters" (Rev 1:12-16). Then in Revelation 14 he has "a golden crown on his head and a sharp sickle in his hand" (14:14). As this mode of apocalyptic presentation of Jesus as the Son of Man unfolds, Jesus acquires the image of a Lion who has conquered (5:5) and a Little Ram[175] who has been slaughtered. When the kings of ten kingdoms make war on the Little Ram (17:14), the Little Ram takes the form of a rider on a white horse with eyes like "a flame of fire," a head with many diadems on it, clothing of a robe dipped in blood, a mouth with a sharp sword extending out from it, and the name "King of kings and Lord of lords" inscribed on his robe and thigh (19:11-16; cf. 1:12-16). These transformations in visible form are characteristic of apocalyptic in the mode that uses earth-materials to describe heavenly beings and focuses on cities, military power, and wealth.

One of the special characteristics of "one like the Son of man" in Revelation is a blending of attributes of "the Ancient of Days" (God) and the angel Gabriel as they are described in Daniel.[176] The head and hair of the heavenly Jesus Messiah is "white as white wool, white as snow" (Rev 1:14), like the Ancient of Days in Dan 7:9. These "creature" characteristics are a matter of making a being who shares attributes characteristic of God "visible" to humans. In addition, however, God's heavenly Messiah Jesus has clothing of a long robe and a golden sash, eyes like a flame of fire, feet of burnished bronze, and a voice like the sound of many waters (Rev 1:13-15; cf. Dan 10:5-6). Beyond this, he has seven stars in his right hand, a sharp, two-edged sword from his mouth (Isa 49:2), and a face like the sun shining in full force.[177] This is

[175] Jesus is referred to without exception as a little ram (*arnion*) in Revelation (5:6, 8, 12, 13; 6:1, 16; 7:9, 10, 14, 17; 12:11; 13:8; 14:1, 4(2), 10; 15:3; 17:14(2); 19:7, 9; 21:9, 14, 22, 23, 27; 22:1, 3; cf. 13:11), rather than as a lamb (*amnos*), which occurs four times in other writings in the NT: John 1:29, 36; Acts 8:32; 1 Pet 1:19; see David E. Aune, *Revelation 1–5* (WBC 52A; Dallas: Word Books, 1997) 367-74, 323 n. 6.d. Many scholars have been reluctant to translate *arnion* as ram since it is a diminutive of *arnēn* meaning "little ram." Scholars regularly present four reasons to translate *arnion* as ram in Revelation: (1) the reference to wrath; (2) the horns; (3) the sign of the ram in the zodiac; (4) the similarity to Dan 8:3 and *1 En*. 90:9, 37; see ibid., 368; J. Massyngberde Ford, *Revelation* (AB 38; Garden City, NY: Doubleday, 1975) 86. There are two more reasons: (5) ten kingdoms who are horns make war on the Little Ram (17:12-14); (6) the image of the Little Ram is related to the image of the Lion of the tribe of Judah (5:5-6). The traditional practice of translating *arnion* as lamb in Revelation results from accommodating Revelation to other writings in the NT, rather than from interpreting its contextual meaning according to the metaphorical mapping in the apocalyptic discourse in Revelation. The appropriate way to translate it so it evokes its natural metaphorical meaning is "little ram."

[176] Adela Yarbro Collins, *Cosmology and Eschatology in Jewish and Christian Apocalypticism* (Leiden: Brill, 1996) 159-97; Collins, *The Apocalyptic Imagination*, 273.

[177] See Aune, ibid., 90-99.

a being whose heavenly attributes of glory, divinity, and cosmic power are visible by means of earthly materials and other phenomena commonly visible to humans on earth.

In the context of the "earthly" attributes of the "one like the Son of Man," God has no human or creaturely "form" in Revelation. In the mode of earth-material apocalyptic, the nature of God is described in relation to earthly materials and things visible on earth, but these descriptions give no "form" to God, in contrast to the form of the one like the Son of Man and the form of other heavenly beings. The one seated on the throne in Revelation "looks like jasper and carnelian" and "around the throne is a rainbow that looks like an emerald" (4:3). Coming from the throne are "flashes of lightning, and rumblings and peals of thunder" (4:5). In front of the throne burn "seven flaming torches, which are the seven spirits of God," and there is also "something like a sea of glass, like crystal" (4:5-6). The description of God is related to earthly substances and to phenomena a person sees on earth, since the mode of presentation is earth-material apocalyptic. It is noticeable, for example, that the seven spirits of God are not "like doves flying around the throne of God" (cf. Mark 1:10). Rather, the spirits of God are described in relation to earthly materials that produce light, namely flaming torches like those that light the streets of cities in the evening. In the midst of all of these descriptions, God has no human or other creaturely form. Instead, all of the "human" and "creaturely" aspects associated with divinity are present in the "one like the Son of Man," who is the primary agent who mediates God's divine powers to the created world. All of the human attributes of God, the "Ancient of Days" (Dan 7), disappear from the portrayal of God in Revelation. These attributes, instead, are present in "the one like the Son of Man," blended together with attributes of the angel Gabriel and other phenomena that give him glory, majesty, and power. God, in contrast, has no "visible" human attributes. Revelation cannot avoid certain images of action and power as it describes the effect of God on the world. For example, God "sits" (4:3; 5:1), has "a right hand" (5:1, 7), and even a face (22:4). But there is no description of them in relation to human form or material substance. God's only visible characteristics are "like" precious stones (jasper and carnelian) that produce a rainbow that looks like an emerald (4:3), since the true nature of God is "glory," which produces light (21:23; 22:5).

In the context of earth-material apocalyptic that brings the throne room of God, the "one like the Son of Man," the one who is "the Lion of the tribe of Judah," and "the slaughtered Little Ram" into view, the actions of God toward the earth gradually lead to a focus on the city of Babylon. The actions of God unfold through the opening of seven seals by "the Little Ram" (6:1–8:1) and the blowing of seven trumpets by seven angels who stand before God (8:2–11:19). Instead of using imagery from Noah and the flood, Sodom and Gomorrah, or Jonah and the Ninevites, Revelation uses imagery from the ten plagues against Egypt as its major resource.[178] The time of Moses, then, rather than the time of Noah, Abraham, Solomon, or Jonah, provides the typology for the events of the end time in Revelation. But it is not the imagery of the Red Sea, God's giving of the law, or rebellion in the wilderness that stands in the foreground. Rather, it is the horrendous time of the ten plagues that God launched against the Egyptians who held the Israelites in slavery that come into the foreground in the account of the end of the world in Revelation. A simplified table displaying the relation looks as follows:[179]

Ten Plagues, Trumpets, and Bowls of Wrath

Ten Plagues: Exodus 7–12	**Seven Trumpets:** Rev 8–9, 11	**Seven Bowls of Wrath:** Rev 15–16
I. Blood in river (7:17-21)	(1) Hail, fire, blood (cf. I, VII)	(1) Boils (cf. VI)
II. Frogs (8:1-7)	(2) Fire, blood (cf. I, VII)	(2) Blood in sea (cf. I)
III. Gnats (8:16-19)	(3) Darkness, wormwood (cf. IX)	(3) Blood in rivers and springs (cf. I)
IV. Flies (8:20-24)	(4) Darkness (cf. IX)	(4) Sun heat (cf. VII)
V. Death of Livestock (9:1-7)	(5) Darkness, smoke, locusts (cf. VII, VIII, IX)	(5) Darkness, pains, sores (cf. VI, IX)
VI. Boils (9:8-12)	(6) Fire, smoke, killing humans (cf. VII, X)	(6) Frogs (cf. II)
VII. Thunder, hail, fire (9:22-26)	(7) Lightning, thunder, earthquake, hail (cf. VII)	(7) Lightning, thunder, earthquake, hail (cf. VII)
VIII. Locusts (10:12-20)		
IX. Darkness (10:21-29)		
X. Death of firstborn humans and livestock (12:29-32)		

From the perspective we have been taking in this chapter on apocalyptic in early Christian discourse, it is informative that no other writing in the NT uses the ten plagues against Egypt for apocalyptic typology. There is reference to "wonders and signs in Egypt" in

[178] See David E. Aune, *Revelation 6–16* (WBC 52B; Nashville: Thomas Nelson Publishers, 1998) 499-506; cf. seven plagues in Pss 78:43-52; 105:27-36; Amos 4:6-13 (ibid., 502-503).

[179] Cf. the more detailed lists in ibid., 500-501.

Stephen's speech at Acts 7:36, which clearly refers to the plagues. But nothing in particular is made of them. Rather, they are part of a "miracle" tradition that highlights wonders and signs "in Egypt, at the Red Sea, and in the wilderness for forty years" (7:36). Along with the shift to earth-material apocalyptic in Revelation comes a shift to God's punishment of Egypt as the typology for the events of destruction (Rev 6–16) that lead to the dramatic destruction of Babylon (Rev 18–19), the city that furnished the military power to destroy Jerusalem and the nation of Israel in that fateful era of the past. For Revelation, the days that lead up to the end time are like the days when the people of Egypt and its Pharaoh ate and drank, married and gave in marriage, until the time when God sent Moses to destroy their power and free the people of Israel from their slavery. At the end of time, God's releasing of plagues on the world, in the midst of which occurs the battle in heaven between Michael and the dragon (Rev 12),[180] establishes the context for the destruction of the wicked city of Babylon (Rev 18–19).[181]

After the destruction of Babylon, God's Messiah, the Little Ram of God, takes the form of a rider named "Faithful and True" and "The Word of God," on a white horse, although his name is known only to himself (19:11-13). In addition to eyes "like a flame of fire" and many diadems on his head, he is "clothed in a robe dipped in blood" (19:12-13). With the armies of heaven following him, a sharp sword from his mouth "strikes down the nations," and he rules them with a rod of iron and "treads the wine press of the fury of the wrath of God the Almighty" (19:14-15). On his robe and thigh are inscribed, "King of kings and Lord of lords" (19:16). His violent actions of judgment create "the great supper of God," where birds come and eat the flesh of kings, captains, the mighty, horses, and their riders (19:17-19). One of the remarkable things about earth-material apocalyptic, then, is the depiction of God's Messiah with military weaponry and dress, engaged in killing with a sword, like earthly armies kill and destroy. In this stream of apocalyptic, heaven itself possesses the earthly materials of warfare to counter the military power of earthly rulers.

After the great supper of God, the dragon, who is "the Devil and Satan," is bound for a thousand years while the Messiah reigns (20:1-4). After the thousand years, the Devil is thrown into the lake of fire and sulfur to be tormented day and night forever (20:7), and Death and Hades are destroyed in the lake of fire (Rev 20).[182] In this context, the first heaven and earth pass away, a new heaven and new earth appear, and the holy city, the new Jerusalem, comes down from heaven "like a

[180] See Aune, *Revelation 6–16*, 663-76; cf. Collins, *The Apocalyptic Imagination*, 275-76.
[181] Aune, ibid., 961-1040.
[182] Ibid., 1069-1108.

bride adorned" (21:1-2).[183] From the perspective of our approach in this chapter, another remarkable feature is the "earthly imagery" of wealth and abundance in the new space that arrives, namely the new Jerusalem from heaven. The city itself is pure gold (21:18), with walls and gates decorated with precious jewels (21:12-21). These walls do not primarily signify the ability of the city to protect its citizens from harm, since its gates will always be open during the day (21:25), but primarily to display its glory and radiance "like a very rare jewel, like jasper, clear as crystal" (21:11). Within this wealthy space is abundant water from "the water of life, bright as crystal, flowing from the throne of God and of the Little Ram through the middle of the street of the city" (22:1-2). Also, there is an eternal supply of food from "the tree of life with its twelve kinds of fruit, producing its fruit each month" not only for food but also for "the healing of the nations" (22:2). In addition, the city is blessed with eternal light, "for the Lord God will be their light, and they will reign forever and ever" (22:5).[184] In contrast to angel-spirit apocalyptic, which leaves the space where believers will "be with the Lord" undefined and undescribed, earth-material apocalyptic describes the new space and time in relation to abundant wealth, never-ending food and drink, and eternal light which even allows the people in the city to see the face of the Lord God (22:4)! In this apocalyptic vision, believers will be blessed in every way it is possible to describe an extraordinary environment of earthly blessing.

Conclusion

One of the most important aspects of apocalyptic in the New Testament is its emerging nature in the context of the ongoing production of Jewish apocalyptic literature during the first and second centuries CE. In contrast to wisdom and prophetic literature, which were conventional modes of biblical literature, apocalyptic was emerging in ways that were not accepted as "canonical" in many Jewish circles of leadership.

A major rhetorical effect of apocalyptic discourse is the periodization of world history. Apocalyptic literature regularly presents the events within these eras as story-summaries containing "scenario" events rather than "historical" events. Since scenario events regularly share structures of activities with one another, they can be told cyclically in different versions, or they may be presented in a manner that leaves their exact sequence unclear. When apocalyptic discourse creates story-summaries, it is regularly presenting the "inside story" about the rela-

[183] Lynn R. Huber, *Like a Bride Adorned: Reading Metaphor in John's Apocalypse* (ESEC 12; New York/London: T & T Clark International, 2007).

[184] Aune, *Revelation 6–16*, 1108-94.

tion of periods of world history to one another. For this reason, these story-summaries become argumentative, giving them syllogistic and enthymematic form and force.

Analysis of apocalyptic discourse in major portions of the New Testament reveals a focus in Paul's undisputed letters on the eras of Adam, Abraham, and Moses, with the era of David coming into view in Romans. There is no reference to or particular interest in the time of Noah, or to Sodom and Gomorrah. The effect of Paul's argumentation about Jesus Messiah as the last Adam, it has been argued, was to reverse the devastating result of the cosmological myth of the sinful angels, which Jewish apocalyptic literature during Paul's time was blaming on Adam. Paul argued that God reversed the devastating result by transforming his flesh-Messiah Jesus into an eternal-spirit Messiah who dwells in the heavens. Believers who become "in Messiah" enter into a "new procreative" environment grounded in God's righteousness that allows the Spirit to enliven their bodies toward "fruit of the Spirit" while they live on earth and to transform them into spirit beings at the end of time.

The Sayings Gospel Q, which was emerging during and after the time of Paul, shows no special interest in the time of Adam or David. Its primary focus is on the eras of Noah and the flood, Sodom and Lot, the Queen of the South during the time of King Solomon, and Jonah and the Ninevites. In addition, it features Abraham, Isaac, and Jacob eating at table in the future kingdom of God, while traditional "sons of Abraham" are excluded from it. Introducing the time of "the Son of Man," a title which never appears in the writings of Paul or any other letter in the NT, the Q sayings feature Jesus defining the time of the mission of his disciples as "the harvest." This definition makes not only the time of Jesus a special apocalyptic era, but it also makes the "mission time" of followers of Jesus a special apocalyptic era.

The Gospel of Mark, in the absence of the Q material, has no reference to Noah, Sodom and Lot, the Queen of the South, or Jonah and the Ninevites. It also has no reference to Adam. Instead of featuring Abraham, Isaac, and Jacob eating at table in the future kingdom of God, it features Jesus using God's identification of himself as "the God of Abraham, Isaac, and Jacob" as proof that God raises the dead. Instead of focusing on past eras, Mark develops a detailed set of scenario events that lead up to the coming of the Son of Man to rescue his elect from the four corners of the earth (Mark 13). In addition, Mark establishes the baptism of Jesus as an apocalyptic moment in which Jesus is sent into his adult ministry equipped with "the Spirit" that comes into him from the open heavens, and he features a moment of transformation of Jesus into a heavenly-like being on a mountain in the middle of his ministry (9:2-8). This momentary transformation creates the context for Jesus to relate his rejection, suffering, death, and resurrection to his return as the Son of Man in the future. The rhetorical effect of these events and discussions is to make the time of Jesus' adult life a special apocalyptic time, framed by Jesus' baptism, transfiguration, and resurrection after his death and burial, in addition to the time of his coming in the future.

The Gospels of Matthew and Luke, containing the Q material, emphasize the eras of Noah, Abraham, Sodom, Gomorrah, Lot, the Queen of the South, and Jonah and the Ninevites. They also feature the time of David as a time of promise for the coming Messiah, especially using this imagery in a context where the spirit enters into Jesus at the time when he is conceived in the womb of Mary. Also as a result of the presence of the Q material, Matthew and Luke feature John the Baptizer as a fiery apocalyptic preacher who sets the stage for an apocalyptic understanding of Jesus' activity. Matthew features the Son of Man returning not only to rescue his elect, but also to judge the unrighteous by sending them to outer darkness where there is weeping and gnashing of teeth. In turn, Luke focuses apocalyptic discourse on Jesus' journey to Jerusalem and death in the city. Then the Acts of the Apostles, focusing on Abraham's promise to the nations, Moses' prediction of a prophet like him who would come after him, and David's apocalyptic vision of the Lord's Messiah sitting at the right hand of God, features mission to the Gentiles as a special apocalyptic time. This focus give Acts an important relation to Paul's letters, even though there is no focus on the time of Adam in the narrative.

One especially interesting result of the focus on special eras of time within world history in NT writings is the relation of Jude and 2 Peter to the Q Sayings. All of them share a focus on Sodom, and Q and 2 Peter also share a focus on Noah. This also gives Jude and 2 Peter a special relation to Matthew and Luke. Jude and 2 Peter, like the Q sayings, do not place the death and resurrection of Jesus in the center of their apocalyptic focus. Instead of emphasizing Jesus' death and resurrection, Jude and 2 Peter emphasize the ungodly influence of intruders into their community, and this signals turmoil prior to the coming of the Lord Jesus to punish those who are unrighteous. 2 Peter is also interesting for its focus on the destruction of all "elements" both in heaven and on earth at the end of time. This represents a transition beyond the stream of angel-spirit apocalyptic in other NT writings toward the earth-material mode of apocalyptic one finds in Revelation. Along with Jude and 2 Peter, 2 Thessalonians presents a mode of apocalyptic that is transitional from the angel-spirit mode in the Gospels, Acts, and undisputed letters of Paul to the violent destruction characteristic of the earth-material apocalyptic in Revelation. In 2 Thessalonians, the Lord Jesus annihilates the lawless one with the breath of his mouth when he comes. This mode of visualizing the coming of the Lord Jesus, along with Jude and 2 Peter, exhibits a transition to the more violent depiction of the function of the Lord Jesus in the future that one finds in Revelation.

Distinguishing between an angel-spirit stream of apocalyptic that does and does not embed an earth-material stream of apocalyptic in it, the chapter ends with an analysis of Revelation as a dramatic instance of earth-material apocalyptic embedded in angel-spirit apocalyptic in first century Christian discourse. Instead of focusing on the eras of Adam, Noah, Abraham, Solomon, or Jonah, it uses extensive imagery from the ten plagues in Egypt during the time of Moses, along with imagery of the Lion of Judah, the Root of David, to present God's powerful destruction of cities that symbolize godless military power and wealth on earth. In addition, it uses the imagery of the Ram of God, which is present in *1 Enoch* and other apocalyptic Jewish literature, reconfiguring this image in terms of "the Little Ram who was slaughtered" as it presents its view of God's destruction of the world from the perspective of heaven. One of the most dramatic images in Revelation, however, is its depiction of the Son of Man with dimensions of earthly substances that includes a two-edged sword coming out of his mouth. In the context of its use of Daniel 7 and 10 for the image of the Lord Jesus Messiah as "one like the Son of Man," the focus on the past era of the ten plagues in Egypt blends with destruction that finally brings an end to the city of Babylon, the place of Daniel's residence. Revelation envisions God bringing total destruction to the city of Babylon in the context of the destruction of the seven bowls of wrath, the seven trumpets, Michael's victory over the Dragon in the heavens, and the great supper of God, which is brought about by the sword of "the King of kings and Lord of lords" riding on his white horse. All of these events create the context for the total destruction of Satan, Death, and Hades, and the emergence of a new heaven and earth, and a new holy city, the city of Jerusalem, coming down out of heaven. A remarkable feature of this new heavenly city is abundant "earthly" wealth and resources. This emphasis is a natural part of the earth-material stream of apocalyptic, but it is absent from the angel-spirit stream of apocalyptic in all other writings in the NT. The closest image to it, undeveloped in any detail, is the image of Abraham, Isaac, and Jacob in Q, Matthew, and Luke, eating at table in the Kingdom.

Overall, then, one can see that early Christian apocalyptic rhetorolect created a view of "world history" among first century believers in Jesus as the Messiah that focused on special eras of past time in relation to the end of time. Through multiple ways of relating the eras of Adam, Noah, Abraham and Lot, Moses, David, Solomon, Jonah, and Daniel in Babylon, first century Christians created highly complex, deeply intertextural apocalyptic story-summaries, scenario-events, and enthymematic arguments. These multiple ways of viewing world history supported a set of beliefs that extended from God's plans for the entire universe before creation to God's plans for the time after the end of this world and the heavens above it. In significant ways, then, early Christian apocalyptic rhetorolect, with its new configurations of God's time and space, made substantive contributions to early Christian reasoning about God, God's Messiah, and life in the world in relation to them, to other people, and to the world God created. If it had not been for the apocalyptic reasoning and argumentation of first century Christians, Christianity probably would not exist today. And indeed, if it did exist without apocalyptic reasoning and argumentation, it is very difficult to imagine what it could be like.

10

Conversations and Prospectives

Introduction

Up to this point, we have analyzed, interpreted, and discussed first century Christian rhetorolects as idealized cognitive models (ICMs).[1] We have used this approach, which emerged out of the discipline of cognitive semantics, because it offers strategies of analysis and interpretation of texts that are exceptionally helpful for moving from 19th and 20th century practices of biblical exegesis and commentary to 21st century sociorhetorical practices of analysis, interpretation, and commentary. Comprehensive essays by David B. Gowler[2] and H.J. Bernard Combrink[3] have assisted the analysis and interpretation in this volume, as well as *Fabrics of Discourse* in 2003.[4] In addition, published or forthcoming collections of essays and special programmatic essays by Duane F. Watson,[5] Gregory Carey, L. Gregory Bloomquist,[6] and Robert L.

[1] George Lakoff, *Women, Fire, and Dangerous Things: What Categories Reveal about the Mind* (Chicago and London: University of Chicago Press, 1987).

[2] David B. Gowler, "The Development of Socio-Rhetorical Criticism," in Vernon K. Robbins, *New Boundaries in Old Territory: Forms and Social Rhetoric in Mark* (ed. D.B. Gowler; ESEC 3; New York: Peter Lang, 1994) 1-35; online: http://userwww.service.emory.edu/%7Edgowler/chapter.htm; idem, "The End of the Beginning: The Continuing Maturation of Socio-Rhetorical Analysis," in Vernon K. Robbins, *Sea Voyages and Beyond* (Blandford Forum, UK: Deo Publishing, forthcoming).

[3] H.J. Bernard Combrink, "The Challenge of Making and Redrawing Boundaries: A Perspective on Socio-Rhetorical Criticism," *Nederduitse Gereformeerde Teologiese Tydskrif* 40 (1999) 18-30; online: http://www.religion.emory.edu/faculty/robbins/SRS/Combrink/ChallengeBoundSRC.pdf; idem, "The Challenges and Opportunities of a Socio-Rhetorical Commentary," *Scriptura* 79 (2002) 106-21; online: http://www.religion.emory.edu/faculty/robbins/SRS/Combrink/CombrinkSRCommentary.pdf; idem, "The Contribution of Socio-Rhetorical Interpretation to the Reformed Interpretation of Scripture," in *Reformed Theology: Identity and Ecumenicity II: Biblical Interpretation in the Reformed Tradition* (ed. W.M.J. Alston & M. Welker; Grand Rapids, MI: Eerdmans, 2007) 91-106.

[4] David B. Gowler, L. Gregory Bloomquist, and Duane F. Watson, *Fabrics of Discourse: Essays in Honor of Vernon K. Robbins* (Harrisburg/London/New York: Trinity Press International, 2003).

[5] Duane F. Watson, "Why We Need Socio-Rhetorical Commentary and What It Might Look Like," in *Rhetorical Criticism and the Bible* (ed. S.E. Porter and D.L. Stamps;

Webb[7] have played an important role. In addition, many participants in the Rhetoric of Religious Antiquity Research Group, which is now a Seminar in the Society of Biblical Literature chaired by David A. deSilva,[8] have produced various essays that were part of the ongoing conversation. These include Russell B. Sisson, Wesley H. Wachob, Charles A. Wanamaker, Gerhard van den Heever, Roy R. Jeal, B. J. Oropeza, Dennis Sylva, Terry Callan, and others.[9] Approaching first century Christian rhetorolects as ICMs, we have been able to work strategically with descriptive-narrative structuring, argumentative-enthymematic structuring, metaphoric mapping, and metonymic mapping in wisdom, prophetic, and apocalyptic discourse both prior to and during the first century CE in biblical, deutero-canonical, pseudepigraphical, and Greco-Roman literature.

JSNTS 195; Sheffield: Sheffield Academic Press, 2002) 129-57; idem (ed.), *The Intertexture of Apocalyptic Discourse in the New Testament* (Symposium Series 14; Atlanta: SBL, 2002); idem (ed.), *The Role of Miracle Discourse in the Argumentation of the New Testament* (Symposium; Atlanta: SBL and Leiden: Brill, 2008).

[6] Gregory Carey and L. Gregory Bloomquist (eds.), *Vision and Persuasion: Rhetorical Dimensions of Apocalyptic Discourse* (St. Louis, MO: Chalice Press, 1999); L. Gregory Bloomquist, "A Possible Direction for Providing Programmatic Correlation of Textures in Socio-Rhetorical Analysis," in S.E. Porter and D.L. Stamps (eds.), *Rhetorical Criticism and the Bible*, 61-96; idem, "Suffering and Joy: Subverted by Joy in Paul's Letter to the Philippians," *Int* 61 (2007) 270-82; idem, "The Role of Argumentation in the Miracle Stories of Luke-Acts: Towards a Fuller Identification of Miracle Discourse for Use in Socio-Rhetorical Analysis," in Watson, *The Role of Miracle Discourse*; and a forthcoming volume on priestly discourse.

[7] Robert L. Webb, "Intertexture and Rhetorical Strategy in First Peter's Apocalyptic Discourse: A Study in Sociorhetorical Interpretation," in *Reading First Peter with New Eyes: Methodological Reassessments of 1 Peter* (ed. Robert L. Webb and Betsy Bauman-Martin; LNTS 364; London: T & T Clark, 2007) 72-110; idem and Duane F. Watson, *Reading 2 Peter with New Eyes: Methodological Reassessments of the Letter of 2 Peter* (Library of New Testament Studies: London: T. & T. Clark, 2008).

[8] Including a forthcoming volume of essays on precreation discourse in *Religion and Theology*.

[9] Selections outside the volumes of collected essays include Russell B. Sisson, "Instructions for 'Broker' Apostles: A Socio-Rhetorical Analysis of Matthew's Mission Discourse," in *Rhetorical Argumentation in Biblical Texts: Essays from the Lund 2000 Conference* (ed. A. Eriksson, T. Olbricht, and Walter Übelacker; ESEC 8; Harrisburg, PA: Trinity Press International, 2002) 174-87; idem, "Overcoming the Fear of Death: Physical Body and Community in Hebrews," *Scriptura* 90 (2005) 670-78; Roy R. Jeal, "Clothes Make the (Wo)Man," *Scriptura* 90 (2005) 685-99; idem, "Blending Two Arts: Rhetorical Words, Rhetorical Pictures and Social Formation in the Letter to Philemon," *Sino-Christian Studies* 5 (June 2008); B.J. Oropeza, *Paul and Apostasy: Eschatology, Perseverance, and Falling Away in the Corinthian Congregation* (WUNT 2. Reihe 15; Tübingen: J.C.B. Mohr [Paul Siebeck], 2000/Wipf & Stock, 2007); Wesley H. Wachob, "The Languages of 'Household' and 'Kingdom' in the Letter of James: A Socio-Rhetorical Study," in *Reading James with New Eyes: Methodological Reassessments of the Letter of James* (ed. R.L. Webb and J.S. Kloppenborg; Library of New Testament Studies 342; London/New York: T. & T. Clark, 2007) 151-68.

In this chapter, we will engage in a series of conversations and prospectives that relate the work in this volume to various ongoing discussions and to research and interpretation that will occupy the second volume. Along the way we will use some insights from cognitive sociology to move beyond a discussion of rhetorolects as ICMs to a discussion of their role in social and collective memory among first century Christians. The writings of Eviatar Zerubavel[10] will function as an important resource,[11] since he has worked energetically with a "sociology of thinking," which he calls cognitive sociology, to exhibit the nature of social memories and the relation of social memories to collective memory.[12] Recent work on NT writings by Philip F. Esler and Samuel Byrskog will be used to focus and add perspective to this step in our discussion. Overall, this chapter will invite many voices into the conversation as this volume comes to a close and we move toward the next volume, which will investigate precreation, priestly, miracle, and creedal rhetorolect in early Christianity.

A Conversation with Jerry L. Sumney and Edith M. Humphrey: Chronology

At a review session of the manuscript of this first volume at the Society of Biblical Literature Meetings in San Diego during November 2007, Jerry Sumney and Edith Humphrey criticized the sequence of chapters in the volume. Since most interpreters consider wisdom discourse to be secondary to apocalyptic as a result of emphases within the teaching of Jesus and the letters of Paul, they argued, apocalyptic should have been the first rather than the last topic of research and discussion. At present, many will know, there is a bitter divide in New Testament studies over the chronological relation of wisdom and apocalyptic discourse in both the Q Sayings Gospel and the teaching of the historical Jesus. Both Sumney and Humphrey construed my discussion in this volume to side with those who argue that wisdom discourse preceded apocalyptic discourse in the teaching of Jesus and the Q Sayings Gospel.

[10] Eviatar Zerubavel's writings became known to me through an email from L. Gregory Bloomquist on November 27, 2007, and from Samuel Byrskog's essay, "A New Quest for the *Sitz im Leben*: Social Memory, the Jesus Tradition and the Gospel of Matthew," *NTS* 52 (2006) 319-36, which Samuel told me about on November 26 at the 2007 AAR/SBL meetings in San Diego.

[11] Eviatar Zerubavel, *Hidden Rhythms: Schedules and Calendars in Social Life* (Chicago: University of Chicago Press, 1981); idem, *The Fine Line: Making Distinctions in Everyday Life* (New York: Free Press, 1991); idem, *Social Mindscapes: An Invitation to Cognitive Sociology* (Cambridge, MA: Harvard University Press, 1997); idem, *Time Maps: Collective Memory and the Social Shape of the Past* (Chicago: University of Chicago Press, 2003).

[12] See Eviatar Zerubavel, "Social Memories: Steps to a Sociology of the Past," *Qualitative Sociology* 18 (1996) 283-99; idem, *Social Mindscapes*, 81-99; cf. Byrskog, "A New Quest."

From my perspective, the presentation of wisdom rhetorolect first in this volume should not be construed as a strategy to enter, either implicitly or explicitly, the debate about the priority of wisdom or apocalyptic in the teaching of Jesus or the Q Sayings Gospel. Rather, the analysis and interpretation first of wisdom rhetorolect is based on insights from cognitive science that can help us understand how the earliest extant Christian writings communicated their message in all kinds of regions and locations in the Mediterranean world. The key is the way in which wisdom rhetorolect in the midst of the other five rhetorolects helped to make the unusual message of the earliest Christians accessible, in other words in certain ways "familiar," in unexpected regions and locations throughout the Mediterranean world.

In terms of chronology, it is likely that apocalyptic rhetorolect provided the earliest distinctive characteristics of first century Christian discourse. To understand how first century Christian discourse works cognitively, however, it is important to begin with wisdom rhetorolect. A noticeable feature of the earliest extant Christian literature is a significant presence of wisdom rhetorolect that functions as a medium for communicating the meanings of prophetic, apocalyptic, precreation, priestly, and miracle rhetorolect. A major issue is how Christian discourse could gradually become a dominant discourse in the Mediterranean world, when other religious discourses did not, and how Christian discourse has been able to spread throughout other regions of the world in succeeding centuries to the present. The answer lies, from the perspective of the analysis and interpretation in this volume, in the multiple ways in which "conceptual blending," namely "cognitive mapping between mental spaces,"[13] occurs among wisdom, prophetic, apocalyptic, precreation, priestly, and miracle rhetorolect in the literature that became "canonical" for the Christian movement in the context of the first four centuries of its existence in the Mediterranean world.

Underlying the decision to analyze and interpret wisdom rhetorolect before the other rhetorolects is a presupposition that first century Christian wisdom rhetorolect was a primary medium for communicating the meanings of Christian thought, belief, and practice in the Mediterranean world. Wisdom rhetorolect provided basic cognitive frames during the first century with which people could negotiate the meanings of other rhetorolects in Mediterranean society and culture, it continued to provide those cognitive frames throughout subsequent centuries, and it provides those cognitive frames today. The issue is how Christian thought, belief, and action were appropriated cogni-

[13] Gilles Fauconnier, *Mappings in Thought and Language* (Cambridge: Cambridge University Press, 1997) 149.

tively by large numbers of people in the Mediterranean world, rather than a chronology that insists that wisdom rhetorolect preceded or succeeded apocalyptic rhetorolect in early Christian discourse. At stake is an approach to first century Christian writings that became "canonical" for Christianity that explains the way in which Christian discourse also works today in multiple regions and cultures throughout the world.

The conclusion of our investigation is that people learn basic cognitive frames of wisdom discourse during childhood in the family household. An interesting issue is the degree of adult development of the cognitive frames of wisdom discourse when people blend other cognitive frames of discourse with them. When people encounter discourses that concern the "adult" world of political decisions (prophetic), "special" revelation (apocalyptic), philosophical discourse (precreation), sacrificial discourse (priestly), and healing discourse (miracle), they negotiate them with frames and modes of wisdom argumentation which they learn from childhood and continually make richer and fuller in significantly individual ways as they grow older. These negotiations among frames and modes occur through conceptual blending that takes the form of "overmapping." Adults place various networks of meanings functioning in the "world of adults" over matrices of more basic cognitive networks of meanings they learn as children.[14] These overmappings reconfigure basic cognitive modes of thought, belief, and action by bringing certain topics and patterns into the foreground. This foregrounding, in turn, pushes other topics and patterns into the background. The suppression of certain topics and patterns does not cause them to disappear. They may be experientially excluded, but they remain in the background to reappear at any time that people's minds, for one reason or another, recruit them. The "adult" modes of thought, belief, and action, therefore, do not completely displace the more basic cognitive modes. Often they do, however, establish significantly new "priorities."

New modes of reasoning can establish new priorities in multiple ways. As people's minds push different selections of topics into the background and bring other selections of topics into the foreground, highly different "blendings" emerge. A major issue in different contexts of communication is the dominance of certain blendings over other blendings. The existence of multiple kinds of blendings creates

[14] These overmappings occur through complex processes associated with "final cultural categories" and the "ideological texture" of people's locations, choices, beliefs, and actions; see Robbins, *Exploring the Texture of Texts*, 86-119; idem, *The Tapestry of Early Christian Discourse: Rhetoric, Society and Ideology* (London/New York: Routledge, 1996) 167-236.

environments where "newly blended" networks of meanings regularly have certain kinds of "familiarity" as a result of the presence of very basic modes of reasoning in them. Nevertheless, noticeable kinds of "strangeness" emerge and attract special attention. Communications of various kinds occur in contexts of strangeness, since those things which are unusual are related in various ways to things that are familiar. Thus through various kinds of blendings things are, as F. Gerald Downing captured in a book title, "strangely familiar"[15] at the same time that they are unusually strange.

Inviting George A. Kennedy into the Conversation: Worldly and Radical Rhetoric

The approach in this volume builds on the observation by George A. Kennedy that there is a significant intermingling of "worldly rhetoric" with "radical rhetoric" in the writings in the NT.[16] In our terms, wisdom rhetorolect is grounded in topics and modes of argumentation Kennedy calls "worldly" rhetoric. Wisdom rhetorolect, therefore, is the "worldly rhetoric" that is a primary means by which the meanings of Christian thought, belief, and practice were communicated to people in the Mediterranean world. From a "sociorhetorical" perspective, in other words, a primary reason for the success of the earliest extant Christian literature was the presence of wisdom rhetorolect that contained major aspects of Mediterranean "worldly" rhetoric in its discourse.[17]

Inviting George Lakoff, Mark Johnson, Gilles Fauconnier, Mark Turner, and Critical Spatiality Theorists into the Conversation

George Lakoff and Mark Johnson have shown that metaphors people live by come from the contexts in which they live with their bodies.[18] Gilles Fauconnier and Mark Turner have shown, in turn, that people think by bringing insights from one domain into another domain, namely through metaphoric reasoning.[19] This means that the metaphors

[15] F. Gerald Downing, *Strangely Familiar* (Manchester, 1985).

[16] George A. Kennedy, *New Testament Interpretation through Rhetorical Criticism* (Chapel Hill and London: University of North Carolina Press, 1984).

[17] Vernon K. Robbins, "Rhetography: A New Way of Seeing the Familiar Text," in *Words Well Spoken: George Kennedy's Rhetoric of the New Testament* (ed. C. Clifton Black and D.F. Watson; Waco: Baylor University Press, 2008) 81-106.

[18] George Lakoff and Mark Johnson, *Metaphors We Live By* (Chicago/London: University of Chicago Press, c1980, 2003); Mark Johnson, *The Body in the Mind: The Bodily Basis of Meaning, Imagination, and Reason* (Chicago/London: University of Chicago Press, 1987).

[19] G. Fauconnier and M. Turner, *The Way We Think: Conceptual Blending and the Mind's Hidden Complexities* (New York: Basic Books, 2002).

people use to think, believe, and act emerge in relation to their bodies in certain contexts.

Wisdom Rhetorolect as Family Household Discourse

When humans are born into the world, they are born into some kind of "family" location. The standard location into which children are born in "civilized" society is the family household. The everyday experiences and activities within the family household establish the basic cognitive frames and modes of thought, belief, and action of "wisdom" in humans. First century Christian wisdom rhetorolect is an adult version of wisdom that was developed by people living in the Mediterranean world during the first century who believed that God worked in a special way through Jesus of Nazareth to reveal a way to live in the world that is especially "fruitful." Early Christian wisdom rhetorolect blends human experiences of the family household, one's intersubjective body, and the geophysical world (firstspace) with the cultural space of God's cosmos (secondspace).[20] The goal of wisdom rhetorolect is to create people who produce good action, thought, will, and speech with the aid of God's wisdom.

This means that while the primary cognitive location of first century Christian wisdom rhetorolect is in the family household, its radicality lies in its blending of God and God's created world with the family household. This creates the primary metaphoric mapping in the discourse. In the lived space of blending (thirdspace) in early Christian wisdom rhetorolect, God functions as heavenly Father over God's children in the world, whose bodies are to produce goodness and righteousness through the medium of God's wisdom, which is understood metaphorically as God's light in the world. In this context, wisdom rhetorolect emphasizes "fruitfulness" (productivity and reproductivity).

The time-space (chronotope)[21] of first century Christian wisdom rhetorolect is "household-created world" time. In this context, wisdom time is production-reproduction time. This is "seasonal" time focused on "productivity" in an ongoing cycle of "birth-growth-death." One of the characteristics internal to this "wisdom" belief system is to place ethical expectations on humans in relation both to their

[20] For first, second, and third space, see the discussions of "Critical Spatiality Theory" in David M. Gunn and Paula M. McNutt, *"Imagining" Biblical Worlds: Studies in Spatial, Social and Historical Constructs in Honor of James W. Flanagan* (London: Sheffield Academic Press, 2002).

[21] For chronotope, see M. M. Bakhtin, *The Dialogic Imagination: Four Essays* (ed. Michael Holquist; trans. Caryl Emerson and Michael Holquist; Austin: University of Texas Press, 1981) 84-258, 425-26; Bula Maddison, "Liberation Story or Apocalypse? Reading Biblical Allusion and Bakhtin Theory in Toni Morrison's *Beloved*," in *Bakhtin and Genre Theory in Biblical Studies* (ed. Roland Boer; Semeia Studies 63; Atlanta: SBL, 2007) 161-74.

time in the cycle of life and to their location in God's created world. Thus, different things are expected from full-grown adults, elderly people, young adults, and children, as well as different things from householders, leaders, overseers, stewards, servants, workers, strangers, and dependents. God's time as "productivity" time, therefore, holds humans responsible for their words and deeds in relation both to "the season of their life" and to their location in God's created world.

Christianity gave its foundational wisdom discourse distinctive features by embedding it in a holy family of God the Father, Jesus the only Son of God, and Mary the earthly mother of Jesus. This configuration of a holy family blends the concept of an earthly household containing a mother and a son with the concept of a world created by God, who is Father both of the universe and of the Messiah (*christos*) Jesus, from whom the followers of Jesus received the name Christian (*christianoi*: Acts 11:26; 26:28; 1 Pet 4:16). When this family discourse blends with God's created world, the concept of Holy Spirit blends with Mary, the mother of Jesus, especially through the stories of Jesus' birth, where Jesus is "from the Holy Spirit" (Matt 1:18, 20; cf. Luke 1:35). This blending creates a framework of belief that gradually overmaps the initial concept of the holy family with the Trinity of Father, Son, and Holy Spirit[22] in the Christian creedal rhetorolect of the fourth century.

Prophetic Rhetorolect as Political Kingdom Discourse

Early Christian prophetic rhetorolect blends the speech and action of a prophet's body in an experiential space of God's kingdom on earth (firstspace) with conceptual space of God's cosmos (secondspace). The goal of prophetic rhetorolect is to create a governed realm on earth where God's righteousness is enacted among all of God's people in the realm with the aid of God's specially transmitted word in the form of prophetic action and speech. The metaphoric mapping of early Christian prophetic rhetorolect focuses on God's "earthly kingdom" over which God is heavenly king, in which Jesus is God's prophet-king Messiah, and in which followers of Jesus are authoritative prophets "anointed" for confrontation of people that leads to their rejection and perhaps even their death.

In the space of blending (thirdspace) in early Christian prophetic rhetorolect, God functions as heavenly King over his righteous kingdom on earth. The nature of prophetic rhetorolect is to confront religious and political leaders who act on the basis of human greed, pride, and power rather than God's justice, righteousness, and mercy for all people in

[22] See how the concept of the holy family of Father, Son, and Holy Mary is still present in conversation and dialogue in Qur'an 5:116.

God's kingdom on the earth. The time-space (chronotope) of first century Christian prophetic rhetorolect is "continued" time in the context of the beginning and ending of kingdoms. This continuation provides the occasion for various people to extend the manner of life into the present and future that certain people lived in the past. Since kingdoms have a beginning, middle, and end in the history of God's world, different challenges exist in relation to responsibilities during the beginnings, highpoint, and final days of a kingdom. In order for a kingdom to come into existence, there must be "a call" of a prophet to take unusual actions that provide a context for God to bring a "special" kingdom into existence on earth. Once the kingdom has come into existence, God calls prophets to confront leaders of that kingdom with their violations of agreements God has made with them to establish their special blessings as they live on earth. During a nation's downfall and end, and immediately after these tragic events, prophets turn more and more to visions as a medium of God's communication with them.

Apocalyptic Rhetoric as Imperial Military Discourse

Early Christian apocalyptic rhetorolect blends human experiences of the emperor and his imperial army (firstspace) with God's heavenly temple city (secondspace), which can only be occupied by holy, undefiled people.[23] The goal of this blending is to call people into action and thought guided by perfect holiness. The presupposition of the rhetorolect is that only perfect holiness and righteousness can bring a person into the presence of God, who destroys all evil and gathers all holiness together in God's presence. Apocalyptic redemption, therefore, means the presence of all of God's holy beings in a realm where God's holiness and righteousness are completely and eternally present. In this context, God is not simply "king," but is "*pantocratōr*," an emperor with "almighty" power over all things.

In the space of blending (thirdspace) in early Christian apocalyptic rhetorolect, God functions as a heavenly emperor who gives commands to emissaries to destroy all the evil in the universe and to create a cosmic environment where holy bodies experience perfect well-being in the presence of God. Apocalyptic rhetorolect, then, features destruction of evil and construction of a cosmic environment of perfect well-being.

The time-space (chronotope) of first century Christian apocalyptic rhetorolect is "partitioned" time in a context of "eternal empire" time. This partitioning creates at least the following "parts" of time: (1) before creation; (2) creation; (3) Adam; (4) Noah; (5) Abraham; (6) Moses;

[23] For "empire" conceptuality in first century Christianity, see Warren Carter, *The Roman Empire and the New Testament: An Essential Guide* (Nashville: Abingdon Press, 2006).

(7) David, Solomon, and the kings of Israel; (8) the time of the nations (exile); and (9) "that time" (the end of times or the end of "time").[24] The issue, then, is not the beginning and ending of kingdoms, as in prophetic rhetorolect, but the beginning and ending of "all time" in the context of eras of time from the beginning to the end.

One of the questions our analysis of apocalyptic discourse raises is the presence or absence of "earth material" substances in the heavens and in God's nature. It appears from our search of the literature that this topic has not attracted serious attention in modern scholarship. The account of creation in Genesis 1 gives the impression that God's nature is intimately associated with light, sound, and "moisture" in the form of breath-vapor, but not with earthly substances like clay, stone, and metal. What one would call "earthly" substances, therefore, are perceived to be "outside" of God's internal nature: part of the realm in and through which God "created" things. The account of creation in Genesis 2 pictures God as "forming" animals and humans from "earth." While this account features "earth" as an important inner substance of animals and humans, it does not bring stone and metals into view, nor does it suggest that God's nature is somehow like earth, stone, or metal. No one would anticipate even from Genesis 2, therefore, that animals, humans, God, or any divine beings could have stone (albeit "precious gem-stone") or metal (albeit "refined/purified metal") as part of their inner substance.

The nature of God as fire in prophetic discourse appears to be the context in which the relation of God's nature to earthly substances, namely "fiery coal" (Isa 6:6; Ezek 1:13) and "precious gem-stone" (Ezek 1:4, 27), came into view. In turn, "living creatures" in heaven are a combination of animal, human, and "purified" metal (Ezek 1:5-25). Earth-material apocalyptic elaborates these images and extends them to living beings on earth who are manifestations of political kingdoms (e.g., Dan 7–11).

If we place our observations about locations in a table that displays not only wisdom, prophetic, and apocalyptic rhetorolect discussed in this volume, but also precreation, priestly, and miracle rhetorolect, which will be the subject of the next volume, we get the following table:

[24] See the twelve parts of "that time" or "the end of times" in *4 Ezra* 14:11-12 and *2 Bar.* 27; 53-70. Also, see *4 Ezra* 14:10-18 for the concept that time grows old and weak.

Discourses/Rhetorolects

Jewish/Christian Religious-Theological Belief Systems	Prophetic	Apocalyptic	Wisdom	Precreation	Priestly	Miracle
Locations						
Special Locations	Kingdom	Heavens	Nature	Primordial Realm	Temple	Earthly Physical Bodies; Sea
Bridging Locations			House-hold (family; school-house)	Household (imperial [emperor's])	House-hold (God's)	
	Eternal Realm (future)	Eternal Realm (future)		Eternal realm (timeless)		

Inviting Timothy Beech into the Conversation: Mediterranean Discourses

In a Ph.D. thesis written at St. Paul University, Ottawa, Canada, under the guidance of L. Gregory Bloomquist, Timothy Beech proposed that first century apocalyptic rhetorolect is a localization of Mediterranean "mantic" discourse along with "oracle" discourse.[25] Then in response to a question at his oral defense of the dissertation, he proposed that Hebrew prophetic discourse also is a localization of Mediterranean "mantic" discourse. This would mean that early Christian prophetic and apocalyptic rhetorolect are both localizations of Mediterranean mantic discourse, alongside Greco-Roman oracle discourse, which is another localization of Mediterranean mantic discourse.

The interchange has caused me to expand the insights of Beech beyond first century Christian prophetic and apocalyptic rhetorolect as localizations of Mediterranean mantic discourse. My provisional conclusion is that first century Christian wisdom and precreation rhetorolect are two localizations of Mediterranean philosophical discourse. Wisdom rhetorolect is a localization of Mediterranean moral philosophical discourse, and precreation rhetorolect is a localization of Mediterranean speculative philosophical discourse. In addition, first century Christian priestly and miracle rhetorolect are two localizations of Mediterranean ritual discourse. This produces the following table, which points toward discussions that will be developed in the second volume:

[25] Timothy Beech, "A Socio-Rhetorical Analysis of the Development and Function of the Noah-Flood Narrative in *Sibylline Oracles* 1-2," Ph.D. dissertation, Saint Paul University, Ottawa, Canada, 2008.

Discourses / Rhetorolects

Mediterranean Discourses	Mantic Discourses (Divine Communications)		Philosophical Discourses (Mental Searching)		Ritual Discourses (Religious Actions)	
Jewish/Christian Religious-Theological Belief Systems	Prophetic	Apocalyptic	Wisdom	Precreation	Priestly	Miracle

Inviting College Students and M.M. Bakhtin into the Conversation: Belief Systems

As I faced the challenge during Spring 2008 of communicating to a new class of Emory College students the nature of early Christian rhetorolects, instead of introducing the word "rhetorolect" I used the combined phrase "Discourses/Belief Systems." The students immediately gravitated to the phrase "belief systems," never using the term "discourse"! As I reflected on this, I realized that I myself had used M.M. Bakhtin's understanding of belief systems in Chapter 4 on wisdom rhetorolect (p. 148, n. 33), where he defines a belief system as "the circle of one's vision" or "conceptual horizon."[26]

It seems to have helped the students that I never once used the term "rhetorolect" in the class room, and I do not insist on using the word "discourse." To them, what I have called rhetorolects throughout this volume are alternative belief systems that blend with one another in early Christian writings.

The college students in my class seem to have no difficulty with the idea that there could be multiple, different belief systems functioning in first century Christian writings and in Christian writings today. Indeed they have become energized by the possibility of multiple belief systems in first century Christian writings, and they would like more class time to "practice" identifying, discussing, and interpreting the major, alternative belief systems that were present, and in some reconfigured way are still present today. They also are intrigued by the way these belief systems blend with one another. They consider this blending to be similar to the blending that occurs when they purchase a "smoothie" at the Cox Hall Food Court. Indeed, they know that when different things are blended together in the smoothies they order, some things remain quite "chunky," while other things blend together so thoroughly that it is almost impossible to identify their particular characteristics, except that they know they are there! Then their next question regularly is, "Exactly how are the belief systems

[26] Bakhtin, *The Dialogical Imagination*, 425. The editors explain that "When the term [Russian: *krugozory*] is used on a global or societal scale we have rendered it as 'belief system'; when it refers to the local vantage point of an individual, as 'conceptual horizon'."

related to inner texture, intertexture, social-cultural texture, ideological texture, and sacred texture?" This takes us to our next conversation.

Inviting *Exploring the Texture of Texts* into the Conversation: Deity, Holy Persons, Spirit Beings

As I was writing this volume, colleagues asked me regularly about the relationship of early Christian rhetorolects to the sociorhetorical textures discussed in publications that appeared in 1996.[27] Gradually I have become convinced that the first century Christian rhetorolects discussed in this volume came into view as a result of applying the analytical strategies of "sacred texture"[28] to the inner, inter-, social-cultural, and ideological texture of writings that emerged during the first four centuries of the Christian era. As a result of this awareness, it is now possible to present an initial discussion and display of the dimensions of the six rhetorolects on the basis of the topics of sacred texture as they were presented in 1996: deity, holy persons, spirit beings, divine history, human redemption, human commitment, religious community, and ethics. Let us begin with deity, holy persons, and spirit beings.[29] Then as we discuss the other topics, we will bring other people into the conversation.

A key to understanding the changing role of deity, holy persons, and spirit beings in the six rhetorolects lies in the studies of Fauconnier and Turner. In their discussion of simplex networks, Fauconnier and Turner introduce the relation of frames to character in blending processes. From our perspective, rhetorolects are cultural frames that are so robust they are idealized cognitive models (ICMs).[30] When Fauconnier and Turner describe a frame in the context of explaining a simplex network, they say: "An especially simple kind of integration network is one in which human cultural and biological history has provided an effective frame that applies to certain kinds of elements as values, and that frame is in one input space and some of those kinds of elements are in the other input space."[31] For an example they use the "readily available frame of human kinship," which is "*the family*, which includes roles for father, mother, child, and so on."[32]

[27] Vernon K. Robbins, *Exploring the Texture of Texts: A Guide to Socio-Rhetorical Interpretation* (Harrisburg, PA: Trinity Press International, 1996); idem, *The Tapestry of Early Christian Discourse: Rhetoric, Society, and Ideology* (London: Routledge, 1996). See the description of the approach in W. Randolph Tate, "Socio-Rhetorical Criticism," in idem, *Interpreting the Bible: A Handbook of Terms and Methods* (Peabody, MA: Hendrickson, 2006) 342-46.

[28] Robbins, *Exploring the Texture of Texts*, 120-31.

[29] Ibid., 120-23.

[30] Lakoff, *Women, Fire, and Dangerous Things*, 68-76.

[31] Fauconnier and Turner, *The Way We Think*, 120.

[32] Ibid.

From our perspective, Fauconnier and Turner's discussion of the family as a human kinship network applies to the experientially grounded (firstspace) frame that first century Christians built up into an ICM we call wisdom rhetorolect. In their discussion, Fauconnier and Turner introduce two human beings, Paul and Sally, who blend through cross-space mapping in a simplex network that is a "Frame to values connection – that is, an organized bundle of role connectors. In this case, the role *father* connects to the value *Paul* and the role *daughter* connects to the value *Sally*."[33] In first century Christian wisdom rhetorolect, there is, first, a frame to values blend that connects the role Heavenly Father to God and the role earthly Son to Jesus. Second, this simplex network has a potentiality of blending with any number of "fathers," "mothers," "sons," and "daughters" with or without specific names in Christian "stories."[34] In this context, the father-son "frame to values" simplex network may blend with people in Christian stories in the form of mirror networks, single-scope networks, double-scope networks,[35] or even multiple-scope integration networks.[36]

The value "Paul" blends into the first century Christian wisdom "family" network when Paul himself sends a letter that says, "For though you might have ten thousand guardians in Christ, you do not have many fathers. Indeed, in Christ Jesus I became your father through the gospel" (1 Cor 4:15). In this communication the role father connects to the value Paul in such a way that it invites the Corinthians to recruit first century Christian wisdom rhetorolect, which supports Paul's speaking to them in an instructive, didactic mode. Paul fills this frame with discourse when he says: "I am not writing this to make you ashamed, but to admonish you as my beloved children.... I appeal to you, then, be imitators of me. For this reason I sent you Timothy, my beloved and faithful child in the Lord, to remind you of my ways in Christ Jesus, as I teach them everywhere in every church" (1 Cor 4:14, 16-17). In this wisdom rhetorolect, the role father connects to the value Paul in such a manner that the role child connects to the value Timothy, who has learned from his "father" Paul and can transmit what he has learned from his father to

[33] Ibid.

[34] I am grateful to Gilles Fauconnier for sharpening this issue for me both in emails before the November, 2007, SBL Conference in San Diego and in the session with him during the meeting. He clarified the importance of the people in the blends in the rhetorolects by responding in particular to my discussion of role, value, identity, and character in Vernon K. Robbins, "Conceptual Blending and Early Christian Imagination," in *Explaining Christian Origins and Early Judaism: Contributions from Cognitive and Social Science* (ed. Petri Luomanen, Ilkka Pyysiäinen, and Risto Uro; Biblical Interpretation Series 89; Leiden/Boston: Brill, 2007) 184-92 [161-95].

[35] Fauconnier and Turner, *The Way We Think*, 122-35.

[36] Ibid., 299-308.

Paul's other "children" (Timothy's "brothers and sisters") in the Corinthian church through an activity of "teaching."

When the frame shifts from human kinship, in which wisdom rhetorolect is grounded, to the readily available frame of political kingship, in which prophetic rhetorolect is gounded, the frame contains "political interlocutors," who function in roles of king, prophet, emissaries, and so on. The existence of the Herodian dynasty during much of the first century CE provided an experientially grounded (firstspace) frame for early Christian prophetic rhetorolect to be built up into an ICM. In this context, the frame to values connection in the story of Israel played a role through people like David and Nathan (2 Sam 7); Uzziah, Jeroboam, and Amos (Amos 1:1); Josiah, Jehoiakin, Zedekiah, and Jeremiah (Jer 1:1-3); and many others. In this "Israelite story," the values David, Uzziah, Jeroboam, Josiah, Jehoiakin, and Zedekiah connect to the role king and the values Nathan, Amos, and Jeremiah connect to the role prophet. First century Christian prophetic rhetorolect, which is grounded in the frame to values connection in the political kingship simplex network, blends into this network the values God connected to the role Heavenly Father-King and the value Jesus connected to the role earthly-Son King-Messiah. In this frame-shifting to prophetic rhetorolect, the wisdom Father-Son frame to values blend does not disappear. Rather, it blends with the prophetic King-Messiah frame to values network in a manner that places the Kingship of God and the Messiahship of Jesus in the foreground, supported by the Fatherhood of God and the Sonship of Jesus in the background.

When the Christian story introduces someone like "Paul" into the prophetic political kingship blend, we begin to see how the different rhetorolects worked in first century Christian discourse. It did not work right to connect either the role "king" or the role "messiah" to the value Paul. Therefore, another role had to be recruited from the network for Paul. One of the natural roles for the value Paul in the "God-King/Jesus-Messiah" network was "prophet," one who receives divine messages from God-King and delivers them to earthly kings, leaders, and members of the political kingdom. Paul, of course, would not be confronting Jesus-Messiah-King, like the prophets of Israel might. Thus the role had to be reconfigured. Paul reconfigured the language of prophet to "apostle" as he localized the prophetic network in his discourse. The reconfiguration worked in the context of Paul's "identity" and "character," to which we must turn next. Paul's identity does not allow the role king or messiah to be connected to him. Therefore, the role prophet is the natural candidate. But Paul's character in his letters is not one that foregrounds his confrontation of kings. In his discourse, therefore, Paul reconfigures the language of "prophet" through a "prophet-wisdom blend" into the language of "apostle," one sent by both God and Messiah Jesus to create "families" belonging to both God and Christ. The prophetic-wisdom blend foregrounds Paul's authority to confront people with a specific message he has been given by God and Messiah Jesus to deliver to people, but it also supports Paul's presentation of this message in a didactic, "fatherly" mode for the purpose of building "family-communities."

Another readily available frame during the first century CE was "imperial domain," which includes roles for emperor, emperor's son, ruling elite, military forces, and elite alliances, all supported by divine sanction and elite values.[37] From our perspective, first century Christians built up both apocalyptic and precreation rhetorolect on this experientially grounded (firstspace) frame. Apocalyptic rhetorolect emphasized the presence of God's ruling elite (Son of man, angels, etc.) while precreation rhetorolect emphasized the presence of God's heavenly household, God's imperial son, and elite alliances established through the emperor's son. We will not discuss precreation rhetorolect here, since this is a major topic for the second volume. When Paul's discourse places him within the apocalyptic imperial domain frame, the role of seer who receives "revelations" connects to the value Paul. Paul received a special "gospel" through "a revelation of Jesus Christ" (Gal 1:12). This enabled him not only to speak as a teacher of "knowledge or prophecy or teaching," but as one who could speak with "a revelation" that would benefit his hearers (1 Cor 14:6). Indeed, Paul had received special "visions and revelations of the Lord" in which he had been caught up into the third heaven (2 Cor 12:2). This allowed him to "speak God's wisdom, in mystery, which God decreed before the ages for our glory," which no earthly rulers understood (1 Cor 2:7).

Blending wisdom with apocalyptic, Paul presents himself and his associates "as servants of Christ and stewards of God's mysteries" (1 Cor 4:1). In addition, Paul knows a special apocalyptic mystery concerning how "we will all be changed, in a moment, in the twinkling of an eye, at the last trumpet" (1 Cor 15:51-52). Indeed, Paul "knows" that at the coming of Christ all who belong to Christ will rise up in the resurrection (1 Cor 15:23; 1 Thess 4:16), after which will come the end, when Christ "hands over the kingdom to God the Father, after he has destroyed every ruler and every authority and power" (1 Cor 15:24). In first century Christian discourse, then, the value Paul not only connects to the roles of teacher of wisdom and prophetic apostle of the gospel, but also to the role of apocalyptic seer of the resurrection of God's Messiah, the coming again of God's Messiah, the resurrection of the dead, and the end time. In other words, multiple frames blend with

[37] Carter, *The Roman Empire and the New Testament*, 1-13.

one another to make a robust belief system filled with networks of human kinship, political kingship, and imperial domain.

When a value like Elizabeth, Zechariah, Mary the mother of Jesus, John the Baptist, Peter, Mary Magdalene, Judas, James, or Stephen is present in a network, identity and character function dynamically to limit, direct, or reconfigure relationships in the blending. As Fauconnier and Turner state: "It is a central aspect of human understanding to think that people have characters that manifest themselves as circumstances change.... Character transports over frames and remains recognizable in all of them."[38] During the first century, Christians found a way for the identity and character of God and Jesus to transport over six major cultural frames: wisdom, prophetic, apocalyptic, precreation, priestly, and miracle. Both the character of God and the character of Jesus became more robust as the six rhetorolects blended with one another. In first century Christian discourse, God functions as Father (wisdom); King (prophetic); Almighty Emperor (apocalyptic; precreation); Holy God (priestly); and Divine Power (miracle) with multiple roles in multiple blends. In turn, Jesus functions as Son (wisdom); Messiah (prophetic); Son of Man (apocalyptic); Word (precreation); High Priest (priestly); and Son of God/Son of David (miracle), again with multiple roles in multiple blends. For first century Christians, the identity and character of both God and Jesus allowed them to function robustly in multiple "cultural roles" in the six different frames (rhetorolects).

Interpreters have much to do, of course, to "update" our understanding of how blending works in relation to identity and character in both God and Jesus in first century Christian writings. But the other major topic is, "What about all the people in the 'story' of Israel as well as the unfolding story of Christianity?" This is where the story-lines discussed in this volume become important in the discussion of blending in rhetorolects. First century Christians were able to find a robust role in at least four of the six rhetorolects for people like Moses. Some people however, like Solomon, only functioned prominently in one rhetorolect (in this instance, wisdom). In other words, first century Christians "presupposed" that God functioned robustly in all six frames (rhetorolects), and they "built up" the character of Jesus to function robustly not only in wisdom, prophetic, and apocalyptic rhetorolect, but also, as we will see in the next volume, in precreation, priestly, and miracle rhetorolect. But they did not try, or not were not able, to build up the character of every "biblical" or "Christian" person in such a way that they functioned dynamically in all six rhetorolects. Rather, "identity" and "character" put certain "biblical" and "Christian" people

[38] Fauconnier and Turner, *The Way We Think*, 249.

either decidedly in the background of certain rhetorolect story-lines, or it eliminated them altogether from a particular story-line.

The relation of frame to identity and character, then, is a highly important issue in analysis and interpretation of conceptual blending in early Christian discourse. Fauconnier and Turner list five character types: saint, diplomat, hooker (prostitute), mediator, and conqueror. Then they say: "Construing *prostitute* as just a general frame, we can investigate character by asking how such a character would perform in that frame."[39] Then they ask how "Mother Teresa, Margaret Thatcher, Cleopatra, or Bill Clinton would operate within the prostitute frame." They observe that Mother Teresa's character (saint) might reveal itself in acceptance of "the sacrifice with fortitude, by never complaining, by trusting God." But "the frame cannot impinge upon her character, for 'To the pure, all things pure'."[40] Therefore, character will prevent her from ever becoming a prostitute. In the case of Mary Magdalene, they suggest, there is a requirement of a change in character from prostitute to saint.[41] This is a very important discussion for the first century Christian rhetorolects. The rhetorolects I have introduced suggest that both God and Jesus somehow fill both the frames and the roles internal to wisdom, prophetic, apocalyptic, precreation, priestly, and miracle rhetorolect. But how do God and Jesus operate within each frame? How many "biblical" people from the "story of Israel" may operate within each frame? Then how do people in the "Christian" story-lines operate within each frame?

One of the key aspects of early Christian discourse is its presentation of Jesus as a character who is transportable over many different frames and activities. The transportability has certain limits, but the nature of the different frames is truly remarkable, since a significant number of the frames have counterfactual relationships to one another.[42] There are frames that present Jesus with seemingly unlimited power, juxtaposed with frames that present Jesus with power so limited that people are able to kill him and bury him. There are frames that limit Jesus to a human personage born on earth, and frames that present Jesus as a cosmic being who existed "before all other things were created." There are frames that limit Jesus to a human personage who "loves even his enemies," and frames that present Jesus as destroying people on earth with a two-edged sword that comes out of his mouth. There are frames that present Jesus as "a friend of prostitutes and tax-collectors," and there are frames that present Jesus as the

[39] Ibid., 253.
[40] Ibid.
[41] Ibid.
[42] Ibid., 31-32, 87-88, 218-19, 224-31, 238-47. I am grateful to L. Gregory Bloomquist for continually pursuing the issue of counterfactuality in the rhetorolects.

perfect, holy high priest in the heavens. On the one hand, the rhetorolects blend Jesus with six major "character types": sage; prophet; end-time seer and judge; eternal being; priest; and miracle worker. On the other hand, the rhetorolects blend Jesus with six major cultural frames: wisdom; prophetic; apocalyptic; precreation; priestly; and miracle.[43]

Deity, Holy Persons, and Spirit Beings

Mediterranean Discourses	Mantic Discourses (Divine Communications)		Philosophical Discourses (Mental Searching)		Ritual Discourses (Religious Actions)	
Jewish/Christian Religious-Theological Belief Systems	Prophetic	Apocalyptic	Wisdom	Precreation	Priestly	Miracle
Deity						
God (Jesus): Robbins, *Exploring*, 120-121;	God as Cosmic King	God as Cosmic Military Emperor	God as Cosmic Father of the Earth	God as Cosmic Emperor Father of All; Jesus as Divine Logos	God as Holy	God as Power
Holy Persons						
Jesus: Robbins, *Exploring*, 121-122	Jesus as Prophet	Jesus as Son of Man	Jesus as Son/Teacher	Emanations from God: Wisdom (Sophia), Word (Logos); Jesus as Light/ Witness to God the Father	Jesus as Sacrifice/ High Priest	Jesus as Healer/ Miracle Worker
Multiple-Role Holy Persons	Moses		Moses		Moses	Moses
	Daniel	Daniel	Daniel			
	Samuel				Samuel	
Other Persons	Prophets, Kings: Isaiah, Jeremiah, Hosea, Amos, David, [Abraham]	Seers: Noah, Daniel, Ezekiel, Joel	Sages, Teachers: Solomon, Job		Priests: Aaron, Levi	Miracle Workers: Elijah, Elisha,
Spirit Beings						
Jesus: Robbins, *Exploring*, 123		[Heavenly Son of Man]	Wisdom	Paraclete, [Light]		
Other Spirit Beings	Angels	Angels			Angels	Angels
		Satan				
		Unclean spirits/ demons				Unclean spirits/ demons

[43] Cf. Robbins, "Conceptual Blending and Early Christian Imagination," 188-89.

In this volume, we have discussed not only how God and Jesus function within the three frames of first century Christian wisdom, prophetic, and apocalyptic discourse. We have also discussed how certain "biblical" people in the story of Israel either function in them or are not included in them during the first century. In addition, we have discussed some of the ways Paul himself functions in the "Christian story-lines" of first century Christian wisdom, prophetic, and apocalyptic rhetorolect. But there is much work left to be done. An initial attempt to display the appearance of major personages (deity, holy persons, and spirit beings) in the six rhetorolects has produced the table above. The table does not try to include the function of people like John the Baptist, Zechariah, Elizabeth, Mary the mother of Jesus, John the Baptist, Herod, Peter, Judas, Mary Magdalene, James, etc. in the frames. Nor does it analyze, describe, and interpret the function of unnamed people like Pharisees, Sadducees, scribes, tax collectors, etc. in the frames. This means that much work remains to be done to describe the manner in which identity and character transport across the frames in the six major first century Christian rhetorolects.

Inviting John D. Caputo into the Conversation: Story-Lines in Divine History

The next "sacred texture" category in *Exploring the Texture of Texts* is "divine history." In this analytical frame, "divine powers direct historical processes and events toward certain results."[44] At this point, it is important to invite John D. Caputo into the conversation. His book *The Weakness of God* programmatically explores the content of names as "events."[45] Of special importance is the way in which "Events are what names 'mean' in the sense of what they are getting at, what they are trying to actualize, the source of their restlessness, the endless ends toward which names reach out, hurling themselves forward toward something, I know not what, toward God knows what."[46] In his presentation, names are "events" that are known by their uncontainabilty, translatability, deliteralization, excess, and evil, and which are beyond being, constitute the "truth" of a name, and have an irreducibly temporal character.[47]

Caputo's discussion explains how and why most of the "events" in the story-lines of the six first century Christian rhetorolects are "names." The issue is a theological hermeneutics which "tries to fol-

[44] Robbins, *Exploring the Texture of Texts*, 123.

[45] John D. Caputo, *The Weakness of God: A Theology of the Event* (Bloomington/Indianapolis: Indiana University Press, 2006).

[46] Ibid., 3.

[47] Ibid., 2–7.

low the tracks of the name of God, to stay on the trail it leaves behind as it makes its way through our lives."[48] Of special importance is his description of a "bipolarity" in theology. In his words, "theology is a house divided against itself … it lacks self-understanding to the point that it is intellectually bipolar, vacillating wildly between the heights of power and the depths of weakness."[49] In my terms, where there is wisdom about loving one's enemy, this wisdom blends conceptually with

Divine History/Story-Lines (Names as Events)

	Prophetic	Apocalyptic	Wisdom	Precreation	Priestly	Miracle
Robbins, *Exploring*, 123-125				Emanations from God: Wisdom (Sophia), Word (Logos)		
		Creation: angel-spirits to watch over all creation	Creation: tree of the knowledge of good and evil			
		Adam: death				
		Noah: flood				
	Abraham					
	Moses	Moses: ten plagues	Moses: Torah		Moses Aaron Levi	Moses: Miracles
	[Elijah, Elisha]					Miracle Workers: Elijah, Elisha
	Samuel				Samuel	
	David		[David: Psalms as Wisdom]			
			Solomon: Proverbs			
	Amos, Isaiah, Jeremiah, Hosea, Micah, etc.					
			Job			
		Jonah				
		Ezekiel				
	Daniel	Daniel: Babylon	Daniel			
		Joel				

power that judges and destroys. Where there is prophetic confrontation that judges, this prophetic confrontation blends conceptually with wisdom that says he who judges shall be judged. The question at any

[48] Ibid., 7.
[49] Ibid., 7-8.

point is what rhetorolects are overmapping one another and how. The real complexity is that two, three, or four "naming" discourses "team up" at times either with or against one or two others that are blended together. We will see in the next volume that where there is love before creation, it blends with judgment in the present. Likewise, where there is sacrifice that redeems, there is killing that judges. The bipolarity is so complex and so convoluted that it blends conceptualities "all which ways" in its attempts to express itself. All of this requires "continual conceptual blending." What Caputo attempts through deconstruction, therefore, this volume attempts through conceptual blending. An initial table of names as events in the six major first century Christian rhetorolects is offered above.

In sociorhetorical terms, these names emerge from the descriptive-narrative structuring in the rhetorolects that produce rhetography,[50] the image-schemas and pictures that invite people's minds to recruit plot-lines and story-lines in the history of the world God produced through his act of creating. In this volume, we have explored three of the six story-lines: wisdom, prophetic, and apocalyptic.

The Story-Line of Wisdom: Creation, Moses, Solomon, and Jesus

Resources for the wisdom story-line lie in Genesis, the Deuteronomic literature, literature attributed to Solomon, the psalms, the prophetic literature, and common knowledge about people who sow grain, bake bread, herd sheep, sweep their houses, and tend vineyards. This means there are four basic rhetorical resources for early Christian wisdom rhetorolect: (1) Torah wisdom; (2) wisdom story; (3) proverbial wisdom, and (4) argumentative wisdom. The resource for Torah wisdom lies primarily in statements that God told to Moses and Moses told to Israel. Resources for wisdom story lie in traditions about people like Joseph and Daniel, but in many other places as well. Resources for proverbial wisdom lie in traditions about Solomon and other people like Job in the Hebrew Bible, in Hellenistic Jewish literature both inside and outside the OT Apocrypha, and in Hellenistic-Roman moral philosophical literature of various kinds. Resources for argumentative wisdom are especially rich in the sphere of Hellenistic literature, both Jewish and Hellenistic-Roman. Sirach 40-48, in particular, exhibits a wisdom story-line of famous people on earth. The resources for early Christian wisdom rhetorolect, therefore, are both deep and wide in the Hebrew Bible, in Hellenistic Jewish literature, and in Hellenistic-Roman literature contemporary with early Christianity. The story-line features God as giver of wisdom and a prestigious line of wise people

[50] Robbins, "Rhetography."

down to Jesus, who possessed special wisdom, and people after Jesus, who continued, and continue today, to present the wisdom of God to others.

The Prophetic Story-Line: Abraham, Moses, Prophets, Kings, Exile

In first century Christian prophetic rhetorolect, God functions as King of the heavens and focuses in a special way on people God has chosen and called to enact and exhibit righteousness and justice on earth. When Jesus functions as God's Messiah on earth, his rule as earthly king blends with the fate of God's prophets. This creates a curious blend of earthly king and earthly prophet, where God authorizes an earthly prophetic king to die a kingly prophetic death. The first century Christian focus on Jesus as an earthly Messiah therefore blends three spaces – God's kingship in heaven, God's kingdom on earth where God's Messiah was killed, and God's special people who believe in Jesus as God's Messiah.

Rather than focusing on people from childhood to adulthood, prophetic rhetorolect focuses on the responsibilities of adult leaders to fulfill God's will to have a special kingdom of righteous people on earth. The effect of prophetic rhetorolect in first century Christian discourse was not only the production of distinctively authorized confrontational modes in the Mediterranean world but also the production of story-lines that validated the authorization. There are three basic rhetorical resources for early Christian prophetic rhetorolect: (1) the story of Abraham; (2) the story of Moses; and (3) stories and oracles of prophets and kings during the time of kings over Israel.

The image-description structuring (rhetography) of early Christian prophetic rhetorolect emphasizes the relation of events in God's renewed kingdom on earth to God's initial inauguration of and communication with a chosen kingdom of Israel. This structuring produces a sequential history that begins with Israel in the past, continues with Israel in exile through the time of the emergence of Christianity, gains new momentum with the story of Jesus in the context of the exile of Israel, and continues after the death and resurrection of Jesus in the lives of Jesus' followers. Instead of simply creating a picture, the story-lines in first century Christian prophetic rhetorolect function as emergent structures for assertions, arguments, and stories based on: (1) specific people (including the speech of "personified scripture"); (2) specific "event-pictures";[51] (3) specific stories; and (4) a series of

[51] An event-picture evokes a situation that implies a specific action or set of actions. Therefore, rather than simply picturing a "situation" like a household, it pictures a context in which an event took place but does not present a story of the event.

events that comprise an "overall story." Since kingdoms have a beginning, middle, and end in the history of God's world, different challenges exist in relation to responsibilities during the beginnings, highpoint, and final days of a kingdom. In order for a kingdom to come into existence, there must be "a call" of a prophet to take unusual actions that provide a context for God to bring a "special" kingdom into existence on earth. Once the kingdom has come into existence, God calls prophets to confront leaders of that kingdom with their violations of agreements God has made with them to establish their special blessings as they live on earth. During a nation's downfall and end, and immediately after these tragic events, prophets turn more and more to visions as a medium of God's communication with them. These dynamics inform the prophetic story-line in God's world. First century Christian prophetic rhetorolect produced multiple story-lines in which John the Baptist, Jesus, and followers of Jesus "continue" the lives of various prophets in the past through their confrontation of immoral and unjust practices, which brings them rejection, suffering, and even death.

The Apocalyptic Story-Line: Adam, Enoch, Noah, Sodom, Gomorrah, Egypt, Son of Man, Resurrection of the Dead

In apocalyptic rhetorolect, the discourse introduces theses, rationales, and conclusions to the hearer/reader through exceptionally picturesque scenes. The specificity and concreteness of apocalyptic discourse lies in revelation to specific people, display of very detailed descriptions of beings (God, beasts, evil personages, good personages), display of spaces (bountiful gardens, beautiful cities, spaces of punishment, spaces of worship, altars, temples, walls), and display of procedures (programmatic destruction of portions of the earth, specific procedures of torture, specific processes of journey of a righteous soul into heaven and then into the paradise of jubilation, specific processes of journeys through the heavens and throughout the cosmos).[52]

Apocalyptic produces a periodization of history that names a sequence of eras. Writings in the New Testament focus especially on six eras in the Hebrew Bible as they create an apocalyptic story of God's world:

[52] John J. Collins, ed., *Apocalypse: The Morphology of a Genre* (Semeia 14; Chico, CA: Scholars Press, 1979); idem, *Jewish Wisdom in the Hellenistic Age* (Louisville: Westminster John Knox, 1997); idem, *The Apocalyptic Imagination: An Introduction to Jewish Apocalyptic Literature* (2nd ed.; Grand Rapids: Eerdmans, 1998); idem, ed., *The Encyclopedia of Apocalypticism* (vol. 1 of *The Origins of Apocalypticism in Judaism and Christianity;* New York: Continuum, 1998); Adela Yarbro Collins, "Early Christian Apocalyptic Literature," *ANRW* 25.6:4666–4711; Gregory Cary and L. Gregory Bloomquist, *Vision and Persuasion: Rhetorical Dimensions of Apocalyptic Discourse* (St. Louis, MO: Chalice, 1999).

1. The time in which Satan, who is understood to be an evil angel cast out of heaven by God, successfully tempted Adam and Eve. Satan, working through Eve, caused God to cast Adam and Eve out of the Garden of Eden, and Satan continually causes people to go astray in the present;
2. God's taking of Enoch into heaven, where he oversaw God's destruction of the world through a flood and the rescue of Noah by means of an ark that floated on the water;
3. God's destruction of Sodom and Gomorrah with fire from heaven;
4. God's sending of ten plagues against the Egyptians;
5. God's empowerment of "one like a son of man" in the heavens to have authority and power over kingdoms on earth;
6. God's development of a process of resurrection of the dead as a way to transport faithful people who have died away from an environment of divine destruction into an environment of eternal well-being.

For the Christian apocalyptic story, these periods of time became important for God's apocalyptic transformations of Jesus, and for the eventual transformation of believers.

In addition to Jesus Christ and believers, the world is a focus of God's activities of transformation in early Christian apocalyptic rhetorolect. Within time, there will come a period when God brings all things to an end and will create a special era beyond time.

Inviting Seanna Coulson into the Conversation: Human Redemption

In the midst of a discussion of deity, holy persons, spirit beings, and divine history, human redemption is a topic of great importance for first century Christian rhetorolects. In *Exploring the Texture of Texts*, I wrote that human redemption

> is the transmission of benefit from the divine to humans as a result of events, rituals, or practices. As a result of things that happen or could happen if people do them, divine powers will transform human lives and take them into a higher level of existence. Perhaps the result will be the changing of the mortal nature of humans – namely, a state of existence that leads to death – into an immortal nature, a state where they will no longer die. Or perhaps a burden of impurity or guilt is removed in such a manner that a person is liberated from powers or practices that are debilitating and destructive.[53]

When I look back on this description of human redemption, I realize that I was describing some of the alternatives within the first cen-

[53] Robbins, *Exploring the Texture of Texts*, 125-26.

tury Christian rhetorolects. What is the view of human redemption in any one rhetorolect? Is it possible to describe the nature of human redemption foregrounded in each of the six major first century Christian rhetorolects?

Especially as I was working with the issue of the nature of human redemption in each of the six rhetorolects, I became aware of the importance of "frame shifting" as Seanna Coulson has discussed it in her book entitled *Semantic Leaps*.[54] She describes frame-shifting as an emergence of meaning "from the integration of linguistic and nonlinguistic knowledge, as meaning and background are intimately intertwined."[55] Thus, she says, "Understanding which space is being built, and consequently which background frames are relevant, often proves crucial for understanding the overall significance of a linguistic utterance."[56]

Frame-shifting is particularly important in first century Christian writings about human redemption. Let us take, for example, Mark 8:34–9:1. This unit begins with:

> If any want to become my followers, let them deny themselves and take up their cross and follow me. [35]For those who want to save their life will lose it, and those who lose their life for my sake, and for the sake of the gospel, will save it. [36]For what will it profit them to gain the whole world and forfeit their life? [37]Indeed, what can they give in return for their life? (Mark 8:34-37)

This appears quite clearly to be some kind of wisdom discourse. There are two rationales (8:35-36) that support a conditional clause (8:34) that presupposes that following Jesus will bring some kind of human redemption. This redemption comes from a paradoxical wisdom about gaining life by losing it, accompanied by the insight that attempting to save one's own life will only lead to losing it. As Robert C. Tannehill has said, "The saying *intends* to be a paradox."[57] This paradoxical wisdom is supported by two rhetorical questions, one that asserts that attempting to gain the whole world will only cause one to forfeit one's life and another that presupposes that there is nothing a person can give in return for their life.

So where can a person recruit meaning for this argumentative sequence? It would seem to lie in some kind of cultural frame of paradoxical wisdom. In a broad Mediterranean context, the cultural frame would seem to lie in some kind of Cynic wisdom like one sees in

[54] Seanna Coulson, *Semantic Leaps: Frame-Shifting and Conceptual Blending in Meaning Construction* (Cambridge: Cambridge University Press, 2001).

[55] Ibid., 31.

[56] Ibid., 32.

[57] Robert C. Tannehill, *The Sword of His Mouth* (SBLSemeiaSup 1; Philadelphia: Fortress Press and Missoula, MT: Scholars Press, 1975) 99.

Epictetus: "If you want to be crucified, just wait. The cross will come. If it seems reasonable to comply, and the circumstances are right, then it's to be carried through, and your integrity maintained" (*Diatr.* 2.2.10).[58] In addition, one finds: "[S]ome persons, like cattle, are interested in nothing but their fodder; for to all of you that concern yourselves with property and lands and slaves and one office or another, all this is nothing but fodder!" (*Diatr.* 2.14.24).[59]

But the cultural frame shifts in Mark 8:38–9:1:

> Those who are ashamed of me and of my words in this adulterous and sinful generation, of them the Son of Man will also be ashamed when he comes in the glory of his Father with the holy angels.' And he said to them, 'Truly I tell you, there are some standing here who will not taste death until they see that the kingdom of God has come with power.' (Mark 8:38–9:1)

A reader who has no ability to shift the frame from paradoxical wisdom to first century Christian apocalyptic rhetorolect will not be able to understand the meaning of these verses. Frame-shifting occurs in the sequence of statements away from paradoxical wisdom that might be informed by a Cynic-Stoic orientation to an apocalyptic view. In other words, in the sequence of statements there is a shift of frame from a perspective where a person achieves some form of "redemption" by learning a particular philosophical view and adopting a particular lifestyle to a perspective where a heavenly figure called "the Son of man" will come to judge people's lives according to principles of God's rule that come from Jewish heritage and will bring in God's kingdom, understood as an era of the end time.

What kind of human redemption is in view in the sequence in Mark 8:34-9:1, then? It is not a redemption that paradoxically comes in the context of a particular philosophical lifestyle on earth, but that comes through action inaugurated by God understood through Jewish heritage, who will redeem not only humans but the entire created world. To understand the sequence more completely, however, it is necessary to analyze and interpret the particular blending of first century Christian wisdom, prophetic, and apocalyptic rhetorolect that occurs in the frame-shifting in these verses. An initial display of alternative forms of human redemption in the six first century Christian rhetorolects looks as follows:

[58] Craig A. Evans, *Mark 8:27–16:20* (WBC 34B; Nashville: Thomas Nelson Publishers, 2001) 25, citing John D. Crossan, *The Historical Jesus: The Life of a Mediterranean Jewish Peasant* (San Francisco: HarperCollins, 1991) 353.

[59] Cited from *Epictetus 1* (trans. W.A. Oldfather; LCL; Cambridge, MA: Harvard University Press, 1979) 313; cf. F. Gerald Downing, *Cynics and Christian Origins* (Edinburgh: T & T Clark, 1992) 17-18.

Human Redemption/Body

	Prophetic	Apocalyptic	Wisdom	Precreation	Priestly	Miracle
Robbins, *Exploring*, 125-126	Commissioned by God; Filled with God's word	Earthly bodies transformed into heavenly forms; Heavenly bodies transformed into visible [earth-like] forms	Enlightened	Born of spirit	Holy	Restored

Inviting Eviatar Zerubavel, Philip Esler, Marco Cinnerelli, and Samuel Byrskog into the Conversation: Individual Commitment, Religious Community, and Ethics

Beyond human redemption as an important topic, a person also finds human commitment, religious community, and ethics to be important in first century Christian discourse.[60] This brings us to important issues in cognitive sociology, which help us to understand "memory-communities" in the Mediterranean world. First century Christian literature played a major role in the production, nurturing, and maintenance of memory-communities. Yet many questions emerge when a person makes an assertion like this. Some of the questions are: What is a memory-community? How do humans create memory-communities? What is the nature of memory-knowledge? What is the function of memory-communities in localized geographical regions? What is their function in large geographical areas containing many localized regions?

Using the language of Eviatar Zerubavel, we are seeking to understand the "social mindscape" of first century Christianity when we talk about memory-communities.[61] This means we are supplementing "conceptual blending" with a "sociology of thinking" that calls attention to "sociomental" topics and issues.[62] At this point, it will be helpful for us to remind ourselves that some form of primary Greek words for wisdom, prophecy, and apocalyptic (revelation) occur in six books in the NT: Matthew, Luke, Romans, 1 Corinthians, Ephesians, and Revelation. In the NT canon, this represents the first and last books (Matthew; Revelation), the two longest Gospels (Matthew; Luke); and the first and longest two letters attributed to Paul (Romans; 1 Corinthians), plus a letter that scholars consider to be a summary of Paul's undisputed letters (Ephesians). This means that these books contain

[60] Robbins, *Exploring the Texture of Texts*, 126-31.

[61] Eviatar Zerubavel, *Social Mindscapes: An Invitation to Cognitive Sociology* (Cambridge, MA: Harvard University Press, 1997).

[62] Ibid., 5.

"primary" language for both "social" and "collective" memory about wisdom, prophetic, and apocalyptic in early Christian discourse.

Sociobiographical Memory and Memory-Communities

The beginning point for Eviatar Zerubavel is a distinction between "personal" and "social" memory. He observes that personal memories are only part of our fund of memory knowledge. To be sure, every human has individual, personal memories, which no one but that person has. But a significant portion of a human's memory knowledge, he proposes, is "social" memory, namely knowledge possessed by "memory-communities," which he variously calls "mnemonic communities," "thought communities," and "cognitive subcultures." In contrast to "personal" memories, he proposes, knowledge that memory-communities possess is "impersonal," namely, knowledge that groups of people who never "personally" experienced the events have at the basis of the "social" knowledge they share in common.[63]

Language, of course, is "the" primary tool that enables social memories to exist among members of memory-communities.[64] The oral production of language and then the interactive relation between oral and written literature are the major means by which humans produce memory-communities. By the end of the first century CE, virtually no one was alive who had "personally" experienced events with Jesus of Nazareth. But many people lived in the context of "social memories" of Jesus of Nazareth that were repeatedly communicated to them through various language media, including hearing portions of the Gospels "performed" orally to them or read aloud to them. In this context, regularized meetings, commemorative times of remembering and celebrating, and established rituals of various kinds produced social memories located in time and space.

Zerubavel's approach helps to explain both the reason for and function of certain quite surprising aspects of the writings in the New Testament. One of the remarkable things about the NT writings, for example, is an absence of reference to John the Baptist in all twenty-one letters and Revelation, and an absence of reference to Jesus as the Son of Man in all twenty-one letters. In addition, there is an absence of reference to Adam in Revelation, in all the Gospels except Luke (3:38), and in all the letters except Romans (5:14), 1 Corinthians (15:22, 45), 1 Timothy (2:13-14), and Jude (14). There are, on the

[63] Ibid., 7-8, 31-34, 46-47, 89-95, 100-102.

[64] Eviatar Zerubavel, "Language and Memory: 'Pre-Columbian' America and the Social Logic of Periodization," *Social Research* 65 (1998) 315-28; idem, *Social Mindscapes*, 7-8, 66-67, 92-93.

other hand, references to Moses in all the Gospels, in Acts, in Romans, 1-2 Corinthians, 2 Timothy, Hebrews, Jude, and Revelation. Still, however, there is no reference to Moses in fifteen (more than half!) of the NT writings. References to Abraham also occur in all the Gospels, in Acts, Romans, 2 Corinthians and Hebrews, and in addition they occur in Galatians, James, and 1 Peter but not in 1 Corinthians, 2 Timothy, Jude, and Revelation! Currently there is a principle in literary-historical biblical interpretation that arguments from "silence" are faulty arguments. Our argument is an argument from "presence," but an argument that looks at this presence with an awareness also of absence in first century Christian writings. This double awareness is energized by cognitive sociology about memory, which calls attention to what people place in the background, minimize, avoid, or even intentionally "forget," in the context of "remembering," which is a process of foregrounding, maximizing, continually calling to attention, and intentionally "remembering" for fear of forgetting.[65]

Throughout this volume we have searched for data that exhibits the selective use of wisdom, prophetic, and apocalyptic personages, imagery, argumentation, and story-lines in first century Christian writings.[66] What is present in and absent from New Testament literature, we have proposed, can help us see processes through which first century Christians used certain language repetitively to produce discourse that guided their thoughts, actions, emotions, and commitments. A remarkable aspect of these writings is their diversity. Many of the writings are highly different from one another. Despite this diversity, however, there is significant unity. Zerubavel's writings can help us describe this diversity and unity in ways that can move us forward into the 21st century with tools of cognitive science to aid us in our work.

Collective Memory and Possible Social Identities

One of the characteristics of early Christian writings is the presence of alternative "possible social identities" in their discourse.[67] As we have said above, the first century Christian rhetorolects blend Jesus with six major "character types": sage; prophet; end-time seer and judge; eternal being; priest; and miracle worker on the basis of six major cultural

[65] Zerubavel, *Social Mindscapes*, 81-99.

[66] See Eviatar Zerubavel, *Time Maps: Collective Memory and the Social Shape of the Past* (Chicago/London: University of Chicago Press, 2003) 1-14.

[67] Marco Cinnirella, "Exploring Temporal Aspects of Social Identity: The Concept of Possible Social Identities," *European Journal of Social Psychology* 28 (1998) 227-48; Philip F. Esler, "'Remember My Fetters': Memorialisation of Paul's Imprisonment," in *Explaining Christian Origins and Early Judaism: Contributions from Cognitive and Social Science* (ed. P. Luomanen, I. Pyysiäinen, and R. Uro; Biblical Interpretation Series 89; Leiden/Boston: Brill, 2007) 231-58.

frames: wisdom; prophetic; apocalyptic; precreation; priestly; and miracle. How many of these social identities are possible for believers to adopt, activate, or reconfigure in their lives? The lines humans draw and the distinctions humans make "vary across cognitive subcultures within the same culture during the same period."[68] Perhaps certain identities are possible for some people in some cultures that are not possible for others in other cultures. Exploring possible social identities in contexts that exhibit the activation of certain identities could shed valuable light on the rhetorical effect of Christian discourse in various contexts throughout various centuries.

In *Exploring the Texture of Texts* and *The Tapestry of Early Christian Discourse,*[69] the exploration of "specific social topics" established an initial framework for exploring possible social identities in first century Christianity. The table below exhibits a beginning point for exploring possible social identities in the context of the six major first century Christian rhetorolects. Much further work awaits to be done on bringing these identities into view in the earliest Christian writings, as well as in writings in Christianity and other religious traditions today.

Human Commitment/Religious Community/Ethics

	Prophetic	Apocalyptic	Wisdom	Precreation	Priestly	Miracle
Robbins, *Exploring*, 126-130	Reformist (*Exploring*, 73)	Revolutionist/ Utopian (*Exploring*, 72-74)	Conversionist (*Exploring*, 72)	Gnostic-Manipulationist/ Conversionist (*Exploring*, 72-73)	Gnostic-Manipulationist/ Utopian (*Exploring*, 73-74)	Thaumaturgical (*Exploring*, 73)

Synchronization of Wisdom, Prophetic, and Apocalyptic Story-Lines in First Century Christian Discourse

Another issue in a discussion of cognitive sociology in relation to Christian discourse is synchronization of social memory in collective memory. According to Zerubavel, "Remembering and re-experiencing the past" are, over time, "fused into one comprehensive event."[70] This fusion produces "a single common collective memory"[71] at the expense of personal and social memories. Individual, diversified social identities become unified, reduced by common forgetting linked to common remembering. This occurs through "synchronization" of social memory with collective memory. Individual writings exhibit

[68] Zerubavel, *Social Mindscapes,* 63.

[69] Robbins, *Exploring the Texture of Texts,* 72-75; idem, *The Tapestry of Early Christian Discourse*, 147-59.

[70] Samuel Byrskog, "A New Quest for the *Sitz im Leben*: Social Memory, the Jesus Tradition and the Gospel of Matthew," *SNTS* 52 (2006) 331 [319–36], citing works of Eviatar Zerubavel.

[71] Zerubavel, *Social Mindscapes*, 95-99.

negotiations of "social memory" with "collective memory," and collective sociotemporal landmarks make it possible to integrate several different personal pasts into a single common past.[72] In addition, "[A] single *common time* (made up of a common past, a common present, and a common future) presupposes unmistakably impersonal, *standard time-reckoning frameworks* such as clock time and the calendar."[73] One of the major processes under way from the first through the fourth centuries CE were various synchronizations of social memory with collective memory. There is much here for investigators of Christianity to explore, analyze, and interpret. A very sketchy beginning point can be a table like the following, which exhibits potentials for synchronization in the story-lines of first century Christian wisdom, prophetic, and apocalyptic rhetorolect.

Synchronization in Process in First Century Christian Discourse

Wisdom	Prophetic	Apocalyptic
Creation: tree of the knowledge of good and evil		Creation: angel-spirits to watch over all creation
		Adam: death
		Noah: flood
	Abraham	Abraham and Lot: Sodom; Gomorrah
Moses: Torah	Moses	Moses: ten plagues
	David	David
Solomon: proverbs		Solomon
	Isaiah	
		Jonah
		Daniel: Babylon

What is gained by a collective memory is also a loss of diversity. Fortunately, writings are the products of a combination of sociobiographical memories, social memories, and collective memory. It is important in our research, analysis, and interpretation during the 21st century to remain in touch with all three kinds of memory not only in Christian writings but in writings throughout broad regions of our world.

A Special Conversation with Eviatar Zerubavel about the Names of the Rhetorolects

Some colleagues have expressed disappointment that I did not find more innovative terms to describe first century Christian rhetorolects. To them, the terms wisdom, prophetic, apocalyptic, precreation,

[72] Ibid., 101.
[73] Ibid., 102.

priestly, and miracle are too "conventional." In retrospect, it may be the case that my analysis and description of first century Christian discourse has a relation to Columbus's description of America when he "discovered" it. In Zerubavel's words: "Whereas Columbus 'viewed' America as a mere extension of the familiar (that is, as a group of islands lying somewhere off the shores of China), Waldseemüller was prepared to re-view it as an altogether new cosmographic entity, and thereby to literally rediscover Columbus's 'Indies' as 'America'."[74] I suppose it is natural that in my "discovery" of first century Christian discourse I have simply "viewed" it as an extension of the familiar, that is, as an extension of modes of biblical and deutero-canonical thought and writing during the Hellenistic-Roman period in the Mediterranean world.

The alternative could have been to "view" first century Christian discourse as "Christian discourse" rather than "emerging" discourse. I see a significant number of my colleagues describing the NT writings as "Christian discourse" rather than as a highly variegated "emerging Mediterranean discourse" during the first century CE. Some of the "issues" that have been raised about my analysis and interpretation of various portions of NT writings concern how certain emphases could be present (like "multiple" apocalyptic conceptions of the time[s] in which Jesus was transformed into a "divine-like" being) when these views do not appear among the early Church fathers and they are not consistent with the Nicene-Constantinopolitan Creed. A primary point of my analysis and interpretation is to exhibit the nature of first century Christian discourse prior to the "cognitive socialization" of it by leaders and writers during the second through the fourth centuries CE.

A major goal of my analysis and interpretation, then, is to view first century Christian discourse as "emerging Mediterranean discourse," rather than as "fully-formed Christian discourse." In other words, I think the NT writings indeed are "extensions of the familiar." When we understand more clearly how they are extensions of the familiar, we are in a position to bring into sharper relief the "new" dimensions in the discourse. In other words, when multiple "discoveries" of the familiar and unfamiliar in first century Christian discourse are synchronized with one another, we can more sharply perceive and more clearly display the nature of "an altogether new cosmographic entity" that emerged by the fourth century CE.

Why describe NT writings as "extensions of the familiar," rather than as "an altogether new cosmographic entity"? It is my conviction that displays of the processes of change, like Zerubavel's display of the steps in the shift from viewing the "New World" as part of Asia to

[74] Zerubavel, *Social Mindscapes,* 27.

viewing it as a continent of the "Americas," is an important part of describing the nature of "the new." Displaying these steps helps us understand how we as humans classify things, attending to certain things as "relevant" while relegating other things to "irrelevance," placing certain things in the foreground and other things in the background, as we create "the story" of Christianity. This understanding can equip us both to understand the past responsibly and to live responsibly in a world bombarded with daily information from multiple forms of media.

Inviting Relational Thinkers to Carry the Conversation into the Twenty-First Century

This volume presents a thesis that the earliest Christian literature was informed by story-lines that presented God's commitment to productivity (wisdom rhetorolect), the necessity for humans to engage in authoritative confrontation about the requirements of God's ways (prophetic rhetorolect), and images of dramatic transformation of the created world (apocalyptic rhetorolect). A key to the thesis is a view that humans blend conceptualities, rather than setting them off from one another. This is likely to be an opposite instinct at the beginning of the twenty-first century, when religious traditions seem to be driven much more by opposition than by reconciliation. It might appear today that the great religious traditions set themselves apart from one another, and indeed internally set everything they do in opposition to what other people do. Actually, the opposite is true. The great religions have become what they are today through processes of dynamic blending of traditions and conceptualities with one another.

It is, in fact, a certain kind of science during the nineteenth and twentieth centuries that has given scholars the impression that Christianity achieved its incredible influence in the world through processes of setting itself off from every other kind of thinking. This kind of science has led many scholars and theologians to argue that Christianity is a "faith" rather than a "religion." This kind of argumentation and theology is a particular kind of Christian rhetoric, a rhetoric that results from blending certain kinds of specialist-oriented science with Christian belief. These specialist-oriented modes of science became highly prominent in a context in Western culture that emphasized the mind over the body. When a specialized focus on only one part of the body, namely the mind, blended with a post-Kantian dualism between body and mind, scientific methods of literary and historical analysis and interpretation began to appear with processes, procedures, and goals that were intentionally extrinsic to the processes, procedures, and goals within the subject of study itself. The goal was to be objective, namely not to allow the processes, procedures, and goals of the subject performing the analysis or the subject under analysis to stand in the way. The goal needed to lie outside both the analyst and the phenomena being analyzed. The analyst needed to be kept out of the analysis, of course, because every analyst is biased, namely the analyst has his or her own self-interests. Ironically, it was considered important to keep the subject of the analysis out of the analysis, because the subject itself is deceptive, namely that which seems to be true is most definitely untrue! In other words, only that which is counterintuitive can be true. Those things which are obvious have to be thoroughly critiqued, tested under stringent procedures of analysis in contexts of attack from every conceivable angle a person can formulate. Only under these conditions, it was argued, can that which is true hold its own, namely to show itself for what it really is.

The present volume presupposes that modernist scientific procedures that exclude the subject from the analysis are insufficient for the tasks of exploration, analysis, and interpretation for the 21st century. While counterintuitive scientific procedures have produced highly valuable information, it is essential for us to engage in multiple kinds of cognitive scientific procedures of exploration, analysis, and interpretation to understand the nature of humans, human society, human history, human culture, and religions which humans have created over the centuries. Only to the extent that we find ways to robustly include subjects, subjectivities, and intersubjectivities[75] in our interpretive analytics will we be able to deal dynamically and responsibly with the issues that face humans as they try to live together with one another throughout the 21st century.

[75] Vernon K. Robbins, "The Rhetorical Full-Turn in Biblical Interpretation and Its Relevance for Feminist Hermeneutics," in *Her Master's Tools? Feminist and Postcolonial Engagements of Historical-Critical Discourse* (ed. C. Vander Stichele and T. Penner; Global Perspectives on Biblical Scholarship 9; Atlanta: SBL and Leiden: Brill, 2005) 109-27.

Index of Authors

Index of Subjects

Index of Biblical and Other References